History of Israel

From Ancient times to 1948

Editor

Silvia Herbert

Scribbles

Year of Publication 2018

ISBN : 9789352979769

Book Published by

Scribbles

(An Imprint of Alpha Editions)

email - alphaedis@gmail.com

Produced by: PediaPress GmbH
Limburg an der Lahn
Germany
http://pediapress.com/

The content within this book was generated collaboratively by volunteers. Please be advised that nothing found here has necessarily been reviewed by people with the expertise required to provide you with complete, accurate or reliable information. Some information in this book may be misleading or simply wrong. Alpha Editions and PediaPress does not guarantee the validity of the information found here. If you need specific advice (for example, medical, legal, financial, or risk management) please seek a professional who is licensed or knowledgeable in that area.

Sources, licenses and contributors of the articles and images are listed in the section entitled "References". Parts of the books may be licensed under the GNU Free Documentation License. A copy of this license is included in the section entitled "GNU Free Documentation License"

The views and characters expressed in the book are those of the contributors and his/her imagination and do not represent the views of the Publisher.

Contents

Articles 1

Prehistory of the Levant 1
Prehistory of the Levant 1

Bronze and Iron Ages 9
History of ancient Israel and Judah 9
Hebrews 31
Israelites 35
Biblical judges 55

Israel and Judah (Iron Age II) 61
Kingdom of Israel (united monarchy) 61
Kingdom of Israel (Samaria) 71
Kingdom of Judah 83

Roman period (64 BCE–4th century CE) 99
History of the Jews in the Roman Empire 99

Crusades and Mongols (1099–1291) 109
Kingdom of Jerusalem 109

Mutasarrifate of Jerusalem 153
Mutasarrifate of Jerusalem 153

British Mandate of Palestine — 163

- Mandatory Palestine 163
- Jewish Agency for Israel 213
- Fifth Aliyah 249
- Tripartite Pact 253
- 1936–1939 Arab revolt in Palestine 266
- White Paper of 1939 312

World War II and the Holocaust — 325

- History of the Jews during World War II 325
- The Holocaust 330
- Aliyah Bet 397
- Jewish insurgency in Mandatory Palestine 413
- United Nations Partition Plan for Palestine 452

Civil War — 475

- 1947–48 Civil War in Mandatory Palestine 475

Arab-Israel War — 519

- 1948 Arab–Israeli War 519

Appendix — 589

- References 589
- Article Sources and Contributors 644
- Image Sources, Licenses and Contributors 647

Article Licenses — 657

Index — 659

Prehistory of the Levant

Prehistory of the Levant

Part of a series on the
History of Israel
Ancient Israel and Judah
<ul><li>Natufian culture</li><li>Prehistory</li><li>Canaan</li><li>Israelites</li><li>United monarchy</li><li>Northern Kingdom</li><li>Kingdom of Judah</li><li>Babylonian rule</li></ul>
Second Temple period (530 BCE–70 CE)
<ul><li>Persian rule</li><li>Hellenistic period</li><li>Hasmonean dynasty</li><li>Herodian dynasty<ul><li>Kingdom</li><li>Tetrarchy</li></ul></li><li>Roman Judea</li></ul>
Middle Ages (70–1517)
<ul><li>Roman Palaestina</li><li>Byzantine Palaestina<ul><li>Prima</li><li>Secunda</li></ul></li><li>Revolt against Constantius Gallus</li><li>Samaritan revolts</li><li>Revolt against Heraclius</li></ul>

- Caliphates
  - Filastin
  - Urdunn
- Kingdom of Jerusalem
- Ayyubid dynasty
- Mamluk Sultanate

Modern history (1517–1948)

- Ottoman rule
  - Eyalet
  - Mutasarrifate
- Old Yishuv
- Zionism
- OETA
- British mandate

State of Israel (1948–present)

- Independence
- Timeline
- Years
- Arab–Israeli conflict
- Start-up Nation

History of the Land of Israel by topic

- Judaism
- Jerusalem
- Zionism
- Jewish leaders
- Jewish warfare
- Nationality

Related

- Jewish history
- Hebrew calendar
- Archaeology
- Museums

Israel portal

- v
- t
- e[1]

Part of a series on the

History of Palestine

Prehistory

- Natufian culture
- Pre-Pottery
- Tahunian
- Ghassulian
- Jericho

Ancient history

- Canaan
- Phoenicia
- Ancient Israel and Judah
- Philistia
- Median Empire
- Achaemenid Empire (Yehud Medinata)

Classical period

- Seleucus
- Antigonus
- Hasmonean dynasty
- Herodian kingdom
- Province of Judea
- Syria Palaestina
- Byzantine Empire (Palaestina Prima / Secunda)

Islamic rule

- Muslim conquest
- Rashidun (Jund Filastin, Jund al-Urdunn)
- Umayyad
- Abbasid
- Fatimid
- Crusader
- Ayyubid
- Mamluk
- Ottoman

Modern era

- British Mandate
- All-Palestine
- Jordanian West Bank
- Egyptian Gaza Strip
- Israel
- Military Governorate
- Israeli Civil Administration
- Palestinian Authority (Gaza Strip) State of Palestine

 **Palestine portal**

- v
- t
- e²

The **prehistory of the Levant** includes the various cultural changes that occurred, as revealed by archaeological evidence, prior to recorded traditions in the area of the Levant. Archaeological evidence suggests that *Homo sapiens* and other hominid species originated in Africa (see hominid dispersal) and that one of the routes taken to colonize Eurasia was through the Sinai desert and the Levant, which means that this is one of the most important and most occupied locations in the history of earth. Not only have many cultures and traditions of humans lived here, but also many species of the genus *Homo*. In addition, this region is one of the centers for the development of agriculture.

Cultures

The earliest traces of the human occupation in the Levant are documented in Ubeidiya Israel in the Jordan Valley of the Southern Levant, dated to the Lower Palaeolithic period, c. 1.4 million years ago. The lithic assemblages relate to the Early Acheulian culture. Later Acheulian sites include Gesher Benot Ya'akov, Tabun Cave and others dated to the time span of c. 1,400,000 – c. 250,000 years ago. This layer contains the world's first signs of domesticated dogs and controlled usage of fire.[3] Lower Palaeolithic human remains from the Southern Levant are scarce; they include isolated teeth from 'Ubeidiya, long bone fragments from Gesher Benot Ya'akov, and a fragmentary skull from Zuttiyeh Cave ("The Galilee Man").

The Middle Palaeolithic period (c. 250,000 – c. 48,000 BCE) is represented in the Levant by the Mousterian culture, known from numerous sites (both caves and open-air sites) through the region. The chronological subdivision of the Mousterian is based on the stratigraphic sequence of the Tabun Cave. Middle Paleolithic human remains include both the Neanderthals (in Kebara Cave, Amud Cave and Tabun), and anatomically modern humans (AMH) from Jebel Qafzeh and Skhul Cave.

The Upper Palaeolithic period is dated in the Levant to c. 48,000 – c. 20,000 BCE.

Epi-Palaeolithic period (c. 20,000 – c. 9,500 cal. BCE) is characterized by significant cultural variability and wide spread of the microlithic technologies. Beginning with the appearance of the Kebaran culture (18,000–12,500 BCE) a microlithic toolkit was associated with the appearance of the bow and arrow into the area. Kebaran shows affinities with the earlier Helwan phase in the Egyptian Fayyum, and may be associated with a movement of people across the Sinai associated with the climatic warming after the Late Glacial Maxima of 20,000 BCE. Kebaran affiliated cultures spread as far as Southern Turkey. The latest part of the period (c. 12,500 – c. 9,500 cal. BCE) is the time of flourishing of the Natufian culture and development of sedentism among the hunter-gatherers.

Natufian

This Culture existed from about 13,000 to 9,800 BCE in the Levant. A lot of archaeological excavations of this culture creates a relatively well defined understanding of these people. Two of the most significant aspects of this Culture were their large community sizes and their sedentary lifestyles. Although the Late Natufian experienced a slight reversal in this trend (possibly a result of the cold climatic period the Younger Dryas) as their community size shrank and they became more nomadic, it is believed that this culture continued through and was the foundation for the Neolithic Revolution.

Neolithic Period

(See full article and more detail here: Neolithic) The Neolithic period is traditionally divided to the Pre-Pottery (A and B) and Pottery phases. PPNA developed from the earlier Natufian cultures of the area. This is the time of the agricultural transition and development of farming economies in the Near East, and the region's first known megaliths (and Earth's oldest known megalith, other than Gobekli Tepe, which is in the Northern Levant and from an unknown culture) with a burial chamber and tracking of the sun or other stars.

In addition, the Levant in the Neolithic and Chalcolithic was involved in large scale, far reaching trade. Obsidian found in the Chalcolithic levels at Gilat, Israel have had their origins traced via elemental analysis to three sources in Southern Anatolia: Hotamis Dağ, Göllü Dağ, and as far east as Nemrut Dağ itself 500 km (310 mi) East of the other two sources. This is indicative of a very large trade circle reaching as far as the Northern Fertile Crescent at Nemrut Dağ and as far north as Hotamis Dağ.

The Ghassulian period created the basis of the Mediterranean economy which has characterised the area ever since. A Chalcolithic culture, the Ghassulian economy was a mixed agricultural system consisting of extensive cultivation of grains (wheat and barley), intensive horticulture of vegetable crops, commercial production of vines and olives, and a combination of transhumance and nomadic pastoralism. The Gassulian culture, according to Juris Zarins, developed out of the earlier Munhata phase of what he calls the *"circum Arabian nomadic pastoral complex"*, probably associated with the first appearance of Semites in this area.

Geographically the area is divided between a coastal plain, hill country to the East and the Jordan Valley joining the Sea of Galilee to the Dead Sea. Rainfall decreases from the north to the south, with the result that the northern region of Israel has generally been more economically developed than the southern one of Judah.

The area's location at the center of three trade routes linking three continents made it the meeting place for religious and cultural influences from Egypt, Syria, Mesopotamia, and Asia Minor:

1. A Coastal Route (the "*Via Maris*"): connecting Gaza and the Philistine coast north to Joppa and Megiddo, travelling north through Byblos to Phoenicia and Anatolia.
2. A Hill Route: travelling through the Negev, Kadesh Barnea, to Hebron and Jerusalem, and thence north to Samaria, Shechem, Shiloh, Beth Shean and Hazor, and thence to Kadesh and Damascus.
3. The "Kings Highway": travelling north from Eilat, east of the Jordan through Amman to Damascus, and connected to the "frankincense road" north from Yemen and South Arabia.

The area seems to have suffered from acute periods of desiccation, and reduced rainfall which has influenced the relative importance of settled versus nomadic ways of living. The cycle seems to have been repeated a number of times during which a reduced rainfall increases periods of fallow, with farmers spending increasing amounts of time with their flocks and away from cultivation. Eventually they revert to fully nomadic cultures, which, when rainfall increases settle around important sources of water and begin to spend increasing amounts of time on cultivation. The increased prosperity leads to a revival of inter-regional and eventually international trade. The growth of villages rapidly proceeds to increased prosperity of market towns and city states, which attract the attention of neighbouring great powers, who may invade to capture control of regional trade networks and possibilities for tribute and taxation. Warfare leads to opening the region to pandemics, with resultant depopulation, overuse of fragile soils and a reversion to nomadic pastoralism.

Early and Middle Bronze Age

The urban development of Canaan lagged considerably behind that of Egypt and Mesopotamia and even that of Syria, where from 3,500 BCE a sizable city developed at Hamoukar. This city, which was conquered, probably by people coming from the Southern Iraqi city of Uruk, saw the first connections between Syria and Southern Iraq that some[4,5] have suggested lie behind the patriarchal traditions. Urban development again began culminating in the Early

Bronze Age development of sites like Ebla, which by 2,300 BCE was incorporated once again into an Empire of Sargon, and then Naram-Sin of Akkad (Biblical Accad). The archives of Ebla show reference to a number of Biblical sites, including Hazor, Jerusalem, and a number of people have claimed, also to Sodom and Gomorrah, mentioned in the patriarchal records. The collapse of the Akkadian Empire, saw the arrival of peoples using Khirbet Kerak Ware pottery,[6] coming originally from the Zagros Mountains, east of the Tigris. It is suspected by some[7] that this event marks the arrival in Syria and Palestine of the Hurrians, people later known in the Biblical tradition possibly as Horites.

The following Middle Bronze Age period was initiated by the arrival of "Amorites" from Syria in Southern Iraq, an event which people like Albright (above) associated with the arrival of Abraham's family in Ur. This period saw the pinnacle of urban development in the area of Syria and Palestine. Archaeologists show that the chief state at this time was the city of Hazor, which may have been the capital of the region of Israel. This is also the period in which Semites began to appear in larger numbers in the Nile delta region of Egypt.

External links

- Joel Ng, Introduction to Biblical Archaeology 2: From Stone to Bronze[8]
- Paul James Cowie, Archaeowiki: Archaeology of the Southern Levant[9]

Bronze and Iron Ages

History of ancient Israel and Judah

<indicator name="pp-default"> 🔒 </indicator>

Part of a series on the
History of Israel

Ancient Israel and Judah
<ul><li>Natufian culture</li><li>Prehistory</li><li>Canaan</li><li>Israelites</li><li>United monarchy</li><li>Northern Kingdom</li><li>Kingdom of Judah</li><li>Babylonian rule</li></ul>
Second Temple period (530 BCE–70 CE)
<ul><li>Persian rule</li><li>Hellenistic period</li><li>Hasmonean dynasty</li><li>Herodian dynasty<ul><li>Kingdom</li><li>Tetrarchy</li></ul></li><li>Roman Judea</li></ul>
Middle Ages (70–1517)
<ul><li>Roman Palaestina</li><li>Byzantine Palaestina<ul><li>Prima</li><li>Secunda</li></ul></li><li>Revolt against Constantius Gallus</li></ul>

- Samaritan revolts
- Revolt against Heraclius
- Caliphates
  - Filastin
  - Urdunn
- Kingdom of Jerusalem
- Ayyubid dynasty
- Mamluk Sultanate

Modern history (1517–1948)

- Ottoman rule
  - Eyalet
  - Mutasarrifate
- Old Yishuv
- Zionism
- OETA
- British mandate

State of Israel (1948–present)

- Independence
- Timeline
- Years
- Arab–Israeli conflict
- Start-up Nation

History of the Land of Israel by topic

- Judaism
- Jerusalem
- Zionism
- Jewish leaders
- Jewish warfare
- Nationality

Related

- Jewish history
- Hebrew calendar
- Archaeology
- Museums

Israel portal

- v
- t
- e [10]

History of ancient Israel and Judah 11

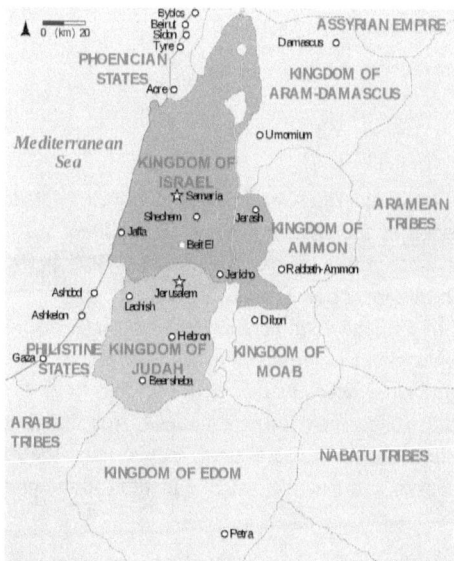

Figure 1: *Approximate map of the Iron Age kingdom of Israel (blue) and kingdom of Judah (yellow), with their neighbors (tan) (9th century BCE)*

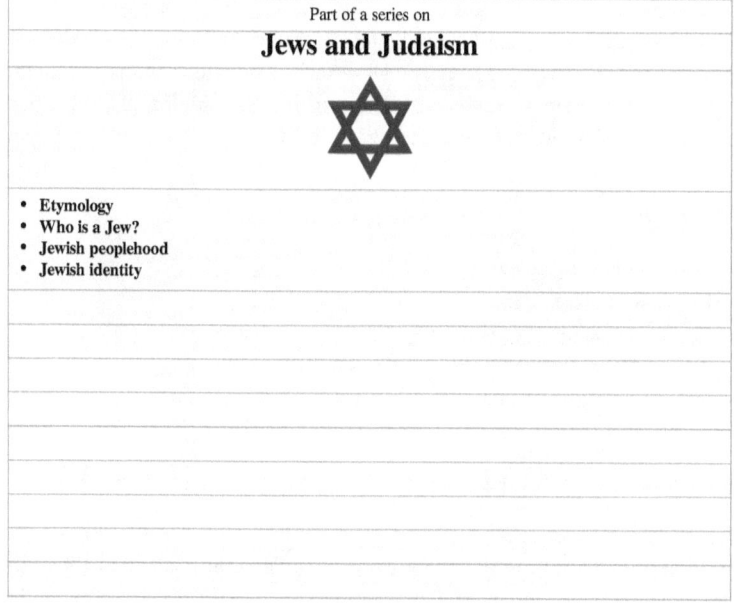

- Category: Jews and Judaism
- Portal: Judaism

- v
- t
- e[11]

The Kingdom of Israel and the Kingdom of Judah were related kingdoms from the Iron Age period of the ancient Levant. The Kingdom of Israel emerged as an important local power by the 10th century BCE before falling to the Neo-Assyrian Empire in 722 BCE. Israel's southern neighbor, the Kingdom of Judah, emerged in the 8th or 9th century BCE and later became a client state of first the Neo-Assyrian Empire and then the Neo-Babylonian Empire before a revolt against the latter led to its destruction in 586 BCE. Following the fall of Babylon to the Achaemenid Empire under Cyrus the Great in 539 BCE, some Judean exiles returned to Jerusalem, inaugurating the formative period in the development of a distinctive Judahite identity in the province of Yehud Medinata.

During the Hellenistic classic period, Yehud was absorbed into the subsequent Hellenistic kingdoms that followed the conquests of Alexander the Great, but in the 2nd century BCE the Judaeans revolted against the Seleucid Empire and created the Hasmonean kingdom. This, the last nominally independent kingdom of Israel, gradually lost its independence from 63 BCE with its conquest by Pompey of Rome, becoming a Roman and later Parthian client kingdom. Following the installation of client kingdoms under the Herodian dynasty, the Province of Judea was wracked by civil disturbances, which culminated in the First Jewish–Roman War, the destruction of the Second Temple, the emergence of Rabbinic Judaism and Early Christianity.

Periods

- Iron Age I: 1200–1000 BCE
- Iron Age II: 1000–586 BCE
- Neo-Babylonian: 586–539 BCE
- Persian: 539–332 BCE
- Hellenistic: 332–53 BCE[12]

Late Bronze Age background (1600–1200 BCE)

The eastern Mediterranean seaboard – the Levant – stretches 400 miles north to south from the Taurus Mountains to the Sinai Peninsula, and 70 to 100 miles east to west between the sea and the Arabian Desert.[13] The coastal plain of the southern Levant, broad in the south and narrowing to the north, is backed in its southernmost portion by a zone of foothills, the Shfela; like the plain this narrows as it goes northwards, ending in the promontory of Mount Carmel. East of the plain and the Shfela is a mountainous ridge, the "hill country of Judah" in the south, the "hill country of Ephraim" north of that, then Galilee and Mount Lebanon. To the east again lie the steep-sided valley occupied by the Jordan River, the Dead Sea, and the wadi of the Arabah, which continues down to the eastern arm of the Red Sea. Beyond the plateau is the Syrian desert, separating the Levant from Mesopotamia. To the southwest is Egypt, to the northeast Mesopotamia. The location and geographical characteristics of the narrow Levant made the area a battleground among the powerful entities that surrounded it.[14]

Canaan in the Late Bronze Age was a shadow of what it had been centuries earlier: many cities were abandoned, others shrank in size, and the total settled population was probably not much more than a hundred thousand.[15] Settlement was concentrated in cities along the coastal plain and along major communication routes; the central and northern hill country which would later become the biblical kingdom of Israel was only sparsely inhabited[16] although letters from the Egyptian archives indicate that Jerusalem was already a Canaanite city-state recognising Egyptian overlordship.[17] Politically and culturally it was dominated by Egypt,[18] each city under its own ruler, constantly at odds with its neighbours, and appealing to the Egyptians to adjudicate their differences.

The Canaanite city state system broke down during the Late Bronze Age collapse,[19] and Canaanite culture was then gradually absorbed into that of the Philistines, Phoenicians and Israelites.[20] The process was gradual[21] and a strong Egyptian presence continued into the 12th century BCE, and, while some Canaanite cities were destroyed, others continued to exist in Iron Age I.[22]

Iron Age I (1200–1000 BCE)

The name "Israel" first appears in the Merneptah Stele c. 1209 BCE: "Israel is laid waste and his seed is no more."[23] This "Israel" was a cultural and probably political entity, well enough established for the Egyptians to perceive it as a possible challenge, but an ethnic group rather than an organised state;[24] Archaeologist Paula McNutt says: "It is probably ... during Iron Age I [that] a population began to identify itself as 'Israelite'," differentiating itself from its neighbours via prohibitions on intermarriage, an emphasis on family history and genealogy, and religion.[25]

In the Late Bronze Age there were no more than about 25 villages in the highlands, but this increased to over 300 by the end of Iron Age I, while the settled

Figure 2: *The Merneptah Stele. While alternative translations exist, the majority of biblical archeologists translate a set of hieroglyphs as "Israel", representing the first instance of the name Israel in the historical record.*

population doubled from 20,000 to 40,000.[26] The villages were more numerous and larger in the north, and probably shared the highlands with pastoral nomads, who left no remains.[27] Archaeologists and historians attempting to trace the origins of these villagers have found it impossible to identify any distinctive features that could define them as specifically Israelite – collared-rim jars and four-room houses have been identified outside the highlands and thus cannot be used to distinguish Israelite sites,[28] and while the pottery of the highland villages is far more limited than that of lowland Canaanite sites, it develops typologically out of Canaanite pottery that came before.[29] Israel Finkelstein proposed that the oval or circular layout that distinguishes some of the earliest highland sites, and the notable absence of pig bones from hill sites, could be taken as markers of ethnicity, but others have cautioned that these can be a "common-sense" adaptation to highland life and not necessarily revelatory of origins.[30] Other Aramaean sites also demonstrate a contemporary absence of pig remains at that time, unlike earlier Canaanite and later Philistine excavations.

In *The Bible Unearthed* (2001), Finkelstein and Silberman summarised recent studies. They described how, up until 1967, the Israelite heartland in

Figure 3: *The Canaanite god Baal, 14th–12th century BCE (Louvre museum, Paris)*

the highlands of western Palestine was virtually an archaeological *terra incognita*. Since then, intensive surveys have examined the traditional territories of the tribes of Judah, Benjamin, Ephraim, and Manasseh. These surveys have revealed the sudden emergence of a new culture contrasting with the Philistine and Canaanite societies existing in the Land of Israel earlier during Iron Age I.[31] This new culture is characterised by a lack of pork remains (whereas pork formed 20% of the Philistine diet in places), by an abandonment of the Philistine/Canaanite custom of having highly decorated pottery, and by the practice of circumcision. The Israelite ethnic identity had originated, not from the Exodus and a subsequent conquest, but from a transformation of the existing Canaanite-Philistine cultures.[32] <templatestyles src="Template:Quote/styles.css"/>

> *These surveys revolutionized the study of early Israel. The discovery of the remains of a dense network of highland villages – all apparently established within the span of few generations – indicated that a dramatic social transformation had taken place in the central hill country of Canaan around 1200 BCE. There was no sign of violent invasion or even the infiltration of a clearly defined ethnic group. Instead, it seemed to be a revolution in lifestyle. In the formerly sparsely populated highlands from the Judean hills in the south to the hills of Samaria in the north, far from the*

Figure 4: *A reconstructed Israelite house, 10th–7th century BCE. Eretz Israel Museum, Tel Aviv.*

Canaanite cities that were in the process of collapse and disintegration, about two-hundred fifty hilltop communities suddenly sprang up. Here were the first Israelites.[33]

Modern scholars therefore see Israel arising peacefully and internally from existing people in the highlands of Canaan.[34]

Iron Age II (1000–587 BCE)

Unusually favourable climatic conditions in the first two centuries of Iron Age II brought about an expansion of population, settlements and trade throughout the region.[35] In the central highlands this resulted in unification in a kingdom with the city of Samaria as its capital, possibly by the second half of the 10th century BCE when an inscription of the Egyptian pharaoh Shoshenq I, the biblical Shishak, records a series of campaigns directed at the area.[36] Israel had clearly emerged by the middle of the 9th century BCE, when the Assyrian king Shalmaneser III names "Ahab the Israelite" among his enemies at the battle of Qarqar (853). At this time Israel was apparently engaged in a three-way contest with Damascus and Tyre for control of the Jezreel Valley and Galilee in the north, and with Moab, Ammon and Aram Damascus in the east for control of Gilead; the Mesha Stele (c. 830), left by a king of Moab, celebrates his success in throwing off the oppression of the "House of Omri" (i.e., Israel). It bears what is generally thought to be the earliest extra-biblical reference to the name *Yahweh*. A century later Israel came into increasing conflict with the expanding Neo-Assyrian Empire, which first split its territory into several smaller units and then destroyed its capital, Samaria (722). Both the biblical and Assyrian sources speak of a massive deportation of people from Israel and their replacement with settlers from other parts of the empire – such population exchanges were an established part of Assyrian imperial policy, a means of breaking the old power structure – and the former Israel never again became an independent political entity.[37]

Judah emerged somewhat later than Israel, probably during the 9th century BCE, but the subject is one of considerable controversy.[38] There are indications that during the 10th and 9th centuries BCE, the southern highlands had been divided between a number of centres, none with clear primacy.[39] During the reign of Hezekiah, between c. 715 and 686 BCE, a notable increase in the power of the Judean state can be observed.[40] This is reflected in archaeological sites and findings, such as the Broad Wall; a defensive city wall in Jerusalem; and the Siloam tunnel, an aqueduct designed to provide Jerusalem with water during an impending siege by the Neo-Assyrian Empire led by Sennacherib; and the Siloam inscription, a lintel inscription found over the doorway of a tomb, has been ascribed to comptroller Shebna. LMLK seals on storage jar handles, excavated from strata in and around that formed by Sennacherib's destruction, appear to have been used throughout Sennacherib's 29-year reign, along with bullae from sealed documents, some that belonged to Hezekiah himself and others that name his servants;

King Ahaz's seal is a piece of reddish-brown clay that belonged to King Ahaz of Judah, who ruled from 732 to 716 BCE. This seal contains not only the name of the king, but the name of his father, King Yehotam. In addition, Ahaz is specifically identified as "king of Judah." The Hebrew inscription, which is set on three lines, reads as follows: "l'hz*y/hwtm*mlk*/yhdh", which translates as "belonging to Ahaz (son of) Yehotam, King of Judah."[41]

In the 7th century Jerusalem grew to contain a population many times greater than earlier and achieved clear dominance over its neighbours.[42] This occurred at the same time that Israel was being destroyed by the Neo-Assyrian Empire, and was probably the result of a cooperative arrangement with the Assyrians to establish Judah as an Assyrian vassal state controlling the valuable olive industry. Judah prospered as a vassal state (despite a disastrous rebellion against Sennacherib), but in the last half of the 7th century BCE, Assyria suddenly collapsed, and the ensuing competition between Egypt and the Neo-Babylonian Empire for control of the land led to the destruction of Judah in a series of campaigns between 597 and 582.

Figure 5: *Reconstruction of the Ishtar Gate of Babylon*

Babylonian period

Babylonian Judah suffered a steep decline in both economy and population[43] and lost the Negev, the Shephelah, and part of the Judean hill country, including Hebron, to encroachments from Edom and other neighbours.[44] Jerusalem, while probably not totally abandoned, was much smaller than previously, and the town of Mizpah in Benjamin in the relatively unscathed northern section of the kingdom became the capital of the new Babylonian province of Yehud Medinata.[45] (This was standard Babylonian practice: when the Philistine city of Ashkalon was conquered in 604, the political, religious and economic elite [but not the bulk of the population] was banished and the administrative centre shifted to a new location).[46] There is also a strong probability that for most or all of the period the temple at Bethel in Benjamin replaced that at Jerusalem, boosting the prestige of Bethel's priests (the Aaronites) against those of Jerusalem (the Zadokites), now in exile in Babylon.[47]

The Babylonian conquest entailed not just the destruction of Jerusalem and its temple, but the liquidation of the entire infrastructure which had sustained Judah for centuries.[48] The most significant casualty was the state ideology of "Zion theology,"[49] the idea that the god of Israel had chosen Jerusalem for his dwelling-place and that the Davidic dynasty would reign there forever.[50] The fall of the city and the end of Davidic kingship forced the leaders of the exile community – kings, priests, scribes and prophets – to reformulate the concepts of community, faith and politics.[51] The exile community in Babylon thus became the source of significant portions of the Hebrew Bible: Isaiah 40–55; Ezekiel; the final version of Jeremiah; the work of the hypothesized priestly source in the Pentateuch; and the final form of the history of Israel from Deuteronomy to 2 Kings.[52] Theologically, the Babylonian exiles were responsible for the doctrines of individual responsibility and universalism (the concept that one god controls the entire world) and for the increased emphasis on purity and holiness. Most significantly, the trauma of the exile experience led to the development of a strong sense of Hebrew identity distinct from other peoples,[53] with increased emphasis on symbols such as circumcision and Sabbath-observance to sustain that distinction.[54]

The concentration of the biblical literature on the experience of the exiles in Babylon disguises the fact that the great majority of the population remained in Judah; for them, life after the fall of Jerusalem probably went on much as it had before.[55] It may even have improved, as they were rewarded with the land and property of the deportees, much to the anger of the community of exiles remaining in Babylon.[56] The assassination around 582 of the Babylonian governor by a disaffected member of the former royal House of David provoked a Babylonian crackdown, possibly reflected in the Book of Lamentations, but the situation seems to have soon stabilised again.[57] Nevertheless, those unwalled cities and towns that remained were subject to slave raids by the Phoenicians and intervention in their internal affairs by Samaritans, Arabs, and Ammonites.[58]

Persian period

When Babylon fell to the Persian Cyrus the Great in 539 BCE, Judah (or Yehud medinata, the "province of Yehud") became an administrative division within the Persian empire. Cyrus was succeeded as king by Cambyses, who added Egypt to the empire, incidentally transforming Yehud and the Philistine plain into an important frontier zone. His death in 522 was followed by a period of turmoil until Darius the Great seized the throne in about 521. Darius introduced a reform of the administrative arrangements of the empire including the collection, codification and administration of local law codes, and it is reasonable to suppose that this policy lay behind the redaction of the Jewish Torah.[59] After 404 the Persians lost control of Egypt, which became Persia's main rival outside Europe, causing the Persian authorities to tighten their administrative control over Yehud and the rest of the Levant.[60] Egypt was eventually reconquered, but soon afterward Persia fell to Alexander the Great, ushering in the Hellenistic period in the Levant.

Yehud's population over the entire period was probably never more than about 30,000 and that of Jerusalem no more than about 1,500, most of them connected in some way to the Temple.[61] According to the biblical history, one of the first acts of Cyrus, the Persian conqueror of Babylon, was to commission Jewish exiles to return to Jerusalem and rebuild their Temple, a task which they are said to have completed c. 515.[62] Yet it was probably not until the middle of the next century, at the earliest, that Jerusalem again became the capital of Judah.[63] The Persians may have experimented initially with ruling Yehud as a Davidic client-kingdom under descendants of Jehoiachin,[64] but by the mid–5th century BCE, Yehud had become, in practice, a theocracy, ruled by hereditary high priests,[65] with a Persian-appointed governor, frequently Jewish, charged with keeping order and seeing that taxes (tribute) were collected and paid.[66] According to the biblical history, Ezra and Nehemiah arrived in Jerusalem in the middle of the 5th century BCE, the former empowered by the Persian king to enforce the Torah, the latter holding the status of governor with a royal commission to restore Jerusalem's walls.[67] The biblical history mentions tension between the returnees and those who had remained in Yehud, the returnees rebuffing the attempt of the "peoples of the land" to participate in the rebuilding of the Temple; this attitude was based partly on the exclusivism that the exiles had developed while in Babylon and, probably, also partly on disputes over property.[68] During the 5th century BCE, Ezra and Nehemiah attempted to reintegrate these rival factions into a united and ritually pure society, inspired by the prophecies of Ezekiel and his followers.[69]

The Persian era, and especially the period between 538 and 400 BCE, laid the foundations for the unified Judaic religion and the beginning of a scriptural canon.[70] Other important landmarks in this period include the replacement of Hebrew as the everyday language of Judah by Aramaic (although Hebrew continued to be used for religious and literary purposes)[71] and Darius's reform of the empire's bureaucracy, which may have led to extensive revisions and reorganizations of the Jewish Torah. The Israel of the Persian period consisted of descendants of the inhabitants of the old kingdom of Judah, returnees from the Babylonian exile community, Mesopotamians who had joined them or had been exiled themselves to Samaria at a far earlier period, Samaritans, and others.[72]

Hellenistic period

On the death of Alexander the Great (322 BCE), Alexander's generals divided the empire among themselves. Ptolemy I, the ruler of Egypt, seized Yehud Medinata, but his successors lost it in 198 to the Seleucids of Syria. At first, relations between Seleucids and Jews were cordial, but the attempt of Antiochus IV Epiphanes (174–163) to impose Hellenic cults on Judea sparked a

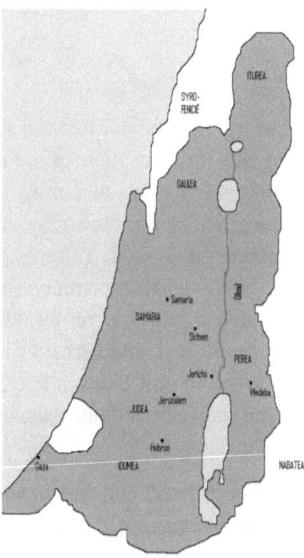

Figure 6: *The Hasmonean kingdom at its largest extent*

national rebellion that ended in the expulsion of the Seleucids and the establishment of an independent Jewish kingdom under the Hasmonean dynasty. Some modern commentators see this period also as a civil war between orthodox and hellenized Jews. Hasmonean kings attempted to revive the Judah described in the Bible: a Jewish monarchy ruled from Jerusalem and including all territories once ruled by David and Solomon. In order to carry out this project, the Hasmoneans forcibly converted one-time Moabites, Edomites, and Ammonites to Judaism, as well as the lost kingdom of Israel.[73] Some scholars argue that the Hasmonean dynasty institutionalized the final Jewish biblical canon.[74]

In 63 BCE the Roman general Pompey conquered Jerusalem and made the Jewish kingdom a client state of Rome. In 40–39 BCE, Herod the Great was appointed King of the Jews by the Roman Senate, and in 6 CE the last ethnarch of Judea was deposed by the emperor Augustus, his territories combined with Idumea and Samaria and annexed as Iudaea Province under direct Roman administration.[75] The name Judea (Iudaea) ceased to be used by Greco-Romans after the revolt of Simon Bar Kochba in 135 CE; the area was henceforth called Syria Palaestina (Greek: Παλαιστίνη, Palaistinē; Latin: Palaestina).

Religion

Iron Age Yahwism

The religion of the Israelites of Iron Age I, like the Ancient Canaanite religion from which it evolved and other religions of the ancient Near East, was based on a cult of ancestors and worship of family gods (the "gods of the fathers").[76,77] With the emergence of the monarchy at the beginning of Iron Age II the kings promoted their family god, Yahweh, as the god of the kingdom, but beyond the royal court, religion continued to be both polytheistic and family-centered.[78] The major deities were not numerous – El, Asherah, and Yahweh, with Baal as a fourth god, and perhaps Shamash (the sun) in the early period.[79] At an early stage El and Yahweh became fused and Asherah did not continue as a separate state cult, although she continued to be popular at a community level until Persian times.[80]

Yahweh, the national god of both Israel and Judah, seems to have originated in Edom and Midian in southern Canaan and may have been brought to Israel by the Kenites and Midianites at an early stage.[81] There is a general consensus among scholars that the first formative event in the emergence of the distinctive religion described in the Bible was triggered by the destruction of Israel by Assyria in c. 722 BCE. Refugees from the northern kingdom fled to Judah, bringing with them laws and a prophetic tradition of Yahweh. This religion was subsequently adopted by the landowners of Judah, who in 640 BCE placed the eight-year-old Josiah on the throne. Judah at this time was a vassal state of Assyria, but Assyrian power collapsed in the 630s, and around 622 Josiah and his supporters launched a bid for independence expressed as loyalty to "Yahweh alone".

The Babylonian exile and Second Temple Judaism

According to the Deuteronomists, as scholars call these Judean nationalists, the treaty with Yahweh would enable Israel's god to preserve both the city and the king in return for the people's worship and obedience. The destruction of Jerusalem, its Temple, and the Davidic dynasty by Babylon in 587/586 BCE was deeply traumatic and led to revisions of the national mythos during the Babylonian exile. This revision was expressed in the Deuteronomistic history, the books of Joshua. Judges, Samuel and Kings, which interpreted the Babylonian destruction as divinely-ordained punishment for the failure of Israel's kings to worship Yahweh to the exclusion of all other deities.[82]

The Second Temple period (520 BCE – 70 CE) differed in significant ways from what had gone before.[83] Strict monotheism emerged among the priests of the Temple establishment during the seventh and sixth centuries BCE, as did beliefs regarding angels and demons.[84] At this time, circumcision, dietary laws, and Sabbath-observance gained more significance as symbols of Jewish identity, and the institution of the synagogue became increasingly important, and most of the biblical literature, including the Torah, was written or substantially revised during this time.[85]

References

Bibliography

- Albertz, Rainer (1994) [Vanderhoek & Ruprecht 1992]. *A History of Israelite Religion, Volume I: From the Beginnings to the End of the Monarchy*[86]. Westminster John Knox Press.<templatestyles src="Module:Citation/CS1/styles.css"></templatestyles>
- Albertz, Rainer (1994) [Vanderhoek & Ruprecht 1992]. *A History of Israelite Religion, Volume II: From the Exile to the Maccabees*[87]. Westminster John Knox Press.<templatestyles src="Module:Citation/CS1/styles.css"></templatestyles>
- Albertz, Rainer (2003a). *Israel in Exile: The History and Literature of the Sixth Century B.C.E.*[88] Society of Biblical Literature.<templatestyles src="Module:Citation/CS1/styles.css"></templatestyles>
- Albertz, Rainer; Becking, Bob, eds. (2003b). *Yahwism After the Exile: Perspectives on Israelite Religion in the Persian Era*[89]. Koninklijke Van Gorcum.<templatestyles src="Module:Citation/CS1/styles.css"></templatestyles>
Becking, Bob. "Law as Expression of Religion (Ezra 7–10)". Missing or empty |title= (help)<templatestyles src="Module:Citation/CS1/styles.css"></templatestyles>
- Amit, Yaira, et al., eds. (2006). *Essays on Ancient Israel in its Near Eastern Context: A Tribute to Nadav Na'aman*[90]. Eisenbrauns.<templatestyles src="Module:Citation/CS1/styles.css"></templatestyles>
- Avery-Peck, Alan, et al., eds. (2003). *The Blackwell Companion to Judaism*[91]. Blackwell.<templatestyles src="Module:Citation/CS1/styles.css"></templatestyles>
Murphy, Frederick J. R. "Second Temple Judaism". Missing or empty |title= (help)<templatestyles src="Module:Citation/CS1/styles.css"></templatestyles>
- Barstad, Hans M. (2008). *History and the Hebrew Bible*[92]. Mohr Siebeck.<templatestyles src="Module:Citation/CS1/styles.css"></templatestyles>
- Becking, Bob, ed. (2001). *Only One God? Monotheism in Ancient Israel and the Veneration of the Goddess Asherah*[93]. Sheffield Academic Press.<templatestyles

src="Module:Citation/CS1/styles.css"></templatestyles>
Dijkstra, Meindert. "El the God of Israel, Israel the People of YHWH: On the Origins of Ancient Israelite Yahwism". Missing or empty |title= (help)<templatestyles src="Module:Citation/CS1/styles.css"></templatestyles> Dijkstra, Meindert. "I Have Blessed You by Yahweh of Samaria and His Asherah: Texts with Religious Elements from the Soil Archive of Ancient Israel". Missing or empty |title= (help)<templatestyles src="Module:Citation/CS1/styles.css"></templatestyles>
- Becking, Bob; Korpel, Marjo Christina Annette, eds. (1999). *The Crisis of Israelite Religion: Transformation of Religious Tradition in Exilic and Post-Exilic Times*[94]. Brill.<templatestyles src="Module:Citation/CS1/styles.css"></templatestyles> Niehr, Herbert. *Religio-Historical Aspects of the Early Post-Exilic Period*.<templatestyles src="Module:Citation/CS1/styles.css"></templatestyles>
- Bedford, Peter Ross (2001). *Temple Restoration in Early Achaemenid Judah*[95]. Brill.<templatestyles src="Module:Citation/CS1/styles.css"></templatestyles>
- Ben-Sasson, H.H. (1976). *A History of the Jewish People*. Harvard University Press. ISBN 0-674-39731-2.<templatestyles src="Module:Citation/CS1/styles.css"></templatestyles>
- Blenkinsopp, Joseph (1988). *Ezra-Nehemiah: A Commentary*[96]. Eerdmans.<templatestyles src="Module:Citation/CS1/styles.css"></templatestyles>
- Blenkinsopp, Joseph; Lipschits, Oded, eds. (2003). *Judah and the Judeans in the Neo-Babylonian Period*[97]. Eisenbrauns.<templatestyles src="Module:Citation/CS1/styles.css"></templatestyles> Blenkinsopp, Joseph. "Bethel in the Neo-Babylonian Period". Missing or empty |title= (help)<templatestyles src="Module:Citation/CS1/styles.css"></templatestyles> Lemaire, André. *Nabonidus in Arabia and Judea During the Neo-Babylonian Period*.<templatestyles src="Module:Citation/CS1/styles.css"></templatestyles>
- Blenkinsopp, Joseph (2009). *Judaism, the First Phase: The Place of Ezra and Nehemiah in the Origins of Judaism*[98]. Eerdmans.<templatestyles src="Module:Citation/CS1/styles.css"></templatestyles>
- Bloch-Smith, Elizabeth (2008). "Bible, Archaeology, and the Social Sciences". In Frederick E. Greenspahn. *The Hebrew Bible: new insights and scholarship*[99]. NYU Press.<templatestyles src="Module:Citation/CS1/styles.css"></templatestyles>
- Brett, Mark G. (2002). *Ethnicity and the Bible*[100]. Brill.<templatestyles src="Module:Citation/CS1/styles.css"></templatestyles>

- Edelman, Diana. "Ethnicity and Early Israel". Missing or empty |title= (help)<templatestyles src="Module:Citation/CS1/styles.css"></templatestyles>
- Bright, John (2000) [1959]. *A History of Israel*[101] (4th ed.). Westminster John Knox Press.<templatestyles src="Module:Citation/CS1/styles.css"></templatestyles>
- Coogan, Michael D., ed. (1998). *The Oxford History of the Biblical World*[102]. Oxford University Press.<templatestyles src="Module:Citation/CS1/styles.css"></templatestyles> Stager, Lawrence E. "Forging an Identity: The Emergence of Ancient Israel". Missing or empty |title= (help)<templatestyles src="Module:Citation/CS1/styles.css"></templatestyles>
- Coogan, Michael D. (2009). *A Brief Introduction to the Old Testament*[103]. Oxford University Press.<templatestyles src="Module:Citation/CS1/styles.css"></templatestyles>
- Coote, Robert B.; Whitelam, Keith W. (1986). "The Emergence of Israel: Social Transformation and State Formation Following the Decline in Late Bronze Age Trade". *Semeia* (37): 107–47.<templatestyles src="Module:Citation/CS1/styles.css"></templatestyles>
- Davies, Philip R. (1992). *In Search of Ancient Israel*[104]. Sheffield.<templatestyles src="Module:Citation/CS1/styles.css"></templatestyles>
- Davies, Philip R. (2009). "The Origin of Biblical Israel"[105]. *Journal of Hebrew Scriptures*. 9 (47). Archived from the original[106] on 28 May 2008.<templatestyles src="Module:Citation/CS1/styles.css"></templatestyles>
- Day, John (2002). *Yahweh and the Gods and Goddesses of Canaan*[107]. Sheffield Academic Press.<templatestyles src="Module:Citation/CS1/styles.css"></templatestyles>
- Dever, William (2001). *What Did the Biblical Writers Know, and When Did They Know It?*[108]. Eerdmans.<templatestyles src="Module:Citation/CS1/styles.css"></templatestyles>
- Dever, William (2003). *Who Were the Early Israelites and Where Did They Come From?*[109]. Eerdmans.<templatestyles src="Module:Citation/CS1/styles.css"></templatestyles>
- Dever, William (2005). *Did God Have a Wife?: Archaeology and Folk Religion in Ancient Israel*[110]. Eerdmans.<templatestyles src="Module:Citation/CS1/styles.css"></templatestyles>
- Dunn, James D.G; Rogerson, John William, eds. (2003). *Eerdmans commentary on the Bible*[111]. Eerdmans.<templatestyles src="Module:Citation/CS1/styles.css"></templatestyles> Rogerson, John William. "Deuteronomy". Miss-

ing or empty |title= (help)
- Edelman, Diana, ed. (1995). *The Triumph of Elohim: From Yahwisms to Judaisms*[112]. Kok Pharos.
- Finkelstein, Israel; Silberman, Neil Asher (2001). *The Bible Unearthed*[113].
- Finkelstein, Israel; Mazar, Amihay; Schmidt, Brian B. (2007). *The Quest for the Historical Israel*[114]. Society of Biblical Literature. Mazar, Amihay. "The Divided Monarchy: Comments on Some Archaeological Issues". Missing or empty |title= (help)
- Gnuse, Robert Karl (1997). *No Other Gods: Emergent Monotheism in Israel*[115]. Sheffield Academic Press.
- Golden, Jonathan Michael (2004a). *Ancient Canaan and Israel: An Introduction*[116]. Oxford University Press.
- Golden, Jonathan Michael (2004b). *Ancient Canaan and Israel: New Perspectives*[117]. ABC-CLIO.
- Goodison, Lucy; Morris, Christine (1998). *Goddesses in Early Israelite Religion in Ancient Goddesses: The Myths and the Evidence*[118]. University of Wisconsin Press.
- Grabbe, Lester L. (2004). *A History of the Jews and Judaism in the Second Temple Period*[119]. T&T Clark International.
- Grabbe, Lester L., ed. (2008). *Israel in Transition: From Late Bronze II to Iron IIa (c. 1250–850 B.C.E.)*[120]. T&T Clark International.
- Killebrew, Ann E. (2005). *Biblical Peoples and Ethnicity: An Archaeological Study of Egyptians, Canaanites, and Early Israel, 1300–1100 B.C.E.*[121] Society of Biblical Literature.
- King, Philip J.; Stager, Lawrence E. (2001). *Life in Biblical Israel*[122]. Westminster John Knox Press. ISBN 0-664-22148-3.
- Kuhrt, Amélie (1995). *The Ancient Near East*

c. *3000–330 BCE*[123]. Routledge.<templatestyles src="Module:Citation/CS1/styles.css"></templatestyles>
- Lemche, Niels Peter (1998). *The Israelites in History and Tradition*[124]. Westminster John Knox Press.<templatestyles src="Module:Citation/CS1/styles.css"></templatestyles>
- Levy, Thomas E. (1998). *The Archaeology of Society in the Holy Land*[125]. Continuum International Publishing.<templatestyles src="Module:Citation/CS1/styles.css"></templatestyles> LaBianca, Øystein S.; Younker, Randall W. "The Kingdoms of Ammon, Moab and Edom: The Archaeology of Society in Late Bronze/Iron Age Transjordan (c. 1400–500 CE)". Missing or empty |title= (help)<templatestyles src="Module:Citation/CS1/styles.css"></templatestyles>
- Lipschits, Oded (2005). *The Fall and Rise of Jerusalem*[126]. Eisenbrauns.<templatestyles src="Module:Citation/CS1/styles.css"></templatestyles>
- Lipschits, Oded, et al., eds. (2006). *Judah and the Judeans in the Fourth Century B.C.E.*[127] Eisenbrauns.<templatestyles src="Module:Citation/CS1/styles.css"></templatestyles> Kottsieper, Ingo. "And They Did Not Care to Speak Yehudit". Missing or empty |title= (help)<templatestyles src="Module:Citation/CS1/styles.css"></templatestyles> Lipschits, Oded; Vanderhooft, David. "Yehud Stamp Impressions in the Fourth Century B.C.E.". Missing or empty |title= (help)<templatestyles src="Module:Citation/CS1/styles.css"></templatestyles>
- Liverani, Mario (2005). *Israel's History and the History of Israel*, London, Equinox.
- Markoe, Glenn (2000). *Phoenicians*[128]. University of California Press.<templatestyles src="Module:Citation/CS1/styles.css"></templatestyles>
- Mays, James Luther, et al., eds. (1995). *Old Testament Interpretation*[129]. T&T Clarke.<templatestyles src="Module:Citation/CS1/styles.css"></templatestyles> Miller, J. Maxwell. "The Middle East and Archaeology". Missing or empty |title= (help)<templatestyles src="Module:Citation/CS1/styles.css"></templatestyles>
- McNutt, Paula (1999). *Reconstructing the Society of Ancient Israel*[130]. Westminster John Knox Press.<templatestyles src="Module:Citation/CS1/styles.css"></templatestyles>
- Merrill, Eugene H. (1995). "The Late Bronze/Early Iron Age Transition and the Emergence of Israel". *Bibliotheca Sacra*. **152** (606): 145–62.<templatestyles src="Module:Citation/CS1/styles.css"></templatestyles>

- Middlemas, Jill Anne (2005). *The Troubles of Temple-less Judah*[131]. Oxford University Press.<templatestyles src="Module:Citation/CS1/styles.css"></templatestyles>
- Miller, James Maxwell; Hayes, John Haralson (1986). *A History of Ancient Israel and Judah*[132]. Westminster John Knox Press. ISBN 0-664-21262-X.<templatestyles src="Module:Citation/CS1/styles.css"></templatestyles>
- Miller, Robert D. (2005). *Chieftains of the Highland Clans: A History of Israel in the 12th and 11th Centuries B.C.*[133] Eerdmans.<templatestyles src="Module:Citation/CS1/styles.css"></templatestyles>
- Moore, Megan Bishop; Kelle, Brad E. (2011). *Biblical History and Israel's Past*[134]. Eerdmans.<templatestyles src="Module:Citation/CS1/styles.css"></templatestyles>
- Nodet, Étienne (1999) [Editions du Cerf 1997]. *A Search for the Origins of Judaism: From Joshua to the Mishnah*[135]. Sheffield Academic Press.<templatestyles src="Module:Citation/CS1/styles.css"></templatestyles>
- Pitkänen, Pekka (2004). "Ethnicity, Assimilation and the Israelite Settlement"[136] (PDF). *Tyndale Bulletin*. **55** (2): 161–82. Archived from the original[137] (PDF) on 17 July 2011.<templatestyles src="Module:Citation/CS1/styles.css"></templatestyles>
- Silberman, Neil Asher; Small, David B., eds. (1997). *The Archaeology of Israel: Constructing the Past, Interpreting the Present*[138]. Sheffield Academic Press.<templatestyles src="Module:Citation/CS1/styles.css"></templatestyles> Hesse, Brian; Wapnish, Paula. "Can Pig Remains Be Used for Ethnic Diagnosis in the Ancient Near East?". Missing or empty |title= (help)<templatestyles src="Module:Citation/CS1/styles.css"></templatestyles>
- Smith, Mark S. (2001). *Untold Stories: The Bible and Ugaritic Studies in the Twentieth Century*. Hendrickson Publishers.<templatestyles src="Module:Citation/CS1/styles.css"></templatestyles>
- Smith, Mark S.; Miller, Patrick D. (2002) [Harper & Row 1990]. *The Early History of God*[139]. Eerdmans.<templatestyles src="Module:Citation/CS1/styles.css"></templatestyles>
- Rendsburg, Gary (2008). "Israel without the Bible". In Frederick E. Greenspahn. *The Hebrew Bible: new insights and scholarship*[99]. NYU Press.<templatestyles src="Module:Citation/CS1/styles.css"></templatestyles>
- Soggin, Michael J. (1998). *An Introduction to the History of Israel and Judah*[140]. Paideia.<templatestyles src="Module:Citation/CS1/styles.css"></templatestyles>
- Thompson, Thomas L. (1992). *Early History*

of the Israelite People[141]. Brill.
- Van der Toorn, Karel (1996). *Family Religion in Babylonia, Syria, and Israel*[118]. Brill.
- Van der Toorn, Karel; Becking, Bob; Van der Horst, Pieter Willem (1999). *Dictionary of Deities and Demons in the Bible*[142] (2d ed.). Koninklijke Brill.
- Vaughn, Andrew G.; Killebrew, Ann E., eds. (1992). *Jerusalem in Bible and Archaeology: The First Temple Period*[143]. Sheffield. Cahill, Jane M. "Jerusalem at the Time of the United Monarchy". Missing or empty |title= (help) Lehman, Gunnar. "The United Monarchy in the Countryside". Missing or empty |title= (help)
- Wylen, Stephen M. (1996). *The Jews in the Time of Jesus: An Introduction*[144]. Paulist Press.
- Zevit, Ziony (2001). *The Religions of Ancient Israel: A Synthesis of Parallactic Approaches*[145]. Continuum.

Further reading

- Avery-Peck, Alan, and Neusner, Jacob, (eds), "The Blackwell Companion to Judaism (Blackwell, 2003)[146]
- Brettler, Marc Zvi, "The Creation of History in Ancient Israel" (Routledge, 1995)[147], and also review at Dannyreviews.com[148]
- Cook, Stephen L., "The social roots of biblical Yahwism" (Society of Biblical Literature, 2004)[149]
- Day, John (ed), "In search of pre-exilic Israel: proceedings of the Oxford Old Testament Seminar" (T&T Clark International, 2004)[150]
- Gravett, Sandra L., "An Introduction to the Hebrew Bible: A Thematic Approach" (Westminster John Knox Press, 2008)[151]
- Grisanti, Michael A., and Howard, David M., (eds), "Giving the Sense:Understanding and Using Old Testament Historical Texts" (Kregel Publications, 2003)[152]
- Hess, Richard S., "Israelite religions: an archaeological and biblical survey" Baker, 2007)[153]

- Kavon, Eli, "Did the Maccabees Betray the Hanukka Revolution?"[154], *The Jerusalem Post*, 26 December 2005
- Lemche, Neils Peter, "The Old Testament between theology and history: a critical survey" (Westminster John Knox Press, 2008)[155]
- Levine, Lee I., "Jerusalem: portrait of the city in the second Temple period (538 B.C.E.–70 C.E.)" (Jewish Publication Society, 2002)[156]
- Na'aman, Nadav, "Ancient Israel and its neighbours" (Eisenbrauns, 2005)[157]
- Penchansky, David, "Twilight of the gods: polytheism in the Hebrew Bible" (Westminster John Knox Press, 2005)[158]
- Provan, Iain William, Long, V. Philips, Longman, Tremper, "A Biblical History of Israel" (Westminster John Knox Press, 2003)[159]
- £Russell, Stephen C., "Images of Egypt in early biblical literature" (Walter de Gruyter, 2009)[160]
- Sparks, Kenton L., "Ethnicity and identity in ancient Israel" (Eisenbrauns, 1998)[161]
- Stackert, Jeffrey, "Rewriting the Torah: literary revision in Deuteronomy and the holiness code" (Mohr Siebeck, 2007)[162]
- Vanderkam, James, "An introduction to early Judaism" (Eerdmans, 2001)[163]

Hebrews

Part of a series on
Jews and Judaism

• Etymology • Who is a Jew? • Jewish peoplehood • Jewish identity
• Category: Jews and Judaism • Portal: Judaism
• v • t • e[164]

Hebrews (Hebrew: עברים or עבריים, Tiberian *Iḇrîm, Iḇriyyîm*; Modern Hebrew *'Ivrim, 'Ivriyyim*; ISO 259-3 *ʕibrim, ʕibriyim*) is a term appearing 34 times within 32 verses[165,166] of the Hebrew Bible. While the term was not an ethnonym,[167,168] it is mostly taken as synonymous with the Semitic-speaking Israelites, especially in the pre-monarchic period when they were still nomadic. However, in some instances it may also be used in a wider sense, referring to the Phoenicians, or to other ancient groups, such as the group known as Shasu of *Yhw* on the eve of the Bronze Age collapse.[169]

By the time of the Roman Empire, Greek *Hebraios* could refer to the Jews in general, as Strong's Hebrew Dictionary puts it "any of the Jewish Nation"[170] and at other times more specifically to the Jews living in Judea. In Early Christianity, the Greek term Ἑβραῖος refers to Jewish Christians as opposed to the gentile Christians and Judaizers (Acts 6:1 among others). Ἰουδαία is the province where the Temple was located.

Figure 7: *Rameses III's tiles depicting Canaanite and Shasu leaders as captives. Most archaeologists as of 2018[171] regard the Hebrews as local Canaanite refugees and Shasu settling down in the hill-country.*

In Armenian, Italian, Modern Greek, Serbian, Bulgarian, Russian, Romanian, and a few other modern languages, there is a pejorative connotation associated with the word corresponding to the word Jew; because of that, in each of these languages, the primary word used is that which corresponds to "Hebrew". The translation of "Hebrew" is used also in the Kurdish language and was once used also in French.

With the revival of the Hebrew language and the emergence of the Hebrew Yishuv, the term has been applied to the Jewish people of this re-emerging society in Israel or anything associated with it.

Etymology

The definitive origin of the term "Hebrew" remains uncertain. The Biblical term *Ivri* (עברי; Hebrew pronunciation: [ʕivˈri]), meaning "to traverse" or "to pass over", is usually rendered as *Hebrew* in English, from the ancient Greek Ἑβραῖος and the Latin *Hebraeus*. The Biblical word *Ivri* has the plural form *Ivrim*, or *Ibrim*.

Genesis 10:21[172] refers to Shem, the elder brother of Ham and Japheth and thus the first-born son of Noah, as the father of the sons of Eber (עבר), which may have a similar meaning.

Figure 8: *Greek painting of three Chaldeans with captive Hebrews*

Some authorsWikipedia:Avoid weasel words argue that *Ibri* denotes the descendants of the biblical patriarch Eber (Hebrew, עבר), son of Shelah, a great-grandson of Noah and an ancestor of Abraham,[173] hence the occasional anglicization *Eberites*.

Since the 19th-century CE discovery of the second-millennium BCE inscriptions mentioning the Habiru, many theories have linked these to the Hebrews. Some scholars argue that the name "Hebrew" is related to the name of those seminomadic Habiru people recorded in Egyptian inscriptions of the 13th and 12th centuries BCE as having settled in Egypt.[174] Other scholars rebut this, proposing that the Hebrews are mentioned in older texts of the 3rd Intermediate Period of Egypt (15th century BCE) as Shasu of *Yhw*.

Use as synonym for "Israelites"

In the Hebrew Bible, the term "Hebrew" is normally used by Israelites when speaking of themselves to foreigners, or is used by foreigners when speaking about Israelites.[175] In fact, the Torah in *parashat Lekh Lekha* ("go!" or "leave!", literally "go for you") calls Abraham *Avram Ha-Ivri* ("Abram the Hebrew"), which translates literally as "Abram the one who stands on the other side." [Gen. 14:13][176]

Figure 9: *Moses (l) and Aaron (r) lead the Jews across the Red Sea while pursued by Pharaoh. Fresco from the Dura-Europos synagogue in Syria, 244–256 CE*

Israelites are defined as the descendants of Jacob, son of Isaac, grandson of Abraham. Eber, an ancestor of Jacob (seven generations removed), is a distant ancestor of many people, including the Israelites, Ishmaelites, Edomites, Moabites, Ammonites, Midianites and Qahtanites.

According to the Jewish Encyclopedia the terms "Hebrews" and "Israelites" usually describe the same people, stating that they were called Hebrews before the conquest of the Land of Canaan and Israelites afterwards.[177] Professor Nadav Na'aman and others say that the use of the word "Hebrew" to refer to Israelites is rare and when used it is used "to Israelites in exceptional and precarious situations, such as migrants or slaves."

Use as synonym for "Jews"

By the Roman period, "Hebrews" could be used to designate the Jews, who use the Hebrew language.[178] The Epistle to the Hebrews was probably written for Jewish Christians.[179]

In some modern languages, including Armenian, Greek, Italian, Romanian, and many Slavic languages, the name *Hebrews* survives as the standard ethnonym for Jews, but in many other languages in which there exist both terms, it is considered derogatory to call modern Jews "Hebrews".Wikipedia:Citation needed Among certain left-wing or liberal circles of Judaic cultural lineage, the word "Hebrew" is used as an alternatively secular description of the Jewish people (e.g., Bernard Avishai's *The Hebrew Republic* or left-wing wishes for a "Hebrew-Arab" joint cultural republican state).

Use in Zionism

Beginning in the late 19th century, the term "Hebrew" became popular among secular Zionists; in this context the word alluded to the transformation of the Jews into a strong, independent, self-confident secular national group ("the New Jew") sought by classical Zionism. This use died out after the establishment of the state of Israel, when "Hebrew" was replaced with "Jew" or "Israeli".

References

- Jewish Encyclopedia[180]
- Jewish History Resource Center[181]

Bibliography

- *Ancient Judaism*, Max Weber, Free Press, 1967, <templatestyles src="Module:Citation/CS1/styles.css" />ISBN 0-02-934130-2

External links

- Media related to Hebrews at Wikimedia Commons

Israelites

<indicator name="pp-default"> 🔒 </indicator>

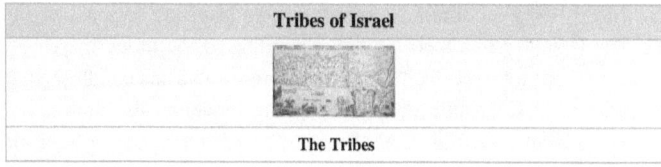

Tribes of Israel
The Tribes

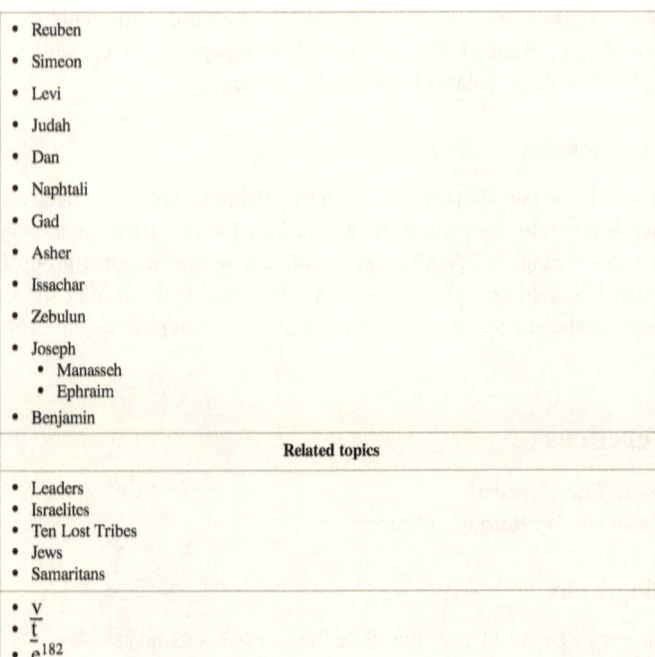

The **Israelites** (/ˈɪzriəlaɪts/; Hebrew: בני ישראל *Bnei Yisra'el*)[183] were a confederation of Iron Age Semitic-speaking tribes of the ancient Near East, who inhabited a part of Canaan during the tribal and monarchic periods.[184,185,186,187,188] According to the religious narrative of the Hebrew Bible, the Israelites' origin is traced back to the Biblical patriarchs and matriarchs Abraham and his wife Sarah, through their son Isaac and his wife Rebecca, and their son Jacob who was later called Israel, whence they derive their name, with his wives Leah and Rachel.

Modern archaeology has largely discarded the historicity of the religious narrative, with it being reframed as constituting an inspiring national myth narrative. The Israelites and their culture, according to the modern archaeological account, did not overtake the region by force, but instead branched out of the indigenous Canaanite peoples that long inhabited the Southern Levant, Syria, ancient Israel, and the Transjordan region[189] through the development of a distinct monolatristic—later cementing as monotheistic—religion centered on Yahweh, one of the Ancient Canaanite deities. The outgrowth of Yahweh-centric belief, along with a number of cultic practices, gradually gave rise to a distinct Israelite ethnic group, setting them apart from other Canaanites.[190,191,192]

Figure 10: *Mosaic of the 12 Tribes of Israel, from a synagogue wall in Jerusalem*

In the Hebrew Bible the term *Israelites* is used interchangeably with the term *Twelve Tribes of Israel*. Although related, the terms Hebrews, Israelites, and Jews are not interchangeable in all instances. "Israelites" (*Yisraelim*) refers specifically to the direct descendants of any of the sons of the patriarch Jacob (later called Israel), and his descendants as a people are also collectively called "Israel", including converts to their faith in worship of the god of Israel, Yahweh. "Hebrews" (*'Ivrim*), on the contrary, is used to denote the Israelites' immediate forebears who dwelt in the land of Canaan, the Israelites themselves, and the Israelites' ancient and modern descendants (including Jews and Samaritans). "Jews" (*Yehudim*) is used to denote the descendants of the Israelites who coalesced when the Tribe of Judah absorbed the remnants of various other Israelite tribes. Thus, for instance, Abraham was a Hebrew but he was not technically an Israelite nor a Jew, Jacob was both a Hebrew and the first Israelite but not a Jew, while David (as a member of the Tribe of Judah) was all three, a Hebrew, an Israelite, and a Judahite (*Yehudi*, Jew). A Samaritan, on the contrary, while being both a Hebrew and an Israelite, is not a Jew.

During the period of the divided monarchy "Israelites" was only used to refer to the inhabitants of the northern Kingdom of Israel, and it is only extended to cover the people of the southern Kingdom of Judah in post-exilic usage.[193]

Figure 11: *The Merneptah stele. While alternative translations exist, the majority of biblical archaeologists translate a set of hieroglyphs as Israel, representing the first instance of the name Israel in the historical record.*

The Israelites are the ethnic stock from which modern Jews and Samaritans originally trace their ancestry.[194,195,196] Modern Jews are named after and also descended from the southern Israelite Kingdom of Judah,[197,198,199,200,201] particularly the tribes of Judah, Benjamin and partially Levi.

Finally, in Judaism, the term "Israelite" is, broadly speaking, used to refer to a lay member of the Jewish ethnoreligious group, as opposed to the priestly orders of Kohanim and Levites. In texts of Jewish law such as the Mishnah and Gemara, the term יהודי (*Yehudi*), meaning Jew, is rarely used, and instead the ethnonym ישראלי (*Yisraeli*), or Israelite, is widely used to refer to Jews. Samaritans commonly refer to themselves and to Jews collectively as Israelites, and they describe themselves as the Israelite Samaritans.[202,203]

Etymology

The term *Israelite* is the English name for the descendants of the biblical patriarch Jacob in ancient times, which is derived from the Greek Ισραηλίτες,[204] which was used to translate the Biblical Hebrew term *b'nei yisrael*, יִשְׂרָאֵל, as either "sons of Israel" or "children of Israel".[205]

The name *Israel* first appears in the Hebrew Bible in Genesis 32:29[206]. It refers to the renaming of Jacob, who, according to the Bible, wrestled with an angel, who gave him a blessing and renamed him *Israel* because he had "striven with God and with men, and have prevailed". The Hebrew Bible etymologizes the name as from *yisra* "to prevail over" or "to struggle/wrestle with", and *el*, "God, the divine".[207,208]

The name *Israel* first appears in non-biblical sources c. 1209 BCE, in an inscription of the Egyptian pharaoh Merneptah. The inscription is very brief and says simply: "Israel is laid waste and his seed is not" (see below). The inscription refers to a people, not to an individual or a nation-state.

Terminology

In modern Hebrew, *b'nei yisrael* ("children of Israel") can denote the Jewish people at any time in history; it is typically used to emphasize Jewish ethnic identity. From the period of the Mishna (but probably used before that period) the term *Yisrael* ("an Israel") acquired an additional narrower meaning of Jews of legitimate birth other than Levites and Aaronite priests (*kohanim*). In modern Hebrew this contrasts with the term *Yisraeli* (English "Israeli"), a citizen of the modern State of Israel, regardless of religion or ethnicity.

The term *Hebrew* has Eber as an eponymous ancestor. It is used synonymously with "Israelites", or as an ethnolinguistic term for historical speakers of the Hebrew language in general.

The Greek term *Ioudaioi* (Jews) was an exonym originally referring to members of the Tribe of Judah, which formed the nucleus of the kingdom of Judah, and was later adopted as a self-designation by people in the diaspora who identified themselves as loyal to the God of Israel and the Temple in Jerusalem.[209,210,211,212]

The Samaritans, who claim descent from the tribes of Ephraim and Manasseh (plus Levi through Aaron for kohens), are named after the Israelite Kingdom of Samaria, but until modern times many Jewish authorities contested their claimed lineage, deeming them to have been conquered foreigners who were settled in the Land of Israel by the Assyrians, as was the typical Assyrian policy to obliterate national identities. Today, Jews and Samaritans both recognize each other as communities with an authentic Israelite origin.

The terms "Jews" and "Samaritans" largely replaced the title "Children of Israel"[213] as the commonly used ethnonym for each respective community.

Historical Israelites

Part of **a series** on the
History of Israel

Ancient Israel and Judah

- Natufian culture
- Prehistory
- Canaan
- Israelites
- United monarchy
- Northern Kingdom
- Kingdom of Judah
- Babylonian rule

Second Temple period (530 BCE–70 CE)

- Persian rule
- Hellenistic period
- Hasmonean dynasty
- Herodian dynasty
  - Kingdom
  - Tetrarchy
- Roman Judea

Middle Ages (70–1517)

- Roman Palaestina
- Byzantine Palaestina
  - Prima
  - Secunda
- Revolt against Constantius Gallus
- Samaritan revolts
- Revolt against Heraclius
- Caliphates
  - Filastin
  - Urdunn
- Kingdom of Jerusalem
- Ayyubid dynasty
- Mamluk Sultanate

Modern history (1517–1948)

- Ottoman rule
  - Eyalet
  - Mutasarrifate
- Old Yishuv
- Zionism
- OETA
- British mandate

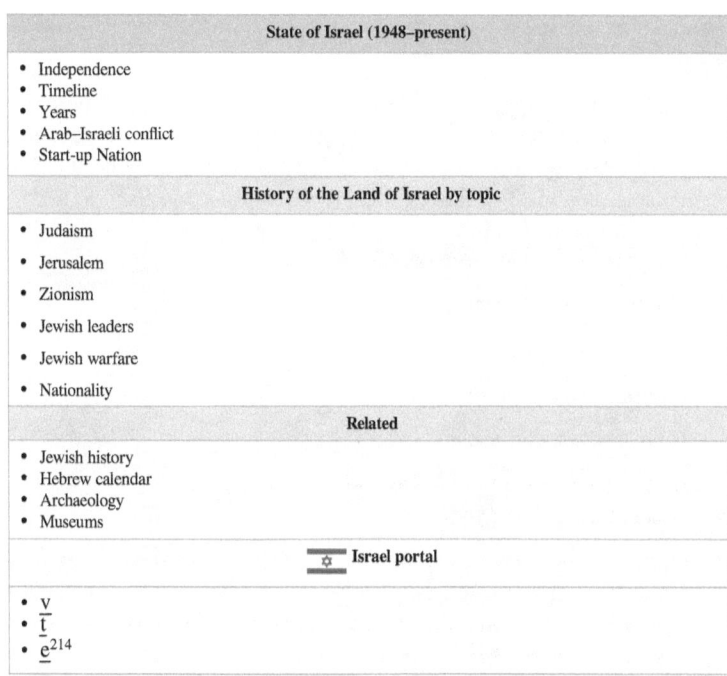

Several theories exist proposing the origins of the Israelites in raiding groups, infiltrating nomads or emerging from indigenous Canaanites driven from the wealthier urban areas by poverty to seek their fortunes in the highland.[215] Various, ethnically distinct groups of itinerant nomads such as the Habiru and Shasu recorded in Egyptian texts as active in Edom and Canaan could have been related to the later Israelites, which does not exclude the possibility that the majority may have had their origins in Canaan proper. The name Yahweh, the god of the later Israelites, may indicate connections with the region of Mount Seir in Edom.[216]

The prevailing academic opinion today is that the Israelites were a mixture of peoples predominantly indigenous to Canaan, although an Egyptian matrix of peoples may also have played a role in their ethnogenesis,[217,218] with an ethnic composition similar to that in Ammon, Edom and Moab,[219] and including Hapiru and Šośu.[220] The defining feature which marked them off from the surrounding societies was a staunch egalitarian organisation focused on Yahweh worship, rather than mere kinship.

The language of the Canaanites may perhaps be best described as an "archaic form of Hebrew, standing in much the same relationship to the Hebrew of the Old Testament as does the language of Chaucer to modern English." The

Canaanites were also the first people, as far as is known, to have used an alphabet.

The name Israel first appears c. 1209 BCE, at the end of the Late Bronze Age and the very beginning of the period archaeologists and historians call Iron Age I, on the Merneptah Stele raised by the Egyptian Pharaoh Merneptah. The inscription is very brief: <templatestyles src="Template:Quote/styles.css"/>

> *Plundered is Canaan with every evil,*
>
> *Carried off is Ashkelon,*
>
> *Seized upon is Gezer,*
>
> *Yeno^cam is made as that which does not exist*
>
> *Israel lies fallow, it has no seed;*
>
> *Ḥurru has become a widow because of Egypt.* UNIQ-ref-0-5d4cfb4109fe789c-QINU

As distinct from the cities named (Ashkelon, Gezer, Yenoam) which are written with a toponymic marker, Israel is written hieroglyphically with a demonymic determinative indicating that the reference is to a human group, variously located in central Palestine or the highlands of Samaria.[221]

Over the next two hundred years (the period of Iron Age I) the number of highland villages increased from 25 to over 300[21] and the settled population doubled to 40,000.[222] By the 10th century BCE a rudimentary state had emerged in the north-central highlands,[223] and in the 9th century this became a kingdom.[224] Settlement in the southern highlands was minimal from the 12th through the 10th centuries BCE, but a state began to emerge there in the 9th century,[225] and from 850 BCE onwards a series of inscriptions are evidence of a kingdom which its neighbours refer to as the "House of David."[226]

After the destruction of the Israelite kingdoms of Samaria and Judah in 720 and 586 BCE respectively,[227] the concepts of Jew and Samaritan gradually replaced Judahite and Israelite. When the Jews returned from the Babylonian captivity, the Hasmonean kingdom was establishedWikipedia:Accuracy dispute#Disputed statement in present-day Israel, consisting of three regions which were Judea, Samaria, and the Galilee. In the pre-exilic First Temple Period the political power of Judea was concentrated within the tribe of Judah, Samaria was dominated by the tribe of Ephraim and the House of Joseph, while the Galilee was associated with the tribe of Naphtali, the most eminent tribe of northern Israel.[228],[229] At the time of the Kingdom of Samaria, the

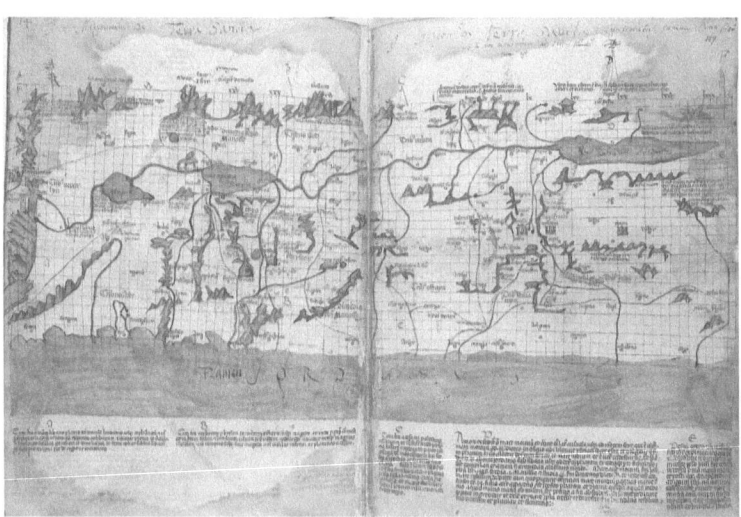

Figure 12: *Map of the Holy Land, Pietro Vesconte, 1321, showing the allotments of the tribes of Israel. Described by Adolf Erik Nordenskiöld as "the first non-Ptolemaic map of a definite country"*

Galilee was populated by northern tribes of Israel, but following the Babylonian exile the region became Jewish. During the Second Temple period relations between the Jews and Samaritans remained tense. In 120 BCE the Hasmonean king Yohanan Hyrcanos I destroyed the Samaritan temple on Mount Gerizim, due to the resentment between the two groups over a disagreement of whether Mount Moriah in Jerusalem or Mount Gerizim in Shechem was the actual site of the Aqedah, and the chosen place for the Holy Temple, a source of contention that had been growing since the two houses of the former united monarchy first split asunder in 930 BCE and which had finally exploded into warfare.Wikipedia:Accuracy dispute#Disputed statement 190 years after the destruction of the Samaritan Temple and the surrounding area of Shechem, the Roman general and future emperor Vespasian launched a military campaign to crush the Jewish revolt of 66 CE, which resulted in the destruction of the Jewish Temple in Jerusalem in 70 CE by his son Titus, and the subsequent exile of Jews from Judea and the Galilee in 135 CE following the Bar Kochba revolt.[230]

Biblical Israelites

The Israelite story begins with some of the culture heroes of the Jewish people, the Patriarchs. The Torah traces the Israelites to the patriarch Jacob, grandson

Figure 13: *Model of the Mishkan constructed under the auspices of Moses, in Timna Park, Israel*

of Abraham, who was renamed Israel after a mysterious incident in which he wrestles all night with God or an angel. Jacob's twelve sons (in order of birth), Reuben, Simeon, Levi, Judah, Dan, Naphtali, Gad, Asher, Issachar, Zebulun, Joseph and Benjamin, become the ancestors of twelve tribes, with the exception of Joseph, whose two sons Mannasseh and Ephraim, who were adopted by Jacob, become tribal eponyms (Genesis 48[231]).[232]

The mothers of Jacob's sons are:

- Leah: Reuben, Simeon, Levi, Judah, Issachar, Zebulun
- Rachel: Joseph (Ephraim and Menasseh), Benjamin
- Bilhah (Rachel's maid): Dan, Naphtali
- Zilpah (Leah's maid): Gad, Asher (Genesis 35:22–26[233])

Jacob and his sons are forced by famine to go down into Egypt, although Joseph was already there, as he had been sold into slavery while young. When they arrive they and their families are 70 in number, but within four generations they have increased to 600,000 men of fighting age, and the Pharaoh of Egypt, alarmed, first enslaves them and then orders the death of all male Hebrew children. A woman from the tribe of Levi hides her child, places him in a woven basket, and sends him down the Nile river. He is named Mosheh, or Moses, by the Egyptians who find him. Being a Hebrew baby, they award a Hebrew woman the task of raising him, the mother of Moses volunteers, and the child and his mother are reunited.[234,235]

At the age of forty Moses kills an Egyptian, after he sees him beating a Hebrew to death, and escapes as a fugitive into the Sinai desert, where he is taken in by the Midianites and marries Zipporah, the daughter of the Midianite priest Jethro. When he is eighty years old, Moses is tending a herd of sheep in solitude on Mount Sinai when he sees a desert shrub that is burning but is not consumed. The God of Israel calls to Moses from the fire and reveals his name, Yahweh (from the Hebrew root word 'HWH' meaning to exist), and tells Moses that he is being sent to Pharaoh to bring the people of Israel out of Egypt.[236]

Yahweh tells Moses that if Pharaoh refuses to let the Hebrews go to say to Pharaoh "Thus says Yahweh: Israel is my son, my first-born and I have said to you: Let my son go, that he may serve me, and you have refused to let him go. Behold, I will slay your son, your first-born". Moses returns to Egypt and tells Pharaoh that he must let the Hebrew slaves go free. Pharaoh refuses and Yahweh strikes the Egyptians with a series of horrific plagues, wonders, and catastrophes, after which Pharaoh relents and banishes the Hebrews from Egypt. Moses leads the Israelites out of bondage[237] toward the Red Sea, but Pharaoh changes his mind and arises to massacre the fleeing Hebrews. Pharaoh finds them by the sea shore and attempts to drive them into the ocean with his chariots and drown them.[238]

Yahweh causes the Red Sea to part and the Hebrews pass through on dry land into the Sinai. After the Israelites escape from the midst of the sea, Yahweh causes the ocean to close back in on the pursuing Egyptian army, drowning them to death. In the desert Yahweh feeds them with manna that accumulates on the ground with the morning dew. They are led by a column of cloud, which ignites at night and becomes a pillar of fire to illuminate the way, southward through the desert until they come to Mount Sinai. The twelve tribes of Israel encamp around the mountain, and on the third day Mount Sinai begins to smolder, then catches fire, and Yahweh speaks the Ten Commandments from the midst of the fire to all the Israelites, from the top of the mountain.[239]

Moses ascends biblical Mount Sinai and fasts for forty days while he writes down the Torah as Yahweh dictates, beginning with Bereshith and the creation of the universe and earth.[240,241] He is shown the design of the Mishkan and the Ark of the Covenant, which Bezalel is given the task of building. Moses descends from the mountain forty days later with the Sefer Torah he wrote, and with two rectangular lapis lazuli[242] tablets, into which Yahweh had carved the Ten Commandments in Paleo–Hebrew. In his absence, Aaron has constructed an image of Yahweh,[243] depicting him as a young Golden Calf, and has presented it to the Israelites, declaring "Behold O Israel, this is your god who brought you out of the land of Egypt". Moses smashes the two tablets and grinds the golden calf into dust, then throws the dust into a stream of water flowing out of Mount Sinai, and forces the Israelites to drink from it.[244]

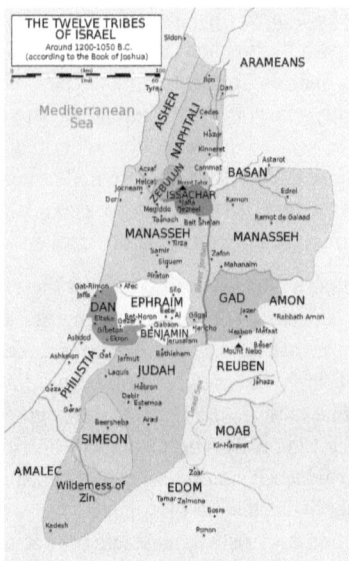

Figure 14: *Map of the twelve tribes of Israel (before the move of Dan to the north), based on the Book of Joshua*

Moses ascends Mount Sinai for a second time and Yahweh passes before him and says: 'Yahweh, Yahweh, a god of compassion, and showing favor, slow to anger, and great in kindness and in truth, who shows kindness to the thousandth generation, forgiving wrongdoing and injustice and wickedness, but will by no means clear the guilty, causing the consequences of the parent's wrongdoing to befall their children, and their children's children, to the third and fourth generation'[245] Moses then fasts for another forty days while Yahweh carves the Ten Commandments into a second set of stone tablets. After the tablets are completed, light emanates from the face of Moses for the rest of his life, causing him to wear a veil so he does not frighten people.[246]

Moses descends Mount Sinai and the Israelites agree to be the chosen people of Yahweh and follow all the laws of the Torah. Moses prophesies if they forsake the Torah, Yahweh will exile them for the total number of years they did not observe the shmita.[247] Bezael constructs the Ark of the Covenant and the Mishkan, where the presence of Yahweh dwells on earth in the Holy of Holies, above the Ark of the Covenant, which houses the Ten Commandments. Moses sends spies to scout out the Land of Canaan, and the Israelites are commanded to go up and conquer the land, but they refuse, due to their fear of warfare and violence. In response, Yahweh condemns the entire generation, including

Moses, who is condemned for striking the rock at Meribah, to exile and death in the Sinai desert.[248]

Before Moses dies he gives a speech to the Israelites where he paraphrases a summary of the mizwoth given to them by Yahweh, and recites a prophetic song called the Ha'azinu. Moses prophesies that if the Israelites disobey the Torah, Yahweh will cause a global exile in addition to the minor one prophesied earlier at Mount Sinai, but at the end of days Yahweh will gather them back to Israel from among the nations when they turn back to the Torah with zeal.[249] The events of the Israelite exodus and their sojourn in the Sinai are memorialized in the Jewish and Samaritan festivals of Passover and Sukkoth, and the giving of the Torah in the Jewish celebration of Shavuoth.[250]

Forty years after the Exodus, following the death of the generation of Moses, a new generation, led by Joshua, enters Canaan and takes possession of the land in accordance with the promise made to Abraham by Yahweh. Land is allocated to the tribes by lottery. Eventually the Israelites ask for a king, and Yahweh gives them Saul. David, the youngest (divinely favored) son of Jesse of Bethlehem would succeed Saul. Under David the Israelites establish the united monarchy, and under David's son Solomon they construct the Holy Temple in Jerusalem, using the 400-year-old materials of the Mishkan, where Yahweh continues to tabernacle himself among them. On the death of Solomon and reign of his son, Rehoboam, the kingdom is divided in two.[251]

The kings of the northern Kingdom of Samaria are uniformly bad, permitting the worship of other gods and failing to enforce the worship of Yahweh alone, and so Yahweh eventually allows them to be conquered and dispersed among the peoples of the earth; and strangers rule over their remnant in the northern land. In Judah some kings are good and enforce the worship of Yahweh alone, but many are bad and permit other gods, even in the Holy Temple itself, and at length Yahweh allows Judah to fall to her enemies, the people taken into captivity in Babylon, the land left empty and desolate, and the Holy Temple itself destroyed.[252]

Yet despite these events Yahweh does not forget his people, but sends Cyrus, king of Persia to deliver them from bondage. The Israelites are allowed to return to Judah and Benjamin, the Holy Temple is rebuilt, the priestly orders restored, and the service of sacrifice resumed. Through the offices of the sage Ezra, Israel is constituted as a holy nation, bound by the Torah and holding itself apart from all other peoples.[253]

Genetics

According to the bible Abraham came from Ur of the Chaldeans[254] and the Israelites are descended from the Chaldaeans.[255] Chaldea was a region of ancient Babylonia in what is now southeastern Iraq, the Chaldeans were Semites, a group of people who spoke language related to Aramic.[256]

The study of (Al-Zahery) suggests the eastern side of fertile crescent as the homeland of the Y-chromosome haplogroup J, furthermore J(xM172) seems to have had its center in Iraq.[257]

In 2000, M. Hammer, et al. conducted a study on 1371 men and definitively established that part of the paternal gene pool of Jewish communities in Europe, North Africa and Middle East came from a common Middle East ancestral population.[258] In another study (Nebel) noted; "In comparison with data available from other relevant populations in the region, Jews were found to be much more closely related to groups in the north of the Fertile Crescent (Kurds, Turks, and Armenians) than to their Arab neighbors."[259]

Bibliography

<templatestyles src="Refbegin/styles.css" />

- Albertz, Rainer (1994) [Vandenhoeck & Ruprecht 1992]. *A History of Israelite Religion, Volume I: From the Beginnings to the End of the Monarchy*[260]. Westminster John Knox Press. ISBN 978-0-664-22719-7.<templatestyles src="Module:Citation/CS1/styles.css"></templatestyles>
- Albertz, Rainer (1994) [Vanderhoek & Ruprecht 1992]. *A History of Israelite Religion, Volume II: From the Exile to the Maccabees*[261]. Westminster John Knox Press. ISBN 978-0-664-22720-3.<templatestyles src="Module:Citation/CS1/styles.css"></templatestyles>
- Albertz, Rainer (2003a). *Israel in Exile: The History and Literature of the Sixth Century B.C.E.*[262] Society of Biblical Literature. ISBN 978-1-58983-055-4.<templatestyles src="Module:Citation/CS1/styles.css"></templatestyles>
- Albertz, Rainer; Becking, Bob, eds. (2003b). *Yahwism After the Exile: Perspectives on Israelite Religion in the Persian Era*[263]. Koninklijke Van Gorcum. ISBN 978-90-232-3880-5.<templatestyles src="Module:Citation/CS1/styles.css"></templatestyles>
- Amit, Yaira; et al., eds. (2006). *Essays on Ancient Israel in its Near Eastern Context: A Tribute to Nadav Na'aman*[264]. Eisenbrauns. ISBN 978-1-57506-128-3.<templatestyles src="Module:Citation/CS1/styles.css"></templatestyles>

- Avery-Peck, Alan; et al., eds. (2003). *The Blackwell Companion to Judaism*[265]. Blackwell. ISBN 978-1-57718-059-3.
- Barstad, Hans M. (2008). *History and the Hebrew Bible*[266]. Mohr Siebeck. ISBN 978-3-16-149809-1.
- Becking, Bob, ed. (2001). *Only One God? Monotheism in Ancient Israel and the Veneration of the Goddess Asherah*[267]. Sheffield Academic Press. ISBN 978-1-84127-199-6.
- Becking, Bob. *Law as Expression of Religion (Ezra 7–10)*.
- Becking, Bob; Korpel, Marjo Christina Annette, eds. (1999). *The Crisis of Israelite Religion: Transformation of Religious Tradition in Exilic and Post-Exilic Times*[268]. Brill. ISBN 978-90-04-11496-8. Niehr, Herbert. *Religio-Historical Aspects of the Early Post-Exilic Period*.
- Bedford, Peter Ross (2001). *Temple Restoration in Early Achaemenid Judah*[269]. Brill. ISBN 978-90-04-11509-5.
- Ben-Sasson, H.H. (1976). *A History of the Jewish People*. Harvard University Press. ISBN 0-674-39731-2.
- Blenkinsopp, Joseph (1988). *Ezra-Nehemiah: A Commentary*[270]. Eerdmans. ISBN 978-0-664-22186-7.
- Blenkinsopp, Joseph; Lipschits, Oded, eds. (2003). *Judah and the Judeans in the Neo-Babylonian Period*[271]. Eisenbrauns. ISBN 978-1-57506-073-6.
- Blenkinsopp, Joseph. *Bethel in the Neo-Babylonian Period*.
- Blenkinsopp, Joseph (2009). *Judaism, the First Phase: The Place of Ezra and Nehemiah in the Origins of Judaism*[272]. Eerdmans. ISBN 978-0-8028-6450-5.
- Brett, Mark G. (2002). *Ethnicity and the Bible*[273]. Brill. ISBN 978-0-391-04126-4.
- Bright, John (2000). *A History of Israel*[274]. Westminster John Knox Press. ISBN 978-0-664-22068-6.

- Cahill, Jane M. *Jerusalem at the Time of the United Monarchy*.
- Coogan, Michael D., ed. (1998). *The Oxford History of the Biblical World*[275]. Oxford University Press. ISBN 978-0-19-513937-2.
- Coogan, Michael D. (2009). *A Brief Introduction to the Old Testament*[276]. Oxford University Press. ISBN 978-0-19-533272-8.
- Coote, Robert B.; Whitelam, Keith W. (1986). "The Emergence of Israel: Social Transformation and State Formation Following the Decline in Late Bronze Age Trade". *Semeia* (37): 107–47.
- Davies, Philip R. *The Origin of Biblical Israel*.
- Davies, Philip R. (1992). *In Search of Ancient Israel*[277]. Sheffield. ISBN 978-1-85075-737-5.
- Davies, Philip R. (2009). "The Origin of Biblical Israel"[278]. *Journal of Hebrew Scriptures*. **9** (47). Archived from the original[279] on May 28, 2008.
- Day, John (2002). *Yahweh and the Gods and Goddesses of Canaan*[280]. Sheffield Academic Press. ISBN 978-0-8264-6830-7.
- Dever, William (2001). *What Did the Biblical Writers Know, and When Did They Know It?*[281]. Eerdmans. ISBN 978-0-8028-2126-3.
- Dever, William (2003). *Who Were the Early Israelites and Where Did They Come From?*[282]. Eerdmans. ISBN 978-0-8028-0975-9.
- Dever, William (2005). *Did God Have a Wife?: Archaeology and Folk Religion in Ancient Israel*[283]. Eerdmans. ISBN 978-0-8028-2852-1.
- Dijkstra, Meindert. *El the God of Israel, Israel the People of YHWH: On the Origins of Ancient Israelite Yahwism*.
- Dijkstra, Meindert. *I Have Blessed You by YHWH of*

Samaria and His Asherah: Texts with Religious Elements from the Soil Archive of Ancient Israel.
- Dunn, James D.G; Rogerson, John William, eds. (2003). *Eerdmans commentary on the Bible*[284]. Eerdmans. ISBN 978-0-8028-3711-0.
- Edelman, Diana. *Ethnicity and Early Israel.*
- Edelman, Diana, ed. (1995). *The Triumph of Elohim: From Yahwisms to Judaisms*[285]. Kok Pharos. ISBN 978-90-390-0124-0.
- Finkelstein, Neil Asher; Silberman (2001). *The Bible Unearthed*[286]. ISBN 978-0-7432-2338-6.
- Finkelstein, Israel; Mazar, Amihay; Schmidt, Brian B. (2007). *The Quest for the Historical Israel*[287]. Society of Biblical Literature. ISBN 978-1-58983-277-0.
- Gnuse, Robert Karl (1997). *No Other Gods: Emergent Monotheism in Israel*[288]. Sheffield Academic Press. ISBN 978-1-85075-657-6.
- Golden, Jonathan Michael (2004a). *Ancient Canaan and Israel: An Introduction*[289]. Oxford University Press. ISBN 978-0-19-537985-3.
- Golden, Jonathan Michael (2004b). *Ancient Canaan and Israel: New Perspectives*[290]. ABC-CLIO. ISBN 978-1-57607-897-6.
- Goodison, Lucy; Morris, Christine (1998). *Goddesses in Early Israelite Religion in Ancient Goddesses: The Myths and the Evidence*[291]. University of Wisconsin Press. ISBN 978-90-04-10410-5.
- Grabbe, Lester L. (2004). *A History of the Jews and Judaism in the Second Temple Period*[292]. T&T Clark International. ISBN 978-0-567-04352-8.
- Grabbe, Lester L., ed. (2008). *Israel in Transition: From Late Bronze II to Iron IIa (c. 1250–850 B.C.E.)*[293]. T&T Clark International. ISBN 978-0-567-02726-9.

- Greifenhagen, F.V (2002). *Egypt on the Pentateuch's ideological map*[294]. Sheffield Academic Press. ISBN 978-0-8264-6211-4.
- Hesse, Brian; Wapnish, Paula (1997). "Can Pig Remains Be Used for Ethnic Diagnosis in the Ancient Near East?". In Silberman, Neil Asher; Small, David B. *The Archaeology of Israel: Constructing the Past, Interpreting the Present*[295]. Sheffield Academic Press. ISBN 1-85075-650-3.
- Joffe, Alexander H. (2006). *The Rise of Secondary States in the Iron Age Levant*[296]. University of Arizona Press.
- Killebrew, Ann E. (2005). *Biblical Peoples and Ethnicity: An Archaeological Study of Egyptians, Canaanites, and Early Israel, 1300–1100 B.C.E.*[297] Society of Biblical Literature. ISBN 978-1-58983-097-4.
- King, Philip J.; Stager, Lawrence E. (2001). *Life in Biblical Israel*[298]. Westminster John Knox Press. ISBN 0-664-22148-3.
- Kottsieper, Ingo. *And They Did Not Care to Speak Yehudit.*
- Kuhrt, Amélie (1995). *The Ancient Near East c. 3000–330 C*[299]. Routledge. ISBN 978-0-415-16763-5.
- Lehman, Gunnar. *The United Monarchy in the Countryside.*
- Lemaire, Andre. *Nabonidus in Arabia and Judea During the Neo-Babylonian Period.*
- Lemche, Niels Peter (1998). *The Israelites in History and Tradition*[300]. Westminster John Knox Press. ISBN 978-0-664-22727-2.
- Levy, Thomas E. (1998). *The Archaeology of Society in the Holy Land*[301]. Continuum International Publishing. ISBN 978-0-8264-6996-0.
- LaBianca, Øystein S.; Younker, Randall W. *The Kingdoms of Ammon, Moab and Edom: The Archaeology of Society in Late Bronze/Iron Age Transjordan (c. 1400–500 CE).*
- Lipschits, Oded (2005). *The Fall and Rise of Jerusalem*[302].

Eisenbrauns. ISBN 978-1-57506-095-8.
- Lipschits, Oded; et al., eds. (2006). *Judah and the Judeans in the Fourth Century B.C.E*[303]. Eisenbrauns. ISBN 978-1-57506-130-6.
- Lipschits, Oded; Vanderhooft, David. *Yehud Stamp Impressions in the Fourth Century B.C.E.*
- Mazar, Amihay. *The Divided Monarchy: Comments on Some Archaeological Issues.*
- Markoe, Glenn (2000). *Phoenicians*[304]. University of California Press. ISBN 978-0-520-22614-2.
- Mays, James Luther; et al., eds. (1995). *Old Testament Interpretation*[305]. T&T Clarke. ISBN 978-0-567-29289-6.
- Miller, J. Maxwell. *The Middle East and Archaeology.*
- McNutt, Paula (1999). *Reconstructing the Society of Ancient Israel*[306]. Westminster John Knox Press. ISBN 978-0-664-22265-9.
- Merrill, Eugene H. (1995). "The Late Bronze/Early Iron Age Transition and the Emergence of Israel". *Bibliotheca Sacra*. **152** (606): 145–62.
- Middlemas, Jill Anne (2005). *The Troubles of Templeless Judah*[307]. Oxford University Press. ISBN 978-0-19-928386-6.
- Miller, James Maxwell; Hayes, John Haralson (1986). *A History of Ancient Israel and Judah*[308]. Westminster John Knox Press. ISBN 0-664-21262-X.
- Miller, Robert D. (2005). *Chieftains of the Highland Clans: A History of Israel in the 12th and 11th Centuries B.C.*[309] Eerdmans. ISBN 978-0-8028-0988-9.
- Murphy, Frederick J. R. *Second Temple Judaism.*
- Nodet, Étienne (1999) [Editions du Cerf 1997]. *A Search for the Origins of Judaism: From Joshua to the Mishnah*[310]. Sheffield

- Academic Press. ISBN 978-1-85075-445-9.
- Pitkänen, Pekka (2004). "Ethnicity, Assimilation and the Israelite Settlement"[311] (PDF). *Tyndale Bulletin.* **55** (2): 161–82. Archived from the original[312] (PDF) on July 17, 2011.
- Rogerson, John William. *Deuteronomy.*
- Silberman, Neil Asher; Small, David B., eds. (1997). *The Archaeology of Israel: Constructing the Past, Interpreting the Present*[313]. Sheffield Academic Press. ISBN 978-1-85075-650-7.
- Smith, Mark S. (2001). *Untold Stories: The Bible and Ugaritic Studies in the Twentieth Century.* Hendrickson Publishers.
- Smith, Mark S.; Miller, Patrick D. (2002) [Harper & Row 1990]. *The Early History of God*[314]. Eerdmans. ISBN 978-0-8028-3972-5.
- Soggin, Michael J. (1998). *An Introduction to the History of Israel and Judah*[315]. Paideia. ISBN 978-0-334-02788-1.
- Stager, Lawrence E. *Forging an Identity: The Emergence of Ancient Israel.*
- Thompson, Thomas L. (1992). *Early History of the Israelite People*[316]. Brill. ISBN 978-90-04-09483-3.
- Van der Toorn, Karel (1996). *Family Religion in Babylonia, Syria, and Israel*[291]. Brill. ISBN 978-90-04-10410-5.
- Van der Toorn, Karel; Becking, Bob; Van der Horst, Pieter Willem (1999). *Dictionary of Deities and Demons in the Bible*[317] (2d ed.). Koninklijke Brill. ISBN 978-90-04-11119-6.
- Tubb, Jonathan N. (1998). *Canaanites*[318]. University of Oklahoma Press. ISBN 0-8061-3108-X.
- Vaughn, Andrew G.; Killebrew, Ann E., eds. (1992). *Jerusalem in Bible and Archaeology: The First Temple Period*[319]. Sheffield. ISBN 978-1-58983-066-0.

- Wylen, Stephen M. (1996). *The Jews in the Time of Jesus: An Introduction*[320]. Paulist Press. ISBN 978-0-8091-3610-0.<templatestyles src="Module:Citation/CS1/styles.css"></templatestyles>
- Zevit, Ziony (2001). *The Religions of Ancient Israel: A Synthesis of Parallactic Approaches*[321]. Continuum. ISBN 978-0-8264-6339-5.<templatestyles src="Module:Citation/CS1/styles.css"></templatestyles>

Biblical judges

שופטים
Judges in the Bible
Italics indicate individuals not explicitly described as judges
Book of Joshua
• *Joshua*
Book of Judges
• Othniel • Ehud • Shamgar • Deborah • Gideon • *Abimelech* • Tola • Jair • Jephthah • Ibzan • Elon • Abdon • Samson
First Book of Samuel
• Eli • Samuel
• v • t • e[322]

The **biblical judges**[323] are described in the Hebrew Bible, and mostly in the Book of Judges, as people who served roles as military leaders in times of crisis, in the period before an Israelite monarchy was established.

Figure 15: *The judge Shamgar slaughters 600 men with an ox goad. From a medieval German manuscript.*

Role

A cyclical pattern is regularly recounted in the Book of Judges to show the need for the various judges: apostasy of the Israelite people, hardship brought on as punishment from God, crying out to the Lord for rescue.[324]Wikipedia:Citing sources

The story of the judges seems to describe successive individuals, each from a different tribe of Israel, described as chosen by God to rescue the people from their enemies and establish justice.

While *judge* is the closest literal translation of the Hebrew term used in the Masoretic text, the position as described is more one of unelected non-hereditary leadership than that of legal pronouncement. However, Cyrus H. Gordon argued that they may have come from among the hereditary leaders of the fighting, landed and ruling aristocracy, like the kings (*basileis*) in Homer.[325] Coogan says that they were most likely tribal or local leaders, contrary to the Deuteronomistic historian's portrayal of them as leaders of all of Israel,[326] but Malamat pointed out that in the text, their authority is described as being recognized by local groups or tribes beyond their own.[327]

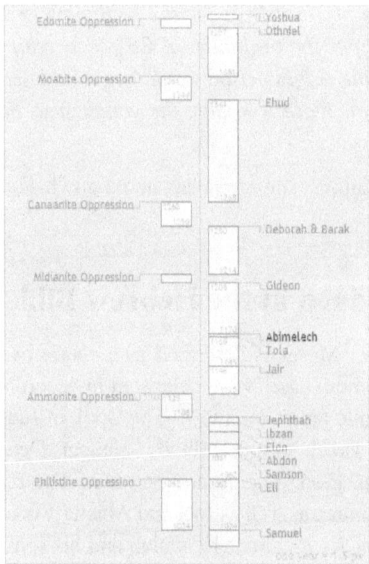

Figure 16: *Timeline of biblical judges (one interpretation)*

Historicity and timeline

The biblical scholar Kenneth Kitchen argues that, from the conquest of Canaan by Joshua until the formation of the first Kingdom of Israel and Judah (c. 1150–1025 BCE), the Israelite tribes may have formed a loose confederation. In this conception, no central government would have existed but in times of crisis, the people would have been led by *ad hoc* chieftains, known as judges (*shoftim*).[328] Wikipedia:Citing sources However, some scholars are uncertain whether such a role existed in ancient Israel.[329]

Working with the chronology in *Judges*, Payne points out that although the timescale of Judges is indicated by Jephthah's statement (Judges 11:26) that Israel had occupied the land for around 300 years, some of the judges overlapped one another. Noting that Deborah's victory has been confirmed as taking place in 1216 from archaeology undertaken at Hazor, he suggests that the period may have lasted from c. 1382 to c. 1063.[330]

Bill T. Arnold and H. G. M. Williamson wrote that if <templatestyles src="Template:Quote/styles.css"/>

> all the figures given in Judges (years of oppression, years the judges led Israel, years of peace achieved by the judges) are treated as consecutive, then the total duration of the events described in Judges is 410 years. If

we accept a date of 1000 BCE for the beginning of David's reign over all Israel, which puts the beginning of Eli's leadership of Israel at about 1100 BCE, then the judges period would begin no later than 1510 BCE – impossible even for those who date the conquest to the fifteenth century BCE[331]

There is also doubt among some scholars about any historicity of the Book of Judges.[332]

Judges mentioned in the Hebrew Bible

In the Hebrew Bible, Moses is described as a *shofet* over the Israelites and appoints others to whom cases were delegated in accordance with the advice of Jethro, his Midianite father-in-law.[333] The Book of Judges mentions twelve leaders who judged Israel: Othniel, Ehud, Shamgar, Deborah, Gideon, Tola, Jair, Jephthah, Ibzan, Elon, Abdon, and Samson. The First Book of Samuel mentions Eli and Samuel, as well as Joel and Abiah (two sons of Samuel). The First Book of Chronicles mentions Kenaniah and his sons. The Second Book of Chronicles mentions Amariah and Zebadiah (son of Ishmael).

The biblical text does not generally describe these leaders as "a judge", but says that they "judged Israel", using the verb שָׁפַט (*š-f-t*).[334] Wikipedia:Citing sources Thus, Othniel "judged Israel" (Judges 3:10), Tola "judged Israel twenty-three years" (Judges 10:2), and Jair judged Israel twenty-two years (Judges 10:3).

References

Bibliography

<templatestyles src="Refbegin/styles.css" />

Arnold, Bill T.; Williamson, H. G. M. (2005). *Dictionary of the Old Testament: Historical Books*. Downers Grove, Illinois: InterVarsity Press. ISBN 978-0-8308-1782-5.<templatestyles src="Module:Citation/CS1/styles.css"></templatestyles>

Boling, Robert G.; Nelson, Richard D. (2006). "Judges". In Attridge, Harold W.; Meeks, Wayne A. *The HarperCollins Study Bible* (rev. ed.). HarperCollins Publishers.<templatestyles src="Module:Citation/CS1/styles.css"></templatestyles>

Brettler, Marc Zvi (2002). *The Book of Judges*. London: Routledge. ISBN 978-0-415-16216-6.<templatestyles src="Module:Citation/CS1/styles.css"></templatestyles>

Coogan, Michael D. (2009). *A Brief Introduction to the Old Testament*. New York: Oxford University Press. ISBN 978-0-19-533272-8.<templatestyles src="Module:Citation/CS1/styles.css"></templatestyles>

Davies, Philip R. (2006) [1992]. *In Search of "Ancient Israel": A Study in Biblical Origins*. London: Continuum. ISBN 978-1-85075-737-5.<templatestyles src="Module:Citation/CS1/styles.css"></templatestyles>

Drum, Walter (1910). "Judges". In Herbermann, Charles G.; Pace, Edward A.; Pallen, Condé B.; Shahan, Thomas J.; Wynne, John J. *Catholic Encyclopedia*. **8**. New York: Encyclopedia Press (published 1913). pp. 547–549.<templatestyles src="Module:Citation/CS1/styles.css"></templatestyles>
This article incorporates text from this public-domain publication.

Gordon, Cyrus H. (1962). *Greek and Hebrew Civilizations*.<templatestyles src="Module:Citation/CS1/styles.css"></templatestyles>

Hauser, Alan J. (1975). "The 'Minor Judges': A Re-Evaluation". *Journal of Biblical Literature*. **94** (2): 190–200. doi: 10.2307/3265729[335]. ISSN 0021-9231[336].<templatestyles src="Module:Citation/CS1/styles.css"></templatestyles>

Kitchen, K. A. (2003). *On the Reliability of the Old Testament*. Grand Rapids, Michigan: William B. Eerdmans Publishing Company. ISBN 978-0-8028-4960-1.<templatestyles src="Module:Citation/CS1/styles.css"></templatestyles>

Malamat, A. (1971). Mazor, Benjamin, ed. *Judges*. Givatayim, Israel: Rutgers University Press. pp. 129–163.<templatestyles src="Module:Citation/CS1/styles.css"></templatestyles>

Payne, J. P. (1996). "Book of Judges". In Marshall, I. Howard; Millard, A. R.; Packer, J. I.; Wiseman, D. J. *New Bible Dictionary* (3rd ed.). Leicester, England: Inter-Varsity Press. ISBN 978-0-8308-1439-8.<templatestyles src="Module:Citation/CS1/styles.css"></templatestyles>

Thompson, Thomas L. (2000). *Early History of the Israelite People: From the Written & Archaeological Sources*. Leiden, Netherlands: Brill. ISBN 978-90-04-11943-7.<templatestyles src="Module:Citation/CS1/styles.css"></templatestyles>

Further reading

<templatestyles src="Refbegin/styles.css" />

Wolf, C. U. (1962). "Judge". *The Interpreter's Dictionary of the Bible*. Abingdon Press.<templatestyles src="Module:Citation/CS1/styles.css"></templatestyles>

Israel and Judah (Iron Age II)

Kingdom of Israel (united monarchy)

The **United Monarchy** (Hebrew: הממלכה המאוחדת) is the name given to the Israelite[337] </ref> kingdom of Israel and Judah, during the reigns of Saul, David and Solomon, as depicted in the Hebrew Bible. This is traditionally dated between 1050 BCE and 930 BCE. On the succession of Solomon's son, Rehoboam, around 930 BCE, the biblical account reports that the country split into two kingdoms: the Kingdom of Israel (including the cities of Shechem and Samaria) in the north and the Kingdom of Judah (containing Jerusalem) in the south.

In contemporary scholarship the united monarchy is generally held to be a literary construction and not a historical reality, pointing to the lack of archaeological evidence. Some scholars argue that there is historical evidence to support its existence. It is generally accepted that a "House of David" existed, but many believe that David could have only been the monarch or chieftain of Judah, which was likely small, and that the northern kingdom was a separate development. There are some dissenters to this view.

Sources

According to standard source criticism, a number of distinct source texts were spliced together to produce the current Books of Samuel. The most prominent in the early parts of the first book are the pro-monarchical source and the anti-monarchical source. In identifying these two sources, two separate accounts can be reconstructed. The anti-monarchical source describes

Figure 17: *Map of the Kingdom of Israel as described in the Hebrew Bible around the narrative time of David and Saul (vassal states and defeated kingdoms in red)*

Samuel as having thoroughly routed the Philistines, yet begrudgingly accepting the people's demand for a ruler, subsequently appointing Saul by cleromancy.Wikipedia:Citation needed

The pro-monarchical source describes the divinely appointed birth of Saul (a single word being changed by a later editor so that it referred to Samuel instead), and his leading of an army to victory over the Ammonites, resulted in the clamouring of the people for him to lead them against the Philistines, whereupon he is appointed king.

Textual critics also point to disparities in the account of David's rise to power as indicative of separate threads being merged later to create a Golden Age of a united monarchy. David is thought by scholars to have been a ruler in Judah, while Israel, comparatively immense and highly developed, continued unfettered. Modern archaeology also supports this view.

Most scholars believe the Books of Samuel exhibit too many anachronisms to have been a contemporary account. For example, there is mention of later armor (1 Samuel 17:4–7, 38–39; 25:13), use of camels (1 Samuel 30:17), cavalry (as distinct from chariotry) (1 Samuel 13:5, 2 Samuel 1:6), and iron picks and axes (as though they were common) (2 Samuel 12:31). The historicity of the conquest described in the Book of Samuel is not attested, and many scholars regard this conquest as legendary in origin, particularly given the lack of evidence for the battles described involving the destruction of the Canaanite peoples. Most scholars believe that Samuel was compiled in the 8th century BCE (rather than the 10th century when most of the events described take place) based on both historical and legendary sources, primarily serving to fill the gap in Israelite history after the events described in Deuteronomy. This gap in the historical record is characteristic of the Late Bronze Age collapse; cultural memories of times before the disaster often became embellished as stories of a "lost golden age", as in the Trojan Epic Cycle.Wikipedia:Citation needed

Biblical narrative
Origin

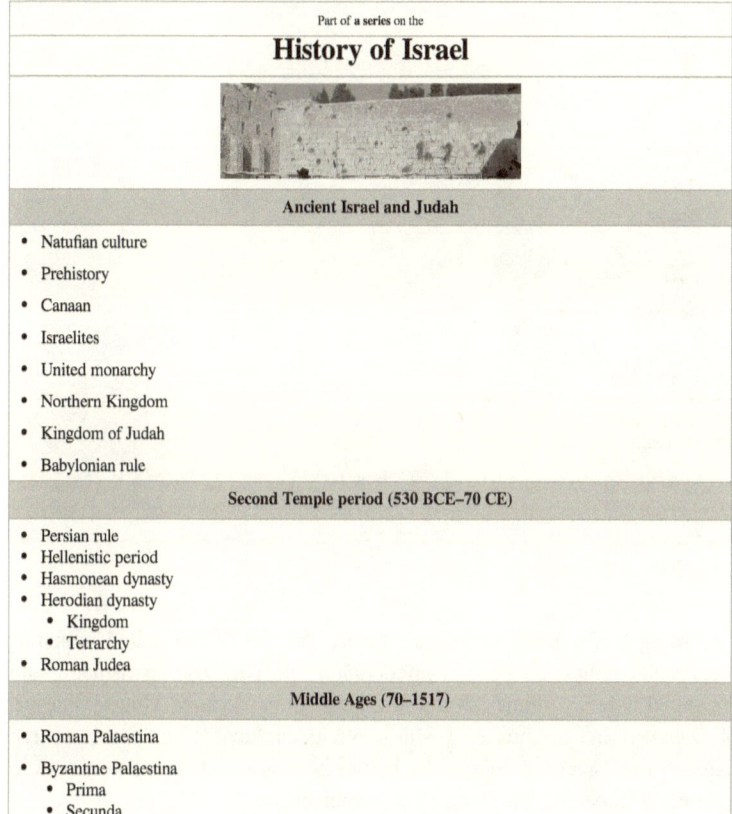

Part of a series on the
History of Israel
Ancient Israel and Judah
• Natufian culture • Prehistory • Canaan • Israelites • United monarchy • Northern Kingdom • Kingdom of Judah • Babylonian rule
Second Temple period (530 BCE–70 CE)

• Persian rule
• Hellenistic period
• Hasmonean dynasty
• Herodian dynasty
  • Kingdom
  • Tetrarchy
• Roman Judea

Middle Ages (70–1517)

• Roman Palaestina
• Byzantine Palaestina
  • Prima
  • Secunda

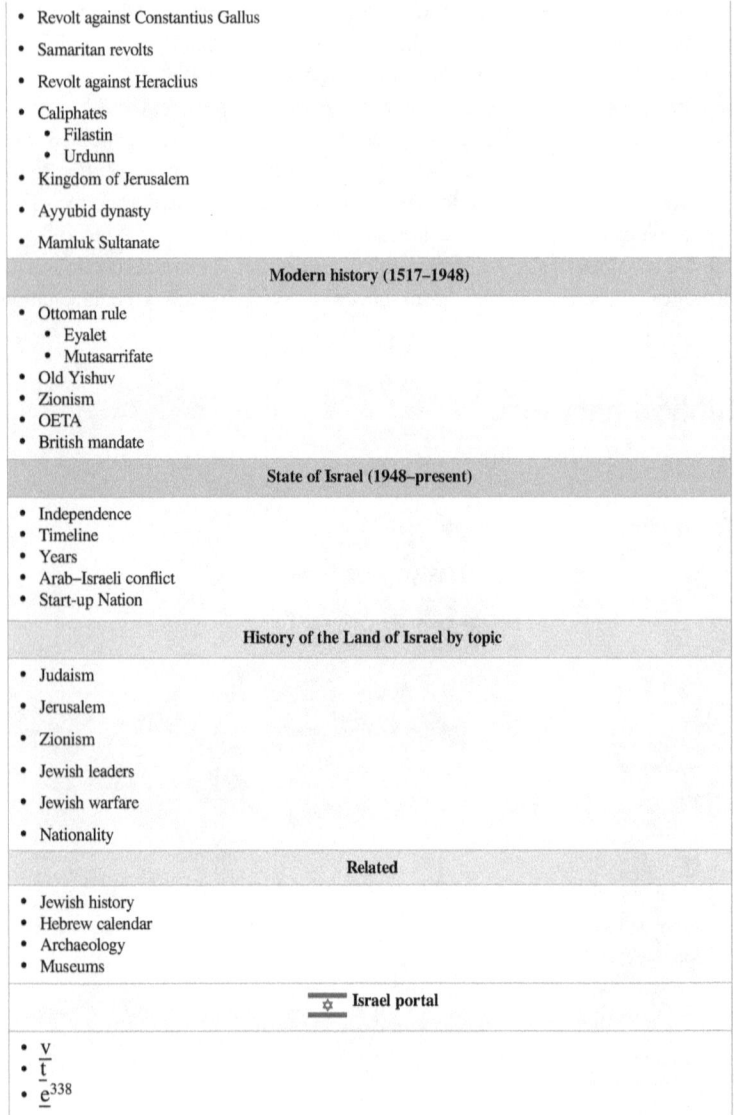

According to the Book of Judges, before the rise of the united monarchy the Israelite tribes lived as a confederation under *ad hoc* charismatic leaders called judges. Abimelech the first judge to be declared king by the men of Shechem and the house of Millo, Wikipedia:Identifying reliable sources reigned over Israel for three years before he was killed during the Battle of Thebez. Wikipedia:Identifying reliable sources

According to the biblical account, the united monarchy was formed when there was a large popular expression in favour of introducing a king to rule over the decentralised Israelite confederacy. Increasing pressure from the Philistines and other neighboring peoples is said by the Bible to have forced the Israelites to unite as state following the anointing of Saul by Samuel. The Bible treats the notion of kingship as having been anathema, it being viewed as the placing of one man in a position of reverence and power that ought to be reserved for God.Wikipedia:Citation needed

Civil war

David and Saul become bitter enemies, at least from Saul's point of view, although sources describe Jonathan, Saul's son, and Michal, Saul's daughter, as assisting David to escape Saul, ultimately leading to a brief reconciliation before Saul's death.Wikipedia:Citation needed

According to the Second Book of Samuel, Saul's disobedience prompts God to curtail his reign and hand his kingdom over to another dynasty. Saul dies in battle against the PhilistinesWikipedia:Citation needed after a reign of just two years.[339] His heir, Ishbaal, rules for only two years before being assassinated. David, heretofore king of Judah only, ends the conspiracy and is appointed king of Israel in Ishbaal's place. Some textual critics and biblical scholars suggest that David was actually responsible for the assassination and that David's innocence was a later invention to legitimize his actions.

Israel rebels against David and appoints David's son Absalom king, forcing David into exile east of the Jordan.Wikipedia:Citation needed David eventually launches a successful counterattack that results in the loss of Absalom. Having retaken Judah and asserted control over Israel, David returns west of the Jordan. Throughout the remainder of his reign, he continues to suppress rebellions that arise among the people of Israel.Wikipedia:Citation needed

This section of the biblical text, and the bulk of the remainder of the Books of Samuel, is thought by textual critics to belong to a single large source known as the Court History of David. Although reflecting the political bias of the kingdom of Judah following the destruction of Israel, the source remains somewhat more neutral than the pro- and antimonarchical sources comprising earlier parts of the text. Israel and Judah are portrayed in this source as quite distinct kingdoms.Wikipedia:Citation needed

Golden Age

Prior to the ascension of Saul, the city of Shiloh is seen as the national capital, at least in the religious sense, a claim that from an archaeological standpoint is considered plausible. Throughout the monarchy of Saul, the capital is located in Gibeah. After Saul's death, Ishbaal rules over the kingdom of Israel from Mahanaim, while David establishes the capital of the kingdom of Judah in Hebron.Wikipedia:Citation needed

Following the civil war with Saul, David forges a strong and unified Israelite monarchy, reigning c. 1000 to 961 BCE and establishing Jerusalem as his national capital in 1006 BCE. Some modern archaeologists, however, believe that the two distinct cultures and geographic entities of Judah and Israel continued uninterrupted, and that if a political union between them did exist, it possibly had no practical effect on their relationship.

In the biblical account, David embarks on successful military campaigns against the enemies of Judah and Israel, defeating such regional entities as the Philistines to secure his borders. Israel grows from kingdom to empire, its sphere of influence—militarily and politically—expanding to control the weaker client states of Philistia, Moab, Edom and Ammon, with Aramaean city-states Aram-Zobah and Aram-Damascus becoming vassal states.Wikipedia:Identifying reliable sources The imperial border is described as stretching from the Mediterranean Sea to the Arabian Desert, from the Red Sea to the Euphrates River. Some modern archaeologists believe that the area under the control of Judah and Israel, excluding the Phoenician territories on the shore of the Mediterranean, did not exceed 34,000 square kilometres (13,000 sq mi), of which the kingdom of Israel encompassed about 24,000 square kilometres (9,300 sq mi).Wikipedia:Citation needed

David is succeeded by his son Solomon, who obtains the throne in a somewhat disreputable manner from rival claimant Adonijah, his elder brother.Wikipedia:Citation needed The reign of Solomon (c. 961 to 922 BCE) proves to be a period of unprecedented peace, prosperity, and cultural development. Solomon embarks on an aggressive campaign of public building, erecting the First Temple in Jerusalem with assistance from the King of Tyre, with whom he has maintained the strong alliance forged by his father.Wikipedia:Citation needed Like the palace of David, Solomon's temple is designed and built with the assistance of Tyrian architects, master craftsmen, skilled labourers, money, jewels, cedar, and other goods obtained in exchange for land ceded to Tyre.Wikipedia:Citation needed

Solomon goes on to rebuild numerous major cities, including Megiddo, Hazor, and Gezer. Some scholars have attributed aspects of archaeological remains excavated from this sites, including six-chambered gates and ashlar palaces, to

Figure 18: *Map showing the Kingdoms of Israel (blue) and Judah (orange), ancient Southern Levant borders and ancient cities such as Urmomium and Jerash. The map shows the region in the 9th century BCE.*

this building programme. However, excavation teams at Meggido later established that these structures are from different time periods. Yigael Yadin subsequently concluded that the stables once believed to have served Solomon's vast collection of horses were actually built by King Ahab in the 9th century BCE.

End

Following Solomon's death in c. 926 BCE, tensions between the northern part of Israel containing the ten northern tribes, and the southern section dominated by Jerusalem and the southern tribes reached boiling point. When Solomon's successor Rehoboam dealt tactlessly with economic complaints of the northern tribes, in about 930 BCE (there are differences of opinion as to the actual year) the United Kingdom of Israel and Judah split into two kingdoms: the northern Kingdom of Israel, which included the cities of Shechem and Samaria, and the southern Kingdom of Judah, which contained Jerusalem; with most of the non-Israelite provinces achieving independence.Wikipedia:Citation needed

The Kingdom of Israel (or Northern Kingdom, or Samaria) existed as an independent state until 722 BCE when it was conquered by the Assyrian Empire, while the Kingdom of Judah (or Southern Kingdom) existed as an independent state until 586 BCE when it was conquered by the Neo-Babylonian Empire.Wikipedia:Citation needed

Biblical chronology

Many alternative chronologies have been suggested, and there is no ultimate consensus between the different factions and scholarly disciplines concerned with this period, as to when it is depicted as having begun or when it ended.

Most bibical scholars follow either of the older chronologies established by William F. Albright or Edwin R. Thiele, or the newer chronology of Gershon Galil, all of which are shown below. All dates are BCE. Thiele's chronology generally corresponds with Galil's chronology below with a difference of at most one year.[340]

Albright/-Thiele dates	Galil dates	Common/-Biblical name	Regnal Name and style	Notes
House of Saul				
c. 1021–1000	c. 1030–1010	Saul	Shaul ben Qysh, Melekh Ysra'el	Killed in battle, suicide
c. 1000	c. 1010–1008	Ishbaal (Ish-boseth)	Ishba'al ben Shaul, Melekh Ysra'el	Assassinated
House of David				
c. 1000–962	c. 1008–970	David	Dawidh ben Yishai, Melekh Ysra'el	Son-in-law of Saul, brother-in-law of Ish-boseth
c. 962–c. 922	c. 970–931	Solomon	Sh'lomoh ben Dawidh, Melekh Ysra'el	Son of David and Bathsheba

Archaeological record

In contemporary scholarship the united monarchy is generally held to be a literary construction and not a historical reality, due to the lack of archeological evidence for it. It is generally accepted that a "House of David" existed, but many believe that David could have only been the monarch or chieftain of Judah, and that the northern kingdom was a separate development. There are some dissenters to this view.Wikipedia:Citation needed

Oded Lipschits wrote in the *Jewish Study Bible* that <templatestyles src="Template:Quote/styles.css"/>

the premonarchic period long ago became a literary description of the mythological roots, the early beginnings of the nation and the way to describe the right of Israel on its land. The archeological evidence also does not support the existence of a united monarchy under David and Solomon as described in the Bible, so the rubric of "united monarchy" is best abandoned, although it remains useful for discussing how the Bible views the Israelite past.

According to Israel Finkelstein and Neil Silberman, authors of *The Bible Unearthed*, ideas of a united monarchy are not accurate history but rather "creative expressions of a powerful religious reform movement," possibly "based on certain historical kernels." Finkelstein and Silberman do accept that David and Solomon were real kings of Judah about the 10th century BCE, but they cite the fact that the earliest independent reference to the Kingdom of Israel dates to about 890 BCE, while that for the kingdom of Judah dates to about 750 BCE. This is supported by Jonathan Tubb, who argues that the story of the united monarchy was fabricated as a Golden Age tale during the Exile. He accepts the historicity of David and Solomon but cautions that "[t]hey must be seen . . . as local folk heroes and not as rulers of international status."

On the other hand, while Amélie Kuhrt does acknowledge that "there are no royal inscriptions from the time of the united monarchy (indeed very little written material altogether), and not a single contemporary reference to either David or Solomon," she concludes that "[a]gainst this must be set the evidence for substantial development and growth at several sites, which is plausibly related to the tenth century." Kenneth Kitchen reaches a similar conclusion, arguing that "the physical archaeology of tenth-century Canaan is consistent with the former existence of a unified state on its terrain."

Excavations at Khirbet Qeiyafa, an Iron Age site located in Judah, found an urbanized settlement radiocarbon dated well before scholars such as Finklestein suggest urbanization began in Judah, supporting existence of a Judahite kingdom. The Israel Antiquities Authority stated: "The excavations at Khirbat Qeiyafa clearly reveal an urban society that existed in Judah already in the late eleventh century BCE. It can no longer be argued that the Kingdom of Judah developed only in the late eighth century BCE or at some other later date." The techniques and interpretations used to reach some conclusions related to Khirbet Qeiyafa have been criticized by some scholars, among them Finkelstein and Alexander Fantalkin of Tel Aviv University.

In August 2015, Israeli archaeologists discovered massive fortifications in the ruins of the ancient city of Gath, supposed birthplace of Goliath. The size of the fortifications show Gath to have been a very large city in the 10th century BCE, perhaps the largest in Canaan at the time. The professor leading the dig, Aren Maeir, estimated that Gath was as much as four times the size of

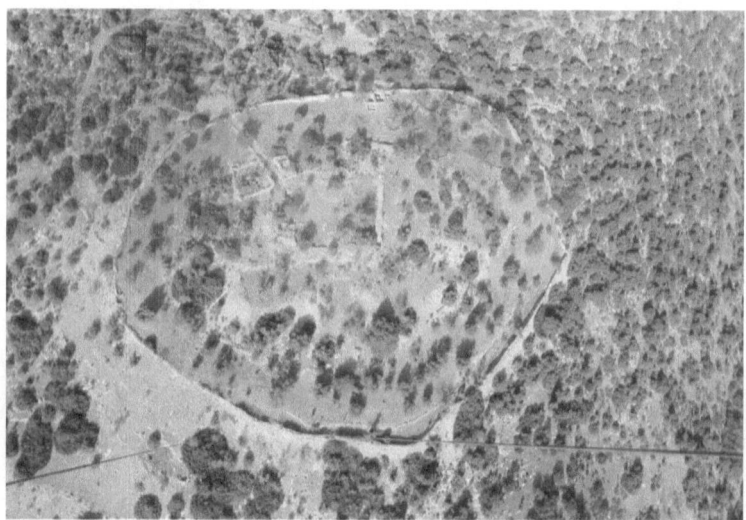

Figure 19: *Aerial view of Khirbet Qeiyafa.*

contemporary Jerusalem, casting doubt that David's kingdom could have been as powerful as described in the Bible.

External links

- The Debate over the Historicity and Chronology of the United Monarchy in Jerusalem[341] by Ong Kar Khalsa
- Jewish Virtual Library[342]
- Newadvent Encyclopedia[343]

Kingdom of Israel (Samaria)

	Kingdom of Israel
	יִשְׂרָאֵל מַמְלֶכֶת
	930 BCE–720 BCE
Status	Kingdom
Capital	Shechem (930 BCE) Penuel (930–909) Tirzah (909–880) Samaria (880–720)
Common languages	Hebrew
Religion	Monolatristic or monotheistic Yahwism Canaanite polytheism Mesopotamian polytheism Folk religion
Government	Monarchy
Historical era	Classical Antiquity
• Jeroboam's Revolt	930 BCE
• Assyrian exile	720 BCE
ISO 3166 code	IL
Preceded by	**Succeeded by**
Kingdom of Israel (united monarchy)	Neo-Assyrian Empire

Today part of	Israel
	Golan Heights
	West Bank
	Jordan
	Lebanon
	Syria

Part of a series on the

History of Israel

Ancient Israel and Judah

- Natufian culture
- Prehistory
- Canaan
- Israelites
- United monarchy
- Northern Kingdom
- Kingdom of Judah
- Babylonian rule

Second Temple period (530 BCE–70 CE)

- Persian rule
- Hellenistic period
- Hasmonean dynasty
- Herodian dynasty
  - Kingdom
  - Tetrarchy
- Roman Judea

Middle Ages (70–1517)

- Roman Palaestina
- Byzantine Palaestina
  - Prima
  - Secunda
- Revolt against Constantius Gallus
- Samaritan revolts
- Revolt against Heraclius
- Caliphates
  - Filastin
  - Urdunn
- Kingdom of Jerusalem
- Ayyubid dynasty
- Mamluk Sultanate

Modern history (1517–1948)

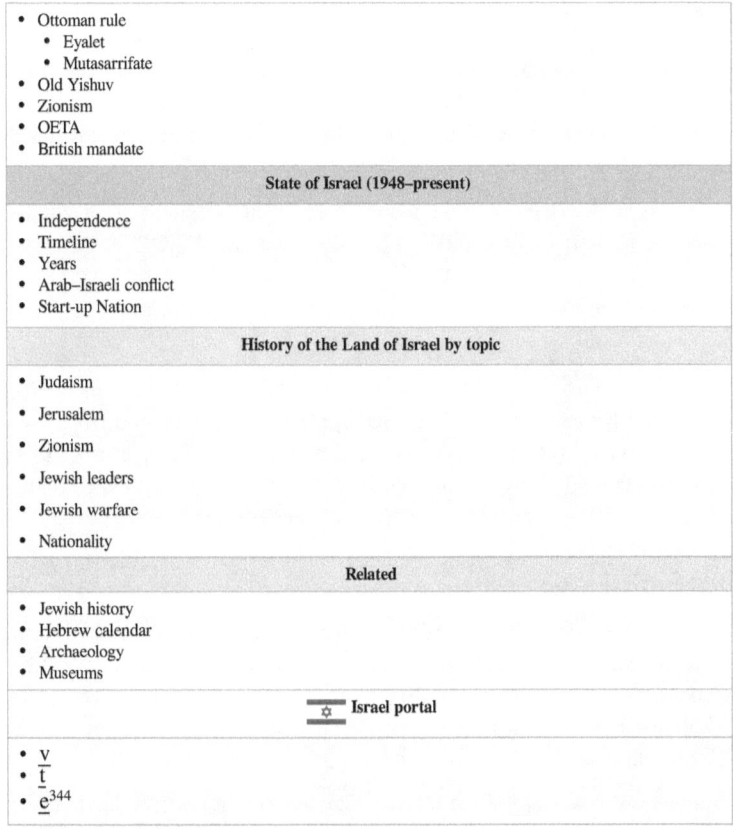

- Ottoman rule
  - Eyalet
  - Mutasarrifate
- Old Yishuv
- Zionism
- OETA
- British mandate

State of Israel (1948–present)

- Independence
- Timeline
- Years
- Arab–Israeli conflict
- Start-up Nation

History of the Land of Israel by topic

- Judaism
- Jerusalem
- Zionism
- Jewish leaders
- Jewish warfare
- Nationality

Related

- Jewish history
- Hebrew calendar
- Archaeology
- Museums

Israel portal

- v
- t
- e[344]

According to the Hebrew Bible, the **Kingdom of Israel** (Hebrew: מַמְלֶכֶת יִשְׂרָאֵל, Modern *Mamlekhet Yisra'el*, Tiberian *Mamléḵeṯ Yiśrā'ēl*) was one of two successor states to the former United Kingdom of Israel and Judah. Historians often refer to the Kingdom of Israel as the "Northern Kingdom" or as the "Kingdom of Samaria" to differentiate it from the Southern Kingdom of Judah.

Modern scholarship, incorporating textual criticism and archaeology, has challenged the biblical account that the northern kingdom of Israel broke off from a united monarchy with the southern kingdom of Judah, suggesting instead that the northern civilization of Israel developed independently of Judah (a comparatively small and rural area), and that it first reached the political, economic, military and architectural sophistication of a kingdom under the Omride dynasty around 884 BCE.[345:169–195]

The Kingdom of Israel existed roughly from 930 BCE until 720 BCE, when it was conquered by the Neo-Assyrian Empire. The major cities of the kingdom were Shechem, Tirzah, and Shomron (Samaria).

Biblical narrative

In the Hebrew Bible, the Kingdom of Israel has been referred to as the "House of Joseph".[346,347] It is also frequently referenced (particularly in poetry) as Ephraim, the tribe whose territory housed the capital cities and the royal families. It has also been referred to as "Israel in Samaria".[348]

According to the Hebrew Bible, the territory of the Kingdom of Israel comprised the territories of the tribes of Zebulun, Issachar, Asher, Naphtali, Dan, Manasseh, Ephraim, Reuben and Gad. Its capital was Samaria according to the Book of Isaiah.

United Monarchy

The United Kingdom of Israel and Judah is said to have existed from about 1030 to about 930 BCE. It was a union of all the twelve Israelite tribes living in the area that presently approximates modern Israel and the other Levantine territories including much of western Jordan, and western Syria.

Division

After the death of Solomon in about 931 BCE, all the Israelite tribes except for Judah and Benjamin (called the ten northern tribes) refused to accept Rehoboam, the son and successor of Solomon, as their king. The rebellion against Rehoboam arose after he refused to lighten the burden of taxation and services that his father had imposed on his subjects.

Jeroboam, who was not of the Davidic line, was sent forth from Egypt by the malcontents. The Tribe of Ephraim and all Israel raised the old cry, "Every man to his tents, O Israel". Rehoboam fled to Jerusalem, and in 930 BCE (some date it in 920 BCE), Jeroboam was proclaimed king over all Israel at Shechem. After the revolt at Shechem at first only the tribe of Judah remained loyal to the house of David. But very soon after the tribe of Benjamin joined Judah. The northern kingdom continued to be called the Kingdom of Israel or Israel, while the southern kingdom was called the Kingdom of Judah. 2 Chronicles 15:9 also says that members of the tribes of Ephraim, Manasseh and Simeon fled to Judah during the reign of Asa of Judah.

Both Eusebius and Josephus place the division in 997 BCE – lunar dates of Venus can be mistaken as 64 years later (c. 930 BCE). (Crossing of sun over Mars as Tamuz would be 10 July 997 BCE.)

Shechem was the first capital of the Kingdom of Israel. Afterwards it was Tirzah. King Omri built his capital in Samaria (1 Kings 16:24), which continued as such until the destruction of the Kingdom by the Assyrians (2 Kings 17:5[349]). During the three-year siege of Samaria by the Assyrians,

Shalmaneser V died and was succeeded by Sargon II of Assyria, who himself records the capture of that city thus: "Samaria I looked at, I captured; 27,280 men who dwelt in it I carried away" into Assyria. Thus, around 720 BCE, after two centuries, the kingdom of the ten tribes came to an end.

Today, among archaeologists, Samaria is one of the most universally accepted archaeological sites from the biblical period[350] At around 850 BCE, the Mesha Stele, written in Old Hebrew alphabet, records a victory of King Mesha of Moab against king Omri of Israel and his son Ahab.

Relations between the kingdoms

For the first sixty years, the kings of Judah tried to re-establish their authority over the northern kingdom, and there was perpetual war between them. For the following eighty years, there was no open war between them, and, for the most part, they were in friendly alliance, co-operating against their common enemies, especially against Damascus.

The conflict between Israel and Judah was resolved when Jehoshaphat, King of Judah, allied himself with the house of Ahab through marriage. Later, Jehosophat's son and successor, Jehoram of Judah, married Ahab's daughter Athaliah, cementing the alliance. However, the sons of Ahab were slaughtered by Jehu following his coup d'état around 840 BCE.

Destruction of the kingdom

In c. 732 BCE, Pekah of Israel, while allied with Rezin, king of Aram, threatened Jerusalem. Ahaz, king of Judah, appealed to Tiglath-Pileser III, the king of Assyria, for help. After Ahaz paid tribute to Tiglath-Pileser Tiglath-Pileser sacked Damascus and Israel, annexing Aram and territory of the tribes of Reuben, Gad and Manasseh in Gilead including the desert outposts of Jetur, Naphish and Nodab. People from these tribes including the Reubenite leader, were taken captive and resettled in the region of the Khabur River system. Tiglath-Pilesar also captured the territory of Naphtali and the city of Janoah in Ephraim and an Assyrian governor was placed over the region of Naphtali. According to 2 Kings 16:9[351] and 15:29[352], the population of Aram and the annexed part of Israel was deported to Assyria.

Israel continued to exist within the reduced territory as an independent kingdom until around 720 BCE, when it was again invaded by Assyria and the rest of the population deported. The Bible relates that the population of Israel was exiled, becoming known as the Ten Lost Tribes, leaving only the Tribe of Judah, the Tribe of Simeon (that was "absorbed" into Judah), the Tribe of Benjamin and the people of the Tribe of Levi who lived among them of the original Israelites nation in the southern Kingdom of Judah. However, in their book

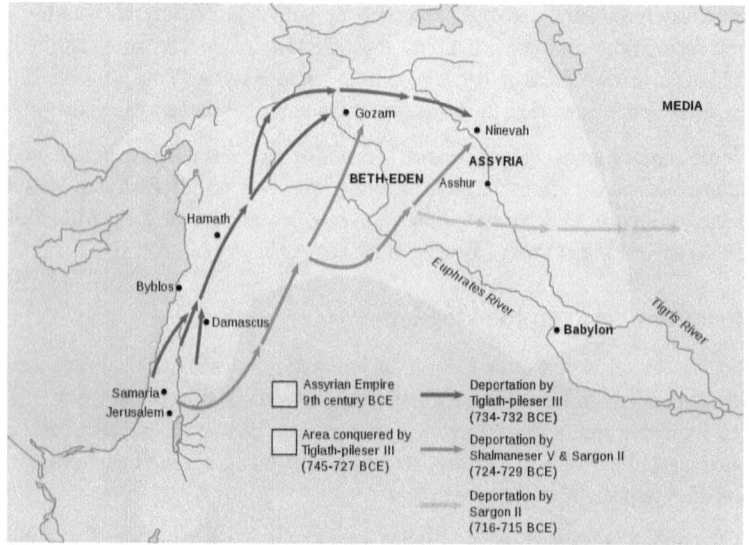

Figure 20: *Deportation of the Northern Kingdom by the Assyrian Empire*

The Bible Unearthed, authors Israel Finkelstein and Neil Asher Silberman estimate that only a fifth of the population (about 40,000) were actually resettled out of the area during the two deportation periods under Tiglath-Pileser III and Sargon II.:[221] Many also fled south to Jerusalem, which appears to have expanded in size fivefold during this period, requiring a new wall to be built, and a new source of water (Siloam) to be provided by King Hezekiah.

The remainder of the northern kingdom was conquered by Sargon II, who captured the capital city Samaria in the territory of Ephraim. He took 27,290 people captive from the city of Samaria resettling some with the Israelites in the Khabur region and the rest in the land of the Medes thus establishing Hebrew communities in Ecbatana and Rages.

The Book of Tobit additionally records that Sargon had taken other captives from the northern kingdom to the Assyrian capital of Nineveh, in particular Tobit from the town of Thisbe in Naphtali.

In medieval Rabbinic fable, the concept of the ten tribes who were taken away from the House of David (who continued the rule of the southern kingdom of Judah), becomes confounded with accounts of the Assyrian deportations leading to the myth of the "Ten Lost Tribes". The recorded history differs from this fable: No record exists of the Assyrians having exiled people from Dan, Asher, Issachar, Zebulun or western Manasseh. Descriptions of the deportation of people from Reuben, Gad, Manasseh in Gilead, Ephraim and Naphtali

Kingdom of Israel (Samaria)

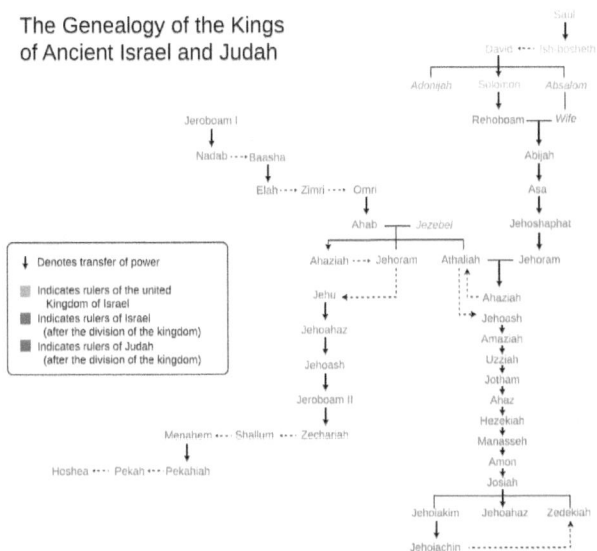

Figure 21: *The genealogy of the kings of the United Kingdom of Israel and Judea, the Kingdom of Israel and the kings of the Kingdom of Judah. Most historians follow either of the older chronologies established by William F. Albright or Edwin R. Thiele, or the newer chronologies of Gershon Galil and Kenneth Kitchen, all of which are shown below. All dates are BC/BCE.*

indicate that only a portion of these tribes were deported and the places to which they were deported are known locations given in the accounts. The deported communities are mentioned as still existing at the time of the composition of the books of Kings and Chronicles and did not disappear by assimilation. 2 Chronicles 30:1-11 explicitly mentions northern Israelites who had been spared by the Assyrians in particular people of Ephraim, Manasseh, Asher, Issachar and Zebulun and how members of the latter three returned to worship at the Temple in Jerusalem during the reign of Hezekiah.

Royal houses

Al-bright	Thiele	Galil	Kitchen	Common/-Biblical name	Regnal Name and style	Notes
				The House of Jeroboam		

Kingdom of Israel (Samaria)

922–901 BCE	931–910 BCE	931–909 BCE	931–911 BCE	Jeroboam I	בֶּן-נְבָט יָרָבְעָם יִשְׂרָאֵל מֶלֶךְ **Yerav'am** ben Nevat, Melekh Yisra'el	Led the rebellion and divided the kingdoms. Reigned in Israel (Northern Kingdom) for 22 years. Death: Natural Causes
901–900 BCE	910–909 BCE	909–908 BCE	911–910 BCE	Nadab	בֶּן-יָרָבְעָם נָדָב יִשְׂרָאֵל מֶלֶךְ **Nadav** ben Yerav'am, Melekh Yisra'el	Reigned in Israel for 2 years. Death: Killed by Baasha, son of Ahijah of the house of Issachar, along with his whole family.

The House of Baasha

900–877 BCE	909–886 BCE	908–885 BCE	910–887 BCE	Baasha	בֶּן-אֲחִיָּה בַּעְשָׁא יִשְׂרָאֵל מֶלֶךְ **Ba'asha** ben Achiyah, Melekh Yisra'el	Reigned over Israel in Tirzah for 24 years. Death: Natural Causes
877–876 BCE	886–885 BCE	885–884 BCE	887–886 BCE	Elah	בֶּן-בַּעְשָׁא אֵלָה יִשְׂרָאֵל מֶלֶךְ **'Elah** ben Ba'asha, Melekh Yisra'el	Reigned over Israel in Tirzah for 2 years. Death: Zimri, one of his officials, got him drunk and killed him at his house in Azra.

The House of Zimri

876 BCE	885 BCE	884 BCE	886 BCE	Zimri	יִשְׂרָאֵל מֶלֶךְ זִמְרִי **Zimri**, Melekh Yisra'el	Reigned over Israel in Tirzah for 7 days. Death: He set his palace on fire when Omri and all the Israelites with him withdrew from Gibbethon and laid siege to Tirzah.

The House of Omri

876–869 BCE	885–874 BCE	884–873 BCE	886–875 BCE	Omri	מֶלֶךְ עָמְרִי יִשְׂרָאֵל **'Omri**, Melekh Yisra'el	Reigned over Israel in Samaria for 12 years. Death: Natural Causes
869–850 BCE	874–853 BCE	873–852 BCE	875–853 BCE	Ahab	בֶּן-עָמְרִי אַחְאָב יִשְׂרָאֵל מֶלֶךְ **Ah'av** ben 'Omri, Melekh Yisra'el	Reigned over Israel in Samaria for 22 years. Death: Shot by an archer during the battle at Ramoth Gilead. He died upon his arrival at Samaria.
850–849 BCE	853–852 BCE	852–851 BCE	853–852 BCE	Ahaziah	בֶּן-אַחְאָב אֲחַזְיָהוּ יִשְׂרָאֵל מֶלֶךְ **'Ahazyahu** ben 'Ah'av, Melekh Yisra'el	Reigned over Israel in Samaria for 2 years. Death: He fell through the lattice of his upper room and injured himself. Elijah the prophet told him he would never leave his bed and would die on it.
849–842 BCE	852–841 BCE	851–842 BCE	852–841 BCE	Joram	בֶּן-אַחְאָב יוֹרָם יִשְׂרָאֵל מֶלֶךְ **Yehoram** ben 'Ah'av, Melekh Yisra'el	Reigned over Israel in Samaria for 12 years. Death: Killed by Jehu, the next king of Israel,

The House of Jehu

842–815 BCE	841–814 BCE	842–815 BCE]	841–814 BCE	Jehu	בֶּן־נִמְשִׁי יֵהוּא יִשְׂרָאֵל מֶלֶךְ **Yehu** ben Nimshi, Melekh Yisra'el	Reigned over Israel in Samaria for 28 years.[353] Death: Natural Causes
815–801 BCE	814–798 BCE	819–804 BCE	814–806 BCE	Jehoahaz	בֶּן־יֵהוּא יְהוֹאָחָז יִשְׂרָאֵל מֶלֶךְ **Yeho'ahaz** ben Yehu, Melekh Yisra'el	Reigned over Israel in Samaria for 17 years. Death: Natural Causes
801–786 BCE	798–782 BCE	805–790 BCE	806–791 BCE	Jehoash (Joash)	בֶּן־יְהוֹאָחָז יוֹאָשׁ יִשְׂרָאֵל מֶלֶךְ **Yeho'ash** ben Yeho'ahaz, Melekh Yisra'el	Reigned over Israel in Samaria for 16 years. Death: Natural Causes
786–746 BCE	782–753 BCE	790–750 BCE	791–750 BCE	Jeroboam II	בֶּן־יוֹאָשׁ יָרָבְעָם יִשְׂרָאֵל מֶלֶךְ **Yerav'am** ben Yeho'ash, Melekh Yisra'el	Reigned over Israel in Samaria for 41 years. Death: Natural Causes. The Book of Jonah or Jonah's journey to Nineveh (when he was swallowed by a whale or fish) happened at that time.
746 BCE	753 BCE	750–749 BCE	750 BCE	Zachariah	בֶּן־יָרָבְעָם זְכַרְיָה יִשְׂרָאֵל מֶלֶךְ **Zekharyah** ben Yerav'am, Melekh Yisra'el	Reigned over Israel in Samaria for 6 months. Death: Shallum son of Jabesh killed him in front of the people and succeeded as king.

The House of Shallum

745 BCE	752 BCE	749 BCE	749 BCE	Shallum	בֶּן־יָבֵשׁ שַׁלּוּם יִשְׂרָאֵל מֶלֶךְ **Shallum** ben Yavesh, Melekh Yisra'el	Reigned over Israel in Samaria for 1 month. Death: Menahem son of Gadi attacked Shallum and assassinated him.

The House of Menahem (also known as the House of Gadi)

745–738 BCE	752–742 BCE	749–738 BCE	749–739 BCE	Menahem	בֶּן־גָּדִי מְנַחֵם יִשְׂרָאֵל מֶלֶךְ **Menachem** ben Gadi, Melekh Yisra'el	Reigned over Israel in Samaria for 10 years. Death: Natural Causes
738–737 BCE	742–740 BCE	738–736 BCE	739–737 BCE	Pekahiah	בֶּן־מְנַחֵם פְּקַחְיָה יִשְׂרָאֵל מֶלֶךְ **Pekahyah** ben Menahem, Melekh Yisra'el	Reigned over Israel in Samaria for 2 years. **Death**: Pekah son of Remaliah, one of the chief officers, took 50 men with him and assassinated the king in his palace at Samaria.

The House of Pekah

737–732 BCE	740–732 BCE	736–732 BCE	737–732 BCE	Pekah	בֶּן־רְמַלְיָהוּ פֶּקַח יִשְׂרָאֵל מֶלֶךְ **Pekah** ben Remalyahu, Melekh Yisra'el	Reigned over Israel in Samaria for 20 years. Death: Hoshea son of Elah conspired against him and assassinated him.
The House of Hoshea							
732–722 BCE	732–722 BCE	732–722 BCE	732–722 BCE]	Hoshea	בֶּן־אֵלָה הוֹשֵׁעַ יִשְׂרָאֵל מֶלֶךְ **Hoshe'a** ben 'Elah, Melekh Yisra'el	Reigned over Israel in Samaria for 9 years.[354] Death: King Shalmanser attacked and captured Samaria. He charged Hoshea of treason and he put him in prison, then, he deported the Israelites to Assyria.

Kingdom of Judah

The Kingdom of Judah continued to exist as an independent state until 586 BCE, when it was conquered by the Neo-Babylonian Empire.

Religion

The religious climate of the Kingdom of Israel appears to have followed two major trends. The first, that of worship of Yahweh, and the second that of worship of Baal as detailed in the Hebrew Bible (1 Kings 16:31[355]) and in the Baal cycle discovered at Ugarit.

According to the Hebrew Bible Jeroboam built two places of worship, one at Bethel and one at far northern Dan, as alternatives to the Temple in Jerusalem.[356] (1 Kings 12:29[357]) He did not want the people of his kingdom to have religious ties to Jerusalem, the capital city of the rival Kingdom of Judah. He erected golden bulls at the entrance to the Temples to represent the national god.[358] The Hebrew Bible, written from the perspective of scribes in Jerusalem, referred to these acts as the way of Jeroboam or the errors of Jeroboam. (1 Kings 12:26-29[359])

The Bible states that Ahab allowed the cult worship of Baal to become an acceptable religion of the kingdom. His wife Jezebel was a devotee to Baal worship. (1 Kings 16:31[355])

Prophets

- Elijah, opponent of religious inventions under Ahab and Jezebel
- Elisha, chosen successor of Elijah
- Amos
- Hosea
- Jonah
- Nahum

List of proposed Assyrian references to Kingdom of Israel (Samaria)

The table below lists all the historical references to the Kingdom of Israel (Samaria) in Assyrian records. King Omri's name takes the Assyrian shape of "Humri", his kingdom or dynasty that of Bit Humri or alike - the "House of Humri/Omri".

Assyrian King	Inscription	Year	Transliteration	Translation
Shalmaneser III	Kurkh Monoliths	853 BCE	KUR sir-'i-la-a-a	"Israel"
Shalmaneser III	Black Obelisk, Calah Fragment, Kurba'il Stone, Ashur Stone	841 BCE	mar Hu-um-ri-i	"[Bit]-Humrite"
Adad-nirari III	Tell al-Rimah Stela	803 BCE	KUR Sa-me-ri-na-a-a	"land of Samaria"
Adad-nirari III	Nimrud Slab	803 BCE	KUR <Bit>-Hu-um-ri-i	"the 'land of Bit-Humri"
Tiglath-Pileser III	Layard 45b+ III R 9,1	740 BCE	[KUR sa-me-ri-i-na-a-a]	["land of Samaria"]
Tiglath-Pileser III	Iran Stela	739–738 BCE	KUR sa-m[e]-ri-i-na-a-[a]	"land of Samaria"
Tiglath-Pileser III	Layard 50a + 50b + 67a	738–737 BCE	URU sa-me-ri-na-a-a	"city of Sarnaria"
Tiglath-Pileser III	Layard 66	732–731 BCE	URU Sa-me-ri-na	"city of Sarnaria")
Tiglath-Pileser III	III R 10,2	731 BCE	KUR E Hu-um-ri-a	"land of Bit-Humri"

Tiglath-Pileser III	ND 4301 + 4305	730 BCE	KUR E Hu-um-ri-a	"land of Bit-Humri"
Shal-maneser V	Babylonian Chronicle ABC1	725 BCE	URU Sa-ma/-ba-ra-'-in	"city of Sarnaria"
Sargon II	Nimrud Prism, Great Summary Inscription	720 BCE	URU Sa-me-ri-na	"city of Samerina"
Sargon II	Palace Door, Small Summary Inscription, Cylinder Inscription, Bull Inscription	720 BCE	KUR Bit-Hu-um-ri-a	"land of Bit-Humri"

External links

- About Israel - The Information Center About Israel[360]
- [[Category:All articles with dead external links[361]]Wikipedia:Link rot Biblical History] The Jewish History Resource Center - Project of the Dinur Center for Research in Jewish History, The Hebrew University of Jerusalem
- Complete Bible Genealogy[362] A synchronized chart of the kings of Israel and Judah

Kingdom of Judah

Kingdom of Judah	
9th or 8th century BCE–586 BCE	
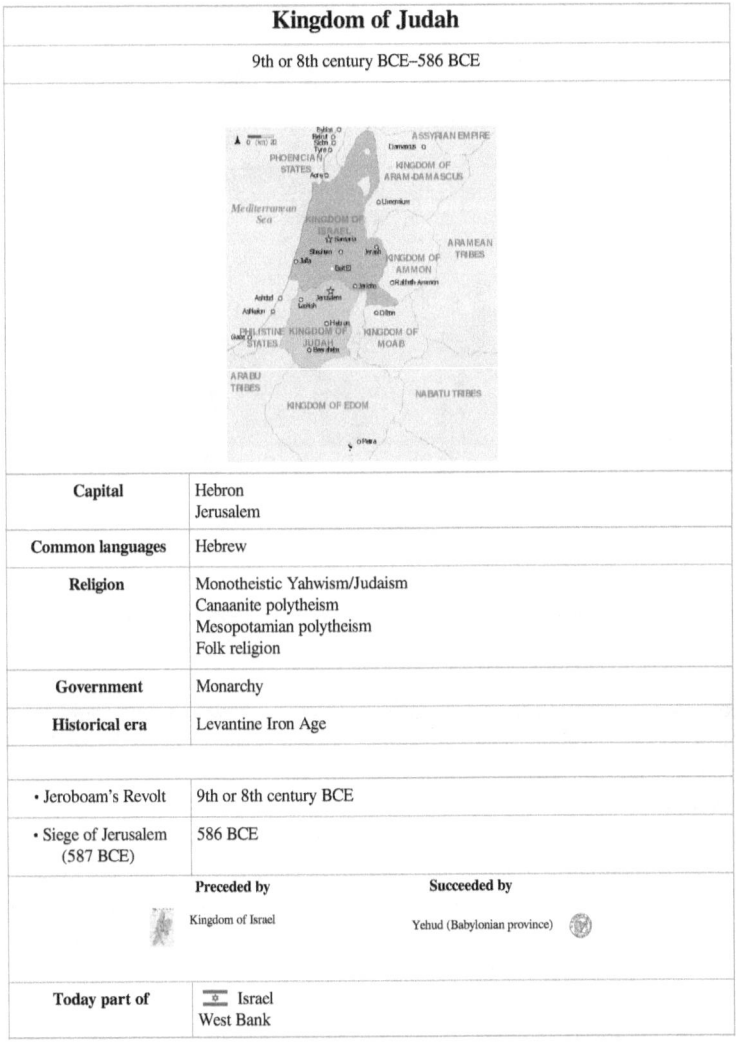	
Capital	Hebron Jerusalem
Common languages	Hebrew
Religion	Monotheistic Yahwism/Judaism Canaanite polytheism Mesopotamian polytheism Folk religion
Government	Monarchy
Historical era	Levantine Iron Age
• Jeroboam's Revolt	9th or 8th century BCE
• Siege of Jerusalem (587 BCE)	586 BCE
Preceded by	Succeeded by
Kingdom of Israel	Yehud (Babylonian province)
Today part of	Israel West Bank

The **Kingdom of Judah** (Hebrew: יְהוּדָה מַמְלֶכֶת, *Mamlekhet Yehudāh*) was an Iron Age kingdom of the Southern Levant. The Hebrew Bible depicts it as the successor to a United Monarchy, but historians are divided about the veracity of this account. In the 10th and early 9th centuries BCE, the territory of Judah appears to have been sparsely populated, limited to small rural settlements, most of them unfortified. Jerusalem, the kingdom's capital, likely did not emerge as a significant administrative center until the end of the 8th

Figure 22: *Mesha Stele c. 850 BCE – An inscribed stone set up c. 840 BCE by Mesha of Moab tells how Chemosh, the God of Moab, had been angry with his people and allowed them to be subjugated to Israel, but at length assisted Mesha to throw off the yoke of Israel and restore the lands of Moab.*

century; before this the archaeological evidence suggests its population was too small to sustain a viable kingdom.[363] In the 7th century its population increased greatly, prospering under Assyrian vassalage (despite Hezekiah's revolt against the Assyrian king Sennacherib), but in 605 the Assyrian Empire was defeated, and the ensuing competition between the Twenty-sixth Dynasty of Egypt and the Neo-Babylonian Empire for control of the Eastern Mediterranean led to the destruction of the kingdom in a series of campaigns between 597 and 582, the deportation of the elite of the community, and the incorporation of Judah into a province of the Neo-Babylonian Empire.

Archaeological record

Significant academic debate exists around the character of the Kingdom of Judah. Little archaeological evidence of an extensive, powerful Kingdom of Judah before the late 8th century BCE has been found; Nimrud Tablet K.3751, dated c. 733 BCE, is the earliest known record of the name Judah (written in Assyrian cuneiform as Yaudaya or KUR.ia-ú-da-a-a).

Archaeologists of the minimalist school doubt the extent of the Kingdom of Judah as depicted in the Bible. Around 1990–2010, an important group of archaeologists and biblical scholars formed the view that the actual Kingdom of Judah bore little resemblance to the biblical portrait of a powerful monarchy. These scholars say the kingdom was no more than a small tribal entity.

However, Yosef Garfinkel has written in a preliminary report published by the Israeli Antiquities Authority that finds at the Khirbet Qeiyafa site support the notion that an urban society already existed in Judah in the late 11th century BCE. Other archaeologists say that the identification of Khirbet Qeiyafa as an Israelite settlement is uncertain.

The status of Jerusalem in the 10th century BCE is a major subject of debate. The oldest part of Jerusalem and its original urban core is the City of David, which does not show evidence of significant Israelite residential activity until the 9th century. However, unique administrative structures such as the Stepped Stone Structure and the Large Stone Structure, which originally formed one structure, contain material culture dated to Iron I. On account of the apparent lack of settlement activity in the 10th century BCE, Israel Finkelstein argues that Jerusalem in the century was a small country village in the Judean hills, not a national capital, and Ussishkin argues that the city was entirely uninhabited. Amihai Mazar contends that if the Iron I/Iron IIa dating of administrative structures in the City of David are correct, (as he believes) "Jerusalem was a rather small town with a mighty citadel, which could have been a center of a substantial regional polity."

Biblical narrative

Part of a series on the
History of Israel
Ancient Israel and Judah
• Natufian culture
• Prehistory
• Canaan
• Israelites
• United monarchy
• Northern Kingdom
• Kingdom of Judah
• Babylonian rule

Second Temple period (530 BCE–70 CE)

- Persian rule
- Hellenistic period
- Hasmonean dynasty
- Herodian dynasty
  - Kingdom
  - Tetrarchy
- Roman Judea

Middle Ages (70–1517)

- Roman Palaestina
- Byzantine Palaestina
  - Prima
  - Secunda
- Revolt against Constantius Gallus
- Samaritan revolts
- Revolt against Heraclius
- Caliphates
  - Filastin
  - Urdunn
- Kingdom of Jerusalem
- Ayyubid dynasty
- Mamluk Sultanate

Modern history (1517–1948)

- Ottoman rule
  - Eyalet
  - Mutasarrifate
- Old Yishuv
- Zionism
- OETA
- British mandate

State of Israel (1948–present)
- Independence - Timeline - Years - Arab–Israeli conflict - Start-up Nation
History of the Land of Israel by topic
- Judaism - Jerusalem - Zionism - Jewish leaders - Jewish warfare - Nationality
Related
- Jewish history - Hebrew calendar - Archaeology - Museums

	Israel portal
• v • t • e³⁶⁴	

According to the Hebrew Bible, the kingdom of Judah resulted from the breakup of the United Kingdom of Israel (1020 to about 930 BCE) after the northern tribes refused to accept Rehoboam, the son of Solomon, as their king. At first, only the tribe of Judah remained loyal to the house of David, but soon after the tribe of Benjamin joined Judah. The two kingdoms, Judah in the south and Israel in the north, coexisted uneasily after the split until the destruction of the Kingdom of Israel by Assyria in c. 722/721.

The major theme of the Hebrew Bible's narrative is the loyalty of Judah, and especially its kings, to Yahweh, which it states is the God of Israel. Accordingly, all the kings of Israel and almost all the kings of Judah were "bad", which in terms of Biblical narrative means that they failed to enforce monotheism. Of the "good" kings, Hezekiah (727–698 BCE) is noted for his efforts at stamping out idolatry (in this case, the worship of Baal and Asherah, among other traditional Near Eastern divinities),³⁶⁵ but his successors, Manasseh of Judah (698–642 BCE) and Amon (642–640 BCE), revived idolatry, drawing down on the kingdom the anger of Yahweh. King Josiah (640–609 BCE) returned to the worship of Yahweh alone, but his efforts were too late and Israel's unfaithfulness caused God to permit the kingdom's destruction by the Neo-Babylonian Empire in the Siege of Jerusalem (587 BCE).

However it is now fairly well established among academic scholars that the Biblical narrative is not an accurate reflection of religious views in either Judah or particularly Israel during this period.

Relations with the Northern Kingdom

Rulers of Judah

- Saul
- David
- Solomon
- Rehoboam
- Abijah
- Asa
- Jehoshaphat
- Jehoram
- Ahaziah
- Athaliah

- J(eh)oash
- Amaziah
- Uzziah/Azariah
- Jotham
- Ahaz
- Hezekiah
- Manasseh
- Amon
- Josiah
- Jehoahaz
- Jehoiakim
- Jeconiah/Jehoiachin
- Zedekiah
- <u>v</u>
- <u>t</u>
- <u>e</u>[366]

For the first sixty years, the kings of Judah tried to re-establish their authority over the northern kingdom, and there was perpetual war between them. Israel and Judah were in a state of war throughout Rehoboam's seventeen-year reign. Rehoboam built elaborate defenses and strongholds, along with fortified cities. In the fifth year of Rehoboam's reign, Shishak, pharaoh of Egypt, brought a huge army and took many cities. In the sack of Jerusalem (10th century BCE), Rehoboam gave them all of the treasures out of the temple as a tribute and Judah became a vassal state of Egypt.

Rehoboam's son and successor, Abijah of Judah continued his father's efforts to bring Israel under his control. He fought the Battle of Mount Zemaraim against Jeroboam of Israel and was victorious with a heavy loss of life on the Israel side. According to the books of Chronicles, Abijah and his people defeated them with a great slaughter, so that 500,000 chosen men of Israel fell slain after which Jeroboam posed little threat to Judah for the rest of his reign and the border of the tribe of Benjamin was restored to the original tribal border.

Abijah's son and successor, Asa of Judah, maintained peace for the first 35 years of his reign, during which time he revamped and reinforced the fortresses originally built by his grandfather, Rehoboam. 2 Chronicles states that at the Battle of Zephath, the Egyptian-backed chieftain Zerah the Ethiopian and his million men and 300 chariots was defeated by Asa's 580,000 men in the Valley of Zephath near Maresha. The Bible does not state whether Zerah was a pharaoh or a general of the army. The Ethiopians were pursued all the way to Gerar, in the coastal plain, where they stopped out of sheer exhaustion. The resulting peace kept Judah free from Egyptian incursions until the time of Josiah some centuries later.

In his 36th year, Asa was confronted by Baasha of Israel, who built a fortress at Ramah on the border, less than ten miles from Jerusalem. The result was that the capital was under pressure and the military situation was precarious. Asa took gold and silver from the Temple and sent them to Ben-Hadad I, king of Aram-Damascus, in exchange for the Damascene king canceling his peace treaty with Baasha. Ben-Hadad attacked Ijon, Dan, and many important cities of the tribe of Naphtali, and Baasha was forced to withdraw from Ramah. Asa tore down the unfinished fortress and used its raw materials to fortify Geba and Mizpah in Benjamin on his side of the border.

Asa's successor, Jehoshaphat, changed the policy towards Israel and instead pursued alliances and co-operation with the northern kingdom. The alliance with Ahab was based on marriage. This alliance led to disaster for the kingdom with the battle of Ramoth-Gilead. He then entered into an alliance with Ahaziah of Israel for the purpose of carrying on maritime commerce with Ophir. But the fleet that was then equipped at Ezion-Geber was immediately wrecked. A new fleet was fitted out without the cooperation of the king of Israel, and although it was successful, the trade was not prosecuted. He subsequently joined Jehoram of Israel in a war against the Moabites, who were under tribute to Israel. This war was successful, with the Moabites being subdued. However, on seeing Mesha's act of offering his own son in a human sacrifice on the walls of Kir-haresheth filled Jehoshaphat with horror and he withdrew and returned to his own land.

Jehoshaphat's successor, Jehoram of Judah formed an alliance with Israel by marrying Athaliah, the daughter of Ahab. Despite this alliance with the stronger northern kingdom, Jehoram's rule of Judah was shaky. Edom revolted, and he was forced to acknowledge their independence. A raid by Philistines, Arabs and Ethiopians looted the king's house and carried off all of his family except for his youngest son, Ahaziah of Judah.

Clash of empires

After Hezekiah became sole ruler in c. 715 BCE, he formed alliances with Ashkelon and Egypt, and made a stand against Assyria by refusing to pay tribute. (Isaiah 30–31[367]; 36:6–9[368]) In response, Sennacherib of Assyria attacked the fortified cities of Judah. (2 Kings 18:13[369]) Hezekiah paid three hundred talents of silver and thirty talents of gold to Assyria – requiring him to empty the temple and royal treasury of silver and strip the gold from the doorposts of Solomon's Temple. (2 Kings 18:14–16[370]) However, Sennacherib besieged Jerusalem[371] (2 Kings 18:17[372]) in 701 BCE, though the city was never taken.

During the long reign of Manasseh (c. 687/686 – 643/642 BCE), Judah was a vassal of Assyrian rulers – Sennacherib and his successors, Esarhaddon and

Figure 23: *Stamped bulla of a servant of King Hezekiah used to seal a papyrus document*

Ashurbanipal after 669 BCE. Manasseh is listed as being required to provide materials for Esarhaddon's building projects, and as one of a number of vassals who assisted Ashurbanipal's campaign against Egypt.

When Josiah became king of Judah in c. 641/640 BCE, the international situation was in flux. To the east, the Neo-Assyrian Empire was beginning to disintegrate, the Neo-Babylonian Empire had not yet risen to replace it, and Egypt to the west was still recovering from Assyrian rule. In this power vacuum, Judah was able to govern itself for the time being without foreign intervention. However, in the spring of 609 BCE, Pharaoh Necho II personally led a sizable army up to the Euphrates to aid the Assyrians. Taking the coast route Via Maris into Syria at the head of a large army, Necho passed the low tracts of Philistia and Sharon. However, the passage over the ridge of hills which shuts in on the south of the great Jezreel Valley was blocked by the Judean army led by Josiah, who may have considered that the Assyrians and Egyptians were weakened by the death of the pharaoh Psamtik I only a year earlier (610 BCE). Presumably in an attempt to help the Babylonians, Josiah attempted to block the advance at Megiddo, where a fierce battle was fought and where Josiah was killed. Necho then joined forces with the Assyrian Ashur-uballit II and together they crossed the Euphrates and lay siege to Harran. The combined forces failed to capture the city, and Necho retreated back to northern Syria. The event also marked the disintegration of the Assyrian Empire.

On his return march to Egypt in 608 BCE, Necho found that Jehoahaz had been selected to succeed his father, Josiah. Necho deposed Jehoahaz, who had been king for only three months, and replaced him with his older brother, Jehoiakim. Necho imposed on Judah a levy of a hundred talents of silver (about $3^3/_4$ tons or about 3.4 metric tons) and a talent of gold (about 34 kilograms (75 lb)). Necho then took Jehoahaz back to Egypt as his prisoner, never to return.

Jehoiakim ruled originally as a vassal of the Egyptians, paying a heavy tribute. However, when the Egyptians were defeated by the Babylonians at Carchemish in 605 BCE, Jehoiakim changed allegiances, paying tribute to Nebuchadnezzar II of Babylon. In 601 BCE, in the fourth year of his reign, Nebuchadnezzar unsuccessfully attempted to invade Egypt and was repulsed with heavy losses. This failure led to numerous rebellions among the states of the Levant which owed allegiance to Babylon. Jehoiakim also stopped paying tribute to Nebuchadnezzar and took a pro-Egyptian position. Nebuchadnezzar soon dealt with these rebellions. According to the Babylonian Chronicles, after invading "the land of Hatti (Syria/Palestine)"[373] in 599 BCE, he lay siege to Jerusalem. Jehoiakim died in 598 BCE during the siege, and was succeeded by his son Jeconiah at an age of either eight or eighteen. The city fell about three months later, on 2 Adar (March 16) 597 BCE. Nebuchadnezzar pillaged both Jerusalem and the Temple, carting all his spoils to Babylon. Jeconiah and his court and other prominent citizens and craftsmen, along with a sizable portion of the Jewish population of Judah, numbering about 10,000 were deported from the land and dispersed throughout the Babylonian Empire. (2 Kings 24:14[374]) Among them was Ezekiel. Nebuchadnezzar appointed Zedekiah, Jehoiakim's brother, king of the reduced kingdom, who was made a tributary of Babylon.

Destruction and dispersion

Despite the strong remonstrances of Jeremiah and others, Zedekiah revolted against Nebuchadnezzar, ceasing to pay tribute to him and entered into an alliance with Pharaoh Hophra. In 589 BCE, Nebuchadnezzar II returned to Judah and again besieged Jerusalem. During this period, many Jews fled to surrounding Moab, Ammon, Edom and other countries to seek refuge. The city fell after a siege which lasted either eighteen or thirty months and Nebuchadnezzar again pillaged both Jerusalem and the Temple, after which he destroyed them both. After killing all of Zedekiah's sons, with the possible exception of one, Nebuchadnezzar took Zedekiah to Babylon, putting an end to the independent Kingdom of Judah. According to the Book of Jeremiah, in addition to those killed during the siege, some 4,600 people were deported after the fall of

Figure 24: *Depiction of Jewish king and soldiers in ancient Judah*

Judah. By 586 BCE much of Judah was devastated, and the former kingdom suffered a steep decline of both economy and population.

Jerusalem apparently remained uninhabited for much of the 6th century, and the centre of gravity shifted to Benjamin, the relatively unscathed northern section of the kingdom, where the town of Mizpah became the capital of the new Babylonian province of Yehud for the remnant of the Jewish population in a part of the former kingdom. This was standard Babylonian practice: when the Philistine city of Ashkelon was conquered in 604 BCE, the political, religious and economic elite (but not the bulk of the population) was banished and the administrative centre shifted to a new location.

Gedaliah was appointed governor of the Yehud Medinata, supported by a Babylonian guard. The administrative centre of the province was Mizpah in Benjamin, not Jerusalem. On hearing of the appointment, many of the Judeans that had taken refuge in surrounding countries were persuaded to return to Judah. However, before long Gedaliah was assassinated by a member of the royal house, and the Chaldean soldiers killed. The population that was left in the land and those that had returned fled to Egypt fearing a Babylonian reprisal, under the leadership of Yohanan ben Kareah, ignoring the urging of the prophet Jeremiah against the move. (2 Kings 25:26[375], Jeremiah 43:5–7[376]) In Egypt, the refugees settled in Migdol, Tahpanhes, Noph, and Pathros, (Jeremiah 44:1[377]) and Jeremiah went with them as a moral guardian.

The numbers that were deported to Babylon and those who made their way to Egypt and the remnant that remained in the land and in surrounding countries is subject to academic debate. The Book of Jeremiah reports that 4600 were exiled to Babylonia. The Books of Kings suggest that it was ten thousand, and later eight thousand.

Re-establishment under Persian rule

In 539 BCE the Achaemenid Empire conquered Babylonia and allowed the exiles to return to Yehud Medinata and rebuild the Temple, which was completed in the sixth year of Darius (515 BCE) (Ezra 6:15[378]) under Zerubbabel, the grandson of the second to last king of Judah, Jeconiah. Yehud Medinata was a peaceful part of the Achaemenid Empire until the fall of the Empire in c. 333 BCE to Alexander the Great.

References

 Wikimedia Commons has media related to *Kingdom of Judah*.

Further reading

- Albertz, Rainer (1994) [Vanderhoek & Ruprecht 1992]. *A History of Israelite Religion, Volume I: From the Beginnings to the End of the Monarchy*[379]. Westminster John Knox Press.<templatestyles src="Module:Citation/CS1/styles.css"></templatestyles>
- Albertz, Rainer (1994) [Vanderhoek & Ruprecht 1992]. *A History of Israelite Religion, Volume II: From the Exile to the Maccabees*[380]. Westminster John Knox Press.<templatestyles src="Module:Citation/CS1/styles.css"></templatestyles>
- Albertz, Rainer (2003a). *Israel in Exile: The History and Literature of the Sixth Century B.C.E.*[381] Society of Biblical Literature.<templatestyles src="Module:Citation/CS1/styles.css"></templatestyles>
- Becking, Bob (2003b). "Law as Expression of Religion (Ezra 7–10)". *Yahwism After the Exile: Perspectives on Israelite Religion in the Persian Era*[382]. Koninklijke Van Gorcum. ISBN 978-9023238805.<templatestyles src="Module:Citation/CS1/styles.css"></templatestyles>
- Amit, Yaira, et al., eds. (2006). *Essays on Ancient Israel in its Near Eastern Context: A Tribute to Nadav Na'aman*[383]. Eisenbrauns.<templatestyles src="Module:Citation/CS1/styles.css"></templatestyles>

- Davies, Philip R. "The Origin of Biblical Israel"[384]. Retrieved 14 February 2015.<templatestyles src="Module:Citation/CS1/styles.css"></templatestyles>
- Barstad, Hans M. (2008). *History and the Hebrew Bible*[385]. Mohr Siebeck.<templatestyles src="Module:Citation/CS1/styles.css"></templatestyles>
- Bedford, Peter Ross (2001). *Temple Restoration in Early Achaemenid Judah*[386]. Brill.<templatestyles src="Module:Citation/CS1/styles.css"></templatestyles>
- Ben-Sasson, H.H. (1976). *A History of the Jewish People*. Harvard University Press. ISBN 0-674-39731-2.<templatestyles src="Module:Citation/CS1/styles.css"></templatestyles>
- Blenkinsopp, Joseph (1988). *Ezra-Nehemiah: A Commentary*[387]. Eerdmans.<templatestyles src="Module:Citation/CS1/styles.css"></templatestyles>
- Blenkinsopp, Joseph; Lipschits, Oded, eds. (2003). *Judah and the Judeans in the Neo-Babylonian Period*[388]. Eisenbrauns.<templatestyles src="Module:Citation/CS1/styles.css"></templatestyles>
- Blenkinsopp, Joseph (2003). "Bethel in the Neo-Babylonian Period". In Oded Lipschits; Joseph Blenkinsopp. *Judah and the Judeans in the Neo-Babylonian Period*[389]. Eisenbrauns. ISBN 978-1575060736.<templatestyles src="Module:Citation/CS1/styles.css"></templatestyles>
- Blenkinsopp, Joseph (2009). *Judaism, the First Phase: The Place of Ezra and Nehemiah in the Origins of Judaism*[390]. Eerdmans.<templatestyles src="Module:Citation/CS1/styles.css"></templatestyles>
- Brett, Mark G. (2002). *Ethnicity and the Bible*[391]. Brill.<templatestyles src="Module:Citation/CS1/styles.css"></templatestyles>
- Bright, John (2000). *A History of Israel*[392]. Westminster John Knox Press.<templatestyles src="Module:Citation/CS1/styles.css"></templatestyles>
- Coogan, Michael D., ed. (1998). *The Oxford History of the Biblical World*[393]. Oxford University Press.<templatestyles src="Module:Citation/CS1/styles.css"></templatestyles>
- Coote, Robert B.; Whitelam, Keith W. (1986). "The Emergence of Israel: Social Transformation and State Formation Following the Decline in Late Bronze Age Trade". *Semeia* (37): 107–47.<templatestyles src="Module:Citation/CS1/styles.css"></templatestyles>
- Davies, Philip R. (1992). *In Search of Ancient Israel*[394]. Sheffield.<templatestyles src="Module:Citation/CS1/styles.css"></templatestyles>

- Davies, Philip R. (2009). "The Origin of Biblical Israel"[395]. *Journal of Hebrew Scriptures*. **9** (47). Archived from the original[396] on 2008-05-28.<templatestyles src="Module:Citation/CS1/styles.css"></templatestyles>
- Dever, William (2001). *What Did the Biblical Writers Know, and When Did They Know It?*[397]. Eerdmans.<templatestyles src="Module:Citation/CS1/styles.css"></templatestyles>
- Dever, William (2003). *Who Were the Early Israelites and Where Did They Come From?*[398]. Eerdmans.<templatestyles src="Module:Citation/CS1/styles.css"></templatestyles>
- Dunn, James D.G; Rogerson, John William, eds. (2003). *Eerdmans commentary on the Bible*[399]. Eerdmans.<templatestyles src="Module:Citation/CS1/styles.css"></templatestyles>
- Edelman, Diana, ed. (1995). *The Triumph of Elohim: From Yahwisms to Judaisms*[400]. Kok Pharos.<templatestyles src="Module:Citation/CS1/styles.css"></templatestyles>
- Finkelstein, Israel; Silberman, Neil Asher (2001). *The Bible Unearthed*[401].<templatestyles src="Module:Citation/CS1/styles.css"></templatestyles>
- Finkelstein, Israel; Mazar, Amihay; Schmidt, Brian B. (2007). *The Quest for the Historical Israel*[402]. Society of Biblical Literature.<templatestyles src="Module:Citation/CS1/styles.css"></templatestyles>
- Golden, Jonathan Michael (2004a). *Ancient Canaan and Israel: An Introduction*[403]. Oxford University Press.<templatestyles src="Module:Citation/CS1/styles.css"></templatestyles>
- Golden, Jonathan Michael (2004b). *Ancient Canaan and Israel: New Perspectives*[404]. ABC-CLIO.<templatestyles src="Module:Citation/CS1/styles.css"></templatestyles>
- Killebrew, Ann E. (2005). *Biblical Peoples and Ethnicity: An Archaeological Study of Egyptians, Canaanites, and Early Israel, 1300–1100 B.C.E.*[405] Society of Biblical Literature.<templatestyles src="Module:Citation/CS1/styles.css"></templatestyles>
- King, Philip J.; Stager, Lawrence E. (2001). *Life in Biblical Israel*[406]. Westminster John Knox Press. ISBN 0-664-22148-3.<templatestyles src="Module:Citation/CS1/styles.css"></templatestyles>
- Kuhrt, Amélie (1995). *The Ancient Near East c. 3000–330 BC*[407]. Routledge.<templatestyles src="Module:Citation/CS1/styles.css"></templatestyles>
- Lemche, Niels Peter (1998). *The Israelites in History and Tradition*[408]. Westminster John Knox Press.<templatestyles src="Module:Citation/CS1/styles.css"></templatestyles>
- Levy, Thomas E. (1998). *The Archaeology of Society in the Holy*

- *Land*[409]. Continuum International Publishing.
- Lipschits, Oded (2005). *The Fall and Rise of Jerusalem*[410]. Eisenbrauns.
- Lipschits, Oded, et al., eds. (2006). *Judah and the Judeans in the Fourth Century B.C.E.*[411] Eisenbrauns.
- McNutt, Paula (1999). *Reconstructing the Society of Ancient Israel*[412]. Westminster John Knox Press.
- Merrill, Eugene H. (1995). "The Late Bronze/Early Iron Age Transition and the Emergence of Israel". *Bibliotheca Sacra*. **152** (606): 145–62.
- Middlemas, Jill Anne (2005). *The Troubles of Templeless Judah*[413]. Oxford University Press.
- Miller, James Maxwell; Hayes, John Haralson (1986). *A History of Ancient Israel and Judah*[414]. Westminster John Knox Press. ISBN 0-664-21262-X.
- Miller, Robert D. (2005). *Chieftains of the Highland Clans: A History of Israel in the 12th and 11th Centuries B.C.*[415] Eerdmans.
- Moore, Megan Bishop; Kelle, Brad E. (2011). *Biblical History and Israel's Past*[416]. Eerdmans. ISBN 978-0-8028-6260-0.
- Pitkänen, Pekka (2004). "Ethnicity, Assimilation and the Israelite Settlement"[417] (PDF). *Tyndale Bulletin*. **55** (2): 161–82. Archived from the original[418] (PDF) on 2011-07-17.
- Silberman, Neil Asher; Small, David B., eds. (1997). *The Archaeology of Israel: Constructing the Past, Interpreting the Present*[419]. Sheffield Academic Press.
- Soggin, Michael J. (1998). *An Introduction to the History of Israel and Judah*[420]. Paideia.
- Van der Toorn, Karel (1996). *Family Religion in Babylonia, Syria, and Israel*[421]. Brill.

- Zevit, Ziony (2001). *The Religions of Ancient Israel: A Synthesis of Parallactic Approaches*[422]. Continuum.

Roman period (64 BCE–4th century CE)

History of the Jews in the Roman Empire

The **history of the Jews in the Roman Empire** traces the interaction of Jews and Romans during the period of the Roman Empire (27 BC – AD 476). Their cultures began to overlap in the centuries just before the Christian Era. Jews, as part of the Jewish diaspora, migrated to Rome and Roman Europe from the Land of Israel, Asia Minor, Babylon and Alexandria in response to economic hardship and incessant warfare over the land of Israel between the Ptolemaic and Seleucid empires. In Rome, Jewish communities enjoyed privileges and thrived economically, becoming a significant part of the Empire's population (perhaps as much as ten percent).

The Roman general Pompey in his eastern campaign established the Roman province of Syria in 64 BC and conquered Jerusalem in 63 BC. Julius Caesar conquered Alexandria c. 47 BC and defeated Pompey in 45 BC. Under Julius Caesar, Judaism was officially recognised as a legal religion, a policy followed by the first Roman emperor, Augustus. Herod the Great was designated 'King of the Jews' by the Roman Senate in c. 40 BC, the Roman province of Egypt was established in 30 BC, and Judea proper, Samaria and Idumea (biblical Edom) were converted to the Roman province of Iudaea in 6 AD. Jewish–Roman tensions resulted in several Jewish–Roman wars, 66-135 AD, which resulted in the destruction of Jerusalem and the Second Temple and institution of the Jewish Tax in 70 and Hadrian's attempt to create a new Roman colony named Aelia Capitolina c. 130.

Around this time, Christianity developed from Second Temple Judaism. In 313, Constantine and Licinius issued the Edict of Milan giving official recognition to Christianity as a legal religion. Constantine the Great moved the Roman capital from Rome to Constantinople ('New Rome') c. 330, sometimes

Figure 25: *Figure of a holy man from the 3rd-century wall paintings at the synagogue of Dura-Europos*

considered the start of the Byzantine Empire, and with the Edict of Thessalonica in 380, Christianity became the state church of the Roman Empire. The Christian emperors persecuted their Jewish subjects and restricted their rights.

Jews in Rome

According to the *Jewish Encyclopedia* article on Rome:[423] <templatestyles src="Template:Quote/styles.css"/>

> Jews have lived in Rome for over 2,000 years, longer than in any other European city. They originally went there from Alexandria, drawn by the lively commercial intercourse between those two cities. They may even have established a community there as early as the second pre-Christian century, for in the year 139 B.C. the pretor Hispanus issued a decree expelling all Jews who were not Italian citizens.

The Jewish Encyclopedia connects the two civil wars raging during the last decades of the first century BC: one in Judea between the two Hasmonean brothers Hyrcanus II and Aristobulus II and one in the Roman republic between Julius Caesar and Pompey, and describes the evolution of the Jewish population in Rome:

Figure 26: *Siege and destruction of Jerusalem by the Romans. Painted c.1504*

<templatestyles src="Template:Quote/styles.css"/>

> ... the Jewish community in Rome grew very rapidly. The Jews who were taken to Rome as prisoners were either ransomed by their coreligionists or set free by their Roman masters, who found their peculiar custom obnoxious. They settled as traders on the right bank of the Tiber, and thus originated the Jewish quarter in Rome.

Even before Rome annexed Judea as a province, the Romans had interacted with Jews from their diasporas settled in Rome for a century and a half. Many cities of the Roman provinces in the eastern Mediterranean contained very large Jewish communities, dispersed from the time of the sixth century BCE.

Rome's involvement in the Eastern Mediterranean dated from 63 BC, following the end of the Third Mithridatic War, when Rome made Syria a province. After the defeat of Mithridates VI of Pontus, the proconsul Pompeius Magnus (Pompey the Great) remained to secure the area, including a visit to the Jerusalem Temple. During the 1st century BC, the Herodian Kingdom was established as a Roman client kingdom and in 6 AD parts became a province of the Roman Empire, named Iudaea Province.[424]

Julius Caesar formulated a policy of allowing Jews to follow their traditional religious practices, a policy which was followed, and extended, by Augustus,

Figure 27: *Relief from the Arch of Titus in Rome depicting a menorah and other objects looted from the Temple of Jerusalem carried in a Roman triumph*

first emperor of Rome, reigned 27 BC - 14 AD. This gave Judaism the status of a *religio licita* (permitted religion) throughout the Empire.

The financial crisis under Caligula (37–41) has been proposed as the "first open break between Rome and the Jews", even though problems were already evident during the Census of Quirinius in 6 and under Sejanus (before 31).[425]

Jewish–Roman wars

In 66 AD, the First Jewish–Roman War began. The revolt was put down by the future Roman emperors Vespasian and Titus. In the Siege of Jerusalem in 70 AD, the Romans destroyed much of the Temple in Jerusalem and, according to some accounts, plundered artifacts from the Temple, such as the Menorah. Jews continued to live in their land in significant numbers, the Kitos War of 115-117 notwithstanding, until Julius Severus ravaged Judea while putting down the Bar Kokhba revolt of 132–136. 985 villages were destroyed and most of the Jewish population of central Judaea was essentially wiped out – killed, sold into slavery, or forced to flee.[426] Banished from Jerusalem, which was renamed Aelia Capitolina, the Jewish population now centered on Galilee,[427] initially at Yavneh.

After the Jewish-Roman wars (66–135), Hadrian changed the name of Iudaea province to *Syria Palaestina* and Jerusalem to *Aelia Capitolina* in an attempt to erase the historical ties of the Jewish people to the region.[428] In addition, after 70, Jews and Jewish Proselytes were only allowed to practice their religion if

Figure 28: *Jewish ritual objects depicted in 2nd century gold glass from Rome*

they paid the Jewish tax, and after 135 were barred from Jerusalem except for the day of Tisha B'Av.

The diaspora

Many of the Judaean Jews were sold into slavery[429] while others became citizens of other parts of the Roman Empire. The book of Acts in the New Testament, as well as other Pauline texts, make frequent reference to the large populations of Hellenised Jews in the cities of the Roman world. These Hellenised Jews were only affected by the diaspora in its spiritual sense, absorbing the feeling of loss and homelessness which became a cornerstone of the Jewish faith, much supported by persecutions in various parts of the world. The policy towards proselytization and conversion to Judaism, which spread the Jewish religion throughout Hellenistic civilization, seems to have ended with the wars against the Romans and the following reconstruction of Jewish values for the post-Temple era.

Of critical importance to the reshaping of Jewish tradition from the Temple-based religion to the traditions of the Diaspora, was the development of the interpretations of the Torah found in the Mishnah and Talmud.

Figure 29: *A pair of putti bearing a menorah, on a cast of a 2nd- or 3rd-century relief (original in the National Museum of Rome)*

Late Roman period

In spite of the failure of the Bar Kokhba revolt, Jews remained in the land of Israel in significant numbers. The Jews who remained there went through numerous experiences and armed conflicts against consecutive occupiers of the Land. Some of the most famous and important Jewish texts were composed in Israeli cities at this time. The Jerusalem Talmud, the completion of the Mishnah and the system of niqqud are examples.

In this period the *tannaim* and *amoraim* were active rabbis who organized and debated the Jewish oral law. A major catalyst in Palestinian Judaism is haNasi, who was a wealthy rabbi and one of the last tannaim, oral interpreters of the Law. He was in good standing with Roman authority figures, which aided in his ascent to being the Patriarch of the Jewish community in Palestine. The decisions of the *tannaim* are contained in the Mishnah, Beraita, Tosefta, and various Midrash compilations. The Mishnah was completed shortly after 200 AD, probably by Judah haNasi. The commentaries of the *amoraim* upon the Mishnah are compiled in the Jerusalem Talmud, which was completed around 400 AD, probably in Tiberias.

In 351, the Jewish population in Sepphoris, under the leadership of Patricius, started a revolt against the rule of Constantius Gallus, brother-in-law of Emperor Constantius II. The revolt was eventually subdued by Gallus' general, Ursicinus.

According to tradition, in 359 Hillel II created the Hebrew calendar, which is a lunisolar calendar based on math rather than observation. Until then, the entire Jewish community outside the land of Israel depended on the observational calendar sanctioned by the Sanhedrin; this was necessary for the proper observance of the Jewish holy days. However, danger threatened the participants in that sanction and the messengers who communicated their decisions to distant communities. As the religious persecutions continued, Hillel determined to provide an authorized calendar for all time to come that was not dependent on observation at Jerusalem.

Julian, the only emperor to reject Christianity after the conversion of Constantine, allowed the Jews to return to "holy Jerusalem which you have for many years longed to see rebuilt" and to rebuild the Temple. However Julian was killed in battle on 26 June 363 in his failed campaign against the Sassanid Empire, and the Third Temple was not rebuilt at that time.

During the Byzantine–Sasanian War of 602–628 many Jews sided against the Eastern Roman Empire in the Jewish revolt against Heraclius, which successfully assisted the invading Persian Sassanids in conquering all of Roman Egypt and Syria. In reaction to this further anti-Jewish measures were enacted throughout the Eastern Roman realm and as far away as Merovingian France.[430] Soon thereafter, 634, the Muslim conquests began, during which many Jews initially rose up again against their Eastern Roman rulers.[431]

Dispersion of the Jews in the Roman Empire

Following the 1st-century Great Revolt and the 2nd-century Bar Kokhba revolt, the destruction of Judea exerted a decisive influence upon the dispersion of the Jewish people throughout the world, as the center of worship shifted from the Temple to Rabbinic authority.

Some Jews were sold as slaves or transported as captives after the fall of Judea, others joined the existing diaspora, while still others remained in Judea and began work on the Jerusalem Talmud. The Jews in the diaspora were generally accepted into the Roman Empire, but with the rise of Christianity, restrictions grew. Forced expulsions and persecution resulted in substantial shifts in the international centers of Jewish life to which far-flung communities often looked, although not always unified, due to the Jewish people's dispersion itself. Jewish communities were thereby largely expelled from Judea and sent to various Roman provinces in the Middle East, Europe and North Africa. The Roman Jewry came to develop a character associated with the urban middle class in the modern age.

Figure 30: *Expulsion of the Jews in the Reign of the Emperor Hadrian (135 CE): How Heraclius turned the Jews out of Jerusalem. (Facsimile of a miniature in the Histoire des Empereurs, 15th-century manuscript, in the Library of the Arsenal, Paris.)*

Further reading

- Barclay, John M. G. 1996. *Jews in the Mediterranean Diaspora from Alexander to Trajan (323 B.C.E.–117 C.E.).* Edinburgh: T. & T. Clark.
- Goodman, Martin. 2000. *State and Society in Roman Galilee, A.D. 132–212.* London and Portland, OR: Vallentine Mitchell.
- Goodman, M. 2004. "Trajan and the Origins of Roman Hostility to the Jews." *Past & Present* 182: 3-29.
- Mclaren, James S. 2013. "The Jews in Rome during the Flavian Period." *Antichthon* 47:156-172.
- Pucci Ben Zeev, Miriam. 1998. *Jewish Rights in the Roman World: The Greek and Roman Documents Quoted by Josephus Flavius.* Tübingen, Germany: Mohr.
- Rutgers, Leonard Victor. 2000. *The Jews in Late Ancient Rome: Evidence of Cultural Interaction in the Roman Diaspora.* Leiden, The Netherlands: Brill.
- Schürer, Emil. 1973. *The History of the Jewish People in the Time of Jesus Christ (175 B.C.–135 A.D.).* Revised and edited by Emil Schürer,

Géza Vermès, Fergus Millar, Matthew Black, and Martin Goodman. 2 vols. Edinburgh: T. & T. Clark.
- Smallwood, E. Mary. 1976. The Jews under Roman Rule. Leiden, The Netherlands: Brill.
- Stern, Menahem, ed. 1974. *Greek and Latin Authors on Jews and Judaism.* 3 vols. Jerusalem: Israel Academy of Sciences and Humanities.
- Varhelyi, Zsuzsanna. 2000. "Jews in Civic Life under the Roman Empire." *Acta antiqua Academiae Scientiarum Hungaricae* 40.1/4:471-478.
- Weitzmann, Kurt, ed. 1979. *Age of Spirituality: Late Antique and Early Christian Art, Third to Seventh Century.* New York: The Museum.

Crusades and Mongols (1099–1291)

Kingdom of Jerusalem

(Latin) Kingdom of Jerusalem
Regnum Hierosolimitanum (Latin) *Roiaume de Jherusalem* (Old French) *Regno di Gerusalemme* (Italian) Βασίλειον τῶν Ἱεροσολύμων (Medieval Greek) הלטיניח ירושלים ממלכח (Hebrew) مملكة القدس (Arabic)
1099–1291
 Flag Coat of arms

Kingdom of Jerusalem

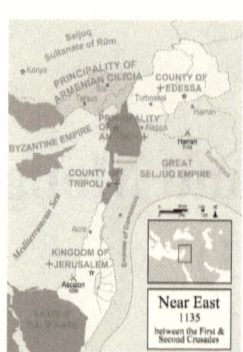

Capital	Jerusalem (1099–1187, 1229–1244) Tyre (1187–1191) Acre (1191–1229, 1244–1291)
Common languages	Latin (official/ceremonial) Old French (popular) Italian Arabic Medieval Greek Western Aramaic
Religion	Catholic Church (official) Eastern Orthodox Church Islam Judaism Samaritanism Druzism
Government	Feudal monarchy
King of Jerusalem	
• 1100–1118	Baldwin I
• 1285–1291	Henry II
Legislature	Haute Cour
Historical era	High Middle Ages
• First Crusade	1095–1099
• Capture of Jerusalem	15 July 1099
• Battle of Montgisard	25 November 1177
• First Fall of Jerusalem	1187
• Third Crusade	1189
• Sixth Crusade	1229
• War of the Lombards	1228–1243
• Final Fall of Jerusalem	1244

Kingdom of Jerusalem

	• Fall of Acre	18 May 1291
Population		
	• 1131[432]	250,000
Currency		Bezant
Preceded by		**Succeeded by**
Fatimid Caliphate		Ayyubid Dynasty
Great Seljuq Empire		Mamluk Sultanate (Cairo)
Today part of		Cyprus Egypt Israel Palestine Jordan Lebanon

Part of a series on the

History of Israel

Ancient Israel and Judah

- Natufian culture
- Prehistory
- Canaan
- Israelites
- United monarchy
- Northern Kingdom
- Kingdom of Judah
- Babylonian rule

Second Temple period (530 BCE–70 CE)

- Persian rule
- Hellenistic period
- Hasmonean dynasty
- Herodian dynasty
  - Kingdom
  - Tetrarchy
- Roman Judea

Middle Ages (70–1517)

- Roman Palaestina
- Byzantine Palaestina
  - Prima
  - Secunda
- Revolt against Constantius Gallus

- Samaritan revolts
- Revolt against Heraclius
- Caliphates
  - Filastin
  - Urdunn
- Kingdom of Jerusalem
- Ayyubid dynasty
- Mamluk Sultanate

Modern history (1517–1948)

- Ottoman rule
  - Eyalet
  - Mutasarrifate
- Old Yishuv
- Zionism
- OETA
- British mandate

State of Israel (1948–present)

- Independence
- Timeline
- Years
- Arab–Israeli conflict
- Start-up Nation

History of the Land of Israel by topic

- Judaism
- Jerusalem
- Zionism
- Jewish leaders
- Jewish warfare
- Nationality

Related

- Jewish history
- Hebrew calendar
- Archaeology
- Museums

Israel portal

- v
- t
- e[433]

The **(Latin) Kingdom of Jerusalem** was a crusader state established in the Southern Levant by Godfrey of Bouillon in 1099 after the First Crusade. The kingdom lasted nearly two hundred years, from 1099 until 1291 when the last remaining possession, Acre, was destroyed by the Mamluks, but its history is divided into two distinct periods. The sometimes so-called **First Kingdom of Jerusalem** lasted from 1099 to 1187, when it was almost entirely overrun by Saladin. After the subsequent Third Crusade, the kingdom was re-established in Acre in 1192, and lasted until that city's destruction in 1291, except for a brief two decades in which Frederick II of Hohenstaufen reclaimed Jerusalem back into Christian hands after the Sixth Crusade. This second kingdom is sometimes called the **Second Kingdom of Jerusalem** or the **Kingdom of Acre**, after its new capital. Most of the crusaders who settled there were of French origin.

Geographic boundaries

At first the kingdom was little more than a loose collection of towns and cities captured during the crusade, but at its height in the mid-12th century, the kingdom encompassed roughly the territory of modern-day Israel, Palestine and the southern parts of Lebanon. From the Mediterranean Sea, the kingdom extended in a thin strip of land from Beirut in the north to the Sinai Desert in the south; into modern Jordan and Syria in the east, and towards Fatimid Egypt in the west. Three other crusader states founded during and after the First Crusade were located further north: the County of Edessa (1097–1144), the Principality of Antioch (1098–1268), and the County of Tripoli (1109–1289). While all three were independent, they were closely tied to Jerusalem. Beyond these to the north and west lay the states of Armenian Cilicia and the Byzantine Empire, with which Jerusalem had a close relationship in the twelfth century. Further east, various Muslim emirates were located which were ultimately allied with the Abbasid caliph in Baghdad. The fragmentation of the Muslim east allowed for the initial success of the crusade, but as the 12th century progressed, the kingdom's Muslim neighbours were united by Nur ad-Din Zangi and Saladin, who vigorously began to recapture lost territory. Jerusalem itself fell to Saladin in 1187, and in the 13th century the kingdom was reduced to a few cities along the Mediterranean coast. In this period, the kingdom was ruled by the Lusignan dynasty of the Kingdom of Cyprus, another crusader state founded during the Third Crusade. Dynastic ties also strengthened with Tripoli, Antioch, and Armenia. The kingdom was soon increasingly dominated by the Italian city-states of Venice and Genoa, as well as the imperial ambitions of the Holy Roman Emperors. Emperor Frederick II (reigned 1220-1250) claimed the kingdom by marriage, but his presence sparked a civil war (1228-1243) among the kingdom's nobility. The kingdom became little more than a pawn in the politics and warfare of the Ayyubid and Mamluk dynasties in Egypt, as well as the Khwarezmian and Mongol invaders. As a relatively minor kingdom, it received little financial or military support from Europe; despite numerous small expeditions, Europeans generally proved unwilling to undertake an expensive journey to the east for an apparently losing cause. The Mamluk sultans Baibars (reigned 1260-1277) and al-Ashraf Khalil (reigned

1290-1293) eventually reconquered all the remaining crusader strongholds, culminating in the destruction of Acre in 1291.

People

The kingdom was ethnically, religiously, and linguistically diverse, although the crusaders themselves and their descendants were an elite Catholic minority. They imported many customs and institutions from their homelands in Western Europe, and there were close familial and political connections with the West throughout the kingdom's existence. The kingdom also inherited "oriental" qualities, influenced by the pre-existing customs and populations. The majority of the kingdom's inhabitants were native Christians, especially Greek and Syriac Orthodox, as well as Sunni and Shi'a Muslims. The native Christians and Muslims, who were a marginalized lower class, tended to speak Greek and Arabic, while the crusaders, who came mainly from France, spoke French. There were also a small number of Jews and Samaritans.

According to the Jewish writer Benjamin of Tudela, who travelled through the kingdom around 1170, there were 1,000 Samaritans in Nablus, 200 in Caesarea and 300 in Ascalon. Since sets a lower bound for the Samaritan population at 1,500, since the contemporary *Tolidah*, a Samaritan chronicle, also mentions communities in Gaza and Acre. Benjamin of Tudela estimated the total Jewish population of 14 cities in the kingdom to be 1,200, making the Samaritan population of the time larger than the Jewish, perhaps for the only time in history.[434]

History

First Crusade and the foundation of the kingdom

The First Crusade was preached at the Council of Clermont in 1095 by Pope Urban II, with the goal of assisting the Byzantine Empire against the invasions of the Seljuk Turks. However, the main objective quickly became the control of the Holy Land. The Byzantines were frequently at war with the Seljuks and other Turkish dynasties for control of Anatolia and Syria. The Sunni Seljuks had formerly ruled the Great Seljuk Empire, but this empire had collapsed into several smaller states after the death of Malik-Shah I in 1092. Malik-Shah was succeeded in the Anatolian Sultanate of Rûm by Kilij Arslan I, and in Syria by his brother Tutush I, who died in 1095. Tutush's sons Fakhr al-Mulk Radwan and Duqaq inherited Aleppo and Damascus respectively, further dividing Syria amongst emirs antagonistic towards each other, as well as Kerbogha, the atabeg of Mosul. This disunity among the Anatolian and Syrian emirs allowed

Figure 31: *After the successful siege of Jerusalem in 1099, Godfrey of Bouillon, leader of the First Crusade, became the first ruler of the Kingdom of Jerusalem.*

the crusaders to overcome any military opposition they faced on the way to Jerusalem.

Egypt and much of Palestine were controlled by the Arab Shi'ite Fatimid Caliphate, which had extended further into Syria before the arrival of the Seljuks. Warfare between the Fatimids and Seljuks caused great disruption for the local Christians and for western pilgrims. The Fatimids, under the nominal rule of caliph al-Musta'li but actually controlled by vizier al-Afdal Shahanshah, had lost Jerusalem to the Seljuks in 1073; they recaptured it in 1098 from the Artuqids, a smaller Turkish tribe associated with the Seljuks, just before the arrival of the crusaders.

The crusaders arrived at Jerusalem in June 1099; a few of the neighbouring towns (Ramla, Lydda, Bethlehem, and others) were taken first, and Jerusalem itself was captured on July 15.[435] On 22 July, a council was held in the Church of the Holy Sepulchre to establish a king for the newly created Kingdom of Jerusalem. Raymond IV of Toulouse and Godfrey of Bouillon were recognized as the leaders of the crusade and the siege of Jerusalem. Raymond was the wealthier and more powerful of the two, but at first he refused to become king, perhaps attempting to show his piety and probably hoping that the other nobles would insist upon his election anyway. The more popular Godfrey did not hesitate like Raymond, and accepted a position as secular leader. Although it is widely claimed that he took the title *Advocatus Sancti Sepulchri* ("advocate" or "defender" of the Holy Sepulchre), this title is used only in a letter that was not written by Godfrey. Instead, Godfrey himself seems to have used the more ambiguous term *princeps*, or simply retained his title of *dux* from Lower Lorraine. According to William of Tyre, writing in the later 12th century when Godfrey had become a legendary hero, he refused to wear "a crown of gold" where Christ had worn "a crown of thorns".[436] Robert the Monk is the only contemporary chronicler of the crusade to report that Godfrey took the title "king".[437,438] Raymond was incensed and took his army to forage away from the city. The new kingdom, and Godfrey's reputation, was secured with the defeat of the Fatimid Egyptian army under al-Afdal Shahanshah at the Battle of Ascalon one month after the conquest, on August 12, but Raymond and Godfrey's continued antagonism prevented the crusaders from taking control of Ascalon itself.[439]

There was still some uncertainty about what to do with the new kingdom. The papal legate Daimbert of Pisa convinced Godfrey to hand over Jerusalem to him as Latin Patriarch, with the intention to set up a theocratic state directly under papal control. According to William of Tyre, Godfrey may have supported Daimbert's efforts, and he agreed to take possession of "one or two other cities and thus enlarge the kingdom" if Daimbert were permitted to rule Jerusalem.[440] Godfrey did indeed increase the boundaries of the kingdom, by capturing Jaffa, Haifa, Tiberias, and other cities, and reducing many others to tributary status. He set the foundations for the system of vassalage in the kingdom, establishing the Principality of Galilee and the County of Jaffa. But his reign was short, and he died of an illness in 1100. His brother Baldwin of Boulogne successfully outmanoeuvred Daimbert and claimed Jerusalem for himself as "King of the Latins of Jerusalem". Daimbert compromised by crowning Baldwin in Bethlehem rather than Jerusalem, but the path for a secular state had been laid.[441] Within this secular framework, a Catholic church hierarchy was established, overtop of the local Eastern Orthodox and Syriac Orthodox authorities, who retained their own hierarchies (the Catholics considered them schismatics and thus illegitimate; and vice versa). Under the Latin Patriarch, there were four suffragan archdioceses and numerous dioceses.[442]

Expansion

During Baldwin I's reign, the kingdom expanded even further. The numbers of European inhabitants increased, as the minor crusade of 1101 brought reinforcements to the kingdom. Baldwin repopulated Jerusalem with Franks and native Christians, after his expedition across the Jordan in 1115.[443] With help

Figure 32: *The funeral of Baldwin I from the book: Les Passages d'outremer faits par les Français contre les Turcs depuis Charlemagne jusqu'en 1462.*

from the Italian city-states and other adventurers, notably King Sigurd I of Norway, Baldwin captured the port cities of Acre (1104), Beirut (1110), and Sidon (1111), while exerting his suzerainty over the other crusader states to the north – Edessa (which he had founded in 1097 during the crusade), Antioch, and Tripoli, which he helped capture in 1109. He successfully defended against Muslim invasions, from the Fatimids at the numerous battles at Ramla and elsewhere in the southwest of the kingdom, and from Damascus and Mosul at the Battle of al-Sannabra in the northeast in 1113.[444] As Thomas Madden says, Baldwin was "the true founder of the kingdom of Jerusalem", who "had transformed a tenuous arrangement into a solid feudal state. With brilliance and diligence, he established a strong monarchy, conquered the Palestinian coast, reconciled the crusader barons, and built strong frontiers against the kingdom's Muslim neighbours."[445]

Baldwin brought with him an Armenian wife, traditionally named Arda (although never named such by contemporaries), whom he had married to gain political support from the Armenian population in Edessa, and whom he quickly set aside when he no longer needed Armenian support in Jerusalem. He bigamously married Adelaide del Vasto, regent of Sicily, in 1113, but was convinced to divorce her as well in 1117; Adelaide's son from her first marriage, Roger II of Sicily, never forgave Jerusalem, and for decades withheld much-needed Sicilian naval support.[446]

Baldwin died without heirs in 1118, during a campaign against Egypt, and the kingdom was offered to his brother Eustace III of Boulogne, who had accompanied Baldwin and Godfrey on the crusade. Eustace was uninterested, and instead the crown passed to Baldwin's relative, probably a cousin, Baldwin of Le Bourg, who had previously succeeded him in Edessa. Baldwin II was an able ruler, and he too successfully defended against Fatimid and Seljuk invasions. Although Antioch was severely weakened after the Battle of Ager Sanguinis in 1119, and Baldwin himself was held captive by the emir of Aleppo from 1122–1124, Baldwin led the crusader states to victory at the Battle of Azaz in 1125. His reign saw the establishment of the first military orders, the Knights Hospitaller and the Knights Templar; the earliest surviving written laws of the kingdom, compiled at the Council of Nablus in 1120; and the first commercial treaty with the Republic of Venice, the Pactum Warmundi, in 1124. The increase of naval and military support from Venice led to the capture of Tyre that year. The influence of Jerusalem was further extended over Edessa and Antioch, where Baldwin II acted as regent when their own leaders were killed in battle, although there were regency governments in Jerusalem as well during Baldwin's captivity.[447] Baldwin was married to the Armenian noblewoman Morphia of Melitene, and had four daughters: Hodierna and Alice, who married into the families of the Count of Tripoli and Prince of Antioch; Ioveta, who became an influential abbess; and the eldest, Melisende, who was his heir and succeeded him upon his death in 1131, with her husband Fulk V of Anjou as king-consort. Their son, the future Baldwin III, was named co-heir by his grandfather.[448]

Edessa, Damascus, and the Second Crusade

Fulk was an experienced crusader and had brought military support to the kingdom during a pilgrimage in 1120. He brought Jerusalem into the sphere of the Angevin Empire, as the father of Geoffrey V of Anjou and grandfather of the future Henry II of England. Not everyone appreciated the imposition of a foreigner as king. In 1132 Antioch, Tripoli, and Edessa all asserted their independence and conspired to prevent Fulk from exercising the suzerainty of Jerusalem over them. He defeated Tripoli in battle, and settled the regency in Antioch by arranging a marriage between the countess, Melisende's niece Constance, and his own relative Raymond of Poitiers.[449] Meanwhile, in Jerusalem, the native crusader nobles opposed Fulk's preference for his Angevin retinue. In 1134 Hugh II of Jaffa revolted against Fulk, allying with the Muslim garrison at Ascalon, for which he was convicted of treason *in absentia*. The Latin Patriarch intervened to settle the dispute, but an assassination attempt was then made on Hugh, for which Fulk was blamed. This scandal allowed

Kingdom of Jerusalem 119

Cruisés (xiᵉ-xiiiᵉ-siècles).

Figure 33: *Crusader warriors*

Melisende and her supporters to gain control of the government, just as her father had intended.[450] Accordingly, Fulk "became so uxorious that...not even in unimportant cases did he take any measures without her knowledge and assistance."[451]

Fulk was then faced with a new and more dangerous enemy: the atabeg Zengi of Mosul, who had taken control of Aleppo and had set his sights on Damascus as well; the union of these three states would have been a serious blow to the growing power of Jerusalem. A brief intervention in 1137–1138 by the Byzantine emperor John II Comnenus, who wished to assert imperial suzerainty over all the crusader states, did nothing to stop the threat of Zengi; in 1139 Damascus and Jerusalem recognized the severity of the threat to both states, and an alliance was concluded which halted Zengi's advance. Fulk used this time to construct numerous castles, including Ibelin and Kerak.[452] After the death of both Fulk and Emperor John in separate hunting accidents in 1143, Zengi invaded and conquered Edessa in 1144. Queen Melisende, now regent for her elder son Baldwin III, appointed a new constable, Manasses of Hierges, to head the army after Fulk's death, but Edessa could not be recaptured, despite Zengi's own assassination in 1146.[453] The fall of Edessa shocked Europe, and a Second Crusade arrived in 1148.

After meeting in Acre in June, the crusading kings Louis VII of France and Conrad III of Germany agreed with Melisende, Baldwin III and the major nobles of the kingdom to attack Damascus. Zengi's territory had been divided amongst his sons after his death, and Damascus no longer felt threatened, so an alliance had been made with Zengi's son Nur ad-Din, the emir of Aleppo. Perhaps remembering attacks launched on Jerusalem from Damascus in previous decades, Damascus seemed to be the best target for the crusade, rather than Aleppo or another city to the north which would have allowed for the recapture of Edessa. The subsequent Siege of Damascus was a complete failure; when the city seemed to be on the verge of collapse, the crusader army suddenly moved against another section of the walls, and were driven back. The crusaders retreated within three days. There were rumours of treachery and bribery, and Conrad III felt betrayed by the nobility of Jerusalem. Whatever the reason for the failure, the French and German armies returned home, and a few years later Damascus was firmly under Nur ad-Din's control.[454]

Civil war

The failure of the Second Crusade had dire long-term consequences for the kingdom. The West was hesitant to send large-scale expeditions; for the next few decades, only small armies came, headed by minor European nobles who desired to make a pilgrimage. The Muslim states of Syria were meanwhile gradually united by Nur ad-Din, who defeated the Principality of Antioch at the Battle of Inab in 1149 and gained control of Damascus in 1154. Nur ad-Din was extremely pious and during his rule the concept of jihad came to be interpreted as a kind of counter-crusade against the kingdom, which was an impediment to Muslim unity, both political and spiritual.[455]

In Jerusalem, the crusaders were distracted by a conflict between Melisende and Baldwin III. Melisende continued to rule as regent long after Baldwin came of age. She was supported by, among others, Manasses of Hierges, who essentially governed for her as constable; her son Amalric, whom she set up as Count of Jaffa; Philip of Milly; and the Ibelin family. Baldwin asserted his independence by mediating disputes in Antioch and Tripoli, and gained the support of the Ibelin brothers when they began to oppose Manasses' growing power, thanks to his marriage to their widowed mother Helvis of Ramla. In 1153 Baldwin had himself crowned as sole ruler, and a compromise was reached by which the kingdom was divided in two, with Baldwin taking Acre and Tyre in the north and Melisende remaining in control of Jerusalem and the cities of the south. Baldwin was able to replace Manasses with one of his own supporters, Humphrey II of Toron. Baldwin and Melisende knew that this situation was untenable. Baldwin soon invaded his mother's possessions, defeated Manasses, and besieged his mother in the Tower of David in Jerusalem. Melisende surrendered and retired to Nablus, but Baldwin appointed her his regent and chief advisor, and she retained some of her influence, especially

Figure 34: *The Tower of David in Jerusalem as it appears today*

in appointing ecclesiastical officials.[456] In 1153, Baldwin launched an offensive against Ascalon, the fortress in the south from which Fatimid Egyptian armies had continually raided Jerusalem since the foundation of the kingdom. The fortress was captured and was added to the County of Jaffa, still in the possession of his brother Amalric.[457]

Byzantine alliance and invasion of Egypt

With the capture of Ascalon the southern border of the kingdom was now secure, and Egypt, formerly a major threat to the kingdom but now destabilized under the reign of several underaged caliphs, was reduced to a tributary state. Nur ad-Din remained a threat in the east, and Baldwin had to contend with the advances of Byzantine emperor Manuel I Comnenus, who claimed suzerainty over the Principality of Antioch. In order to bolster the defences of the kingdom against the growing strength of the Muslims, Baldwin III made the first direct alliance with the Byzantine Empire, by marrying Theodora Comnena, a niece of emperor Manuel; Manuel married Baldwin's cousin Maria.[458] As William of Tyre put it, it was hoped that Manuel would be able "to relieve from his own abundance the distress under which our realm was suffering and to change our poverty into superabundance".[459]

When Baldwin died childless in 1162, a year after his mother Melisende, the kingdom passed to his brother Amalric, who renewed the alliance negotiated by Baldwin. In 1163 the chaotic situation in Egypt led to a refusal to pay

Figure 35: *Byzantine Emperor Manuel I Comnenus, who became a close ally of the Kingdom of Jerusalem.*

tribute to Jerusalem, and requests were sent to Nur ad-Din for assistance; in response, Amalric invaded, but was turned back when the Egyptians flooded the Nile at Bilbeis. The Egyptian vizier Shawar again requested help from Nur ad-Din, who sent his general Shirkuh, but Shawar quickly turned against him and allied with Amalric. Amalric and Shirkuh both besieged Bilbeis in 1164, but both withdrew due to Nur ad-Din's campaigns against Antioch, where Bohemond III of Antioch and Raymond III of Tripoli were defeated at the Battle of Harim. It seemed likely that Antioch itself would fall to Nur ad-Din, but he withdrew when Emperor Manuel sent a large Byzantine force to the area. Nur ad-Din sent Shirkuh back to Egypt in 1166, and Shawar again allied with Amalric, who was defeated at the Battle of al-Babein. Despite the defeat, both sides withdrew, but Shawar remained in control with a crusader garrison in Cairo.[460] Amalric cemented his alliance with Manuel by marrying Manuel's niece Maria Komnene in 1167, and an embassy led by William of Tyre was sent to Constantinople to negotiate a military expedition, but in 1168 Amalric pillaged Bilbeis without waiting for the naval support promised by Manuel. Amalric accomplished nothing else, but his actions prompted Shawar to switch sides again and seek help from Shirkuh. Shawar was promptly assassinated, and when Shirkuh died in 1169, he was succeeded by his nephew Yusuf, better known as Saladin. That year, Manuel sent a large Byzantine fleet of some 300 ships to assist Amalric, and the town of Damietta was placed under siege. However, the Byzantine fleet sailed with enough provisions for only three months. By the time that the crusaders were ready supplies were already running out and the fleet retired. Each side sought to blame the other for the failure, but both knew that they could not take Egypt without the other's assistance: the alliance was maintained, and plans for another campaign in Egypt were made, which ultimately were to come to naught.[461]

In the end, Nur ad-Din was victorious and Saladin established himself as Sultan of Egypt. Saladin soon began to assert his independence from Nur ad-Din, and with the death of both Amalric and Nur ad-Din in 1174, he was well-placed to begin exerting control over Nur ad-Din's Syrian possessions as well.[462] Upon the death of the pro-western Emperor Manuel in 1180, the Kingdom of Jerusalem lost its most powerful ally.

The subsequent events have often been interpreted as a struggle between two opposing factions, the "court party", made up of Baldwin's mother, Amalric's first wife Agnes of Courtenay, her immediate family, and recent arrivals from Europe who were inexperienced in the affairs of the kingdom and who were in favour of war with Saladin; and the "noble party", led by Raymond of Tripoli and the lesser nobility of the kingdom, who favoured peaceful coexistence with the Muslims. This is the interpretation offered by William of Tyre, who was firmly placed in the "noble" camp, and his view was taken up by subsequent historians; in the 20th century, Marshall W. Baldwin,[463] Steven Runciman,[464] and Hans E. Mayer[465] favoured this interpretation. Peter W. Edbury, on the other hand, argues that William, as well as the thirteenth-century authors who continued William's chronicle in French and were allied to Raymond's supporters in the Ibelin family, cannot be considered impartial.[466] Although the events were clearly a dynastic struggle, "the division was not between native barons and newcomers from the West, but between the king's maternal and paternal kin."[467]

Miles of Plancy was briefly *bailli* or regent during Baldwin IV's minority. Miles was assassinated in October 1174, and Count Raymond III of Tripoli, Amalric's first cousin, became regent. It is highly probable that Raymond or his supporters engineered the assassination.[468] Baldwin reached his majority in 1176, and despite his illness he no longer had any legal need for a regent. Since Raymond was his nearest relative in the male line with a strong claim to the throne, there was concern about the extent of his ambitions, although he had no direct heirs of his own. To balance this, the king turned from time to time to his uncle, Joscelin III of Edessa, who was appointed seneschal in 1176; Joscelin was more closely related to Baldwin than Raymond was, but had no claim to the throne himself.[469]

As a leper, Baldwin had no children and could not be expected to rule much longer, so the focus of his succession passed to his sister Sibylla and his younger half-sister Isabella. Baldwin and his advisors recognised that it was essential for Sibylla to be married to a Western nobleman in order to access support from

European states in a military crisis; while Raymond was still regent, a marriage was arranged for Sibylla and William of Montferrat, a cousin of Louis VII of France and of Frederick Barbarossa, Holy Roman Emperor. It was hoped that by allying with a relative of the western emperor, Frederick would come to the kingdom's aid.[470] Jerusalem looked again towards the Byzantine Empire for help, and Emperor Manuel was looking for a way to restore his empire's prestige after his defeat at the Battle of Myriokephalon in 1176; this mission was undertaken by Raynald of Châtillon.[471] After William of Montferrat arrived in 1176, he fell ill and died in June 1177, leaving Sibylla widowed and pregnant with the future Baldwin V. Raynald was then named regent.[472]

Soon afterwards, Philip of Flanders arrived in Jerusalem on pilgrimage; he was Baldwin IV's cousin, and the king offered him the regency and command of the army, both of which Philip refused, although he objected to the appointment of Raynald as regent. Philip then attempted to intervene in the negotiations for Sibylla's second husband, and suggested one of his own retinue, but the native barons refused his suggestion. In addition, Philip seemed to think he could carve out a territory of his own in Egypt, but he refused to participate with the planned Byzantine-Jerusalem expedition. The expedition was delayed and finally cancelled, and Philip took his army away to the north.[473]

Most of the army of Jerusalem marched north with Philip, Raymond III, and Bohemond III to attack Hama, and Saladin took the opportunity to invade the kingdom. Baldwin proved to be an effective and energetic king as well as being a brilliant military commander: he defeated Saladin at the Battle of Montgisard in September 1177 despite being greatly outnumbered and having to rely on a levee-en-masse. Although Baldwin's presence despite his illness was inspirational, direct military decisions were actually made by Raynald.[474]

Hugh III of Burgundy was expected to come to Jerusalem and marry Sibylla, but Hugh was unable to leave France due to the political unrest there in 1179–1180 following the death of Louis VII. Meanwhile, Baldwin IV's stepmother Maria, mother of Isabella and stepmother of Sibylla, married Balian of Ibelin. At Easter in 1180, Raymond and his cousin Bohemond III of Antioch attempted to force Sibylla to marry Balian's brother Baldwin of Ibelin. Raymond and Bohemond were King Baldwin's nearest male relatives in the paternal line, and could have claimed the throne if the king died without an heir or a suitable replacement. Before Raymond and Bohemond arrived, Agnes and King Baldwin arranged for Sibylla to be married to a Poitevin newcomer, Guy of Lusignan, whose older brother Amalric of Lusignan was already an established figure at court.[475] Internationally, the Lusignans were useful as vassals of Baldwin and Sibylla's cousin Henry II of England. Baldwin betrothed eight-year-old Isabella to Humphrey IV of Toron, stepson of the powerful Raynald of Châtillon, thereby removing her from the influence of the Ibelin family and that of her mother.[476]

The dispute between the two factions in the kingdom affected the election of a new Patriarch in 1180. When Patriarch Amalric died on 6 October 1180, the two most obvious choices for his successor were William of Tyre and Heraclius of Caesarea. They were fairly evenly matched in background and education, but politically they were allied with opposite parties, as Heraclius was one of Agnes of Courtenay's supporters. The canons of the Holy Sepulchre asked the king for advice, and Heraclius was chosen through Agnes' influence. There were rumours that Agnes and Heraclius were lovers, but this information comes from the partisan 13th-century continuations of William of Tyre's history, and there is no other evidence to substantiate such a claim.[477]

At the end of 1181, Raynald of Châtillon raided south into Arabia, in the direction of Medina, although he did not make it that far. It was probably around this time that Raynald also attacked a Muslim caravan. The kingdom had a truce with Saladin at the time, and Raynald's actions have been seen as an independent act of brigandage; it is possible that he was trying to prevent Saladin from moving his forces north to take control of Aleppo, which would have strengthened Saladin's position.[478] In response, Saladin attacked the kingdom in 1182, but was defeated at Belvoir Castle. King Baldwin, although quite ill, was still able to command the army in person. Saladin attempted to besiege Beirut from land and sea, and Baldwin raided Damascene territory, but neither side did significant damage. In December 1182, Raynald launched a naval expedition on the Red Sea, which made it as far south as Rabigh. The expedition was defeated and two of Raynald's men were actually taken to Mecca to be executed in public. Like his earlier raids, Raynald's expedition is usually seen as selfish and ultimately fatal for Jerusalem, but according to Bernard Hamilton it was actually shrewd strategy, meant to damage Saladin's prestige and reputation.[479]

In 1183 a general tax was levied throughout the kingdom, which was unprecedented in Jerusalem and almost all of medieval Europe to that point. The tax helped pay for larger armies for the next few years. More troops were certainly needed, since Saladin was finally able to gain control of Aleppo, and with peace in his northern territories he could focus on Jerusalem in the south. King Baldwin was so incapacitated by his leprosy that it was necessary to appoint a regent, and Guy of Lusignan was chosen, as he was Baldwin's legal heir and the king was not expected to live. The inexperienced Guy led the Frankish army against Saladin's incursions into the kingdom, but neither side made any real gains, and Guy was criticized by his opponents for not striking against Saladin when he had the chance.[480]

In October 1183 Isabella married Humphrey of Toron at Kerak, during a siege by Saladin, who perhaps hoped to take some valuable prisoners. As King Baldwin, although now blind and crippled, had recovered enough to resume his reign and his command of the army, Guy was removed from the regency and his five-year-old step-son, King Baldwin's nephew and namesake Baldwin, was crowned as co-king in November. King Baldwin himself then went to relieve the castle, carried on a litter, and attended by his mother. He was reconciled with Raymond of Tripoli and appointed him military commander. The siege was lifted in December and Saladin retreated to Damascus.[481] Saladin attempted another siege in 1184, but Baldwin repelled that attack as well, and Saladin raided Nablus and other towns on the way home.[482]

In October 1184, Guy of Lusignan led an attack on the Bedouin nomads from his base in Ascalon. Unlike Raynald's attacks on caravans, which may have had some military purpose, Guy attacked a group that was usually loyal to Jerusalem and provided intelligence about the movements of Saladin's troops. At the same time, King Baldwin contracted his final illness and Raymond of Tripoli, rather than Guy, was appointed as his regent. His nephew Baldwin was paraded in public, wearing his crown as Baldwin V. Baldwin IV finally succumbed to his leprosy in May 1185.[483]

Meanwhile, the succession crisis had prompted a mission to the west to seek assistance. In 1184, Patriarch Heraclius travelled throughout the courts of Europe, but no help was forthcoming. Heraclius offered the "keys of the Holy Sepulchre, those of the Tower of David and the banner of the Kingdom of Jerusalem", but not the crown itself, to both Philip II of France and Henry II of England; the latter, as a grandson of Fulk, was a first cousin of the royal family of Jerusalem, and had promised to go on crusade after the murder of Thomas Becket. Both kings preferred to remain at home to defend their own territories, rather than act as regent for a child in Jerusalem. The few European knights who did travel to Jerusalem did not even see any combat, since the truce with Saladin had been re-established. William V of Montferrat was one of the few who came to his grandson Baldwin V's aid.[484]

Baldwin V's rule, with Raymond of Tripoli as regent and his great-uncle Joscelin of Edessa as his guardian, was short. He was a sickly child and died in the summer of 1186. Raymond and his supporters went to Nablus, presumably in an attempt to prevent Sibylla from claiming the throne, but Sibylla and her supporters went to Jerusalem, where it was decided that the kingdom should pass to her, on the condition that her marriage to Guy be annulled. She agreed but only if she could choose her own husband and king, and after being crowned, she immediately crowned Guy with her own hands. Raymond had refused to attend the coronation, and in Nablus he suggested that Isabella and Humphrey should be crowned instead, but Humphrey refused to agree to

Figure 36: *17th-century interpretation of Guy of Lusignan (right) being held captive by Saladin (left), clad in a traditional (Islamic) royal garment, painted by Jan Lievens.*

this plan which would have certainly started a civil war. Humphrey went to Jerusalem and swore allegiance to Guy and Sibylla, as did most of Raymond's other supporters. Raymond himself refused to do so and left for Tripoli; Baldwin of Ibelin also refused, gave up his fiefs, and left for Antioch.[485]

Loss of Jerusalem and the Third Crusade

Raymond of Tripoli allied with Saladin against Guy and allowed a Muslim garrison to occupy his fief in Tiberias, probably hoping that Saladin would help him overthrow Guy. Saladin, meanwhile, had pacified his Mesopotamian territories, and was now eager to attack the crusader kingdom; he did not intend to renew the truce when it expired in 1187. Before the truce expired, Raynald of Chatillon, the lord of Oultrejourdain and of Kerak and one of Guy's chief supporters, recognized that Saladin was massing his troops, and attacked Muslim caravans in an attempt to disrupt this. Guy was on the verge of attacking Raymond, but realized that the kingdom would need to be united in the face of the threat from Saladin, and Balian of Ibelin effected a reconciliation between the two during Easter in 1187. Saladin attacked Kerak again in April, and in May, a Muslim raiding party ran into the much smaller embassy on its way to negotiate with Raymond, and defeated it at the Battle of Cresson near Nazareth.

Figure 37: *The Near East, c. 1190, at the outset of the Third Crusade.*

Raymond and Guy finally agreed to attack Saladin at Tiberias, but could not agree on a plan; Raymond thought a pitched battle should be avoided, but Guy probably remembered the criticism he faced for avoiding battle in 1183, and it was decided to march out against Saladin directly. On July 4, 1187, the army of the kingdom was utterly destroyed at the Battle of Hattin. Raymond of Tripoli, Balian of Ibelin, and Reginald of Sidon escaped, but Raynald was executed by Saladin and Guy was imprisoned in Damascus.[486]

Over the next few months Saladin easily overran the entire kingdom. Only the port of Tyre remained in Frankish hands, defended by Conrad of Montferrat, the paternal uncle of Baldwin V, who had coincidentally arrived just in time from Constantinople. The fall of Jerusalem essentially ended the first Kingdom of Jerusalem. Much of the population, swollen with refugees fleeing Saladin's conquest of the surrounding territory, was allowed to flee to Tyre, Tripoli, or Egypt (whence they were sent back to Europe), but those who could not pay for their freedom were sold into slavery, and those who could were often robbed by Christians and Muslims alike on their way into exile. The capture of the city led to the Third Crusade, launched in 1189 and led by Richard the Lionheart, Philip Augustus and Frederick Barbarossa, though the last drowned en route.[487]

Guy of Lusignan, who had been refused entry to Tyre by Conrad, began to besiege Acre in 1189. During the lengthy siege, which lasted until 1191, Patriarch Heraclius, Queen Sibylla and her daughters, and many others died of disease. With the death of Sibylla in 1190, Guy now had no legal claim to the kingship, and the succession passed to Sibylla's half-sister Isabella. Isabella's mother Maria and the Ibelins (now closely allied to Conrad) argued that Isabella and Humphrey's marriage was illegal, as she had been underage at the time; underlying this was the fact that Humphrey had betrayed his wife's cause in 1186. The marriage was annulled amid some controversy. Conrad, who was now the nearest kinsman to Baldwin V in the male line, and had already proved himself a capable military leader, then married Isabella, but Guy refused to concede the crown.[488]

When Richard arrived in 1191, he and Philip took different sides in the succession dispute. Richard backed Guy, his vassal from Poitou, while Philip supported Conrad, a cousin of his late father Louis VII. After much ill-feeling and ill-health, Philip returned home in 1191, soon after the fall of Acre. Richard defeated Saladin at the Battle of Arsuf in 1191 and the Battle of Jaffa in 1192, recovering most of the coast, but could not recover Jerusalem or any of the inland territory of the kingdom. It has been suggested that this may have actually been a strategic decision by Richard rather than a failure as such, as he may have recognized that Jerusalem in particular was in fact a strategic liability as long as the crusaders were obligated to defend it, as it was isolated from the sea where Western reinforcements could arrive.[489] Conrad was unanimously elected king in April 1192, but was murdered by the Hashshashin only days later. Eight days after that, the pregnant Isabella was married to Count Henry II of Champagne, nephew of Richard and Philip, but politically allied to Richard. As compensation, Richard sold Guy the island of Cyprus, which Richard had captured on the way to Acre, although Guy continued to claim the throne of Jerusalem until his death in 1194.[490]

The crusade came to an end peacefully, with the Treaty of Ramla negotiated in 1192; Saladin allowed pilgrimages to be made to Jerusalem, allowing the crusaders to fulfill their vows, after which they all returned home. The native crusader barons set about rebuilding their kingdom from Acre and the other coastal cities.

The Kingdom of Acre

For the next hundred years, the Kingdom of Jerusalem clung to life as a tiny kingdom hugging the Syrian coastline. Its capital was moved to Acre and controlled most of the coastline of present-day Israel and southern and central Lebanon, including the strongholds and towns of Jaffa, Arsuf, Caesarea, Tyre, Sidon, and Beirut. At best, it included only a few other significant cities, such as Ascalon and some interior fortresses, as well as suzerainty over Tripoli and Antioch. The new king, Henry of Champagne, died accidentally in 1197, and Isabella married for a fourth time, to Aimery of Lusignan, Guy's brother. Aimery had already inherited Cyprus from Guy, and had been crowned king by Frederick Barbarossa's son, Emperor Henry VI. Henry led a crusade in 1197 but died along the way. Nevertheless, his troops recaptured Beirut and Sidon for the kingdom before returning home in 1198.[491,492] A five-year truce was then concluded with the Ayyubids in Syria in 1198.[493]

The Ayyubid empire had fallen into civil war after the death of Saladin in 1193. His sons claimed various parts of his empire: az-Zahir took control of Aleppo, al-Aziz Uthman held Cairo, while his eldest son, al-Afdal, retained Damascus. Saladin's brother Al-Adil Sayf ad-Din (often called "Saphadin" by the crusaders) acquired al-Jazira (northern Mesopotamia), and al-Adil's son al-Mu'azzam took possession of Karak and Transjordan. In 1196, al-Afdal was driven out of Damascus by al Adil in alliance with Uthman. When Uthman died in 1198, al Afdal returned to power as regent in Egypt for Uthman's infant son. Allied with az-Zahir, he then attacked his uncle in Damascus. The alliance fell apart, and al-Adil then defeated al Afdal in Egypt and annexed the country. In 1200 Al-Adil proclaimed himself Sultan of Egypt and Syria, entrusting Damascus to al-Mu'azzam and al-Jazira to another son, al-Kamil. Following a second unsuccessful siege of Damascus by the two brothers, Al Afdal accepted a fief consisting of Samosata and a number of other towns. Az-Zahir of Aleppo submitted to his uncle in 1202, thus re-uniting the Ayyubid territories.[494]

Meanwhile, schemes were hatched to reconquer Jerusalem through Egypt. A Fourth Crusade was planned after the failure of the Third, but it resulted in the sack of Constantinople in 1204, and most of the crusaders involved never arrived in the kingdom. Aimery, however, not knowing of the diversion to Constantinople, raided Egypt in advance of the expected invasion.[495] Both Isabella and Aimery died in 1205 and again an underage girl, Isabella and Conrad's daughter Maria of Montferrat, became queen of Jerusalem. Isabella's half-brother John of Ibelin, the Old Lord of Beirut governed as regent until 1210 when Maria married an experienced French knight, John of Brienne.[496] Maria died in childbirth in 1212, and John of Brienne continued to rule as regent for their daughter Isabella II.[497]

Fifth Crusade and Frederick II

The Fourth Lateran Council in 1215 called for a new, better-organized crusade against Egypt. In late 1217 Andrew II of Hungary and Leopold VI, Duke of Austria arrived in Acre and, along with John of Brienne, raided territory further inland, including Mount Tabor, but without success.[498] After the departure of the Hungarians, the remaining crusaders set about refortifying Caesarea and

Figure 38: *Frederick II (left) meets al-Kamil (right). Nuova Cronica by Giovanni Villani (14th century).*

the Templar fortress of Château Pèlerin throughout the winter of 1217 and spring of 1218.[499]

In the spring of 1218 the Fifth Crusade began in earnest when German crusader fleets landed at Acre. Along with King John, who was elected leader of the crusade, the fleets sailed to Egypt and besieged Damietta at the mouth of the Nile in May. The siege progressed slowly, and the Egyptian sultan al-Adil died in August 1218, supposedly of shock after the crusaders managed to capture one of Damietta's towers. He was succeeded by his son al-Kamil. In the autumn of 1218 reinforcements arrived from Europe, including the papal legate Pelagius of Albano. In the winter the crusaders were affected by floods and disease, and the siege dragged on throughout 1219, when Francis of Assisi arrived to attempt to negotiate a truce. Neither side could agree to terms, despite the Ayyubid offer of a thirty-year truce and the restoration of Jerusalem and most of the rest of the former kingdom. The crusaders finally managed to starve out the city and captured it in November. Al-Kamil retreated to the nearby fortress of al-Mansurah, but the crusaders remained in Damietta throughout 1219 and 1220, awaiting the arrival of Holy Roman Emperor Frederick II, while King John returned to Acre briefly to defend against al-Mu'azzam, who was raiding the kingdom from Damascus in John's absence. Still expecting the emperor's imminent arrival, in July 1221, the crusaders set off towards Cairo, but they were stopped by the rising Nile, which al-Kamil allowed to flood by breaking the dams along its course. The sultan easily defeated the trapped crusader army and regained Damietta. Emperor Frederick had, in fact, never left Europe at all.[500]

After the failure of the crusade, John travelled throughout Europe seeking assistance, but found support only from Frederick, who then married John and Maria's daughter Isabella II in 1225. The next year, Isabella died giving birth to their son Conrad IV, who succeeded his mother to the throne although he never appeared in the east. Frederick had reneged on his promise to lead the Fifth Crusade, but was now eager to cement his claim to the throne through Conrad. There were also plans to join with al-Kamil in attacking al-Mu'azzam in Damascus, an alliance which had been discussed with Egyptian envoys in Italy. But after continually delaying his departure for the Holy Land, including suffering an outbreak of disease in his fleet, he was excommunicated by Pope Gregory IX in 1227. The crusaders, led not by Frederick but by his representatives Richard Filangieri, Henry IV, Duke of Limburg, and Hermann of Salza, Grand Master of the Teutonic Knights, arrived in the east late in 1227, and while waiting for the emperor they set about refortifying Sidon, where they built the sea castle, and Montfort, which later became the headquarters of the Teutonic Knights. The Ayyubids of Damascus did not dare attack, as al-Mu'azzam had suddenly died not long before. Frederick finally arrived on the Sixth Crusade in September 1228, and claimed the regency of the kingdom in the name of his infant son.[501]

Frederick immediately came into conflict with the native nobles of Outremer, some of whom resented his attempts to impose Imperial authority over both Cyprus and Jerusalem. The Cypriot nobles were already quarrelling amongst themselves about the regency for Henry I of Cyprus, who was still a child. The High Court of Cyprus had elected John of Ibelin as regent, but Henry's mother Alice of Champagne wished to appoint one of her supporters; Alice and her party, members or supporters of the Lusignan dynasty, sided with Frederick, whose father had crowned Aimery of Lusignan king in 1197. At Limassol, Frederick demanded that John give up not only the regency of Cyprus, but also John's own lordship of Beirut on the mainland. John argued that Frederick had no legal authority to make such demands and refused to give up either title. Frederick then imprisoned John's sons as hostages to guarantee John's support for his crusade.[502]

John did accompany Frederick to the mainland, but Frederick was not well-received there; one of his few supporters was Balian, Lord of Sidon, who had welcomed the crusaders the year before and now acted as an ambassador to the Ayyubids. The death of al-Mu'azzam negated the proposed alliance with al-Kamil, who along with his brother al-Ashraf had taken possession of Damascus (as well as Jerusalem) from their nephew, al-Mu'azzam's son an-Nasir Dawud. However, al-Kamil presumably did not know of the small size of Frederick's army, nor the divisions within it caused by his excommunication, and wished to avoid defending his territories against another crusade. Frederick's presence alone was sufficient to regain Jerusalem, Bethlehem, Nazareth, and a number of surrounding castles without a fight: these were recovered in February 1229, in return for a ten-year truce with the Ayyubids and freedom of worship for Jerusalem's Muslim inhabitants. The terms of the treaty were unacceptable to the Patriarch of Jerusalem Gerald of Lausanne, who placed the city under interdict. In March, Frederick crowned himself in the Church of the Holy Sepulchre, but because of his excommunication and the interdict Jerusalem was never truly reincorporated into the kingdom, which continued to be ruled from Acre.[503]

Meanwhile, in Italy, the Pope had used Frederick's excommunication as an excuse to invade his Italian territories; the papal armies were led by Frederick's former father-in-law John of Brienne. Frederick was forced to return home in 1229, leaving the Holy Land "not in triumph, but showered with offal" by the citizens of Acre.[504]

War of the Lombards and the Barons' Crusade

Nevertheless, Frederick sent an Imperial army in 1231, under Richard Filangieri, who occupied Beirut and Tyre, but was unable to gain control of Acre. John's supporters formed a commune in Acre, of which John himself was elected mayor in 1232. With the help of the Genoese merchants, the commune recaptured Beirut. John also attacked Tyre, but was defeated by Filangieri at the Battle of Casal Imbert in May 1232.

On Cyprus, King Henry I came of age in 1232 and John's regency was no longer necessary. Both John and Filangieri raced back to Cyprus to assert their authority, and the imperial forces were defeated at the Battle of Agridi on June 15. Henry became undisputed king of Cyprus, but continued to support the Ibelins over the Lusignans and the imperial party. On the mainland, Filangieri had the support of Bohemund IV of Antioch, the Teutonic Knights, the Knights Hospitaller, and the Pisan merchants. John was supported by his nobles on Cyprus, and by his continental holdings in Beirut, Caesarea, and Arsuf, as well as by the Knights Templar and the Genoese. Neither side could make any headway, and in 1234 Gregory IX excommunicated John and his supporters. This was partly revoked in 1235, but still no peace could be made. John died in 1236 and the war was taken up by his son Balian of Beirut and his nephew Philip of Montfort.[505]

Meanwhile, the treaty with the Ayyubids was set to expire in 1239. Plans for a new crusade to be led by Frederick came to nothing, and Frederick himself

Figure 39: *Coronation of Maria of Montferrat and John of Brienne, King of Jerusalem and Latin Emperor of Constantinople*

was excommunicated by Gregory IX again in 1239. However, other European nobles took up the cause, including Theobald IV, Count of Champagne and King of Navarre, Peter of Dreux, and Amaury VI of Montfort, who arrived in Acre in September 1239. Theobald was elected leader of the crusade at a council in Acre, attended by the most of the important nobles of the kingdom, including Walter of Brienne, John of Arsuf, and Balian of Sidon. The arrival of the crusade was a brief respite from the Lombard War; Filangieri remained in Tyre and did not participate. The council decided to refortify Ascalon in the south and attack Damascus in the north.

The crusaders may have been aware of the new divisions among the Ayyubids; al-Kamil had occupied Damascus in 1238 but had died soon afterwards, and his territory was inherited by his family. His sons al-Adil abu Bakr and as-Salih Ayyub inherited Egypt and Damascus. Ayyub marched on Cairo in an attempt to drive out al-Adil, but during his absence al-Kamil's brother as-Salih Isma'il took over Damascus, and Ayyub was taken prisoner by an-Nasir Dawud. The crusaders, meanwhile, marched to Ascalon. Along the way, Walter of Brienne captured livestock intended to resupply Damascus, as the Ayyubids had probably learned of the crusaders' plans to attack it. The victory was short-lived, however, as the crusaders were then defeated by the Egyptian army at Gaza in November 1239. Henry II, Count of Bar was killed and Amaury of Montfort captured. The crusaders returned to Acre, possibly because the native barons of the kingdom were suspicious of Filangieri in Tyre. Dawud took advantage of the Ayyubid victory to recapture Jerusalem in December, the ten-year truce having expired.

Although Ayyub was Dawud's prisoner, the two now allied against al-Adil in Egypt, which Ayyub seized in 1240. In Damascus, Isma'il recognized the threat of Dawud and Ayyub against his own possessions, and turned to the crusaders for assistance. Theobald concluded a treaty with Isma'il, in return for territorial concessions that restored Jerusalem to Christian control, as well as much of the rest of the former kingdom, even more territory than Frederick had recovered in 1229. Theobald, however, was frustrated by the Lombard War, and returned home in September 1240. Almost immediately after Theobald's departure, Richard of Cornwall arrived. He completed the rebuilding of Ascalon, and also made peace with Ayyub in Egypt. Ayyub confirmed Isma'il's concessions in 1241, and prisoners taken at Gaza were exchanged by both sides. Richard returned to Europe in 1241.[506]

Although the kingdom had essentially been restored, the Lombard War continued to occupy the kingdom's nobility. As the Templars and Hospitallers supported opposite sides, they also attacked each other, and the Templars broke the treaty with the Ayyubids by attacking Nablus in 1241. Conrad proclaimed that he had come of age in 1242, eliminating both Frederick's claim to the regency and the need for an imperial guardian to govern in his place, although he had not yet turned 15, the age of majority according to the customs of Jerusalem. Through Conrad, Frederick tried to send an imperial regent, but the anti-imperial faction in Acre argued that Jerusalem's laws allowed them to appoint their own regent. In June the *Haute Cour* granted the regency to Alice of Champagne, who, as the daughter of Isabella I, was Conrad's great-aunt and his closest relative living in the kingdom. Alice ordered Filangieri to be arrested, and along with the Ibelins and Venetians, besieged Tyre, which fell in July 1243. The Lombard War was over, but the king was still absent, as Conrad never came to the east. Alice was prevented from exercising any real power as regent by Philip of Montfort, who took control of Tyre, and Balian of Beirut, who continued to hold Acre.

Crusade of Louis IX

The Ayyubids were still divided between Ayyub in Egypt, Isma'il in Damascus, and Dawud in Kerak. Isma'il, Dawud, and al-Mansur Ibrahim of Homs went to war with Ayyub, who hired the Khwarazmians to fight for him. The Khwarazmians were nomadic Turks from central Asia, who had recently been displaced by the Mongols further to the east and were now residing in Mesopotamia. With Ayyub's support they sacked Jerusalem in the summer of

1244, leaving it in ruins and useless to both Christians and Muslims. In October, the Khwarazmians, along with the Egyptian army under the command of Baibars, were met by the Frankish army, led by Philip of Montfort, Walter of Brienne, and the masters of the Templars, Hospitallers, and Teutonic Knights, along with al-Mansur and Dawud. On October 17 the Egyptian-Khwarazmian army destroyed the Frankish-Syrian coalition, and Walter of Brienne was taken captive and later executed. By 1247, Ayyub had reoccupied most of the territory that had been conceded in 1239, and had also gained control of Damascus.[507]

A new crusade was discussed at the Council of Lyon in 1245 by Pope Innocent IV. The council deposed Frederick II, so no help could be expected from the empire, but King Louis IX of France had already vowed to go on crusade. Louis arrived in Cyprus in 1248, where he gathered an army of his own men, including his brothers Robert of Artois, Charles of Anjou, and Alphonse of Poitiers, and those of Cyprus and Jerusalem, led by the Ibelin family John of Jaffa, Guy of Ibelin, and Balian of Beirut. Once again the target was Egypt. Damietta was captured without resistance when the crusaders landed in June 1249, but the crusade halted there until November, by which time the Egyptian sultan Ayyub had died and had been succeeded by his son Turanshah. In February, the crusaders were defeated at the Battle of al-Mansurah, where Robert of Artois was killed. The crusaders were unable to cross the Nile, and, suffering from disease and lack of supplies, retreated towards Damietta in April. They were defeated along the way at the Battle of Fariskur, with Louis being taken captive by Turanshah. During Louis' captivity, Turanshah was overthrown by his Mamluk soldiers, led by the general Aybak, who then released Louis in May in return for Damietta and a large ransom. For the next four years Louis resided in Acre, and helped refortify that city along with Caesarea, Jaffa, and Sidon. He also made truces with the Ayyubids in Syria, and sent embassies to negotiate with the Mongols, who were beginning to threaten the Muslim world. before returning home in 1254. He left behind a large garrison of French soldiers in Acre, under the command of Geoffrey of Sergines.[508]

In the midst of these events, Alice of Champagne had died in 1246 and had been replaced as regent by her son King Henry I of Cyprus, for whom John of Jaffa served as *bailli* in Acre. During Louis IX's stay in Acre, Henry I died in 1253, and was succeeded in Cyprus by his infant son Hugh II. Hugh was technically regent of Jerusalem as well, both for Conrad and for Conrad's son Conradin after Conrad died in 1254. Both Cyprus and Jerusalem were governed by Hugh's mother Plaisance of Antioch, but John remained *bailli* for Hugh in Acre. John made peace with Damascus and attempted to regain Ascalon; the Egyptians, now ruled by the Mamluk sultanate, besieged Jaffa in

1256 in response. John defeated them, and afterwards gave up the bailliage to his cousin John of Arsuf.[509]

War of Saint Sabas

In 1256 the commercial rivalry between the Venetian and Genoese merchant colonies broke out into open warfare. In Acre, the two colonies disputed possession of the monastery of Saint Sabas. The Genoese, assisted by the Pisan merchants, attacked the Venetian quarter and burned their ships, but the Venetians drove them out. The Venetians were then expelled from Tyre by Philip of Monfort. John of Arsuf, John of Jaffa, John II of Beirut, the Templars, and the Teutonic Knights supported the Venetians, who also convinced the Pisans to join them, while the Hospitallers supported the Genoese. In 1257 the Venetians conquered the monastery and destroyed its fortifications, although they were unable to expel the Genoese completely. They blockaded the Genoese quarter, but the Genoese were supplied by the Hospitallers, whose complex was nearby, and by Philip of Montfort who sent food from Tyre. In August 1257, John of Arsuf tried to end the war by granting commercial rights in Acre to Ancona, an Italian ally of Genoa, but aside from Philip of Montfort and the Hospitallers, the rest of the nobles continued to support Venice. In June 1258, Philip and the Hospitallers marched on Acre while a Genoese fleet attacked the city by sea. The naval battle was won by Venice, and the Genoese were forced to abandon their quarter and flee to Tyre with Philip. The war also spread to Tripoli and Antioch, where the Embriaco family, descended from Genoese crusaders, were pitted against Bohemond VI of Antioch, who supported the Venetians. In 1261 the Patriarch, Jacques Pantaleon, organised a council to re-establish order in the kingdom, though the Genoese did not return to Acre.[510]

Mongols

It was during this period that the Mongols arrived in the Near East. Their presence further east had already displaced the Khwarazmians, and embassies had been sent by various popes as well as Louis IX to ally or negotiate with them, but they were uninterested in alliances. They sacked Baghdad in 1258, and Aleppo and Damascus in 1260, destroying both the Abbasid caliphate and the last vestiges of the Ayyubid dynasty. Hethum I of Armenia and Bohemond VI of Antioch had already submitted to the Mongols as vassals. Some of the Mongols were Nestorian Christians, including Kitbuqa, one of the generals at the sieges of Baghdad and Damascus, but despite this, the nobles of Acre refused to submit. As the kingdom was by now a relatively unimportant state, the Mongols paid little attention to it, but there were a few skirmishes in 1260: the forces of Julian of Sidon killed the nephew of Kitbuqa, who responded by sacking Sidon, and John II of Beirut was also captured by the Mongols during another raid. The apparently inevitable Mongol conquest was stalled when Hulagu, the Mongol commander in Syria, returned home after the death of his brother Möngke Khan, leaving Kitbuqa with a small garrison. The Mamluks of Egypt then sought, and were granted, permission to advance through Frankish territory, and defeated the Mongols at the Battle of Ain Jalut in September 1260. Kitbuqa was killed and all of Syria fell under Mamluk control. On the way back to Egypt, the Mamluk sultan Qutuz was assassinated by the general Baibars, who was far less favourable than his predecessor to alliances with the Franks.[511]

Fall of Acre

John of Arsuf had died in 1258 and was replaced as *bailli* by Geoffrey of Sergines, Louis IX's lieutenant in Acre. Plaisance died in 1261, but as her son Hugh II was still underage, Cyprus passed to his cousin Hugh of Antioch-Lusignan, whose mother Isabella of Cyprus, Alice of Champagne and Hugh I of Cyprus' daughter and Hugh II's aunt, took over the regency in Acre. She appointed as *bailli* her husband Henry of Antioch (who was also Plaisance's uncle), but died in 1264. The regency in Acre was then claimed by Hugh of Antioch-Lusignan and his cousin Hugh of Brienne, and Hugh II died in 1267 before he reached the age of majority. Hugh of Antioch-Lusignan won the dispute and succeeded Hugh II on Cyprus as Hugh III. When Conradin was executed in Sicily in 1268, there was no other Hohenstaufen heir to succeed him, and Hugh III inherited the Kingdom of Jerusalem as well in 1269. This was disputed by another branch of the Lusignan family: Maria of Antioch, daughter of Bohemond IV of Antioch and Melisende of Lusignan (herself a daughter of Isabella I and Amalric II), claimed the throne as the oldest living relative of Isabella I, but for the moment her claim was ignored. By this time, the Mamluks under Baibars were taking advantage of the kingdom's constant disputes, and began conquering the remaining crusader cities along the coast. In 1265, Baibars took Caesarea, Haifa and Arsuf, and Safad and Toron in 1266. In 1268 he captured Jaffa and Beaufort, and then besieged and destroyed Antioch.[512]

Hugh III and Baibars made a one-year truce after these conquests; Baibars knew that Louis IX was planning another crusade from Europe, and assumed that the target would once again be Egypt. But instead the crusade was diverted to Tunis, where Louis died. Baibars was free to continue his campaigns: in 1270 he had the Assassins kill Philip of Montfort, and in 1271 he captured the Hospitaller and Teutonic Knights strongholds of Krak des Chevaliers and Montfort Castle. He also besieged Tripoli, but abandoned it in May when

Figure 40: *Krak des Chevaliers, Syria. UNESCO World Heritage Site*

Prince Edward of England arrived, the only part of Louis IX's crusade to arrive in the east. Edward could do nothing except arrange a ten-year truce with Baibars, who nevertheless attempted to have him assassinated as well. Edward left in 1272, and despite the Second Council of Lyon's plans for another crusade in 1274, no further large-scale expedition ever arrived. Hugh III's authority on the mainland began to break down; he was an unpopular king, and Beirut, the only territory left outside of Acre and Tyre, started to act independently. Its heiress, Isabella of Ibelin (widow of Hugh II), actually placed it under Baibars' protection. Finding the mainland ungovernable, Hugh III left for Cyprus, leaving Balian of Arsuf as *bailli*. Then in 1277, Maria of Antioch sold her claim to the kingdom to Charles of Anjou, who sent Roger of San Severino to represent him. The Venetians and Templars supported the claim, and Balian was powerless to oppose him. Baibars died in 1277 and was succeeded by Qalawun. In 1281 the ten-year truce expired and was renewed by Roger. Roger returned to Europe after the Sicilian Vespers in 1282, and was replaced by Odo Poilechien. Hugh III attempted to re-assert his authority on the mainland by landing at Beirut in 1283, but this was ineffective and he died in Tyre in 1284. He was succeeded briefly by his son John II, who died soon after in 1285, and was succeeded by his brother, Hugh III's other son Henry II. That year Qalawun captured the Hospitaller fortress of Marqab. Charles of Anjou also died in 1285, and the military orders and the commune of Acre accepted

Henry II as king; Odo Poilechen refused to recognize him, but was allowed to hand Acre over to the Templars rather than Henry directly, and the Templars then handed it to the king. War broke out between the Venetians and Genoese again in 1287, and Tripoli fell to Qalawun in 1289. Although it was only a matter of time before Acre also fell, the end of the crusader kingdom was actually instigated in 1290 by newly arrived crusaders, who rioted in Acre and attacked the city's Muslim merchants. Qalawun died before he could retaliate, but his son al-Ashraf Khalil arrived to besiege Acre in April 1291. Acre was defended by Henry II's brother Amalric of Tyre, the Hospitallers, Templars, and Teutonic Knights, the Venetians and Pisans, the French garrison led by Jean I de Grailly, and the English garrison led by Otton de Grandson, but they were vastly outnumbered. Henry II himself arrived in May during the siege, but the city fell on May 18. Henry, Amalric, Otton, and Jean escaped, as did a young Templar named Roger de Flor, but most of the other defenders did not, including the master of the Templars Guillaume de Beaujeu. Tyre fell without a fight the next day, Sidon fell in June, and Beirut in July.[513]

The crusaders moved their headquarters north to cities such as Tortosa, but lost that too, and were forced to relocate their headquarters offshore to Cyprus. Some naval raids and attempts to retake territory were made over the next ten years, but with the loss of the island of Arwad in 1302/1303, the Kingdom of Jerusalem ceased to exist on the mainland. The kings of Cyprus for many decades hatched plans to regain the Holy Land, but without success. For the next seven centuries, up to today, a veritable multitude of European monarchs have used the title of King of Jerusalem.

Life in the early kingdom

The Latin population of the kingdom was always small; although a steady stream of settlers and new crusaders continually arrived, most of the original crusaders who fought in the First Crusade simply went home. According to William of Tyre, "barely three hundred knights and two thousand foot soldiers could be found" in the kingdom in 1100 during Godfrey's siege of Arsuf.[514] From the very beginning, the Latins were little more than a colonial frontier exercising rule over the native Muslim, Greek and Syriac population, who were more numerous. But Jerusalem came to be known as Outremer, the French word for "overseas", and as new generations grew up in the kingdom, they began to think of themselves as natives, rather than immigrants. Although they never gave up their core identity as Western Europeans or Franks, their clothing, diet, and commercialism integrated much Oriental, particularly Byzantine, influence. As the chronicler Fulcher of Chartres wrote around 1124,

> For we who were Occidentals now have been made Orientals. He who was a Roman or Frank has in this land been made into a Galilaean, or

an inhabitant of Palestine. He who was of Rheims or Chartres has now become a citizen of Tyre or Antioch. We have already forgotten the places of our birth; already these are unknown to many of us or not mentioned any more.[515]

The crusaders and their descendants often learned to speak Greek, Arabic, and other eastern languages, and intermarried with the native Christians (whether Greek, Syriac, or Armenian) and sometimes with converted Muslims.[516] Nonetheless, the Frankish principalities remained a distinctive Occidental colony in the heart of Islam.

Fulcher, a participant in the First Crusade and chaplain of Baldwin I, continued his chronicle up to 1127. Fulcher's chronicle was very popular and was used as a source by other historians in the west, such as Orderic Vitalis and William of Malmesbury. Almost as soon as Jerusalem had been captured, and continuing throughout the 12th century, many pilgrims arrived and left accounts of the new kingdom; among them are the English Saewulf, the Russian Abbot Daniel, the Frank Fretellus, the Byzantine Johannes Phocas, and the Germans John of Würzburg and Theoderich.[517] Aside from these, thereafter there is no eyewitness to events in Jerusalem until William of Tyre, archbishop of Tyre and chancellor of Jerusalem, who began writing around 1167 and died around 1184, although he includes much information about the First Crusade and the intervening years from the death of Fulcher to his own time, drawn mainly from the writings of Albert of Aix and Fulcher himself. From the Muslim perspective, a chief source of information is Usamah ibn Munqidh, a soldier and frequent ambassador from Damascus to Jerusalem and Egypt, whose memoirs, *Kitab al i'tibar*, include lively accounts of crusader society in the east. Further information can be gathered from travellers such as Benjamin of Tudela and Ibn Jubayr.

Crusader society and demographics

The Kingdom at first was virtually bereft of a loyal subject population and had few knights to implement the laws and orders of the realm. With the arrival of Italian trading firms, the creation of the military orders, and immigration by European knights, artisans, and farmers, the affairs of the Kingdom improved and a feudal society developed, similar to but distinct from the society the crusaders knew in Europe. The nature of this society has long been a subject of debate among crusade historians.

In the 19th and early 20th centuries, French scholars, such as E. G. Rey, Gaston Dodu, and René Grousset believed that the crusaders, Muslims and Christians lived in a totally integrated society. Ronnie Ellenblum claims this view was influenced by French imperialism and colonialism; if medieval French crusaders

Figure 41: *Crusaders coin, Acre, 1230.*

Figure 42: *Crusaders coin, Acre, circa 1230.*

could integrate themselves into local society, then certainly modern French colonies in the Levant could thrive.[518] In the mid-20th century, scholars such as Joshua Prawer, R. C. Smail, Meron Benvenisti, and Claude Cahen argued instead that the crusaders lived totally segregated from the native inhabitants, who were thoroughly Arabicized and/or Islamicized and were a constant threat to the foreign crusaders. Prawer argued further that the kingdom was an early attempt at colonization, in which the crusaders were a small ruling class, who were dependent on the native population for survival but made no attempt to integrate with them.[519] For this reason, the rural European society to which the crusaders were accustomed was replaced by a more secure urban society in the pre-existing cities of the Levant.[520]

According to Ellenblum's interpretation the inhabitants of the Kingdom (Latin Christians living alongside native Greek and Syriac Christians, Shia and Sunni Arabs, Sufis, Bedouin, Turks, Druze, Jews, and Samaritans) all had major differences between each other as well as with the crusaders. Relations between eastern Christians and the Latin crusaders were "complex and ambiguous", not simply friendly or hostile. The Turks were the common enemy for everyone, as they were only very recent arrivals in the Levant, and although they had imposed their rule prior to the arrival of the crusaders, it is unlikely that they were thoroughly Islamicized as Prawer and others believed. The eastern Christians, at least, probably felt closer ties to their fellow Christian crusaders than to either Turkic overlords or Muslim Arabs.[521]

Although the crusaders came upon an ancient urban society, Ellenblum argues that they neither completely abandoned their rural European lifestyle, nor was European society completely rural to begin with. Crusader settlement in the Levant resembled the types of colonization and settlement that were already being practiced in Europe, a mixture of urban and rural civilization centred around fortresses. The crusaders were neither totally integrated with the native population, nor did they segregate themselves in the cities away from the rural natives, but rather that they settled in both urban and rural areas; specifically, they settled in areas that had traditionally been inhabited by the eastern Christians. Areas that were traditionally Muslim had very little crusader settlement, just as they already had very few native Christian inhabitants.[522]

Into this mixed society the crusaders adapted existing institutions and introduced their own familiar customs from Europe. As in Europe the nobles had their own vassals and were themselves vassals to the king. Agricultural production was regulated by the *iqta*, a Muslim system of land ownership and payments roughly (though far from exactly) equivalent to the feudal system of Europe, and this system was not heavily disrupted by the crusaders.[523]

As Hans Mayer says, "the Muslim inhabitants of the Latin Kingdom hardly ever appear in the Latin chronicles", so information on their role in society is difficult to find. The crusaders "had a natural tendency to ignore these matters as simply without interest and certainly not worthy of record."[524] Although Muslims, as well as Jews and Eastern Christians, had virtually no rights in the countryside, where they were essentially the property of the crusader lord who owned the land,[525] tolerance for other faiths was in general no higher or lower than that found elsewhere in the Middle East. Greeks, Syriacs, and Jews continued to live as they had before, subject to their own laws and courts, with their former Muslim overlords simply replaced by the crusaders; Muslims now joined them at the lowest level of society. The *ra'is*, the leader of a Muslim or Syriac community, was a kind of vassal to whatever noble owned his land, but as the crusader nobles were absentee landlords the *ra'is* and their communities had a high degree of autonomy.[526]

Arab-Andalusian geographer and traveler Ibn Jubayr, who was hostile to the Franks, described the Muslims living under the Christian crusaders' Kingdom of Jerusalem in the late 12th-century:

<templatestyles src="Template:Quote/styles.css"/>

> *We left Tibnin by a road running past farms where Muslims live who do very well under the Franks-may Allah preserve us from such a temptation! The regulations imposed on them are the handing over of half of the grain crop at the time of harvest and the payment of a poll tax of one dinar and seven qirats, together with a light duty on their fruit trees. The Muslims own their own houses and rule themselves in their own way. This is the way the farms and big villages are organized in Frankish territory. Many Muslims are sorely tempted to settle here when they see the far from comfortable conditions in which their brethren live in the districts under Muslim rule. Unfortunately for the Muslims, they have always reason for complaint about the injustices of their chiefs in the lands governed by their coreligionists, whereas they can have nothing but praise for the conduct of the Franks, whose justice they can always rely on.*[527]

In the cities, Muslims and Eastern Christians were free, although no Muslims were permitted to live in Jerusalem itself. They were second-class citizens and played no part in politics or law, and owed no military service to the crown, although in some cities they may have been the majority of the population. Likewise, citizens of the Italian city-states owed nothing as they lived in autonomous quarters in the port cities.[528]

There were an unknown number of Muslim slaves living in the Kingdom. There was a very large slave market in Acre which functioned throughout the twelfth and thirteenth centuries. Although Christians, both Western and Eastern, were by law prohibited from being sold into slavery, the native Christians were often indistinguishable from the Muslim population and the Italian merchants were sometimes accused of selling them along with Muslim slaves.[529] Slavery was less common than ransom, especially for prisoners of war; the large numbers of prisoners taken during raids and battles every year ensured that ransom money flowed freely between the Christian and Muslim states.[530] Escape for prisoners and slaves was probably not difficult, as the inhabitants of the countryside were majority Muslim, and fugitive slaves were always a problem. The only legal means of manumission was conversion to (Catholic) Christianity. No Christian, whether Western or Eastern, was permitted by law to be sold into slavery.[531]

The nomadic Bedouin tribes were considered to be the property of the king and under his protection. They could be sold or alienated just like any other property, and later in the 12th century they were often under the protection of a lesser noble or one of the military orders.[532]

21st century positions on the question of cultural integration or cultural apartheid remains debated. Interactions between the Franks and the native Muslims and Christians, though muddled, prevailed on practical coexistence. Though likely overstated, the accounts of Usamah Ibn-Munqidh of Shaizar's travels through Antioch and Jerusalem described a level of aristocratic exchange elevated above ethnic prejudice.[533] Contact between Muslims and Christians came on the administrative or personal level (on the basis of taxes or translation), not communal or cultural, representative of a hierarchical lord over subject relationship.[534] Evidence of inter-cultural integration remains scarce, but evidence of inter-cultural cooperation and complex social interaction proves more common. Key use of the word dragoman, literally translator, with Syriac administrators and Arabic headsmen represented the direct need for negotiation of interests on both sides.[535] Comments on households with Arabic-speaking Christians and a few Arabized Jews and Muslims represent a less dichotomous relationship than the mid-20th-century historians depicted.[536] Rather, the commonality of Frankish Christians having non-Frankish priests, doctors, and other roles within households and inter-cultural communities presents the lack of standardized discrimination. Jersulamite William of Tyre complained about a trend to hire Jewish or Muslim medical practitioners over their Latin and Frankish counterparts. Evidence even indicates alterations to Frankish cultural and social customs regarding hygiene (notorious amongst Arabs for their lack of washing and knowledge of bathhouse culture), going so far as to ensure water supplies for domestic use in addition to irrigation.[537]

Population

It is impossible to give an accurate estimate of the population of the kingdom. Josiah Russell calculates that all of Syria had about 2.3 million people at the time of the crusades, with perhaps eleven thousand villages; most of these, of course, were outside of crusader rule even at the greatest extent of all four crusader states.[538] It has been estimated by scholars such as Joshua Prawer and Meron Benvenisti that there were at most 120,000 Franks and 100,000 Muslims living in the cities, with another 250,000 Muslim and Eastern Christian peasants in the countryside. The crusaders accounted for 15–25% of the total population.[539] Benjamin Z. Kedar estimates that there were between 300,000 and 360,000 non-Franks in the Kingdom, 250,000 of whom were villagers in the countryside, and "one may assume that Muslims were in the majority in some, possibly most parts of the kingdom of Jerusalem..."[540] As Ronnie Ellenblum points out, there simply is not enough existing evidence to accurately count the population and any estimate is inherently unreliable.[541] Contemporary chronicler William of Tyre recorded the census of 1183, which was intended to determine the number of men available to defend against an invasion, and to determine the amount of tax money that could be obtained from the inhabitants, Muslim or Christian. If the population was actually counted, William did not record the number.[542] In the 13th century, John of Ibelin drew up a list of fiefs and the number of knights owed by each, but this gives no indication of the non-noble, non-Latin population.

The Mamluks, led by Baibars, eventually made good their pledge to cleanse the entire Middle East of the Franks. With the fall of Antioch (1268), Tripoli (1289), and Acre (1291), those Christians unable to leave the cities were massacred or enslaved and the last traces of Christian rule in the Levant disappeared.[543,544]

Economy

The urban composition of the area, combined with the presence of the Italian merchants, led to the development of an economy that was much more commercial than it was agricultural. Palestine had always been a crossroads for trade; now, this trade extended to Europe as well. European goods, such as the woolen textiles of northern Europe, made their way to the Middle East and Asia, while Asian goods were transported back to Europe. Jerusalem was especially involved in the silk, cotton and spice trade; other items that first appeared in Europe through trade with crusader Jerusalem included oranges and sugar, the latter of which chronicler William of Tyre called "very necessary for the use and health of mankind." In the countryside, wheat, barley, legumes, olives, grapes, and dates were grown. The Italian city-states made enormous profits

Figure 43: *Crusader coins of the Kingdom of Jerusalem. Left: Denier in European style with Holy Sepulchre (1162–75). Center: Kufic gold bezant (1140–80). Right: gold bezant with Christian symbol (1250s). Gold coins were first copied dinars and bore Kufic script, but after 1250 Christian symbols were added following Papal complaints (British Museum).*

from this trade, thanks to commercial treaties like the *Pactum Warmundi*, and it influenced their Renaissance in later centuries.

Jerusalem collected money through tribute payments, first from the coastal cities which had not yet been captured, and later from other neighbouring states such as Damascus and Egypt, which the crusaders could not conquer directly. After Baldwin I extended his rule over Oultrejordain, Jerusalem gained revenue from the taxation of Muslim caravans passing from Syria to Egypt or Arabia. The money economy of Jerusalem meant that their manpower problem could be partially solved by paying for mercenaries, an uncommon occurrence in medieval Europe. Mercenaries could be fellow European crusaders, or, perhaps more often, Muslim soldiers, including the famous Turcopoles.

Education

Jerusalem was the center of education in the kingdom. There was a school in the Church of the Holy Sepulchre, where the basic skills of reading and writing Latin were taught;[545] the relative wealth of the merchant class meant that their children could be educated there along with the children of nobles – it is likely that William of Tyre was a classmate of future king Baldwin III. Higher education had to be undertaken at one of the universities in Europe;[546] the development of a university was impossible in the culture of crusader Jerusalem, where warfare was far more important than philosophy or theology. Nonetheless, the nobility and general Frankish population were noted for the high literacy: lawyers and clerks were in abundance, and the study of law, history, and other academic subjects was a beloved pastime of the royal family and

Figure 44: *Main entrance to the Church of the Holy Sepulchre.*

the nobility.[547] Jerusalem had an extensive library not only of ancient and medieval Latin works but of Arabic literature, much of which was apparently captured from Usamah ibn Munqidh and his entourage after a shipwreck in 1154.[548] The Holy Sepulchre contained the kingdom's scriptorium and the city had a chancery where royal charters and other documents were produced. Aside from Latin, the standard written language of medieval Europe, the populace of crusader Jerusalem communicated in vernacular forms of French and Italian; Greek, Armenian, and even Arabic were used by Frankish settlers.

Art and architecture

In Jerusalem itself the greatest architectural endeavour was the expansion of the Church of the Holy Sepulchre in western Gothic style. This expansion consolidated all the separate shrines on the site into one building, and was completed by 1149. Outside of Jerusalem, castles and fortresses were the major focus of construction: Kerak and Montreal in Oultrejordain and Ibelin near Jaffa are among the numerous examples of crusader castles.

Crusader art was a mix of Western, Byzantine, and Islamic styles. The major cities featured baths, interior plumbing, and other advanced hygienic tools which were lacking in most other cities and towns throughout the world. The foremost example of crusader art are perhaps the Melisende Psalter, an illuminated manuscript commissioned between 1135 and 1143 and now located in

Figure 45: *Melisende Psalter Folio 9v - The Harrowing of Hell*

the British Library, and the sculpted Nazareth Capitals. Paintings and mosaics were popular forms of art in the kingdom, but many of these were destroyed by the Mamluks in the 13th century; only the most durable fortresses survived the reconquest.

Government and legal system

Immediately after the First Crusade, land was distributed to loyal vassals of Godfrey, forming numerous feudal lordships within the kingdom. This was continued by Godfrey's successors. The number and importance of the lordships varied throughout the twelfth and thirteenth centuries, and many cities were part of the royal domain. The king was assisted by a number of officers of state. The king and the royal court were normally located in Jerusalem, but due to the prohibition on Muslim inhabitants, the capital was small and underpopulated. The king just as often held court at Acre, Nablus, Tyre, or wherever else he happened to be. In Jerusalem, the royal family lived firstly on the Temple Mount, before the foundation of the Knights Templar, and later in the palace complex surrounding the Tower of David; there was another palace complex in Acre.

Because the nobles tended to live in Jerusalem rather than on estates in the countryside, they had a larger influence on the king than they would have had in Europe. The nobles, along with the bishops, formed the *haute cour* (high court), which was responsible for confirming the election of a new king (or a regent if necessary), collecting taxes, minting coins, allotting money to the king, and raising armies. The *haute cour* was the only judicial body for the nobles of the kingdom, hearing criminal cases such as murder, rape, and treason, and simpler feudal disputes such as recovery of slaves, sales and purchases of fiefs, and default of service. Punishments included forfeiture of land and exile, or in extreme cases death. The first laws of the kingdom were, according to tradition, established during Godfrey of Bouillon's short reign, but were more probably established by Baldwin II at the Council of Nablus in 1120. Benjamin Z. Kedar argued that the canons of the Council of Nablus were in force in the 12th century but had fallen out of use by the thirteenth. Marwan Nader questions this and suggests that the canons may not have applied to the whole kingdom at all times.[549] The most extensive collection of laws, together known as Assizes of Jerusalem, were written in the mid-13th century, although many of them are purported to be twelfth-century in origin.[550]

There were other, lesser courts for non-nobles and non-Latins; the *Cour des Bourgeois* provided justice for non-noble Latins, dealing with minor criminal offences such as assault and theft, and provided rules for disputes between non-Latins, who had fewer legal rights. Special courts such as the *Cour de la Fond* (for commercial disputes in the markets) and the *Cour de la Mer* (an admiralty court) existed in the coastal cities. The extent to which native Islamic and Eastern Christian courts continued to function is unknown, but the *ra'is* probably exercised some legal authority on a local level. The *Cour des Syriens* judged non-criminal matters among the native Christians (the "Syriacs"). For criminal matters non-Latins were to be tried in the *Cour des Bourgeois* (or even the *Haute Cour* if the crime was sufficiently severe).[551]

The Italian communes were granted almost complete autonomy from the very early days of the Kingdom, thanks to their military and naval support in the years following the First Crusade. This autonomy included the right to administer their own justice, although the kinds of cases that fell under their jurisdiction varied at different times.[552]

The king was recognised as head of the Haute Cour, although he was legally only *primus inter pares*.

Legacy

After the loss of all territory in the Levant in 1291, there were late attempts at further crusades, nominally proposing to recapture Jerusalem, but with the rise of the Ottoman Empire their character was more and more that of a desperate defensive war rarely reaching beyond the Balkans (Alexandrian Crusade,

Smyrniote crusades). Henry IV of England made a pilgrimage to Jerusalem in 1393/4, and he later vowed to lead a crusade to recapture the city, but he did not undertake such a campaign before his death in 1413. The Levant remained under Ottoman control from 1517 until the Partition of the Ottoman Empire in 1918.

With the Fall of Ruad in 1303, the Kingdom of Jerusalem lost its final outpost on the Levantine coast, its possession closest to the Holy Land now being Cyprus. Henry II of Jerusalem retained the title of king of Jerusalem until his death in 1324, and the title continued to be claimed by his successors, the kings of Cyprus. The title of "king of Jerusalem" was also continuously used by the Angevin kings of Naples, whose founder, Charles of Anjou, had in 1277 bought a claim to the throne from Mary of Antioch. Thereafter, this claim to the Kingdom of Jerusalem was treated as a tributary of the crown of Naples, which often changed hands by testament or conquest rather than direct inheritance. As Naples was a papal fief, the Popes often endorsed the title of King of Jerusalem as well as of Naples, and the history of these claims is that of the Neapolitan Kingdom. In 1441, control of the Kingdom of Naples was lost to Alfonso V of Aragon and the title thus was claimed by the kings of Spain, and after the War of the Spanish Succession both by the House of Bourbon and the House of Habsburg. The title is still in *de facto* use by the Spanish Crown, currently held by Felipe VI of Spain. It was also claimed by Otto von Habsburg as Habsburg pretender until 1958, and by the kings of Italy until 1946.

Sources

Wikimedia Commons has media related to *Kingdom of Jerusalem*.

Primary sources

- Fulcher of Chartres, *A History of the Expedition to Jerusalem, 1095–1127*, trans. Frances Rita Ryan. University of Tennessee Press, 1969.
- William of Tyre, *A History of Deeds Done Beyond the Sea*, trans. E.A. Babcock and A.C. Krey. Columbia University Press, 1943.
- Philip K. Hitti, trans., *An Arab-Syrian Gentleman and Warrior in the Period of the Crusades; Memoirs of Usamah ibn-Munqidh* (Kitab al i'tibar). New York, 1929

Secondary sources

- Bernard Hamilton, *The Leper King & His Heirs*. Cambridge, 2000.
- Carole Hillenbrand, *The Crusades: Islamic Perspectives*. Routledge, 2000.
- P.M. Holt, *The Age of the Crusades: The Near East from the Eleventh Century to 1517*. Longman, 1989.
- Humphreys, R. S. (1997) *From Saladin to the Mongols: The Ayyubids of Damascus, 1193-1260*, SUNY Press
- Benjamin Z. Kedar, Hans Eberhard Mayer & R. C. Smail, ed., *Outremer: Studies in the history of the Crusading Kingdom of Jerusalem presented to Joshua Prawer*. Yad Izhak Ben-Zvi Institute, 1982.
- John L. La Monte, *Feudal Monarchy in the Latin Kingdom of Jerusalem, 1100–1291*. Cambridge, Massachusetts, 1932.
- Hans E. Mayer, *The Crusades*. Oxford University Press, 1965 (trans. John Gillingham, 1972).
- Pernoud, Régine, *The Crusaders: The Struggle for the Holy Land*[553]. Ignatius Press, 2003.
- Joshua Prawer, *The Latin Kingdom of Jerusalem: European Colonialism in the Middle Ages*. London, 1972.
- Joshua Prawer, *Crusader Institutions*. Oxford University Press, 1980.
- Jonathan Riley-Smith, *The Feudal Nobility and the Kingdom of Jerusalem, 1174–1277*. The Macmillan Press, 1973.
- Jonathan Riley-Smith, *The First Crusade and the Idea of Crusading*. University of Pennsylvania, 1991.
- Jonathan Riley-Smith, ed., *The Oxford History of the Crusades*. Oxford, 2002.
- Steven Runciman, *A History of the Crusades*. Cambridge University Press, 1951–54.
- Kenneth Setton, ed., *A History of the Crusades*. Madison, 1969–1989 (available online[554]).
- Steven Tibble, *Monarchy and Lordships in the Latin Kingdom of Jerusalem, 1099–1291*. Clarendon Press, 1989.
- Jerusalem, Latin Kingdom of (1099–1291)[555] – Article in the Catholic Encyclopedia

Mutasarrifate of Jerusalem

Mutasarrifate of Jerusalem

<indicator name="pp-default"> 🔒 </indicator>

Mutasarrifate of Jerusalem Kudüs-i Şerif Mutasarrıflığı	
Mutasarrifate of the Ottoman Empire	
← 🌙 1872–1917 🇬🇧 →	
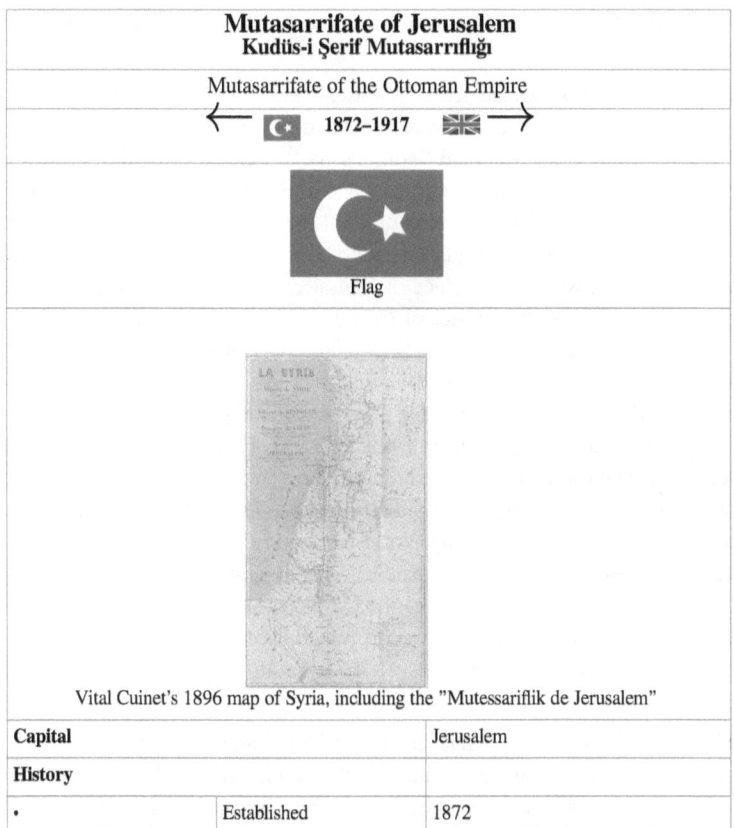 Flag	
Vital Cuinet's 1896 map of Syria, including the "Mutessariflik de Jerusalem"	
Capital	Jerusalem
History	
•	Established	1872

	British conquest	1917
Area		
	1862	12,486 km² (4,821 sq mi)
Population		
	1897[556]	298,653
Today part of		Egypt Israel Jordan Palestine

The **Mutasarrifate of Jerusalem** (*Ottoman Turkish: Kudüs-i Şerif Mutasarrıflığı*; Arabic: متصرفية القدس الشريف), also known as the **Sanjak of Jerusalem**, was an Ottoman district with special administrative status established in 1872.[557] The district encompassed Jerusalem as well as Bethlehem, Hebron, Jaffa, Gaza and Beersheba. During the late Ottoman period, the Mutasarrifate of Jerusalem, together with the Sanjak of Nablus and Sanjak of Akka (Acre), formed the region that was commonly referred to as "Southern Syria" or "Palestine".[558]

The district was separated from Damascus and placed directly under Constantinople in 1841,[557] and formally created as an independent province in 1872 by Grand Vizier Mahmud Nedim Pasha.[557] Scholars provide a variety of reasons for the separation, including increased European interest in the region, and strengthening of the southern border of the Empire against the Khedivate of Egypt.[557] Initially, the Mutasarrifate of Acre and Mutasarrifate of Nablus were combined with the province of Jerusalem, with the combined province being referred to in the register of the court of Jerusalem as the "Jerusalem Eyalet",[559] and referred to by the British consul as creation of "Palestine into a separate eyalet".[560] However, after less than two months,[560] the sanjaks of Nablus and Acre were separated and added to the Vilayet of Beirut, leaving just the Mutasarrifate of Jerusalem. In 1906, the Kaza of Nazareth was added to the Jerusalem Mutasarrifate, as an exclave, primarily in order to allow the issuance of a single tourist permit to Christian travellers. The area was conquered by the Allied Forces in 1917 during World War I and a military Occupied Enemy Territory Administration (OETA South) set up to replace the Ottoman administration. OETA South consisted of the Ottoman sanjaks of Jerusalem, Nablus and Acre. The military administration was replaced by a British civilian administration in 1920 and the area of OETA South was incorporated into the British Mandate of Palestine in 1923.

The political status of the Mutasarrifate of Jerusalem was unique to other Ottoman province since it came under the direct authority of the Ottoman capital Constantinople. The inhabitants identified themselves primarily on religious terms, 84% being Muslim Arabs. The district's villages were normally inhabited by farmers while its towns were populated by merchants, artisans, landowners and money-lenders. The elite consisted of the religious leadership, wealthy landlords and high-ranking civil servants.

History

In 1841, the district was separated from Damascus and placed directly under Constantinople[557] and formally created as an independent Mutasarrifate in 1872. Before 1872, the Mutasarrifate of Jerusalem was officially a *sanjak* within the Syria Vilayet (created in 1864, following the Tanzimat reforms).

The southern border of the Mutasarifate of Jerusalem was redrawn in 1906, at the instigation of the British, who were interested in safeguarding their imperial interests and in making the border as short and patrollable as possible.[561]

In the mid-19th century the inhabitants of Palestine identified themselves primarily in terms of religious affiliation. The population was 84% Muslim Arabs, 10% Christian Arabs, 5% Jewish, and 1% Druze Arabs. Towards the end of the 19th century, the idea that the region of Palestine or the Mutasarifate of Jerusalem formed a separate political entity became widespread among the district's educated Arab classes. In 1904, former Jerusalem official Najib Azuri formed in Paris, France the *Ligue de la Patrie Arabe* ("Arab Fatherland League") whose goal was to free Ottoman Syria and Iraq from Turkish domination. In 1908, Azuri proposed the elevation of the *mutassarifate* to the status of *vilayet* to the Ottoman Parliament after the 1908 Young Turk Revolution.

The area was conquered by the Allied Forces in 1917 during World War I and a military Occupied Enemy Territory Administration (OETA South) set up to replace the Ottoman administration. OETA South consisted of the Ottoman sanjaks of Jerusalem, Nablus and Acre. The military administration was replaced by a British civilian administration in 1920 and the area of OETA South became the territory of the British Mandate of Palestine in 1923, with some border adjustments with Lebanon and Syria.

Boundaries

Below are six contemporary Ottoman maps showing the "Quds Al-Sharif Sancağı" or "Quds Al-Sharif Mutasarrıflığı". The fourth map shows the 1860 borders between Ottoman Syria and the Khedivate of Egypt, although the border was moved to the current Israel-Egypt border in 1906, and the area north of the Negev Desert is labelled "Filastin" (Palestine).

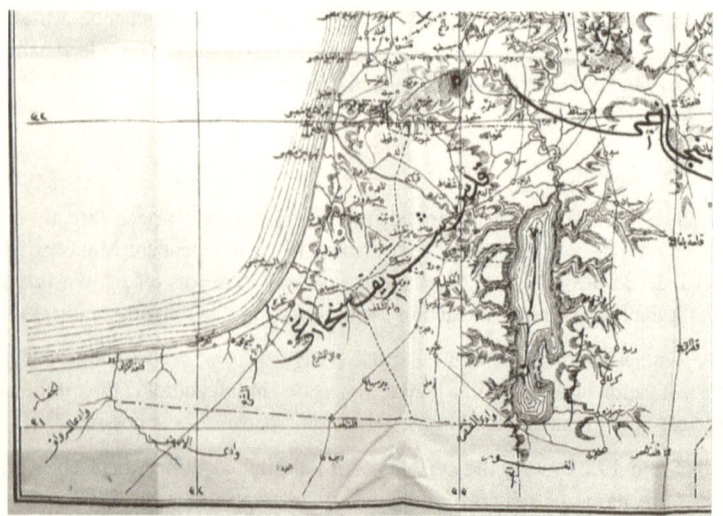

Figure 46: *1883*

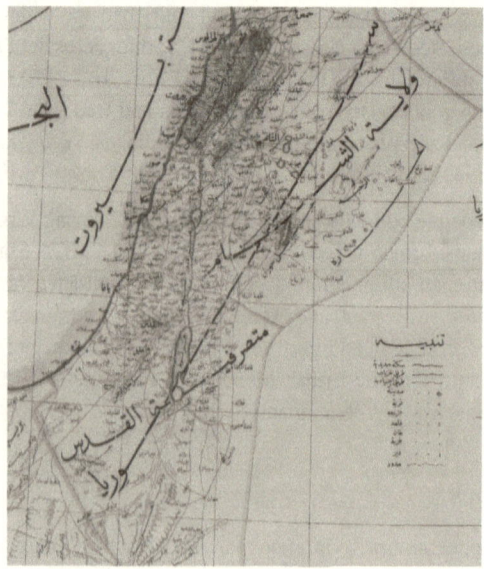

Figure 47: *1893*

Figure 48: *1889*

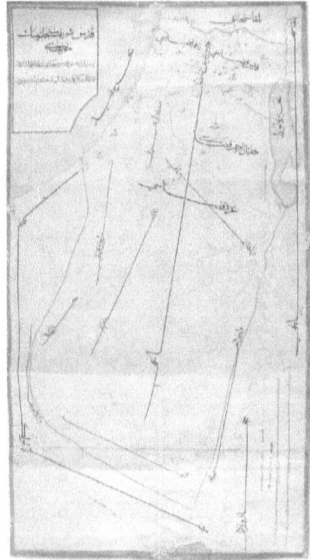

Figure 49: *c.1900*

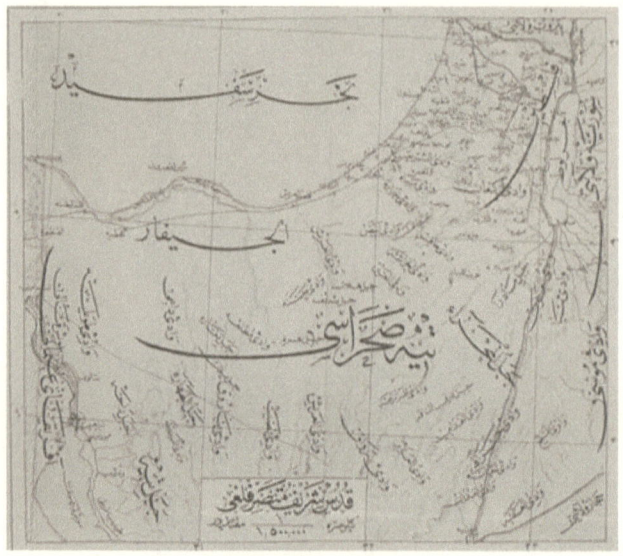

Figure 50: *1907*

Figure 51: *1907*

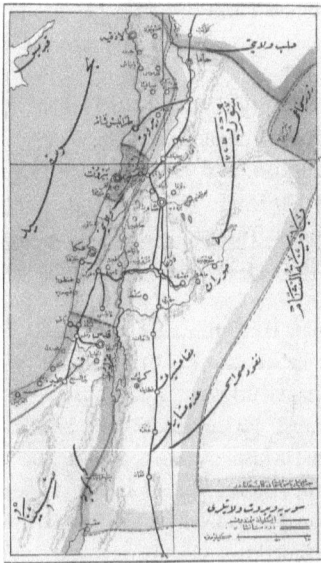

Figure 52: *1912-13*

The division was bounded on the west by the Mediterranean, on the east by the River Jordan and the Dead Sea, on the north by a line from the mouth of the river Auja to the bridge over the Jordan near Jericho, and on the south by a line from midway between Gaza and Arish to Aqaba.[562]

Administrative divisions

Administrative divisions of the Mutasarrifate (1872-1909):

1. **Beersheba Kaza** (Ottoman Turkish: قضا بءرالسبع; Turkish: *Birüsseb' kazası*; Arabic: قضاء بئر السبع), which included two sub-districts and a municipality:
   - a-Hafir (Ottoman Turkish: ناحيه حفير; Turkish: *Hafır nahiyesi*; Arabic: ناحية عوجة الحفير), created in 1908 as a middle point between Beersheba and Aqaba, close to the newly agreed border with Sinai
   - al-Mulayha, created in 1908 as a midway point between Hafir and Aqaba
   - Beersheba (Ottoman Turkish: بلدية بءرالسبع; Turkish: *Birüsseb' belediyesi*; Arabic: بلدية بئر السبع), created in 1901
2. **Gaza Kaza** (Ottoman Turkish: قضا غزه; Turkish: *Gazze kazası*; Arabic: قضاء غزة), which included three sub-districts and a municipality:
   - Al-Faluja (Ottoman Turkish: ناحيه فلوجه; Turkish: *Felluce nahiyesi*; Arabic: ناحية الفالوجة), created in 1903

- Khan Yunis (Ottoman Turkish: ناحيه خان يونس; Turkish: *Hanyunus nahiyesı*; Arabic: ناحية خان يونس), created in 1903 and became a municipality in 1917
- al-Majdal (Ottoman Turkish: ... ناحيه; Turkish: *Mücdel nahiyesı*; Arabic: ناحية المجدل), created in 1880
- Gaza (Ottoman Turkish: بلدية غزّه; Turkish: *Gazze belediyesı*; Arabic: بلدية غزة), created in 1893

3. **Hebron Kaza** (Ottoman Turkish: قضا خليل الرحمن; Turkish: *Halilü'r Rahman kazası*; Arabic: قضاء الخليل), which included two sub-districts and a municipality:
    - Bayt 'Itab (Ottoman Turkish: ناحيه بيت اعطاب; Turkish: *Beyt-i a'tâb nahiyesı*; Arabic: ناحية بيت عطاب), created in 1903
    - Bayt Jibrin (Ottoman Turkish: ناحيه بيت جبرين; Turkish: *Beyt-i Cireyn nahiyesı*; Arabic: ناحية بيت جبرين), created in 1903
    - Hebron (Ottoman Turkish: بلدية خليل الرحمن; Turkish: *Halilü'r Rahman belediyesı*; Arabic: بلدية الخليل), created in 1886

4. **Jaffa Kaza** (Ottoman Turkish: قضا يافه; Turkish: *Yafa kazası*; Arabic: قضاء يافَا), which included two sub-districts and a municipality:
    - Ni'lin (Ottoman Turkish: ناحيه نعلين; Turkish: *Na'leyn nahiyesı*; Arabic: ناحية نعلين), created in 1903
    - Ramla (Ottoman Turkish: ناحيه رمله; Turkish: *Remle nahiyesı*; Arabic: ناحية الرملة), created in 1880, became municipality before 1888 and re-established as sub-district in 1889
    - Lydda (Ottoman Turkish: بلدية ...; Turkish: *Lod belediyesı*; Arabic: ... بلدية)

5. **Jerusalem Kaza** (Ottoman Turkish: قضا قدس; Turkish: *Kudüs-i Şerif kazası*; Arabic: قضاء القدس الشريف), which included four sub-districts and two municipalities:
    - Abwein (Ottoman Turkish: ناحيه ...; Turkish: *Abaveyn nahiyesı*; Arabic: ناحية عبوين), created in 1903;
    - Bethlehem (Ottoman Turkish: ناحيه بيت اللحم; Turkish: *Beytü'l lahim nahiyesı*; Arabic: ناحية بيت لحم), created in 1883 and became a municipality in 1894;
    - Ramallah (Ottoman Turkish: ناحيه رام الله; Turkish: *Ramallah nahiyesı*; Arabic: ناحية رام الله), created in 1903 and became a municipality in 1911,
    - Saffa (Ottoman Turkish: ناحيه صفا; Turkish: *Safa nahiyesı*; Arabic: ناحية صفًا),
    - Jerusalem (Ottoman Turkish: بلدية قدس; Turkish: *Kudüs-i Şerif belediyesı*; Arabic: بلدية القدس الشريف), created in 1867 and
    - Beit Jala (Ottoman Turkish: بلدية ...; Turkish: ... *belediyesı*; Arabic: بلدية بيت جالا), created in 1912.

6. **Nazareth Kaza** (Ottoman Turkish: قضا الْنَاصِرَة; Turkish: *Nasra kazası*; Arabic: قضاء الْنَاصِرَة), established 1906.

Mutasarrıfs of Jerusalem

The Mutasarrıfs of Jerusalem were appointed by the Porte to govern the district. They were usually experienced civil servants who spoke little or no Arabic, but knew a European language - most commonly French - in addition to Ottoman Turkish.

Pre-separation from Damascus

- Sureyya Pasha 1857–63
- Izzet Pasha 1864–67
- Nazif Pasha 1867–69
- Kamil Pasha 1869–71
- Ali Bey 1871–72

Post-separation from Damascus

- Nazif Pasha (same as above) 1872–73
- Kamil Pasha (same as above) 1873–75
- Ali Bey (same as above) 1874–76
- Faik Bey 1876–77
- Şerif Mehmed Rauf Paşa 1877–89
- Resad Pasha 1889–90
- Ibrahim Hakki Pasha 1890–97
- Mehmet Tevfik Biren 1897–01
- Mehmet Cavit Bey 1901–02
- Osman Kazim Bey 1902–04
- Ahmed Resid Bey 1904–06
- Ali Ekrem Bolayır 1906–08

Post Young Turk Revolution

List of mutasarrıfs after the 1908 Young Turk Revolution:

- Subhi Bey 1908–09
- Nazim Bey 1909–10
- Azmi Bey 1910–11
- Cevdet Bey 1911–12
- Muhdi Bey 1912
- Tahir Hayreddin Bey 1912–13
- Ahmed Macid Bey 1913–15

Bibliography

<templatestyles src="Refbegin/styles.css" />

- Abu-Manneh, Butrus (1999). "The Rise of the Sanjak of Jerusalem in the Late Nineteenth Century". In Ilan Pappé. *The Israel/Palestine Question*[563]. Routledge. ISBN 978-0-415-16948-6. Retrieved 2013-06-28.<templatestyles src="Module:Citation/CS1/styles.css"></templatestyles>

British Mandate of Palestine

Mandatory Palestine

<indicator name="pp-default"> 🔒 </indicator>

Mandatory Palestine	
1920–1948	
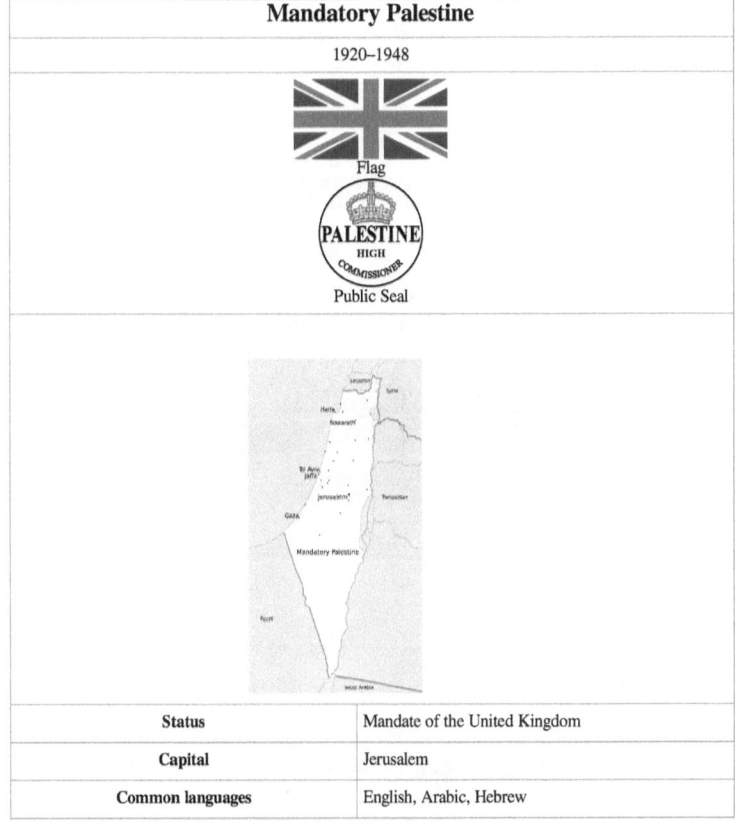	
Status	Mandate of the United Kingdom
Capital	Jerusalem
Common languages	English, Arabic, Hebrew

Religion	Islam, Judaism, Christianity, Baha'i Faith, Druze faith
High Commissioner	
• 1920–1925 (first)	Sir Herbert L. Samuel
• 1945–1948 (last)	Sir Alan G. Cunningham
Historical era	Interwar period, World War II
• Mandate assigned	25 April 1920
• Britain officially assumes control	29 September 1923
• Creation of the state of Israel declared	14 May 1948
Currency	Egyptian pound (until 1927) Palestine pound (from 1927)

Preceded by	Succeeded by
	Israel
Occupied Enemy Territory Administration	Jordanian annexation of the West Bank
	All-Palestine Protectorate

Today part of	Israel
	Palestine
	Governance of the Gaza Strip

Part of a series on the
History of Israel

Ancient Israel and Judah

- Natufian culture
- Prehistory
- Canaan
- Israelites
- United monarchy
- Northern Kingdom
- Kingdom of Judah
- Babylonian rule

Second Temple period (530 BCE–70 CE)

- Persian rule
- Hellenistic period
- Hasmonean dynasty
- Herodian dynasty
  - Kingdom
  - Tetrarchy
- Roman Judea

Middle Ages (70–1517)

- Roman Palaestina
- Byzantine Palaestina
  - Prima
  - Secunda
- Revolt against Constantius Gallus
- Samaritan revolts
- Revolt against Heraclius
- Caliphates
  - Filastin
  - Urdunn
- Kingdom of Jerusalem
- Ayyubid dynasty
- Mamluk Sultanate

Modern history (1517–1948)

- Ottoman rule
  - Eyalet
  - Mutasarrifate
- Old Yishuv
- Zionism
- OETA
- British mandate

State of Israel (1948–present)

- Independence
- Timeline
- Years
- Arab–Israeli conflict
- Start-up Nation

History of the Land of Israel by topic

- Judaism
- Jerusalem
- Zionism
- Jewish leaders
- Jewish warfare
- Nationality

Related

- Jewish history
- Hebrew calendar
- Archaeology
- Museums

Israel portal

- v
- t
- e[564]

Part of a series on the
History of Palestine

Prehistory
- Natufian culture
- Pre-Pottery
- Tahunian
- Ghassulian
- Jericho

Ancient history
- Canaan
- Phoenicia
- Ancient Israel and Judah
- Philistia
- Median Empire
- Achaemenid Empire (Yehud Medinata)

Classical period
- Seleucus
- Antigonus
- Hasmonean dynasty
- Herodian kingdom
- Province of Judea
- Syria Palaestina
- Byzantine Empire (Palaestina Prima / Secunda)

Islamic rule
- Muslim conquest
- Rashidun (Jund Filastin, Jund al-Urdunn)
- Umayyad
- Abbasid
- Fatimid
- Crusader
- Ayyubid
- Mamluk

- Ottoman

Modern era

- British Mandate
- All-Palestine
- Jordanian West Bank
- Egyptian Gaza Strip
- Israel
- Military Governorate
- Israeli Civil Administration
- Palestinian Authority (Gaza Strip)
  State of Palestine

                        Palestine portal

- v
- t
- e[565]

Mandatory Palestine[566] (Arabic: فلسطين *Filasṭīn*; Hebrew: פָּלֶשְׂתִּינָה ("א") *Pālēśtīnā (EY)*, where "EY" indicates "Eretz Yisrael", Land of Israel) was a geopolitical entity established between 1920 and 1923 in the region of Palestine as part of the Partition of the Ottoman Empire under the terms of the British Mandate for Palestine.

During the First World War (1914–18), an Arab uprising and the British Empire's Egyptian Expeditionary Force under General Edmund Allenby drove the Turks out of the Levant during the Sinai and Palestine Campaign.[567] The United Kingdom had agreed in the McMahon–Hussein Correspondence that it would honour Arab independence if they revolted against the Ottomans, but the two sides had different interpretations of this agreement, and in the end, the UK and France divided up the area under the Sykes–Picot Agreement—an act of betrayal in the eyes of the Arabs. Further complicating the issue was the Balfour Declaration of 1917, promising British support for a Jewish "national home" in Palestine. At the war's end the British and French set up a joint "Occupied Enemy Territory Administration" in what had been Ottoman Syria. The British achieved legitimacy for their continued control by obtaining a mandate from the League of Nations in June 1922. The formal objective of the League of Nations mandate system was to administer parts of the defunct Ottoman Empire, which had been in control of the Middle East since the 16th century, "until such time as they are able to stand alone."[568] The civil Mandate administration was formalised with the League of Nations' consent in 1923 under the British Mandate for Palestine, which covered two administrative areas. The land west of the Jordan River, known as Palestine, was under direct British administration until 1948. The land east of the Jordan, a semi-autonomous region known as Transjordan, under the rule of the Hashemite family from the Hijaz, gained independence in 1946.[569]

During the British Mandate period the area experienced the ascent of two major nationalist movements, one among the Jews and the other among the Arabs. The competing national interests of the Arab and Jewish populations of Palestine against each other and against the governing British authorities matured into the Arab Revolt of 1936–1939 and the Jewish insurgency in Palestine before culminating in the Civil War of 1947–1948. The aftermath of the Civil War and the consequent 1948 Arab–Israeli War led to the establishment of the 1949 cease-fire agreement, with partition of the former Mandatory Palestine between the newborn state of Israel with a Jewish majority, the Arab West Bank annexed by the Jordanian Kingdom and the Arab All-Palestine Government in the Gaza Strip under the protectorate of Egypt.

History of Palestine under the British Mandate

1920s

Following its occupation by British troops in 1917–1918, Palestine was governed by the Occupied Enemy Territory Administration. In July 1920 a civilian administration headed by a High Commissioner replaced the military administration.[570] The first High Commissioner, Herbert Samuel, a Zionist and a recent British cabinet minister, arrived in Palestine on 20 June 1920 to take up his appointment from 1 July.

Following the arrival of the British, the inhabitants established Muslim-Christian Associations in all the major towns.[571] In 1919 they joined to hold the first Palestine Arab Congress in Jerusalem.[572] Its aimed primarily at representative government and opposition to the Balfour Declaration.

The Zionist Commission formed in March 1918 and became active in promoting Zionist objectives in Palestine. On 19 April 1920, elections took place for the Assembly of Representatives of the Palestinian Jewish community.[573] The Zionist Commission received official recognition in 1922 as representative of the Palestinian Jewish community.Wikipedia:Citation needed

One of the first actions of the newly installed civil administration in 1921 had been to grant Pinhas Rutenberg—a Jewish entrepreneur—concessions for the production and distribution of electrical power. Rutenberg soon established an electric company whose shareholders were Zionist organisations, investors, and philanthropists. Palestinian-Arabs saw it as proof that the British intended to favour Zionism. The British administration claimed that electrification would enhance the economic development of the country as a whole, while at the same time securing their commitment to facilitate a Jewish National Home through economic—rather than political—means.[574]

Figure 53: *The formal transfer of Jerusalem to British rule. A native priest reads the proclamation from the steps of the Tower of David.*

Figure 54: *The arrival of Sir Herbert Samuel. From left to right: T. E. Lawrence, Emir Abdullah, Air Marshal Sir Geoffrey Salmond, Sir Herbert Samuel, Sir Wyndham Deedes and others.*

Figure 55: *An Arab "protest gathering" in session, in the Rawdat el Maaref hall, 1929. From left to right : unknown – Amin al-Husayni – Musa al-Husayni – Raghib al-Nashashibi – unknown*

Samuel tried to establish self-governing institutions in Palestine, as required by the mandate, but the Arab leadership refused to co-operate with any institution which included Jewish participation.[575] When Grand Mufti of Jerusalem Kamil al-Husayni died in March 1921, High Commissioner Samuel appointed his half-brother Mohammad Amin al-Husseini to the position. Amin al-Husseini, a member of the al-Husayni clan of Jerusalem, was an Arab nationalist and Muslim leader. As Grand Mufti, as well as in the other influential positions that he held during this period, al-Husseini played a key role in violent opposition to Zionism. In 1922, al-Husseini was elected President of the Supreme Muslim Council which had been established by Samuel in December 1921.[576] The Council controlled the Waqf funds, worth annually tens of thousands of pounds[577] and the orphan funds, worth annually about £50,000, as compared to the £600,000 in the Jewish Agency's annual budget.[578] In addition, he controlled the Islamic courts in Palestine. Among other functions, these courts had the power to appoint teachers and preachers.

The 1922 Palestine Order in Council[579] established a Legislative Council, which was to consist of 23 members: 12 elected, 10 appointed, and the High Commissioner. Of the 12 elected members, eight were to be Muslim Arabs, two Christian Arabs, and two Jews.[580] Arabs protested against the distribution

Figure 56: *Arab revolt against the British*

of the seats, arguing that as they constituted 88% of the population, having only 43% of the seats was unfair. Elections took place in February and March 1923, but due to an Arab boycott, the results were annulled and a 12-member Advisory Council was established.[581]

In October 1923, Britain provided the League of Nations with a report on the administration of Palestine for the period 1920–1922, which covered the period before the mandate.[582]

1930s: Arab armed insurgency

In 1930, Sheikh Izz ad-Din al-Qassam arrived in Palestine from Syria and organised and established the Black Hand, an anti-Zionist and anti-British militant organisation. He recruited and arranged military training for peasants and by 1935 he had enlisted between 200 and 800 men. The cells were equipped with bombs and firearms, which they used to kill Zionist settlers in the area, as well as engaging in a campaign of vandalism of the settlers-planted trees and British constructed rail-lines. In November 1935, two of his men engaged in a firefight with a Palestine police patrol hunting fruit thieves and a policeman was killed. Following the incident, British police launched a manhunt and surrounded al-Qassam in a cave near Ya'bad. In the ensuing battle, al-Qassam was killed.

The Arab revolt

The death of al-Qassam on 20 November 1935 generated widespread outrage in the Arab community. Huge crowds accompanied Qassam's body to his grave in Haifa. A few months later, in April 1936, the Arab national general strike broke out. The strike lasted until October 1936, instigated by the Arab Higher Committee, headed by Amin al-Husseini. During the summer of that year, thousands of Jewish-farmed acres and orchards were destroyed, Jewish civilians were attacked and killed, and some Jewish communities, such as those in Beisan and Acre, fled to safer areas. (Gilbert 1998, p. 80) The violence abated for about a year while the British sent the Peel Commission to investigate. (Khalidi 2006, pp. 87–90)

During the first stages of the Arab Revolt, due to rivalry between the clans of al-Husseini and Nashashibi among the Palestinian Arabs, Raghib Nashashibi was forced to flee to Egypt after several assassination attempts ordered by Amin al-Husseini.

Following the Arab rejection of the Peel Commission recommendation, the revolt resumed in autumn of 1937. Over the next 18 months, the British lost control of Nablus and Hebron. British forces, supported by 6,000 armed Jewish auxiliary police,[583] suppressed the widespread riots with overwhelming force. The British officer Charles Orde Wingate (who supported a Zionist revival for religious reasons) organised Special Night Squads composed of British soldiers and Jewish volunteers such as Yigal Alon, which "scored significant successes against the Arab rebels in the lower Galilee and in the Jezreel valley"(Black 1991, p. 14) by conducting raids on Arab villages. (Shapira 1992, pp. 247, 249, 350) The Jewish militia Irgun used violence also against Arab civilians as "retaliatory acts", attacking marketplaces and buses.

By the time the revolt concluded in March 1939, more than 5,000 Arabs, 400 Jews, and 200 British had been killed and at least 15,000 Arabs were wounded. The Revolt resulted in the deaths of 5,000 Palestinian Arabs and the wounding of 10,000. In total, 10% of the adult Arab male population was killed, wounded, imprisoned, or exiled. (Khalidi 2001, p. 26) From 1936 to 1945, while establishing collaborative security arrangements with the Jewish Agency, the British confiscated 13,200 firearms from Arabs and 521 weapons from Jews.

The attacks on the Jewish population by Arabs had three lasting effects: First, they led to the formation and development of Jewish underground militias, primarily the Haganah, which were to prove decisive in 1948. Secondly, it became clear that the two communities could not be reconciled, and the idea of partition was born. Thirdly, the British responded to Arab opposition with the White Paper of 1939, which severely restricted Jewish land purchase and

Figure 57: *Jewish demonstration against White Paper in Jerusalem in 1939*

immigration. However, with the advent of World War II, even this reduced immigration quota was not reached. The White Paper policy also radicalised segments of the Jewish population, who after the war would no longer cooperate with the British.

The revolt had a negative effect on Palestinian Arab leadership, social cohesion, and military capabilities and contributed to the outcome of the 1948 War because "when the Palestinians faced their most fateful challenge in 1947–49, they were still suffering from the British repression of 1936–39, and were in effect without a unified leadership. Indeed, it might be argued that they were virtually without any leadership at all".

Partition proposals

In 1937, the Peel Commission proposed a partition between a small Jewish state, whose Arab population would have to be transferred, and an Arab state to be attached to Jordan. The proposal was rejected outright by the Arabs. The two main Jewish leaders, Chaim Weizmann and David Ben-Gurion, had convinced the Zionist Congress to approve equivocally the Peel recommendations as a basis for more negotiation.[584,585,586,587,588] In a letter to his son in October 1937, Ben-Gurion explained that partition would be a first step to "possession of the land as a whole".[589,590] The same sentiment was recorded

Figure 58: *Australian soldiers in Tel Aviv in 1942*

by Ben-Gurion on other occasions, such as at a meeting of the Jewish Agency executive in June 1938,[591] as well as by Chaim Weizmann.[592]

Following the London Conference (1939) the British Government published a White Paper which proposed a limit to Jewish immigration from Europe, restrictions on Jewish land purchases, and a program for creating an independent state to replace the Mandate within ten years. This was seen by the Yishuv as betrayal of the mandatory terms, especially in light of the increasing persecution of Jews in Europe. In response, Zionists organised *Aliyah Bet*, a program of illegal immigration into Palestine. Lehi, a small group of extremist Zionists, staged armed attacks on British authorities in Palestine. However, the Jewish Agency, which represented the mainstream Zionist leadership, still hoped to persuade Britain to allow resumed Jewish immigration, and cooperated with Britain in World War II.

World War II

Allied and Axis activity

On 10 June 1940, Italy declared war on the British Commonwealth and sided with Germany. Within a month, the Italians attacked Palestine from the air, bombing Tel Aviv and Haifa,[593] inflicting multiple casualties.

In 1942, there was a period of great concern for the Yishuv, when the forces of German General Erwin Rommel advanced east across North Africa towards the Suez Canal and there was fear that they would conquer Palestine. This period was referred to as the "200 days of dread". This event was the direct cause for the founding, with British support, of the Palmach[594] – a highly trained regular unit belonging to Haganah (a paramilitary group which was mostly made up of reserve troops).

As in most of the Arab world, there was no unanimity amongst the Palestinian Arabs as to their position regarding the belligerents in World War II. A number of leaders and public figures saw an Axis victory as the likely outcome and a way of securing Palestine back from the Zionists and the British. Even though Arabs were not highly regarded by Nazi racial theory, the Nazis encouraged Arab support as a counter to British hegemony.[595] SS-Reichsfuehrer Heinrich Himmler was keen to exploit this, going so far as to enlist the aid of the Grand Mufti of Jerusalem, Mohammad Amin al-Husseini, sending him the following telegram on 2 November 1943:

To the Grand Mufti: The National Socialist movement of Greater Germany has, since its inception, inscribed upon its flag the fight against the world Jewry. It has therefore followed with particular sympathy the struggle of freedom-loving Arabs, especially in Palestine, against Jewish interlopers. In the recognition of this enemy and of the common struggle against it lies the firm foundation of the natural alliance that exists between the National Socialist Greater Germany and the freedom-loving Muslims of the whole world. In this spirit I am sending you on the anniversary of the infamous Balfour declaration my hearty greetings and wishes for the successful pursuit of your struggle until the final victory – Reichsfuehrer S.S. Heinrich Himmler

The Mufti al-Husseini would spend the rest of the war in Nazi Germany and the occupied areas in Europe.Wikipedia:Citation needed

Mobilisation

On 3 July 1944, the British government consented to the establishment of a Jewish Brigade, with hand-picked Jewish and also non-Jewish senior officers. On 20 September 1944, an official communiqué by the War Office announced the formation of the Jewish Brigade Group of the British Army. The Jewish brigade then was stationed in Tarvisio, near the border triangle of Italy, Yugoslavia, and Austria, where it played a key role in the Berihah's efforts to help Jews escape Europe for Palestine, a role many of its members would continue after the brigade was disbanded. Among its projects was the education and care of the Selvino children. Later, veterans of the Jewish Brigade became key participants of the new State of Israel's Israel Defense Forces.

Figure 59: *Jewish Brigade headquarters under the Union Flag and Jewish flag.*

From Palestine Regiment, two platoons, one Jewish, under the command of Brigadier Ernest Benjamin, and another Arab were sent to join allied forces on the Italian Front, having taken part of final offensive there.

Besides Jews and Arabs from Palestine, in total by mid-1944 the British had assembled a multiethnic force consisting of volunteer European Jewish refugees (from German-occupied countries), Yemenite Jews and Abyssinian Jews.[596]

The Holocaust and immigration quotas

In 1939, as a consequence of the White Paper of 1939, the British reduced the number of immigrants allowed into Palestine. World War II and the Holocaust started shortly thereafter and once the 15,000 annual quota was exceeded, Jews fleeing Nazi persecution were interned in detention camps or deported to places such as Mauritius.

Starting in 1939, a clandestine immigration effort called Aliya Bet was spearheaded by an organisation called Mossad LeAliyah Bet. Tens of thousands of European Jews escaped the Nazis in boats and small ships headed for Palestine. The Royal Navy intercepted many of the vessels; others were unseaworthy and were wrecked; a Haganah bomb sunk the SS *Patria*, killing 267 people; two more were sunk by Soviet submarines. The motor schooner *Struma* was torpedoed and sunk in the Black Sea by a Soviet submarine in February 1942 with the loss of nearly 800 lives. The last refugee boats to try to reach Palestine during the war were the *Bulbul*, *Mefküre* and *Morina* in August 1944. A Soviet submarine sank the motor schooner *Mefküre* by torpedo and shellfire and

Figure 60: *Jerusalem on VE Day, 8 May 1945*

machine-gunned survivors in the water, killing between 300 and 400 refugees. Illegal immigration resumed after World War II.

After the war 250,000 Jewish refugees were stranded in displaced persons (DP) camps in Europe. Despite the pressure of world opinion, in particular the repeated requests of US President Harry S. Truman and the recommendations of the Anglo-American Committee of Inquiry that 100,000 Jews be immediately granted entry to Palestine, the British maintained the ban on immigration.

Beginning of Zionist insurgency

The Jewish Lehi (Fighters for the Freedom of Israel) and Irgun (National Military Organisation) movements initiated violent uprisings against the British Mandate in 1940s. On 6 November 1944, Eliyahu Hakim and Eliyahu Bet Zuri (members of Lehi) assassinated Lord Moyne in Cairo. Moyne was the British Minister of State for the Middle East and the assassination is said by some to have turned British Prime Minister Winston Churchill against the Zionist cause. After the assassination of Lord Moyne, the Haganah kidnapped, interrogated, and turned over to the British many members of the Irgun ("The Hunting Season"), and the Jewish Agency Executive decided on a series of measures against "terrorist organisations" in Palestine.[597] Irgun ordered its members not to resist or retaliate with violence, so as to prevent a civil war.

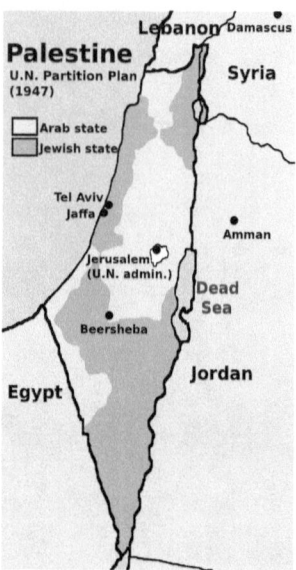

Figure 61: *The UN Partition Plan.*

After World War II: Insurgency and the Partition Plan

The three main Jewish underground forces later united to form the Jewish Resistance Movement and carry out several attacks and bombings against the British administration. In 1946, the Irgun blew up the King David Hotel in Jerusalem, the headquarters of the British administration, killing 92 people. Following the bombing, the British Government began interning illegal Jewish immigrants in Cyprus. In 1948 the Lehi assassinated the UN mediator Count Bernadotte in Jerusalem. Yitzak Shamir, future prime minister of Israel was one of the conspirators.

The negative publicity resulting from the situation in Palestine caused the Mandate to become widely unpopular in Britain, and caused the United States Congress to delay granting the British vital loans for reconstruction. The British Labour party had promised before its election to allow mass Jewish migration into Palestine but reneged on this promise once in office. Anti-British Jewish militancy increased and the situation required the presence of over 100,000 British troops in the country. Following the Acre Prison Break and the retaliatory hanging of British Sergeants by the Irgun, the British announced their desire to terminate the mandate and to withdraw by no later than the beginning of August 1948.[598]

The Anglo-American Committee of Inquiry in 1946 was a joint attempt by Britain and the United States to agree on a policy regarding the admission of Jews to Palestine. In April, the Committee reported that its members had arrived at a unanimous decision. The Committee approved the American recommendation of the immediate acceptance of 100,000 Jewish refugees from Europe into Palestine. It also recommended that there be no Arab, and no Jewish State. The Committee stated that "in order to dispose, once and for all, of the exclusive claims of Jews and Arabs to Palestine, we regard it as essential that a clear statement of principle should be made that Jew shall not dominate Arab and Arab shall not dominate Jew in Palestine." U.S. President Harry S Truman angered the British Government by issuing a statement supporting the 100,000 refugees but refusing to acknowledge the rest of the committee's findings. Britain had asked for U.S assistance in implementing the recommendations. The U.S. War Department had said earlier that to assist Britain in maintaining order against an Arab revolt, an open-ended U.S. commitment of 300,000 troops would be necessary. The immediate admission of 100,000 new Jewish immigrants would almost certainly have provoked an Arab uprising.[599]

These events were the decisive factors that forced Britain to announce their desire to terminate the Palestine Mandate and place the Question of Palestine before the United Nations, the successor to the League of Nations. The UN created UNSCOP (the UN Special Committee on Palestine) on 15 May 1947, with representatives from 11 countries. UNSCOP conducted hearings and made a general survey of the situation in Palestine, and issued its report on 31 August. Seven members (Canada, Czechoslovakia, Guatemala, Netherlands, Peru, Sweden, and Uruguay) recommended the creation of independent Arab and Jewish states, with Jerusalem to be placed under international administration. Three members (India, Iran, and Yugoslavia) supported the creation of a single federal state containing both Jewish and Arab constituent states. Australia abstained.

On 29 November 1947, the UN General Assembly, voting 33 to 13, with 10 abstentions, adopted a resolution recommending the adoption and implementation of the *Plan of Partition with Economic Union* as **Resolution 181 (II).**, while making some adjustments to the boundaries between the two states proposed by it. The division was to take effect on the date of British withdrawal. The partition plan required that the proposed states grant full civil rights to all people within their borders, regardless of race, religion or gender. It is important to note that the UN General Assembly is only granted the power to make recommendations, therefore, UNGAR 181 was not legally binding.[600] Both the U.S. and the Soviet Union supported the resolution. Haiti, Liberia, and the Philippines changed their votes at the last moment after concerted pressure from the U.S. and from Zionist organisations. The five members of the Arab League, who were voting members at the time, voted against the Plan.

The Jewish Agency, which was the Jewish state-in-formation, accepted the plan, and nearly all the Jews in Palestine rejoiced at the news.

The partition plan was rejected out of hand by Palestinian Arab leadership and by most of the Arab population. Meeting in Cairo on November and December 1947, the Arab League then adopted a series of resolutions endorsing a military solution to the conflict.

Britain announced that it would accept the partition plan, but refused to enforce it, arguing it was not accepted by the Arabs. Britain also refused to share the administration of Palestine with the UN Palestine Commission during the transitional period. In September 1947, the British government announced that the Mandate for Palestine would end at midnight on 14 May 1948.[601]

Some Jewish organisations also opposed the proposal. Irgun leader Menachem Begin announced, "The partition of the Homeland is illegal. It will never be recognised. The signature by institutions and individuals of the partition agreement is invalid. It will not bind the Jewish people. Jerusalem was and will forever be our capital. Eretz Israel will be restored to the people of Israel. All of it. And for ever." These views were publicly rejected by the majority of the nascent Jewish state.Wikipedia:Citation needed

Termination of the Mandate

When the UK announced the independence of Transjordan in 1946, the final Assembly of the League of Nations and the General Assembly both adopted resolutions welcoming the news.[602] The Jewish Agency objected, claiming that Transjordan was an integral part of Palestine, and that according to Article 80 of the UN Charter, the Jewish people had a secured interest in its territory.

During the General Assembly deliberations on Palestine, there were suggestions that it would be desirable to incorporate part of Transjordan's territory into the proposed Jewish state. A few days before the adoption of Resolution 181 (II) on 29 November 1947, U.S. Secretary of State Marshall noted frequent references had been made by the Ad Hoc Committee regarding the desirability of the Jewish State having both the Negev and an "outlet to the Red Sea and the Port of Aqaba." According to John Snetsinger, Chaim Weizmann visited President Truman on 19 November 1947 and said it was imperative that the Negev and Port of Aqaba be under Jewish control and that they be included in the Jewish state. Truman telephoned the US delegation to the UN and told them he supported Weizmann's position. However, the Trans-Jordan memorandum excluded territories of the Emirate of Transjordan from any Jewish settlement.[603]

Figure 62: *British leaving Haifa in 1948*

Immediately after the UN resolution, the 1947-1948 Civil War in Mandatory Palestine broke out between the Arab and Jewish communities, and British authority began to break down. On 16 December 1947, the Palestine Police Force withdrew from the Tel Aviv area, home to more than half the Jewish population, and turned over responsibility for the maintenance of law and order to Jewish police. As the civil war raged on, British military forces gradually withdrew from Palestine, although they occasionally intervened in favour of either side. As they withdrew, they handed over control to local authorities and locally raised police forces were charged with maintaining law and order. The areas they withdrew from often quickly became war zones. The British maintained strong presences in Jerusalem and Haifa, even as Jerusalem came under siege by Arab forces and became the scene of fierce fighting, though the British occasionally intervened in the fighting, largely to secure their evacuation routes, including by proclaiming martial law and enforcing truces. The Palestine Police Force was largely inoperative, and government services such as social welfare, control of water supplies, and postal services were withdrawn. In April 1948, the British withdrew from most of Haifa but retained an enclave in the port area to be used in the evacuation of British forces, and temporarily retained RAF Ramat David airbase to cover their retreat, leaving behind a volunteer police force to maintain order. The city was quickly captured by the Haganah in the Battle of Haifa. Following the victory, British

Figure 63: *Hoisting of the Yishuv flag in Tel Aviv, 1 January 1948*

forces in Jerusalem announced that they had no intention of assuming control of any local administrations, but would not permit any actions that would hamper the safe and orderly withdrawal of British forces from Palestine, and would set up military courts to try persons who interfered.[604] Although by this time British authority in most of Palestine had broken down, with most of the country in control of the Jews and Arabs, the British air and sea blockade of Palestine remained firmly in place.

The British had notified the U.N. of their intent to terminate the mandate not later than 1 August 1948.[605] However, early in 1948, the United Kingdom announced its firm intention to end its mandate in Palestine on 14 May. In response, President Harry S Truman made a statement on 25 March proposing UN trusteeship rather than partition, stating that "unfortunately, it has become clear that the partition plan cannot be carried out at this time by peaceful means... unless emergency action is taken, there will be no public authority in Palestine on that date capable of preserving law and order. Violence and bloodshed will descend upon the Holy Land. Large-scale fighting among the people of that country will be the inevitable result."

By 14 May 1948, the only British forces remaining in Palestine were in the Haifa area and in Jerusalem. On that same day, the British garrison in Jerusalem withdrew, and High Commissioner Alan Cunningham left the city for Haifa, where he was to leave the country by sea. The Jewish Leadership, led by future Prime Minister, David Ben-Gurion, declared the establishment of a Jewish State in Eretz-Israel, to be known as the State of Israel,[606] on the afternoon of 14 May 1948 (5 Iyar 5708 in the Hebrew calendar), to come into force at midnight of that day.[607,608] On the same day, the Provisional Government of Israel asked the US Government for recognition, on the frontiers specified in the UN Plan for Partition. The United States immediately replied, recognizing "the provisional government as the de facto authority."

On 15 May 1948, the Palestine Mandate ended and the State of Israel came into being. The Palestine Government formally ceased to exist, the status of British forces still in the process of withdrawal from Haifa changed to occupiers of foreign territory, the Palestine Police Force formally stood down and was disbanded, with the remaining personnel evacuated alongside British military forces, the British blockade of Palestine was lifted, and all Mandatory Palestine passports ceased to give British protection. The 1948 Palestinian exodus occurred in the period leading up to the end of the Mandate and subsequently.[609,610]

Over the next few days, approximately 700 Lebanese, 1,876 Syrian, 4,000 Iraqi, 2,800 Egyptian troops crossed over the borders and into Palestine.[611] Around 4,500 Transjordanian troops, commanded partly by 38 British officers who had resigned their commissions in the British army only weeks earlier, including overall commander, General John Bagot Glubb, entered the Corpus separatum region encompassing Jerusalem and its environs (in response to the Haganah's Operation Kilshon)[612] and moved into areas designated as part of the Arab state by the UN partition plan.

Politics

Name

<templatestyles src="Multiple_image/styles.css" />

1927 Mandatory Palestine postage stamp

1941 Mandatory Palestine coin

1927 Mandatory Palestine revenue stamp

1927 Mandatory Palestine coin

"Palestine" is shown in English, Arabic (فلسطين) and Hebrew; the latter includes the acronym א״י for *Eretz Yisrael* (Land of Israel).

The name given to the Mandate's territory was "Palestine", in accordance with European traditions.Wikipedia:Citation needed The term Palestine was coined in the Western culture from the name of Palaestina province of the Roman (Syria-Palaestina) and later Byzantine Empire (Palaestina Prima and Palaestina Secunda).Wikipedia:Citation needed The Mandate charter stipulated that Mandatory Palestine would have three official languages, namely English, Arabic and Hebrew.

In 1926, the British authorities formally decided to use the traditional Arabic and Hebrew equivalents to the English name, i.e. *filasṭīn* (فلسطين) and *pālēśtīnā* (פלשתינה) respectively. The Jewish leadership proposed that the proper Hebrew name should be *Ērēts Yiśrā'el* (ארץ) Land=ישראל of Israel). The final compromise was to add the initials of the Hebrew proposed name, Alef-Yud, within parenthesis, (א״י) whenever the Mandate's name was mentioned in Hebrew in official documents. The Arab leadership saw this compromise as a violation of the mandate terms. Some Arab politicians suggested that there should be a similar Arabic concession, such as "Southern Syria" (سوريا الجنوبية). The British authorities rejected this proposal.[613] The divergent tendencies regarding the nature and purpose of the mandate are visible already in the discussions concerning the name for this new entityWikipedia:Citation needed. According to the Minutes of the Ninth Session of the League of Nations' Permanent Mandate Commission:

> Colonel Symes explained that the country was described as "Palestine" by Europeans and as "Falestin" by the Arabs. The Hebrew name for the country was the designation "Land of Israel", and the Government,

to meet Jewish wishes, had agreed that the word "Palestine" in Hebrew characters should be followed in all official documents by the initials which stood for that designation. As a set-off to this, certain of the Arab politicians suggested that the country should be called "Southern Syria" in order to emphasise its close relation with another Arab State.[614] Wikipedia:No original research#Primary, secondary and tertiary sources

Arab community

<templatestyles src="Multiple_image/styles.css" />

Front cover

Biographical pages

Passports from the British Mandate era.

The resolution of the San Remo Conference contained a safeguarding clause for the existing rights of the non-Jewish communities. The conference accepted the terms of the Mandate with reference to Palestine, on the understanding that there was inserted in the memorandum a legal undertaking by the Mandatory Power that it would not involve the surrender of the rights hitherto enjoyed by the non-Jewish communities in Palestine.[615] The draft mandates for Mesopotamia and Palestine, and all of the post-war peace treaties contained clauses for the protection of religious groups and minorities. The mandates invoked the compulsory jurisdiction of the Permanent Court of International Justice in the event of any disputes.

Article 62 (LXII) of the Treaty of Berlin, 13 July 1878 dealt with religious freedom and civil and political rights in all parts of the Ottoman Empire.[616] The guarantees have frequently been referred to as "religious rights" or "minority rights". However, the guarantees included a prohibition against discrimination in civil and political matters. Difference of religion could not be alleged against any person as a ground for exclusion or incapacity in matters relating to the enjoyment of civil or political rights, admission to public employments, functions, and honours, or the exercise of the various professions and industries, "in any locality whatsoever."

A legal analysis performed by the International Court of Justice noted that the Covenant of the League of Nations had provisionally recognised the communities of Palestine as independent nations. The mandate simply marked a transitory period, with the aim and object of leading the mandated territory to become an independent self-governing State.[617] Judge Higgins explained that the Palestinian people are entitled to their territory, to exercise self-determination, and to have their own State."[618] The Court said that specific guarantees regarding freedom of movement and access to the Holy Sites contained in the Treaty of Berlin (1878) had been preserved under the terms of the Palestine Mandate and a chapter of the United Nations Partition Plan for Palestine.[619]

According to historian Rashid Khalidi, the mandate ignored the political rights of the Arabs. The Arab leadership repeatedly pressed the British to grant them national and political rights, such as representative government, over Jewish national and political rights in the remaining 23% of the Mandate of Palestine which the British had set aside for a Jewish homeland. The Arabs reminded the British of President Wilson's Fourteen Points and British promises during the First World War. The British however made acceptance of the terms of the mandate a precondition for any change in the constitutional position of the Arabs. A legislative council was proposed in The Palestine Order in Council, of 1922[620] which implemented the terms of the mandate. It stated that: "No Ordinance shall be passed which shall be in any way repugnant to or inconsistent with the provisions of the Mandate." For the Arabs, this was unacceptable, as they felt that this would be "self murder". As a result, the Arabs boycotted the elections to the Council held in 1923, which were subsequently annulled.[621] During the whole interwar period, the British, appealing to the terms of the mandate, which they had designed themselves, rejected the principle of majority rule or any other measure that would give an Arab majority control over the government of Palestine.

The terms of the mandate required the establishment of self-governing institutions in both Palestine and Transjordan. In 1947, Foreign Secretary Bevin admitted that during the previous twenty-five years the British had done their best to further the legitimate aspirations of the Jewish communities without prejudicing the interests of the Arabs, but had failed to "secure the development of self-governing institutions" in accordance with the terms of the Mandate.[622]

Figure 64: *A 1930 protest in Jerusalem against the British Mandate by Arab women. The sign reads "No dialogue, no negotiations until termination [of the Mandate]".*

Palestinian Arab leadership and national aspirations

Under the British Mandate, the office of "Mufti of Jerusalem", traditionally limited in authority and geographical scope, was refashioned into that of "Grand Mufti of Palestine". Furthermore, a Supreme Muslim Council (SMC) was established and given various duties, such as the administration of religious endowments and the appointment of religious judges and local muftis. In Ottoman times, these duties had been fulfilled by the bureaucracy in Istanbul.(Khalidi 2006, p. 63) In dealings with the Palestinian Arabs, the British negotiated with the elite rather than the middle or lower classes.(Khalidi 2006, p. 52) They chose Hajj Amin al-Husseini to become Grand Mufti, although he was young and had received the fewest votes from Jerusalem's Islamic leaders.(Khalidi 2006, pp. 56–57) One of the mufti's rivals, Raghib Bey al-Nashashibi, had already been appointed mayor of Jerusalem in 1920, replacing Musa Kazim, whom the British removed after the Nabi Musa riots of 1920,(Khalidi 2006, pp. 63, 69)(Segev 2000, pp. 127–144) during which he exhorted the crowd to give their blood for Palestine.(Morris 2001, p. 112) During the entire Mandate period, but especially during the latter half, the rivalry between the mufti and al-Nashashibi dominated Palestinian politics. Khalidi ascribes the failure of the Palestinian leaders to enroll mass support, because of their experiences during the Ottoman Empire period, as they were then part of the ruling elite and accustomed to their commands being obeyed. The idea of mobilising the masses was thoroughly alien to them.(Khalidi 2006, p. 81)

There had already been rioting and attacks on and massacres of Jews in 1921 and 1929. During the 1930s, Palestinian Arab popular discontent with Jewish immigration grew. In the late 1920s and early 1930s, several factions of Palestinian society, especially from the younger generation, became impatient with the internecine divisions and ineffectiveness of the Palestinian elite and engaged in grass-roots anti-British and anti-Zionist activism, organised by groups such as the Young Men's Muslim Association. There was also support for the radical nationalist Independence Party (*Hizb al-Istiqlal*), which called for a boycott of the British in the manner of the Indian Congress Party. Some took to the hills to fight the British and the Jews. Most of these initiatives were contained and defeated by notables in the pay of the Mandatory Administration, particularly the mufti and his cousin Jamal al-Husseini. A six-month general strike in 1936 marked the start of the great Arab Revolt.(Khalidi 2006, pp. 87–90)

Jewish Yishuv

The conquest of the Ottoman Syria by the British forces in 1917, found a mixed community in the region, with Palestine, the southern part of the Ottoman Syria, containing a mixed population of Muslims, Christians, Jews and Druze. In this period, the Jewish community (Yishuv) in Palestine was composed of traditional Jewish communities in cities (the *Old Yishuv*), which had existed for centuries,[623] and the newly established agricultural Zionist communities (the *New Yishuv*), established since the 1870s. With the establishment of the Mandate, the Jewish community in Palestine formed the Zionist Commission to represent its interests.

In 1929, the Jewish Agency for Palestine took over from the Zionist Commission its representative functions and administration of the Jewish community. During the Mandate period, the Jewish Agency was a quasi-governmental organisation that served the administrative needs of the Jewish community. Its leadership was elected by Jews from all over the world by proportional representation. The Jewish Agency was charged with facilitating Jewish immigration to Palestine, land purchase and planning the general policies of the Zionist leadership. It ran schools and hospitals, and formed the Haganah. The British authorities offered to create a similar *Arab Agency* but this offer was rejected by Arab leaders.[624]

In response to numerous Arab attacks on Jewish communities, the Haganah, a Jewish paramilitary organisation, was formed on 15 June 1920 to defend

Figure 65: *Jewish immigration to Mandatory Palestine from 1920 to 1945*

Jewish residents. Tensions led to widespread violent disturbances on several occasions, notably in 1921 (see Jaffa riots), 1929 (primarily violent attacks by Arabs on Jews—see 1929 Hebron massacre) and 1936–1939. Beginning in 1936, Jewish groups such as Etzel (Irgun) and Lehi (Stern Gang) conducted campaigns of violence against British military and Arab targets.

Jewish immigration

During the Mandate, the Yishuv or Jewish community in Palestine, grew from one-sixth to almost one-third of the population. According to official records, 367,845 Jews and 33,304 non-Jews immigrated legally between 1920 and 1945. It was estimated that another 50–60,000 Jews and a marginal number of Arabs, the latter mostly on a seasonal basis, immigrated illegally during this period.[625] Immigration accounted for most of the increase of Jewish population, while the non-Jewish population increase was largely natural. Of the Jewish immigrants, in 1939 most had come from Germany and Czechoslovakia, but in 1940–1944 most came from Romania and Poland, with an additional 3,530 immigrants arriving from Yemen during the same period.[626]

Initially, Jewish immigration to Palestine met little opposition from the Palestinian Arabs. However, as anti-Semitism grew in Europe during the late 19th and early 20th centuries, Jewish immigration (mostly from Europe) to Palestine began to increase markedly. Combined with the growth of Arab nationalism in the region and increasing anti-Jewish sentiments the growth of Jewish population created much Arab resentment. The British government placed limitations on Jewish immigration to Palestine. These quotas were controversial, particularly in the latter years of British rule, and both Arabs and Jews disliked the policy, each for their own reasons.

Jewish immigrants were to be afforded Palestinian citizenship:

Article 7. The Administration of Palestine shall be responsible for enacting a nationality law. There shall be included in this law provisions framed so as to facilitate the acquisition of Palestinian citizenship by Jews who take up their permanent residence in Palestine.

Jewish national home

In 1919, the General Secretary (and future President) of the Zionist Organisation, Nahum Sokolow, published *History of Zionism (1600–1918)*. He also represented the Zionist Organisation at the Paris Peace Conference.

" "
> The object of Zionism is to establish for the Jewish people a home in Palestine secured by public law." ... It has been said and is still being obstinately repeated by anti-Zionists again and again, that Zionism aims at the creation of an independent "Jewish State" But this is fallacious. The "Jewish State" was never part of the Zionist programme. The Jewish State was the title of Herzl's first pamphlet, which had the supreme merit of forcing people to think. This pamphlet was followed by the first Zionist Congress, which accepted the Basle programme—the only programme in existence.
>
> — Nahum Sokolow, History of Zionism[627]

One of the objectives of British administration was to give effect to the Balfour Declaration of 1917, which was also set out in the preamble of the mandate, as follows:

Whereas the Principal Allied Powers have also agreed that the Mandatory should be responsible for putting into effect the declaration originally made on November 2nd, 1917, by the Government of His Britannic Majesty, and adopted by the said Powers, in favour of the establishment in Palestine of a national home for the Jewish people, it being clearly understood that nothing should be done which might prejudice the civil and religious rights of existing non-Jewish communities in Palestine, or the rights and political status enjoyed by Jews in any other country.

The United Nations Special Committee on Palestine said the Jewish National Home, which derived from the formulation of Zionist aspirations in the 1897 Basle program has provoked many discussions concerning its meaning, scope and legal character, especially since it had no known legal connotation and there are no precedents in international law for its interpretation. It was used in the Balfour Declaration and in the Mandate, both of which promised the establishment of a "Jewish National Home" without, however, defining its meaning. A statement on "British Policy in Palestine," issued on 3 June 1922 by the Colonial Office, placed a restrictive construction upon the Balfour Declaration. The statement included "the disappearance or subordination of the Arabic population, language or customs in Palestine" or "the imposition of Jewish nationality upon the inhabitants of Palestine as a whole", and made it clear that in the eyes of the mandatory Power, the Jewish National Home was to be founded in Palestine and not that Palestine as a whole was to be converted into a Jewish National Home. The Committee noted that the construction, which restricted considerably the scope of the National Home, was made prior to the confirmation of the Mandate by the Council of the League of Nations and was formally accepted at the time by the Executive of the Zionist Organisation.[628]

In March 1930, Lord Passfield, the Secretary of State for the Colonies, had written a Cabinet Paper[629] which said:

In the Balfour Declaration there is no suggestion that the Jews should be accorded a special or favoured position in Palestine as compared with the Arab inhabitants of the country, or that the claims of Palestinians to enjoy self-government (subject to the rendering of administrative advice and assistance by a Mandatory as foreshadowed in Article XXII of the Covenant) should be curtailed in order to facilitate the establishment in Palestine of a National Home for the Jewish people." ... Zionist leaders have not concealed and do not conceal their opposition to the grant of any measure of self-government to the people of Palestine either now or for many years to come. Some of them even go so far as to claim that that provision of Article 2 of the Mandate constitutes a bar to compliance with the demand of the Arabs for any measure of self-government. In view of the provisions of Article XXII of the Covenant and of the promises made to the Arabs on several occasions that claim is inadmissible.

The League of Nations Permanent Mandates Commission took the position that the Mandate contained a dual obligation. In 1932 the Mandates Commission questioned the representative of the Mandatory on the demands made by the Arab population regarding the establishment of self-governing institutions, in accordance with various articles of the mandate, and in particular Article 2. The Chairman noted that "under the terms of the same article, the mandatory Power had long since set up the Jewish National Home."

In 1937, the Peel Commission, a British Royal Commission headed by Earl Peel, proposed solving the Arab–Jewish conflict by partitioning Palestine into two states. The two main Jewish leaders, Chaim Weizmann and David Ben-Gurion, had convinced the Zionist Congress to approve equivocally the Peel recommendations as a basis for more negotiation.[630] The US Consul General at Jerusalem told the State Department that the Mufti had refused the principle of partition and declined to consider it. The Consul said that the Emir Abdullah urged acceptance on the ground that realities must be faced, but wanted modification of the proposed boundaries and Arab administrations in the neutral enclave. The Consul also noted that Nashashibi sidestepped the principle, but was willing to negotiate for favourable modifications.

A collection of private correspondence published by David Ben Gurion contained a letter written in 1937 which explained that he was in favour of partition because he didn't envision a partial Jewish state as the end of the process. Ben Gurion wrote "What we want is not that the country be united and whole, but that the united and whole country be Jewish." He explained that a first-class Jewish army would permit Zionists to settle in the rest of the country with or without the consent of the Arabs.[631] Benny Morris said that both Chaim Weizmann and David Ben Gurion saw partition as a stepping stone to further expansion and the eventual takeover of the whole of Palestine.[632] Former Israeli Foreign Minister and historian Schlomo Ben Ami writes that 1937 was the same year that the "Field Battalions" under Yitzhak Sadeh wrote the "Avner Plan", which anticipated and laid the groundwork for what would become in 1948, Plan D. It envisioned going far beyond any boundaries contained in the existing partition proposals and planned the conquest of the Galilee, the West Bank, and Jerusalem.[633]

In 1942, the Biltmore Program was adopted as the platform of the World Zionist Organisation. It demanded "that Palestine be established as a Jewish Commonwealth."

In 1946 an Anglo-American Committee of Inquiry noted that the demand for a Jewish State went beyond the obligations of either the Balfour Declaration or the Mandate and had been expressly disowned by the Chairman of the Jewish Agency as recently as 1932. The Jewish Agency subsequently refused to accept the subsequent Morrison-Grady Plan as the basis for discussion. A spokesman for the agency, Eliahu Epstein, told the US State Department that the Agency could not attend the London conference if the Grady-Morrison proposal was on the agenda. He stated that the Agency was unwilling to be placed in a position where it might have to compromise between the Grady-Morrison proposals on the one hand and its own partition plan on the other. He stated that the Agency had accepted partition as the solution for Palestine which it favoured.[634]

Land ownership

After transition to the British rule, much of the agricultural land in Palestine (about one third of the whole territory) was still owned by the same landowners as under Ottoman rule, mostly powerful Arab clans and local Muslim sheikhs. Other lands had been held by foreign Christian organisations (most notably the Greek Orthodox Church), as well as Jewish private and Zionist organisations, and to lesser degree by small minorities of Bahai's, Samaritans and Circassians.

As of 1931, the territory of the British Mandate of Palestine was 26,625,600 dunams (26,625.6 km^2), of which 8,252,900 dunams (8,252.9 km^2) or 33%

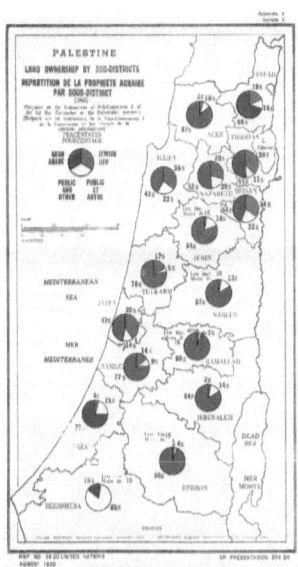

Figure 66: *Map of Palestine Land ownership by sub-district (1945) originally published in the Village Statistics, 1945*

were arable. Official statistics show that Jews privately and collectively owned 1,393,531 dunams (1,393.53 km^2), or 5.23% of Palestine's total in 1945.[635] The Jewish owned agricultural land was largely located in the Galilee and along the coastal plain. Estimates of the total volume of land that Jews had purchased by 15 May 1948 are complicated by illegal and unregistered land transfers, as well as by the lack of data on land concessions from the Palestine administration after 31 March 1936. According to Avneri, Jews held 1,850,000 dunams (1,850 km^2) of land in 1947, or 6.94% of the total. Stein gives the estimate of 2,000,000 dunams (2,000 km^2) as of May 1948, or 7.51% of the total. According to Fischbach, By 1948, Jews and Jewish companies owned 20% percent of all cultivable land in the country.

Nevertheless, the amount of land owned by Jews is easier to calculate than that owned by Arabs. It is difficult to reckon the total amount of land owned by Arabs (Muslim, Christian and Druze) in Mandatory Palestine.Wikipedia:Citation needed The 1945 UN estimate shows that Arab ownership of arable land was on average 68% of a district, ranging from 15% ownership in the Beer-Sheba district to 99% ownership in the Ramallah district. These data cannot be fully understood without comparing them to those of neighbouring countries: in Iraq, for instance, still in 1951 only 0.3 per cent of registered land (or 50 per cent of the total amount) was categorised as 'private property'.[636]

Land ownership by district

The following table shows the 1945 land ownership of mandatory Palestine by district:

Land ownership of Palestine in 1945 by district

District	Sub-district	Arab-owned	Jewish-owned	Public / other
Haifa	Haifa	42%	35%	23%
Galilee	Acre	87%	3%	10%
	Beisan	44%	34%	22%
	Nazareth	52%	28%	20%
	Safad	68%	18%	14%
	Tiberias	51%	38%	11%
Lydda	Jaffa	47%	39%	14%
	Ramle	77%	14%	9%
Samaria	Jenin	84%	<1%	16%
	Nablus	87%	<1%	13%
	Tulkarm	78%	17%	5%
Jerusalem	Hebron	96%	<1%	4%
	Jerusalem	84%	2%	14%
	Ramallah	99%	<1%	1%
Gaza	Beersheba	15%	<1%	85%
	Gaza	75%	4%	21%

Data from the Land Ownership of Palestine[637]

Land ownership by corporation

The table below shows the land ownership of Palestine by large Jewish Corporations (in square kilometres) on 31 December 1945.

Land ownership of Palestine by large Jewish Corporations (in square kilometres) on 31 December 1945

Corporations	Area
JNF	660.10
PICA	193.70
Palestine Land Development Co. Ltd.	9.70

Hemnuta Ltd	16.50
Africa Palestine Investment Co. Ltd.	9.90
Bayside Land Corporation Ltd.	8.50
Palestine Kupat Am. Bank Ltd.	8.40
Total	906.80
Data is from Survey of Palestine (vol. I, p. 245).[638]	

Land ownership by type

The land owned privately and collectively by Jews, Arabs and other non-Jews can be classified as urban, rural built-on, cultivable (farmed), and uncultivable. The following chart shows the ownership by Jews, Arabs and other non-Jews in each of the categories.

Land ownership of Palestine (in square kilometres) on 1 April 1943

Category	Arab / non-Jewish ownership	Jewish ownership	Total
Urban	76.66	70.11	146.77
Rural built-on	36.85	42.33	79.18
Cereal (taxable)	5,503.18	814.10	6,317.29
Cereal (not taxable)	900.29	51.05	951.34
Plantation	1,079.79	95.51	1,175.30
Citrus	145.57	141.19	286.76
Banana	2.30	1.43	3.73
Uncultivable	16,925.81	298.52	17,224.33
Total	24,670.46	1,514.25	26,184.70
Data is from Survey of Palestine (vol. II, p. 566).[639] By the end of 1946, Jewish ownership had increased to 1624 km^2.[640]			

List of Mandatory land laws

- Land Transfer Ordinance of 1920
- 1926 Correction of Land Registers Ordinance
- Land Settlement Ordinance of 1928
- Land Transfer Regulations of 1940

In February 1940, the British Government of Palestine promulgated the *Land Transfer Regulations* which divided Palestine into three regions with different restrictions on land sales applying to each. In Zone "A", which included the hill-country of Judea as a whole, certain areas in the Jaffa sub-District, and in the Gaza District, and the northern part of the Beersheba sub-District, new

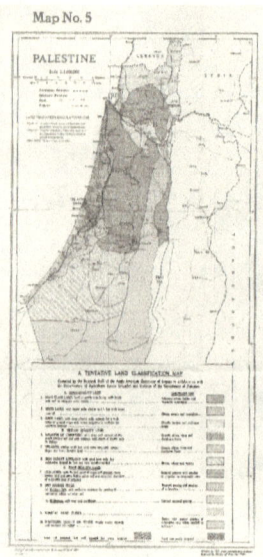

Figure 67: *Land classification as prescribed in 1940.*

agreements for sale of land other than to a Palestinian Arab were forbidden without the High Commissioner's permission. In Zone "B", which included the Jezreel Valley, eastern Galilee, a parcel of coastal plain south of Haifa, a region northeast of the Gaza District, and the southern part of the Beersheba sub-District, sale of land by a Palestinian Arab was forbidden except to a Palestinian Arab with similar exceptions. In the "free zone", which consisted of Haifa Bay, the coastal plain from Zikhron Ya'akov to Yibna, and the neighbohood of Jerusalem, there were no restrictions. The reason given for the regulations was that the Mandatory was required to "ensur[e] that the rights and positions of other sections of the population are not prejudiced," and an assertion that "such transfers of land must be restricted if Arab cultivators are to maintain their existing standard of life and a considerable landless Arab population is not soon to be created"[641]

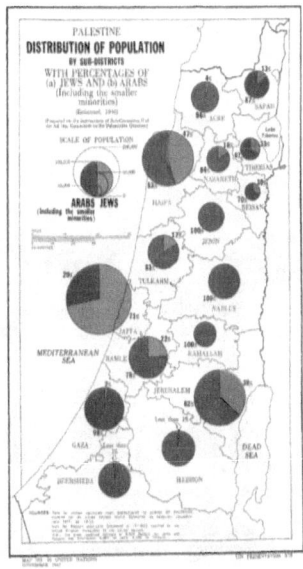

Figure 68: *Population distribution at the end of the Mandate*

Demographics

British censuses and estimations

In 1920, the majority of the approximately 750,000 people in this multi-ethnic region were Arabic-speaking Muslims, including a Bedouin population (estimated at 103,331 at the time of the 1922 census and concentrated in the Beersheba area and the region south and east of it), as well as Jews (who comprised some 11% of the total) and smaller groups of Druze, Syrians, Sudanese, Somalis, Circassians, Egyptians, Copts, Greeks, and Hejazi Arabs.

- The first census of 1922 showed a population of 757,182, of whom 78% were Muslim, 11% Jewish and 10% Christian.
- The second census, of 1931, gave a total population of 1,035,154 of whom 73.4% were Muslim, 16.9% Jewish and 8.6% Christian.

A discrepancy between the two censuses and records of births, deaths and immigration, led the authors of the second census to postulate the illegal immigration of about 9,000 Jews and 4,000 Arabs during the intervening years.[642]

There were no further censuses but statistics were maintained by counting births, deaths and migration. By the end of 1936 the total population was approximately 1,300,000, the Jews being estimated at 384,000. The Arabs had also increased their numbers rapidly, mainly as a result of the cessation

Figure 69: *Christian Arab boys at Jerusalem YMCA, 1938.*

of the military conscription imposed on the country by the Ottoman Empire, the campaign against malaria and a general improvement in health services. In absolute figures their increase exceeded that of the Jewish population, but proportionally, the latter had risen from 13 per cent of the total population at the census of 1922 to nearly 30 per cent at the end of 1936.[643]

Some components such as illegal immigration could only be estimated approximately. The White Paper of 1939, which placed immigration restrictions on Jews, stated that the Jewish population "has risen to some 450,000" and was "approaching a third of the entire population of the country". In 1945, a demographic study showed that the population had grown to 1,764,520, comprising 1,061,270 Muslims, 553,600 Jews, 135,550 Christians and 14,100 people of other groups.

Year	Total	Muslim	Jewish	Christian	Other
1922	752,048	589,177 (78%)	83,790 (11%)	71,464 (10%)	7,617 (1%)
1931	1,036,339	761,922 (74%)	175,138 (17%)	89,134 (9%)	10,145 (1%)
1945	1,764,520	1,061,270 (60%)	553,600 (31%)	135,550 (8%)	14,100 (1%)

| Average compounded population growth rate per annum, 1922–1945 | 3.8% | 2.6% | 8.6% | 2.8% | 2.7% |

By district

The following table gives the religious demography of each of the 16 districts of the Mandate in 1945.

		Demography of Palestine in 1945 by district						
District	Sub-District	Muslim	Percentage	Jewish	Percentage	Christian	Percentage	Total
Haifa	Haifa	95,970	38%	119,020	47%	33,710	13%	253,450
Galilee	Acre	51,130	69%	3,030	4%	11,800	16%	73,600
	Beisan	16,660	67%	7,590	30%	680	3%	24,950
	Nazareth	30,160	60%	7,980	16%	11,770	24%	49,910
	Safad	47,310	83%	7,170	13%	1,630	3%	56,970
	Tiberias	23,940	58%	13,640	33%	2,470	6%	41,470
Lydda	Jaffa	95,980	24%	295,160	72%	17,790	4%	409,290
	Ramle	95,590	71%	31,590	24%	5,840	4%	134,030
Samaria	Jenin	60,000	98%	negligible	<1%	1,210	2%	61,210
	Nablus	92,810	98%	negligible	<1%	1,560	2%	94,600
	Tulkarm	76,460	82%	16,180	17%	380	1%	93,220
Jerusalem	Hebron	92,640	99%	300	<1%	170	<1%	93,120
	Jerusalem	104,460	41%	102,520	40%	46,130	18%	253,270
	Ramallah	40,520	83%	negligible	<1%	8,410	17%	48,930
Gaza	Beersheba	6,270	90%	510	7%	210	3%	7,000
	Gaza	145,700	97%	3,540	2%	1,300	1%	150,540
Total		1,076,780	58%	608,230	33%	145,060	9%	1,845,560

Government and institutions

Under the terms of the August 1922 Palestine Order in Council, the Mandate territory was divided into administrative regions known as districts and administer by the office of the British High Commissioner for Palestine.[644]

Britain continued the *millet* system of the Ottoman Empire whereby all matters of a religious nature and personal status were within the jurisdiction of Muslim

Figure 70: *Jerusalem city hall, 1939*

courts and the courts of other recognised religions, called confessional communities. The High Commissioner established the Orthodox Rabbinate and retained a modified *millet* system which only recognised eleven religious communities: Muslims, Jews and nine Christian denominations (none of which were Christian Protestant churches). All those who were not members of these recognised communities were excluded from the *millet* arrangement. As a result, there was no possibility, for example, of marriages between confessional communities, and there were no civil marriages. Personal contacts between communities were nominal.

Apart from the Religious Courts, the judicial system was modelled on the British one, having a High Court with appellate jurisdiction and the power of review over the Central Court and the Central Criminal Court. The five consecutive Chief Justices were:

- Thomas Haycraft (1921–1927)
- Michael McDonnell (1927–1936)
- Harry Herbert Trusted (1936–1941) (afterwards Chief Justice of the Federated Malay States, 1941)
- Frederick Gordon-Smith (1941–1944)
- William James Fitzgerald (1944–1948

Economy

Between 1922 and 1947, the annual growth rate of the Jewish sector of the economy was 13.2%, mainly due to immigration and foreign capital, while that of the Arab was 6.5%. Per capita, these figures were 4.8% and 3.6% respectively. By 1936, the Jewish sector earned 2.6 times as much as Arabs. Compared to other Arab countries, the Palestinian Arab individuals earned slightly more.

The Jaffa Electric Company was founded in 1923 by Pinhas Rutenberg, and was later absorbed into a newly created Palestine Electric Company. Palestine Airways was founded in 1934, Angel Bakeries in 1927, and the Tnuva dairy in 1926. Electric current mainly flowed to Jewish industry, following it to its nestled locations in Tel Aviv and Haifa. Although Tel Aviv had by far more workshops and factories, the demand for electric power for industry was roughly the same for both cities by the early 1930s.[645]

The country's largest industrial zone was in Haifa, where many housing projects were built for employees.

On the scale of the UN Human Development Index determined for around 1939, of 36 countries, Palestinian Jews were placed 15th, Palestinian Arabs 30th, Egypt 33rd and Turkey 35th. The Jews in Palestine were mainly urban, 76.2% in 1942, while the Arabs were mainly rural, 68.3% in 1942. Overall, Khalidi concludes that Palestinian Arab society, while overmatched by the Yishuv, was as advanced as any other Arab society in the region and considerably more than several.

Education

Under the British Mandate, the country developed economically and culturally. In 1919 the Jewish community founded a centralised Hebrew school system, and the following year established the Assembly of Representatives, the Jewish National Council and the Histadrut labour federation. The Technion university was founded in 1924, and the Hebrew University of Jerusalem in 1925.

Literacy rates in 1932 were 86% for the Jews compared to 22% for the Palestinian Arabs, but Arab literacy rates steadily increased thereafter. Palestinian Arabs compared favourably in this respect to residents of Egypt and Turkey, but unfavourably to the Lebanese.

Gallery

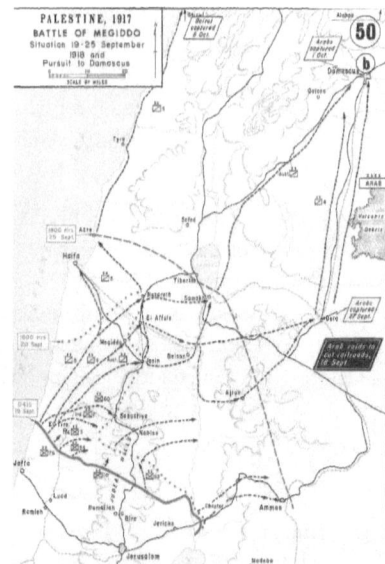

Figure 71: *General Allenby's final attacks of the Palestine Campaign gave Britain control of the area*

Figure 72: *Field Marshal Allenby entering Jerusalem with British troops on 11 December 1917*

Figure 73: *General Watson meeting with the Mayor of Jerusalem in December 1917*

Figure 74: *The surrender of Jerusalem by the Ottomans to the British on 9 December 1917 following the Battle of Jerusalem*

Figure 75: *Main post office, Jaffa Road, Jerusalem*

Figure 76: *Rockefeller Museum, built in Jerusalem during the British Mandate*

Figure 77: *Main post office, Jaffa*

Figure 78: *Anglo-Palestine Bank*

Figure 79: *Western Wall, 1933*

Figure 80: *Supreme Military Tribunal of the British Mandate, Kiryat Shmuel, Jerusalem*

Figure 81: *YMCA in Jerusalem, built during the British Mandate*

Figure 82: *"Bevingrad" in Jerusalem, Russian Compound behind barbed wire*

Figure 83: *Mandate-era mailbox, Jerusalem*

Figure 84: *1941 currency coin*

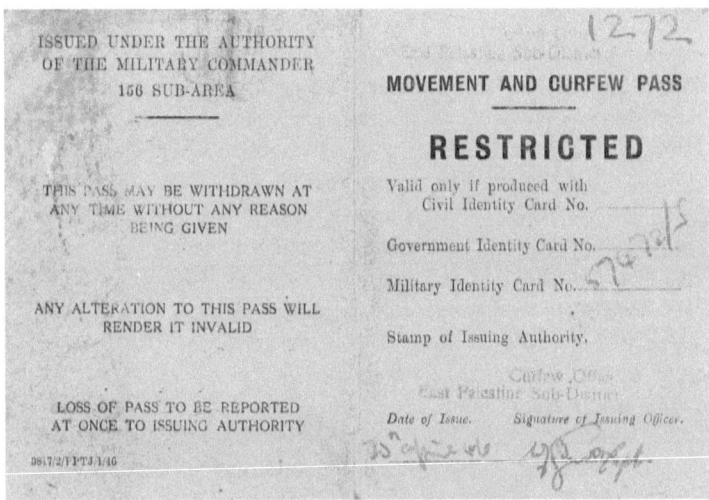

Figure 85: *Movement and curfew pass, issued under the authority of the British Military Commander, East Palestine, 1946*

Quotes

Bibliography

- Pappé, Ilan (15 August 1994). "Introduction"[646]. *The Making of the Arab–Israeli Conflict, 1947–1951*[647]. I.B.Tauris. ISBN 978-1-85043-819-9. Retrieved 2 May 2009.<templatestyles src="Module:Citation/CS1/styles.css"></templatestyles>
- Khalidi, Rashid (2006). *The Iron Cage: The Story of the Palestinian Struggle for Statehood*[648]. Beacon Press. ISBN 978-0-8070-0308-4. Retrieved 2 May 2009.<templatestyles src="Module:Citation/CS1/styles.css"></templatestyles>
- Khalidi, Rashid (2007) [1st ed. 2001]. "The Palestinians and 1948: the underlying causes of failure"[649]. In Eugene L. Rogan & Avi Shlaim. *The War for Palestine: Rewriting the History of 1948*[650] (2nd ed.). Cambridge University Press. ISBN 978-0-521-69934-1. Retrieved 2 May 2009.<templatestyles src="Module:Citation/CS1/styles.css"></templatestyles>
- Khalidi, Walid (1987) [Original in 1971]. *From Haven to Conquest: Readings in Zionism and the Palestine Problem Until 1948*[651]. Institute for Palestine Studies. ISBN 978-0-88728-155-6. Retrieved 2 May 2009.<templatestyles src="Module:Citation/CS1/styles.css"></templatestyles>

- Morris, Benny (2001) [1999]. *Righteous Victims: A History of the Zionist–Arab Conflict, 1881–1999*[652]. New York: Alfred A. Knopf. ISBN 978-0-679-74475-7. Retrieved 2 May 2009.<templatestyles src="Module:Citation/CS1/styles.css"></templatestyles>
- Aruri, Naseer Hasan (1972). *Jordan: A Study in Political Development 1923–1965*[653]. The Hague: Martinus Nijhoff Publishers. ISBN 978-90-247-1217-5. Retrieved 2 May 2009.<templatestyles src="Module:Citation/CS1/styles.css"></templatestyles>
- Biger, Gideon (2004). *The Boundaries of Modern Palestine, 1840–1947*[654]. London: Routledge. ISBN 978-0-7146-5654-0. Retrieved 2 May 2009.<templatestyles src="Module:Citation/CS1/styles.css"></templatestyles>
- Louis, Wm. Roger (1969). "The United Kingdom and the Beginning of the Mandates System, 1919–1922". *International Organization*. **23** (1): 73–96. doi: 10.1017/s0020818300025534[655].<templatestyles src="Module:Citation/CS1/styles.css"></templatestyles>
- Segev, Tom (2001) [Original in 2000]. "Nebi Musa, 1920"[656]. *One Palestine, Complete: Jews and Arabs Under the British Mandate*[657]. Trans. Haim Watzman. London: Henry Holt and Company. ISBN 978-0-8050-6587-9. Retrieved 2 May 2009.<templatestyles src="Module:Citation/CS1/styles.css"></templatestyles>
- Stein, Kenneth W. (1987) [Original in 1984]. *The Land Question in Palestine, 1917–1939*[658]. University of North Carolina Press. ISBN 978-0-8078-4178-5. Retrieved 2 May 2009.<templatestyles src="Module:Citation/CS1/styles.css"></templatestyles>
- Gilbert, Martin (1998). *Israel: a history*[659]. Doubleday. ISBN 978-0-385-40401-3. Retrieved 2 May 2009.<templatestyles src="Module:Citation/CS1/styles.css"></templatestyles>
- Shapira, Anita (1992). *Land and Power: The Zionist Resort to Force, 1881–1948*[660]. trans. William Templer. Oxford University Press. ISBN 978-0-19-506104-8. Retrieved 2 May 2009.<templatestyles src="Module:Citation/CS1/styles.css"></templatestyles>
- Black, Ian (1991). *Israel's Secret Wars: A History of Israel's Intelligence Services*. Morris, Benny. Grove Press. ISBN 978-0-8021-1159-3.<templatestyles src="Module:Citation/CS1/styles.css"></templatestyles>
- Avneri, Aryeh L. (1984). *The Claim of Dispossession: Jewish Land-Settlement and the Arabs, 1878–1948*[661]. Transaction Publishers. ISBN 978-0-87855-964-0. Retrieved 2 May 2009.<templatestyles src="Module:Citation/CS1/styles.css"></templatestyles>
- Khalaf, Issa (1991). *Politics in Palestine: Arab Factionalism and Social Disintegration, 1939–1948*[662]. State University of New York Press.

ISBN 978-0-7914-0708-0. Retrieved 6 May 2009.<templatestyles src="Module:Citation/CS1/styles.css"></templatestyles>
- Bayliss, Thomas (1999). *How Israel Was Won: A Concise History of the Arab–Israeli Conflict.* Lexington Books. <templatestyles src="Module:Citation/CS1/styles.css" />ISBN 978-0-7391-0064-6
- Bethell, Nicholas *The Palestine Triangle: the Struggle Between the British, the Jews and the Arabs, 1935–48*, London: Deutsch, 1979 <templatestyles src="Module:Citation/CS1/styles.css" />ISBN 0-233-97069-X.
- El-Eini, Roza I.M. (2006). *Mandated Landscape: British Imperial Rule in Palestine, 1929–1948*[663]. London: Routledge. ISBN 978-0-7146-5426-3. Retrieved 5 May 2009.<templatestyles src="Module:Citation/CS1/styles.css"></templatestyles>
- Hughes, Matthew, ed. (2004). *Allenby in Palestine: The Middle East Correspondence of Field Marshal Viscount Allenby June 1917 – October 1919.* Army Records Society. **22**. Phoenix Mill, Thrupp, Stroud, Gloucestershire: Sutton Publishing Ltd. ISBN 978-0-7509-3841-9.<templatestyles src="Module:Citation/CS1/styles.css"></templatestyles>
- Katz, Shmuel (1973). *Battleground: Fact and Fantasy in Palestine*[648]. Bantam Books. ISBN 978-0-929093-13-0. Retrieved 2 May 2009.<templatestyles src="Module:Citation/CS1/styles.css"></templatestyles>
- Paris, Timothy J. (2003). *Britain, the Hashemites and Arab Rule, 1920–1925: The Sherifian Solution.* London: Routledge. <templatestyles src="Module:Citation/CS1/styles.css" />ISBN 0-7146-5451-5
- Sherman, A J (1998).*Mandate Days: British Lives in Palestine, 1918–1948*, Thames & Hudson. <templatestyles src="Module:Citation/CS1/styles.css" />ISBN 0-8018-6620-0
- Vareilles, Guillaume (2010). *Les frontières de la Palestine, 1914–1947*, Paris, L'Harmattan. <templatestyles src="Module:Citation/CS1/styles.css" />ISBN 978-2-296-13621-2

Further reading

- Wright, Quincy, *The Palestine Problem*[664], Political Science Quarterly, Vol. 41, No. 3 (September, 1926), pp. 384–412, via JSTOR
- Hanna, Paul Lamont, " British Policy in Palestine[665]", Washington, D.C., American Council on Public Affairs, (1942)
- Miller, Rory, ed. *Britain, Palestine and Empire: The Mandate Years* (2010)
- Ravndal, Ellen Jenny. "Exit Britain: British Withdrawal From the Palestine Mandate in the Early Cold War, 1947–1948," *Diplomacy and Statecraft,* (Sept 2010) 21#3 pp. 416–433.

- Roberts, Nicholas E. "Re-Remembering the Mandate: Historiographical Debates and Revisionist History in the Study of British Palestine," *History Compass* (March 2011) 9#3 pp. 215–230.
- Kamel, Lorenzo. "Whose Land? Land Tenure in Late Nineteenth- and Early Twentieth-Century Palestine", "British Journal of Middle Eastern studies" (April 2014), 41, 2, pp. 230–242.

Primary sources

- Golani, Motti, ed. *The End of the British Mandate for Palestine, 1948: The Diary of Sir Henry Gurney* (2009).

External links

- Media related to British Mandate of Palestine at Wikimedia Commons

Jewish Agency for Israel

Jewish Agency for Israel

Hebrew: ישראל לארץ היהודית הסוכנות (HaSochnut HaYehudit L'Eretz Yisra'el)	
Founded	1929
Tax ID no.	23-7254561
Legal status	501(c)(3)
Purpose	To inspire Jews throughout the world to connect with their people, heritage, and land, and empower them to build a thriving Jewish future and a strong Israel.
Headquarters	Jerusalem
Coordinates	31.777°N 35.216°E[666] Coordinates: 31.777°N 35.216°E[666]
Chairman-Elect	Isaac Herzog
Chairman of the Board of Governors	Michael Siegal[667]
Director-General	Alan Hoffmann
Deputy Chair of the Executive	David Breakstone
Revenue <templatestyles src="Nobold/styles.css"/>(2016)	$381,438,000
Expenses <templatestyles src="Nobold/styles.css"/>(2016)	$333,228,000
Endowment	$1,345,000 (2016)
Employees <templatestyles src="Nobold/styles.css"/>(2016)	1,140[668]
Volunteers <templatestyles src="Nobold/styles.css"/>(2016)	25,000
Website	www<wbr/>.jewishagency<wbr/>.org[669]

The **Jewish Agency for Israel** (Hebrew: ישראל, לארץ היהודית הסוכנות *HaSochnut HaYehudit L'Eretz Yisra'el*) is the largest Jewish nonprofit organization in the world. Its mission is to "inspire Jews throughout the world to connect with their people, heritage, and land, and empower them to build a thriving Jewish future and a strong Israel."

It is best known as the primary organization fostering the immigration ("Aliyah") and absorption of Jews and their families from the Jewish diaspora

Figure 86: *Jewish Agency headquarters, Jerusalem*

into Israel. Since 1948 the Jewish Agency for Israel has brought 3 million immigrants to Israel, and offers them transitional housing in "absorption centers" throughout the country.

The Jewish Agency played a central role in the founding and the development of the State of Israel. David Ben Gurion served as the Chairman of its Executive Committee from 1935, and in this capacity on May 14, 1948 he proclaimed independence for the State of Israel. He became Israel's first Prime Minister. In the years before and after the founding of the state, the Jewish Agency oversaw the establishment of about 1,000 towns and villages in Mandate Palestine. It serves as the main link between Israel and Jewish communities around the world.

As of 2017[670] the Jewish Agency operates and/or funds programs worldwide that:

- bring Jews to Israel on "Israel Experiences" trips, such as Masa Israel Journey and Onward Israel
- bring "Israel in your community" through a variety of Jewish education and communal programs, such as Shlichim (emissaries), Partnership2Gether and programming for Jews in Russian-language countries

- help vulnerable Israelis (both Jewish and Arab) and encourage "Jewish Social Action" in programs such as Youth Villages, Youth Futures, Young Activism, and Amigour subsidized housing
- facilitate Aliyah and help immigrants integrate into Israeli society. For example, it conducts intensive Hebrew-language immersion programs in Israel and residential programs for immigrants aged 18 to 35.

Part of a series on
Aliyah
Jewish immigration to the Land of Israel
Concepts
<ul><li>Promised Land</li><li>Gathering of Israel</li><li>Diaspora<ul><li>Negation</li></ul></li><li>Homeland for the Jewish people</li><li>Zionism</li><li>Jewish question</li><li>Law of Return</li></ul>
Pre-Modern Aliyah
<ul><li>Return to Zion</li><li>Old Yishuv</li><li>Perushim</li></ul>
Aliyah in modern times
<ul><li>First</li><li>Second</li><li>during World War I</li><li>Third</li><li>Fourth</li><li>Fifth</li><li>Aliyah Bet</li><li>Bricha</li><li>from Muslim countries<ul><li>Yemen</li><li>Iraq</li><li>Morocco</li><li>Lebanon</li></ul></li></ul>

- from the Soviet Union
  - post-Soviet
- from Ethiopia
- from Latin America

Absorption
<ul><li>Revival of the Hebrew language<ul><li>Ulpan</li><li>Hebraization of surnames</li></ul></li><li>Kibbutz</li><li>Youth village</li><li>Immigrant camps</li><li>Ma'abarot</li><li>Development town</li><li>Austerity</li></ul>
Organizations
<ul><li>World Zionist Organization</li><li>Jewish National Fund</li><li>Jewish Agency for Israel</li><li>Youth Aliyah</li><li>Mossad LeAliyah Bet</li><li>El Al</li><li>Ministry of Aliyah and Integration</li><li>Nefesh B'Nefesh</li><li>Am Yisrael Foundation</li></ul>
Related topics
<ul><li>Yishuv</li><li>Sabra</li><li>Yerida</li><li>Jewish refugees</li><li>History of the Jews in the Land of Israel</li><li>Demographic history of Palestine (region)</li><li>Historical Jewish population comparisons</li><li>Yom HaAliyah</li></ul>
<ul><li>v</li><li>t</li><li>e[671]</li></ul>

By law, the Jewish Agency is a para-statal organization, but it does not receive core funding from the Israeli government.Wikipedia:Please clarify The Jewish Agency is funded by the Jewish Federations of North America, Keren Hayesod, major Jewish communities and federations, and foundations and donors from Israel and around the world. The dozens of programs it supports or operates benefit well over a million Israelis and Jews worldwide every year.Wikipedia:Citation needed

In 2008 the Jewish Agency won the Israel Prize for its historical contribution to Israel and to the worldwide Jewish community.

Current programs

As of 2016, The Jewish Agency sponsors dozens of programs that connect Jews to Israel and to each other. The Agency organizes the programs into four different categories: Israel Experiences, Israel in Your Community (Jewish and Zionist education in the Jewish diaspora), Jewish Social Action (helping vulnerable Israelis), and Aliyah.

Some programs:

Israel experiences

The Israel Experience programs bring young Jews from around the globe to Israel to get to know the country and deepen their Jewish identities.

- **Taglit-Birthright Israel** provides ten-day educational trips to Israel for Jews ages 18 to 26 from around the world, completely free of charge. The Jewish Agency is the largest organizational partner in the initiative and is directly involved in bringing over 9,000 participants on Taglit-Birthright each year, with a special focus on facilitating Taglit-Birthright experiences and related programming for communities in need and for Russian-speaking Jews in the former Soviet Union and Germany.[672]
- **Onward Israel**[673] organizes 6- to 10-week professional internships in Israel for students and young professionals who have previously visited Israel on Taglit-Birthright or another group tour. Participants come in groups, all from the same community or organization.[674]
- **Masa Israel Journey** is a public-service organization founded in 2004 by the Government of Israel's Office of the Prime Minister, together with The Jewish Agency. It includes a portfolio of more than 200 programs in Israel for Jews aged 18–30, including study programs, service programs, and career development. Programs last from 2–12 months. It sponsors over 10,000 participants per year. Masa provides significant scholarships to participants, performs outreach, and operates alumni activities.
- **Israel Tech Challenge**[675] is a partnership of The Jewish Agency with the National Cyber Bureau and other partners and donors. It offers trips to Israel of varying lengths for students and young professionals (aged 18–30) with knowledge in the field of computer science and programming. The programs offer visits with Israeli hi-tech professionals and academics, along with experience or training in coding, cyber security and/or data science.

- **Machon Le'Madrichim** trains, in Israel, Jewish counselors of Zionist youth movements around the world, to give them tools for running educational Zionist programs in their home communities when they return. It was founded in 1946 by the World Zionist Organization. As of 2013, it had 12,000 alumni from South America, the United States, South Africa, Australia, North Africa, and Europe.
- **Na'ale** allows Jewish teenagers from the diaspora to study in Israel and earn a high school diploma. Students start the program in ninth or tenth grade and graduate after the twelfth grade with a full Israeli matriculation certificate (*bagrut*). During the first year, students follow an intensive Hebrew-language program so that they become able to speak, read and write in Hebrew. The program is fully subsidized by the Israeli government. The Na'ale scholarship includes: fully subsidized tuition, free ticket to Israel, room and board, health insurance, trips, and extra curricular activities. Na'ale offers a variety of schools all over Israel from which candidates may choose, including secular, national religious, ultra-orthodox, kibbutz, and urban boarding schools.

Jewish and Zionist education outside Israel

In its mission to strengthen the ties between Israel and worldwide Jewry and to promote Jewish culture and identity, The Jewish Agency sends out *shlichim*, or emissaries, to Jewish communities across the globe; partners with Israel and Diaspora communities, and operates and/or funds Jewish educational programs for Russian-speaking Jews and their children. It also supports Jewish inclusion and diversity programs.[676]

- **Israel Fellows to Hillel** are Israeli young adults who have completed army service and university study. The Campus Fellows travel for two years to North American university campuses with the goal of empowering student leadership and promoting positive engagement with Israel. According to The Jewish Agency, the aims of an Israel Fellow are to "create an ongoing Israel presence for Jewish students and the broader community . . . . partner with student organizations, campus study abroad offices, Jewish and Israel studies departments, local Jewish federations, Israeli consulates, and Jewish Community Centers . . . [and] follow through with Taglit-Birthright trip alumni via one-on-one meetings and special programs and events to keep them active and encourage them to continue their Jewish journeys while in college." In 2014–15, 70 Fellows were sent to campuses in North America, South America, and other regions.[677]
- **Shlichim** (Jewish Agency "emissaries") are active in communal organizations, Jewish schools, community centers, synagogues and youth movements. There are also Summer Shlichim who serve in Jewish summer

camps. They serve as a central resource for Israel education in the local community. In the 2014-15 program year, The Jewish Agency sent 1,120 short-term emissaries to summer camps, and 295 long-term emissaries to countries around the world (not including the Israel Fellows).

- **Programs for Russian-speaking Jewry** The organization has developed special outreach to Russian Jewry, because they have largely been separated from Jewish communities even after the fall of the Soviet Union. Only an estimated 20 percent of the 800,000 Jews across former Soviet states are engaged in Jewish life. And Russian Jews who have emigrated to other countries have often been separated from Jewish community life. The Agency runs programs for them (in the former Soviet Union, North America, Germany, Australia, and Israel) that fall are organized into four areas: (1) Camping, youth education, and counselor training (2) leadership training (3) visits to Israel (4) Focus on facilitation of Aliyah from the former Soviet Union and Germany.

- **FSU Summer and Winter Camps** introduce young Russian-speaking Jews in the former Soviet Union to their Jewish heritage. Staffed by trained local counselors and Russian-speaking Israeli counselors, participants are introduced to Jewish history, Jewish customs and practices, and Israel. The Agency organizes counselors to follow up with attendees in year-round Jewish educational activities. In 2015, some 6,800 participants in the former Soviet Union attended sleepaway camps and 455 went to day camps.

- **Partnership2Gether** (P2G, previously known as Partnership 2000) is the "peoplehood platform" that connects some 450 Jewish and Israeli communities in 46 partnerships. The program has more than 350,000 participants each year. Its goals are to "connect the global Jewish family, increase Jewish identity, strengthen Israeli society, create living bridges to Israel and understanding of life in the Jewish state, and increase understanding of the rich variety of religious expression and renewal around the world."

- **The Global School Twinning Network** connects schools in Israel to Jewish schools around the world, usually as part of a P2G partnership. Students share projects and communicate via Skype and Facebook. The Network includes 668 schools in 334 pairings, serving about 52,000 children and teens.[678]

- **Support for Religious Streams:** In 2014, The Jewish Agency allocated $2.8 million to 30 educational programs in Israel under the auspices of the Reform, Conservative, and Modern Orthodox movements. Their goal is to "help Israelis understand the varied expressions of Judaism outside Israel, and help Jews worldwide feel that their styles of Jewish expression can find a home in Israel."

Figure 87: *Clergy in the Conservative Judaism movement read from a Torah scroll.*

- **The Emergency Assistance Fund** provides for physical security improvements, such as video surveillance & CCTV, alarms, locks, gates, and reinforced walls/doors/windows, at synagogues, Jewish community centers, schools, and camps so that Jewish communal life can continue in greater safety. Jewish institutions outside Israel and North America are eligible for assistance. Recipients have included institutions in Argentina, Brazil, Greece, South Africa, and others. In 2014, allocations totaled $2 million, to 95 communities in 25 countries.
- **Jewish People Policy Institute** was established in 2002 as an independent professional policy planning think tank to promote the identity, culture, prosperity, and continuity of the Jewish people. JPPI holds annual conferences and meetings that explore the Jewish condition. Participants have included Dennis Ross, Shimon Peres, Natan Sharansky, Malcolm Hoenlein, and Tzipi Livni. The Institute conducts meetings, publishes reports and position papers, and produces contingency plans that help the development of Jewish communities around the world.

Jewish social action

The Jewish Agency also helps vulnerable populations in Israel and around the world.

- **Youth Futures** is a community-based initiative for mentoring at-risk pre-teens and adolescents. Each Youth Futures "Mentor" works with 16 at-risk children over the course of three years, teaching skills for academic improvement and social integration. In 2014–15, approximately 350 trained Youth Futures staff members worked with 5,000 children and teens, plus 7,000 of their family members, in 200 schools in 35 communities in Israel. In addition to secular and traditional Jews, Youth Futures serves Arab, Bedouin, Druze, and Ultra-Orthodox communities.
- **Youth Villages** provide safe, cost-effective boarding school settings for 850 young people ages 12 to 18 who have severe emotional, behavioral and family problems. The four Jewish Agency Youth Villages provide intensive, holistic services and help the youths succeed in and complete high school, and enter the Israeli army with their peers.[679]
- **Project TEN** brings together young Israelis and their Jewish peers from across the globe to work on sustainable projects in developing regions. Participants spend three months working in onsite service projects in vulnerable communities. Project TEN is a service-learning program designed to build participants' Jewish identities while they serve others. In 2016, Project TEN runs volunteer centers in Winneba, Ghana; Oaxaca, Mexico; Gondar, Ethiopia; Kibbutz Harduf, Israel; and Arad, Israel. In 2015 the program involved 200 volunteers around the world.
- **Mechinot: Post-High School Service Learning** programs provide Israeli 18–19-year-olds with a 6-month opportunity for Jewish study, volunteering, skill-building, and personal development in the period between their graduation from high school and their induction to the IDF. The programs encourage a mix of self-reliance and communal responsibility; they give the high school graduates a framework in which to develop leadership abilities, and increase their chances of acceptance to a more high-level or elite army unit. This preparation can improve their career trajectory for the long-term. Participants live, work, and study together in small groups with inspiring role models. There are four clusters of such programs: (a) **Derech Eretz**, **Alma**, and **Harel** are pre-army mechinot, or preparatory programs, for young people from Israel's outlying regions with few educational or professional opportunities, or from socio-economically depressed neighborhoods.[680] (b) **Kol Ami** brings together Israeli and Diaspora Jews. The Diaspora participants stay for three months, during which the entire group explores issues of the Jewish people and Israel; the Israelis stay on for another three months of army preparation. (c) **Aharai! B'Ir**, whose

curriculum is similar to that of Derech Eretz, but differs in that it is a day program, based in urban settings, and therefore meets the needs of those Israeli high school graduates whose families are so poor that the young people must stay at home to work or care for family members until their army inductions. (d) **Post-Army Mechinot** helps just-released IDF soldiers transition into civilian life and learn vocational skills.

- **Young Activism** includes programs that train and support young-adult Israeli volunteers, who go on to create their own social entrepreneurship projects, thus widening the circles of influence. The Young Activism programs include (a) support for **Young Communities**, groups of idealistic young Israelis who commit to settling long-term in Israel's high-need areas and creating programs that increase local quality of life. (b) **Choosing Tomorrow**, which encourages university students in Israel's outlying areas to create Young Communities and settle long-term in the region (c) **Ketzev**, which provides extra training and mentoring to some of the Young Communities to help them build self-sustaining "social entrepreneurship" businesses, that provide cultural or educational benefits to customers. (d) **Click**, which provides micro-grants to individual volunteers or very small groups, to help them launch small-scale local projects. (e) The **Young Adults' Hub** in Arad, where dozens of Israelis and Diaspora Jews receive subsidized housing in exchange for their volunteer activities for the city.
- **Net@**[681] gives high-performing teenagers an opportunity to rise above their families' socio-economic backgrounds by training them for four years in marketable computer skills, leading to certification as computer and network technicians through Cisco Systems. The program is in addition to the participants' high school course load and also increases their English comprehension skills. In 2014, around 1,100 teens participated in the program, and another 400 children participated in Net@ Junior.
- **Loan Funds** assist entrepreneurs and business owners in Israel to open or expand their businesses, through loans with highly attractive conditions as well as comprehensive business guidance. The Jewish Agency acts as a partial guarantor for the loans, to support those businesses that otherwise would have a difficult time qualifying for loans or presenting the necessary collateral for them. The various funds have different eligibility criteria, with some focusing on stimulating the economy in specific regions of Israel, and others focusing on specific populations of business owners, such as Israeli Arabs, Ethiopian-Israelis, immigrants, etc.
- **The Fund for Victims of Terror** provides two forms of financial assistance to those who have been wounded, or had family members killed, in a terrorist attack or war against Israel. It provides immediate assistance in the 24–48 hours after the attack, and it provides subsidies for long-term rehabilitation needs. In 2014, the fund provided emergency grants to 120

families impacted by Operation Protective Edge, and more than 1 million shekels (around $250,000 according to the exchange rate at the time) to 80 families with long-term effects from Operation Pillar of Defense.
- **Amigour**[682] is a Jewish Agency subsidiary that provides housing for Israel's elderly. In 2014 it operated 57 facilities that housed 7,500 seniors, mainly Holocaust survivors. Additionally, it operates 13,000 public housing apartments that provide government-subsidized housing to 40,000 single-parent families, elderly, and new immigrants.

Aliyah

The Jewish Agency still brings thousands of Jews to move to Israel each year. In 2014, The Agency helped a total of nearly 26,500 *olim* (immigrants) make Aliyah, the highest number in 13 years. They noted significant growth in immigration from Ukraine and France. The Agency continues to support these *olim* as they integrate into Israeli society.

- **Aliyah of Rescue** is The Jewish Agency's Aliyah infrastructure that brings Jews suffering persecution or economic distress to Israel.[683] The services include covert operations to help Jews move out of Middle Eastern and North African countries with which Israel does not have diplomatic relations.
- **Pre-Aliyah Services** are provided by The Jewish Agency to prospective immigrants around the world. Agency *shlichim*, or emissaries, give guidance on issues such as education, housing, health and employment opportunities in Israel. For those who do not have an emissary nearby, The Agency provides assistance online and on the phone through its Global Service Center. Additionally, The Agency is responsible for verifying that each potential immigrant is eligible for Aliyah under Israel's Law of Return and, once eligibility is proven, for facilitating the receipt of the Aliyah visa via the local Israeli embassy or consulate.[684]
- **Absorption Centers** around the country offer temporary housing for new immigrants and provide space for Hebrew instruction, preparation for life and employment in Israel, events, activities and cultural presentations. 17 of The Agency's 22 Absorption Centers cater specifically to Ethiopian *olim* and provide services tailored to the needs of the Ethiopian community. The other 5 house immigrants from around the world, primarily the FSU, South America, and the Middle East.[685]
- *Ulpan*: **Intensive Hebrew Language Programs** for new immigrants include five hours of immersive language instruction, five days a week, for five months. The programs are offered free of charge to all new immigrants. Ulpan instructors are certified by the Ministry of Education.[686]

Figure 88: *The Arab city of Umm al-Fahm in northern Israel*

- **Centers for Young Adults** provide *ulpan* classes, accommodations and a range of services to ease absorption for *olim* ages 18–35. These Centers include the Ulpan Etzion network for college graduates and young professionals; Beit Brodetzky in Tel Aviv and Ulpan Kinneret in Tiberias, for high school graduates looking for job or army preparation; and Kibbutz Ulpan, combining Hebrew instruction with volunteer work on ten different kibbutzim.[687] It also includes Selah, a program for high school graduates from the Former Soviet Union, and TAKA, which combines *ulpan* studies with pre-academic preparatory courses for immigrants headed to Israeli colleges who wish to polish their skills.[688]
- **Wings** encompasses an array of services including practical guidance and personal mentorship for young immigrants who join the IDF as lone soldiers, far from their families.[689]

Services for Israeli Arabs and Minorities

As part of its efforts to strengthen Israeli society and to support vulnerable populations in Israel, The Jewish Agency has, for many years, supported or operated programs that encourage co-existence between Israeli Jews and Israeli Arabs, and programs designed specifically to serve Israel's non-Jewish citizens, and they continue to create new ones.[690] Some of the programs:

- **Youth Futures**, the mentorship program for middle-school students, is active in 36 locations around Israel. Some localities served by Youth Futures are Jewish, while others are mixed and, in recent years, The Jewish Agency has begun to serve children and families living in completely non-Jewish locales: East Jerusalem (100% Arab participants), Tel-Aviv Jaffa (32% of participants are Arab), Acco and Matte Asher (34%), Lod (57% Arab/Bedouin), Horfeish (100% Druze), and El Kassum (100% Bedouin).
- **Choosing Tomorrow**, one of The Agency's "Young Activism" social entrepreneurship training programs, includes three groups of Arab university and college students (total 40 students) who are being trained to create their own social-welfare programs that will specifically benefit their local (Arab) communities. These groups are in Be'er Sheva, the Jezre'el Valley, and a group at the Alkassemy Arab College. Additionally, Choosing Tomorrow groups in the Negev work to improve medical services to the Bedouin population, by teaching Arabic to local doctors and helping them understand and connect with Bedouin culture.
- **Community Food Co-op in Beit Ja'an**. The Jewish Agency is in the process of creating a network of Food Co-operatives all over Israel, a new market chain that will reduce food costs and encourage neighborhood volunteerism. As of April 2016, stores have opened in Sderot and Arad, and one of the next two is planned for the Druze town of Beit Ja'an.
- **Desert Stars** is a social entrepreneurship incubator for Bedouin high school students who wish to act as leaders in their communities to create positive social change.
- **Net@** is a program supported by The Jewish Agency. In its chapters in Ramle, Nazareth, Acre, Jerusalem, and Tel Aviv-Jaffa, Jewish and Arab teenagers study computers together, volunteer in community computer labs together, and serve as mentors together to junior-high school participants. In addition, Net@ has all-Arab chapters in Umm Al Fahm, Yirka, and Tira. 25% of all counselors in Net@ are Israeli Arab.
- **Acharai Pre-Army Academy** (*Mechinah*) includes a mixed Jewish-Druze group in which soon-to-be-enlisted young Israelis of both religions work together to volunteer, promote co-existence, and prepare for their IDF service.
- **Atidim** is a national Israeli program provides scholarships and educational activities to gifted students, funded in part by The Jewish Agency. Most programs serve both Jewish and non-Jewish students, and there are some programs dedicated specifically to the Arab sector. All told, in 2014 Atidim programs included more than 2,340 non-Jewish participants, including Druze, Bedouin, Arabs and other non-Jewish Israelis. Additionally the alumni association includes hundreds of Arab, Druze, and Bedouin graduates.

Figure 89: *Druze Israeli soldiers in the "Herev" Battalion, an elite IDF Unit in the Northern Command.*

- **Jewish Agency scholarship funds** benefit Arab recipients as well as Jewish ones.
- **Jewish Agency Loan Funds** often help Israeli-Arab small business owners to receive bank loans at favorable rates. The 9 different funds act as guarantors. One of the Funds specifically aims to assist small business owners who are Arab, ultra-Orthodox, female, Ethiopian, or immigrants.

Emergency projects

During the 2006 Lebanon War, the Jewish Agency moved 50,000 children from northern Israel to 50 residential camps out of the rocket range. 12,000 children went to Jewish Agency-equipped camp-style day care held in community centers. After a number of absorption centers were hit by rockets, The Jewish Agency moved 2,100 new immigrants to safety and distributed 2,700 bomb shelter kits. The Jewish Agency established a micro-business loan fund in the north to boost the local economy.

The Jewish Agency has played an important role in supporting the residents of Sderot and the surrounding area, which has been the target of many rockets launched from Gaza. More than 12,000 children have enjoyed respite activities in the center and north of the country (during Operation Protective Edge); 300 educators have been trained to work with children living through trauma

Figure 90: *Bomb shelter in Sderot, Israel*

(during Operation Cast Lead); supplemental educational activities have been offered to more than 2,000 students; the S.O.S. Emergency Fund for Victims of Terror has helped more than 200 people whose lives were directly affected by the Kassam attacks; 100 bomb shelters were renovated in the region during Cast Lead and 500 during Operation Protective Edge; and 500 students received scholarships (during Cast Lead) to study at Sapir College in Sderot, with more scheduled to receive scholarships as of the aftermath of Operation Protective Edge.

During the Israel-Gaza conflict of 2014 (Operation Protective Edge) The Jewish Agency arranged for children from Israeli areas in the line of fire to enjoy "days of respite" for fun activities in regions less likely to experience air raids. According to the organization's Annual Report for 2014-15, they provided 73,500 such experiences. Additionally they provided 2,000 hours of therapy for new immigrants, provided mental health intervention and financial support to 340 "lone soldiers," gave 120 grants from the Fund for the Victims of Terror, and distributed 1,300 scholarships in March 2015 to students who live 0–4 km, or study 0–40 km, from the Gaza border.

Figure 91: *Jewish immigrants of the Second Aliyah, 1912*

History

Name

Established as the **Palestine Office** (of the Zionist Organization) in 1908, the organization became the **Zionist Commission**, later **Palestine Zionist Executive**, which was designated in 1929 as the "Jewish agency" provided for in the League of Nations' Palestine Mandate[691] and was thus again renamed as **The Jewish Agency for Palestine**. After the establishment of the State it received its current name, **The Jewish Agency for Israel**.

1908–1928: Beginnings as an arm of the World Zionist Organization

The Jewish Agency began as the **Palestine Office** (Hebrew: המשרד הארץ- ישראלי, *HaMisrad HaEretz Yisraeli*, lit. "Office for the Land of Israel"), founded in Jaffa in 1908, as the operational branch of the Zionist Organization (ZO) in Ottoman-controlled Palestine under the leadership of Arthur Ruppin.[692] The main tasks of the Palestine Office were to represent the Jews of Palestine in dealings with the Turkish sultan and other foreign dignitaries, to aid Jewish immigration, and to buy land for Jews to settle.

The Palestine Office was established under the inspiration of Theodore Herzl's vision for a solution to "the Jewish question": the issue of anti-Semitism and the place of Jews in the world. In his pamphlet "The Jewish State," Herzl envisioned the Jewish people settled as an independent nation on its own land,

Figure 92: *Haim Weizmann, founder and director of the Zionist Commission (a precursor of The Jewish Agency), leader of the Zionist Organization, and first President of the State of Israel*

taking its place among the other nation-states of the world. The Palestine Office, which eventually became The Jewish Agency, was based upon Herzl's organizational ideas for how to bring a Jewish state into being.[693]

The influx of Jews to Palestine on the Second Aliyah (1904-1914) made the purchase of land particularly urgent. With the aid of the Jewish National Fund (JNF), the Palestine Office bought land for newcomers in two locations: Chavat Kinneret (near the Sea of Galilee), and Kibbutz Ruhama (near Sderot of today). Kibbutz Ruhama was specifically designated for Russian Jews from the Second Aliyah. Over the following decades, the Palestine Office established hundreds more *moshavim* and kibbutzim throughout Palestine.[694] The Palestine Office continued to purchase land together with JNF (In Hebrew: *Keren Kayemet L'Yisrael*, KKL).

With the outbreak of World War I, the anticipated disintegration of the Ottoman Empire raised hopes among Zionists for increased Jewish immigration and eventual sovereignty in Palestine.[695] In 1918, Great Britain conquered the region and it fell under British military rule.[696]

Following the promulgation of the pro-Zionist Balfour Declaration of 1917, Dr. Chaim Weizmann, president of the British Zionist Federation[697] formed

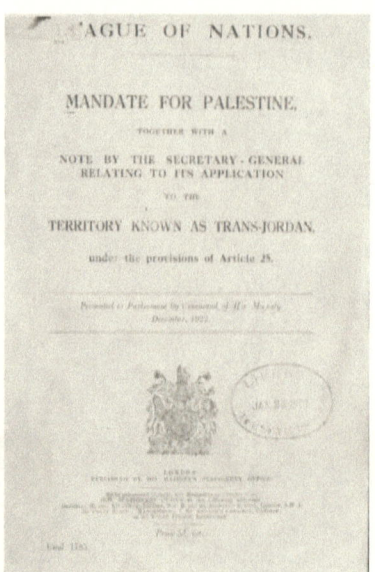

Figure 93: *The front page of the Mandate for Palestine and Transjordan memorandum, presented to UK Parliament in December 1922, prior to it coming into force in 1923. The British control of the region lasted until 1948.*

the **Zionist Commission** in March 1918 to go to Palestine and make recommendations to the British government. The Commission reached Palestine on 14 April 1918 and proceeded to study conditions and to report to the British government,[698] and was active in promoting Zionist objectives in Palestine. Weizmann was instrumental in restructuring the ZO's Palestine office into departments for agriculture, settlement, education, land, finance, immigration, and statistics. The Palestine Office was merged into the Zionist Commission, headed by Chaim Weizmann.[699]

On 25 April 1920, the Principal Allied Powers agreed at the San Remo conference to allocate the Ottoman territories to the victorious powers and assigned Palestine, Transjordan and Iraq as Mandates to Britain, with the Balfour Declaration being incorporated into the Palestine Mandate. The League of Nations formally approved these mandates in 1922.[700] Article 4 of the Mandate provided for "the recognition of an appropriate Jewish agency as a public body for the purpose of advising and co-operating with the Administration of Palestine in such economic, social and other matters as may affect the establishment of the Jewish National Home and the interests of the Jewish population of Palestine."[701] The ZO leaders had contributed to the drafting of the Mandate. In November 1921, the Zionist Commission became the **Zionist Exec-**

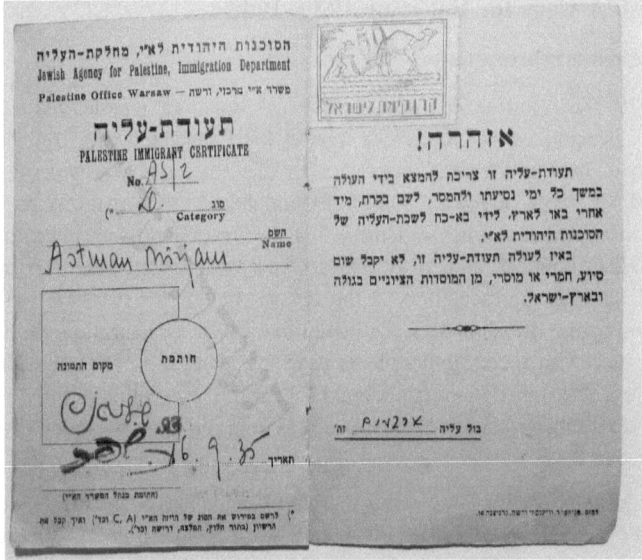

Figure 94: *Palestine immigrant certificate issued in Warsaw (16-9-1935) by the Jewish Agency.*

utiveWikipedia:Accuracy dispute#Disputed statement and was designated as the **Jewish agency for Palestine** for the purpose of Article 4 of the Palestine Mandate.[702,703]

In 1921 Ze'ev Jabotinsky was elected to the Executive but he resigned in 1923, accusing Weizmann of not being vigorous enough with the Mandatory Government. Other issues between the Revisionists and the agency were the distribution of entry permits, Weizmann's support for the Zionist Labour Movement, and the proposal to expand the Agency. The Revisionists broke completely with Agency in 1935, but rejoined ZO in 1947. In 1951 the ZO/JA included all Zionist organizations except Herut.[704]

The **Palestine Zionist Executive** was charged with facilitating Jewish immigration to Palestine, land purchase, and planning the general policies of the Zionist leadership. It ran schools and hospitals, and formed a defence force, the Haganah. Chaim Weizmann was the leader of both the World Zionist Organization and the Palestine Zionist Executive until 1929. The arrangement enabled the ZO to issue entry permits to new immigrants.

Jewish Agency for Palestine 1929–1948

Non-Zionists representation

In 1929, the Palestine Zionist Executive was renamed, restructured and officially inaugurated as **The Jewish Agency for Palestine** by the 16th Zionist Congress, held in Zurich, Switzerland.[705] The new body was larger and included a number of Jewish non-Zionist individuals and organizations, who were interested in Jewish settlement in Palestine. They were philanthropic rather than political, and many opposed talk of a Jewish State. With this broader Jewish representation,[706] the Jewish Agency for Palestine was recognized by the British in 1930, in lieu of the Zionist Organization, as the appropriate Jewish agency under the terms of the Mandate.[707] The 16th Zionist Congress determined that in the event of the future dissolution of the Agency, the Zionist Organisation would replace it as representative of the Jews for the purpose of the Mandate.

There was strong opposition within the ZO when the idea of enlargement of the Board of Governors of the Jewish Agency was first raised in 1924 to include non-Zionist Jews, and the idea was accepted by the Zionist Congress only in 1927.[708]

Even though non-Zionists took part in the Agency, it was still closely tied to the Zionist Organization. The President of the ZO served as the chair of the Executive Council and the Assembly of The Jewish Agency, and half of the members of the Agency's governing bodies were chosen by the ZO, ensuring a unified policy and close cooperation between the two organizations.[709,710] The change was Chaim Weizmann's initiative and was established on the principle of parity between Zionist and non-Zionist Jews working together in the building of a Jewish national home.[711]

Those participating included Sholem Asch, H.N. Bialik, Leon Blum, Albert Einstein, Immanuel Löw, Lord Melchett and Herbert Samuel.[712] American non-Zionists received 44 of the 112 seats allotted to non-Zionists.[713] The British Board of Deputies joined as a constituent body.[714]

Weizmann was criticized for being too pro-British. When the 1930 White Paper was published recommending restricting Jewish immigration, his position became untenable and he resigned from the ZO and The Jewish Agency. He protested that the British had betrayed their commitment expressed in the Balfour Declaration and that he could no longer work with them.[715] Nahum Sokolow, who had been elected to succeed Weizmann, remained in his position. Arthur Ruppin succeeded Sokolow as Chairman of the Jewish Agency in 1933 and David Ben-Gurion and Moshe Shertok joined the executive. In 1935, Ben-Gurion was elected Chairman of the Agency to succeed Ruppin.[716]

Figure 95: *David Ben-Gurion was Chairman of the Executive of the Jewish Agency from 1935–1948. Upon the founding of the State of Israel, he left his position to become the first Prime Minister of the state.*

In 1937 The Peel Commission published its report into the disturbances of the year before. For the first time, partition and the setting up of a Jewish State was recommended. The 1937 Zionist Congress rejected the Commission's conclusions, a majority insisting that the Balfour Declaration referred to all of Palestine and Transjordan, but the executive was authorized to continue exploring what the "precise terms" were. This decision revealed differences within the Jewish Agency, with the non-Zionists disagreeing with the decision and some calling for a conference of Jews and Arabs.[717]

In 1947 the last non-Zionist member of the Jewish Agency, Wemer Senator, resigned[718] and while the 50 percent participation of non-Zionists in the Agency before had not worked in practice, the Jewish Agency and the World Zionist Organization now became de facto identical.[719]

Organization

From 1929 to 1948, the Jewish Agency was organized into four departments: the Government Department (performing foreign relations on behalf of the Jewish community of Palestine); the Security Department; the Aliyah Department, and the Education Department. The Jewish Agency Executive included David Ben-Gurion as chairman, and Rabbi Yehuda Leib Maimon and Yitzhak

Figure 96: *Offices of the Jewish Agency in Jerusalem following car bomb 11 March 1948*

Gruenbaum, among others. The Jewish Agency was (and is still) housed in a fortress-like building in the Rehavia neighborhood of Jerusalem. The land for the Rehavia neighborhood had been purchased in 1922 by the Palestine Land Development Corporation, and construction of The Jewish Agency headquarters was paid for by the ZO. The three-winged structure with a large open courtyard was designed by Yochanan Rattner. Along with The Jewish Agency it also houses the headquarters of the JNF and Keren Hayesod-United Israel Appeal. On March 11, 1948, a bomb planted in the courtyard of the building by Arab militants killed 13 and wounded many others.[720] The Keren Hayesod wing was completely destroyed.[721] Leib Yaffe, director-general of Keren Hayesod, was among those killed in the bombing.[722]

The building continues to serve as the headquarters of The Jewish Agency as of 2014. The organization also has satellite sites worldwide.

Pre-State Immigration and Settlement 1934–1948

Throughout the years 1934–1948, in a phenomenon known as the *Ha'apala* (ascension), The Jewish Agency facilitated clandestine immigration beyond the British quotas. In 1938 it established *HaMosad LeAliyah Bet* (המוסד לעלייה ב׳, lit. *Institution for Immigration B*), which took charge of the effort. Overall, in these years, The Agency, in partnership with other organizations, helped

Figure 97: *Recha Freier, founder of Youth Aliyah, circa 1964. Youth Aliyah saved more than 5,000 young European Jews by bringing them to Palestine in the years preceding the Holocaust.*

over 150,000 people in their attempt to enter Palestine, organizing a total of 141 voyages on 116 ships.[723] The potential immigrants were Jews fleeing Nazi atrocities in Europe and, after the war, refugees from DP camps who sought a home in Palestine. Most of the Ma'apilim ships (of the Ha'apala movement) were intercepted by the British, but a few thousand Jews did manage to slip past the authorities. The operation as a whole also helped to unify the long-standing Jewish community in Palestine as well as the newcomer Jewish refugees from Europe.[724]

In these years The Agency made use of the "tower and stockade" (Hebrew: ומגדל) חומה) method to establish dozens of new Jewish settlements literally overnight, without obtaining permission from the Mandate authorities. These settlements were built on land purchased by the JNF and relied on an Ottoman law stating that any building with a full roof could not be torn down.[725] In 1933 The Jewish Agency negotiated a Ha'avara (Transfer) Agreement with Nazi Germany under which approximately 50,000 German Jews were allowed to immigrate to Palestine and retain some of their assets as German export goods.[726]

In 1943 The Jewish Agency's Henrietta Szold joined Recha Freier in developing the Youth Aliyah program, which between 1933 and 1948 rescued more

Figure 98: *Survivors of the Buchenwald concentration camp arriving in Palestine in 1945. Since their immigration was illegal, they were arrested by the British.*

5,000 young Jews from Europe, brought them to Palestine, and educated them in special boarding schools.[727,728,729] According to Professor Dvora Hacohen, between 1933 and 2011 the Youth Aliyah movement helped over 300,000 young people make Aliyah.

When World War II broke out, The Jewish Agency established a committee to aid European Jewry by finding them entry permits to Palestine, sending them food, and maintaining contact. The Agency also helped recruit 40,000 members of the Palestinian Jewish community (a full 8 percent of the Jewish population of Palestine) to be trained by the British military and aid in the Allies' struggle against the Nazis; most served in the Middle East and Africa, but some served behind enemy lines in Europe, among them a group of 32 parachutists that included Hannah Szenes. In total, 800 were killed in their efforts.[730]

When World War II ended The Agency continued to aid illegal immigration to Palestine through *HaMossad LeAliyah Bet* in an effort known as the *Bricha*. Between 1945 and 1948 The Jewish Agency send 66 ships of refugees to Palestine.[731] Most were intercepted by British authorities, who placed the illegal immigrants, who had just survived the Holocaust, in detention camps in Palestine and later in Cyprus. Only with the establishment of the State of Israel were the detainees allowed to enter the country.[732]

Figure 99: *David Ben-Gurion, Chairman of the Jewish Agency, declaring the establishment of the State of Israel, in Tel Aviv, May 14, 1948. Ben-Gurion became Israel's first Prime Minister.*

Resistance, and Formation of Israel's First Government

Frustrated with Great Britain's continued anti-Zionist stance, The Jewish Agency helped put together an agreement signed by the Hagannah, the Irgun, and the Lehi to form a United Resistance Movement against the British.[733] In 1946 British troops raided Jewish Agency headquarters as part of Operation Agatha, a broad effort to quash Jewish resistance in Palestine. Important figures in The Agency including Moshe Sharett, head of The Agency's political department, and Dov Yosef, member of The Agency's Executive Committee, were arrested and imprisoned in Latrun.[734]

The United Nations recommended the partition of Palestine on 29 November 1947. Meanwhile, The Jewish Agency collaborated with the Jewish National Council to set up a People's Council (*Mo'ezet Ha'am*) and National Administration (*Minhelet Ha'am*).[735] After the declaration of independence on 14 May 1948, these two bodies formed the provisional government of the State of Israel.[736]

Figure 100: *Yemenite Jews arriving in Israel through Operation Magic Carpet.*

The Jewish Agency for Israel

Post-State immigration, settlement, and infrastructure

Following the establishment of the State of Israel in 1948, The Jewish Agency for Israel shifted its focus to facilitating economic development and absorbing immigrants. Organizationally, it changed its structure: The Aliyah Department remained, as well as the Education Department (which promoted Jewish and Zionist education in the diaspora), but the Security and Government Departments were replaced by the Department of Agriculture and Settlement, and by the Israel Department (supporting activities that help vulnerable populations within Israel).

The Agency's budget in 1948 was IL 32 million; its funding came from Keren Hayesod, the JNF, fund-raising drives, and loans.[737]

In 1949, The Jewish Agency brought 239,000 Holocaust survivors, from DP camps in Europe and detention camps in Cyprus, to Israel.[738] In the years following Israel's founding, Jews in many Arab countries suffered from violence and persecution, and fled or were driven from their homes.[739] The Agency helped to airlift 49,000 Yemenite Jews to Israel on Operation Magic Carpet, and over the next few years brought hundreds of thousands of Jewish refugees to Israel from Northern Africa, Turkey, Iraq, and Iran.

Between 1948 and 1952, about 700,000 immigrants arrived in the new state. The Jewish Agency helped these immigrants acclimate to Israel and begin to build new lives. It established schools to teach them Hebrew, beginning with Ulpan Etzion in 1949. (The first student to register for Ulpan Etzion was Ephraim Kishon.[740]) It also provided them with food, housing, and vocational training. For a time the construction of new housing could not keep up with demand, and many of the new immigrants were placed in temporary *ma'abarot*, or transit camps.

In 1952 the "Zionist Organization-Jewish Agency for Israel Status Law" was passed by the Knesset formalizing the roles of each group.[741] It was agreed that the WZO and The Jewish Agency would continue to supervise Aliyah, absorption, and settlement, while the state would handle all other matters previously dealt with by The Agency including security, education, and employment.[742] Article 4 of the Status Law stipulated that the World Zionist Organization (clarified in Article 3 as "also the Jewish Agency") is an "authorized agency" of the State, establishing its ongoing parastatal rather than purely nongovernmental status.[743]

In the early years of the state The Jewish Agency aided in the establishment of a variety of different institutions that developed the country's economic and cultural infrastructure. These included El Al, the national airline; Binyanei HaUma, the national theater and cultural center; and museums, agricultural, and land development companies.[744]

In the years after 1948, The Agency's Department of Agricultural Settlement established an additional 480 new towns and villages throughout Israel. It provided them with equipment, livestock, irrigation infrastructure, and expert guidance. By the late 1960s these towns produced 70% of Israel's total agricultural output.

The Agency also focused its energies on Jews outside of Israel. The Department for Education and Culture in the Diaspora and the Department of Torah Education and Culture in the Diaspora were created to help replace the loss of centers of Jewish learning destroyed by the Holocaust. They trained Hebrew teachers; sent Israelis abroad to supplement Diaspora schools, camps, and youth organizations; and trained cantors, shochatim (ritual slaughterers) and mohelim (ritual circumcisers) in Diaspora communities.[745]

Immigration and absorption, 1967–1990s

Jewish pride and euphoria following Israel's dramatic victory in the Six Day War of 1967 prompted a new wave of immigration.[746] In order to aid in the absorption of this influx of immigrants, the Israeli government's Ministry for Absorption was created in June 1968, taking over some aspects of absorption from The Agency and the ZO.[747]

Figure 101: *Ethiopian Jews arriving in Israel from Addis Ababa, through Operation Solomon, 1991*

In the 1980s The Jewish Agency began to bring the Ethiopian Jewish Community to Israel. On Operation Moses and Operation Joshua more than 8,000 immigrants were airlifted out of Ethiopia.[748] In 1991 about 14,400 Ethiopian Jews were flown to Israel in the space of 36 hours on Operation Solomon.[749] Since then, a steady trickle of immigrants have been brought to Israel from Ethiopia by The Jewish Agency. The Agency has taken charge of housing them in absorption centers, teaching them Hebrew, helping them find employment and in general easing their integration into Israeli society. In 2013 most of the "*olim*," or new immigrants, in absorption centers are from Ethiopia.

With the collapse of the Soviet Union in the late 1980s, Russian and Eastern European Jews began to stream to Israel in the tens of thousands. In 1990, about 185,000 immigrants arrived from the FSU; in the following year, nearly 150,000 came; and for the rest of the decade a steady average of 60,000 immigrants from the region made their way to Israel every year.[750] Since the fall of the Berlin Wall in 1989, nearly a million Jews and their family members from the former Soviet Union have made Aliyah, presenting tremendous absorption challenges.[751] The Jewish Agency has helped them to integrate through a variety of programs including Hebrew language instruction, placement in absorption centers, and job training.

Figure 102: *Participants on a Taglit-Birthright trip to Israel, 2012*

Program expansion, 1990s–2009

In 1994, The Jewish Agency, together with the United Jewish Communities and Keren Hayesod-United Israel Appeal, established Partnership 2000. Now known as Partnership2Gether or P2G, the program connects 45 Israeli communities with over 500 Jewish communities around the globe in a "sister city"-style network. Diaspora participants travel to Israel and vice versa, and are hosted by their partner communities; schools are connected through the Global Twinning Network; global Jewish communities support loan funds helping entrepreneurs and small business owners in their partner cities; and young Jewish adults in Israel on long-term programs meet with their Israeli peers for dialogue and workshops.[752]

The Jewish Agency provides Jewish communities outside Israel a continuum of programming to "bring Israel" to local worldwide Jewish communities. They do this in part through "*shlichim*," or emissaries. *Shlichim* are Israeli educators or cultural ambassadors, who spend an extended period of time (2 months to 5 years) abroad to "bring Israel" to the community. *Shlichim* are also posted at college campuses in organizations like Hillel or active in youth organizations.

Other Jewish Agency-sponsored programs that are instrumental in inspiring Jewish youth with a connection to Israel are "Israel Experiences" (educational visits to Israel) such as Taglit-Birthright Israel, a 10-day visit to Israel provided free-of-charge to young Jewish adults. The Jewish Agency is an important organizational partner in the Taglit-Birthright initiative.

In 2004, The Jewish Agency and the Government of Israel together created (and continue to co-sponsor as of 2016) Masa Israel Journey[753], which provides stipends to young Jews between the ages of 18–30 who would like to study, volunteer, or perform internships in Israel for a period of 5–12 months.

During this period, the Jewish Agency's Israel Department focused (and continues to focus) on strengthening Israel's periphery, namely the Galilee region in the north and the Negev in the South. The emergence of the high-tech industry in Israel created a significant socio-economic disparity between the center of country and the outer regions. Thus, the Jewish Agency sought (and continues to seek) to "lessen cultural and economic gaps."

For example, its Youth Futures program, founded in 2006, includes a holistic approach to dealing with at-risk youth in Israel: each child, referred to the program by a teacher or social worker, is connected to a "Mentor" who is responsible for connecting the child to resources and community services. The Jewish Agency is also a significant partner in the Net@ program offered by Cisco Systems. Program participants are Israeli high school students in socio-economically disadvantaged areas, who study the Cisco computer curriculum and earn certification as computer technicians; they also engage in volunteering and study democratic values.

Strategic plans

At the February 2010 Board of Governors meeting, Natan Sharansky announced a shift in the priorities of The Jewish Agency from Aliyah to strengthening Jewish identity for young adults around the world.

From 1948 until 2009, The Jewish Agency was organized into departments: the Aliyah and Absorption department, which was responsible for the immigration and integration of Jews coming to Israel; the Education department, which worked to deepen the connection of Jews worldwide to Israel; and the Israel department, which focused on improving the lives of socio-economically vulnerable Israelis. (A fourth department, for Agriculture and Settlement, had been in operation starting in 1948, but had closed long before 2009.)

In order to increase efficiency, The Jewish Agency, under the leadership of its new Chairman of the Executive, Natan Sharansky, decided to restructure the organization. The three main departments were reorganized into the following six program units:

- **Israel Experiences** – provides opportunities for young Jews from around the world to encounter Israel and meet Israelis, and for Israelis to meet them
- **Shlichim and Israel Fellows** – sends Israeli emissaries to Diaspora communities worldwide to strengthen Jewish identity and connection to Israel
- **Russian-Speaking Jewry** – runs programs for Russian-speaking Jews of all ages around the world, with a focus on Jewish education and building Jewish communal leadership
- **Social Activism** – aids the vulnerable in Israel and around the world, and trains young Jews and Israelis to engage in social activism
- **Partnerships** – oversees Partnership2Gether, connecting Jewish communities in Israel and the Diaspora to learn from each other and to build a sense of global Jewish peoplehood
- **Aliyah, Absorption, and Special Operations** – aids all immigrants with the Aliyah (resettlement in Israel) process and integration both before and after their arrival, and rescues Jews from areas of distress to bring them to Israel

Each program unit reports directly to The Jewish Agency's Director General. Additionally, The Agency's support units – such as human resources, marketing, and finance – which had until 2009 existed independently for each department, were trimmed and consolidated into single units that serve the entire organization.

Along with the organizational restructuring came a new focus. As the first decade of the 21st century came to a close, The Agency noted that most of global Jewry was now located in democratic, stable societies that were relatively friendly to Jewish residents. As "Aliyah of Rescue" became urgent for decreasing numbers of Jews, new challenges were arising for world Jewry, most notably, Agency leaders remarked, the need to engage young Jews in Jewish culture and to help Israeli Jews and those who live outside Israel to understand each other and feel connected to what they call the "global Jewish family." While continuing "Aliyah of Rescue" operations, The Agency decided to focus its primary energies on fostering a strong relationship between world Jewry and Israel, and on encouraging Aliyah based on a love for the country, what it calls "Aliyah of Choice."[754] Its main vehicle for doing so would be to bring Jews from around the world to Israel on short- and long-term tourist programs to allow them to get to know the country and to give Israelis the opportunity to get to know them and vice versa.[755] Parallel to these efforts, The Agency decided to increase its investment in strengthening Jewish communities around the globe. Its goals would be to grow local Jewish leadership, to strengthen Jewish identity, and to deepen the connection of communities worldwide to Israel and to the Jewish people as a whole.[756]

Figure 103: *Natan Sharansky, Chairman of the Executive of The Jewish Agency for Israel, in 2016*

Governance

The Jewish Agency Executive is charged with administering the operations of The Jewish Agency, subject to the control of the Board of Governors. It has 26 members, of which 24 are chosen by the Board of Governors. The Executive is composed in the following manner: 12 members designated by WZO and 12 members designated jointly by JFNA/UIA and Keren Hayesod. In addition, the World Chairperson of Keren Hayesod and the Chairperson of the JFNA Executive are ex-officio members in the Executive. The current Chairperson of the Executive is Mr. Natan Sharansky.

Over the years the Executive board has included many prominent members of Israeli society. Some of the famous Israelis who have served on the board include: M. D. Eder – 1922; Frederick Kisch – 1922–31; Haim Arlosoroff – 1931–33; Moshe Shertok – 1933–48;[757] Arthur Ruppin – 1933–35; David Ben-Gurion (Chairman of the Executive) – 1935–48.

Past Chairmen of the Executive

Source:

- Frederick Hermann Kisch – 1923–31
- Haim Arlosoroff – 1931–33
- Arthur Ruppin – 1933–35

- David Ben Gurion – 1935–48
- Berl Locker – 1948–56
- Zalman Shazar – 1956–61
- Moshe Sharett – 1961–65
- Louis Arie Pincus – 1965–74
- Pinhas Sapir – 1974–75[758]
- Yosef Almogi 1974–75Wikipedia:Accuracy dispute#Disputed statement
- Arieh Dulzin – 1974 1978–87
- Simha Dinitz – 1987–94
- Avraham Burg – 1995–99
- Sallai Meridor – 1999–2005
- Ze'ev Bielski – 2005–09
- Natan Sharansky – 2009–18
- Isaac Herzog – 2018–[759]

The Board of Governors, which meets not less than three times a year, is the central policy-making body of The Jewish Agency. The 120 Governors play a crucial role in the governance of the Agency in overseeing budgets and operations and in recommending policy to the Agency. Members of the Board are elected to serve for a two-year term in the following manner: 60 of the members (50 percent) are designated by WZO; 36 of the members (30 percent) are designated by JFNA/UIA; 24 members (20 percent) are designated by Keren Hayesod. The Board of Governors determines policy of The Jewish Agency for Israel and manages, supervises, controls, and directs its operations and activities. The current chairperson of the Board of Governors, as of July 2014, is Mr. Charles (Chuck) Horowitz Ratner.

The Assembly, which meets at least once every two years, is the supreme governing body of The Jewish Agency. It has 518 delegates who are elected in the following manner: 259 of the members (50 percent) are designated by the WZO; 155 of the members (30 percent) are designated by the Jewish Federations of North America/United Israel Appeal (JFNA/UIA); and 104 of the members (20 percent) are designated by Keren Hayesod. The Assembly is responsible for determining basic policies and goals of The Jewish Agency; receiving and reviewing reports from the Board of Governors; making recommendations on major issues; and adopting resolutions on the above.

The Director General is responsible, under the direction of the Chairperson of the Executive, for the implementation of policies established by the Assembly, the Board of Governors and the Executive. In addition, he/she is responsible for all operations and administration of The Jewish Agency, including implementation of long-term strategic goals. The current Director General is Alan Hoffmann, who was previously the Director General of The Jewish Agency's

Figure 104: *Alan Hoffmann, Jewish Agency Director General*

Education Department. He is the first immigrant to hold the position of Director General.

Funding and budget

The Jewish Agency is funded by the Jewish Federations of North America, Keren Hayesod, major Jewish communities and federations, and foundations and donors from Israel and around the world. At the same time, one Jewish Federation has stopped funding the Jewish Agency.

The organization's total operating budget in 2013 was US$355,833,000, and its projected operating budget for 2014 is US$369,206,000.

Due to the volatile U.S. dollar, the global economic crisis and the Madoff scandal, The Jewish Agency for Israel has recently been forced to make significant cuts to its budget. The Board of Governors voted to cut $45 million in November 2008 and an additional $26 million at the February 2009 meeting.

Jewish Agency International Development, the organization's main fundraising arm in North America, is a registered 501(c)(3).[760]

Figure 105: *Jewish Agency headquarters in Jerusalem*

Awards and recognition

On May 8, 2008, at the Israeli government's 60th Independence Day celebration, the Jewish Agency for Israel was awarded the Israel Prize for lifetime achievement & special contribution to society and the State of Israel.

External links

 Wikimedia Commons has media related to *Jewish Agency for Israel*.

- Official Jewish Agency Website[669]
- https://www.facebook.com/JewishAgency
- https://twitter.com/JewishAgency
- https://www.youtube.com/user/JewishAgencydotorg
- Taglit-Birthright[761] Official Website
- Onward Israel[673] Official Website
- MyIsraelSummer[762] Official Website (Jewish Agency portal)
- Project Ten[763] Official Website (Program is a Jewish Agency initiative)
- Partnership2Gether[764] Official Website
- Connect Israel[765] (Jewish Agency program)
- Makom[766] (creates Jewish Agency educational content)
- Jewish People Policy Planning Institute[767] Official Website
- The Central Zionist Archives[768] in Jerusalem. Collections of the Jewish Agency for Israel.
- Masa Israel Journey[769] Official Website
- Israel Tech Challenge[675] Official Website
- Net@[681] (a program of The Jewish Agency, Cisco, and Appleseeds Academy)
- Amigour[682] (Jewish Agency subsidiary)

Fifth Aliyah

Part of a series on
Aliyah

Jewish immigration to the Land of Israel
Concepts
• Promised Land • Gathering of Israel • Diaspora   • Negation • Homeland for the Jewish people • Zionism • Jewish question • Law of Return
Pre-Modern Aliyah
• Return to Zion • Old Yishuv • Perushim
Aliyah in modern times

• First
• Second
• during World War I
• Third
• Fourth
• Fifth
• Aliyah Bet
• Bricha
• from Muslim countries
  • Yemen
  • Iraq
  • Morocco
  • Lebanon
• from the Soviet Union
  • post-Soviet
• from Ethiopia
• from Latin America

Absorption

- Revival of the Hebrew language
  - Ulpan
  - Hebraization of surnames
- Kibbutz
- Youth village
- Immigrant camps
- Ma'abarot
- Development town
- Austerity

Organizations
• World Zionist Organization
• Jewish National Fund
• Jewish Agency for Israel
• Youth Aliyah
• Mossad LeAliyah Bet
• El Al
• Ministry of Aliyah and Integration
• Nefesh B'Nefesh
• Am Yisrael Foundation

Related topics
• Yishuv
• Sabra
• Yerida
• Jewish refugees
• History of the Jews in the Land of Israel
• Demographic history of Palestine (region)
• Historical Jewish population comparisons
• Yom HaAliyah

- $\underline{v}$
- $\underline{t}$
- $\underline{e}$[770]

The **Fifth Aliyah** (Hebrew: החמישית העלייה, *HaAliyah HaHamishit*) refers to the fifth wave of the Jewish immigration to Palestine from Europe and Asia between the years 1929 and 1939,[771] with the arrival of 225,000 to 300,000 Jews.[772] The Fifth immigration wave began after the 1929 Palestine riots, and after the comeback from the economic crisis in Mandatory Palestine in 1927, during the period of the Fourth Aliyah. The end of this immigration wave was with the start of World War II.

This wave of immigration began as a pioneering one, but with the onset of racial persecution in Nazi Germany attained the character of a mass migration between 1933 and 1939, with at least 55,000 Jews from Central Europe immigrating to Palestine or residing there as semi-permanent residents.[773] The riots in the British Mandate during 1936 had weakened the immigration wave, but during the years 1938-1939 thousands of immigrants came, some of them illegally.

The causes for the Immigration

- The rise to power of Hitler and the Nazi Party caused enormous disruption to the lives of Jews in Germany and Eastern Europe. As Nazi persecution tightened its grip on the Jewish population, many who wished to leave Germany were prevented by the immigration laws of the Third Reich, forcing them to stay and suffer from the titanic wave of overt anti-semitism sweeping the country. In an attempt to ameliorate this problem, a transmission agreement (Haavara) was reached in August 1933 between the Jewish agency and the Nazi authorities, stipulating that Jews leaving Germany be reimbursed for their assets, even though German law at that time required Jews to give up their assets in order to leave. In addition to these provisions, an allowance was also made for the importation of German merchandise to Palestine. While not destined to be a permanent arrangement, the Haavara Agreement served interests on both sides of the dispute and helped facilitate continued Jewish immigration to the region.
- The exchange of the British colonial administrator - the new British colonial administrator, Arthur Wauchope, was pro-Zionist, granting many immigration permits and encouraging the Jewish economy and Zionist settlement.
- The economic growth in Palestine - the transmission agreement with Germany bringing large amounts of money was a starting point to the recovery of the Jewish economy in Palestine after the crisis of the late 1920s.Wikipedia:Citation needed
- The closing of gates to the United States - in 1921 the United States decided to condense immigration, and even during the period of the Fifth Aliyah the US kept its gates closed to the majority of immigrants, despite the persecution of the Jews in Europe.
- Anti-semitism in the world prevailed - many more regimes in mainly European countries adopted a policy of anti-semitism which encouraged riots, persecution and the economic and social limitations on Jews.Wikipedia:Citation needed

Gallery

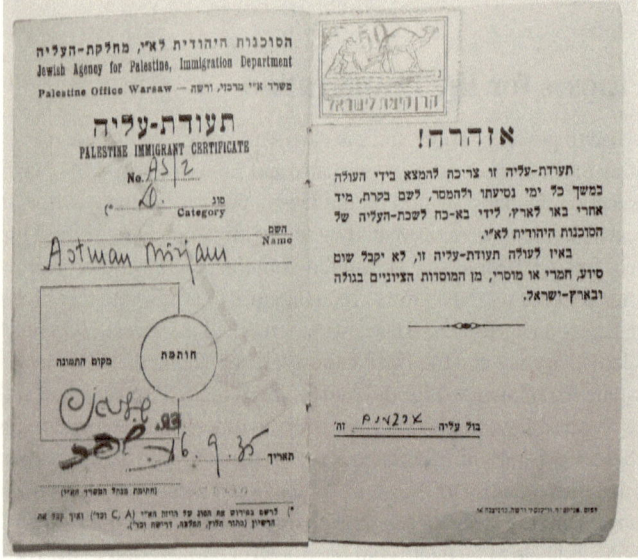

Figure 106: *Palestine immigrant certificate issued in Warsaw (16-9-1935) by the Jewish Agency*

References

 Wikimedia Commons has media related to *Fifth Aliyah*.

Tripartite Pact

<indicator name="pp-default"> 🔒 </indicator>

Tripartite Pact

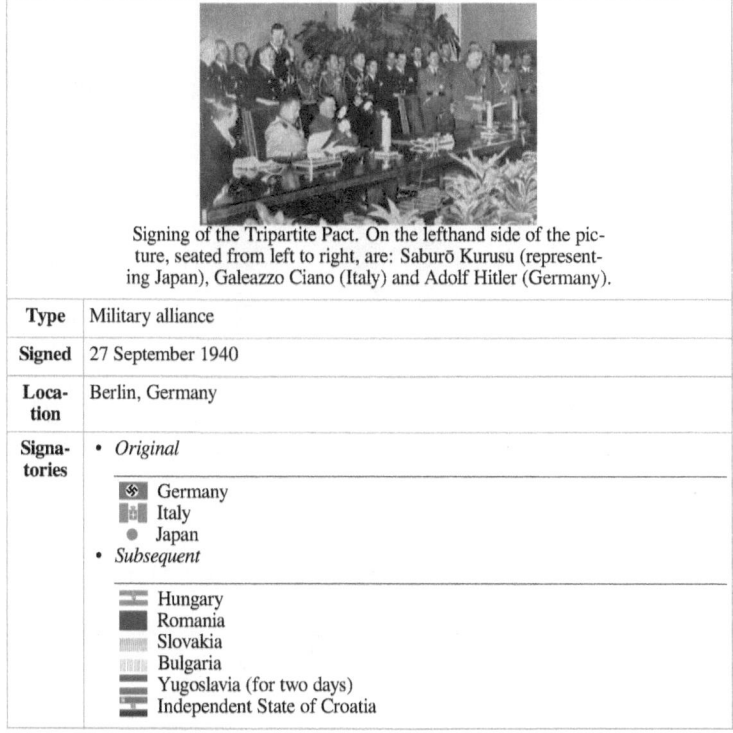

Signing of the Tripartite Pact. On the lefthand side of the picture, seated from left to right, are: Saburō Kurusu (representing Japan), Galeazzo Ciano (Italy) and Adolf Hitler (Germany).

Type	Military alliance
Signed	27 September 1940
Location	Berlin, Germany

Signatories	• *Original*
	    Germany
	    Italy
	    Japan
	• *Subsequent*
	    Hungary
	    Romania
	    Slovakia
	    Bulgaria
	    Yugoslavia (for two days)
	    Independent State of Croatia

The **Tripartite Pact**, also known as the **Berlin Pact**, was an agreement between Germany, Italy and Japan signed in Berlin on 27 September 1940 by, respectively, Joachim von Ribbentrop, Galeazzo Ciano and Saburō Kurusu. It was a defensive military alliance that was eventually joined by Hungary (20 November 1940), Romania (23 November 1940), Bulgaria (1 March 1941) and Yugoslavia (25 March 1941), as well as by the German client state of Slovakia (24 November 1940). Yugoslavia's accession provoked a *coup d'état* in Belgrade two days later, and Italy and Germany responded by invading Yugoslavia (with Bulgarian, Hungarian and Romanian assistance) and partitioning the country. The resulting Italo-German client state known as the Independent State of Croatia joined the pact on 15 June 1941.

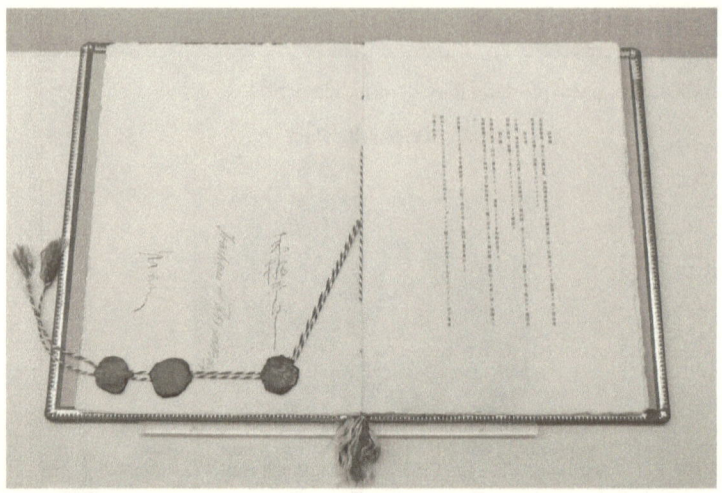

Figure 107: *Japanese version of the Tripartite Pact, 27 September 1940.*

The Tripartite Pact was directed primarily at the United States. Its practical effects were limited, since the Italo-German and Japanese operational theatres were on opposite sides of the world and the high contracting powers had disparate strategic interests. Some technical cooperation was carried out, and the Japanese declaration of war on the United States propelled, although it did not require, a similar declaration of war from all the other signatories of the Tripartite Pact.

Text

<templatestyles src="Template:Quote/styles.css"/>

> The Governments of Japan, Germany, and Italy consider it as the condition precedent of any lasting peace that all nations in the world be given each its own proper place, have decided to stand by and co-operate with one another in their efforts in Greater East Asia and the regions of Europe respectively wherein it is their prime purpose to establish and maintain a new order of things, calculated to promote the mutual prosperity and welfare of the peoples concerned. It is, furthermore, the desire of the three Governments to extend cooperation to nations in other spheres of the world that are inclined to direct their efforts along lines similar to their

own for the purpose of realizing their ultimate object, world peace. Accordingly, the Governments of Japan, Germany and Italy have agreed as follows:

ARTICLE 1. Japan recognizes and respects the leadership of Germany and Italy in the establishment of a new order in Europe.

ARTICLE 2. Germany and Italy recognize and respect the leadership of Japan in the establishment of a new order in Greater East Asia.

ARTICLE 3. Japan, Germany, and Italy agree to cooperate in their efforts on aforesaid lines. They further undertake to assist one another with all political, economic and military means if one of the Contracting Powers is attacked by a Power at present not involved in the European War or in the Japanese-Chinese conflict.

ARTICLE 4. With a view to implementing the present pact, joint technical commissions, to be appointed by the respective Governments of Japan, Germany and Italy, will meet without delay.

ARTICLE 5. Japan, Germany and Italy affirm that the above agreement affects in no way the political status existing at present between each of the three Contracting Powers and Soviet Russia.

ARTICLE 6. The present pact shall become valid immediately upon signature and shall remain in force ten years from the date on which it becomes effective. In due time, before the expiration of said term, the High Contracting Parties shall, at the request of any one of them, enter into negotiations for its renewal.

In faith whereof, the undersigned duly authorized by their respective governments have signed this pact and have affixed hereto their signatures.

Done in triplicate at Berlin, the 27th day of September, 1940, in the 19th year of the fascist era, corresponding to the 27th day of the ninth month of the 15th year of Showa (the reign of Emperor Hirohito).

Background

Although Germany and Japan technically became allies with the signing of Anti-Comintern Pact of 1936, the 1939 Molotov–Ribbentrop Pact between Germany and the Soviet Union came as a surprise to Japan. In November 1939, Germany and Japan signed the "Agreement for Cultural Cooperation between Japan and Germany", which restored the "reluctant alliance" between them.

Figure 108: *The Japanese embassy in Berlin clad in the flags of the three signatories of the Tripartite Pact in September 1940.*

Later signatories

In a ceremonial speech following the signing of the pact on 27 September, Ribbentrop may have suggested that the signatories were open to accepting new signatories in the future. The *Deutsche Allgemeine Zeitung* (DAZ) reported his words as follows:

> *The purpose of the Pact is, above all things, to help restore peace to the world as quickly as possible. Therefore any other State which wishes to accede to this bloc (der diesem Block beitreten will), with the intention of contributing to the restoration of peaceful conditions, will be sincerely and gratefully made welcome and will participate in the economic and political reorganisation.*

The official *Deutsches Nachrichtenbüro* (DNB), however, as well as most of the press, reported a slightly different version, in which the words "having good will towards the pact" (*der diesem Pakt wohlwollend gegenübertreten will*[774]) instead of "accede to" were used. It is likely that initially it was not envisaged that other nations would join the treaty, and that Ribbentrop misspoke. The official record in the DNB therefore corrected his words to remove any reference to "accession" by other states, but produced an awkward wording in the process.[775]

The Italian foreign minister, Ciano, was resolutely opposed to the idea of adding smaller states to the pact as late as 20 November 1940, arguing in his diary that they weakened the pact and were useless bits of diplomacy.[775]

Hungary

The Kingdom of Hungary was the fourth state to sign the pact and the first to join it after 27 September 1940. The Hungarian ambassador in Berlin, Döme Sztójay, telegraphed his foreign minister, István Csáky, immediately after news of the signing and of Ribbentrop's speech had reached him. He urged Csáky to join the pact, even claiming that it was the expectation of Germany and Italy that he would do so. He considered it especially important that Hungary sign the pact before Romania did. In response, Csáky asked Sztójay and the ambassador in Rome, Frigyes Villani, to make enquiries regarding Hungary's accession and its potential obligations under the pact. On 28 September, the German secretary of state for foreign affairs, Ernst von Weizsäcker, informed Hungary that Ribbentrop had meant not a "formal accession" but merely "an attitude in the spirit of the Pact". The Italian answer was similar. Nonetheless, within the week the Hungarian government had sent out formal notice of its "spiritual adherence" to the pact.[775]

In the week after Hungary's "spiritual adherence", the Balkan situation changed. Germany granted a Romanian request to send troops to guard the Ploieşti oil fields, and Hungary granted a German request to allow its troops to transit Hungary to get to Romania. On 7 October 1940, the first German troops arrived in Ploieşti. It is probable that Romania's accession to the pact had been delayed until the German troops were in place, lest the Soviets take preemptive action to secure the oil fields for themselves. In turn, Hungary's accession had been delayed until Romania's had been negotiated. On 9 October or thereabouts, Weizsäcker delivered a message from Ribbentrop to Sztójay informing him that Hitler now wanted "friendly states" to join the pact. In a telephone conversation with Ciano on 9 or 10 October, Ribbentrop claimed that Hungary had sent a second request to join the pact. Mussolini reluctantly consented. On 12 October, Ribbentrop informed Sztójay that both Italy and Japan had consented to Hungary's accession. Since the Hungarian regent, Miklós Horthy, had specifically instructed Sztójay to ask that Hungary be the first new state to accede to the pact, Ribbentrop granted the request.[775]

Romania

The Kingdom of Romania had joined the Allied Powers in World War I and had received Transylvania from Austria–Hungary. After Germany and Italy awarded parts of Transylvania back to Hungary and Southern Dobruja back to

Bulgaria and after the Soviet Union had taken Bessarabia and Northern Bukovina, the Fascist Iron Guard party came to power and Romania joined the Tripartite Pact on November 23, 1940. This was due to the Romanian desire for protection against the Soviet Union.

In Marshal Ion Antonescu's affidavit read out at the IG Farben Trial (1947–48), he stated that the agreement on entering the pact had been concluded before his visit to Berlin on 22 November 1940.[776]

Slovakia

On 14 March 1939, the Slovak Republic was declared in the midst of the dismemberment of Czechoslovakia. Hitler invited Monsignor Jozef Tiso to be the new nation's leader. Soon after it was formed, Slovakia was involved in a war with neighboring Hungary. Although Slovakia had signed a "Protection Treaty" with Nazi Germany, Germany refused to intervene. The war resulted in territorial gains by Hungary at Slovakia's expense. Even so, Slovakia supported the German invasion of Poland in 1939.

Shortly after the signing of the Tripartite Pact, following the Hungarian lead, Slovakia sent messages of "spiritual adherence" to Germany and Italy.[775]

On 24 November 1940, the day after Romania signed the pact, the Slovak prime minister and foreign minister, Vojtech Tuka, went to Berlin to meet Ribbentrop. There, he signed Slovakia's accession to the Tripartite Pact. The purpose of this was to increase Tuka's standing in Slovakia relative to that of his rival, Tiso, although the Germans had no intention of permitting Tiso to be removed.[777]

Bulgaria

The Kingdom of Bulgaria had been an ally of Germany and on the losing side in World War I. From the beginning, the Germans pressured Bulgaria to join the Tripartite Pact. On 17 November 1940, Tsar Boris III and Foreign Minister Ivan Popov met with Adolf Hitler in Germany. According to Hermann Neubacher, Germany's special envoy to the Balkans, Bulgaria's relation to the Axis powers was completely settled at this meeting. On 23 November, however, the Bulgarian ambassador in Berlin, Peter Draganov, informed the Germans that while Bulgaria had agreed in principle to join the pact, it wished to delay its signing for the time being.[778]

The meeting with Hitler precipitated a visit to Bulgaria by the Soviet diplomat Arkady Sobolev on 25 November. He encouraged the Bulgarians to sign a mutual assistance pact that had first been discussed in October 1939. He offered Soviet recognition of Bulgarian claims in Greece and Turkey. The Bulgarian

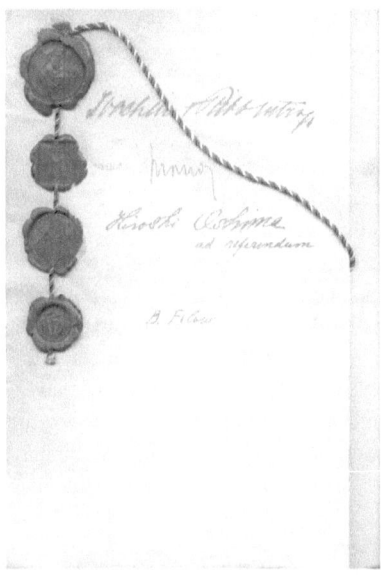

Figure 109: *Official protocol of Bulgaria's accession into the Tripartite Pact.*

government, however, was disturbed by the subversive actions of the Bulgarian Communist Party in response to these talks, apparently at Soviet urging.[779]

On 26 December 1940, the far-right politician Alexander Tsankov introduced a motion in the National Assembly urging the government to immediately accede to the Tripartite Pact. It was voted down.[780]

Bulgaria's hand was finally forced by Germany's desire to intervene in the Italo-Greek War. This would require moving troops through Bulgaria. With no possibility of resisting Germany militarily, Prime Minister Bogdan Filov signed Bulgaria's accession to the pact in Vienna on 1 March 1941. He announced that this was done partly in gratitude for Germany's assistance to Bulgaria in obtaining the Treaty of Craiova with Romania, and that it would not affect Bulgaria's relations with Turkey or the Soviet Union. Later that day, Ribbentrop promised Filov that after the fall of Greece, Bulgaria would obtain an Aegean coastline between the Struma and Maritsa rivers.[781]

According to Article 17 of the Tarnovo Constitution, treaties had to be ratified by the National Assembly. In the case of the Tripartite Pact, the government sought to have the treaty ratified without debate or discussion. Seventeen opposition deputies submitted an interpellation and one, Ivan Petrov, asked why the Assembly had not been consulted in advance and whether the pact involved

Bulgaria in war. They were ignored. The pact was ratified by a vote of 140 to 20.[781]

Yugoslavia

On 25 March 1941 in Vienna, Dragiša Cvetković, Prime Minister of the Kingdom of Yugoslavia, signed the Tripartite Pact. On 27 March, the regime was overthrown in a military *coup d'état* with British support. Seventeen-year-old King Peter was declared to be of age. The new Yugoslav government under Prime Minister and General Dušan Simović, refused to ratify Yugoslavia's signing of the Tripartite Pact, and started negotiations with Great Britain and the Soviet Union. The enraged Hitler issued Directive 25 as an answer to the coup, and then simultaneously attacked Yugoslavia and Greece starting on 6 April. The German Air Force bombed Belgrade for three days and nights. German ground troops moved in, and Yugoslavia capitulated on 17 April.

Croatia

The Independent State of Croatia (*Nezavisna Država Hrvatska*, or NDH) signed the Tripartite Pact on 15 June 1941.[782]

Potential signatories

Soviet Union

Just prior to the formation of the Tripartite Pact, the Soviet Union was informed of its existence, and the potential of its joining.[783] Vyacheslav Molotov was thus sent to Berlin to discuss the pact and the possibility of the Soviet Union joining it.[783] The Soviets considered joining the Tripartite Pact to be an update of existing agreements with Germany.[783] During the visit to Berlin, Molotov agreed in principle to the Soviet Union joining the pact so long as some details, such as Soviet annexation of Finland, could be worked out.[783] The Soviet government sent a revised version of the pact to Germany on 25 November.[783] To demonstrate the benefits of partnership, the Soviet Union made large economic offerings to Germany.[783]

However, the Germans had no intention of allowing the Soviets to join the pact. They were already making preparations for their invasion of the Soviet Union and were committed to doing so regardless of any action the Soviets took. <templatestyles src="Template:Quote/styles.css"/>

> *Political conversations designed to clarify the attitude of Russia in the immediate future have been started. Regardless of the outcome of these conversations, all preparations for the East previously ordered orally are*

to be continued. [Written] directives on that will follow as soon as the basic elements of the army's plan for the operation have been submitted to me and approved by me. —Adolf Hitler[783]

When they received the Soviet proposal in November, they simply did not reply. They did, however, accept the new economic offerings, and signed an agreement for such on 10 January 1941.[783]

Finland

Military co-operation between Finland and Nazi Germany started in late 1940 after Finland had lost a significant amount of her territory to Soviet aggression in the Winter War. Finland joined Operation Barbarossa on 25 June 1941, starting the Continuation War. In November, Finland signed the Anti-Comintern Pact (an anti-communist agreement directed against the Soviet Union) with many other countries allied with Germany. Soon after this Germany suggested Finland sign the Tripartite Pact. However, the Finnish government refused, because Finland saw its war as a "separate war" from the Second World War, and it saw its objectives as different from those of Nazi Germany. Finland also wanted to maintain diplomatic relations with the Allied Powers, the United States in particular. During the Second World War, Germany asked Finland several times to sign the pact, but always the Finnish government declined the offer. Diplomatic relations between Finland and the United States were maintained until June 1944, although the US ambassador had already been recalled earlier. The United Kingdom, however, declared war on Finland on 6 December 1941 in support of its ally, the Soviet Union.

At the request of the German command, the Finns established a winter warfare school in Kankaanpää. It began its first two-month course for German officers and NCOs in December 1941. In the summer of 1942, the German-speaking Finnish instructors taught a course on forest warfare. General Waldemar Erfurth, the German liaison to the Finnish general headquarters, considered the school an outstanding success. It was also attended by some Hungarian officers.[784]

Thailand

Japan attacked Thailand at 02:00 local time on 8 December 1941. The Japanese ambassador, Teiji Tsubokami, told the Thai foreign minister, Direk Jayanama, that Japan only wanted permission for its troops to pass through Thailand to attack the British in Malaya and Burma. At 07:00, Prime Minister Plaek Phibunsongkhram (Phibun) held an emergency cabinet meeting in Bangkok and soon after a ceasefire was ordered. Phibun then met with Tsubokami, who offered him four options: to conclude a defensive–offensive alliance with Japan, to join the Tripartite Pact, to cooperate in Japanese military

Figure 110: *Luang Wichitwathakan (centre, standing) and German diplomats, 1943*

operations, or to agree to the joint defence of Thailand. Military cooperation was chosen, the Tripartite Pact rejected.[785]

According to the post-war memoires of Direk Jayanama, Phibun planned to later sign the pact, but Direk's opposition prevented this.[786]

Tripartite relations, 1940–1943

The "joint technical commissions" required by the pact were established by an agreement of 20 December 1940. They were to consist of a general commission in each capital, consisting of the host foreign minister and the other two partners' ambassadors. Under the general commission were to be military and economic commissions. On 15 December 1941 the first meeting of all three commissions in one capital, Berlin, took place, labelled a "Tripartite Pact Conference". It was decided there to form a "Permanent Council of the Tripartite Pact Powers", but nothing happened for two months. Only the Italians, whom the Japanese mistrusted, pushed for greater collaboration.[788]

On 18 January 1942, the German and Italian governments signed two secret operational agreements, one with the Imperial Japanese Army and another with the Imperial Japanese Navy. These agreements divided the world along longitude 70° east into two major operational zones, but it had almost no military significance. Chiefly, it committed the powers to cooperation in matters of commerce, intelligence and communication.[788]

Figure 111: *China's declaration of war against Germany and Italy (9 December 1941) was made on the grounds that the Tripartite Pact banded the allies together "into a block of aggressor states working closely together to carry out their common program of world conquest and domination".*[787]

On 24 February 1942 the Permanent Council met under the chairmanship of Ribbentrop, who announced that "the propaganda effect is one of the main reasons for our meetings". The representatives set up a propaganda commission and then adjourned indefinitely. The military commission in Berlin met only two or three times by 1943, and there were no trilateral naval talks at all. Germany and Japan conducted separate naval discussions, and Italy consulted the Japanese independently for its planned assault on Malta in 1942.[788]

The economic relationship between the Tripartite powers was fraught with difficulty. Japan would not grant economic concessions to Germany in 1941, lest they ruin its negotiations with the United States. In January 1942 negotiations on economic cooperation began, but an agreement was not signed until 20 January 1943 in Berlin. Italy was invited to sign a similar agreement in Rome at the same time, for propaganda purposes, but none of the supplementary Berlin protocols applied to Italo-Japanese relations.[788]

"No separate peace" agreement

Japan first pressed Germany to join the war with the United States on 2 December 1941, only two days after notifying Berlin of its intention to go to war. Receiving no response, Japan approached Italy. At 04:00 on the morning of 5 December, Ribbentrop gave the Japanese ambassador a proposal—which had already been approved by Italy—to join the war and prosecute it jointly. On 11 December 1941, the same day as the German declaration of war against the United States and the Italian declaration, the three powers signed an agreement—already hammered out on 8 December—barring any separate peace with the United States or Britain. It was "intended as a propaganda accompaniment to the declaration of war".[788] <templatestyles src="Template:Quote/styles.css"/>

> ARTICLE I. Italy, Germany and Japan will henceforth conduct in common and jointly a war which has been imposed on them by the United States of America and England, by all means at their disposal and until the end of hostilities.
>
> ARTICLE II. Italy, Germany and Japan undertake each for himself that none of the parties to the present accord will conclude either armistice or peace, be it with the United States or with England without complete and reciprocal agreement [of the three signatories to this pact].
>
> ARTICLE III. Italy, Germany and Japan, even after the victorious conclusion of this war, will collaborate closely in the spirit of the Tripartite Pact, concluded Sept. 21, 1940, in order to realize and establish an equitable new order in the world.
>
> ARTICLE IV. The present accord is effective immediately on its signature and remains in force for the duration of the Tripartite Pact, signed Sept. 27, 1940. The high contracting parties of this accord will at an opportune moment agree among themselves the means of implementing Article III above of this accord.

Sources

<templatestyles src="Refbegin/styles.css" />

- Bán, András D. (2004). *Hungarian–British Diplomacy, 1938–1941: The Attempt to Maintain Relations*. Translated by Tim Wilkinson. London: Frank Cass. ISBN 0714656607.<templatestyles src="Module:Citation/CS1/styles.css"></templatestyles>

- Chinvanno, Anuson (1992). *Thailand's Policies towards China, 1949–54*. Macmillan.
- Flood, E. Thadeus (1970). "Review of *Thailand and the Second World War* by Direk Chayanam". *The Journal of Asian Studies*. **29** (4): 988–90. doi: 10.2307/2943163[789].
- Boog, Horst; Rahn, Werner; Stumpf, Reinhard; et al., eds. (2001). *Germany and the Second World War, Volume 6: The Global War*[790]. Oxford University Press. Retrieved 29 November 2014.
- DiNardo, R. L. (1996). "The Dysfunctional Coalition: The Axis Powers and the Eastern Front in World War II". *The Journal of Military History*. **60** (4): 711–30. doi: 10.2307/2944662[791].
- Giurescu, Dinu C. (2000). *Romania in the Second World War (1939–1945)*. Boulder, CO: East European Monographs.
- Jelínek, Yeshayahu (1971). "Slovakia's Internal Policy and the Third Reich, August 1940 – February 1941". *Central European History*. **4** (3): 242–70. doi: 10.1017/s0008938900015363[792].
- Kolanović, Nada Kisić (2006). "The NDH's Relations with Southeast European Countries, Turkey and Japan, 1941–45". *Totalitarian Movements and Political Religions*. **7** (4): 473–92. doi: 10.1080/14690760600963248[793].
- Macartney, C. A. (1956). *October Fifteenth: A History of Modern Hungary, 1929–1945*. vol. 1. Edinburgh: Edinburgh University Press.
- Miller, Marshall Lee (1975). *Bulgaria during the Second World War*. Stanford, CA: Stanford University Press.
- Weinberg, Gerhard L. (1994). *A World at Arms: A Global History of World War II*. Cambridge University Press. ISBN 978-0-521-61826-7.

External links

 Wikimedia Commons has media related to *Tripartite Pact*.

- Signing of the Tripartite Pact[794] on YouTube

1936–1939 Arab revolt in Palestine

<indicator name="pp-default"> 🔒 </indicator>

1936–39 Arab revolt in Mandatory Palestine
Part of Intercommunal violence in Mandatory Palestine
 British soldiers on an armoured train car with two Palestinian Arab prisoners
Date: April 1936 – August 1939 **Location**: 🇬🇧 Mandatory Palestine **Result**: Revolt suppressed
Belligerents

🇬🇧 United Kingdom
▪ British Army
Palestine Police Force
Jewish Settlement Police
Jewish Supernumerary Police
Special Night Squads
 	
Jewish National Council Yishuv
• 🌿 Haganah
  • FOSH
  • Peulot Meyuhadot
• Irgun
 	
• NDF (from 1937)
  • Arab "peace bands"
	▪ Arab Higher Committee (1936 – October 1937)
	• Local rebel factions (*fasa'il*)
	• Volunteers from Arab world
	▪ Central Committee of National Jihad in Palestine (October 1937 – 1939)
	• Bureau of the Arab Revolt in Palestine (late 1938 – 1939)
	Society for the Defense of Palestine

Commanders and leaders

🇬🇧 General Arthur Grenfell Wauchope High Commissioner and Commander-in-chief (1932–38) 🇬🇧 Sir Harold MacMichael High Commissioner (1938–44) Lt.-General John Dill GOC (1936–37) Lt.-General Archibald Wavell GOC (1937–38) Lt.-General Robert Haining GOC (1938–39) Major-General Bernard Montgomery Commander, 8th Infantry Div., 1938–39 Air Commodore Roderic Hill AOC, Palestine and Transjordan (1936–38) Air Commodore Arthur Harris AOC, Palestine and Transjordan (1938–39) Admiral Dudley Pound Commander-in-Chief, British Mediterranean Fleet (1936–39)	*Political leadership* Mohammed Amin al-Husayni (exiled) Raghib al-Nashashibi (defected) Izzat Darwaza (exiled) *Local rebel commanders* Abd al-Rahim al-Hajj Muhammad (General Commander) † Arif Abd al-Raziq Regional Commander) (exiled) Abu Ibrahim al-Kabir (Regional Commander) Yusuf Abu Durra Regional Commander) ✡ Fakhri 'Abd al-Hadi (defected) Abdallah al-Asbah † Issa Battat † Mohammed Saleh al-Hamad † Yusuf Hamdan † Ahmad Mohamad Hasan † Abd al-Qadir al-Husayni (exiled) Wasif Kamal Abdul Khallik † Hamid Suleiman Mardawi † Ibrahim Nassar Mustafa Osta † Mohammad Mahmoud Rana'an Farhan al-Sa'di ✡ Hasan Salama
Eliyahu Golomb Haganah Commander	*Arab volunteer commanders*: Fawzi al-Qawuqji (expelled) Sa'id al-'As † Muhammad al-Ashmar
Raghib al-Nashashibi (from 1937)	
Strength	
25,000[795] to 50,000[796] British soldiers 20,000 Jewish policemen, supernumeraries and settlement guards[797] 15,000 Haganah fighters[798] 2,883 Palestine Police Force, all ranks (1936)[799] 2,000 Irgun militants[800]	1,000–3,000 in 1936–37 between 2,500 and 7,500 in 1938 (plus an additional 6,000 to 15,000 part-timers)[801]
Casualties and losses	
British Security Forces: 262 killed c. 550 wounded[802] **Jews:** c. 300 killed[803] 4 executed	**Arabs:** c. 5,000 killed c. 15,000 wounded 108 executed 12,622 detained 5 exiled

The **1936–1939 Arab revolt in Palestine**, later came to be known as "**The Great Revolt**", was a nationalist uprising by Palestinian Arabs in Mandatory Palestine against the British administration of the Palestine Mandate, demanding Arab independence and the end of the policy of open-ended Jewish immigration and land purchases with the stated goal of establishing a "Jewish National Home".[804] The dissent was directly influenced by the Qassamite rebellion, following the killing of Sheikh Izz ad-Din al-Qassam in 1935, as well as the declaration by Hajj Amin al-Husseini of 16 May 1936 as 'Palestine Day' and calling for a General Strike. The revolt was branded by many in the Jewish Yishuv as "immoral and terroristic", often comparing it to fascism and nazism. Ben Gurion however described Arab causes as fear of growing Jewish economic power, opposition to mass Jewish immigration and fear of the English identification with Zionism.[805]

The general strike lasted from April to October 1936, initiating the violent revolt. The revolt consisted of two distinct phases.[806] The first phase was directed primarily by the urban and elitist Higher Arab Committee (HAC) and was focused mainly on strikes and other forms of political protest. By October 1936, this phase had been defeated by the British civil administration using a combination of political concessions, international diplomacy (involving the rulers of Iraq, Saudi Arabia, Transjordan and Yemen) and the threat of martial law. The second phase, which began late in 1937, was a violent and peasant-led resistance movement provoked by British repression in 1936[807] that increasingly targeted British forces. During this phase, the rebellion was brutally suppressed by the British Army and the Palestine Police Force using repressive measures that were intended to intimidate the Arab population and undermine popular support for the revolt. During this phase, a more dominant role on the Arab side was taken by the Nashashibi clan, whose NDP party quickly withdrew from the rebel Arab Higher Committee, led by the radical faction of Amin al-Husseini, and instead sided with the British – dispatching "Fasail al-Salam" (the "Peace Bands") in coordination with the British Army against nationalist and Jihadist Arab "Fasail" units (literally "bands").

According to official British figures covering the whole revolt, the army and police killed more than 2,000 Arabs in combat, 108 were hanged, and 961 died because of what they described as "gang and terrorist activities". In an analysis of the British statistics, Walid Khalidi estimates 19,792 casualties for the Arabs, with 5,032 dead: 3,832 killed by the British and 1,200 dead because of "terrorism", and 14,760 wounded. Over ten percent of the adult male Palestinian Arab population between 20 and 60 was killed, wounded, imprisoned or exiled.[808] Estimates of the number of Palestinian Jews killed range from 91[809] to several hundred.[810]

The Arab revolt in Mandatory Palestine was unsuccessful, and its consequences affected the outcome of the 1948 Palestine war.[811] It caused the British Mandate to give crucial support to pre-state Zionist militias like the Haganah, whereas on the Palestinian Arab side, the revolt forced the flight into exile of the main Palestinian Arab leader of the period, the Grand Mufti of Jerusalem – Haj Amin al-Husseini.Wikipedia:Accuracy dispute#Disputed statement

Figure 112: *Funeral of Jews from Givat Ada that were killed in 1936.*

Origins

In 1930 Sheikh Izz ad-Din al-Qassam organized and established the Black Hand, an anti-Zionist and anti-British militant organization. He recruited and arranged military training for peasants and by 1935 he had enlisted between 200 and 800 men. They were engaged in a campaign of vandalizing trees planted by farmers and British-constructed rail lines. In November 1935, two of his men engaged in a firefight with the Palestine Police patrol hunting fruit thieves and a policeman was killed. Following the incident, the police launched a manhunt and surrounded al-Qassam in a cave near Ya'bad. In the ensuing battle, al-Qassam was killed.

The death of al-Qassam generated widespread outrage among Palestinian Arabs. Huge crowds accompanied Qassam's body to his grave in Haifa.[812]

The dissent in Palestine was influenced also by the discovery in October 1935 at the port of Jaffa of a large arms shipment destined for the Haganah, sparking Arab fears of a Jewish military takeover of Palestine,[813,814] Jewish immigration also peaked in 1935, just months before Palestinian Arabs began a full-scale, nationwide revolt.[815] In the four years between 1933 and 1936 more than 164,000 Jewish immigrants arrived in Palestine, and between 1931 and 1936 the Jewish population more than doubled from 175,000 to 370,000 people,

Figure 113: *Result of terrorist acts and government measures. Remains of a burnt Jewish passenger bus at Balad Esh-Sheikh outside Haifa. Picture taken between 1934 and 1938.*

increasing the Jewish population share from 17% to 27%, and bringing about a significant deterioration in relations between Palestinian Arabs and Jews.[816]

The uprising began with the 1936 Anabta shooting, a 15 April 1936 roadblock that stopped a convoy of trucks on the Nablus to Tulkarm road during which the (probably Qassamite)[817] assailants shot two Jewish drivers, Israel Khazan, who was killed instantly, and Zvi Dannenberg, who died five days later.[818,819,820] The next day members of the militant Jewish faction, the Irgun, shot and killed two Arab workers sleeping in a hut near Petah Tikva in a revenge attack.[821] Then the funeral for Khazan in Tel Aviv on 17 April attracted a huge crowd, and some Jews beat up Arab bystanders and destroyed property.[822] This was followed by the Bloody Day in Jaffa, in which an Arab mob rampaged through a residential area killing Jews and destroying property.[823] An Arab general strike and revolt ensued that lasted until October 1936.

During the summer of that year, thousands of Jewish-farmed acres and orchards were destroyed, Jewish civilians were attacked and murdered, and some Jewish communities, such as those in Beisan and Acre, fled to safer areas.

Economic background

Economic factors played a major role in the outbreak of the Arab revolt.[824] Palestine's fellahin, the country's peasant farmers, comprised over two-thirds of the indigenous Arab population and from the 1920s onwards they were pushed off the land in increasingly large numbers into urban environments where they often encountered only poverty and social marginalisation. Many were crowded into shanty towns in Jaffa and Haifa where they found succor and encouragement in the teachings of the charismatic preacher Izz ad-Din al-Qassam who worked among the poor in Haifa. The revolt was thus a popular uprising that produced its own leaders and developed into a national revolt.

World War I left Palestine, especially the countryside, deeply impoverished. The Ottoman and then the Mandate authorities levied high taxes on farming and agricultural produce and during the 1920s and 1930s this together with a fall in prices, cheap imports, natural disasters and paltry harvests all contributed to the increasing indebtedness of the fellahin. The rents paid by tenant fellah increased sharply, owing to increased population density, and transfer of land from Arabs to the Jewish settlement agencies, such as the Jewish National Fund, increased the number of fellahin evicted while also removing the land as a future source of livelihood. By 1931 the 106,400 dunums of low-lying Category A farming land in Arab possession supported a farming population of 590,000 whereas the 102,000 dunums of such land in Jewish possession supported a farming population of only 50,000. The problem of 'landless' Arabs grew particularly grave after 1931, causing High Commissioner Wauchope to warn that this 'social peril ... would serve as a focus of discontent and might even result in serious disorders.'

Although the Mandatory government introduced measures to limit the transfer of land from Arabs to Jews these were easily circumvented by willing buyers and sellers. The failure of the authorities to invest in economic growth and healthcare and the Zionist policy of ensuring that their investments were directed only to facilitate expansion of the Yishuv further compounded matters. The government did, however, set the minimum wage for Arab workers below that for Jewish workers, which meant that those making capital investments in the Yishuv's economic infrastructure, such as Haifa's electricity plant, the Shemen oil and soap factory, the Grands Moulins flour mills and the Nesher cement factory, could take advantage of cheap Arab labour pouring in from the countryside. After 1935 the slump in the construction boom and further concentration by the Yishuv on an exclusivist Hebrew labour programme removed most of the sources of employment for rural migrants. By 1935 only 12,000 Arabs (5% of the workforce) worked in the Jewish sector, half of these in agriculture, whereas 32,000 worked for the Mandate authorities and 211,000 were either self-employed or worked for Arab employers.[825]

Figure 114: *Feminist activist Tarab Abdul Hadi, organiser of the Palestinian Arab Women's Association.*

The ongoing disruption of agrarian life in Palestine, which had been continuing since Ottoman times, thus created a large population of landless peasant farmers who subsequently became mobile wage workers who were increasingly marginalised and impoverished; these became willing participants in nationalist rebellion.

Political and socio-cultural background

Initially, the conflict with Zionism helped to make Palestinian Arab society more conservative in cultural, social, religious and political affairs because people were highly motivated to preserve their distinct heritage and identity against the dual impact of British colonialism and Jewish innovation.[826] Traditionally, the Arabs had an elite, but not a real leadership. Both of these things changed over the course of the 1930s. During this period new political organizations and new types of activist began to appear, marking the involvement of a far broader cross-section of the population; in particular, nationalism, which had been long-rooted in rural society began to take hold in urban society.[827]

Youth organisations proliferated at this time; these included the Young Men's Muslim Association, which from 1931 agitated for armed resistance against the Zionists, the Youth Congress Party, which expressed pan-Arab sentiments, and the Palestinian Boy Scout Movement, founded early in 1936, which became active in the general strike.

Women's organisations, which had been active in social matters, became politically involved from the end of the 1920s, with an Arab Women's Congress held in Jerusalem in 1929 attracting 200 participants, and an Arab Women's Association (later Arab Women's Union) being established at the same time, both organised by feminist Tarab Abdul Hadi.

From the beginning of the 1930s new political parties began to appear, including the Independence Party, which called for an Indian Congress Party-style boycott of the British,[828] the pro-Nashashibi National Defence Party, the pro-Husayni Palestinian Arab Party the pro-Khalidi Arab-Palestinian Reform Party, and the National Bloc, based mainly around Nablus.[829]

A few militant secret societies, which advocated armed struggle were formed; these included the Green Hand, which was active in the hills around Safad, but eliminated by the British in 1931, the Organization for Holy Struggle, led by Abd al-Qadir al-Husayni and active in the Hebron area, which was later to play an important role in the 1948 Palestine War, and the Young Rebels or Avenging Youth, active in the Tulkarm and Qalqilyah area from 1935.

Traditional feasts such as Nebi Musa began to acquire a political and nationalist dimension and new national memorial days were introduced or gained new significance; among them Balfour Day (2 November, marking the Balfour Declaration of 1917), the anniversary of the Battle of Hattin (4 July, marking Saladin's recapture of Jerusalem), and beginning in 1930 May 16 was celebrated as Palestine Day.

The expansion of education, the development of civil society and of transportation, communications, and especially of broadcasting and other media, all facilitated these changes.[830]

Regional political background

A number of political changes in neighbouring Arab countries illustrated to the Palestinian Arabs what could be achieved in a Western colony through political pressure and negotiating skill.[831]

In Syria a general strike took place from 20 January to 6 March 1936 spreading to all the major towns, and political demonstrations held throughout the country gave fresh momentum to the Syrian national movement. Although French reprisals were harsh the government agreed on 2 March to the formation of a Syrian delegation to travel to Paris to negotiate a Franco-Syrian Treaty of Independence.[832] This demonstrated that determined economic and political pressure could challenge a fragile imperial administration.[833]

Figure 115: *June 1936 cartoon in Falastin contrasting the actions of Wauchope in 1936 against those of Allenby in 1917*

In Egypt on 2 March 1936 a series of formal negotiations between the United Kingdom and Egypt began leading to the Anglo-Egyptian Treaty of 1936, which granted independence to Egypt, but allowed the British to keep forces in the Suez Canal Zone.[834]

In Iraq a general strike in July 1931, accompanied by organised demonstrations in the streets, led to independence for the former British mandate territory under prime minister Nuri as-Said, and full membership of the League of Nations in October 1932.[835]

Timeline

Arab General Strike and armed insurrection

The strike began on 19 April in Nablus, where an Arab National Committee was formed,[837,838] and by the end of the month National Committees had been formed in all of the towns and some of the larger villages. On 21 April the leaders of the five main parties accepted the decision at Nablus and called for a general strike of all Arabs engaged in labour, transport and shopkeeping for the following day.

Figure 116: *Khalil al-Sakakini called the revolt a "life-and-death struggle.'*[836]

While the strike was initially organised by workers and local committees, under pressure from below, political leaders became involved to help with co-ordination.[839] This led to the formation on 25 April 1936 of the Arab Higher Committee (AHC). The Committee resolved "to continue the general strike until the British Government changes its present policy in a fundamental manner"; the demands were threefold: (1) the prohibition of Jewish immigration; (2) the prohibition of the transfer of Arab land to Jews; (3) the establishment of a National Government responsible to a representative council.[840]

About one month after the general strike started, the leadership group declared a general non-payment of taxes in explicit opposition to Jewish immigration.[843]

In the countryside, armed insurrection started sporadically, becoming more organised with time.[844] One particular target of the rebels was the Mosul–Haifa oil pipeline of the Iraq Petroleum Company constructed only a few years earlier to Haifa from a point on the Jordan River south of Lake Tiberias.[845] This was repeatedly bombed at various points along its length. Other attacks were on railways (including trains) and on civilian targets such as Jewish settlements, secluded Jewish neighbourhoods in the mixed cities, and Jews, both individually and in groups.[846]

The measures taken against the strike were harsh at the beginning and grew harsher as it went along involving house searches without warrants, night raids,

Figure 117: *David Ben-Gurion told mourners at a funeral held on 20 April 1936 for nine victims of rioting in Jaffa the previous day that Jews would only be safe "in communities which are 100% Jewish and built on Jewish land."*[841,842]

preventive detention, caning, flogging, deportation, confiscation of property, and torture.[847] As early as May 1936 the British formed armed Jewish units equipped with armoured vehicles to serve as auxiliary police.[848]

The British government in Palestine was convinced that the strike had the full support of the Palestinian Arabs and they could see "no weakening in the will and spirit of the Arab people."[849] Air Vice-Marshall Richard Peirse, commander of British forces in Palestine and Transjordan from 1933 to 1936, reported that because the rebel armed bands were supported by villagers,

> *It was quickly evident that the only way to regain the initiative from the rebels was by initiating measures against the villagers from which the rebels and saboteurs came ... I therefore initiated, in co-operation with the Inspector-General of Police R. G. B. Spicer, village searches. Ostensibly, these searches were undertaken to find arms and wanted persons, actually the measures adopted by the Police on the lines of similar Turkish methods, were punitive and effective.*

In reality the measures created a sense of solidarity between the villagers and the rebels. The pro-Government Mayor of Nablus complained to the High Commissioner that, "During the last searches effected in villages properties

Figure 118: *Arab strike 1936. Car with brooms to sweep away tacks thrown by strikers.*

were destroyed, jewels stolen, and the Holy Qur'an torn, and this has increased the excitement of the fellahin." However, Moshe Shertok of the Jewish Agency even suggested that all villages in the area of an incident should be punished.[850]

On 2 June, an attempt by rebels to derail a train bringing the 2nd Battalion Bedfordshire and Hertfordshire Regiment from Egypt led to the railways being put under guard, placing a great strain on the security forces.[851] In response to this situation on 4 June the government rounded up a large number of Palestinian leaders and sent them to a detention camp at Auja al-Hafir in the Negev desert.

The Battle of Nur Shams on 21 June marked an escalation with the largest engagement of British troops against Arab militants so far in this Revolt.

During July, Arab volunteers from Syria and Transjordan, led by Fawzi al-Qawukji, helped the rebels to divide their formations into four fronts, each led by a District Commander who had armed platoons of 150–200 fighters, each commanded by a platoon leader.[852]

A Statement of Policy issued by the Colonial Office in London on 7 September declared the situation a: "direct challenge to the authority of the British Government in Palestine" and announced the appointment of Lieutenant-General John Dill as supreme military commander. By the end of September 20,000 British troops in Palestine were deployed to "round up Arab bands".

In June 1936 the British involved their clients in Transjordan, Iraq, Saudi Arabia and Egypt in an attempt to pacify the Palestinian Arabs and on 9 October the rulers made an appeal for the strike to be ended.[853] A more pressing concern may have been the approaching citrus harvest and the soaring prices that were available because of the disruption caused to the Spanish citrus harvest by the Spanish Civil War.

Peel commission

The strike was called off on 11 October 1936 and the violence abated for about a year while the Peel Commission deliberated. The Royal Commission was announced on 18 May 1936 and its members were appointed on 29 July, but the Commission did not arrive in Palestine until 11 November.[854]

The Commission, which concluded that 1,000 Arab rebels had been killed during the strike, later described the disturbances as "an open rebellion of the Palestinian Arabs, assisted by fellow-Arabs from other countries, against Mandatory rule" and noted two unprecedented features of the revolt: the support of all senior Arab officials in the political and technical departments in the Palestine administration (including all of the Arab judges) and the "interest and sympathy of the neighbouring Arab peoples", which had resulted in support for the rebellion in the form of volunteers from Syria and Iraq.[855]

In the early 1920s the first High Commissioner of Palestine, Herbert Samuel, failed to create a unified political structure embracing both Palestinian Arabs and Palestinian Jews in constitutional government with joint political institutions.[857] This failure facilitated internal institutional partition in which the Jewish Agency exercised a degree of autonomous control over the Jewish settlement and the Supreme Muslim Council performed a comparable role for Muslims. Thus, well before Lord Peel arrived in Palestine on 11 November 1936, the groundwork for territorial partition as proposed by the Royal Commission in its report on 7 July 1937 had already been done.

Peel's main recommendation was for partition of Palestine into a small Jewish state (based on current Jewish land ownership population and incorporating the country's most productive agricultural land), a residual Mandatory area, and a larger Arab state linked to Transjordan. A second and more radical proposal was for transfer of 225,000 Palestinian Arabs from the Jewish state to the Arab state and Transjordan. It is likely that Zionist leaders played a role in persuading Peel to accept the notion of transfer, which had been a strand of Zionist ideology from its inception.[858]

The Arab Higher Committee rejected the recommendations immediately, as did the Jewish Revisionists. Initially, the religious Zionists, some of the General Zionists, and sections of the Labour Zionist movement opposed the recommendations. Ben-Gurion was delighted by the Peel Commission's support

Figure 119: *Lord Peel arrives in Mandatory Palestine 11 November 1936. Privately, Peel believed that most Jews would remain in the Diaspora.*[856]

Figure 120: *Fields on fire at the Gan-Shmuel Kibbutz. Picture taken between 1936 and 1939.*

for transfer, which he viewed as the foundation of "national consolidation in a free homeland." Subsequently, the 2 main Jewish leaders, Chaim Weizmann and Ben Gurion had convinced the Zionist Congress to approve equivocally the Peel recommendations as a basis for further negotiation, and to negotiate a modified Peel proposal with the British.

The British government initially accepted the Peel report in principle. However, with war clouds looming over Europe, they realized that to attempt to implement it against the will of the Palestinian Arab majority would rouse up the entire Arab world against Britain. The Woodhead Commission considered three different plans, one of which was based on the Peel plan. Reporting in 1938, the Commission rejected the Peel plan primarily on the grounds that it could not be implemented without a massive forced transfer of Arabs (an option that the British government had already ruled out). With dissent from some of its members, the Commission instead recommended a plan that would leave the Galilee under British mandate, but emphasised serious problems with it that included a lack of financial self-sufficiency of the proposed Arab State. The British Government accompanied the publication of the Woodhead Report by a statement of policy rejecting partition as impracticable due to "political, administrative and financial difficulties".[859]

Resumed Revolt (September 1937 – August 1939)

With the failure of the Peel Commission's proposals the revolt resumed during the autumn of 1937 marked by the assassination on 26 September of Acting District Commissioner of the Galilee Lewis Andrews by Arab gunmen in Nazareth.[860] On 30 September, regulations were issued allowing the Government to detain political deportees in any part of the British Empire, and authorizing the High Commissioner to outlaw associations whose objectives he regarded as contrary to public policy. Haj Amin al-Husseini was removed from the leadership of the Supreme Moslem Council and the General Waqf Committee, the local National Committees and the Arab Higher Committee were disbanded; five Arab leaders were arrested and deported to the Seychelles; and in fear of arrest Jamal el-Husseini fled to Syria and Haj Amin el-Husseini to Lebanon;[861] all frontiers with Palestine were closed, telephone connections to neighbouring countries were withdrawn, press censorship was introduced and a special concentration camp was opened near Acre.[862]

In November 1937, the Irgun formally rejected the policy of Havlagah and embarked on a series of indiscriminate attacks against Arab civilians as a form of what the group called "active defense" against Arab attacks on Jewish civilians. The British authorities set up military courts, which were established for the trial of offenses connected with the carrying and discharge of firearms, sabotage and intimidation. Despite this, however, the Arab campaign of murder and sabotage continued and Arab gangs in the hills took on the appearance of organized guerrilla fighters.

Violence continued throughout 1938. In July 1938, when the Palestine Government seemed to have largely lost control of the situation, the garrison was strengthened from Egypt, and in September it was further reinforced from England. The police were placed under the operational control of the army commander, and military officials superseded the civil authorities in the enforcement of order. In October the Old City of Jerusalem, which had become a rebel stronghold, was reoccupied by the troops. By the end of the year a semblance of order had been restored in the towns, but terrorism continued in rural areas until the outbreak of the Second World War.

Despite cooperation of the Yishuv with the British to quell the revolt, some incidents towards the end of the conflict indicated a coming change in relations. On 12 June 1939, A British explosives expert was killed trying to defuse an Irgun bomb near a Jerusalem post office. On 26 August, two British police officers, Inspector Ronald Barker and Inspector Ralph Cairns, commander of the Jewish Department of the C.I.D., were killed by an Irgun mine in Jerusalem.

In the final fifteen months of the revolt alone there were 936 murders and 351 attempted murders; 2,125 incidents of sniping; 472 bombs thrown and detonated; 364 cases of armed robbery; 1,453 cases of sabotage against government and commercial property; 323 people abducted; 72 cases of intimidation; 236 Jews killed by Arabs and 435 Arabs killed by Jews; 1,200 rebels killed by the police and military and 535 wounded.[863]

Response

Role of the Mandate Government and the British Army

Military law allowed swift prison sentences to be passed.[864] Thousands of Arabs were held in administrative detention, without trial, and without proper sanitation, in overcrowded prison camps.

The British had already formalised the principle of collective punishment in Palestine in the 1924–1925 Collective Responsibility and Punishment Ordinances and updated these ordinances in 1936 with the Collective Fines Ordinance. These collective fines (amounting to £1,000,000 over the revolt[865]) eventually became a heavy burden for poor Palestinian villagers, especially when the army also confiscated livestock, destroyed properties, imposed long curfews and established police posts, demolished houses and detained some or all of the Arab men in distant detention camps.

Full martial law was not introduced but in a series of Orders in Council and Emergency Regulations, 1936–37 'statutory' martial law, a stage between

Figure 121: *The Arab revolt of 1936–39 in Palestine*

Figure 122: *A Jewish bus equipped with wire screens to protect passengers against rocks and grenades thrown by Arab insurgents.*

Figure 123: *Jews evacuate the Old City of Jerusalem after Arab riots in 1936.*

Figure 124: *British soldiers of the Coldstream Guards "cleansing" Jerusalem of Arabs participating in the revolt, 1938*

semi-military rule under civil powers and full martial law under military powers, and one in which the army and not the civil High Commissioner was preeminent was put in place.[866] Following the Arab capture of the Old City of Jerusalem in October 1938, the army effectively took over Jerusalem and then all of Palestine.

The main form of collective punishment employed by the British forces was destruction of property. Sometimes entire villages were reduced to rubble, as happened to Mi'ar in October 1938; more often several prominent houses were blown up and others were trashed inside. The biggest single act of destruction occurred in Jaffa on 16 June 1936, when large gelignite charges were used to cut long pathways through the old city, destroying 220–240 buildings and rendering up to 6,000 Arabs homeless. Scathing criticism for this action from Palestine Chief Justice Sir Michael McDonnell was not well received by the administration and the judge was soon removed from the country.[867] Villages were also frequently punished by fines and confiscation of livestock. The British even used sea mines from the battleship HMS *Malaya* to destroy houses.

In addition to actions against property, a large amount of brutality by the British forces occurred, including beatings, torture and extrajudicial killings. A surprisingly large number of prisoners were "shot while trying to escape". Several incidents involved serious atrocities, such as massacres at al-Bassa and Halhul. Desmond Woods, an officer of the Royal Ulster Rifles, described the massacre at al-Bassa:

> Now I will never forget this incident ... We were at al-Malikiyya, the other frontier base and word came through about 6 o'clock in the morning that one of our patrols had been blown up and Millie Law [the dead officer] had been killed. Now Gerald Whitfeld [Lieutenant-Colonel G.H.P. Whitfeld, the battalion commander] had told these mukhtars that if any of this sort of thing happened he would take punitive measures against the nearest village to the scene of the mine. Well the nearest village to the scene of the mine was a place called al-Bassa and our Company C were ordered to take part in punitive measures. And I will never forget arriving at al-Bassa and seeing the Rolls Royce armoured cars of the 11th Hussars peppering Bassa with machine gun fire and this went on for about 20 minutes and then we went in and I remembered we had lighted braziers and we set the houses on fire and we burnt the village to the ground ... Monty had him [the battalion commander] up and he asked him all about it and Gerald Whitfeld explained to him. He said "Sir, I have warned the mukhtars in these villages that if this happened to any of my officers or men, I would take punitive measures against them and I did this and I would've lost

control of the frontier if I hadn't." Monty said "All right but just go a wee bit easier in the future."

As well as destroying the village the RUR and men from the Royal Engineers collected around fifty men from al-Bassa and blew some of them up with explosion under a bus. Harry Arrigonie, a policeman who was present said that about twenty men were put onto a bus; those who tried to escape were shot and then the driver of the bus was forced to drive over a powerful land mine buried by the soldiers which completely destroyed the bus, scattering the mutilated bodies of the prisoners everywhere. The other villagers were then forced to bury the bodies in a pit.

Despite these measures Lieutenant-General Haining, the General Officer Commanding, reported secretly to the Cabinet on 1 December 1938 that "practically every village in the country harbours and supports the rebels and will assist in concealing their identity from the Government Forces."[868] Haining reported the method for searching villages:

A cordon round the area to be searched is first established either by troops or aircraft and the inhabitants are warned that anybody trying to break through the cordon is likely to be shot. As literally hundreds of villages have been searched, in some cases more than once, during the past six months this procedure is well-known and it can be safely assumed that cordon-breakers have good reasons for wishing to avoid the troops. A number of such cordon-breakers have been shot during searches and it is probable that such cases form the basis of the propaganda that Arab prisoners are shot in cold blood and reported as "killed while trying to escape". After the cordon is established the troops enter the village and all male inhabitants are collected for identification and interrogation.

The report was issued in response to growing concern at the severity of the military measures amongst the general public in Great Britain, among members of the British Government, and among governments in countries neighbouring Palestine.

In addition to actions against villages the British Army also conducted punitive actions in the cities. In Nablus in August 1938 almost 5,000 men were held in a cage for two days and interrogated one after another.[869] During their detention the city was searched and then each of the detainees was marked with a rubber stamp on his release. At one point a night curfew was imposed on most of the cities.

It was common British army practice to make local Arabs ride with military convoys to prevent mine attacks and sniping incidents: soldiers would tie the hostages to the bonnets of lorries, or put them on small flatbeds on the front of trains. The army told the hostages that any of them who tried to run away would be shot. On the lorries, some soldiers would brake hard at the end of a journey and then casually drive over the hostage, killing or maiming him, as Arthur Lane, a Manchester Regiment private recalled:

> ... when you'd finished your duty you would come away nothing had happened no bombs or anything and the driver would switch his wheel back and to make the truck waver and the poor wog on the front would roll off into the deck. Well if he was lucky he'd get away with a broken leg but if he was unlucky the truck behind coming up behind would hit him. But nobody bothered to pick up the bits they were left. You know we were there we were the masters we were the bosses and whatever we did was right ... Well you know you don't want him any more. He's fulfilled his job. And that's when Bill Usher [the commanding officer] said that it had to stop because before long they'd be running out of bloody rebels to sit on the bonnet.

British troops also left Arab wounded on the battlefield to die and maltreated Arab fighters taken in battle, so much so that the rebels tried to remove their wounded or dead from the field of battle. Sometimes, soldiers would occupy villages, expel all of the inhabitants and remain for months. The Army even burned the bodies of "terrorists" to prevent their funerals becoming the focus of protests.[870]

Nevertheless, it has been argued that British behaviour overall was good compared to most other examples where a foreign army suppressed a popular insurgency.

Tegart forts

Sir Charles Tegart was a senior police officer brought into Palestine from the colonial force of British India on 21 October 1937.[871] Tegart and his deputy David Petrie (later head of MI5) advised a greater emphasis on foreign intelligence gathering and closure of Palestine's borders.[872] Like many of those enrolled in the Palestinian gendarmerie, Tegart had served in Great Britain's repression of the Irish War of Independence, and the security proposals he introduced exceeded measures adopted down to this time elsewhere in the British Empire. 70 fortresses were erected throughout the country at strategic choke points and near Palestinian villages which, if assessed as "bad", were subjected to collective punishment.[873,874] Accordingly, from 1938 Gilbert Mackereth, the British Consul in Damascus, corresponded with Syrian and Transjordan authorities regarding border control and security to counteract arms smuggling and "terrorist" infiltration and produced a report for Tegart on the activities of the Palestine Defence Committee in Damascus. Tegart recommended the construction of a frontier road with a barbed wire fence, which became known as

Figure 125: *A surviving police Tegart fort at Latrun devised by Sir Charles Tegart, who also introduced border fences and Arab Investigation Centres.*

Tegart's wall, along the borders with Lebanon and Syria to help prevent the flow of insurgents, goods and weapons. Tegart encouraged close co-operation with the Jewish Agency.[875] It was built by the Histadrut construction company Solel Boneh. The total cost was £2 million. The Army forced the fellahin to work on the roads without pay.[876]

Tegart introduced Arab Investigation Centres where prisoners were subjected to beatings, foot whipping, electric shocks, denailing and what is now known as "waterboarding". Tegart also imported Doberman Pinschers from South Africa and set up a special centre in Jerusalem to train interrogators in torture.[877]

Role of the Royal Air Force

The Royal Air Force developed close air support into its then most refined form during the Arab Revolt.[878] Air patrols had been found effective in keeping convoys and trains free from attack, but this did not help to expose insurgents to battle conditions likely to cause their defeat. From the middle of June 1936 wireless vehicles accompanied all convoys and patrols. During rebel attacks these vehicles could issue emergency "XX calls" (XX with a coded location),

Figure 126: *Pillbox built along the route of Tegart's wall, still standing today near Goren industrial zone, northern Israel*

which were given priority over all other radio traffic, to summon aerial reinforcements. Bombers, which were usually airborne within five minutes, could then either attack insurgents directly or "fix" their position for infantry troops. Forty-seven such XX calls were issued during the revolt, causing heavy losses to the rebels. In the June 1936 Battle of Nur Shams British planes attacked Arab irregulars with machine gun fire.

This use of air power was so successful that the British were able to reduce the regular garrison.

In 1936 an Air Staff Officer in Middle East Command based in the Kingdom of Egypt, Arthur Harris, known as an advocate of "air policing",[879] commented on the revolt saying that "one 250 lb. or 500 lb. bomb in each village that speaks out of turn" would satisfactorily solve the problem.[880] In 1937 Harris was promoted to Air Commodore and in 1938 he was posted to Palestine and Trans-Jordan as Air Officer Commanding the RAF contingent in the region until September 1939. "Limited" bombing attacks on Arab villages were carried out by the RAF,[881] although at times this involved razing whole villages.[882] Harris described the system by which recalcitrant villages were kept under control by aerial bombardment as "Air-Pin".[883]

Figure 127: *The Royal Navy used naval mines from HMS Malaya to destroy Palestinian houses.*

Aircraft of the RAF were also used to drop propaganda leaflets over Palestinian towns and villages telling the fellahin that they were the main sufferers of the rebellion and threatening an increase in taxes.

Low flying RAF squadrons were able to produce detailed intelligence on the location of road blocks, sabotaged bridges, railways and pipelines.[884] RAF aerial photographs were also used to build up a detailed map of Arab population distribution.

Although the British Army was responsible for setting up the Arab counter-insurgent forces (known as the peace bands) and supplying them with arms and money these were operated by RAF Intelligence, commanded by Patrick Domville.[885,886]

At the beginning of the revolt RAF assets in the region comprised a bomber flight at RAF Ramleh, an RAF armoured car flight at Ramleh, fourteen bomber squadrons at RAF Amman, and a RAF armoured car company at Ma'an.

Role of the Royal Navy

At the beginning of the Revolt crew from the Haifa Naval Force's two cruisers were used to carry out tasks ashore, manning two howitzers and naval lorries equipped with QF 2 pounder naval guns and searchlights used to disperse Arab snipers.[887] From the end of June two destroyers were used to patrol the coast of Palestine in a bid to prevent gun running. These searched as many as 150 vessels per week and were an effective preventive measure. At the request of the Army additional naval platoons landed in July to help protect Haifa and Jewish settlements in the surrounding countryside. The Navy also relieved the Army of duties in Haifa by using nine naval platoons to form the *Haifa Town Force* and in August three naval platoons were landed to support the police.

Following publication of the Peel Commission's report in July 1937 HMS *Repulse* sailed to Haifa where landing parties were put ashore to maintain calm. Various other naval vessels continued with this role until the end of the revolt.

Following the Irgun's detonation of a large bomb in a market in Haifa on 6 July 1938 the High Commissioner signalled the Commander-in-Chief of the Mediterranean Fleet, Admiral Sir Dudley Pound, requesting the assistance of naval vessels capable of providing landing parties. Pound dispatched HMS *Repulse* and diverted HMS *Emerald* to Haifa, which arrived the same day and landed five platoons, one to each police district. HMS *Repulse* relieved HMS *Emerald* the following day and after another bomb was detonated on 10 July five platoons from the ship, made up of sailors and Royal Marines, dispersed mobs and patrolled the city.

On 11 July provision of three platoons from *Repulse* released men of the West Kent Regiment for a punitive mission against Arabs who had attacked a Jewish colony near Haifa. By 17 July the *Repulse* established a Company Headquarters where seamen and Royal Marines manned a 3.7-inch howitzer. Sailors, Royal Marines, and men of the Suffolk Regiment, who had embarked on the *Repulse*, accompanied foot patrols of the Palestine Police Force.

The *Repulse*, HMS *Hood* and HMS *Warspite* provided howitzer crews which were sent ashore to combat gun running near the border with Lebanon. Detained Arabs were used to build emplacements and the howitzers were moved quickly between these positions by day and night to confuse bandits as to the likely direction of fire. Periodically, the guns were used to fire warning rounds close to the vicinity of villages believed to have rebel sympathies.

Strategic importance of Haifa

Britain had completed the modern deep-sea port in Haifa in 1933 and finished laying a pipeline from the Iraqi oilfields to Haifa in 1935,[888] shortly before the outbreak of the revolt. A refinery for processing oil from the pipeline was completed by Consolidated Refineries Ltd, a company jointly owned by British Petroleum and Royal Dutch Shell, in December 1939.[889]

These facilities enhanced the strategic importance of Palestine and of Haifa in particular in Britain's control of the eastern Mediterranean. The threat to British control of the region posed by the Italian invasion of Abyssinia in October 1935 and the deteriorating situation in Europe toward the end of the 1930s probably made British policy makers more willing to make concessions

Figure 128: *Reuven Zaslany (Shiloah), later first director of Mossad, worked closely with British intelligence during the Arab Revolt.*

to Arab governments on the Palestine issue following the furore over the recommendations of the Peel Commission.

Role of the British intelligence services

The Arab Revolt was the last major test of Britain's security services in the Middle East before World War II.[890] The development and deployment of intelligence-led counterinsurgency strategies was integral to the restoration of British imperial control in Palestine as the revolt had demonstrated to the British authorities how a popular rebellion could undermine intelligence gathering operations and thereby impair their ability to predict and respond to intercommunal disorder. The rebellion had brought together urban nationalism and peasant economic grievances arising from rural poverty and landlessness, which was blamed on British misrule. Accordingly, the Palestinian revolt targeted the political and economic apparatus of the British colonial state, including the communications network, pipelines, police stations, army outposts and British personnel. It was this aspect of the revolt, rather than attacks on Jews or violence between rivals for leadership of the national movement, that most concerned the high commissioner. The mandate authorities were further disturbed by the unity of purpose displayed during the six-month general strike and by the resurgence of pan-Arab nationalism as evidenced by the rise of the Istiqlal Party.

In response to these challenges the British army command ("I" Branch) and battalion headquarters across Palestine issued a daily intelligence bulletin every afternoon detailing political developments. Special Service Officers (SSOs) assigned to intelligence gathering reported directly to their local command headquarters and their cars were equipped with wireless transmitters so that high grade intelligence could be reported directly to "I" Branch immediately. These sources of intelligence gradually became more important than those of the C.I.D. in Palestine, which had been dependent on Arab informers, and which were no longer reliable.

In September 1937, the Jewish Agency appointed Reuven Zaslany liaison officer for intelligence and security affairs between the Political Department of the Jewish Agency and the intelligence arms of the Royal Air Force and the C.I.D.[891] Zaslany sifted through intelligence collected by Jewish-controlled field operatives and forwarded it to the British military. He was a frequent visitor at the headquarters of British intelligence and the army, the police and C.I.D. and he also travelled to Damascus to liaise with the Arab opposition's peace bands and with the British Consul in Iraq. Colonel Frederick Kisch, a British army officer and Zionist leader, was appointed chief liaison officer between the British army and the Jewish Agency Executive with Zaslany as his deputy. Zaslany also worked as interpreter for Patrick Domville, head of RAF Intelligence in Palestine (who was described by Haganah leader Dov Hos as the "best Zionist informer on the English"), until the latter was posted to Iraq in 1938, and through him became acquainted with many of the British intelligence officers.[892]

In 1937 the Jewish Agency's intelligence groups were responsible for bugging the Peel Commission hearings in Palestine.[893] Eventually, the Arab Revolt convinced the Agency that a central intelligence service was required and this led to the formation of a counter-intelligence agency known as the *Ran* (headed by Yehuda Arazi, who also helped to smuggle rifles, machine guns and ammunition from Poland to Palestine) and thereafter in 1940 to the creation of SHAI, the forerunner of Mossad.[894,895,896]

British and Jewish co-operation

The *Haganah* (Hebrew for "defence"), a Jewish paramilitary organisation, actively supported British efforts to suppress the uprising, which reached 10,000 Arab fighters at their peak during the summer and fall of 1938. Although the British administration did not officially recognise the *Haganah*, the British security forces cooperated with it by forming the Jewish Settlement Police,

1936–1939 Arab revolt in Palestine 293

Figure 129: *Men of Captain Orde Wingate's Special Night Squads, possibly in Kfar Tavor.*

Figure 130: *Ghaffirs watching a settlement in Nesher near Haifa. British authorities provided the guns and uniforms.*

Jewish Supernumerary Police, and Special Night Squads. The Special Night Squads engaged in activities described by colonial administrator Sir Hugh Foot, as 'extreme and cruel' involving torture, whipping, abuse and execution of Arabs.

The British authorities maintained, financed and armed the Jewish police from this point onward until the end of the Mandate,[897] and by the end of September 1939 around 20,000 Jewish policeman, supernumeraries and settlement guards had been authorised to carry arms by the government,[898] which also distributed weapons to outlying Jewish settlements,[899] and allowed the Haganah to acquire arms.[900] Independently of the British, *Ta'as*, the Haganah's clandestine munitions industry, developed an 81-mm mortar and manufactured mines and grenades, 17,500 of the latter being produced for use during the revolt.[901,902]

In June 1937, the British imposed the death penalty for unauthorised possession of weapons, ammunition, and explosives, but since many Jews had permission to carry weapons and store ammunition for defence this order was directed primarily against Palestinian Arabs and most of the 112 executed in Acre Prison were hanged for illegal possession of arms.[903]

In principle all of the joint units functioned as part of the British administration, but in practice they were under the command of the Jewish Agency and "intended to form the backbone of a Jewish military force set up under British sponsorship in preparation for the inevitable clash with the Arabs."[904] The Agency and the Mandate authorities shared the costs of the new units equally. The administration also provided security services to Jewish commercial concerns at cost.

Jewish and British officials worked together to co-ordinate manhunts and collective actions against villages and also discussed the imposition of penalties and sentences. Overall, the Jewish Agency was successful in making "the point that the Zionist movement and the British Empire were standing shoulder to shoulder against a common enemy, in a war in which they had common goals."[905]

The rebellion also inspired the Jewish Agency to expand the intelligence-gathering of its Political Department and especially of its Arab Division, with the focus changing from political to military intelligence.[906] The Arab Division set up a network of Jewish controllers and Arab agents around the country. Some of the intelligence gathered was shared with the British administration, the exchange of information sometimes being conducted by Moshe Shertok, then head of the Jewish Agency, directly with the high commissioner himself. Shertok also advised the administration on political affairs, on one occasion convincing the high commissioner not to arrest Professor Joseph Klausner, a

Revisionist Maximalist activist who had played a key role in the riots of 1929, because of the likely negative consequences.

Forces of the Jewish settlement

Table 1: Security forces and infrastructure created during the Arab revolt

Joint British-Yishuv	Independent Yishuv	Other Yishuv defence infrastructure
Jewish Supernumerary Police	Mobile units (mobile arm of the Haganah)	Ta'as † (weapons manufacture)
Jewish Settlement Police	Fosh (field companies)	Rekhesh † (arms procurement)
Mobile Guards (mobile arm of the Settlement Police)	Hish (field corps)	Ran (counter intelligence)
Special Night Squads	Special Operations Squads	Community ransom (defence tax)
Tegart forts and Tegart's wall	Guards	Tower and stockade settlement

† Ta'as and Rekhesh were developed and expanded during the Arab Revolt but already existed before 1936 and of course the Haganah had been in operation from the earliest days of the Mandate.

Haganah intelligence services

There was no single body within the Jewish settlement capable of co-ordinating intelligence gathering before 1939.[907] Until then there were four separate organisations without any regular or formal liaison. These were an underground militia, forerunner of the first official information service, *Sherut Yediot* (Shai); the *Arab Platoon* of the Palmach, which was staffed by Jews who were Arab-speaking and Arab-looking; *Rekhesh*, the arms procurement service, which had its own intelligence gathering capabilities, and likewise the *Mossad LeAliyah Bet*, the illegal immigration service. In mid-1939 the effort to co-ordinate the activities of these groups was led by Shaul Avigur and Moshe Shertok.

Role of the Revisionist Zionists

In 1931, a Revisionist underground splinter group broke off from Haganah, calling itself the *Irgun* organisation (or *Etzel*). The organisation took its orders from Revisionist leader Ze'ev Jabotinsky who was at odds with the dominant Labour Zionist movement led by David Ben-Gurion.[908] The rift between the two Zionist movements further deteriorated in 1933 when two Revisionists were blamed for the murder of Haim Arlosoroff, who had negotiated the Haavara Agreement between the Jewish Agency and Nazi Germany. The agreement brought 52,000 German Jews to Palestine between 1933 and 1939, and generated $30,000,000 for the then almost bankrupt Jewish Agency, but in addition to the difficulties with the Revisionists, who advocated a boycott of Germany, it caused the Yishuv to be isolated from the rest of world Jewry.[909,910,911]

Ultimately, however, the events of the Arab Revolt blurred the differences between the gradualist approach of Ben-Gurion and the Maximalist Iron Wall approach of Jabotinsky and turned militarist patriotism into a bipartisan philosophy.[912] Indeed, Ben-Gurion's own Special Operations Squads conducted a punitive operation in the Arab village of Lubya firing weapons into a room through a window killing two men and one woman and injuring three people, including two children.[913]

From October 1937 the Irgun instituted a wave of bombings against Arab crowds and buses.[914] For the first time in the conflict massive bombs were placed in crowded Arab public places, killing and maiming dozens. These attacks substantially increased Arab casualties and sowed terror among the population. The first attack was on 11 November 1937, killing two Arabs at the bus depot near Jaffa Street in Jerusalem and then on 14 November, a day later commemorated as the "Day of the Breaking of the *Havlagah* (restraint)," Arabs were killed in simultaneous attacks around Palestine. More deadly attacks followed: on 6 July 1938 21 Arabs were killed and 52 wounded by a bomb in a Haifa market; on 25 July a second market bomb in Haifa killed at least 39 Arabs and injured 70; a bomb in Jaffa's vegetable market on 26 August killed 24 Arabs and wounded 39. The attacks were condemned by the Jewish Agency.

The Arab leader Mohammad Amin al-Husayni and his associates also received funding from Fascist Italy during the revolt as the Italians were in dispute with the United Kingdom over Abyssinia and wished not only to disrupt the British rear[915] but also to extend Italian influence in the region.[916] Files seized at the German High Command in Flansburg reveal that the Arab riots "only through funds made available by Germany to the Grand Mufti of Jerusalem was it possible to carry out the revolt in Palestine."

Role of the "Peace bands"

The "peace bands" (*fasa'il al-salam*) or "Nashashibi units" were made up of disaffected Arab peasants recruited by the British administration and the Nashashibis in late 1938 to battle against Arab rebels during the revolt.[917] Despite their peasant origins the bands were representative mainly of the interests of landlords and rural notables. Some peace bands also sprang up in the Nablus area, on Mount Carmel (a stronghold of the Druze who largely opposed the rebellion after 1937), and around Nazareth without connection to the Nashashibi-Husayni power struggle.[918]

From December 1937 the main opposition figures among the Arabs approached the Jewish Agency for funding and assistance,[919] motivated by the assassination campaign pursued by the rebels at the behest of the Husseini leadership. In October 1937, shortly after Mohammad Amin al-Husayni, the leader of the Arab Higher Committee, had fled from Palestine to escape British retribution, Raghib al-Nashashibi had written to Moshe Shertok stating his full willingness to co-operate with the Jewish Agency and to agree with whatever policy it proposed. From early in 1938 the Nashashibis received funding specifically to conduct anti-rebel operations, with Raghib al-Nashashibi himself receiving £5,000. The British also supplied funding to the peace bands and sometimes directed their operations.

Fakhri Nashashibi was particularly successful in recruiting peace bands in the Hebron hills, on one occasion in December 1938 gathering 3,000 villagers for a rally in Yatta, also attended by the British military commander of the Jerusalem District General Richard O'Connor.

Just two months earlier, on 15 October 1938, rebels had seized the Old City and barricaded the gates.[920] O'Connor had planned the operation by which men of the Coldstream Guards, Royal Northumberland Fusiliers and Black Watch recaptured the Old City, killing 19 rebels. He was later to win fame as the field commander for Operation *Compass* in World War II, in which his forces completely destroyed a much larger Italian army—a victory which nearly drove the Axis from Africa, and in turn, led Adolf Hitler to send the German Africa Corps under Erwin Rommel to try to reverse the situation.

Towards the end of the revolt in May 1939 the authorities dissolved the peace bands and confiscated their arms. However, because members of the bands had become tainted in the eyes of the Palestinian Arabs, and some were under sentence of death, they had little choice but to continue the battle against the national movement's leadership, which they did with the continuing help of the Zionist movement.[921]

Figure 131: *Rebels, some mounted on horses, posing with their rifles and a Palestinian flag emblazoned with a cross and crescent, 1937*

Role of rebel leaders

At least 282 rebel leaders took part in the Arab Revolt, including four Christians.[922] Rebel forces consisted of loosely organized bands known as *fasa'il*[923,924] (sing: *fasil*). The leader of a *fasil* was known as a *qa'id al-fasil* (pl. *quwwa'id al-fasa'il*), which means "band commander".[925] The Jewish press often referred to them as "brigands", while the British authorities and media called them "bandits", "terrorists", "rebels" or "insurgents", but never "nationalists".[926] *Ursabat* (meaning "gangs") was another Arabic term used for the rebels, and it spawned the British soldiers' nickname for all rebels, which was *Oozlebart*.

According to historian Simon Anglim, the rebel groups were divided into general categories: *mujahadeen* and *fedayeen*. The former were guerrillas who engaged in armed confrontations, while the latter committed acts of sabotage.[927] According to later accounts of some surviving rebel leaders from the Galilee, the *mujahideen* maintained little coordination with the nominal hierarchy of the revolt. Most ambushes were the result of a local initiative undertaken by a *qa'id* or a group of *quwwa'id* from the same area.

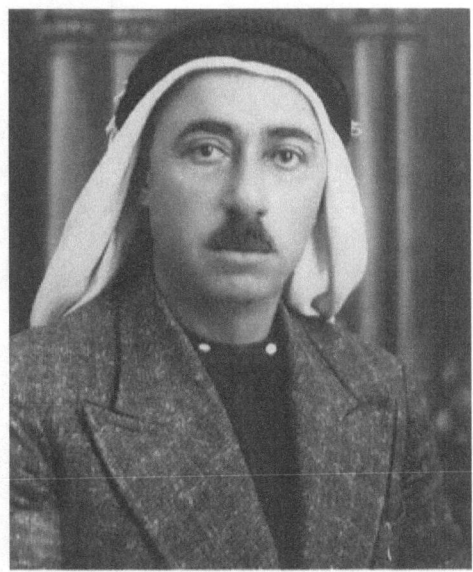

Figure 132: *Abd al-Rahim al-Hajj Muhammad was designated the "General Commander of the Revolt" by the Central Committee of National Jihad in Palestine*

Galilee

Abdul Khallik was an effective peasant leader appointed by Fawzi al-Qawuqji who caused great damage and loss of life in the Nazareth District and was thus a significant adversary of the Mandate and Jewish settlement authorities.[928] He was trapped by British troops in a major engagement on 2 October 1938 and was killed whilst trying to lead his men to safety.[929] Abu Ibrahim al-Kabir was the main Qassamite rebel leader in the Upper Galilee and was the only active rebel leader on the ground who was a member of the Damascus-based Central Committee of National Jihad. Abdallah al-Asbah was a prominent commander active in the Safad region of northeastern Galilee. He was killed by British forces who besieged him and his comrades near the border with Lebanon in early 1937.

Jabal Nablus area

Abd al-Rahim al-Hajj Muhammad from the Tulkarm area was a deeply religious, intellectual man and as a fervent anti-Zionist, he was deeply committed to the revolt.[930] He was regarded second to Qawukji in terms of leadership ability and maintained his independence from the exiled rebel leadership in Damascus.[931] He personally led his *fasa'il* and carried out nighttime attacks

Figure 133: *Farhan al-Sa'di following his arrest by British Mandatory police, 1937. He was later executed. Al-Sa'di was a key actor in setting off the revolt with his April 1936 attack on a bus, which left two Jewish passengers dead.*

against British targets in the revolt's early stage in 1936. When the revolt was renewed in April 1937, he established a more organised command hierarchy consisting of four main brigades who operated in the north-central highlands (Tulkarm-Nablus-Jenin area).[932] He competed for the position of General Commander of the Revolt with Aref Abdul Razzik, and the two served the post in rotation from September 1938 to February 1939, when al-Hajj Muhammad was confirmed as the sole General Commander.[933]

Al-Hajj Muhammad refused to carry out political assassinations at the behest of political factions, including al-Husayni, once stating "I dont work for Husayniya ('Husanyni-ism'), but for wataniya ('nationalism')."[934] He is still known by Palestinians as a hero and martyr and is regarded as a metonym "for a national movement that was popular, honourable, religious, and lofty in its aims and actions."[935] He was shot dead in a firefight with British forces outside the village of Sanur on 27 March 1939, after Farid Irsheid's peace band informed the authorities of his location.[936,937,938]

Yusuf Abu Durra, a Qassamite leader in the Jenin area, was born in Silat al-Harithiya and before becoming a rebel worked as a Gazoz vendor.[939] He was said to be a narrow-minded man who thrived on extortion and cruelty and thus became greatly feared. Yusuf Hamdan was Durra's more respected lieutenant and later a leader of his own unit; he was killed by an army patrol in 1939 and buried in al-Lajjun. Durra himself was apprehended by the Arab Legion in Transjordan on 25 July 1939 and subsequently hanged.

Fakhri Abdul Hadi of Arrabah worked closely with Fawzi al-Qawukji in 1936, but later defected to the British authorities. He bargained for a pardon by offering to collaborate with the British on countering rebel propaganda. Once on the payroll of the British consul in Damascus, Gilbert Mackereth, he carried out many attacks against the rebels in 1938–1939 as leader of his own "peace band".[940,941]

> *Aref had a little mare*
> *Its coat as white as snow*
> *And where that mare and Aref went*
> *We're jiggered if we know.* – British Army verse.

Aref Abdul Razzik of Tayibe was responsible for the area south of Tulkarm and was known for evading capture whilst being pursued by the security forces.[942] He signed his bulletins as 'The Ghost of Sheikh Qassam'. Razzik assumed a place in British army folklore and the troops sang a song about him. Razzik was capable and daring and gained a reputation as one of the army's problem heroes.

Jerusalem area

Issa Battat was a peasant leader in the southern hills below Jerusalem who caused enormous damage to security patrols in his area.[943] He was killed by a patrol of armed police in a battle near Hebron in 1937.[944]

Arab volunteers

In the first phase of the revolt, around 300 volunteers, mostly veterans of the Ottoman Army and/or rebels from the Great Syrian Revolt (1925–27), deployed in northern Palestine. Their overall commander was Fawzi al-Qawuqji and his deputies were Said al-As and Muhammad al-Ashmar. Qawuqji also led the volunteer force's Iraqi and Transjordanian battalions, and al-Ashmar was commander of the Syrian battalion, which largely consisted of volunteers from Damascus's al-Midan Quarter, Hama and Homs. The Druze ex-Ottoman officer, Hamad Sa'ab, commanded the Lebanese battalion.[945]

Figure 134: *Jewish protest demonstration against the Palestine White Paper (18 May 1939). Result of an evening riot in Zion Circus, broken signs windows, etc. Wikipedia: Citation needed*

Outcome

Casualties

Despite the intervention of up to 50,000 British troops and 15,000 Haganah men, the uprising continued for over three years. By the time it concluded in September 1939, more than 5,000 Arabs, over 300 Jews, and 262 Britons had been killed and at least 15,000 Arabs were wounded.

Impact on the Jewish Yishuv

In the overall context of the Jewish settlement's development in the 1930s the physical losses endured during the revolt were relatively insignificant. Although hundreds were killed and property was damaged no Jewish settlement was captured or destroyed and several dozen new ones were established. Over 50,000 new Jewish immigrants arrived in Palestine. In 1936 Jews made up about one-third of the population.[946]

The hostilities contributed to further disengagement of the Jewish and Arab economies in Palestine, which were intertwined to some extent until that time. Development of the economy and infrastructure accelerated. For example,

Figure 135: *Jewish protest demonstrations against the 1939 Palestine White Paper. One of the big posters displayed the previous day.*

whereas the Jewish city of Tel Aviv relied on the nearby Arab seaport of Jaffa, hostilities dictated the construction of a separate Jewish-run seaport for Tel Aviv, inspiring the delighted Ben-Gurion to note in his diary "we ought to reward the Arabs for giving us the impetus for this great creation."[947] Metal works were established to produce armoured sheeting for vehicles and a rudimentary arms industry was founded. The settlement's transportation capabilities were enhanced and Jewish unemployment was relieved owing to the employment of police officers, and replacement of striking Arab labourers, employees, craftsman and farmers by Jewish workers. Most of the important industries in Palestine were owned by Jews and in trade and the banking sector they were much better placed than the Arabs.

As a result of collaboration with the British colonial authorities and security forces many thousands of young men had their first experience of military training, which Moshe Shertok and Haganah leader Eliyahu Golomb cited as one of the fruits of the Haganah's policy of havlagah (restraint).[948]

Although the Jewish settlement in Palestine was dismayed by the publication of the 1939 White Paper restricting Jewish immigration, David Ben-Gurion remained undeterred, believing that the policy would not be implemented, and in fact Neville Chamberlain had told him that the policy would last at the very most only for the duration of the war.[949] In the event the White Paper quotas were exhausted only in December 1944, over five and a half years later, and in the same period the United Kingdom absorbed 50,000 Jewish refugees and the British Commonwealth (Australia, Canada and South Africa) took many thousands more.[950] During the War over 30,000 Jews joined the British forces and even the Irgun ceased operations against the British until 1944.[951]

Impact on the Palestinian Arabs

The revolt weakened the military strength of Palestinian Arabs in advance of their ultimate confrontation with the Jewish settlement in the 1947–48 Civil War in Mandatory Palestine and was thus counterproductive.[952] During the uprising, British authorities attempted to confiscate all weapons from the Arab population. This, and the destruction of the main Arab political leadership in the revolt, greatly hindered their military efforts in the 1948 Palestine war, where imbalances between the Jewish and Arab economic performance, social cohesion, political organisation and military capability became apparent.

The Mufti, Hajj Amin al-Husseini and his supporters directed a Jihad against any person who did not obey the Mufti. Their national struggle was a religious holy war, and the incarnation of both the Palestinian Arab nation and Islam was Hajj Amin al-Husseini. Anyone who rejected his leadership was a heretic and his life was forfeit. After the Peel report publication, the murders of Arabs leaders who opposed the Mufti were accelerated. Pressed by the assassination campaign pursued by the rebels at the behest of the Husseini leadership, the opposition had a security cooperation with the Jews. The flight of wealthy Arabs, which occurred during the revolt, was also replicated in 1947–49.

Thousands of Palestinian houses were destroyed, and massive financial costs were incurred because of the general strike and the devastation of fields, crops and orchards. The economic boycott further damaged the fragile Palestinian Arab economy through loss of sales and goods and increased unemployment.

Clearly, the revolt did not achieve its goals, although it is "credited with signifying the birth of the Arab Palestinian identity."[953] It is generally credited with forcing the issuance of the White Paper of 1939 in which Britain retreated from the partition arrangements proposed by the Peel Commission in favour of the creation of a binational state within ten years, although The League of Nations commission held that the White Paper was in conflict with the terms of the Mandate as put forth in the past. The White Paper of 1939 was regarded by many as incompatible with the commitment to a Jewish National Home in Palestine, as proclaimed in the 1917 Balfour Declaration. Al-Husseini rejected the new policy, although it seems that the ordinary Palestinian Arab accepted the White Paper of 1939. His biographer, Philip Mattar wrote that

Figure 136: *London Conference, St. James' Palace, February 1939. Palestinian delegates (foreground), left to right: Fu'ad Saba, Yaqub Al-Ghussein, Musa Alami, Amin Tamimi, Jamal Al-Husseini, Awni Abdul Hadi, George Antonious, and Alfred Roch. Facing are the British, with Neville Chamberlain presiding. To his right is Lord Halifax, and to his left, Malcolm MacDonald.*

in that case, the Mufti preferred his personal interests and the ideology rather than the practical considerations.

Impact on the British Empire

As the inevitable war with Germany approached, British policy makers concluded that although they could rely on the support of the Jewish population in Palestine, who had no alternative but to support Britain, the support of Arab governments and populations in an area of great strategic importance for the British Empire was not assured.[954] Prime Minister Neville Chamberlain concluded "if we must offend one side, let us offend the Jews rather than the Arabs."

In February 1939 Secretary of State for Dominion Affairs Malcolm MacDonald called together a conference of Arab and Zionist leaders on the future of Palestine at St. James's Palace in London but the discussions ended without agreement on 27 March. The government's new policy as published in White Paper of 17 May had been determined already and despite Jewish protests and Irgun attacks the British remained resolute.

There was a growing feeling among British officials that there was nothing left for them to do in Palestine. Perhaps the ultimate achievement of the Arab Revolt was to make the British sick of Palestine.[955] Major-General Bernard "Monty" Montgomery concluded, "the Jew murders the Arab and the Arab murders the Jew. This is what is going on in Palestine now. And it will go on for the next 50 years in all probability."[956]

Historiography

The 1936–39 Arab Revolt has been and still is marginalized in both Western and Israeli historiography on Palestine, and even progressive Western scholars have little to say about the anti-colonial struggle of the Palestinian Arab rebels against the British Empire.[957] According to Swedenberg's analysis, for instance, the Zionist version of Israeli history acknowledges only one authentic national movement: the struggle for Jewish self-determination that resulted in the Israeli Declaration of Independence in May 1948. Swedenberg writes that the Zionist narrative has no room for an anticolonial and anti-British Palestinian national revolt. Zionists often describe the revolt as a series of "events" (Hebrew מאורעות (תרצ"ו-תרצ"ט) "תרצ"ו-תרצ"ט" "riots", or "happenings".

The appropriate description was debated by Jewish Agency officials, who were keen not to give a negative impression of Palestine to prospective immigrants.[958] In private, however, David Ben-Gurion was unequivocal: the Arabs, he said, were "fighting dispossession ... The fear is not of losing land, but of losing the homeland of the Arab people, which others want to turn into the homeland of the Jewish people."

References

<templatestyles src="Refbegin/styles.css" />

- Antonius, George (1938) *The Arab Awakening. The Story of the Arab National Movement*. Hamish Hamilton. (1945 edition)
- Adelman, Jonathan R. (2008). *The Rise of Israel: A History of a Revolutionary State*. Routledge. <templatestyles src="Module:Citation/CS1/styles.css" />ISBN 978-0-415-77510-6
- Anglim, Simon. (2005). *Orde Wingate, the Iron Wall and Counter-Terrorism in Palestine 1937–39*. Strategic and Combat Studies Institute. <templatestyles src="Module:Citation/CS1/styles.css" />ISBN 978-1874346395
- Arielli, Nir (2010). *Fascist Italy and the Middle East, 1933–40*. Palgrave. <templatestyles src="Module:Citation/CS1/styles.css" />ISBN 978-0-230-23160-3

- Bajohr, Frank (2002). *"Aryanisation" in Hamburg: The Economic Exclusion of Jews and the Confiscation of their Property in Nazi Germany*. Berghahn Books. <templatestyles src="Module:Citation/CS1/styles.css" />ISBN 978-1-57181-485-2
- Bar-On, Mordechai (2004). *A Never-ending Conflict: A Guide to Israeli Military History*. Greenwood. <templatestyles src="Module:Citation/CS1/styles.css" />ISBN 978-0-275-98158-7
- Ben-Ami, Shlomo (2005). *Scars of War, Wounds of Peace: The Israeli-Arab Tragedy* Weidenfeld & Nicolson. <templatestyles src="Module:Citation/CS1/styles.css" />ISBN 978-0-297-84883-7
- Black, Ian and Morris, Benny (1991). *Israel's Secret Wars: A History of Israel's Intelligence Services*. Grove Weidenfeld. <templatestyles src="Module:Citation/CS1/styles.css" />ISBN 978-0-8021-3286-4
- Black, Jeremy (2006). *A Military History of Britain: From 1775 to the Present*. Greenwood Publishing. <templatestyles src="Module:Citation/CS1/styles.css" />ISBN 978-0-275-99039-8
- Bowyer Bell, John (1996). *Terror Out of Zion: The Fight for Israeli Independence*. Transaction Publishers. <templatestyles src="Module:Citation/CS1/styles.css" />ISBN 978-1-56000-870-5
- Cleveland, William L. (2000). *A History of the Modern Middle East*. Westview Press. <templatestyles src="Module:Citation/CS1/styles.css" />ISBN 978-0-8133-3489-9
- Cohen, Hillel (2009). *Army of Shadows: Palestinian Collaboration with Zionism, 1917–1948*. University of California Press. <templatestyles src="Module:Citation/CS1/styles.css" />ISBN 978-0-520-25989-8
- Commins, David Dean (2004). *Historical dictionary of Syria*. Scarecrow Press. <templatestyles src="Module:Citation/CS1/styles.css" />ISBN 978-0-8108-4934-1
- Ferrier, Ronald W. and Bamberg, J. H. (1994). *The History of the British Petroleum Company: 1928–1954. The Anglo-Iranian Years*. Cambridge University Press. <templatestyles src="Module:Citation/CS1/styles.css" />ISBN 978-0-521-25950-7
- Friling, Tuvia (2005). *Arrows in the Dark: David Ben-Gurion, the Yishuv leadership, and Rescue Attempts During the Holocaust*. University of Wisconsin Press. <templatestyles src="Module:Citation/CS1/styles.css" />ISBN 978-0-299-17550-4
- Fry, Michael G., MacKereth, Gilbert & Rabinovich, Itamar (1985). *Despatches from Damascus: Gilbert MacKereth and British Policy in the Levant, 1933–1939*. Dayan Center for Middle Eastern and African Studies, Shiloah Institute, Tel Aviv University. <templatestyles src="Module:Citation/CS1/styles.css" />ISBN 978-965-224-004-0

- Gettleman, Marvin E. and Schaar, Stuart (2003). *The Middle East and Islamic World Reader*. Grove Press. ISBN 978-0-8021-3936-8
- Gilbert, Martin (1998). *Israel: A History*. Black Swan. ISBN 978-0-552-99545-0
- Goren, Tamir (2004). The Judaization of Haifa at the Time of the Arab Revolt. *Middle Eastern Studies*, Volume 40, Issue 4 July, pp. 135–152
- Harouvi, Eldad (1999). 'Reuven Zaslany (Shiloah) and the Covert Cooperation with British Intelligence During the Second World War'. In *Carmel, Hési (Ed.). *Intelligence for Peace: The Role of Intelligence in Times of Peace*. Routledge. ISBN 978-0-7146-4950-4
- Harris, Sir Arthur (1998). *Bomber Offensive*, pp. 30–48. Greenhill Books. ISBN 978-1-85367-314-6
- Horne, Edward (2003). *A Job Well Done: A History of the Palestine Police Force, 1920–1948*. Book Guild. ISBN 978-1-85776-758-2 (First published 1982 by the Palestine Police)
- Hughes, Matthew (2009) The banality of brutality: British armed forces and the repression of the Arab Revolt in Palestine, 1936–39, *English Historical Review* Vol. CXXIV No. 507, pp. 314–354.
- Hughes, Matthew (2009). "The practice and theory of British counterinsurgency: the histories of the atrocities at the Palestinian villages of al-Bassa and Halhul, 1938–1939." *Small Wars & Insurgencies*. 20 (3&4), September 2009, pp. 528–550.
- Johnson, Loch K. (2010). *The Oxford Handbook of National Security Intelligence*. Oxford University Press. ISBN 978-0-19-537588-6
- Kaplan, Eric. 2005. *The Jewish Radical Right: Revisionist Zionism and Its Ideological Legacy*. University of Wisconsin Press. ISBN 978-0-299-20380-1
- 'Kayyālī, Abd al-Wahhāb (1978). *Palestine: A Modern History*. Routledge. ISBN 978-0-85664-635-5
- Kelly, Matthew (2017). *The Crime of Nationalism: Britain, Palestine, and Nation-Building on the Fringe of Empire*. Oakland, California: University of California Press. ISBN 0-520-29149-2.
- Khalidi, Rashid (2001). The Palestinians and 1948: the underlying causes of failure. In Eugene Rogan and Avi Shlaim (eds.). *The War for Palestine* (pp. 12–36). Cambridge: Cambridge University Press.

- ISBN 978-0-521-79476-3
- Khalidi, Walid (1987). *From Haven to Conquest: Readings in Zionism and the Palestine Problem Until 1948*. Institute for Palestine Studies. ISBN 978-0-88728-155-6
- Kimmerling, Baruch (1989). *The Israeli State and Society: Boundaries and Frontiers*. SUNY Press. ISBN 978-0-88706-849-2
- Kimmerling, Baruch and Migdal, Joseph S. (2003). *The Palestinian People: A History*. Harvard University Press. ISBN 978-0-674-01129-8. ISBN 978-0-674-01129-8.
- Krämer, Gudrun (2008). *A History of Palestine: From the Ottoman Conquest to the Founding of the State of Israel*. Princeton University Press. ISBN 978-0-691-11897-0
- Laffin, John (1979). *The Israeli Mind*. Cassell. ISBN 978-0-304-30399-1
- Levenberg, Haim (1993). *Military Preparations of the Arab Community in Palestine: 1945–1948*. London: Routledge. ISBN 978-0-7146-3439-5
- Millman, Brock (1998). *The Ill-made Alliance: Anglo-Turkish Relations, 1934–1940*. McGill-Queen's Press. ISBN 978-0-7735-1603-8
- Morewood, Stephen (2004). *The British Defence of Egypt, 1935–1940: Conflict and Crisis in the Eastern Mediterranean*. Routledge. ISBN 978-0-7146-4943-6
- Morris, Benny (1999). *Righteous Victims: A History of the Zionist-Arab Conflict, 1881–1999*. John Murray. ISBN 978-0-7195-6222-8
- Nashif, Esmail (2008). *Palestinian Political Prisoners: Identity and Community*. Taylor & Francis. ISBN 978-0-415-44498-9
- Nicosia, Francis R. (2008). *Zionism and Anti-Semitism in Nazi Germany*. Cambridge University Press. ISBN 978-0-521-88392-4
- Norris, Jacob (2008). Repression and Rebellion: Britain's Response to the Arab Revolt in Palestine of 1936–39. *The Journal of Imperial and Commonwealth History* 36(1):25–45.
- Omissi, David E. (1990). *Air Power and Colonial Control: the Royal Air Force, 1919–1939*. Manchester University Press.

- src="Module:Citation/CS1/styles.css" />ISBN 978-0-7190-2960-8
- Patai, Raphael (1971). *Encyclopedia of Zionism and Israel*, Herzl Press.
- Palestine Royal Commission Report Presented by the Secretary of State for the Colonies to Parliament by Command of His Majesty, July 1937, Cmd. 5479[959]. His Majesty's Stationery Office., London, 1937. 404 pages + maps.
- Rotter, Andrew John (2008). *Hiroshima: The World's Bomb*. Oxford University Press. <templatestyles src="Module:Citation/CS1/styles.css" />ISBN 978-0-19-280437-2
- Sacharov, Eliahu (2004). *Out of the Limelight: Events, Operations, Missions, and Personalities in Israeli History*. Gefen Publishing House Ltd. <templatestyles src="Module:Citation/CS1/styles.css" />ISBN 978-965-229-298-8
- Segev, Tom (1991) *The Seventh Million*. Henry Holt & Co. <templatestyles src="Module:Citation/CS1/styles.css" />ISBN 978-0-8050-6660-9
- Segev, Tom (2000). *One Palestine Complete: Jews and Arabs Under the British Mandate*. Abacus. <templatestyles src="Module:Citation/CS1/styles.css" />ISBN 978-0-349-11286-2
- Shapira, Anita (1999). *Land and Power: The Zionist Resort to Force, 1881–1948*. Stanford University Press. <templatestyles src="Module:Citation/CS1/styles.css" />ISBN 978-0-8047-3776-0
- Stewart, Ninian (2002). *The Royal Navy and the Palestine Patrol*. Taylor and Francis. <templatestyles src="Module:Citation/CS1/styles.css" />ISBN 978-0-7146-8254-9
- Swedenburg, Ted (2004). "The Role of the Palestinian Peasantry in the Great Revolt (1936–1939)", reprinted in Hourani, Albert H., et al., *The Modern Middle East* I.B. Tauris, pp. 467–503. <templatestyles src="Module:Citation/CS1/styles.css" />ISBN 978-1-86064-963-9.
- Swedenburg, Ted (2003). *Memories of Revolt. The 1936–1939 Rebellion and the Palestinian National Past*. The University of Arkansas Press. <templatestyles src="Module:Citation/CS1/styles.css" />ISBN 978-1-55728-763-2
- Thomas, Martin (2008). *Empires of Intelligence: Security Services and Colonial Disorder After 1914*. University of California Press. <templatestyles src="Module:Citation/CS1/styles.css" />ISBN 978-0-520-25117-5
- Thomas, Martin (2007). *The French Empire Between the Wars: Imperialism, Politics and Society*. Manchester University Press. <templatestyles src="Module:Citation/CS1/styles.css" />ISBN 978-0-7190-7755-5
- Tripp, Charles (2002). *A History of Iraq*. Cambridge University Press. <templatestyles src="Module:Citation/CS1/styles.css" />ISBN 978-0-521-52900-6

- Wasserstein, Bernard (2004). *Israel and Palestine*. Profile Books. <templatestyles src="Module:Citation/CS1/styles.css" />ISBN 978-1-86197-558-4
- White Paper of 1939: Palestine: Statement of Policy Presented by the Secretary of State for the Colonies to Parliament by Command of His Majesty, May 1939, Cmd 6019[960]. His Majesty's Stationery Office, London, 1939.
- Yazbak, Mahmoud (2000). From Poverty to Revolt: Economic Factors in the Outbreak of the 1936 Rebellion in Palestine. *Middle Eastern Studies*, 36(3), pp. 93–113.

External links

Media related to 1936–1939 Arab revolt in Palestine at Wikimedia Commons
- The Arab Revolt in Palestine[961] – A Zionist point of view
- The First Intifada: Rebellion in Palestine 1936–1939[962] – A view from British historian Charles Townshend.

White Paper of 1939

White Paper of 1939	
\multicolumn{2}{c}{1939 White Paper cmd 6019}	
Created	May 1939
Ratified	23 May 1939[963]
Purpose	Statement of British policy in Mandatory Palestine

The **White Paper of 1939**[964] was a policy paper issued by the British government under Neville Chamberlain in response to the 1936–39 Arab Revolt. Following its formal approval in the House of Commons on 23 May 1939,[965,966] it acted as the governing policy for Mandatory Palestine from 1939 until the British departure in 1948, the matter of the Mandate meanwhile having been referred to the United Nations.[967]

The policy, first drafted in March 1939, was prepared by the British government unilaterally as a result of the failure of the Arab-Zionist London Conference.[968] The paper called for the establishment of a Jewish national home in an independent Palestinian state within 10 years, rejecting the idea of partitioning Palestine. It also limited Jewish immigration to 75,000 for 5 years, and ruled that further immigration was to be determined by the Arab majority (section II). Restrictions were put on the rights of Jews to buy land from Arabs (section III).

The proposal did not meet the political demands proposed by Arab representatives during the London Conference and was officially rejected by the representatives of Palestine Arab parties acting under the influence of Haj Amin Eff el Husseini while more moderate Arab opinion represented in the National Defence Party was prepared to accept the White Paper.

White Paper of 1939

Figure 137: *London Conference, St. James's Palace, February 1939. Arab Palestinian delegates (foreground), left to right: Fu'ad Saba, Yaqub Al-Ghussein, Musa Al-Alami, Amin Tamimi, Jamal Al-Husseini, Awni Abdul Hadi, George Antonious, and Alfred Roch. Facing the Arab Palestinians are the British, with Sir Neville Chamberlain presiding. To his right is Lord Halifax, and to his left, Malcolm MacDonald*

Zionist groups in Palestine immediately rejected the White Paper. There was a campaign of attacks on government property, which lasted for several months. On 18 May a Jewish general strike was called.[969]

Key provisions were ultimately never to be implemented, initially because of Churchill's opposition following the change in government, and later because of preoccupation with World War II.[970]

Background

During World War I, the British had made two promises regarding territory in the Middle East. Britain had promised the Hashemite governors of Arabia, through Lawrence of Arabia and the Hussein-McMahon Correspondence, independence for a united Arab country covering Syria in exchange for their supporting the British against the Ottoman Empire. The Ottoman Caliphate had declared a military jihad in support of the Germans and it was hoped that an alliance with the Arabs would quell the chances of a general Muslim uprising in British-held territories in Africa, India, and the Far East.[971] Great

Britain had also negotiated the Sykes-Picot Agreement, agreeing to partition the Middle East between Britain and France.

A variety of strategic factors, such as securing Jewish support in Eastern Europe as the Russian front collapsed, culminated in the Balfour Declaration, 1917, with Britain promising to create and foster a Jewish national home in Palestine. These broad delineations of territory and goals for both the creation of a Jewish homeland in Palestine, and Arab self-determination was approved in the San Remo conference.

In June 1922 the League of Nations approved the Palestine Mandate with effect from September 1923. The Palestine Mandate was an explicit document regarding Britain's responsibilities and powers of administration in Palestine including 'secur[ing] the establishment of the Jewish national home', and 'safeguarding the civil and religious rights of all the inhabitants of Palestine'. In September 1922, the British government presented a memorandum to the League of Nations stating that Transjordan would be excluded from all the provisions dealing with Jewish settlement, in accordance with Article 25 of the Mandate, and this memorandum was approved on 23 September. Due to stiff Arab opposition and pressure against Jewish immigration, Britain redefined Jewish immigration by restricting its flow according to the country's economic capacity to absorb the immigrants. In effect annual quotas were put in place as to how many Jews could immigrate, while Jews possessing a large sum of money (£500) were allowed to enter the country freely.

Following Adolf Hitler's rise to power, a growing number of European Jews were prepared to spend the money necessary to enter Palestine. The 1935 Nuremberg Laws stripped the 500,000 German Jews of their citizenship. Jewish migration was impeded by Nazi restrictions on the transfer of finances abroad (departing Jews had to abandon their property), but the Jewish Agency was able to negotiate an agreement allowing Jews resident in Germany to buy German goods for export to Palestine thus circumventing the restrictions.

The large numbers of Jews entering PalestineWikipedia:Please clarify led to the 1936–39 Arab revolt in Palestine. Britain responded to the Arab revolt by appointing a Royal Commission, known as the Peel Commission which traveled out to Palestine and undertook a thorough study of the issues. The Peel Commission recommended in 1937 that Palestine be partitioned into two states, one Arab the other Jewish. In January 1938, the Woodhead Commission explored the practicalities of partition. The Woodhead Commission considered three different plans, one of which was based on the Peel plan. Reporting in 1938, the Commission rejected the Peel plan primarily on the grounds that it could not be implemented without a massive forced transfer of Arabs (an option that the British government had already ruled out). With dissent from some of its members, the Commission instead recommended a plan that would leave the Galilee under British mandate, but emphasised serious problems with it that included a lack of financial self-sufficiency of the proposed Arab State. The British Government accompanied the publication of the Woodhead Report by a statement of policy rejecting partition as impracticable due to "political, administrative and financial difficulties".[972] It proposed a substantially smaller Jewish state, including the coastal plain only. An international conference (Évian Conference) convened by the United States in July 1938, failed to find any agreement to deal with the rapidly growing number of Jewish refugees.

London Conference

In February 1939 the British called the London Conference to negotiate an agreement between Arabs and Jews in Palestine. The Arab delegates attended on condition that they would not meet directly with the Jewish representatives, which would constitute recognition of Jewish claims over Palestine. So the British government held separate meetings with the two sides. The conference ended in failure on March 17.[973]

In the wake of World War II, the British believed that Jewish support was guaranteed or unimportant. However they feared that the Arab world might turn against them. This geopolitical consideration was, in Raul Hilberg's word, "decisive"[974] to British policies. Egypt, Iraq and Saudi Arabia were independent and allied with Britain.

Content

The main points of the White Paper were:

- **Section I. The Constitution**: It stated that with over 450,000 Jews having now settled in the mandate, the Balfour Declaration about "a national home for the Jewish people" had been met and called for an independent Palestine established within 10 years, governed jointly by Arabs and Jews:

His Majesty's Government believe that the framers of the Mandate in which the Balfour Declaration was embodied could not have intended that Palestine should be converted into a Jewish State against the will of the Arab population of the country. [...] His Majesty's Government therefore now declare unequivocally that it is not part of their policy that Palestine should become a Jewish State. They would indeed regard it as contrary to their obligations to the Arabs under the Mandate, as well as to the assurances which have been given to the Arab people in the past, that the Arab population of Palestine should be made the subjects of a Jewish State against their will.

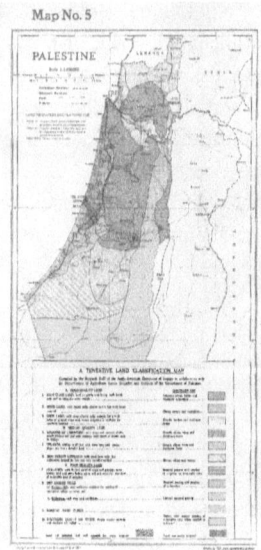

Figure 138: *Land classification and boundaries of land transfer regions as prescribed in 1940.*

The objective of His Majesty's Government is the establishment within 10 years of an independent Palestine State in such treaty relations with the United Kingdom as will provide satisfactorily for the commercial and strategic requirements of both countries in the future. [..] The independent State should be one in which Arabs and Jews share government in such a way as to ensure that the essential interests of each community are safeguarded.

- **Section II. Immigration**: Jewish immigration to Palestine under the British Mandate was to be limited to 75,000 over the next five years, after which it would depend on Arab consent:

His Majesty's Government do not [..] find anything in the Mandate or in subsequent Statements of Policy to support the view that the establishment of a Jewish National Home in Palestine cannot be effected unless immigration is allowed to continue indefinitely. If immigration has an adverse effect on the economic position in the country, it should clearly be restricted; and equally, if it has a seriously damaging effect on the political position in the country, that is a factor that should not be ignored. Although it is not difficult to contend that the large number of Jewish immigrants who have been admitted so far have been absorbed economically, the fear of the Arabs that this influx will continue indefinitely until the Jewish population is in a position to dominate them has produced consequences which are extremely grave for Jews and Arabs alike and for the peace and prosperity of Palestine. The lamentable disturbances of the past three years are only the latest and most sustained manifestation of this intense Arab apprehension [...] it cannot be denied that fear of indefinite Jewish immigration is widespread amongst the Arab population and that this fear has made possible disturbances which have given a serious setback to economic progress, depleted the Palestine exchequer, rendered life and property insecure, and produced a bitterness between the Arab and Jewish populations which is deplorable between citizens of the same country. If in these circumstances immigration is continued up to the economic absorptive capacity of the country, regardless of all other considerations, a fatal enmity between the two peoples will be perpetuated, and the situation in Palestine may become a permanent source of friction amongst all peoples in the Near and Middle East.

Jewish immigration during the next five years will be at a rate which, if economic absorptive capacity permits, will bring the Jewish population up to approximately one third of the total population of the country. Taking into account the expected natural increase of the Arab and Jewish populations, and the number of illegal Jewish immigrants now in the country, this would allow of the admission, as from the beginning of April this year, of some 75,000 immigrants over the next four years. These immigrants would, subject to the criterion of economic absorptive capacity, be admitted as follows: For each of the next five years a quota of 10,000 Jewish immigrants will be allowed on the understanding that a shortage one year may be added to the quotas for subsequent years, within the five-year period, if economic absorptive capacity permits. In addition, as a contribution towards the solution of the Jewish refugee problem, 25,000 refugees will be admitted as soon as the High Commissioner is satisfied that adequate provision for their maintenance is ensured, special consideration being given to refugee children and dependents. The existing machinery for ascertaining economic absorptive capacity will be retained, and the High Commissioner will have the ultimate responsibility for deciding the limits of economic capacity. Before each periodic decision is taken, Jewish and Arab representatives will be consulted. After the period of five years, no further Jewish immigration will be permitted unless the Arabs of Palestine are prepared to acquiesce in it.

- **Section III. Land**: Previously no restriction had been imposed on the transfer of land from Arabs to Jews, while now the *White Paper* stated:

Figure 139: *Jewish demonstration against White Paper in Jerusalem, 1939*

> *The Reports of several expert Commissions have indicated that, owing to the natural growth of the Arab population and the steady sale in recent years of Arab land to Jews, there is now in certain areas no room for further transfers of Arab land, whilst in some other areas such transfers of land must be restricted if Arab cultivators are to maintain their existing standard of life and a considerable landless Arab population is not soon to be created. In these circumstances, the High Commissioner will be given general powers to prohibit and regulate transfers of land.*

Reactions and effects

Parliamentary Approval

On 22 May 1939 the House of Commons debated a motion that the White Paper was inconsistent with the terms of the Mandate. It was defeated by 268 votes to 179. The following day the House of Lords accepted the new policy without a vote.[975]

During the debate, Lloyd George called the White Paper an "act of perfidy" while Winston Churchill voted against the government of his party. The Liberal MP James Rothschild stated during the parliamentary debate that "for the majority of the Jews who go to Palestine it is a question of migration or of physical extinction".[976]

Figure 140: *Jewish demonstration against White Paper in Tel Aviv, 1939, from the collection of the National Library of Israel.*

Figure 141: *Jewish demonstration against White Paper in Tel Aviv, 1939, from the collection of the National Library of Israel.*

Some supporters of the Conservative Wikipedia:Citation needed Government were opposed to the policy on the grounds that it appeared in their view to contradict the Balfour Declaration. Several government MPs either voted against the proposals or abstained, including Cabinet Ministers such as the illustrious Jewish Secretary of State for War Leslie Hore-Belisha.

League of Nations

The supervising authority of the League of Nations, the Permanent Mandates Commission abstained unanimously from endorsing the White Paper,Wikipedia:Citation needed though four out of seven members thought the new policy was inconsistent with that mandate.[977] The League of Nations commission rejected the White Paper because it was in conflict with the terms of the Mandate as put forth in the past. The outbreak of the Second World War suspended any further deliberations.

Arab Reactions

The Arab Higher Committee initially argued that the independence of a future Palestine Government would prove to be illusory, as the Jews could prevent its functioning by withholding participation, and in any case real authority would still be in the hands of British officials. The limitations on Jewish immigration were also held to be insufficient, as there was no guarantee immigration would not resume after five years. In place of the policy enunciated in the White Paper, the Arab Higher Committee called for "a complete and final prohibition" of Jewish immigration and a repudiation of the Jewish national home policy altogether.Wikipedia:Citation needed

In June 1939,[978] Hajj Amin al-Husayni initially "astonished" the other members of the Arab Higher Committee by turning down the White Paper. Al-Husayni, according to Benny Morris, turned the advantageous proposal down for the entirely selfish reason that "it did not place him at the helm of the future Palestinian state."[979]

In July 1940, after two weeks of meetings with the British representative S. F. Newcombe,[980] the leader of the Palestinian Arab delegates to the London Conference, Jamal al-Husseini and fellow delegate Musa al-Alami, agreed to the terms of the White Paper and both signed a copy of it in the presence of the Prime Minister of Iraq, Nuri as-Said.[981]

Zionist Reactions

Zionist groups in Palestine immediately rejected the White Paper and began a campaign of attacks on government property and Arab civilians which lasted for several months. On 18 May a Jewish general strike was called.

On 27 February 1939, in response to enthusiastic Arab demonstrations following reports that the British were proposing to allow Palestine independence on the same terms as Iraq, a coordinated Irgun bombing campaign across the country killed 38 Arabs and wounded 44.[982]

In response to the White Paper, the right-wing Zionist militant group Irgun began formulating plans for a rebellion to evict the British and establish an independent Jewish state. Ze'ev Jabotinsky, the founder of Irgun, who had been exiled from Palestine by the British, proposed a plan for a revolt to take place in October 1939, which he sent to the Irgun High Command in six coded letters. Under Jabotinsky's plan, he, together with other "illegals", would arrive in Palestine by boat, and the Irgun would help him and other passengers escape. Next, the Irgun would raid and occupy Government House, as well as other British centers of power in Palestine, raise the Jewish national flag, and hold them for at least 24 hours even at a heavy cost. Simultaneously, Zionist leaders in Western Europe and the United States would proclaim an independent Jewish state in Palestine, and would function as a government-in-exile. Irgun seriously considered carrying out the plan, but was concerned over the heavy losses it would doubtless incur. Irgun leader Avraham Stern (who would later break from Irgun to form Lehi), formed a plan for 40,000 armed Jewish fighters recruited in Europe to sail to Palestine and join the rebellion. The Polish government supported his plan, and began training Jews and setting aside weaponry for them. However, the outbreak of World War II in September 1939 quickly put an end to these plans.[983,984]

After the outbreak of war in September 1939, the head of the Jewish Agency for Palestine David Ben-Gurion declared: 'We will fight the White Paper as if there is no war, and fight the war as if there is no White Paper.'[985]

Subsequent events

On 13 July the authorities announced the suspension of all Jewish immigration into Palestine until March 1940. The reason given for this decision was the increase in illegal immigrants arriving.[986]

In March 1940, the British High Commissioner for Palestine issued an edict dividing Palestine into three zones.

> *In Zone A, consisting of about 63 percent of the country including the stony hills, land transfers save to a Palestinian Arab were in general forbidden.*

In Zone B. consisting of about 32 percent of the country, transfers from a Palestinian Arab save to another Palestinian Arab were severely restricted at the discretion of the High Commissioner. In the remainder of Palestine, consisting of about five percent of the country-which, however, includes the most fertile areas - land sales remained unrestricted.[987]

In December 1942, when extermination of the Jews became public knowledge, there were 34,000 immigration certificates remaining. In February 1943, the British government announced that the remaining certificates could be used as soon as practicable to rescue Jewish children from southeastern Europe, particularly Bulgaria. This plan was partly successful but many people who received certificates were not able to emigrate (but those in Bulgaria survived).[988] In July it was announced that any Jewish refugee who reached a neutral country in transit would be given clearance for Palestine.[989] During 1943 about half the remaining certificates were distributed,[990] and by the end of the war there were 3,000 certificates left.[991]

At the end of World War II, the British Labour Party conference voted to rescind the White Paper and establish a Jewish state in Palestine, however the Labour Foreign Minister, Ernest Bevin persisted with the policy and it remained in effect until the British departed Palestine in May 1948.

After the war, the determination of Holocaust survivors to reach Palestine led to large scale illegal Jewish migration to Palestine. British efforts to block the migration led to violent resistance by the Zionist underground.

Illegal immigrants detained by the British Government were interned in camps on Cyprus. The immigrants had no citizenship and could not be returned to any country. Those interned included a large number of children and orphans.

From October 1946, the British Government, under the 'severest pressure' from the USA, relented and allowed 1,500 Jewish migrants a month into Palestine.[992] The gesture was in deference to the recommendations of the Anglo-American Committee of Inquiry.[993] Half of those admitted came from the prison camps for illegal immigrants in Cyprus due to fears that a growing Jewish presence in Cyprus would lead to an uprising there.[994]

The Provisional Council of Israel's first constitutional act was a Proclamation that "All legislation resulting from the British Government's White Paper of May, 1939, will at midnight tonight become null and void. This includes the immigration provisions as well as the land transfer regulations of February, 1940."

Bibliography

- Khalaf, Issa (1991). *Politics in Palestine: Arab Factionalism and Social Disintegration, 1939-1948*[995]. SUNY Press. ISBN 978-0-7914-0707-3.<templatestyles src="Module:Citation/CS1/styles.css"></templatestyles>
- Hurewitz, JC (1968). *The Struggle for Palestine*. Westport, CT: Greenwood Press. ISBN 0837101115.<templatestyles src="Module:Citation/CS1/styles.css"></templatestyles>
- Caplan, Neil (2015). *Futile Diplomacy, Volume 2: Arab-Zionist Negotiations and the End of the Mandate*[996]. Routledge. ISBN 978-1-317-44195-3.<templatestyles src="Module:Citation/CS1/styles.css"></templatestyles>
- Cohen, Michael (2014). *Britain's Moment in Palestine: Retrospect and Perspectives, 1917-1948*[997]. Routledge. ISBN 978-1-317-91364-1.<templatestyles src="Module:Citation/CS1/styles.css"></templatestyles>

External links

- 23 May 1939 House of Lords debate[998] in *Hansard*
- British White Paper of 1939[999] at Yale University
- Peel Commission Report (July 1937)[1000] at Jewish Virtual Library

World War II and the Holocaust

History of the Jews during World War II

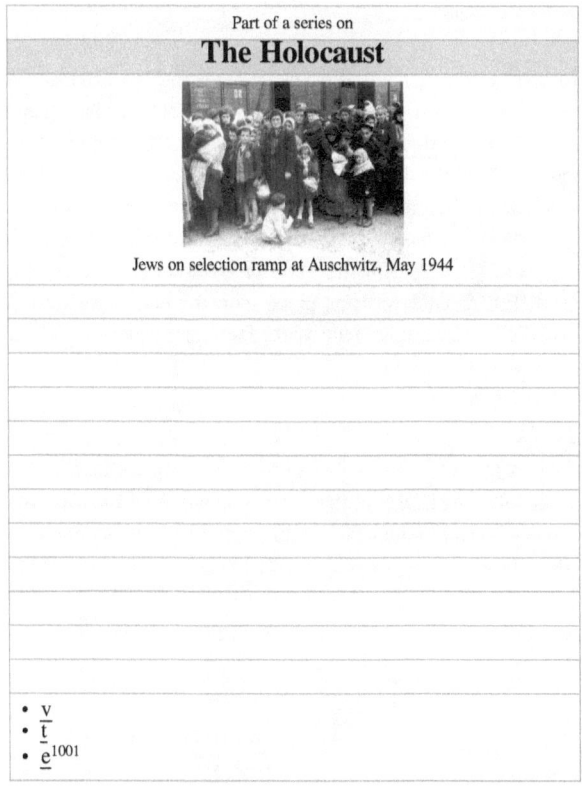

Jews on selection ramp at Auschwitz, May 1944

- v
- t
- e[1001]

The **history of the Jews during World War II** is almost synonymous with the Jewish persecution and murder of unprecedented scale in modern times in political Europe inclusive of European North Africa (pro-Nazi Vichy-North Africa and Italian Libya). The massive scale of the Holocaust which happened during World War II heavily affected the Jewish nation and world public opinion, which only understood the dimensions of the Final Solution after the war. The genocide, known as *HaShoah* in Hebrew, aimed at the elimination of the Jewish people on the European continent. It was a broadly organized operation led by Nazi Germany, in which approximately six million Jews were murdered methodically and with horrifying cruelty. During the Holocaust in occupied Poland, more than one million Jews were murdered in gas chambers of the Auschwitz concentration camp alone. The murder of the Jews of Europe affected Jewish communities in Albania, Austria, Belarus, Belgium, Bosnia & Herzegovina, Channel Islands, Croatia, Czech Republic, Estonia, France, Germany, Greece, Hungary, Italy, Latvia, Libya, Lithuania, Luxembourg, Macedonia, Moldova, The Netherlands, Norway, Poland, Romania, Russia, Serbia, Slovakia, and Ukraine.

Leading to World War II, nearly all Jewish firms in Nazi Germany had either collapsed under financial pressure and declining profits, or had been forced to sell out to the Nazi German government as part of the "Aryanization" policy inaugurated in 1937. As the war started, massacres of Jews took place originally as part of Operation Tannenberg against the Polish nation. The much larger and methodical mass killings of Jews began with the onset of Operation Barbarossa. Led by *Einsatzkommandos* and the Orpo battalions, the destruction of European Jews took place with the active participation of local Auxiliary Police including Belarusian, Estonian, Latvian, Lithuanian, and Ukrainian *Schutzmannschaften*.

History

The following figures of the Federal Agency for Civic Education (Germany) show the annihilation of the Jewish population of Europe by (pre-war) country as percentage points:[1002]

Country	Estimated Pre-War Jewish population	Estimated killed	Percent killed
Poland	3,400,000	3,000,000	88.25%
Russian SFSR	3,000,000	1,000,000	33.3%
Romania	757,000	287,000	38%

Hungary	445,000	270,000	60.7%
Czechoslovakia	357,000	260,000	73%
Germany	500,000	165,000	33%
Lithuania	150,000	145,000	96.7%
Netherlands	140,000	102,000	72.9%
France	300,000	76,000	25.33%
Latvia	93,500	70,000	74.9%
Austria	206,000	65,000	31.5%
Yugoslavia	68,500	60,000	87.6%
Greece	70,000	58,800	84%
Belgium	90,000	25,000	27.8%
Italy	46,000	7,500	16.3%
Luxembourg	3,600	1,200	33.3%
Estonia	4,300	1,000	23%
Norway	1,800	758	42.1%
Bulgaria	48,400	142	0.3%
Denmark	7,800	116	1.49%
Albania	200	100	50%
Finland	2200	7	0.32%
Total	**9,689,500**	**5,594,623**	**57.74%**

Before the onset of war, the first pogrom in Nazi Germany was *Kristallnacht*, often called *Pogromnacht*, or "night of broken glass," in which Jewish homes were ransacked in numerous German cities along with 11,000 Jewish shops, towns and villages,[1003] as civilians and SA stormtroopers destroyed buildings with sledgehammers, leaving the streets covered in smashed windows — the origin of the name "Night of Broken Glass." Jews were beaten to death; 30,000 Jewish men were taken to concentration camps; and 1,668 synagogues ransacked with 267 set on fire. Following Operation Barbarossa launched on 22 June 1941, in the city of Lviv in the occupied territory of the General Government, Ukrainian nationalists organized two large pogroms in July 1941, in which around 6,000 Jews were murdered.

In Lithuania, local militant groups engaged in anti-Jewish pogroms on July 25 and 26, 1941 around Kaunas even before the Nazi forces arrived, killing about 3,800 Jews and burning synagogues and Jewish shops. Perhaps the deadliest of these Holocaust-era pogroms was the Iaşi pogrom in Romania, in which as many as 14,000 Jews were killed by Romanian citizens, police, and military officials.

By December 1941, Adolf Hitler decided to completely exterminate European Jews. In January 1942, during the Wannsee conference, several Nazi leaders discussed the details of the "Final Solution of the Jewish question" (*Endlösung der Judenfrage*). Dr. Josef Bühler urged Reinhard Heydrich to proceed with the "Final Solution" in the General Government. They began to systematically deport Jewish populations from the ghettos and all occupied territories to the seven camps designated as *Vernichtungslager,* or extermination camps: Auschwitz, Birkenau was the Extermination Camp site Belzec, Chelmno, Majdanek, Sobibór and Treblinka II. Sebastian Haffner published the analysis in 1978 that Hitler from December 1941 accepted the failure of his goal to dominate Europe forever on his declaration of war against the United States, but that his withdrawal and apparent calm thereafter was sustained by the achievement of his second goal—the extermination of the Jews.

Even as the German Nazi war machine faltered in the last years of the war, precious military resources such as fuel, transport, munitions, soldiers, and industrial resources were still being heavily diverted away from the war and towards the death camps. By the end of the war, more than half of Jewish population of Europe had been killed in the Holocaust. Poland, home of the largest Jewish community in the world before the war, had over 90% of its Jewish population, or about 3,000,000 Jews, murdered by the Nazis. Greece, Yugoslavia, Lithuania, Czechoslovakia, the Netherlands, and Latvia each had over 70% of their Jewish population killed.

Hungary and Albania lost around half of their Jewish populations, the Soviet Union, Germany, Austria and Luxembourg lost over one third of its Jews, Belgium and France each saw around a quarter of their Jewish populations killed.

During the war, Spain became an unlikely haven for several thousand Jews. They were mainly from Western Europe, fleeing deportation to concentration camps from occupied France, but also Sephardic Jews from Eastern Europe, especially in Hungary. Trudy AlexyWikipedia:Manual of Style/Words to watch#Unsupported attributions refers to the "absurdity" and "paradox of refugees fleeing the Nazis' Final Solution to seek asylum in a country where no Jews had been allowed to live openly as Jews for over four centuries."[1004]

Jews in the Allied Forces

Approximately 1.5 million Jews served in the regular Allied militaries during World War II.[1005]

Approximately 550,000 American Jews served in the various branches of the United States armed services. Roughly 52,000 received U.S. military awards. Another 500,000 served in the Red Army, and more than 160,000 earned citations, with over 150 receiving the Hero of the Soviet Union award. Some

Figure 142: *Servicemen of the 20th Air Force stationed in Guam during World War II participate in a Rosh Hashanah service.*

100,000 Jews served in the Polish Army during the German invasion, and thousands served in the Free Polish Forces, including about 10,000 in Anders' Army. Over 60,000 Jews served in the British Armed Forces (excluding dominion or colonial personnel), including 14,000 in the Royal Air Force and 15,000 in the Royal Navy. About 30,000 Jews from Palestine also served in the British military.[1006,1007,1008]

Jewish partisans also fought throughout occupied Europe and were organized into groups such as the Bielski partisans, United Partisan Organization and the Parczew partisans. Jewish Partisans took part in the Warsaw Ghetto Uprising, the Warsaw uprising and many other battles throughout the war.

External links

 Wikimedia Commons has media related to *Jews in World War II*.

- About the Holocaust[1009] A thematic and chronological narrative of the Holocaust with related video, photos, documents and more from Yad Vashem

The Holocaust

<indicator name="pp-default"> 🔒 </indicator>

The Holocaust	
Part of World War II	
 Hungarian Jews arriving at Auschwitz II-Birkenau in German-occupied Poland, May 1944. Most were "selected" to go straight to the gas chambers. (from the Auschwitz Album)	
Location	Nazi Germany and its occupied territories
Date	1941–1945 (1933–1945, according to a broader definition[1010])
Target	European Jews; broader definitions include the Roma, "incurably sick",[1011] Slavs, Soviet POWs, and others.[1012]</ref>
Attack type	Genocide, ethnic cleansing
Deaths	Around 6 million Jews; using broadest definition, 17 million victims overall.[1013]
Perpetrators	Nazi Germany and its allies

The Holocaust, also referred to as **the Shoah**,[1014] was a genocide during World War II in which Nazi Germany, aided by its collaborators, systematically murdered some six million European Jews, around two-thirds of the Jewish population of Europe,[1015]</ref> between 1941 and 1945.[1016] Jews were targeted for extermination as part of a larger event involving the persecution and murder of other groups, including in particular the Roma and "incurably sick",[1017] as well as ethnic Poles and other Slavs, Soviet citizens, Soviet prisoners of war, political opponents, gay men and Jehovah's Witnesses, resulting in up to 17 million deaths overall.[1018]</ref>

Germany implemented the persecution in stages. Following Adolf Hitler's rise to power in 1933, the government passed laws to exclude Jews from civil society, most prominently the Nuremberg Laws in 1935. Starting in 1933, the Nazis built a network of concentration camps in Germany for political opponents and people deemed "undesirable". After the invasion of Poland in 1939, the regime set up ghettos to segregate Jews. Over 42,000 camps, ghettos, and other detention sites were established.[1019]

The deportation of Jews to the ghettos culminated in the policy of extermination the Nazis called the "Final Solution to the Jewish Question", discussed by senior Nazi officials at the Wannsee Conference in Berlin in January 1942. As German forces captured territories in the East, all anti-Jewish measures were radicalized. Under the coordination of the SS, with directions from the highest leadership of the Nazi Party, killings were committed within Germany itself, throughout German-occupied Europe, and across all territories controlled by the Axis powers. Paramilitary death squads called *Einsatzgruppen* in cooperation with Wehrmacht police battalions and local collaborators murdered around 1.3 million Jews in mass shootings between 1941 and 1945. By mid-1942, victims were being deported from the ghettos in sealed freight trains to extermination camps where, if they survived the journey, they were killed in gas chambers. The killing continued until the end of World War II in Europe in May 1945.

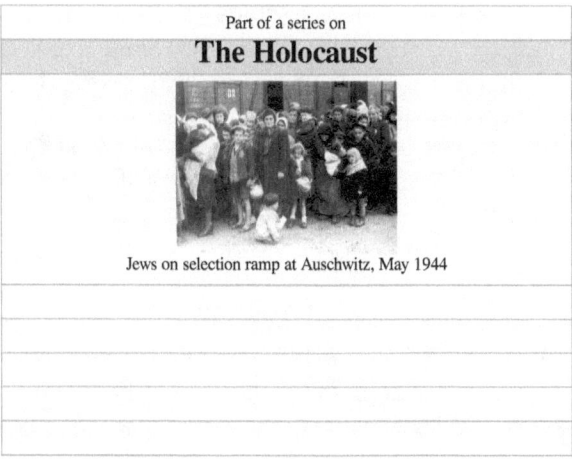

Jews on selection ramp at Auschwitz, May 1944

- v
- t
- e[1020]

Terminology and scope

Terminology

The term *holocaust* comes from the Greek ὁλόκαυστος *holókaustos*: *hólos*, "whole" and *kaustós*, "burnt offering".[1021,1022]</ref> The *Century Dictionary* defined it in 1904 as "a sacrifice or offering entirely consumed by fire, in use among the Jews and some pagan nations".[1023]</ref>

The biblical term *shoah* ,(שואה) meaning "destruction", became the standard Hebrew term for the murder of the European Jews, first used in a pamphlet in 1940, *Sho'at Yehudei Polin* ("Sho'ah of Polish Jews"), published by the United Aid Committee for the Jews in Poland. In October 1941 the magazine *The American Hebrew* used the phrase "before the Holocaust", apparently to refer to the situation in Europe,[1024] and in May 1943 *The New York Times*, discussing the Bermuda Conference, referred to the "hundreds of thousands of European Jews still surviving the Nazi Holocaust".[1025] The Library of Congress created a new category, "Holocaust, Jewish (1939–1945)" in 1968;[1026] the term was popularized in the United States by the NBC miniseries *Holocaust* (1978), about a fictional family of German Jews.[1027] As non-Jewish groups began to count themselves as victims of the Holocaust too, many Jews chose to use the terms *Shoah* or *Churban* instead.[1024,1028]</ref> The Nazis used the phrase "Final Solution to the Jewish Question" (*die Endlösung der Judenfrage*).[1029]

Definition

Most Holocaust historians define the Holocaust as the German state policy, enacted between 1941 and 1945, to exterminate the European Jews.[1030]

Martin Gilbert (*The Holocaust: The Jewish Tragedy*, 1985): "the systematic attempt to destroy all European Jewry—an attempt now known as the Holocaust".[1031]

Peter Hayes (*How Was It Possible? A Holocaust Reader*, 2015): "The Holocaust, the Nazi attempt to eradicate the Jews of Europe, has come to be regarded as the emblematic event of Twentieth Century ... Hitler's ideology depicted the Jews as uniquely dangerous to Germany and therefore uniquely destined to disappear completely from the Reich and all territories subordinate to it. The threat posted by supposedly corrupting but generally powerless Sinti and Roma was far less, and therefore addressed inconsistently in the Nazi realm. Gay men were defined as a problem only if they were German or having sex with Germans or having sex with Germans and considered 'curable' in most cases. ... Germany's murderous intent toward the handicapped inhabitants of European mental institutions ... was more comprehensive ... but here, too, implementation was uneven and life-saving exceptions permitted, especially in Western Europe. Not only were some Slavs—Slovaks, Croats, Bulgarians, some Ukrainians—allotted a favored place in Hitler's New Order, but the fate of most of the other Slavs the Nazis derided as sub-humans ... consisted of enslavement and gradual attrition, not the prompt massacre meted out to the Jews after 1941."[1032]

Raul Hilberg (*The Destruction of the European Jews*, 2003): "With the passage of time, the response of the entire Jewish community to its massive loss became a pervasive problem. At the beginning there was little memorialization. No special observances were held, no major monuments were erected, and not many efforts were made to record the meaning of Auschwitz and Treblinka. Little by little, some documents were gathered and books were written, and after about two decades the annihilation of the Jews was given a name: Holocaust."[1033] Ronnie S. Landau (*The Nazi Holocaust: Its History and Meaning*, 1992): "The Holocaust involved the deliberate, systematic murder of approximately 6 million Jews in Nazi-dominated Europe between 1941 and 1945."[1016]

Michael Marrus (*Perspectives on the Holocaust*, 2015): "The Holocaust, the murder of close to six million Jews by the Nazis during the Second World War ...".[1034]

Timothy D. Snyder (*Bloodlands: Europe Between Hitler and Stalin*, 2010): "In this book the term *Holocaust* signifies the final version of the Final Solution, the German policy to eliminate the Jews of Europe by murdering them. Although Hitler certainly wished to remove the Jews from Europe in a Final Solution earlier, the Holocaust on this definition begins in summer 1941, with the shooting of Jewish women and children in the occupied Soviet Union. The term *Holocaust* is sometimes used in two other ways: to mean all German killing policies during the war, or to mean all oppression of Jews by the Nazi regime. In this book, *Holocaust* means the murder of the Jews in Europe, as carried out by the Germans by guns and gas between 1941 and 1945."[1035]

United States Holocaust Memorial Museum (2017): "The Holocaust was the systematic, bureaucratic, state-sponsored persecution and murder of six million Jews by the Nazi regime and its collaborators."</ref> In *Teaching the Holocaust* (2015), Michael Gray offers three definitions:

- the persecution and murder of Jews by the Nazis and their collaborators between 1933 and 1945; this definition views the events of *Kristallnacht* in Germany in 1938 as an early phase of the Holocaust;[1010]
- the systematic mass murder of Jews by the Nazis and their collaborators between 1941 and 1945; this acknowledges the shift in German policy in 1941 toward the extermination of the Jewish people;[1010]
- the persecution and murder of several groups by the Nazis and their collaborators between 1933 and 1945; this includes all the Nazis' victims.[1010]

The third definition fails, Gray writes, to acknowledge that only the Jewish people were singled out for annihilation.[1010] Donald Niewyk and Francis Nicosia, in *The Columbia Guide to the Holocaust* (2000), favour a definition that focuses on the Jews, Roma, and Aktion T4 victims: "The Holocaust—that is, Nazi genocide—was the systematic, state-sponsored murder of entire groups determined by heredity. This applied to Jews, Gypsies, and the handicapped."[1011]

Distinctive features

Genocidal state

<templatestyles src="Multiple_image/styles.css" />

German-occupied Europe, 1942

Concentration and extermination camps, and ghettos. Territories of the Axis Powers are in olive green.

The logistics of the mass murder turned the country into what Michael Berenbaum called "a genocidal state". Bureaucrats identified who was a Jew, confiscated property, and scheduled trains that deported Jews. Companies fired Jews and later employed them as slave labour. Universities dismissed Jewish faculty and students. German pharmaceutical companies tested drugs on camp prisoners; other companies built the crematoria.[1036] As prisoners entered the death camps, they were ordered to surrender all personal property, which was catalogued and tagged before being sent to Germany for reuse or recycling.[1037] Through a concealed account, the German National Bank helped launder valuables stolen from the victims.[1038]

The industrialization and scale of the murder was unprecedented. The killings were systematically conducted in virtually all areas of occupied Europe—more than 20 occupied countries.[1039] Close to three million Jews in occupied Poland and between 700,000 and 2.5 million Jews in the Soviet Union were killed. Hundreds of thousands more died in the rest of Europe.[1040] Victims were transported in sealed freight trains from all over Europe to extermination camps equipped with gas chambers.[1041] The stationary facilities grew out of Nazi experiments with poison gas during the Aktion T4 mass murder ("euthanasia") programme against the disabled and mentally ill, which began in 1939. The Germans set up six extermination camps in Poland: Auschwitz-Birkenau (established October 1941); Majdanek (October 1941); Chełmno (December 1941); and in 1942 the three Operation Reinhard camps at Belzec, Sobibor, and Treblinka.[1042]

Eberhard Jäckel writes that it was the first time a state had thrown its power behind the idea that an entire people should be wiped out.[1043] </ref> Anyone with three or four Jewish grandparents was to be exterminated,[1044] and complex rules were devised to deal with *Mischlinge* (half and quarter Jews, or "mixed breeds").[1045] Without the help of local collaborators, the Germans would not have been able to extend the Holocaust across most of Europe;[1046] over 200,000 people are estimated to have been Holocaust perpetrators.[1047] Saul Friedländer writes: "Not one social group, not one religious community, not one scholarly institution or professional association in Germany and throughout Europe declared its solidarity with the Jews." Some Christian churches declared, according to Friedländer, "that converted Jews should be regarded as part of the flock, but even then only up to a point".[1048] Discussions at the Wannsee Conference in January 1942 make it clear that the German "final solution of the Jewish question" was intended eventually to include Britain and all the neutral states in Europe, including Ireland, Switzerland, Turkey, Sweden, Portugal, and Spain.[1049]

Figure 143: *The 23 defendants during the Doctors' trial, Nuremberg, 9 December 1946 – 20 August 1947*

Medical experiments

Medical experiments conducted on camp inmates by the SS were another distinctive feature.[1050] At least 7,000 prisoners were subjected to experiments; most died as a result, during the experiments or later.[1051] Twenty-three senior physicians and other medical personnel were charged at Nuremberg, after the war, with crimes against humanity. They included the head of the German Red Cross, tenured professors, clinic directors, and biomedical researchers.[1052] Experiments took place at Auschwitz, Buchenwald, Dachau, Natzweiler, Neuengamme, Ravensbrück, Sachsenhausen, and elsewhere. Some dealt with sterilization of men and women, the treatment of war wounds, ways to counteract chemical weapons, research into new vaccines and drugs, and the survival of harsh conditions.[1051]

The most notorious physician was Josef Mengele, an SS officer who became the Auschwitz camp doctor on 30 May 1943.[1053] Interested in genetics[1053] and keen to experiment on twins, he would pick out subjects from the new arrivals during "selection" on the ramp, shouting "*Zwillinge heraus!*" (twins step forward!).[1054] They would be measured, killed, and dissected. One of Mengele's assistants said in 1946 that he was told to send organs of interest to the directors of the "Anthropological Institute in Berlin-Dahlem". This is thought to refer to Mengele's academic supervisor, Otmar von Verschuer, director from October 1942 of the Kaiser Wilhelm Institute of Anthropology, Human Heredity, and Eugenics in Berlin-Dahlem.[1055,1054,1056,1057]</ref> Mengele's experiments included placing subjects in pressure chambers, testing drugs on them, freezing them, attempting to change their eye color by injecting chemicals into children's eyes, and amputations and other surgeries.[1058]

Origins

Antisemitism and the völkisch movement

Throughout the Middle Ages in Europe, Jews were subjected to antisemitism based on Christian theology, which blamed them for killing Jesus. Even after the Reformation, Catholicism and Lutheranism continued to persecute Jews, accusing them of blood libels and subjecting them to pogroms and expulsions.[1059,1060] The second half of the 19th century saw the emergence in the German empire and Austria-Hungary of the *völkisch* movement, which was developed by such thinkers as Houston Stewart Chamberlain and Paul de Lagarde. The movement embraced a pseudo-scientific racism that viewed Jews as a race whose members were locked in mortal combat with the Aryan race for world domination.[1061] These ideas became commonplace throughout Germany,[1062] with the professional classes adopting an ideology that did not see humans as racial equals with equal hereditary value.[1063] Although the *völkisch* parties had support in elections at first, by 1914 they were no longer influential. This did not mean that antisemitism had disappeared; instead it was incorporated into the platforms of several mainstream political parties.[1062]

Germany after World War I, Hitler's world view

The political situation in Germany and elsewhere in Europe after World War I (1914–1918) contributed to the rise of virulent antisemitism. Many Germans did not accept that their country had been defeated, which gave birth to the stab-in-the-back myth. This insinuated that it was disloyal politicians, chiefly Jews and communists, who had orchestrated Germany's surrender. Inflaming the anti-Jewish sentiment was the apparent over-representation of Jews in the leadership of communist revolutionary governments in Europe, such as Ernst Toller, head of a short-lived revolutionary government in Bavaria. This perception contributed to the canard of Jewish Bolshevism.

The economic strains of the Great Depression led some in the German medical establishment to advocate murder (euphemistically called "euthanasia") of the "incurable" mentally and physically disabled as a cost-saving measure to free up funds for the curable.[1064] By the time the National Socialist German

Workers' Party, or Nazi Party,[1065] </ref> came to power in 1933, there was already a tendency to seek to save the racially "valuable", while ridding society of the racially "undesirable".[1066] The party had originated in 1920[1067] as an offshoot of the *völkisch* movement, and it adopted that movement's antisemitism.[1068] Early antisemites in the party included Dietrich Eckart, publisher of the *Völkischer Beobachter*, the party's newspaper, and Alfred Rosenberg, who wrote antisemitic articles for it in the 1920s. Rosenberg's vision of a secretive Jewish conspiracy ruling the world would influence Hitler's views of Jews by making them the driving force behind communism.[1069] The origin and first expression of Hitler's antisemitism remain a matter of debate.[1070] Central to his world view was the idea of expansion and *lebensraum* (living space) for Germany. Open about his hatred of Jews, he subscribed to the common antisemitic stereotypes.[1071] From the early 1920s onwards, he compared the Jews to germs and said they should be dealt with in the same way. He viewed Marxism as a Jewish doctrine, said he was fighting against "Jewish Marxism", and believed that Jews had created communism as part of a conspiracy to destroy Germany.[1072]

Rise of Nazi Germany

Dictatorship and repression (1933–1939)

With the establishment of the Third Reich in 1933, German leaders proclaimed the rebirth of the *Volksgemeinschaft* ("people's community").[1073] Nazi policies divided the population into two groups: the *Volksgenossen* ("national comrades") who belonged to the *Volksgemeinschaft*, and the *Gemeinschaftsfremde* ("community aliens") who did not. Enemies were divided into three groups: the "racial" or "blood" enemies, such as the Jews and Roma; political opponents of Nazism, such as Marxists, liberals, Christians, and the "reactionaries" viewed as wayward "national comrades"; and moral opponents, such as gay men, the "work-shy", and habitual criminals. The latter two groups were to be sent to concentration camps for "re-education", with the aim of eventual absorption into the *Volksgemeinschaft*. "Racial" enemies could never belong to the *Volksgemeinschaft*; they were to be removed from society.[1074]

Before and after the March 1933 *Reichstag* elections, the Nazis intensified their campaign of violence against opponents.[1075] They set up concentration camps for extrajudicial imprisonment.[1076] One of the first, at Dachau, opened on 9 March 1933.[1077] Initially the camp contained mostly Communists and Social Democrats.[1078] Other early prisons were consolidated by mid-1934 into purpose-built camps outside the cities, run exclusively by the SS.[1079] The

Figure 144: *Nazi boycott of Jewish businesses: SA troopers urge a boycott outside the Nathan Israel Department Store, Berlin, 1 April 1933. All signs read: "Germans! Defend yourselves! Don't buy from Jews."*

initial purpose of the camps was to serve as a deterrent by terrorizing Germans who did not conform.[1080]

Throughout the 1930s, the legal, economic, and social rights of Jews were steadily restricted.[1081] On 1 April 1933, there was a boycott of Jewish businesses.[1082] On 7 April 1933, the Law for the Restoration of the Professional Civil Service was passed, which excluded Jews and other "non-Aryans" from the civil service.[1083] Jews were disbarred from practising law, being editors or proprietors of newspapers, or joining the Journalists' Association. Jews were not allowed to own farms.[1084] In Silesia, in March 1933, a group of men entered the courthouse and beat up Jewish lawyers; Friedländer writes that, in Dresden, Jewish lawyers and judges were dragged out of courtrooms during trials.[1085] Jewish students were restricted by quotas from attending schools and universities.[1083] Jewish businesses were targeted for closure or "Aryanization", the forcible sale to Germans; of the approximately 50,000 Jewish-owned businesses in Germany in 1933, about 7,000 were still Jewish-owned in April 1939. Works by Jewish composers,[1086] authors, and artists were excluded from publications, performances, and exhibitions.[1087] Jewish doctors were dismissed or urged to resign. The *Deutsches Ärzteblatt* (a medical journal) reported on 6 April 1933: "Germans are to be treated by Germans only."[1088]

Figure 145: *The poster reads: "60,000 RM is what this person with hereditary illness costs the community in his lifetime. Fellow citizen, that is your money too. Read Neues Volk, the monthly magazine of the Office of Racial Policy of the NSDAP."*

Sterilization Law, *Aktion T4*

The Nazis used the phrase *Lebensunwertes Leben* (life unworthy of life) in reference to the disabled and mentally ill.[1089] On 14 July 1933, the Law for the Prevention of Hereditarily Diseased Offspring (*Gesetz zur Verhütung erbkranken Nachwuchses*), the Sterilization Law, was passed, allowing for compulsory sterilization.[1090,1091] The *New York Times* reported on 21 December that year: "400,000 Germans to be sterilized".[1092] There were 84,525 applications from doctors in the first year. The courts reached a decision in 64,499 of those cases; 56,244 were in favor of sterilization.[1093] Estimates for the number of involuntary sterilizations during the whole of the Third Reich range from 300,000 to 400,000.[1094]

In October 1939 Hitler signed a "euthanasia decree" backdated to 1 September 1939 that authorized *Reichsleiter* Philipp Bouhler, the chief of Hitler's Chancellery, and Karl Brandt, Hitler's personal physician, to carry out a program of involuntary "euthanasia"; after the war this program was named *Aktion T4*.[1095]

It was named after Tiergartenstraße 4, the address of a villa in the Berlin borough of Tiergarten, where the various organizations involved were headquartered.[1096] T4 was mainly directed at adults, but the "euthanasia" of children was also carried out.[1097] Between 1939 and 1941, 80,000 to 100,000 mentally ill adults in institutions were killed, as were 5,000 children and 1,000 Jews, also in institutions. In addition there were specialized killing centres, where the deaths were estimated at 20,000, according to Georg Renno, the deputy director of Schloss Hartheim, one of the "euthanasia" centers, or 400,000, according to Frank Zeireis, the commandant of the Mauthausen concentration camp.[1098] Overall, the number of mentally and physically handicapped murdered was about 150,000.[1099]

Although not ordered to take part, psychiatrists and many psychiatric institutions were involved in the planning and carrying out of *Aktion T4* at every stage.[1100] After protests from the German Catholic and Protestant churches, Hitler ordered the cancellation of the T4 program in August 1941,[1101] although the disabled and mentally ill continued to be killed until the end of the war.[1099] The medical community regularly received bodies and body parts for research. Eberhard Karl University received 1,077 bodies from executions between 1933 and 1945. The neuroscientist Julius Hallervorden received 697 brains from one hospital between 1940 and 1944: "I accepted these brains of course. Where they came from and how they came to me was really none of my business."[1102]

Nuremberg Laws, Jewish emigration

On 15 September 1935, the Reichstag passed the Reich Citizenship Law and the Law for the Protection of German Blood and German Honor, known as the Nuremberg Laws. The former said that only those of "German or kindred blood" could be citizens. Anyone with three or more Jewish grandparents was classified as a Jew. The second law said: "Marriages between Jews and subjects of the state of German or related blood are forbidden." Sexual relationships between them were also criminalized; Jews were not allowed to employ German women under the age of 45 in their homes.[1103] The laws referred to Jews but applied equally to the Roma and black Germans.[1104]

Nazi racial policy aimed at forcing Jews to emigrate.[1105] Fifty thousand German Jews had left Germany by the end of 1934,[1106] and by the end of 1938, approximately half the German Jewish population had left the country.[1105] Among the prominent Jews who left was the conductor Bruno Walter, who fled after being told that the hall of the Berlin Philharmonic would be burned down if he conducted a concert there.[1107] Albert Einstein, who was abroad when Hitler came to power, never returned to Germany. He was expelled from the Kaiser Wilhelm Society and the Prussian Academy of Sciences, and

Figure 146: *Jewish refugees being marched away by British police at Croydon airport in March 1939. They were put on a flight to Warsaw.*

his citizenship was revoked.[1108] Other Jewish scientists, including Gustav Hertz, lost their teaching positions and left the country.[1109] In March 1938 Germany annexed Austria. Austrian Nazis broke into Jewish shops, stole from Jewish homes and businesses, and forced Jews to perform humiliating acts such as scrubbing the streets or cleaning toilets.[1110] Jewish businesses were "Aryanized", and all the legal restrictions on Jews in Germany were imposed.[1111] In August, Adolf Eichmann was put in charge of the Central Agency for Jewish Emigration. About 100,000 Austrian Jews had left the country by May 1939, including Sigmund Freud and his family.[1112]

The Évian Conference was held in July 1938 by 32 countries as an attempt to help the increased refugees from Germany, but aside from establishing the largely ineffectual Intergovernmental Committee on Refugees, little was accomplished and most countries participating did not increase the number of refugees they would accept.[1113]

Figure 147: *The synagogue in Siegen burning, 10 November 1938.*

Kristallnacht

On 7 November 1938, Herschel Grynszpan, a Polish Jew, shot the German diplomat Ernst vom Rath in the German Embassy in Paris, in retaliation for the expulsion of his parents and siblings from Germany.[1114,1115] </ref> When vom Rath died on 9 November, the government used his death as a pretext to instigate a pogrom against the Jews throughout the Third Reich. The government claimed it was spontaneous, but in fact it had been ordered and planned by Hitler and Goebbels, although with no clear goals, according to David Cesarani; the result, he writes, was "murder, rape, looting, destruction of property, and terror on an unprecedented scale".[1116,1117]

Known as *Kristallnacht* (or "Night of Broken Glass"), the attacks were partly carried out by the SS and SA,[1118] but ordinary Germans joined in; in some areas the violence began before the SS or SA arrived.[1119] Over 7,500 Jewish shops (out of 9,000) were looted and attacked, and over 1,000 synagogues damaged or destroyed. Groups of Jews were forced by the crowd to watch their synagogues burn; in Bensheim they were forced to dance around it and in Laupheim to kneel before it.[1120] At least 90 Jews died. The damage was estimated at 39 million Reichmarks.[1121] Cesarani writes that "[t]he extent of the desolation stunned the population and rocked the regime."[1116] Thirty-thousand Jews were sent to the Dachau, Buchenwald and Sachsenhausen concentration camps.[1122] Many were released within weeks; by early 1939, 2,000 remained in the camps.[1123] German Jewry was held collectively responsible for restitution of the damage; they also had to pay an "atonement tax" of over a billion Reichmarks. Insurance payments for damage to their property were confiscated by the government. A decree on 12 November 1938 barred Jews from most of the remaining occupations they had been allowed to hold.[1124] *Kristallnacht* marked the end of any sort of public Jewish activity and culture, and Jews stepped up their efforts to leave the country.[1125]

Territorial solution and resettlement

Before World War II, Germany considered mass deportation from Europe of German, and later European, Jewry.[1126] Among the areas considered for possible resettlement were British Palestine[1127] and French Madagascar.[1128] After the war began, German leaders considered deporting Europe's Jews to Siberia.[1129] Palestine was the only location to which any German relocation plan produced results, via the Haavara Agreement between the Zionist Federation of Germany and the German government.[1130] This resulted in the transfer of about 60,000 German Jews and $100 million from Germany to Palestine, but it ended with the outbreak of World War II.[1131] In May 1940 Madagascar became the focus of new deportation efforts[1128] because it had unfavorable living conditions that would hasten deaths.[1132] Several German leaders had discussed the idea in 1938, and Adolf Eichmann's office was ordered to carry out resettlement planning, but no evidence of planning exists until after the fall of France in June 1940.[1133] But the inability to defeat Britain prevented the movement of Jews across the seas,[1134] and the end of the Madagascar Plan was announced on 10 February 1942.[1135]

World War II

German-occupied Poland

When Germany invaded Poland in September 1939, it gained control of about 2 million Jews in the occupied territory. The rest of Poland was occupied by the Soviet Union, which had control of the rest of Poland's pre-war population of 3.3–3.5 million Jews.[1136] German plans for Poland included expelling gentile Poles from large areas, confining Jews, and settling Germans on the emptied lands. To help the process along, Reinhard Heydrich, head of the Reich Security Main Office, ordered that the "leadership class" in Poland be killed and the Jews expelled from the Polish areas annexed by Nazi Germany.[1137]

The Germans initiated a policy of sending Jews from all territories they had recently annexed (Austria, Czechoslovakia, and western Poland) to the central section of Poland, which they called the General Government. There the Jews

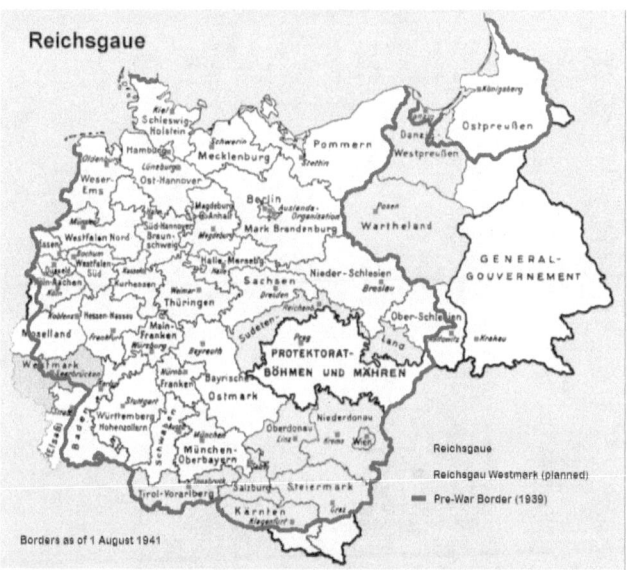

Figure 148: *Nazi Germany before Operation Barbarossa of 1941, including occupied Poland and the General Government territory*

were concentrated in ghettos in major cities,[1138] chosen for their railway lines to facilitate later deportation.[1139] Food supplies were restricted, public hygiene was difficult, and the inhabitants were often subjected to forced labour.[1140] In the labour camps and ghettos at least half a million Jews died of starvation, disease, and poor living conditions.[1141] Jeremy Black writes that the ghettos were not intended, in 1939, as a step towards the extermination of the Jews. Instead, they were viewed as part of a policy of creating a territorial reservation to contain them.[1142,1143,1144] Adolf Eichmann was assigned to remove Jews from Germany, Austria, and the Protectorate of Bohemia and Moravia to the reservation.[1145] Although the idea was to remove 80,000 Jews, Eichmann had managed to send only 4,700 by March 1940, and the plan was abandoned in April.[1146] By mid-October the idea of a Jewish reservation had been revived by Heinrich Himmler, because of the influx of Germanic settlers into the Warthegau.[1147] Resettlement continued until January 1941 under Odilo Globocnik,[1148] and included both Jews and Poles.[1149] By that time 95,000 Jews were already concentrated in the area,[1150] but the plan to deport up to 600,000 additional Jews to the Lublin reservation failed for logistical and political reasons.[1151]</ref>

Figure 149: *German passport stamped with a "J"; this passport was used to escape Europe in 1940*

Other occupied countries

Germany invaded Norway in April 1940. The country was completely occupied by June.[1152] There were about 1,800 Jews in Norway, persecuted by the Norwegian Nazis. In late 1940, the Jews were banned from some occupations, and in 1941 all Jews had to register their property with the government.[1153] Also in 1940, Germany invaded Denmark.[1152] The country was overrun so quickly that there was no chance of organizing resistance. Consequently, the Danish government stayed in power and the Germans found it easier to work through it. Because of this, few measures were taken against the Danish Jews before 1942.[1154]

The Germans invaded the Netherlands, Luxembourg, Belgium, and France in May 1940. In the Netherlands, the Germans installed Arthur Seyss-Inquart as *Reichskommissar*, who quickly began to persecute the approximately 140,000 Dutch Jews. Jews were forced out of their jobs and had to register with the government. Non-Jewish Dutch citizens protested these measures and in February 1941 staged a strike that was quickly crushed.[1155] After Belgium's surrender at the end of May 1940, it was ruled by a German military governor, Alexander von Falkenhausen, who enacted anti-Jewish measures against the approximately 90,000 Jews in Belgium, many of whom were refugees from Germany or Eastern Europe.[1156] France had approximately 300,000 Jews, divided between the German-occupied northern part of France, and the unoccupied collaborationist southern areas under the Vichy regime. The occupied regions were under the control of a military governor, and there, anti-Jewish measures were not enacted as quickly as they were in the Vichy-controlled areas.[1157] In July 1940, the Jews in the parts of Alsace-Lorraine that had been annexed to Germany were expelled into Vichy France.[1158]

Yugoslavia and Greece were invaded in April 1941, and both countries surrendered before the end of the month. Germany and Italy divided Greece into occupation zones but did not eliminate it as a country. Yugoslavia was dismembered, with regions in the north being annexed by Germany, and regions along the coast made part of Italy. The rest of the country was divided into a puppet state of Croatia, which was nominally an ally of Germany, and Serbia, which was governed by a combination of military and police administrators. There were approximately 80,000 Jews in Yugoslavia when it was invaded. The ruling party in Croatia, the Ustashe, not only killed Jews but murdered and expelled Orthodox Christian Serbs and Muslims.[1159] One difference between the Germans and the Croatians was the fact that the Ustashe allowed its Jewish and Serbian victims to convert to Catholicism so they could escape death. Serbia was declared free of Jews in August 1942.[1160]

Germany's allies

Italy introduced some antisemitic measures, but there was less antisemitism there than in Germany, and Italian-occupied countries were generally safer for Jews than German-occupied territories. In some areas, the Italian authorities even tried to protect Jews, such as in the Croatian areas of the Balkans. But while Italian forces in Russia were not as vicious towards Jews as the Germans, they did not try to stop German atrocities either. There were no deportations of Italian Jews to Germany while Italy remained an ally.[1161] Several forced labor camps for Jews were established in Italian-controlled Libya. Almost 2,600 Libyan Jews were sent to camps, where 562 died.

Vichy France's government implemented anti-Jewish measures in French Algeria and the two French Protectorates of Tunisia and Morocco.[1162] Tunisia had 85,000 Jews when the Germans and Italians arrived in November 1942. An estimated 5,000 Jews were subjected to forced labor. Finland was pressured in 1942 to hand over its 150–200 non-Finnish Jews to Germany. After opposition from the government and public, eight non-Finnish Jews were deported in late 1942; only one survived the war.[1163] Japan had little antisemitism in its society and did not persecute Jews in most of the territories it controlled. Jews in Shanghai were confined, but despite German pressure they were not killed.[1164]

Figure 150: *Bodies being pulled out of a death train carrying Romanian Jews from the Iaşi pogrom*

Romania implemented anti-Jewish measures in May and June 1940 as part of its efforts towards an alliance with Germany. Jews were forced from government service, pogroms were carried out, and by March 1941 all Jews had lost their jobs and had their property confiscated.[1165] After Romania joined the invasion of the Soviet Union in June 1941, at least 13,266 Jews were killed in the Iaşi pogrom,[1166] and Romanian troops carried out massacres in Romanian-controlled territory, including the Odessa massacre of 20,000 Jews in Odessa in late 1941. Romania also set up concentration camps under its control in Transnistria, where 154,000–170,000 Jews were deported from 1941 to 1943.[1165]

Anti-Jewish measures were introduced in Slovakia, which would later deport its Jews to German concentration and extermination camps.[1167] Bulgaria introduced anti-Jewish measures in 1940 and 1941, including the requirement to wear a yellow star, the banning of mixed marriages, and the loss of property. Bulgaria annexed Thrace and Macedonia, and in February 1943 agreed to deport 20,000 Jews to Treblinka. All 11,000 Jews from the annexed territories were sent to their deaths, and plans were made to deport additional 6,000–8,000 Bulgarian Jews from Sofia to meet the quota.[1168] When the plans became public, the Orthodox Church and many Bulgarians protested, and King Boris III canceled the deportation of Jews native to Bulgaria.[1169] Instead, they

Figure 151: *The Todesstiege ("stairs of death") at the granite quarry in Mauthausen concentration camp in Austria (opened 1938); inmates were forced to carry heavy rocks up the stairs.*[1173]

were expelled to the interior, pending further decision.[1168] Although Hungary expelled Jews who were not citizens from its newly annexed lands in 1941, it did not deport most of its Jews[1170] until the German invasion of Hungary in March 1944. Between 15 May and 9 July 1944, 440,000 Hungarian Jews were deported to Auschwitz.[1171] In Budapest, nearly 80,000 Jews were killed by the Hungarian Arrow Cross battalions in late 1944.[1172]

Concentration and labor camps

The Third Reich first used concentration camps as places of unlawful incarceration of political opponents and other "enemies of the state". Large numbers of Jews were not sent there until after *Kristallnacht* in November 1938.[1174] Although death rates were high, the camps were not designed as killing centers.[1175] After war broke out in 1939, new camps were established, some outside Germany in occupied Europe. In January 1945, the SS reports had over 700,000 prisoners in their control, of which close to half had died by the end of May 1945 according to most historians. Most wartime prisoners of the camps were not Germans but belonged to countries under German occupation.[1176] It is estimated that the Germans established over 42,000 detention sites throughout Europe, including ghettos, concentration camps, prisoner-of-war camps, labour camps, and extermination camps.

After 1942, the economic functions of the camps, previously secondary to their penal and terror functions, came to the fore. Forced labour of camp prisoners became commonplace and companies utilized their cheap labour.[1174] The guards became much more brutal, and the death rate increased as the guards not only beat and starved prisoners, but killed them more frequently.[1176] Extermination through labour was a policy—camp inmates would literally be worked to death, or to physical exhaustion, at which point they would be gassed or shot.[1177] The Germans estimated the average prisoner's lifespan in a concentration camp at three months, due to lack of food and clothing, constant epidemics, and frequent punishments for the most minor transgressions.[1178] The shifts were long and often involved exposure to dangerous materials.[1179]

Prisoner transportation between camps was often carried out in freight cars with the prisoners packed very tightly. Long delays would take place, with the prisoners confined in the cars on sidings for days.[1180] In mid-1942 labor camps began requiring newly arrived prisoners to be placed in quarantine for four weeks.[1181] Some camps tattooed prisoners with an identification number on arrival, but not all did.[1182] Prisoners wore colored triangles on their uniforms, with the color of the triangle denoting the reason for their incarceration. Red signified a political prisoner, Jehovah's Witnesses had purple triangles, "asocials" and criminals wore black or green. Badges were pink for gay men and yellow for Jews.[1183] Jews had a second yellow triangle that was worn with their original triangle, with the two forming a six-pointed star.[1184,1185]

Ghettos

Main ghettos: Białystok, Budapest, Kraków, Kovno, Łódź, Lvov, Riga, Vilna, Warsaw.

After invading Poland, the Germans established ghettos in the incorporated territories and General Government to confine Jews.[1138] The ghettos were formed and closed off from the outside world at different times and for different reasons.[1186,1187] For example, the Łódź ghetto was closed in April 1940,[1138] to force the Jews inside to give up money and valuables;[1188] the Warsaw ghetto was closed for health considerations (for the people outside, not inside, the ghetto),[1189] but this did not happen until November 1940;[1138] and the Kraków ghetto was not established until March 1941.[1190] The Warsaw Ghetto contained 380,000 people[1138] and was the largest ghetto in Poland; the Łódź Ghetto was the second largest,[1191] holding between 160,000[1192] to

Figure 152: *Polish Jews captured by Germans during the Warsaw Ghetto Uprising, May 1943*

223,000.[1193] Because of the long drawn-out process of establishing ghettos, it is unlikely that they were originally considered part of a systematic attempt to eliminate Jews completely.[1194]

The Germans required each ghetto to be run by a *Judenrat*, or Jewish council.[1195] Councils were responsible for a ghetto's day-to-day operations, including distributing food, water, heat, medical care, and shelter. The Germans also required councils to confiscate property, organize forced labor, and, finally, facilitate deportations to extermination camps.[1196] The councils' basic strategy was one of trying to minimize losses, by cooperating with German authorities, bribing officials, and petitioning for better conditions or clemency.[1197]

Eventually, the Germans ordered the councils to compile lists of names of deportees to be sent for "resettlement".[1198] Although most ghetto councils complied with these orders,[1199] many councils tried to send the least useful workers or those unable to work.[1200] Leaders who refused these orders were shot. Some individuals or even complete councils committed suicide rather than cooperate with the deportations.[1201] Others, like Chaim Rumkowski, who became the "dedicated autocrat" of Łódź,[1202] argued that their responsibility was to save the Jews who could be saved and that therefore others had to be sacrificed.[1203] The councils' actions in facilitating Germany's persecution and

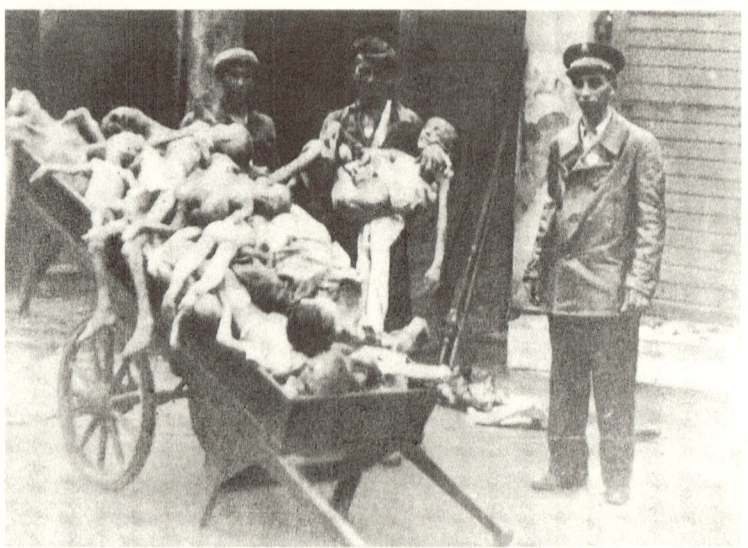

Figure 153: *Bodies of children in the Warsaw Ghetto*

murder of ghetto inhabitants was important to the Germans.[1204] When cooperation crumbled, as happened in the Warsaw ghetto after the Jewish Combat Organisation displaced the council's authority, the Germans lost control.[1205]

Ghettos were intended to be temporary until the Jews were deported to other locations, which never happened. Instead, the inhabitants were sent to extermination camps. The ghettos were, in effect, immensely crowded prisons serving as instruments of "slow, passive murder."[1206] Though the Warsaw Ghetto contained 30% of Warsaw's population, it occupied only 2.5% of the city's area, averaging over 9 people per room.[1207] Between 1940 and 1942, starvation and disease, especially typhoid, killed many in the ghettos.[1208] Over 43,000 Warsaw ghetto residents, or one in ten of the total population, died in 1941; in Theresienstadt, more than half the residents died in 1942.[1206]

Himmler ordered the closing of ghettos in Poland in mid-July 1942, with most inhabitants going to extermination camps. Those Jews needed for war production would be confined at concentration camps.[1209] The deportations from the Warsaw Ghetto began on 22 July; over the almost two months of the *Aktion*, until 12 September, the Warsaw ghetto went from approximately 350,000 inhabitants to about 65,000. Those deported were transported in freight trains to the Treblinka extermination camp.[1210] Similar deportations happened in other ghettos, with many ghettos totally emptied.[1211]

The Holocaust

Figure 154: *Jewish woman chased by men and youth armed with clubs during the Lviv pogroms, July 1941, then occupied Poland, now Ukraine*

The first ghetto uprisings occurred in mid-1942 in small community ghettos.[1212] Although there were armed resistance attempts in both the larger and smaller ghettos in 1943, in every case they failed against the overwhelming German military force, and the remaining Jews were either killed or deported to the death camps.[1213]

Pogroms

A number of deadly pogroms occurred during the Holocaust.[1214] The Germans encouraged some, and others were spontaneous.[1215] Some, such as the Iași pogrom, were in lands controlled by Germany's allies.[1216] In the series of Lviv pogroms committed in occupied Poland,[1217] other scholars are less sure.[1218] </ref> some 6,000 Polish Jews were murdered in the streets in July 1941, on top of 3,000 arrests and mass shootings by *Einsatzgruppe C*.[1218] During the Jedwabne pogrom of July 1941, in the presence of the German officers, several hundred Jews were murdered by some local Poles, with some being burned alive in a barn.[1219,1220] </ref>

Figure 155: *German police shooting women and children from the Mizocz Ghetto, 14 October 1942*

Death squads

Germany invaded the Soviet Union in June 1941.[1221] German propaganda portrayed the war against the Soviet Union as both an ideological war between German National Socialism and Jewish Bolshevism and a racial war between the Germans and the Jewish, Romani and Slavic *Untermenschen* ("subhumans").[1222]

Local populations in some occupied Soviet territories actively participated in the killings of Jews and others. Besides participating in killings and pogroms, they helped identify Jews for persecution and rounded up Jews for German actions.[1223] German involvement ranged from active instigation and involvement to more generalized guidance.[1224] In Lithuania, Latvia, and western Ukraine locals were deeply involved in the murder of Jews from the beginning of the German occupation. Some of these Latvian and Lithuanian units also participated in the murder of Jews in Belarus. In the south, Ukrainians killed about 24,000 Jews and some went to Poland to serve as concentration and death-camp guards.[1223] Military units from some countries allied to Germany also killed Jews. Romanian units were given orders to exterminate and wipe out Jews in areas they controlled.[1225] Ustaše militia in Croatia persecuted and murdered Jews, among others.[1160] Many of the killings were carried out in public, a change from previous practice.[1226]

The mass killings of Jews in the occupied Soviet territories were assigned to four SS formations called *Einsatzgruppen* ("task groups"), which were under

The Holocaust

Figure 156: *The mass murder of 2,749 Jews on the beach near Liepāja, Latvia, 15–17 December 1941*

Heydrich's overall command. Similar formations had been used to a limited extent in Poland in 1939, but the ones operating in the Soviet territories were much larger.[1227] The *Einsatzgruppen*'s commanders were ordinary citizens: the great majority were professionals and most were intellectuals.[1228] By the winter of 1941–1942, the four *Einsatzgruppen* and their helpers had killed almost 500,000 people.[1229]

The largest massacre of Jews by the mobile killing squads in the Soviet Union was at a ravine called Babi Yar outside Kiev,[1230] where 33,771 Jews were killed in a single operation on 29–30 September 1941.[1231,1232] </ref> A mixture of SS and Security Police, assisted by Ukrainian police, carried out the killings.[1233] Although they did not actively participate in the killings, men of the German 6th Army helped round up the Jews of Kiev and transport them to be shot.[1234] By the end of the war, around two million are thought to have been victims of the *Einsatzgruppen* and their helpers in the local population and the German Army. Of those, about 1.3 million were Jews and up to a quarter of a million Roma.[1235]

Figure 157: *Copy of the Wannsee Conference minutes; this page lists the number of Jews in every European country.*

Gas vans

As the mass shootings continued in Russia, the Germans began to search for new methods of mass murder. This was driven by a need to have a more efficient method than simply shooting millions of victims. Himmler also feared that the mass shootings were causing psychological problems in the SS. His concerns were shared by his subordinates in the field.[1236] In December 1939 and January 1940, another method besides shooting was tried. Experimental gas vans equipped with gas cylinders and a sealed compartment were used to kill the disabled and mentally-ill in occupied Poland.[1237] Similar vans, but using the exhaust fumes rather than bottled gas, were introduced to the Chełmno extermination camp in December 1941,[1238] and some were used in the occupied Soviet Union, for example in smaller clearing actions in the Minsk ghetto.[1239] They also were used for murder in Yugoslavia.[1240]

Final Solution

Wannsee Conference

SS-*Obergruppenführer* Reinhard Heydrich, head of the Reich Main Security Office (*Reichssicherheitshauptamt* or RSHA), convened what became known as the Wannsee Conference on 20 January 1942 at a villa, am Grossen Wannsee No. 56/58, in Berlin's Wannsee suburb.[1241,1242] The meeting had been scheduled for 9 December 1941, and invitations had been sent on 29 November, but it had been postponed.[1243] Christian Gerlach argues that Hitler announced his decision to annihilate the Jews on or around 12 December 1941, probably on 12 December during a speech to Nazi Party leaders. This was one day after he declared war on the United States and five days after the attack on Pearl Harbour by Japan. Joseph Goebbels, the Reich Minister of Propaganda, noted of Hitler's speech: "He warned the Jews that if they were to cause another world war, it would lead to their destruction. ... Now the world war has come. The destruction of the Jews must be its necessary consequence."[1244,1245]</ref>

The 15 men present at Wannsee included Adolf Eichmann (head of Jewish affairs for the RSHA and the man who organized the deportation of Jews), Heinrich Müller (head of the Gestapo), and other party leaders and department heads.[1246] Thirty copies of the minutes were made. Copy no. 16 was found by American prosecutors in March 1947 in a German Foreign Office folder.[1247] Written by Eichmann and stamped "Top Secret", the minutes were written in "euphemistic language" on Heydrich's instructions, according to Eichmann's later testimony.[1248] The conference had several purposes. Discussing plans for a "final solution to the Jewish question" (*"Endlösung der Judenfrage"*), and a "final solution to the Jewish question in Europe" (*"Endlösung der europäischen Judenfrage"*), it was intended to share information and responsibility, coordinate efforts and policies (*"Parallelisierung der Linienführung"*), and ensure that authority rested with Heydrich. There was also discussion about whether to include the German *Mischlinge* (half-Jews).[1249] Heydrich told the meeting: "Another possible solution of the problem has now taken the place of emigration, i.e. the evacuation of the Jews to the East, provided that the Fuehrer gives the appropriate approval in advance." He continued:

Under proper guidance, in the course of the final solution the Jews are to be allocated for appropriate labor in the East. Able-bodied Jews, separated according to sex, will be taken in large work columns to these areas for work on roads, in the course of which action doubtless a large portion will be eliminated by natural causes.

The possible final remnant will, since it will undoubtedly consist of the most resistant portion, have to be treated accordingly because it is the product of natural selection and would, if released, act as the seed of a new Jewish revival (see the experience of history.) In the course of the practical execution of the final solution, Europe will be combed through from west to east. Germany proper, including the Protectorate of Bohemia and Moravia, will have to be handled first due to the housing problem and

Figure 158: *Entrance to Auschwitz II-Birkenau, an extermination camp*

additional social and political necessities. The evacuated Jews will first be sent, group by group, to so-called transit ghettos, from which they will be transported to the East.

These evacuations were regarded as provisional or "temporary solutions" ("*Ausweichmöglichkeiten*").[1250,1251]

Translation, Avalon Project: "These actions are, however, only to be considered provisional, but practical experience is already being collected which is of the greatest importance in relation to the future final solution of the Jewish question."</ref> The final solution would encompass the 11 million Jews living not only in territories controlled by Germany, but elsewhere in Europe and adjacent territories, such as Britain, Ireland, Switzerland, Turkey, Sweden, Portugal, Spain, and Hungary, "dependent on military developments".[1250] There was little doubt what the final solution was, writes Peter Longerich: "the Jews were to be annihilated by a combination of forced labour and mass murder".[1252]

Extermination camps, gas chambers

Killing on a mass scale using gas chambers or gas vans was the main difference between the extermination and concentration camps.[1253] From the end of 1941, the Germans built six extermination camps in occupied Poland:

Figure 159: *One of the Sonderkommando photographs shows women being sent to the gas chamber, Auschwitz-Birkenau, August 1944.*

Auschwitz II-Birkenau, Majdanek, Chełmno, and the three Operation Reinhard camps at Bełzec, Sobibor, and Treblinka II. Maly Trostenets, a concentration camp in the Reichskommissariat Ostland, became a killing centre in 1942. Gerlach writes that over three million Jews were murdered in 1942, the year that "marked the peak" of the mass murder of Jews.[1254] At least 1.4 million of these were in the General Government area of Poland.[1255]

Using gas vans, Chełmno had its roots in the Aktion T4 euthanasia program.[1256] Majdanek began as a POW camp, but in August 1942 it had gas chambers installed.[1257] A few other camps are occasionally named as extermination camps, but there is no scholarly agreement on the additional camps; commonly mentioned are Mauthausen in Austria[1258] and Stutthof.[1259] There may also have been plans for camps at Mogilev and Lvov.[1260]

Victims usually arrived at the camps by train.[1261] Almost all arrivals at the Operation Reinhard camps of Treblinka, Sobibór, and Bełżec were sent directly to the gas chambers,[1262] with individuals occasionally selected to replace dead workers.[1263,1264] At Auschwitz, the camp officials usually subjected individuals to selections.[1265] About 25%[1266] of the new arrivals deemed fit to work were sent to slave labour.[1265] Those selected for death at all camps were told to undress and hand their valuables to camp workers.[1267] They were then herded naked into the gas chambers. To prevent panic, they were told the gas chambers were showers or delousing chambers.[1268] The procedure at Chełmno was slightly different. Victims there were placed in a mobile gas van and asphyxiated, while being driven to prepared burial pits in the nearby forests. There the corpses were unloaded and buried.[1269]

Death figures in extermination camps

Camp name	Killed	Ref
Auschwitz II	1,100,000	
Bełżec	600,000	
Chełmno	320,000	
Majdanek	78,000	
Maly Trostinets	65,000	
Sobibór	250,000	
Treblinka	870,000	

At Auschwitz, after the chambers were filled, the doors were shut and pellets of Zyklon-B were dropped into the chambers through vents,[1270] releasing toxic prussic acid, or hydrogen cyanide.[1271] Those inside died within 20 minutes; the speed of death depended on how close the inmate was standing to a gas vent, according to the commandant Rudolf Höss, who estimated that about one-third of the victims died immediately.[1272] Johann Kremer, an SS doctor who oversaw the gassings, testified that: "Shouting and screaming of the victims could be heard through the opening and it was clear that they fought for their lives."[1273] The gas was then pumped out, the bodies were removed, gold fillings in their teeth were extracted, and women's hair was cut.[1274] The work was done by the *Sonderkommando*, work groups of mostly Jewish prisoners.[1275] At Auschwitz, the bodies were at first buried in deep pits and covered with lime, but between September and November 1942, on the orders of Himmler, they were dug up and burned. In early 1943, new gas chambers and crematoria were built to accommodate the numbers.[1276]

At the three Reinhard camps the victims were killed by the exhaust fumes of stationary diesel engines.[1262] Gold fillings were pulled from the corpses before burial, but the women's hair was cut before death. At Treblinka, to calm the victims, the arrival platform was made to look like a train station, complete with fake clock.[1277] Majdanek used Zyklon-B gas in its gas chambers.[1278] In contrast to Auschwitz, the three Reinhard camps were quite small.[1279] Most of the victims at these camps were buried in pits at first. Sobibór and Bełżec began exhuming and burning bodies in late 1942, to hide the evidence, as did Treblinka in March 1943. The bodies were burned in open fireplaces and the remaining bones crushed into powder.[1280]

Figure 160: *Captured members of the Jewish resistance, Warsaw Ghetto, 1943.*

Jewish resistance

Peter Longerich observes that in ghettos in Poland by the end of 1942, "there was practically no resistance".[1281] Raul Hilberg accounts for this compliant attitude by evoking the history of Jewish persecution: as had been the case before, appealing to their oppressors and complying with orders might avoid inflaming the situation until the onslaught abated.[1282,1283] Hilberg cautions against overstating the extent of Jewish resistance, arguing that by turning isolated incidents into resistance, it elevates the slaughter of innocent people into some kind of battle, and diminishes the heroism of those who took active measures to resist the Germans. He asserts that the blending of the passive majority with the active few is a way of deflecting questions about the survival strategies and leadership of the Jewish community.[1284]</ref> Timothy Snyder notes that it was only during the three months after the deportations of July–September 1942 that agreement on the need for armed resistance was reached.[1285,1286]

Several groups were formed, such as the Jewish Fighting Organization in the Warsaw Ghetto and the United Partisan Organization in Vilna.[1287] Over 100 revolts and uprisings occurred in at least 19 ghettos and elsewhere in Eastern Europe. The best known is the Warsaw Ghetto Uprising of 1943, when around 1,000 poorly armed Jewish fighters held the SS at bay for four weeks.[1288,1289] while the Germans reported 16 dead.[1290] The Germans reported around 14,000 Jews killed[1291] </ref> and between 53,000[1292] and 56,000 deported.[1290]</ref> During a revolt in Treblinka on 2 August 1943, inmates killed five or six guards and set fire to camp buildings; several managed to escape.[1293,1294]

In the Białystok Ghetto on 16 August 1943, Jewish insurgents revolted when the Germans announced mass deportations. The fighting lasted five days.[1295] On 14 October 1943, Jews in Sobibór, including Jewish-Soviet prisoners of war, attempted an escape,[1296] killing 11 SS officers and a couple of Ukrainian camp guards.[1297] Around 300 prisoners escaped, but 100 were recaptured and shot.[1298,1296] In October 1944, Jewish members of the *Sonderkommando* at Auschwitz attacked their guards and blew up Crematorium IV with explosives that had been smuggled in. Three German guards were killed, one of whom was stuffed into an oven. The *Sonderkommando* attempted a mass breakout, but all were killed.[1299]

Estimates of Jewish participation in partisan units throughout Europe range from 20,000 to 100,000.[1300] In the occupied Polish and Soviet territories, thousands of Jews fled into the swamps or forests and joined the partisans,[1301] although the partisan movements did not always welcome them.[1302] An estimated 20,000 to 30,000 joined the Soviet partisan movement.[1303] One of the famous Jewish groups was the Bielski partisans in Belarus, led by the Bielski brothers.[1301] Jews also joined Polish forces, including the Home Army. According to Timothy Snyder, "more Jews fought in the Warsaw Uprising of August 1944 than in the Warsaw Ghetto Uprising of April 1943".[1304,1305] Zionist Jews formed the *Armee Juive* (Jewish Army), which participated in armed resistance under a Zionist flag, smuggled Jews out of the country,[1306] and participated in the liberation of Paris and other cities.[1307] As many as 1.5 million Jewish soldiers fought in the Allied armies, including 500,000 in the Red Army, 550,000 in the U.S. Army, 100,000 in the Polish army, and 30,000 in the British army. About 200,000 Jewish soldiers serving in the Red Army died in the war, either in combat or after capture. The Jewish Brigade, a unit of 5,000 Jewish volunteers from the British Mandate of Palestine, fought in the British Army.[1308]</ref>

Flow of information about the mass murder

The Polish government-in-exile in London learned about the extermination camps from the Polish leadership in Warsaw, who from 1940 "received a continual flow of information about Auschwitz", according to historian Michael Fleming.[1309] On 6 January 1942, the Soviet Minister of Foreign Affairs, Viacheslav Molotov, sent out diplomatic notes about German atrocities. The notes were based on reports about bodies surfacing from poorly covered graves in pits and quarries, as well as mass graves found in areas the Red Army had liberated, and on witness reports from German-occupied areas.[1310]

Escapes from the camps were few, but not unknown.[1311] In February 1942, Szlama Ber Winer escaped from the Chełmno concentration camp in Poland, and passed detailed information about it to the Oneg Shabbat group in the Warsaw Ghetto. His report, known by his pseudonym as the Grojanowski Report, had reached London by June 1942. Also in 1942, Jan Karski reported to the Allies on the plight of Jews after being smuggled into the Warsaw Ghetto twice.[1312,1313,1314] but other sources state that he smuggled himself into a transit camp where Jews were sent on to Bełżec.[1313] </ref> On 27 April 1942, Viacheslav Molotov sent out another note about atrocities.[1310] In late July or early August 1942, Polish leaders learned about the mass killings taking place inside Auschwitz. The Polish Interior Ministry prepared a report, *Sprawozdanie 6/42*,[1309,1315] which said at the end:

> *There are different methods of execution. People are shot by firing squads, killed by an "air hammer", and poisoned by gas in special gas chambers. Prisoners condemned to death by the Gestapo are murdered by the first two methods. The third method, the gas chamber, is employed for those who are ill or incapable of work and those who have been brought in transports especially for the purpose/Soviet prisoners of war, and, recently Jews.*[1309]

The report was sent to Polish officials in London by courier and had reached them by 12 November 1942, when it was translated into English and added to another report, "Report on Conditions in Poland". Dated 27 November, this was forwarded to the Polish Embassy in the United States.[1316] On 10 December 1942, the Polish Foreign Affairs Minister, Edward Raczyński, addressed the fledgling United Nations on the killings; the address was distributed with the title *The Mass Extermination of Jews in German Occupied Poland*. He told them about the use of poison gas; about Treblinka, Bełżec and Sobibor; that the Polish underground had referred to them as extermination camps; and that tens of thousands of Jews had been killed in Bełżec in March and April 1942.[1317] One in three Jews in Poland were already dead, he estimated, from a population of 3,130,000.[1318] Raczyński's address was covered by the *New York Times* and *The Times* of London. Winston Churchill received it, and Anthony Eden presented it to the British cabinet. On 17 December 1942, 11 Allies issued the Joint Declaration by Members of the United Nations condemning the "bestial policy of cold-blooded extermination".[1319]

The British and American governments were reluctant to publicize the intelligence they had received. Although the information was felt to be correct, the stories were so extreme that they feared the public would discount them

Figure 161: *Photos from The Black Book of Poland, published in London in 1942 by the Polish government-in-exile*

as exaggerations and that the credibility of both governments would be undermined.[1320] In addition, the US government hesitated to emphasize the atrocities for fear of turning the war into a war about the Jews. Antisemitism and isolationism were common in the US before its entry into the war, and the government wanted to avoid too great a focus on Jewish suffering to keep isolationism from gaining ground.[1321]

Climax, Holocaust in Hungary

<templatestyles src="Multiple_image/styles.css" />

Jews from Carpathian Ruthenia arriving at Auschwitz, May 1944

Jews from Hungary arriving at Auschwitz, summer 1944

Most of the Jewish ghettos of General Government were liquidated in 1942–1943, and their populations shipped to the camps for extermination.[1322,1323,1324] </ref> About 42,000 Jews were shot during the Operation Harvest Festival on 3–4 November 1943. At the same time, rail shipments arrived regularly from western and southern Europe at the extermination camps.[1325] Few Jews were shipped from the occupied Soviet territories to the camps: the killing of Jews in this zone was mostly left in the hands of the SS, aided by locally recruited auxiliaries.[1326,1327] </ref>

Shipments of Jews to the camps had priority over anything but the army's needs on the German railways, and continued even in the face of the increasingly dire military situation at the end of 1942.[1328] Army leaders and economic managers complained about this diversion of resources and the killing of skilled Jewish workers,[1329] but Nazi leaders rated ideological imperatives above economic considerations.[1330]

By 1943 it was evident to the armed forces leadership that Germany was losing the war.[1331] The mass murder continued nevertheless, reaching a "frenetic" pace in 1944.[1332] Auschwitz was gassing up to 6,000 Jews a day by spring that year. On 19 March 1944, Hitler ordered the military occupation of Hungary and dispatched Eichmann to Budapest to supervise the deportation of the country's Jews.[1333] From 22 March, Jews were required to wear the yellow star; forbidden from owning cars, bicycles, radios or telephones; then forced into ghettos.[1334] From 15 May to 9 July, 440,000 Jews were deported from Hungary to Auschwitz-Birkenau, almost all to the gas chambers.[1335,1336,1337]</ref> A month before the deportations began, Eichmann offered to exchange one million Jews for 10,000 trucks and other goods from the Allies, the so-called "blood for goods" proposal.[1338] *The Times* called it "a new level of fantasy and self-deception".[1339]

Figure 162: *Bodies of 2,000–3,000 prisoners evacuated from Buchenwald in 40 sealed boxcars on 7 April 1945, arriving at Dachau on 28 April*

Death marches

By mid-1944 those Jewish communities within easy reach of the Nazi regime had been largely exterminated,[1340] in proportions ranging from about 25 percent in France[1341] to more than 90 percent in Poland.[1342] On 5 May Himmler claimed in a speech that "the Jewish question has in general been solved in Germany and in the countries occupied by Germany".[1343]

As the Soviet armed forces advanced, the camps in eastern Poland were closed down, with surviving inmates shipped to camps closer to Germany.[1344] Efforts were made to conceal evidence of what had happened. The gas chambers were dismantled, the crematoria dynamited, and the mass graves dug up and the corpses cremated.[1345] Local commanders continued to kill Jews, and to shuttle them from camp to camp by forced "death marches". Already sick after months or years of violence and starvation, some were marched to train stations and transported for days at a time without food or shelter in open freight cars, then forced to march again at the other end to the new camp. Others were marched the entire distance to the new camp. Those who lagged behind or fell were shot. Around 250,000 Jews died during these marches.[1346]

Figure 163: *Fritz Klein, the camp doctor, standing in a mass grave at Bergen-Belsen after the camp's liberation by the British 11th Armoured Division, April 1945*

Liberation

The first major camp to be encountered by Allied troops, Majdanek, was discovered by the advancing Soviets on 25 July 1944.[1347] Treblinka, Sobibór, and Bełżec were never liberated, but were destroyed by the Germans in 1943.[1348] Auschwitz was liberated, also by the Soviets, on 27 January 1945;[1349] Buchenwald by the Americans on 11 April;[1350] Bergen-Belsen by the British on 15 April;[1351] Dachau by the Americans on 29 April;[1352] Ravensbrück by the Soviets on 30 April;[1353] and Mauthausen by the Americans on 5 May.[1354] The Red Cross took control of Theresienstadt on 4 May, days before the Soviets arrived.[1355,1356]

The Soviets found 7,600 inmates in Auschwitz.[1357] Some 60,000 prisoners were discovered at Bergen-Belsen by the British 11th Armoured Division; 13,000 corpses lay unburied, and another 10,000 people died from typhus or malnutrition over the following weeks. The BBC's war correspondent, Richard Dimbleby, described the scenes that greeted him and the British Army at Belsen, in a report so graphic that the BBC declined to broadcast it for four days and did so, on 19 April, only after Dimbleby had threatened to resign:[1358]

<templatestyles src="Template:Quote/styles.css"/>

Here over an acre of ground lay dead and dying people. You could not see which was which. ... The living lay with their heads against the corpses and around them moved the awful, ghostly procession of emaciated, aimless people, with nothing to do and with no hope of life, unable to move out of your way, unable to look at the terrible sights around them ... Babies had been born here, tiny wizened things that could not live. ... A mother, driven mad, screamed at a British sentry to give her milk for her child, and thrust the tiny mite into his arms. ... He opened the bundle and found the baby had been dead for days. This day at Belsen was the most horrible of my life.

—Richard Dimbleby, 15 April 1945[1359]

Victims and death toll

Overview

Victims	Killed	Source
Jews	5.9 million	Hayes[1360]
Soviet POWs	2–3 million	Berenbaum[1361]
Ethnic Poles	1.8–1.9 million	Piotrowski
Roma	90,000–220,000	Berenbaum[1362]
Disabled	150,000	Niewyk & Nicosia[1099]
Jehovah's Witnesses	1,400–2,500	USHMM Milton[1363]
Gay men	Unknown	USHMM

Most historians define the Holocaust as the German genocide of the European Jews, carried out between 1941 and 1945. Donald Niewyk and Francis Nicosia, writing in *The Columbia Guide to the Holocaust* (2000), favour a definition that focuses on the Jews, Roma and handicapped (Aktion T4 victims), because they were targets of Nazi efforts to destroy entire groups based on heredity.[1011]

The broadest definition of the Holocaust would include ethnic Poles, Soviet citizens, Soviet prisoners of war, gay men, and political opponents, and would raise the death toll to 17 million.[1013] A research project started in 2000, led by Geoffrey Megargee and Martin Dean for the United States Holocaust Memorial Museum, estimated in 2013 that 15–20 million people had died or been imprisoned in the sites they have identified to date.[1364]

Jews

Figures in Peter Hayes (2015), based on Wolfgang Benz, Jean Ancel and Yitzak Arad[1360]

Country (1945)	Death toll of Jews
Albania	591
Austria	65,459
Baltic states	272,000
Belgium	28,518
Bulgaria	11,393
Croatia	32,000
Czechoslovakia	143,000
Denmark	116
France	76,134
Germany	165,000
Greece	59,195
Hungary	502,000
Italy	6,513
Luxembourg	1,200
Netherlands	102,000
Norway	758
Poland	2,100,000
Romania	220,000
Serbia	10,700
Soviet Union	2,100,000
Total	5,896,577

According to the Yad Vashem Holocaust Martyrs' and Heroes' Remembrance Authority in Jerusalem, "[a]ll the serious research" confirms that between five and six million Jews died. Early postwar calculations were 4.2 to 4.5 million from Gerald Reitlinger;[1365] 5.1 million from Raul Hilberg; and 5.95 million from Jacob Lestschinsky.[1366] In 1986 Lucy S. Dawidowicz used the pre-war census figures to estimate 5.934 million.[1367] Yehuda Bauer and Robert Rozett in the *Encyclopedia of the Holocaust* (1990) estimate 5.59–5.86 million.[1368] A 1996 study led by Wolfgang Benz suggested 5.29 to 6.2 million, based on comparing pre- and post-war census records and surviving German documentation on deportations and killings. Martin Gilbert arrived at a minimum of 5.75 million.[1369] The figures include over one million children.[1370]

The Jews killed represented around one third of the world population of Jews,[1371] and about two-thirds of European Jewry, based on an estimate of 9.7 million Jews in Europe at the start of the war.[1372,1368] Much of the uncertainty stems from the lack of a reliable figure for the number of Jews in Europe in 1939, numerous border changes that make avoiding double-counting of victims difficult, lack of accurate records from the perpetrators, and uncertainty about whether deaths occurring months after liberation, but caused by the persecution, should be counted.[1365]

Almost all Jews within areas occupied by the Germans were killed. There were 3,020,000 Jews in the Soviet Union in 1939, and the losses were 1–1.1 million.[1373] Around one million Jews were killed by the *Einsatzgruppen* in the occupied Soviet territories.[1374,1375] Of Poland's 3.3 million Jews, about 90 percent were killed.[1342] Many more died in the ghettos of Poland before they could be deported.[1376] The death camps accounted for half the number of Jews killed; 80–90 percent of death-camp victims are estimated to have been Jews.[1367] At Auschwitz-Birkenau the Jewish death toll was 1.1 million;[1377] Treblinka 870,000–925,000; Bełżec 434,000–600,000; Chełmno 152,000–320,000; Sobibór 170,000–250,000; and Majdanek 79,000.

Roma

Because the Roma are traditionally a private people with a culture based on oral history, less is known about their experience during the Holocaust than that of any other group.[1378] Bauer writes that this can be attributed to the Roma's distrust and suspicion, and to their humiliation because some of the taboos in Romani culture regarding hygiene and sex were violated at Auschwitz.[1379]

The Roma were subject to discrimination under the Nuremberg racial laws.[1380] The Germans saw them as hereditary criminals and "asocials", and this was reflected in their classification in the concentration camps, where they were usually counted among the asocials and given black triangles to wear.[1381] According to Niewyk and Nicosia, at least 130,000 died, out of nearly one million in German-occupied Europe.[1378] The United States Holocaust Memorial Museum calculates at least 220,000. Ian Hancock, who specializes in Romani history and culture, argues for between 500,000 and 1,500,000.[1382] The Roma refer to the genocide as the *Porajmos*.[1383]

The treatment of the Roma was not consistent across German-occupied territories, with those in France and the Low Countries subject to restrictions on movement and some confinement to collection camps. Those in Central and Eastern Europe were sent to concentration camps and murdered by soldiers and execution squads.[1384] Before being sent to the camps, they were herded into ghettos, including several hundred into the Warsaw Ghetto. Further east,

Figure 164: *Roma waiting to be deported from Asperg, Germany, 22 May 1940*

teams of *Einsatzgruppen* tracked down Romani encampments and murdered the inhabitants on the spot, leaving no records of the victims. They were also targeted by allies of the Germans, such as the Ustaše regime in Croatia, where a large number were killed in the Jasenovac concentration camp;[1384] the total killed in Croatia numbered around 28,000.[1385] After the Germans occupied Hungary, 1,000 Roma were deported to Auschwitz.[1386]

In May 1942 the Roma were placed under similar labour and social laws to the Jews. On 16 December 1942 Heinrich Himmler issued a decree that "Gypsy Mischlinge [mixed breeds], Roma Gypsies, and members of the clans of Balkan origins who are not of German blood" should be sent to Auschwitz, unless they had served in the *Wehrmacht*. This was adjusted on 15 November 1943, when Himmler ordered that, in the occupied Soviet areas, "sedentary Gypsies and part-Gypsies are to be treated as citizens of the country. Nomadic Gypsies and part-Gypsies are to be placed on the same level as Jews and placed in concentration camps." Bauer argues that this adjustment reflected Nazi ideology that the Roma, originally an Aryan population, had been "spoiled" by non-Romani blood.[1387]

Figure 165: *Czesława Kwoka, one of many Polish children murdered in Auschwitz by the Nazis*

Slavs

The Nazis considered the Slavs as subhuman, or *Untermenschen*.[1388,1389] In a secret memorandum dated 25 May 1940, Heinrich Himmler stated that it was in German interests to foster divisions between the ethnic groups in the East. He also wanted to restrict non-Germans in the conquered territories to schools that would only teach them how to write their own name, count up to 500, and obey Germans.[1390,1391] Himmler's *Generalplan Ost* (General Plan East), agreed to by Hitler in the summer of 1942,[1392] involved exterminating, expelling, or enslaving all or most Slavs from their lands over a period of 20–30 years to make living space for Germans.[1393] In 1992 Rudolph Rummel estimated the number of Slavs murdered by the Germans to be 10,547,000.[1394]

Ethnic Poles

German planners in November 1939 called for "the complete destruction" of all Poles.[1395] Poland under German occupation was to be cleared of Poles and settled by German colonists.[1396] The Polish political leadership and other leaders were the targets of an organized campaign of murder (Intelligenzaktion and AB-Aktion).[1397] But German planners decided against a genocide of ethnic Poles on the same scale as against Jews, at least in the short term,[1398] and planned to completely Germanize the Polish territories by removing or allowing to die of mistreatment 80-85% of the Polish population.[1399]

Between 1.8 and 1.9 million non-Jewish Polish citizens perished at German hands during the course of the war, about four-fifths of whom were ethnic Poles with the rest ethnic Ukrainians and Belarusians. At least 200,000 of these victims died in concentration camps with around 146,000 killed in Auschwitz. Many others died as a result of general massacres or uprisings

The Holocaust

Figure 166: *Execution of Poles by Einsatzkommando, Leszno, October 1939*

such as the Warsaw Uprising, where between 120,000 and 200,000 civilians were killed.[1400]

During the occupation, the Germans adopted a policy of restricting food rations and medical services as well as the degradation of sanitation and public hygiene.[1401] The death rate rose from a rate of 13 in 1000 before the war to 18 in 1000 during the war.[1402] Around 6 million of the victims of World War II were Polish citizens, both Jewish and non-Jewish,[1403] </ref> and over the course of the war Poland lost 20 percent of its pre-war population.[1404] Over 90 percent of the death toll came through non-military losses, through various deliberate actions by Germany and the Soviet Union.[1400] Polish children were also kidnapped by Germans in order to be "Germanized", with perhaps as many as 200,000 children being stolen from their families for this purpose.[1405]

Soviet citizens and POWs

Soviet civilian populations in the occupied areas were also heavily persecuted outside of events taking place in the frontline warfare of the Eastern Front.[1406] Villages throughout the Soviet Union were destroyed by German troops.[1407] Germans rounded up civilians for forced labour in Germany as well as causing famines by taking foodstuffs.[1408]

In Belarus, Germany imposed a regime that deported some 380,000 people for slave labour and killed hundreds of thousands of civilians. More than 600 villages had their entire populations killed and at least 5,295 Belarusian settlements were destroyed by the Germans. According to Timothy Snyder, of

Figure 167: *Naked Soviet POWs in the Mauthausen concentration camp, date unknown*

"the nine million people who were on the territory of Soviet Belarus in 1941, some 1.6 million were killed by the Germans in actions away from battlefields, including about 700,000 prisoners of war, 500,000 Jews, and 320,000 people counted as partisans (the vast majority of whom were unarmed civilians)".[1409] The United States Holocaust Memorial Museum has estimated that 3.3 million of the 5.7 million Soviet POWs died in German custody. The death rates decreased as the POWs were needed to work as slaves to help the German war effort; by 1943, half a million of them had been deployed as slave labour.[1361]

Political opponents

German communists, socialists and trade unionists were among the earliest opponents of the Nazis, and they were also among the first to be sent to concentration camps.[1410] Before the invasion of the Soviet Union, Hitler issued the Commissar Order, which ordered the execution of all political commissars and Communist Party members captured. *Nacht und Nebel* ("Night and Fog") was a directive of Hitler in December 1941, resulting in the kidnapping and disappearance of political activists throughout the German occupied territories.[1411]

Figure 168: *Pink-triangle memorial in Nollendorfplatz, Berlin*

Gay men

Around 50,000 German gay men were jailed between 1933 and 1945, and 5,000–15,000 are estimated to have been sent to concentration camps. It is not known how many homosexuals died during the Holocaust.[1412] James Steakley writes that what mattered in Germany was criminal intent or character, rather than acts, and the *"gesundes Volksempfinden"* ("healthy sensibility of the people") became the guiding legal principle.[1413]

In 1936 Himmler created the Reich Central Office for the Combating of Homosexuality and Abortion.[1414] The Gestapo raided gay bars, tracked individuals using the address books of those they arrested, used the subscription lists of gay magazines to find others, and encouraged people to report suspected homosexual behavior and to scrutinize the behavior of their neighbors.[1413] Lesbians were left relatively unaffected; the Nazis saw them as "asocials", rather than sexual deviants.

The men convicted between 1933 and 1944 were sent to camps for "rehabilitation", where they were identified by pink triangles.[1413] Hundreds were castrated, sometimes "voluntarily" to avoid criminal sentences.[1415] Steakley writes that the full extent of gay suffering was slow to emerge after the war. Many victims kept their stories to themselves because homosexuality remained criminalized in postwar Germany.[1413]

Jehovah's Witnesses

Because they refused to pledge allegiance to the Nazi party or to serve in the military, Jehovah's Witnesses were sent to concentration camps where they were given the option of renouncing their faith and submitting to the state's authority.[1416] They were marked out by purple triangles. The United States Holocaust Memorial Museum estimates between 2,700 and 3,300 were sent to concentration camps, but Sybil Milton states the number in the camps was 10,000.[1363] Between 1,400 and 2,500 died while in the camps.[1363] Historian Detlef Garbe writes that "no other religious movement resisted the pressure to conform to National Socialism with comparable unanimity and steadfastness."[1417]

Persons of color

The number of Afro-Germans in Germany when the Nazis came to power is variously estimated at 5,000–25,000.[1418] It is not clear whether these figures included Asians. Although blacks, including prisoners of war, in Germany and German-occupied Europe were subjected to incarceration, sterilization, murder, and other abuse, there was no programme to kill them all as there was for the Jews.

Motivation

Motivation of perpetrators

In his 1965 essay "Command and Compliance", which originated in his work as an expert witness for the prosecution at the Frankfurt Auschwitz Trials, the German historian Hans Buchheim wrote there was no coercion to murder Jews and others, and all who committed such actions did so out of free will. Buchheim wrote that chances to avoid executing criminal orders "were both more numerous and more real than those concerned are generally prepared to admit", and that he found no evidence that SS men who refused to carry out criminal orders were sent to concentration camps or executed.[1419] Moreover, SS rules prohibited acts of gratuitous sadism, as Himmler wished for his men to remain "decent"; acts of sadism were carried out on the initiative of those who were either especially cruel or wished to prove themselves ardent National Socialists. Finally, he argued that those of a non-criminal bent who committed crimes did so because they wished to conform to the values of the group they had joined and were afraid of being branded "weak" by their colleagues if they refused.[1420]

Figure 169: *Holocaust perpetrators Heinrich Himmler, Reinhard Heydrich and Karl Wolff at the Berghof, from silent color film shot by Eva Braun, May 1939*

Similarly, in *Ordinary Men* (1992), Christopher Browning examined the deeds of German Reserve Police Battalion 101 of the *Ordnungspolizei* ("order police"), used to commit massacres and round-ups of Jews, as well as mass deportations to the death camps. The members of the battalion were middle-aged men of working-class background from Hamburg, who were too old for regular military duty. They were given no special training. During the murder of 1,500 Jews from Józefów, their commander allowed them to opt out of direct participation. Fewer than 12 men out of a battalion of 500 did so. Influenced by the Milgram experiment on obedience, Browning argued that the men killed out of peer pressure, not bloodlust.[1421]

German public

In his 1983 book, *Popular Opinion and Political Dissent in the Third Reich*, Ian Kershaw examined the *Alltagsgeschichte* (history of everyday life) in Bavaria during the Nazi period. The most common viewpoint of Bavarians was indifference towards what was happening to the Jews, he wrote. Most Bavarians were vaguely aware of the genocide, but they were vastly more concerned about the war. Kershaw argued that "the road to Auschwitz was built by hate, but paved with indifference".[1422,1423]

Figure 170: *Defendants in the dock at the Nuremberg trials. The main target of the prosecution was Hermann Göring (at the left edge on the first row of benches), considered to be the most important surviving official in the Third Reich after Hitler's death. Göring later committed suicide.*

Kershaw's assessment faced criticism from historians Otto Dov Kulka and Michael Kater. Kater maintained that Kershaw had downplayed the extent of popular antisemitism. Although most of the "spontaneous" antisemitic actions of Nazi Germany had been staged, Kater argued that these had involved substantial numbers of Germans, and therefore it was wrong to view the extreme antisemitism of the Nazis as coming solely from above.[1424] Kulka argued that "passive complicity" would be a better term than "indifference".[1425]

Focusing on the views of Germans opposed to the Nazi regime, the German historian Christof Dipper, in his essay "*Der Deutsche Widerstand und die Juden*" (1983), argued that the majority of the anti-Nazi national-conservatives were antisemitic. No one in the German resistance supported the Holocaust, but Dipper wrote that the national conservatives did not intend to restore civil rights to the Jews after the planned overthrow of Hitler.[1424]

Aftermath

Trials

The Nuremberg trials were a series of military tribunals, held by the Allied forces after World War II in Nuremberg, Germany, to prosecute prominent members of the political, military, and economic leadership of Nazi Germany. The first of these trials was the 1945–1946 trial of the major war criminals before the International Military Tribunal (IMT).[1426] This tribunal tried 22 political and military leaders of the Third Reich,[1427] except for Adolf Hitler, Heinrich Himmler, and Joseph Goebbels, all of whom had committed suicide several months before.[1426]

The prosecution entered indictments against 24 major war criminals[1428] </ref> and seven organizations—the leadership of the Nazi party, the Reich Cabinet, the Schutzstaffel (SS), Sicherheitsdienst (SD), the Gestapo, the Sturmabteilung (SA) and the "General Staff and High Command". The indictments were for: participation in a common plan or conspiracy for the accomplishment of a crime against peace; planning, initiating and waging wars of aggression and other crimes against peace; war crimes; and crimes against humanity. The tribunal passed judgements ranging from acquittal to death by hanging.[1429] Eleven defendants were executed, including Joachim von Ribbentrop, Wilhelm Keitel, Alfred Rosenberg, and Alfred Jodl. Ribbentrop, the judgement declared, "played an important part in Hitler's 'final solution of the Jewish question'".[1430]

Further trials at Nuremberg took place between 1946 and 1949, which tried a further 185 defendants.[1431] West Germany initially tried few ex-Nazis, but after the 1958 *Einsatzgruppen* trial, the government set up a governmental agency to investigate crimes.[1432] Other trials of Nazis and collaborators took place in Western and Eastern Europe414-428}} In 1960, Israeli Mossad agents kidnapped Adolf Eichmann in Argentina and brought him to Israel to stand trial for war crimes. The trial ended in his conviction in December 1961, and his execution in May 1962. Eichmann's trial and death revived interest in war criminals and the Holocaust in general.[1433]

Reparations

In March 1951, the government of Israel requested $1.5 billion from the Federal Republic of Germany to finance the rehabilitation of 500,000 Jewish survivors, arguing that Germany had stolen $6 billion from the European Jews. Israelis were divided about the idea of taking money from Germany. The Conference on Jewish Material Claims Against Germany (known as the Claims Conference) was opened in New York, and after negotiations, the claim was reduced to $845 million.[1434]

In 1988, West Germany allocated another $125 million for reparations. Companies such as BMW, Deutsche Bank, Ford, Opel, Siemens, and Volkswagen faced lawsuits for their use of forced labour during the war. In response, Germany set up the "Remembrance, Responsibility and Future" Foundation in 2000, which paid €4.45 billion to former slave laborers (up to €7,670 each). In 2013, Germany agreed to provide €772 million to fund nursing care, social services, and medication for 56,000 Holocaust survivors around the world. The French state-owned railway company, the SNCF, agreed in 2014 to pay $60 million to Jewish-American survivors, around $100,000 each, for its role in the transport of 76,000 Jews from France to extermination camps between 1942 and 1944.[1435]

Uniqueness question

In *Is the Holocaust Unique?* (1995), Shimon Samuels described the acrimonious debate in Holocaust scholarship between "specifists" and "universalists". The former fear debasement of the Holocaust by invidious comparisons. The latter consider it immoral to hold the Holocaust as beyond comparison.[1436] Peter Novick argued that it is "deeply offensive" to view the Holocaust as unique: What else can all of this possibly mean except 'your catastrophe, unlike ours, is ordinary' ... "[1437]

Historian Dan Stone wrote in 2010 that the idea of the Holocaust as unique has been overtaken by attempts to place it in the context of early-20th-century Stalinism, ethnic cleansing, war, and the Nazis' plans for "demographic reordering" after the war.[1438] Specifist arguments continue nevertheless to inform the views of many specialists. A 2015 view from a historian of the Third Reich, Richard J. Evans:

<templatestyles src="Template:Quote/styles.css"/>

> *Thus although the Nazi 'Final Solution' was one genocide among many, it had features that made it stand out from all the rest as well. Unlike all the others it was bounded neither by space nor by time. It was launched not against a local or regional obstacle, but at a world-enemy seen as operating on a global scale. It was bound to an even larger plan of racial reordering and reconstruction involving further genocidal killing on an almost unimaginable scale, aimed, however, at clearing the way in a particular region – Eastern Europe – for a further struggle against the Jews and those the Nazis regarded as their puppets. It was set in motion by ideologues who saw world history in racial terms. It was, in part, carried out by industrial methods. These things all make it unique.*
>
> —Richard Evans, The Third Reich in History and Memory[1041]

Sources

Works cited

Amar, Tarik Cyril (2015). *The Paradox of Ukrainian Lviv: A Borderland City between Stalinists, Nazis, and Nationalists*. Ithaca, NY: Cornell University Press. ISBN 1501700839.

Arad, Yitzhak (1987). *Belzec, Sobibor, Treblinka: The Operation Reinhard Death Camps*. Bloomington, IN: Indiana University Press. ISBN 978-0-253-21305-1.

—— (2009). *The Holocaust in the Soviet Union*. Lincoln, NE: University of Nebraska Press. ISBN 978-0-8032-4519-8.

Arad, Yitzhak; Gutman, Yisrael; Margaliot, Abraham, eds. (2014) [1981]. *Documents on the Holocaust: Selected Sources on the Destruction of the Jews of Germany and Austria, Poland, and the Soviet Union*. Pergamon Press/Elsevier. ISBN 978-0-803-25937-9.

Bajohr, Frank; Pohl, Dieter (2008). *Massenmord und schlechtes Gewissen: Die deutsche Bevölkerung die NS-Führung und der Holocaust*. Frankfurt am Main: Fischer Taschenbuch Verlag.

Bauer, Yehuda (1997) [1979]. "Forms of Jewish Resistance". In Niewyk, Donald L. *The Holocaust: Problems and Perspectives of Interpretation*. Boston: Houghton Mifflin. pp. 116–132. ISBN 0-669-41700-9.

—— (1998) [1994]. "Gypsies". In Gutman, Yisrael; Berenbaum, Michael. *Anatomy of the Auschwitz Death Camp*. Bloomington, IN: Indiana University Press. pp. 441–455. ISBN 0-253-20884-X.

—— (2001) [1982]. *A History of the Holocaust* (Revised ed.). New York: Franklin Watts. ISBN 0-531-15576-5.

Bauer, Yehuda (1994). *Jews for Sale?: Nazi-Jewish Negotiations, 1933–1945*. New Haven: Yale University Press. ISBN 9780300059137.

——— (2002). *Rethinking the Holocaust*. New Haven, CT: Yale University Press. ISBN 0-300-09300-4.

Bauer, Yehuda; Rozett, Robert (1990). "Appendix". In Gutman, Israel. *Encyclopedia of the Holocaust*. New York: Macmillan Library Reference. pp. 1797–1802. ISBN 0-02-896090-4.

Baumel, Judith Tydor (2001). "Concentration Camps". In Laqueur, Walter. *The Holocaust Encyclopedia*. New Haven, CT: Yale University Press. pp. 133–135. ISBN 0-300-08432-3.

Bazyler, Michael J. (2005) [2003]. *Holocaust Justice: The Battle for Restitution in America's Courts*. New York and London: New York University Press. ISBN 978-0814729380.

Bell, Martin (2017). *War and the Death of News*. London: Oneworld Publications. ISBN 978-1-7860-7109-5.

Ben-Rafael, Eliezer; Glöckner, Olaf; Sternberg, Yitzhak (2011). *Jews and Jewish Education in Germany Today*. Leiden: Brill. ISBN 978-90-04-25329-2.

Benz, Wolfgang (1996). *Dimension des Völkermords. Die Zahl der jüdischen Opfer des Nationalsozialismus* (in German). Dtv. ISBN 3-423-04690-2.

Berenbaum, Michael (2002). "Foreword". In Braham, Randolph L.; Miller, Scott. *The Nazis' Last Victims: The Holocaust in Hungary*. Detroit: Wayne State University Press. p. 9.

——— (2006). *The World Must Know: The History of the Holocaust as Told in the United States Holocaust Memorial Museum* (2nd ed.). Washington, DC: United States Holocaust Memorial Museum. ISBN 978-0-8018-8358-3.

Bergen, Doris (2016). *War & Genocide: A Concise History of the Holocaust* (Third ed.). Lanham, MD: Rowman & Littlefield. ISBN 978-1-4422-4228-9.<templatestyles src="Module:Citation/CS1/styles.css"></templatestyles>

Berghahn, Volker R. (1999). "Germans and Poles, 1871–1945". In Bullivant, Keith; Giles, Geoffrey J.; Pape, Walter. *Yearbook of European Studies. Germany and Eastern Europe: Cultural Identities and Cultural Differences*[1439]. **13**. Amsterdam and Atlanta, GA: Rodopi. pp. 15–36. ISBN 978-9042006881.<templatestyles src="Module:Citation/CS1/styles.css"></templatestyles>

Biddiss, Michael (2001). "Nuremberg trials". In Dear, Ian; Foot, Richard D. *The Oxford Companion to World War II*. Oxford: Oxford University Press. pp. 643–646. ISBN 0-19-280670-X.<templatestyles src="Module:Citation/CS1/styles.css"></templatestyles>

Black, Jeremy (2016). *The Holocaust: History and Memory*. Bloomington, IN: Indiana University Press. ISBN 978-0-253-02214-1.<templatestyles src="Module:Citation/CS1/styles.css"></templatestyles>

Bloxham, Donald (2009). *The Final Solution: A Genocide*. Oxford, UK: Oxford University Press. ISBN 978-0-19-955034-0.<templatestyles src="Module:Citation/CS1/styles.css"></templatestyles>

Braham, Randolph L. (2011). "Hungary: The Controversial Chapter of the Holocaust". In Braham, Randolph L.; vanden Heuvel, William Jacobus. *The Auschwitz Reports and the Holocaust in Hungary*. Boulder, CO: Social Science Monographs. pp. 29–49.<templatestyles src="Module:Citation/CS1/styles.css"></templatestyles>

Browning, Christopher (2001). "Madagascar Plan". In Laqueur, Walter. *The Holocaust Encyclopedia*. New Haven, CT: Yale University Press. pp. 407–409. ISBN 0-300-08432-3.<templatestyles src="Module:Citation/CS1/styles.css"></templatestyles>

—— (1986). "Nazi Ghettoization Policy in Poland: 1939–41". *Central European History*. **19** (4): 343–368. doi:10.1017/s0008938900011158[1440]. JSTOR 4546081[1441].<templatestyles src="Module:Citation/CS1/styles.css"></templatestyles>

—— (1998) [1992]. *Ordinary Men: Reserve Police Battalion 101 and the Final Solution in Poland*. New York: HarperPerennial. ISBN 0-06-099506-8.<templatestyles src="Module:Citation/CS1/styles.css"></templatestyles>

―― (2004). *The Origins of the Final Solution: The Evolution of Nazi Jewish Policy, September 1939 – March 1942*. Jerusalem: Yad Vashem.

Buchheim, Hans (1968). "Command and Compliance". In Helmut Krausnick; Hans Buchheim; Broszat, Martin; Jacobsen, Hans-Adolf. *The Anatomy of the SS State*. New York: Walker and Company. pp. 303–396.

Burleigh, Michael (2001). *The Third Reich: A New History*. New York: Hill and Wang. ISBN 0-8090-9326-X.

Burleigh, Michael; Wippermann, Wolfgang (1991). *The Racial State: Germany 1933–1945*. Cambridge, UK: Cambridge University Press. ISBN 0-521-39802-9.

Cesarani, David (2004). *Becoming Eichmann: Rethinking the Life, Crimes, and Trial of a 'Desk Murderer'*. [New York]: Da Capo Press. ISBN 978-0-306-81476-1.

―― (2016). *Final Solution: The Fate of the Jews 1933–1949*. New York: St. Martin's Press. ISBN 978-1-250-00083-5.

Chase, Edward T. (1999) [1984]. "Preface". *The Transfer Agreement: The Dramatic Story of the Pact Between the Third Reich and Jewish Palestine*. Cambridge, Massachusetts: Brookline Books. ISBN 978-0914153139.

Conot, Robert (1984). *Justice at Nuremberg*. New York: Carroll & Graf. ISBN 978-0-88184-032-2.

Crowe, David M. (2008). *The Holocaust: Roots, History, and Aftermath*. Boulder, CO: Westview Press. ISBN 978-0-8133-4325-9.

Dawidowicz, Lucy (1986) [1975]. *The War Against the Jews: 1933–1945* (Tenth Anniversary ed.). New York: Bantam. ISBN 0-553-34532-X.

Dwork, Deborah; van Pelt, Robert Jan (2003). *Holocaust: A History*. New York: W. W. Norton. ISBN 0-393-05188-9.

Edelheit, Abraham J. (1994). *History of the Holocaust: A Handbook and Dictionary*[1442]. Westview Press. ISBN 0813322405.

Evans, Richard J. (1989). *In Hitler's Shadow: West German Historians and the Attempt to Escape from the Nazi Past*. New York: Pantheon. ISBN 0-679-72348-X.

―――― (2002). *Lying About Hitler: The Holocaust, History and the David Irving Trial*. New York: Basic Books. ISBN 0-465-02153-0.

―――― (2004) [2003]. *The Coming of the Third Reich*. New York: Penguin. ISBN 1-59420-004-1.

―――― (2005). *The Third Reich in Power*. New York: Penguin. ISBN 1-59420-074-2.

―――― (2008). *The Third Reich at War*. New York: Penguin. ISBN 978-1-59420-206-3.

―――― (2015). *The Third Reich in History and Memory*. London: Abacus. ISBN 978-0-349-14075-9.

Fritzsche, Peter (2009). *Life and Death in the Third Reich*[1443]. Harvard University Press. pp. 38–39. ISBN 0674033744.

Fischel, Jack R. (1998). *The Holocaust*. Westport, CT: Greenwood Press. ISBN 0-313-29879-3.

―――― (2010). *Historical Dictionary of the Holocaust* (Second ed.). Lanham, MD: Scarecrow Press. ISBN 978-0-8108-6774-1.

Fischer, Conan (2002). *The Rise of the Nazis*. New Frontiers in History (Second ed.). Manchester, UK: Manchester University Press. ISBN 0-7190-6067-2.

Fischer, Klaus (1998) [1995]. *Nazi Germany: A New History*. New York: Barnes & Noble. ISBN 0-7607-0736-7.

Fisher, Ronit (2001). "Medical Experimentation". In Laqueur, Walter. *The Holocaust Encyclopedia*. New Haven: Yale University Press. pp. 410–414. ISBN 0-300-08432-3.

Fleming, Michael (Spring 2014a). "Allied Knowledge of Auschwitz: A (Further) Challenge to the 'Elusiveness' Narrative". *Holocaust and Genocide Studies*. **28** (1): 31–57. doi: 10.1093/hgs/dcu014[1444].

Fleming, Michael (2014b). *Auschwitz, the Allies and Censorship of the Holocaust*. Cambridge: Cambridge University Press. ISBN 978-1-1070-6279-5.

Friedlander, Henry (1994). "Step by Step: The Expansion of Murder, 1939–1941". *German Studies Review*. **17** (3): 495–507. doi: 10.2307/1431896[1445]. JSTOR 1431896[1446].

Friedländer, Saul (1997). *Nazi Germany and the Jews: The Years of Persecution 1933–1939*. New York: Harper Collins. ISBN 0-06-019042-6.

——— (2007). *The Years of Extermination: Nazi Germany and the Jews 1939–1945*. New York: Harper Perennial. ISBN 978-0-06-093048-6.

Friling, Tuvia; Ioanid, Radu; Ionesc, Mihail E., eds. (2004). *Final Report, International Commission on the Holocaust in Romania*[1447] (pdf). Iași: Polirom. ISBN 973-681-989-2.

Fritz, Stephen (2011). *Ostkrieg: Hitler's War of Extermination in the East*. Lexington, KY: University Press of Kentucky. ISBN 978-0-8131-3416-1.

Garbe, Detlef (2001). "Social Disinterest, Governmental Disinformation, Renewed Persecution, and Now Manipulation of History?". In Hans Hesse. *Persecution and Resistance of Jehovah's Witnesses During the Nazi-Regime 1933–1945*. Bremen: Edition Temmen. pp. 251–265.

Gellately, Robert (2001). *Backing Hitler: Consent and Coercion in Nazi Germany*. Oxford: Oxford University Press. ISBN 0-19-820560-0.

Gellately, Robert; Stoltzfus, Nathan (2001). *Social Outsiders in Nazi Germany*. Princeton University Press. ISBN 978-0691086842.

Gerlach, Christian (December 1998). "The Wannsee Conference, the fate of German Jews, and Hitler's decision in principle to exterminate all European Jews". *The Journal of Modern History*. **70** (4): 759–812. doi: 10.1086/235167[1448].

—— (2016). *The Extermination of the European Jews*. Cambridge: Cambridge University Press. ISBN 0-521-70689-0.

Gilbert, Martin (2001). "Final Solution". In Dear, Ian; Foot, Richard D. *The Oxford Companion to World War II*. Oxford, UK: Oxford University Press. pp. 285–292. ISBN 0-19-280670-X.

—— (1985). *The Holocaust: A History of the Jews of Europe During the Second World War*. New York: Henry Holt. ISBN 0-8050-0348-7.

Giles, Geoffrey J. (1992). "The Most Unkindest Cut of All: Castration, Homosexuality and Nazi Justice". *Journal of Contemporary History*. **27** (1): 41–61. doi: 10.1177/002200949202700103[1449]. JSTOR 260778[1450].

Gray, Michael (2015). *Teaching the Holocaust: Practical Approaches for Ages 11–18*. Abingdon and New York: Routledge. ISBN 978-1-317-65082-9.

Gutman, Israel (1994). *Resistance: The Warsaw Ghetto Uprising*. Boston, MA: Houghton Mifflin. ISBN 0-395-60199-1.

Hanauske-Abel, Hartmut M. (7 December 1996). "Not a slippery slope or sudden subversion: German medicine and National Socialism in 1933". *BMJ*. **313** (7070): 1453–1463. doi: 10.1136/bmj.313.7070.1453[1451]. JSTOR 29733730[1452].

Hancock, Ian (2004). "Romanies and the Holocaust: A Reevaluation and Overview". In Dan Stone. *The Historiography of the Holocaust*. New York, NY: Palgrave-Macmillan. pp. 383–396.

Harran, Marilyn J. (2000). *The Holocaust Chronicle*. Lincolnwood, IL: Publications International. ISBN 0-7853-2963-3.

Hayes, Peter, ed. (2015). *How Was It Possible?: A Holocaust Reader*. Lincoln, NE: University of Nebraska Press.

Hilberg, Raul (2003). *The Destruction of the European Jews* (3rd ed.). New Haven, CT: Yale University Press.

—— (1980). "The Ghetto as a Form of Government". *Annals of the American Academy of Political and Social Science*. **450**: 98–112. doi: 10.1177/000271628045000109[1453]. JSTOR 1042561[1454].

—— (1993) [1992]. *Perpetrators Victims Bystanders: The Jewish Catastrophe 1933–1945*. New York: HarperPerennial. ISBN 0-06-099507-6.

—— (1996). *The Politics of Memory: The Journey of a Holocaust Historian*. Chicago, IL: Ivan R. Dee. ISBN 1566631165.

Hildebrand, Klaus (1984). *The Third Reich*. Translated by Falla, P. S. London: George Allen & Unwin. ISBN 0-04-943033-5.

Hitchcock, William I. (2008). *The Bitter Road to Freedom: A New History of the Liberation of Europe*. New

York: Free Press. ISBN 978-0-7432-7381-7.

Huttenbach, Henry R. (2016) [1991]. "The Romani Porajmos: The Nazi Genocide of Gypsies in Germany and Eastern Europe". In Crowe, David; Kolsti, John. *The Gypsies of Eastern Europe*. Abingdon and New York: Routledge. pp. 31–50. ISBN 978-1-315-49024-3.

Jones, Adam (2006). *Genocide: A Comprehensive Introduction*. London: Routledge. ISBN 0-415-35384-X.

Kennedy, David M., ed. (2007). *The Library of Congress World War II Companion*. New York: Simon & Schuster. ISBN 978-0-7432-5219-5.

Kershaw, Ian (1998). *Hitler 1889–1936: Hubris*. New York: W. W. Norton. ISBN 978-0-393-32035-0.

——— (2000). *Hitler 1936–1945: Nemesis*. New York: W. W. Norton. ISBN 978-0-393-32252-1.

Kochanski, Halik (2012). *The Eagle Unbowed: Poland and the Poles in the Second World War*. Cambridge, MA: Harvard University Press. ISBN 978-0-674-06814-8.

Kwiet, Konrad (2004). "Forced Labour of German Jews in Nazi Germany". In Cesarani, David. *Holocaust: Concepts in Historical Studies: Volume II: From the Persecution of the Jews to Mass Murder*. London: Routledge. pp. 59–81. ISBN 0-415-27511-3.

Landau, Ronnie S. (2016) [1992]. *The Nazi Holocaust: Its History and Meaning*. London: I.B. Tauris. ISBN 978-1-78076-971-4.

Laqueur, Walter (2001). "Jewish Brigade". In Laqueur, Walter. *The Holocaust Encyclopedia*. New Haven: Yale University Press. p. 351. ISBN 0-300-08432-3.

Lichtblau, Eric (1 March 2013). "The Holocaust Just Got More Shocking"[1455]. *The New York Times*. Retrieved 2 March 2013.

Lifton, Robert J. (2000) [1986]. *The Nazi Doctors: Medical Killing and the Psychology of Genocide* (2000 ed.). New York: Basic Books. ISBN 978-0-465-04905-9.

Löb, Ladislaus (2009). *Rezso Kasztner. The Daring Rescue of Hungarian Jews: A Survivor's Account*. London: Random House/Pimlico.

Longerich, Peter (2010). *Holocaust: The Nazi Persecution and Murder of the Jews*. Oxford, UK: Oxford University Press. ISBN 978-0-19-280436-5.

────── (2012). *Heinrich Himmler*. Oxford, UK: Oxford University Press. ISBN 978-0-19-959232-6.

Lukas, Richard C. (2012). *The Forgotten Holocaust: The Poles under German Occupation 1939–1944* (Third ed.). New York: Hippocrene Books. ISBN 978-0-7818-1302-0.

Lusane, Clarence (2003). *Hitler's Black Victims: The Historical Experience of Afro-Germans, European Blacks, Africans and African Americans in the Nazi Era*. London; New York: Routledge.

Lustigman, Marsha; Lustigman, Michael M. (16 October 1994). "Bibliographic Classification of Documents Dealing with the Subject 'Holocaust'". Alexandria, VA: 5th ASIS SIG/CR Classification Research Workshop: 111–120. doi:10.7152/acro.v5i1.1378[1456] (inactive 2018-05-29).

Maier, Charles S. (1997) [1988]. *The Unmasterable Past: History, Holocaust, and German National Identity* (Reprint ed.). Cambridge, MA: Harvard University Press. ISBN 0-674-92977-2.

Marrus, Michael R. (1987). *The Holocaust in History*. New York: Meridian. ISBN 0-452-00953-7.

——— (2015). "Series Preface". In Marrus, Michael R. *The Nazi Holocaust. Part 1: Perspectives on the Holocaust*. Westport and London: Meckler.<templatestyles src="Module:Citation/CS1/styles.css"></templatestyles>

Matthäus, Jürgen (2004). "Operation Barbarossa and the Onset of the Holocaust, June–December 1941". *The Origins of the Final Solution: The Evolution of Nazi Jewish Policy, September 1939 – March 1942*. Lincoln, NE: University of Nebraska Press. pp. 244–308. ISBN 0-8032-1327-1.<templatestyles src="Module:Citation/CS1/styles.css"></templatestyles>

Mazower, Mark (2008). *Hitler's Empire: Nazi Rule in Occupied Europe*. New York: Penguin. ISBN 978-1-59420-188-2.<templatestyles src="Module:Citation/CS1/styles.css"></templatestyles>

McKale, Donald M. (2002). *Hitler's Shadow War: The Holocaust and World War II*. New York: Cooper Square Press. ISBN 0-8154-1211-8.<templatestyles src="Module:Citation/CS1/styles.css"></templatestyles>

Michman, Dan (2012) [2010]. "Jews". In Hayse, Peter; Roth, John K. *The Oxford Handbook of Holocaust Studies*. Oxford, UK: Oxford University Press. pp. 185–202. ISBN 978-0-19-966882-3.<templatestyles src="Module:Citation/CS1/styles.css"></templatestyles>

Milton, Sybil (2001). "Jehovah's Witnesses". In Laqueur, Walter. *The Holocaust Encyclopedia*. New Haven: Yale University Press. pp. 346–350. ISBN 0-300-08432-3.<templatestyles src="Module:Citation/CS1/styles.css"></templatestyles>

Montague, Patrick (2012). *Chelmno and the Holocaust: A History of Hitler's First Death Camp*. Chapel Hill, NC: University of North Carolina Press. ISBN 978-0-8078-3527-2.<templatestyles src="Module:Citation/CS1/styles.css"></templatestyles>

Müller-Hill, Benno (1999). "The Blood from Auschwitz and the Silence of the Scholars". *History and Philosophy of the Life Sciences*. **21** (3): 331–365. JSTOR 23332180[1457].<templatestyles src="Module:Citation/CS1/styles.css"></templatestyles>

Naimark, Norman M. (2001). *Fires of Hatred: Ethnic Cleansing in Twentieth-Century Europe*. Cambridge, MA: Harvard University Press. ISBN 0-674-00313-6.<templatestyles src="Module:Citation/CS1/styles.css"></templatestyles>

Niewyk, Donald L.; Nicosia, Francis R. (2000). *The Columbia Guide to the Holocaust*. New York: Columbia

University Press. ISBN 0-231-11200-9.

Noakes, Jeremy; Pridham, Geoffrey (1983). *Nazism: A History in Documents and Eyewitness Accounts, 1919–1945*. Schocken Books.

Novick, Peter (2000) [1999]. *The Holocaust in American Life*. New York: Houghton Mifflin. ISBN 0-618-08232-8.

Peukert, Detlev (1987) [1982]. *Inside Nazi Germany: Conformity, Opposition and Racism In Everyday Life*. Translated by Deveson, Richard. New Haven, CT: Yale University Press. ISBN 0-300-04480-1.

——— (1994). "The Genesis of the 'Final Solution' from the Spirit of Science". In Crew, David F. *Nazism and German Society, 1933–1945*. London: Routledge. pp. 274–299. ISBN 0-415-08240-4.

Piotrowski, Tadeusz (1998). *Poland's Holocaust: Ethnic Strife, Collaboration With Occupying Forces and Genocide in the Second Republic, 1918–1947*. Jefferson, NC: McFarland & Company.

Piper, Franciszek (1998b) [1994]. "Gas chambers and Crematoria". In Gutman, Yisrael; Berenbaum, Michael. *Anatomy of the Auschwitz Death Camp*. Bloomington, IN: Indiana University Press. pp. 157–182. ISBN 0-253-20884-X.

——— (1998a) [1994]. "The Number of Victims". In Gutman, Yisrael; Berenbaum, Michael. *Anatomy of the Auschwitz Death Camp*. Bloomington, IN: Indiana University Press. pp. 61–80. ISBN 0-253-20884-X.

Polonsky, Antony (2001). "Polish Jewry". In Laqueur, Walter. *The Holocaust Encyclopedia*. New Haven, CT: Yale University Press. pp. 486–493. ISBN 0-300-08432-3.

Proctor, Robert (1988). *Racial Hygiene: Medicine Under the Nazis.* Cambridge, MA: Harvard University Press. ISBN 0-674-74578-7.

Rees, Laurence (2005). *Auschwitz: A New History.* New York: Public Affairs. ISBN 1-58648-303-X.

Rhodes, Richard (2002). *Masters of Death: The SS-Einsatzgruppen and the Invention of the Holocaust.* New York: Alfred A. Knopf. ISBN 978-0375409004.

Roseman, Mark (2003). *The Villa, The Lake, The Meeting: Wannsee and the Final Solution.* London: Penguin Books. ISBN 9-780-1419-2831-9.

Rozett, Robert (1990). "Railways, German". In Gutman, Israel. *Encyclopedia of the Holocaust.* New York: Macmillan Library Reference. pp. 1221–1223. ISBN 0-02-896090-4.

Rozett, Robert; Spector, Shmuel, eds. (2013). *Encyclopedia of the Holocaust.* Abingdon and New York: Routledge. ISBN 1135969574.

Rummel, R. J. (1992). *Democide: Nazi Genocide and Mass Murder*[1458]. New Brunswick, NJ: Transaction Publications.

Samuels, Simon (2009). "Applying the Lessons of the Holocaust". In Alan S. Rosenbaum. *Is the Holocaust Unique? Perspectives on Comparative Genocide.* Boulder, CO Philadelphia, PA: Westview Press Perseus Books Group distributor. pp. 259–270. ISBN 978-0-8133-4406-5.

Snyder, Louis (1976). *Encyclopedia of the Third Reich.* New York: McGraw Hill. ISBN 0-07-059525-9.

Snyder, Timothy (2010). *Bloodlands: Europe Between Hitler and Stalin.* New York: Basic Books. ISBN 978-0-465-00239-9.

Steakley, James (January–February 1974). "Homosexuals and the Third Reich"[1459]. *The Body Politic* (11).<templatestyles src="Module:Citation/CS1/styles.css"></templatestyles>

Spector, Shmuel (1 January 1990). "Aktion 1005—Effacing the murder of millions". *Holocaust and Genocide Studies.* **5** (2): 157–173. doi: 10.1093/hgs/5.2.157[1460].<templatestyles src="Module:Citation/CS1/styles.css"></templatestyles>

Stone, Dan (2010). *Histories of the Holocaust.* Oxford New York: Oxford University Press. ISBN 978-0-19-956679-2.<templatestyles src="Module:Citation/CS1/styles.css"></templatestyles>

Strous, Rael D. (2007). "Psychiatry during the Nazi Era: Ethical Lessons for the Modern Professional"[1461]. *Annals of General Psychiatry.* **6** (8): 8. doi: 10.1186/1744-859X-6-8[1462]. PMC 1828151[1463]. PMID 17326822[1464].<templatestyles src="Module:Citation/CS1/styles.css"></templatestyles>

Szafranski, Jan (1960). "Poland's Losses in World War II". *1939-1945 War Losses in Poland.* Warsaw: Wydawnictwo Zachodnie. pp. 39–72.<templatestyles src="Module:Citation/CS1/styles.css"></templatestyles>

Tec, Nechama (2001). "Resistance in Eastern Europe". In Laqueur, Walter. *The Holocaust Encyclopedia.* New Haven: Yale University Press. pp. 543–550. ISBN 0-300-08432-3.<templatestyles src="Module:Citation/CS1/styles.css"></templatestyles>

Trunk, Isaiah (1996) [1972]. *Judenrat: The Jewish Councils in Eastern Europe under Nazi Occupation.* Lincoln, NE: University of Nebraska Press. ISBN 0-8032-9428-X.<templatestyles src="Module:Citation/CS1/styles.css"></templatestyles>

United States Holocaust Memorial Museum (1996). *Historical Atlas of the Holocaust.* New York: Macmillan. ISBN 0-02-897451-4.<templatestyles src="Module:Citation/CS1/styles.css"></templatestyles>

Wachsmann, Nikolaus (2015). *Kl: A History of the Nazi Concentration Camps.* New York: Farrar, Straus and Giroux. ISBN 978-0-374-11825-9.<templatestyles src="Module:Citation/CS1/styles.css"></templatestyles>

Weinberg, David (2001). "France". In Laqueur, Walter. *The Holocaust Encyclopedia.* New Haven: Yale University Press. pp. 213–222. ISBN 0-300-08432-3.<templatestyles src="Module:Citation/CS1/styles.css"></templatestyles>

Yahil, Leni (1990). *The Holocaust: The Fate of European Jewry, 1932–1945*. New York: Oxford University Press. ISBN 978-0-19-504523-9.

Zimmerman, Joshua D. (2015). *The Polish Underground and the Jews, 1939–1945*. New York: Cambridge University Press. ISBN 978-1-1070-1426-8.

Zuccotti, Susan (1993). *The Holocaust, the French, and the Jews*. New York: Basic Books. ISBN 0-465-03034-3.

Zweig, Ronald (2001). "Reparations, German". In Laqueur, Walter. *The Holocaust Encyclopedia*. New Haven: Yale University Press. pp. 530–532. ISBN 0-300-08432-3.

Further reading

Books

- Benz, Wolfgang (2001). "Death Toll". In Laqueur, Walter. *The Holocaust Encyclopedia*. New Haven: Yale University Press. pp. 137–145. ISBN 0-300-08432-3.
- Dwork, Deborah; van Pelt, Robert Jan (2008). *Auschwitz: 1270 to the Present* (Revised and expanded ed.). New York: Norton. ISBN 978-0-393-32291-0.
- Fleming, Gerald (1994) [1984]. *Hitler and the Final Solution*. Berkeley & Los Angeles, CA: University of California Press. ISBN 0-520-06022-9.
- Keren, Nili (2001). "Children". In Laqueur, Walter. *The Holocaust Encyclopedia*. New Haven, CT: Yale University Press. ISBN 0-300-08432-3.
- Kershaw, Ian (2008). *Hitler, the Germans, and the Final Solution*. New Haven, CT: Yale University Press. ISBN 978-0-300-15127-5.

External links

- Global Directory of Holocaust Museums[1465].
- H-Holocaust[1466], H-Net discussion list for librarians, scholars and advanced students.
- Online documents available from the Dwight D. Eisenhower Presidential Library[1467].
- The Wiener Library for the Study of the Holocaust & Genocide[1468].
- "Common Questions about the Holocaust"[1469], United States Holocaust Memorial Museum
- "Wannsee Protocol, January 20, 1942"[1470], Avalon Project.
- Stills from Soviet documentary "The Atrocities committed by German Fascists in the USSR" ((1)[1471]; (2)[1472]; (3)[1473])
- Nazi Concentration and Prison Camps (1945)[1474], Nuremberg Trials Documentary]
- The Holocaust Chronicle[1475]
- Holocaust Education & Archive Research Team[1476]
- "Human laboratory animals"[1477]. *Life* magazine, 22(8), 24 February 1947, pp. 81–84.

Aliyah Bet

Part of a series on
Aliyah

Jewish immigration to the Land of Israel
Concepts
<ul><li>Promised Land</li><li>Gathering of Israel</li><li>Diaspora<ul><li>Negation</li></ul></li><li>Homeland for the Jewish people</li><li>Zionism</li><li>Jewish question</li><li>Law of Return</li></ul>
Pre-Modern Aliyah
<ul><li>Return to Zion</li><li>Old Yishuv</li><li>Perushim</li></ul>
Aliyah in modern times
<ul><li>First</li><li>Second</li><li>during World War I</li><li>Third</li><li>Fourth</li><li>Fifth</li><li>Aliyah Bet</li><li>Bricha</li><li>from Muslim countries<ul><li>Yemen</li><li>Iraq</li><li>Morocco</li><li>Lebanon</li></ul></li><li>from the Soviet Union<ul><li>post-Soviet</li></ul></li><li>from Ethiopia</li><li>from Latin America</li></ul>
Absorption

- Revival of the Hebrew language
  - Ulpan
  - Hebraization of surnames
- Kibbutz
- Youth village
- Immigrant camps
- Ma'abarot
- Development town
- Austerity

Organizations

- World Zionist Organization
- Jewish National Fund
- Jewish Agency for Israel
- Youth Aliyah
- Mossad LeAliyah Bet
- El Al
- Ministry of Aliyah and Integration
- Nefesh B'Nefesh
- Am Yisrael Foundation

Related topics

- Yishuv
- Sabra
- Yerida
- Jewish refugees
- History of the Jews in the Land of Israel
- Demographic history of Palestine (region)
- Historical Jewish population comparisons
- Yom HaAliyah

- v
- t
- e[1478]

Aliyah Bet (Hebrew: ב' עלייה, "Aliyah 'B'" – bet being the second letter of the Hebrew alphabet) was the code name given to illegal immigration by Jews, most of whom were Holocaust survivors and refugees from Nazi Germany, to Mandatory Palestine between 1934-48, in violation of the restrictions laid out in the British White Paper of 1939.

In modern-day Israel it has also been called by the Hebrew term ***Ha'pala*** (Hebrew: הַעְפָּלָה; *ascension*). The *Aliyah Bet* is distinguished from the *Aliyah Aleph* ("Aliyah 'A'", Aleph being the first letter of the Hebrew alphabet) which refers to the limited Jewish immigration permitted by British authorities during the same period. The name Aliya B is also shortened name for Aliya Bilty Legalit (Hebrew: בלתי-לגאלית עלייה - illegal immigration).

Organization

During *Ha'pala*, several Jewish organizations worked together to facilitate immigration beyond the established quotas. As persecution of Jews intensified in Europe during the Nazi era, the urgency driving the immigration also became more acute. Those who participated in the immigration efforts consistently refused to term it "illegal", instead calling it "clandestine."Wikipedia:Citation needed

Ha'pala occurred in two phases. First, from 1934-42, was an effort to enable European Jews to escape Nazi persecution and genocide. From 1945-48, in a stage known as *Bricha*, it was an effort to find homes for Jewish survivors of the Nazi crimes (Sh'erit ha-Pletah) who were among the millions of displaced persons ("DPs") languishing in refugee camps in occupied Germany.Wikipedia:Citation needed

During the first phase, several organizations (including Revisionists) led the effort; after World War II, the Mossad LeAliyah Bet ("the Institute for Aliyah B"), an arm of the Haganah, took charge.Wikipedia:Citation needed

Routes

Post-World War II, *Ha'pala* journeys typically started in the DP camps and moved through one of two collection points in the American occupation sector, Bad Reichenhall and Leipheim. From there, the refugees travelled in disguised trucks, on foot, or by train to ports on the Mediterranean Sea, where ships brought them to Palestine. Most of the ships had names such as *Lo Tafchidunu* ("You can't frighten us") and *La-Nitzahon* ("To the victory") designed to inspire and rally the Jews of Palestine. Some were named after prominent figures in the Zionist movement, and people who had been killed while supporting Aliyah Bet. More than 70,000 Jews arrived in Palestine on more than 100 ships.

American sector camps imposed no restrictions on the movements out of the camps, and American, French, and Italian officials often turned a blind eye to the movements. Several UNRRA officials (in particular Elizabeth Robertson in Leipheim) acted as facilitators of the emigration. The British government vehemently opposed the movement, and restricted movement in and out of their camps. The British set up armed naval patrols to prevent immigrants from landing in Palestine.Wikipedia:Citation needed

Figure 171: *The journey of Aliyah Bet Group 14*

History

Over 100,000 people attempted to illegally enter Palestine. There were 142 voyages by 120 ships. Over half were stopped by the British patrols. The Royal Navy had eight ships on station in Palestine, and additional ships were tasked with tracking suspicious vessels heading for Palestine. Most of the intercepted immigrants were sent to internment camps in Cyprus: (Karaolos near Famagusta, Nicosia, Dhekelia, and Xylotymbou. Some were sent to the Atlit detention camp in Palestine, and some to Mauritius. The British held as many as 50,000 people in these camps (see Jews in British camps on Cyprus). Over 1,600 drowned at sea. Only a few thousand actually entered Palestine.Wikipedia:Citation needed

The pivotal event in the *Ha'apala* program was the incident of the *SS Exodus* in 1947. The *Exodus* was intercepted and boarded by a British patrol. Despite significant resistance from its passengers, *Exodus* was forcibly returned to Europe. Its passengers were eventually sent back to Germany. This was publicized, to the great embarrassment of the British government.Wikipedia:Citation needed

One account of Aliyah Bet is given by journalist I. F. Stone in his 1946 book *Underground to Palestine,* a first-person account of traveling with European displaced persons attempting to reach the Jewish homeland.

Some 250 American veterans, including Murray Greenfield (of the ship *Hatikva*), from World War II volunteered to sail ten ships ("The Jews' Secret Fleet") from the United States to Europe to load 35,000 survivors of the Holocaust (half of the illegal immigrants to Palestine), only to be deported to detention camps on Cyprus.

Timeline

Before World War II

- In 1934, the first attempt to bring in a large number of illegal immigrants by sea happened when some 350 Jews sailed on the *Vallos*, a chartered ship, without the permission of Jewish Agency, who feared illegal immigration would cause the British to restrict legal immigration. She arrived off the coast of Palestine on 25 August, and the passengers disembarked with the help of the Haganah, which received special permission to assist them.

- On 29 July 1939, the *Colorado*, flying under the Panamanian flag and carrying 378 Jewish refugees from Europe is intercepted by the British; the illegal immigrants are arrested and taken into Haifa.

- On 19 August, the *Aghios Nicolaus*, a Greek owned ship, transfers 840 immigrants to smaller vessels off the coast and sends them to shore.

- On 23 August, the *Parita*, carrying some 700 refugees on board, is deliberately beached at Tel-Aviv by the passengers, the captain and crew having fled in a small boat.

During the war

- On 2 September, the *Tiger Hill*, a 1,499 ton ship built in 1887, is intercepted and fired on by Royal Navy gunboats off Tel Aviv, killing two passengers; the ship is beached on the shore with 1,205 immigrants on board; the *Tiger Hill* had sailed from Constanţa, Romania, on 3 August 1939, with about 750 immigrants on board and had taken on board the passengers from the *Frossoula*, another illegal immigrant ship that was marooned in Lebanon.

- On 16 September, the *Rudnitchan* transfers 364 Jewish refugees into five lifeboats outside the territorial waters of the Mandate and sends them ashore as illegal immigrants.

- On 19 September, the *Noemi Julia*, sailing from Sulina in Romania with 1,130 Jewish refugees from Europe on board is intercepted in the Mediterranean by a British warship and forced to Haifa port; fearing that they would be sent back, the illegal immigrants engage in passive resistance; the British authorities bring them ashore and hold them in a detention camp; they are released a month later.

- On 24-25 November 1939, a large group of immigrants traveled by train from Vienna to Bratislava and about 10 days later sailed from there on the riverboat *Uranus* down the Danube. At the Romanian border, the three smaller riverboats to which they had been transferred on December 14 on entering Yugoslavia were intercepted and the immigrants were forced to disembark at the old fortress town of Kladovo.[1479]. About 1,100 refugees were stranded there. In May 1941, they were still in Yugoslavia, where 915 of them were caught and eventually killed by the invading Nazis.

- On 18 May 1940 the old Italian paddle steamer *Pencho* sailed from Bratislava, with 514 passengers, mostly Betar members. The *Pencho* sailed down the Danube to the Black Sea and into the Aegean Sea. On 9 October, her engines failed and she was wrecked off Mytilene, in the Italian-ruled Dodecanese Islands. The Italians rescued the passengers and took them to Rhodes. All but two were then placed in an internment camp at Ferramonti di Tarsia in southern Italy. They were held there until Allied forces liberated the area in September 1943.

- In October 1940, 1,770 Jewish refugees sailed from Tulcea to Haifa in two ships. The *Pacific* arrived off Haifa on 1 November, followed a few days later by the *Milos*. The Royal Navy intercepted each ship and escorted it into Haifa, where British authorities detained the refugees before transferring them to a requisitioned French ocean liner, the *Patria*, for deportation to Mauritius. They were followed from Tulcea by another 1,634 refugees aboard the *Atlantic*, which arrived on 24 November off Haifa, where the Royal Navy escorted her into harbour. On November 25 the British had just started transferring *Atlantic*'s refugees to *Patria* when Haganah agents planted a bomb aboard the French liner with the intention of disabling her to prevent her from sailing. However, the bomb quickly sank *Patria*, killing 260 people and wounding 172. The survivors were allowed to stay in Palestine on humanitarian grounds.

- In October 1940, a large group of refugees were allowed to leave Vienna. The exodus was organized by Berthold Storfer, a Jewish businessman who worked under Adolf Eichmann. They took four river boats, *Uranus*, *Schönbrunn*, *Helios*, and *Melk*, down the Danube to Romania, where the *Uranus* passengers, about 1,000, boarded the *Pacific*, and sailed on 11 October 1940. They arrived at Haifa on 1 November, followed by the *Milos*. The British transferred all the immigrants to the French liner SS *Patria* to take them for internment to Mauritius. To stop the *Patria* from sailing, the Haganah smuggled a bomb aboard. The explosion holed her side, capsizing her and killing 267 people. The British, by order of Winston Churchill, allowed the survivors to remain in Palestine.Wikipedia:Citation needed

- In December 1940 the *Salvador*, a small Bulgarian schooner formerly named *Tsar Krum*, left Burgas with 327 refugees. On December 12 the *Salvador* was wrecked in a violent storm in the Sea of Marmara, near Istanbul. 223 persons, including 66 children, lost their lives. The survivors were taken to Istanbul. 125 survivors were deported back to Bulgaria, and the remaining 70 left on the *Darien* (No. 66).

- On 11 December 1941, the *Struma* sailed from Constanţa carrying between 760 and 790 refugees. Three days later she reached Istanbul, where Turkey detained her and her passengers for 10 weeks. On 23 February 1942, Turkish authorities towed her back into the Black Sea and cast her adrift. Early the next day the Soviet submarine *Shch-213* torpedoed and sank her. Between 767 and 791 people were killed, and there was only one survivor.

- On 20 September 1942, the *Europa* sailed from Romania with 21 passengers. She was wrecked in the Bosphorus.

- On 21 April 1944, the "Belasitza" sailed from Romania with 273 passengers including 120 children, who went from Istanbul to Palestine by sealed train.

- On 5 August 1944, *Bulbul*, *Mefküre* and *Morino* sailed from Constanţa carrying about 1,000 refugees between them. In the night the Soviet submarine *Shch-215* sank *Mefküre* by torpedo and shellfire, and then machine-gunned survivors in the water. Between 289 and 394 refugees plus seven crew were aboard *Mefküre*; only the crew and five refugees survived. *Bulbul* rescued the few survivors and took them to Turkey.

After VE Day

- On 28 August 1945 the Italian fishing vessel *Dalin*, made in Monopoli, carrying 35 immigrants, landed at Caesarea, disembarked its passengers, and returned to Italy.

- On 4 September 1945, the *Natan*, carrying 79 immigrants, landed in Palestine, carrying seamen and radio operators from the Palmach and Jewish Agency emissaries on the return trip to Italy. On October 1, 1945, the *Natan* again ran the blockade arrived at Shefayim with 73 immigrants.

Figure 172: *Yisrael Meir Lau (aged 8) in the arms of Elazar Schiff, survivors of Buchenwald concentration camp on their arrival at Haifa, 15 July 1945*

- On 9 September 1945, the *Gabriela*, carrying 40 passengers, arrived undetected in Palestine.
- On 17 September 1945, the *Peter*, carrying 168 immigrants, landed in Palestine undetected by the British. She again slipped into Palestine undetected and arrived at Shefayim on 22 October, this time carrying 174 passengers.
- On 23 November 1945, the *Berl Katznelson*, carrying 220 Jewish refugees, arrived in Shefayim. As the ship was landing immigrants she was intercepted by the Royal Navy sloop HMS *Peacock*. Of the passengers, 200 reached the beach and escaped, and 20 were arrested.
- On 14 December 1945, the ship *Hannah Senesh*, carrying 252 passengers, was beached at Nahariya after evading Royal Navy patrols. The passengers were brought ashore via a rope bridge, and evaded capture.
- On 17 January 1946, the *Enzo Sereni*,[1480] carrying 908 passengers, was intercepted by the destroyer HMS *Talybont* and escorted to Haifa.
- On 13 March 1946 the schooner *Wingate*[1481], carrying 248 passengers, ran the blockade and attempted to land. British Palestine Police opened fire from the shore, killing a female Palmach member. The ship was captured and escorted to Haifa by the destroyer HMS *Chevron*.

- On 27 March 1946 the steamer *Tel Hai*, carrying 736 passengers, was intercepted by the destroyer HMS *Chequers* 140 miles out at sea as it approached Palestine.

- On 13 May 1946, the *Max Nordau*, carrying 1,754 immigrants, was captured by the destroyers HMS *Jervis* and HMS *Chequers*. The same day, the ships *Dov Hos* (675 passengers) and *Eliahu Golomb* (735 passengers) arrived in Palestine legally. The British had blockaded the *Dov Hos* after it had arrived in La Spezia, but the passengers responded with a hunger strike and a threat to blow her up, compelling the British to give them entry permits.

- On 8 June 1946, the *Haviva Reik*, carrying 462 passengers, was intercepted by HMS *Saumarez* on 8 June 1946. Some 150 people had previously transferred from the *Haviva Reik* to the *Rafi* off the Palestinian coast, and the crew had disembarked.

- On 26 June 1946, the *Josiah Wedgwood*, carrying 1,259 passengers, was intercepted by HMS *Venus*.

- On 20 July 1946, the *Haganah*, carrying 2,678 passengers, departed from France, and transferred 1,108 of its passengers to the small steamer *Biriah* west of Crete. The *Biriah* was intercepted by HMS *Virago* on 2 July. The *Haganah* picked up a new party of refugees at Bakar, Yugoslavia, and set sail for Palestine, this time also carrying 2,678 passengers total. She was found at sea with its engines broken down and no electrical power, and was towed to Haifa by HMS *Venus*. Her passengers were arrested and interned.Wikipedia:Citation needed

- On 11 August 1946, the *Yagur*, carrying 758 passengers, was intercepted by the destroyer HMS *Brissenden*, with passive resistance from the immigrants.

- On 12 August 1946, the *Henrietta Szold*, carrying 536 passengers, was intercepted. The same day, the British announced that illegal immigrants would be sent to Cyprus and other areas under detention. The first British deportation ship sailed for Cyprus on the same day, with 500 illegal immigrants on board.

- On 13 August 1946, two immigration ships were intercepted: *Katriel Jaffe* (604 passengers) by HMS *Talybont*, and *Twenty Three* (790 passengers) by HMS *Brissenden*. There was desperate resistance on board *Twenty Three*. The same day, two British ships with 1,300 Jewish detainees on board set sail for Cyprus. A crowd of about 1,000 Jews attempted to break into the Haifa port area, and British troops responded with live fire, killing three people and wounding seven.

- On 16 August 1946, the yawl *Amiram Shochat*, carrying 183 passengers, evaded the British blockade and landed near Caesarea.
- On 2 September 1946, the *Dov Hos*, this time named the *Arba Cheruyot*, carrying 1,024 passengers, was seized by the destroyers HMS *Childers* and HMS *Chivalrous*. The boarding was strongly resisted, and two people drowned after jumping off the ship.
- On 22 September 1946, the brigantine *Palmach*, 611 passengers, was seized by the minesweeper HMS *Rowena*. The Royal Navy tried to board the ship four times before finally seizing her, and one passenger was killed.
- On 20 October 1946, the *Eliahu Golomb*, renamed the *Braha Fuld*, carrying 806 passengers, was captured off Lebanon by the destroyer HMS *Chaplet* and minesweeper HMS *Moon*.
- On 19 October, the *Latrun* (1,279 passengers), was intercepted by HMS *Chivalrous* and the minesweeper HMS *Octavia*. Four people had died *en route*, and the ship was leaking and listing heavily when she was intercepted.
- On 9 November 1946, the *HaKedosha* (600 passengers), foundered in a gale and sank. The passengers were rescued by the *Knesset Israel*. The *Knesset Israel*, carrying a total of 3,845 passengers, was intercepted by the destroyers HMS *Haydon* and HMS *Brissenden* and minesweepers HMS Octavia and HMS *Espiegle* and taken to Haifa. The interception met no resistance, but in Haifa when the British tried to transfer them to transport ships to take them to Cyprus the refugees resisted fiercely, two were killed and 46 injured.
- On 5 December 1946, the *Rafiah* (785 passengers), was wrecked on Syrina Island in bad weather. The survivors were rescued by two Royal Navy and one Greek warship, and were taken to Cyprus. Women and children were taken to Palestine.
- On 9 February 1947, the wooden brigantine *Lanegev* (647 passengers) was captured by HMS *Chieftain* after a battle which left one refugee dead.
- On 17 February 1947, the steamer *HaMapil HaAlmoni* (807 passengers) was intercepted by HMS *St Austell Bay*, captured after a violent battle, and taken in tow by the minesweeper HMS *Welfare*.
- On 27 February 1947, the *Haim Arlosoroff*, after the name of an assassinated leader of the Jewish Agency (1,378 passengers) was intercepted by Royal Navy destroyer HMS *Chieftain*, and the passengers put up fierce resistance. The ship ran aground at Bat Galim, south of Haifa, just opposite a British Army camp. The passengers were arrested and deported to Cyprus.[1482]

Figure 173: *Haganah ship Medinat HaYehudim ("Jewish State") in Haifa port, 1947*

Figure 174: *SS Exodus arriving at Haifa port, 20 July 1947*

Figure 175: *United States lands Jewish refugees in Nahariya, 1948*

- On 9 March 1947, the *Ben Hecht* (597 passengers), the only ship sponsored by the Irgun, was captured without resistance by the destroyers HMS *Chieftain*, HMS *Chevron* and HMS *Chivalrous*.

- On 12 March 1947, the *Shabtai Luzinsky* (823 passengers) ran the blockade and beached itself north of Gaza, where the passengers disembarked, and most escaped a British Army cordon. Hundreds of local residents came down to the beach to mingle with passengers who evaded arrest. Many residents were mistaken for refugees, arrested, and sent to Cyprus, with some 460 locals returned home the following week.

- On 30 March 1947, the *Moledet* (1,588 passengers) developed a list and suffered engine failure some 50 miles outside Palestinian waters and issued an SOS. Passengers were transferred to the destroyers HMS *Haydon* and HMS *Charity*, minesweeper HMS *Octavia* and frigate HMS *St Brides Bay*, and the Royal Navy towed *Moledet* to Haifa.

- On 13 April 1947, the *Theodor Herzl* (2,641 passengers) was intercepted by HMS *Haydon* and HMS *St Brides Bay*. Passengers resisted heavily; three were killed and 27 were injured.

- On 23 April 1947, the *Shear Yashuv* (768 passengers) was intercepted by destroyer HMS *Cheviot*.

- On 17 May 1947, the *Hatikva* (1,414 passengers) was intercepted, rammed and captured by the destroyers HMS *Venus* and HMS *Brissenden*.

- On 23 May 1947, the immigrant ship *Mordei Hagetaot*, carrying 1,457 immigrants, was intercepted and boarded by the Royal Navy off southern Palestine. All of its passengers were arrested.
- On 31 May 1947, the Haganah ship *Yehuda Halevy*, carrying 399 immigrants, arrived in Palestine under escort after being intercepted by the Royal Navy. The immigrants were immediately transferred to Cyprus.
- On 18 July 1947, the ship SS *Exodus*, carrying 4,515 immigrants, was intercepted by the cruiser HMS *Ajax* and a flotilla of destroyers. She was rammed and boarded but the immigrants resisted the boarding, and had put up barriers and barbed wire to impede boarding. Two passengers and a crewman were bludgeoned to death, several dozen were injured, and the ship was taken over. The *Exodus* was towed to Haifa, where the immigrants were forced onto three deportation ships and taken to France. When the deportation ships docked in Port-de-Bouc, the passengers refused to disembark after the French government announced that it would only allow the immigrants off the ships if they consented. The immigrants were then taken to Germany, forcibly taken off the ships, and sent back to DP camps.
- On 28 July 1947, the *14 Halalei Gesher Haziv*, carrying 685 Eastern European Jews was intercepted by HMS *Rowena*. The *Shivat Zion*, carrying 411 North African Jews, was intercepted without resistance by the minesweeper. HMS *Providence*.
- On 27 September 1947, the *Af Al Pi Chen* (434 passengers), was intercepted by HMS *Talybont* and taken after violent resistance. One person was killed and ten were injured.
- On 2 October 1947, the *Medinat HaYehudim* (2,664 passengers) was intercepted by the Royal Navy. The same day, the *Geulah*, with 1,385 passengers, was intercepted by HMS *Chaplet*.
- On 15 November 1947, the *Peter*, renamed the *Aliyah* and carrying 182 passengers, ran the British blockade and beached near Netanya. The passengers, all specially-picked youths, quickly disembarked and escaped.
- On 16 November 1947, the *Kadima*, a larger ship carrying 794 immigrants, was intercepted by the Royal Navy and brought to Haifa, where its passengers were transferred to the British transport ship HMT *Runnymede Park* and taken to Cyprus.

Figure 176: *Film about Ha'apala after World War II*

After the UN Partition Resolution

- On 4 December 1947, the *HaPortzim* ran the blockade and landed its 167 passengers at the mouth of the Yarkon River.

- On 22 December 1947, the *Lo Tafchidunu* (884 passengers) was intercepted by HMS *Verulam* and taken in tow by the sloop HMS *Mermaid*.

- On 28 December 1947, the *29 BeNovember* (680 passengers) was intercepted by HMS *Chevron*.

- On 1 January 1948, the *HaUmot HaMeuhadot* (537 passengers) ran the blockade and beached herself at Nahariya. 131 passengers were caught, the rest evaded arrest. The same day, the *Atzmaut* (7,612 passengers) and the *Kibbutz Galuyot* (7,557 passengers) were intercepted by the cruisers HMS *Mauritius* and HMS *Phoebe* and taken to Cyprus.

- On 31 January 1948, the *35 Giborei Kfar Etzion* (280 passengers) was intercepted by HMS *Childers*.

- On 12 February 1948, the *Yerushalayim Hanezura* (679 passengers) was intercepted by HMS *Cheviot*.

- On 20 February 1948, the *Lekommemiyut* (696 passengers) was intercepted by HMS *Childers*.

- On 28 February 1948, the *Bonim v'Lochamim* formerly the *Enzo Sereni*, (982 passengers) was intercepted off Cape Carmel by HMS *Venus* .

- On 29 March 1948, the *Yehiam* (771 passengers) was intercepted by the destroyer HMS *Verulam*.

Figure 177: *Graves of the 223 Jewish passengers of Salvador who drowned during a storm at sea in 1940, Mount Herzl, Jerusalem.*

- On 12 April 1948, the *Tirat Zvi* (817 passengers) was intercepted by HMS *Virago*.

- On 24 April 1948, the *Mishmar HaEmek* (782 passengers) was intercepted by HMS *Chevron* off Haifa.

- On 26 April 1948, the *Nakhson* (553 passengers) was intercepted off Haifa by the sloop HMS *Pelican* after fierce resistance which left a number of people injured.

Conclusion

The success of *Aliyah Bet* was modest when measured in terms of the numbers who succeeded in entering Palestine. But it proved to be a unifying force both for the Jewish community in Palestine (the Yishuv) and for the Holocaust-survivor refugees in Europe (Sh'erit ha-Pletah).

The immigrants who drowned in the sea and whose bodies were found were buried in the National Cemetery in Mount Herzl in Jerusalem.

Further reading

- Greenfield, Murray S.; Hochstein, Joseph M. (1987). *The Jews' Secret Fleet: The Untold Story of North American Volunteers Who Smashed the British Blockade of Palestine*. Jerusalem and New York: Gefen Publishing House. ISBN 978-965-229-517-0.<templatestyles src="Module:Citation/CS1/styles.css"></templatestyles>
- Stewart, Ninian (2002). *The Royal Navy and the Palestine Patrol*. London and Portland OR: Frank Cass Publishing. ISBN 0-7146-5210-5.<templatestyles src="Module:Citation/CS1/styles.css"></templatestyles>

External links

Media related to Aliyah Bet at Wikimedia Commons
- Aliyah Bet and Machal Virtual Museum[1483]
- "Aliyah During World War II and its Aftermath"[1484], *Jewish Virtual Library*
- United States Holocaust Memorial Museum - Aliyah Bet[1485]
- Aliyah Bet Voyages Aliyah Bet Project[1486] Aliyah Bet Voyages includes pictures and details of the boats of Aliyah Bet, ports of origin, dates of sailing, dates of arrival in Palestine and the number of immigrants on board.
- The background to Aliyah Bet[1487]

Jewish insurgency in Mandatory Palestine

<indicator name="pp-default"> 🔒 </indicator>

Jewish insurgency in Mandatory Palestine
Part of Sectarian conflict in Mandatory Palestine

Palestine Railway K class 2-8-4T steam locomotive and freight train derailed from the Jaffa and Jerusalem line after being sabotaged by Jewish insurgents in 1946

Date	1939; 1944–48
Location	British Mandatory Palestine
Result	Zionist victory[1488] • British forces unable to defeat Irgun[1489] • Insurgency turned British public opinion against the deployment in Palestine, leading to Britain's withdrawal

Belligerents	
🇬🇧 United Kingdom • British Army • Royal Navy • Royal Air Force • Royal Marines • Palestine Police Force • Arab Legion (auxiliaries)	Yishuv • Irgun (1939, 1944–48) • Lehi (1944–48) • Haganah (1945–47) • Palmach (1945–47)
Commanders and leaders	
Sir Evelyn Barker Sir Alan Cunningham Harold MacMichael Sir Gordon MacMillan John Vereker, 6th Viscount Gort John Rymer-Jones William Nicol Gray	Menachem Begin Amichai Paglin Yitzhak Shamir Eitan Livni Nathan Yellin-Mor Moshe Sneh Yisrael Galili
Strength	
British police: 4,000 policemen British Armed Forces: 100,000 troops (peak strength)	Haganah: 21,000 troops Irgun: 4,000 troops Palmach: 3,000 troops Lehi: 500 troops Total forces: About 28,500
Casualties and losses	
338 British soldiers, police officers, and civilians killed[1490]	50-100 militants and civilians killed 2,755 arrested 11 executed

The **Jewish insurgency in Mandatory Palestine** (known in the United Kingdom as the **Palestine Emergency**)[1491] involved paramilitary actions carried out by Jewish underground groups against the British forces and officials in Mandatory Palestine. The tensions between Jewish militant underground organizations and the British mandatory authorities rose from 1938 and intensified with the publication of the White Paper of 1939, which outlined new government policies to place further restrictions on Jewish immigration and land purchases and declared the intention of giving independence to Palestine, with an Arab majority, within ten years. Though World War II brought relative calm, the tensions again escalated into an armed struggle towards the end of the war, when it became clear that the Axis Powers were close to defeat. The conflict with the British lasted until the eruption of the civil war and to some degree also until the termination of the British Mandate for Palestine and the establishment of the State of Israel in May 1948.

The armed conflict escalated during the final phase of the World War II, when the Irgun declared a revolt in February 1944, ending the hiatus in operations it had begun in 1940.[1492] Starting from the assassination of Lord Moyne in 1944, the Haganah actively opposed the Irgun and Lehi, in a period of inter-Jewish fighting known as The Hunting Season. However, in autumn 1945, after the end of the war the Haganah began a period of co-operation with the two other underground organizations, forming the Jewish Resistance Movement.[1493] The Haganah refrained from direct confrontation with British forces, and concentrated its efforts on attacking British immigration control, while Irgun and Lehi attacked military and police targets. The Resistance Movement dissolved in recriminations in July 1946 following the King David Hotel bombing, with Irgun and Lehi acting independently, while the main underground militia Haganah acted mainly in supporting Jewish immigration to Mandatory Palestine. After the UN partition plan resolution was passed on 29 November 1947, the civil war between Palestinian Jews and Arabs eclipsed the previous tensions of both with the British.

Within Britain there were deep divisions over Palestine policy. Dozens of British soldiers, Jewish militants and civilians died during the campaigns of insurgency. The conflict led to heightened antisemitism in the UK and, in August 1947, after the hanging of two abducted British sergeants, to widespread anti-Jewish rioting across the UK.[1494] The conflict caused tensions in Britain's relationship with the United States.

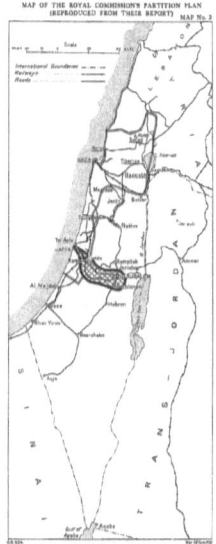

Figure 178: *Peel Commission Partition Plan, July 1937*

Background

Between the World Wars

Although both the 1917 Balfour Declaration and the terms of the League of Nations British Mandate of Palestine called for a national home for the Jewish people in Palestine, the British did not accept any linkage between Palestine and the situation of European Jews. After the Nuremberg Laws of 1935 many German Jews sought refuge abroad, and by the end of 1939 some 80,000 had been given refuge in Great Britain itself.[1495]

In 1936–37, soon after the start of the Arab uprising in Palestine, Earl Peel led a commission to consider a solution. The Peel Commission proposed a partition of Palestine that involved the compulsory resettlement of some Arab and Jewish inhabitants. It was not acceptable either to the Arab or to the Jewish leaders, though David Ben-Gurion remarked in 1937, "The compulsory transfer of the Arabs from the valleys of the proposed Jewish state could give us something which we have never had, even when we stood on our own during the days of the First and Second Temples." The twentieth Zionist Congress resolved in August 1937 that: ".. the partition plan proposed by the Peel Commission is not to be accepted"; but it wished ".. to carry on negotiations in order to clarify the exact substance of the British government's proposal for the foundation of a Jewish state in Palestine".[1496]

A further attempt was made in the Woodhead Commission, also known as the "Palestine Partition Commission", whose report was published in late 1938. A government statement (Cmnd 5843) followed on 11 November 1938.[1497] It concluded that: "His Majesty's Government, after careful study of the Partition Commission's report, have reached the conclusion that this further examination has shown that the political, administrative and financial difficulties involved in the proposal to create independent Arab and Jewish States inside Palestine are so great that this solution of the problem is impracticable." The brief St. James Conference followed in early 1939.

Britain also attended the international Évian Conference in 1938 on the issue of providing for refugees from Germany. Palestine was not discussed as a refuge because it might worsen the ongoing Arab revolt; Zionists naturally hoped that Palestine would be the principal destination for all such refugees.

British immigration restrictions and the 1939 White Paper

In the 1920s, the British imposed restrictions on Jewish immigration to Palestine and the ability of Jews to buy land, claiming that these decisions were taken due to concerns over the economic absorptive capacity of the country. In the 1930s, British authorities set a quota for immigration certificates, and authorized the Jewish Agency to hand them out at its discretion. Shortly before the outbreak of World War II, the British introduced the White Paper of 1939. The White Paper rejected the concept of partition of Palestine into Jewish and Arab states, and announced that the country would be turned into an independent binational state with an Arab majority. It severely curtailed Jewish immigration, allowing for only 75,000 Jews to migrate to Palestine from 1940 to 1944, consisting of a yearly quota of 10,000 per year and a supplementary quota for 25,000 to cover refugee emergencies spread out over the same period. Afterwards, further Jewish immigration would depend on consent of the Arab majority. Sales of Arab land to Jews were to be restricted.

In reaction to British restrictions, illegal immigration to Palestine began. Initially, Jews entered Palestine by land, mainly by slipping across the northern border, where they were aided by the border settlements. In the early 1930s, when crossing the northern border became more difficult, other routes were found. Thousands of Jews came to Palestine on student or tourist visas, and never returned to their countries of origin. Jewish women often entered into fictitious marriages with residents of Palestine to be granted entry for family reunification purposes. In 1934, the first seaborne attempt to bring Jews to Palestine happened when some 350 Jews of the HeHalutz movement in Poland who were unwilling to wait for certificates sailed to Palestine on the *Vallos*, a chartered ship. Two more ships carrying illegal immigrants arrived in 1937, and several more arrived in 1938 and 1939. These voyages were mainly organized by the Revisionist Zionist Organization and the Irgun. Until 1938, the Jewish Agency opposed illegal immigration, fearing that it would impact the number of immigration certificates issued.

Overall, between 1929 and 1940, a period of mass Jewish immigration known as the Fifth Aliyah occurred despite British restrictions. Nearly 250,000 Jews (of whom 20,000 later left) immigrated to Palestine, many of them illegally.

During World War II (1939–44)

The Second World War erupted when Mandatory authorities of Palestine were at the final stages of subduing the armed Arab revolt of 1936–1939. All Jewish organizations, including the Zionists in Europe also played a major role in the Jewish resistance to the Nazis in Europe, automatically allied with the Allied forces, including the British.

The Yishuv temporarily put aside its differences with the British regarding the White Paper, deciding that defeating the Nazis was a more urgent goal. The leader of Palestine's Jews, David Ben-Gurion, issued a call for Jews to "support the British as if there is no White Paper and oppose the White Paper as if there is no war".[1498] During the war, Palestinian Jews volunteered in large numbers to serve in the British Army, serving mainly in North Africa. Of the 470,000 Jews in Palestine at the time, some 30,000 served in the British Army during the war.[1499] There was a Jewish battalion attached to the British Army's 1st Battalion, Royal East Kent Regiment stationed in Palestine.

With the decline of the Arab Revolt by September 1939, the tensions among Jews and Arabs eased as well. During the war, among the Palestinian Arabs, the Nashashibi clan supported the British, while another Arab Palestinian faction, led by exiled Amin al-Husseini, supported the Axis powers. Haj Amin al-Husseini became the most prominent Arab collaborator with the Axis powers.

The Palestine Regiment was formed in 1942, combining three Jewish and one Arab battalions, reaching altogether 3,800 volunteers. It was involved in activities at the Mediterranean scene of the war, sustaining casualties during the North African Campaign. The Special Interrogation Group was also formed in 1942 as a commando unit composed of German-speaking Palestinian Jews. It performed commando and sabotage operations during the Western Desert Campaign.

The Jewish underground group Irgun ceased all anti-British activities by September 1939, and supported the British. An Irgun unit was sent to assist British forces fighting in the Middle East. In 1941, Irgun's David Raziel was killed while fighting in the Kingdom of Iraq with the British against that country's pro-Axis regime. Irgun also provided the British with intelligence from Eastern Europe and North Africa, and allowed members to enlist in the British Army.[1500]

However, in August 1940, Irgun member Avraham Stern formed Lehi, a breakaway group which favored armed struggle against the British to force them out of Palestine and immediately establish a Jewish state. Stern was unaware of the Nazis' intent to exterminate the Jews, and believed that Hitler wanted to make Germany *judenrein* through emigration. Stern proposed an alliance with Nazi Germany, offering the Germans help in conquering the Middle East and driving out the British in exchange for the establishment of a Jewish state in Palestine, which would then take in European Jewry.[1501] This proposal, which never received a reply, cost Lehi and Stern much support.[1502] Stern became a pariah among the Jews in Palestine, and was himself killed by British police in 1942.

During the war, a special paratrooper unit in the British Army composed of Jewish men and women from Palestine was active. The unit's members were sent into occupied Europe, mainly by airdrop, to help organize and participate in local resistance activities on the ground. Some 250 men and women volunteered, of whom 110 underwent training and 37 were infiltrated.

In December 1942, when the mass murder of European Jewry became known to the Allies, the British continued to refuse to change their policy of limited immigration, or to admit Jews from Nazi controlled Europe in numbers outside the quota imposed by the White paper, and the Royal Navy prevented ships with Jewish refugees from reaching Palestine. Some ships carrying Jewish refugees were turned back towards Europe, although in one instance, about 2,000 Jews who were fleeing Europe by sea were detained in a camp in Mauritius, and were given the option of emigrating to Palestine after the war.[1503] The British also stopped all attempts by Palestinian Jews to bribe the Nazis into freeing European Jews. At the time that The Holocaust became known to the Allies, there were 34,000 Jewish immigration certificates for Palestine remaining. In 1943, about half the remaining certificates were distributed, and by the end of the war, 3,000 certificates remained.[1504]

In September 1944, the Jewish Brigade was formed, based on the Palestine Regiment core. The brigade consisted of nearly 5,000 volunteers, including three former Palestine Regiment battalions, the 200th Field Regiment, Royal Artillery and several supporting units. The brigade was dispatched to participate in the Italian campaign in late 1944 and later took part in the Spring 1945 offensive in Italy against the German forces.

History

British restrictions on Jewish immigration

During the 1945 British election, Labour pledged that if they returned to power, they would revoke the White Paper of 1939, permit free Jewish immigration to Palestine and even the transfer of Arabs, and turn Palestine into a Jewish national home that would gradually evolve into an independent state.[1505] However, the new Labour Foreign Secretary, Ernest Bevin, decided to maintain heavy restrictions on Jewish immigration. Before the war, Bevin had been the head of Britain's largest trade-union, the TGWU and in this capacity had led a campaign to prevent German Jews being allowed to migrate to Britain. Bevin favored the White Paper's policy of turning Palestine into an Arab state with a Jewish minority that would have political and economic rights, and feared that the creation of a Jewish state would inflame Arab opinion and jeopardize Britain's position as the dominant power in the Middle East. Bevin also believed that displaced Holocaust survivors should be resettled in Europe instead of Palestine.[1506,1507]

Due to the British immigration restrictions, the Jewish Agency Executive turned to illegal immigration. Over the next few years tens of thousands of Jews sailed towards Palestine in overcrowded vessels in a program known as Aliyah Bet, despite the almost certain knowledge that it would lead to incarceration in a British prison camp (most ships were intercepted). The overwhelming majority were European Jews, including many Holocaust survivors, although some North African Jews were also involved.

In Europe former Jewish partisans led by Abba Kovner began to organize escape routes taking Jews from Eastern Europe down to the Mediterranean where the Jewish Agency organized ships to illegally carry them to Palestine.[1508] British officials in the occupied German zones tried to halt Jewish immigration by refusing to recognize the Jews as a national group and demanding that they return to their places of origin. The British government put diplomatic pressure on Poland, the source of a large number of the Jewish refugees, to clamp down on Jewish emigration, as Poland freely permitted Jews to leave without visas or exit permits, but their efforts proved futile.[1509,1510] In 1947, British Secret Intelligence Service (MI6) launched Operation Embarrass, a clandestine operation to blow up ships in Italian ports that were preparing to take Jewish refugees to Palestine, by having operatives attach limpet mines to the hulls of vessels. From summer 1947 to early 1948, five such attacks were carried out, destroying one ship and damaging two others. Two other British mines were discovered before they detonated.[1511]

In the early stages of illegal immigration, small coastal craft were used to bring in Jewish refugees, but large vessels were soon used. In total, some 60 ships were employed, including 10 ships acquired as war surplus from US boneyards. Among the crews were Jewish American and Canadian volunteers. In order to prevent Jewish illegal migrants reaching Palestine a naval blockade was established to stop boats carrying illegal migrants, and there was extensive intelligence gathering and diplomatic pressure on countries through which the migrants were passing or from whose ports the ships were coming. When an illegal immigrant ship was spotted, it would be approached by warships, and would often maneuver violently to avoid being boarded. British boarding parties consisting of Royal Marines and Paratroopers would then be sent to take control of the ship. On 27 ships, they were met with some level of resistance, including 13 cases of violent resistance, during which boarding parties were opposed by passengers armed with weapons such as clubs, iron bars, axes, firebombs, scalding steam hoses, and pistols. Royal Navy ships would ram transports, and boarding parties forced their way onto the ships and engaged in close-quarters hand-to-hand fighting to gain control. In five instances, firearms were used. During these encounters, two Royal Navy warships were damaged in collisions with immigrant ships. Seven British soldiers were killed during battles to take control of immigrant ships – most of whom drowned after being pushed overboard by passengers. Six passengers were also killed. From 1945 to 1948, some 80,000 illegal immigrants attempted to enter Palestine. About 49 illegal immigrant ships were captured and 66,000 people were detained. Some 1,600 others drowned at sea.

In 1945, the Atlit detainee camp was reopened. The camp had been built in the 1930s to hold illegal Jewish immigrants fleeing Europe, and during World War II it had been used to hold Jewish refugees fleeing the Holocaust, who were often held for an extended period of time before being released. As more and more illegals began arriving in Palestine, the camp was reopened. In October 1945, a raid by the Palmach freed 208 inmates. One week after the King David hotel bombing in July 1946, four ships carrying 6,000 illegal immigrants arrived in Haifa, completely overflowing the Atlit camp.[1512] The British government, which had known for some time that it would be unable to contain Jewish immigration, established internment camps on the island of Cyprus to detain all illegal immigrants. About 53,000 Jews, mostly Holocaust survivors, passed through these holding facilities.

British officials in the liberated zones tried to halt Jewish immigration, and did not recognize the Jews as a national group, demanding that they return to their places of origin. Jewish concentration camp survivors (displaced persons or DPs) were forced to share accommodation with non-Jewish DPs some of whom were former Nazi collaborators, now seeking asylum. In some cases former Nazis were given positions of authority in the camps, which they used to abuse the Jewish survivors.[1513] Food supplies to Jewish concentration camp survivors in the British zone were cut to prevent them from assisting Jews fleeing Eastern Europe. In the British zone they were refused support on the grounds that they were not displaced by the war.[1514]

Troops in the U.S. zone were also not helping survivors but in 1945, U.S. President Harry S. Truman sent a personal representative, Earl G. Harrison, to investigate the situation of the Jewish survivors in Europe. Harrison reported,

> [S]ubstantial unofficial and unauthorized movements of people must be expected, and these will require considerable force to prevent, for the patience of many of the persons involved is, and in my opinion with justification, nearing the breaking point. It cannot be overemphasized that many of these people are now desperate, that they have become accustomed under German rule to employ every possible means to reach their end, and that the fear of death does not restrain them.

The Harrison report changed U.S. policy in the occupied zones, and U.S. policy increasingly focused on helping Jews escape Eastern Europe. Jews escaping post-war anti-Semitic attacks in Eastern Europe learned to avoid the British zone and generally moved through American zones.

In April 1946, the Anglo-American Committee of Enquiry reported that given a chance, half a million Jews would immigrate to Palestine:

> In Poland, Hungary and Rumania, the chief desire is to get out.... The vast majority of the Jewish displaced persons and migrants, however, believe that the only place which offers a prospect is Palestine."[1515]

A survey of Jewish DPs found 96.8% would choose Palestine.[1516]

The Anglo-American Committee recommended that 100,000 Jews be immediately admitted into Palestine. U.S. President Truman pressured the British to accede to this demand. Despite British government promises to abide by the committee's decision, the British decided to persist with restrictions on Jewish migration. Foreign Secretary Bevin remarked that the American pressure to admit 100,000 Jews into Palestine was because "they do not want too many of them in New York". Prime Minister Clement Attlee announced that 100,000 Jews would not be permitted into Palestine long as the "illegal armies" of Palestine (meaning the Jewish militias) were not disbanded.[1517]

In October 1946, in fulfillment of the recommendation of the Anglo-American Committee, Britain decided to allow a further 96,000 Jews into Palestine at a rate of 1,500 a month. Half this monthly quota was allocated to Jews in the prisons on Cyprus, due to fears that if the number of Jewish prisoners in the Cyprus camps kept growing, it would eventually lead to an uprising there.[1518]

On July 18, 1947, the Royal Navy intercepted the Exodus-1947 a ship laden with 4,515 refugees en route to Palestine. The passengers resisted violently,

Figure 179: *Irgun's declaration of revolt, February 1, 1944*

and the boarding ended with two passengers and one crewman dead. Foreign Secretary Ernest Bevin decided that rather than being sent to Cyprus, the immigrants on board the Exodus would be returned to the ship's port of origin in France. Bevin believed that sending illegal immigrants to Cyprus, where they then qualified for inclusion into legal immigration quotas to Palestine, only encouraged more illegal immigration. By forcing them to return to their port of origin, Bevin hoped to deter future illegal immigrants. However, the French government announced that it would not permit the disembarkation of passengers unless it was voluntary on their part. The passengers refused to disembark, spending weeks in difficult conditions. The ship was then taken to Germany, where the passengers were forcibly removed at Hamburg and returned to DP camps. The event became a major media event, influencing UN deliberations, damaging Britain's international image and prestige, and exacerbating the already poor relationship between Britain and the Jews.

Lehi and Irgun begin an insurgency campaign

There is a general agreement among historians that the Jewish underground in Palestine refrained from an opened struggle against Britain, as long as the joint enemy of Germany was still at large. This approach changed towards the beginning of 1944, with withdrawal of Axis forces from the Mediterranean and the advances of the Red Army in Eastern Front. With the general feeling that the Axis forces in Europe were nearing their defeat, the Irgun decided to shift its policy from cease-fire to an active campaign of violence, as long as it would not be hurting the war effort against the Nazi Germany.

In the autumn of 1943, the Irgun approached Lehi and proposed jointly carrying out an insurrection. In February 1944, the Irgun now led by Menachem Begin, ended the wartime truce and declared an uprising. Begin believed that the only way to save European Jewry was to compel the British to leave Palestine as fast as possible and open the country to unrestricted Jewish immigration. Irgun and Lehi began a bombing campaign against British intelligence, immigration, and tax collection offices, and police stations. However, they avoided attacks against British soldiers and military targets until the war was over, as they did not want to hurt the war effort against Germany in any way.

In November 1944, the Lehi (Stern Gang) assassinated Lord Moyne, the British minister in Cairo. The Jewish Agency Executive condemned terror attacks and after Ben-Gurion made a Histadrut address condemning 'murder, robbery, blackmail and theft' and insisting there be no compromises with terrorists within the ranks, a campaign known as The Hunting Season was conducted by the Haganah with British assistance from November 1944 to February 1945, often helped by the British, rounded up Irgun members.

Jewish Agency and Lehi leaders met in secret before the start of the Season. While the exact contents of the meeting were disputed by both sides, it is known that Lehi suspended its activities for six months, and the Season was not extended to Lehi.[1519,1520] Some 1,000 Irgun members were arrested, 250 of whom were interned in camps in Africa. They were released in July 1948, two months after Israeli independence.

The Jewish Resistance Movement and after, 1945–47

After the end of World War II, Lehi, Haganah and other groups joined in the anti-British Jewish Resistance Movement in 1945–46.

In October 1945, the Haganah entered into an alliance with the Irgun and ceased cooperation with the British. In November 1945, units from the Palmach, the Haganah's elite fighting force, as well as Lehi, carried out the Night of the Trains, sabotaging railway networks across Palestine, and blowing up British guard boats in Jaffa and Haifa. The operation symbolized the founding of the Jewish Resistance Movement. In December 1945, Irgun carried out attacks against the British Intelligence Offices and raided a British Army camp.

In 1946, attacks against the British intensified, and now included military targets. On June 16, 1946, Haganah forces carried out attacks against bridges linking Palestine to the neighboring Arab countries, hoping to stop the transfer of weapons to the Palestinian Arabs.Wikipedia:Accuracy dispute#Disputed

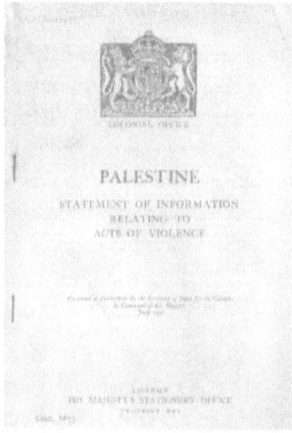

Figure 180: *British Government Statement of Information regarding the attacks*

statement This operation, known as the Night of the Bridges, as well as other attacks around this time, prompted the British to launch Operation Agatha, also known as the *Black Sabbath*. British military and police forces imposed curfews around the country and conducted searches for arms caches and militants in Jerusalem, Tel Aviv, Haifa, and in several dozen Jewish settlements. The British raided the Jewish Agency headquarters in Jerusalem, confiscating large amounts of paperwork, and arrested Jews suspected of being involved with "terrorism", including leading members of the Jewish Agency, holding them without trial.[1521] The British hoped to deter the Haganah, as well as the more extreme Jewish underground groups Irgun and Lehi, from carrying out further attacks. The Haganah stopped carrying out anti-British operations, officially withdrawing from the Jewish Resistance Movement on July 1, 1946. From then on, the Haganah would focus mainly on organizing illegal Jewish immigration to Palestine through its Mossad LeAliyah Bet branch. However, Irgun and Lehi reacted by intensifying their attacks. As a response to Operation Agatha, Irgun carried out the King David Hotel bombing, an attack on the building where the central branches of the civil and military administration of Palestine were based, killing 91 people.[1522] Although the Haganah had initially approved the attack, this had been withdrawn, a fact which the Haganah's contact with the Irgun failed to make clear. The approval had also been based on the attack being carried out in the evening, whereas it was carried out at the height of the working day when the hotel was most busy. The Irgun blamed the British for not evacuating the hotel, in spite of a warning sent by telephone. The British government stated that no warning had been received by anyone in a position to act on it. Rather than contacting the British authorities, the warning had been sent to the hotel's own switchboard, where it was ignored, perhaps because hoax warnings were rife at the time. Due to the Irgun not understanding how temperature affected the fuses, the bomb exploded early. Pedestrians outside the hotel were killed as well as people inside it.

The commander of the British forces in Palestine, General Sir Evelyn Barker, who was having an affair with the Katy Antonius, the wife of the late George Antonius (a leading Arab Nationalist), responded to the King David Hotel bombing by ordering British personnel to boycott all:

"Jewish establishments, restaurants, shop, and private dwellings. No British soldier is to have social intercourse with any Jew.... I appreciate that these measures will inflict some hardship on the troops, yet I am certain that if my reasons are fully explained to them they will understand their propriety and will be punishing the Jews in a way the race dislikes as much as any, by striking at their pockets and showing our contempt of them "[1523]

Barker, whose forces participated in the capture of the Bergen Belsen concentration camp, made many antisemitic comments in his letters to Katy Antonius[1524] and was relieved of his post a few weeks after issuing the statement. A few months after his return to England, Barker was sent a letter bomb by the Irgun, but detected it before it exploded.

The Jewish Agency was issuing constant complaints to the British administration about antisemitic remarks by British soldiers:

"they frequently said "Bloody Jew" or "pigs", sometimes shouted "Heil Hitler", and promised they would finish off what Hitler had begun. Churchill wrote that most British military officers in Palestine were strongly pro-Arab."[1525]

A major insurgency erupted, and the Jewish underground was engaged in constant attacks against British military and police forces. The Jewish Agency Executive, led by David Ben-Gurion, the leading authority of the Jews in Palestine, stayed out of the campaign, but mostly refused to cooperate with the British authorities.[1526] The Jewish civilian population, which was hostile to the British, was also largely uncooperative. The main perpetrators of these attacks were the militant groups Lehi (also known as the Stern Gang) and Irgun. The two groups, which financed their campaigns through bank robberies, extortions, and private donations, attacked British military and police installations, government offices, and ships being used to deport illegal migrants, often with bombs. In at least one case, a police station was attacked with a large truck bomb. They also sabotaged infrastructure such as railroads, bridges, and oil installations. Some 90 economic targets were attacked, among them 20 trains which were damaged or derailed and five train stations which were attacked, and about dozen attacks against the oil industry were carried out, including a March 1947 Lehi raid on the Shell Oil refinery in Haifa which destroyed some 16,000 tons of petroleum. Jewish insurgents regularly staged killings of British soldiers and police officers throughout Palestine, employing booby traps, ambushes, snipers, vehicle bombings, and shooting attacks. British armored vehicles faced attacks by remotely detonated IEDs disguised as milestones which blew vehicles off the road and killed or injured occupants. They were seen by the insurgents as their most cost-effective weapon. The Jewish civilian population of Palestine, encouraged by Zionist groups, engaged in riots, strikes, and demonstrations against the British authorities. The British Army, which eventually had one soldier for every five Jews in Palestine, responded with extensive search operations and raids to arrest militants and uncover illegal arms caches. They regularly imposed curfews, cordons, and collective punishments, and enacted a series of draconian emergency regulations which allowed for arbitrary arrests, to the point that some observers called Palestine a police state. They supplemented their large operations with smaller ones that had the advantage of surprise, including surprise searches of houses and apartments, random identity and baggage checks on public transportation, mobile checkpoints established quickly following attacks, night patrols, and small-scale raids mounted immediately on new intelligence. The British even deployed special forces in the conflict. Although these operations never managed to quell the insurgency, they did succeed in keeping the insurgents off-balance. In 1947, the British withdrew their personnel into barbed-wire enclosures known as "Bevingrads" for their own security. Even then, Irgun managed to penetrate one such security zone in March 1947 and stage a bombing attack on the British Officers' Club in Jerusalem, in the heart of a security zone. Despite extensive efforts, the British were never able to stop the insurgency.[1527] British security forces found it extremely difficult to detect and counter activities by Irgun and Lehi due to the structure of these groups; they were divided into individual cells, whose members were unknown to those in other cells. Furthermore, the extreme loyalty of the operatives of these groups made it almost impossible for British intelligence to infiltrate them, and made it difficult for British interrogators to extract information from captured members.

In addition to the militant campaign in Palestine, Irgun and Lehi attacked British targets in Europe and launched bombing attacks Britain itself. In late 1946 and early 1947, Irgun carried out a series of sabotage attacks on British Army transportation routes in occupied Germany. At around the same time, an attempt was made by Lehi to drop a bomb on the House of Commons from a chartered plane flown from France; this attempt was stopped just before it was to be carried out, when French police discovered Lehi members preparing to cross the English Channel in a plane that was found to be carrying a large bomb. In October 1946, Lehi bombed the British Embassy in Rome, injuring three people. A number of bombs exploded in London, including one at London's Colonial Club, an establishment catering to soldiers and students from British colonies in Africa and the West Indies. The bombing caused no fatalities but injured some servicemen. An attempt was also made to destroy the Colonial Office in London with a large bomb, which malfunctioned after its timer broke. According to a senior police official, it would have caused a death rate similar to that of the King David Hotel bombing had it gone off. Some 21 letter bombs were addressed to senior British political figures, including Prime Minister Clement Attlee and Foreign Secretary Ernest Bevin. Many were intercepted, while others reached their targets but were discovered before they could go off.[1528] An Irgun explosives factory was also discovered in London.

The British arrested thousands during their counterinsurgency campaign, often imposing severe prison terms, including for weapons-related offenses. They also began using flogging as a judicial punishment. However, in late December 1946, after an Irgun member was flogged, the group, delivering on a previous threat, abducted and flogged several British soldiers in return, an event that became known as the Night of the Beatings. While this caused the British to end the use of flogging, they then began to apply the death penalty against convicted insurgents. Within months, four imprisoned Jewish fighters, including three Irgun men that had been arrested during the Night of the Beatings, were hanged. In some instances, Irgun abducted British soldiers and police officers, and in one instance a judge, and threatened to kill them if executions took place. This tactic succeeded in stopping a few executions. In May 1947, a large prison break was staged when Irgun fighters, in a coordinated attack, blasted a large hole the prison wall, and Jewish prisoners blasted their way out through the doors with smuggled explosives. Some 28 Jewish prisoners and 182 Arab prisoners escaped. During the operation, nine fighters and escapees were killed, most of them when a getaway truck ran into a British roadblock, and five Irgun fighters and eight escapees were captured. Three out of the five fighters captured were sentenced to death in June; Irgun responded by kidnapping two British sergeants from the Intelligence Corps and threatening to kill them should the sentences be carried out. The British Army carried out extensive search operations. The Haganah cooperated with the British search effort.[1529] Efforts to locate the hostages proved fruitless. The British authorities decided to carry out the executions despite the danger to the hostages. On July 29, 1947, the three were executed, and the next day the two British sergeants were killed in response. Their bodies were then hanged from trees in an orange grove near Netanya, and were booby-trapped with a bomb, which later injured a British officer attempting to cut one of the bodies down. Following this incident, British soldiers and police officers attacked civilians in Tel Aviv, killing five people, and a wave of anti-Semitic rioting swept Britain over the course of several days; the rioting began in Liverpool and spread to other major British cities, including London, Manchester, Cardiff, Derby and Glasgow, causing widespread damage to Jewish property.[1530,1531] Following this incident, the British government ordered an end to the use of the death penalty in Palestine.

Propaganda campaign

The insurgency was coupled with a local and international propaganda campaign to gain sympathy abroad. The Yishuv authorities publicized the plight of Holocaust survivors and British attempts to stop them from migrating to Palestine, hoping to generate negative publicity against Britain around the world. Ben-Gurion publicly stated that the Jewish insurgency was "nourished by despair", that Britain had "proclaimed war against Zionism", and that British policy was "to liquidate the Jews as a people." Of particular significance was the British interceptions of the blockade runners carrying Jewish immigrants. The SS Exodus incident in particular became a major media event. Propaganda against the British over their treatment of the refugees was disseminated around the world, including claims that the *Exodus* was a "floating Auschwitz". In one incident, after a baby died at sea aboard an Aliyah Bet ship, the body was publicly displayed to the press after the ship docked in Haifa for transfer of the passengers to Cyprus, and journalists were told that "the dirty Nazi-British assassins suffocated this innocent victim with gas."

Through a well-organized international propaganda campaign, Irgun and Lehi reached out to potential international supporters, particularly in the United States and especially among American Jews, who became increasingly sympathetic to the Zionist cause and hostile to Britain. Their propaganda claimed that: Britain's restrictions on Jewish immigration were a violation of international law, as it violated the terms of the mandate; British rule in Palestine was oppressive and had turned the country into a police state; British policies were Nazi-like and anti-Semitic; the insurgency was Jewish self-defence; and the insurgents were winning and British withdrawal from Palestine was inevitable. This propaganda, coupled with statements and actions by British officials and members of the security forces interpreted as anti-Semitic, gained the insurgents international credibility and served to further tarnish Britain's image.

Britain was at this time negotiating a loan from the United States vital to its economic survival. Its treatment of Jewish survivors generated bad publicity, and encouraged the U.S. Congress to stiffen its terms. Many American Jews were initially politically active in pressing Congress for a suspension of the loan guarantees, but Jewish groups and politicians later retracted their support and came out in favor of the loan, fearing accusations of disloyalty to the United States. U.S. President Harry S. Truman put extensive pressure on the British government over its handling of the Palestine situation. The post-war conflict in Palestine caused more damage to Anglo-American relations than any other issue.[1532]

The British decide to leave Palestine

From October 1946, opposition leader, Winston Churchill, began calling for Palestine to be given to the United Nations.[1533]

During the insurgency, the British government organized a conference in London between Zionist and Arab representatives, and attempted to mediate a solution. However, these talks proved fruitless. The Arabs were unwilling to accept any solution except a unified Palestine under Arab rule, and while the Zionists adamantly refused this proposal, instead suggesting partition. After realizing that the Arabs and the Jews were both unwilling to compromise, Bevin began considering turning the Palestine question over to the United Nations.[1534]

Britain increasingly began to see its attempts to suppress the Jewish insurgency as a costly and futile exercise, and its resolve began to weaken. British security forces, which were constantly taking casualties, were unable to suppress the insurgents due to their hit-and-run tactics, poor intelligence, and a noncooperative civilian population. The insurgents were also making the country ungovernable; the King David hotel bombing resulted in the deaths of a large number of civil servants and the loss of many documents, devastating the mandatory administration, while IED attacks on British vehicles began to limit the British Army's freedom of movement throughout the country. The Acre Prison break and the floggings and hangings of British soldiers by the Irgun humiliated the British authorities and further demonstrated their failure to control the situation. At the same time, attacks carried out on economic targets cost Britain almost £2 million in economic damage; meanwhile, Britain was paying about £40 million a year to keep its troops in Palestine, while at the same time the country was going through a deep economic crisis as a result of World War II, with widespread power cuts and strict rationing, and was heavily dependent on American economic aid. There were also indications, such as several successful bombings in London and the letter-bombing campaign against British politicians, that the insurgents were beginning to take the war home to Britain. In addition, British treatment of Holocaust survivors and tactics in Palestine were earning Britain bad publicity around the world, particularly in the United States, and earned the British government constant diplomatic harassment from the Truman administration.

In January 1947, all non-essential British civilians were evacuated from Palestine. On February 14, 1947, British Foreign Secretary Ernest Bevin informed the House of Commons that the Palestine question would be referred to the United Nations. Meanwhile, depending on perspective, a low-level guerrilla war, or campaigns of terrorism, continued through 1947 and 1948. Eventually, Jewish insurgency against the British was overshadowed by the Jewish-Arab fighting of the 1947–48 Civil War in Mandatory Palestine, which started following the UN vote in favor of the United Nations Partition Plan for Palestine.

In 1947, the United States chapter of the United Jewish Appeal raised $150 million in its annual appeal – at that time the largest sum of money ever raised by a charity dependent on private contributions. Half was earmarked for Palestine. *The Times* reported that Palestine brought more dollars into the sterling zone than any other country, save Britain.[1535]

In April 1947 the issue was formally referred to the UN. By this time over 100,000 British soldiers were stationed in Palestine. Referral to the UN led to a period of uncertainty over Palestine's future. A United Nations committee, the United Nations Special Committee on Palestine (UNSCOP) was sent to investigate the problem. On August 31, 1947, UNSCOP recommended that Palestine be partitioned into Jewish and Arab states. On September 20, 1947, the British cabinet voted to evacuate Palestine.[1536]

Although the insurgency played a major role in persuading the British to quit Palestine, other factors also influenced British policy. Britain, facing a deep economic crisis and heavily dependent on the United States, was facing a massive financial burden over its many colonies, military bases, and commitments abroad. At the same time, Britain had also lost the centerpiece of the rationale of its Middle East policy after the end of the British Raj in Colonial India. Britain's Middle East policy had been centered around protecting the flanks of its sea lines of communication to India. After the British Raj ended, Britain no longer needed Palestine. Finally, Britain still had alternative locations such as Egypt, Libya, and Kenya to base its troops.

Partition and civil war

The United Nations Special Committee on Palestine recommended partition, and on 29 November 1947 the United Nations General Assembly voted to recommend partition of Palestine into two states – an Arab and a Jewish one. The partition resolution (181) intended administration of Palestine to be in the hands of five UN representatives and assumed free Jewish immigration into the Jewish area even before the creation of a Jewish state:

> *The mandatory power shall use its best endeavours to ensure that an area situated in the territory of the Jewish state, including a seaport and hinterland adequate to provide facilities for a substantial immigration, shall*

be evacuated at the earliest possible date and in any event not later than 1 February 1948.[1537]

Britain refused to comply with these conditions on the grounds that the decision was unacceptable to the Arabs. It neither allowed Jewish immigration outside the monthly quota, nor granted control to the UN representatives (who became known as the "five lonely pilgrims"). A statement issued by the British Ambassador to the UN stated that the inmates on Cyprus would be released with the termination of the mandate.[1538] The British also refused to cooperate with the UN commission that was sent to monitor the transition; when the commission's six members arrived in Palestine in January 1948, British High Commissioner Alan Cunningham allotted them an unventilated Jerusalem basement from which to work out of. They were gradually reduced to foraging for food and drink, and prevented from carrying out their duties.

Over the remaining period of British rule, British policy was to ensure that the Arabs did not resist Britain or blame it for partition. Convinced that partition was unworkable, the British refused to assist the UN in any way that might require British forces to remain on Palestinian soil (to implement it) or turn their army into a target for Arab forces. On the other side, "The Yishuv perceived the peril of an Arab invasion as threatening its very existence. Having no real knowledge of the Arabs' true military capabilities, the Jews took Arab propaganda literally, preparing for the worst and reacting accordingly."[1539]

As the British began to withdraw during the closing months of the mandate, civil war erupted in Palestine between the Jews and Arabs. During this period, as well as restricting Jewish immigration, Britain handed over strategic military and police positions to the Arabs as they abandoned them, and froze Jewish Agency assets in London banks. However, the British generally stayed out of the fighting and only intervened occasionally. Even so, they were still sometimes caught in the crossfire or deliberately attacked for their weapons. There is little evidence that Bevin, despite his hostility to Zionism, wanted to strangle the incipient Jewish state at birth. Instead, his main concern seems to have been to ensure that Egypt retained control of the parts of the Negev they were occupying, so that Britain had a land link between Egypt and Jordan.

On 22 February 1948, as part of the civil war, Arab militants detonated a truck laden with explosives in Ben Yehuda Street in Jerusalem, killing about 60 people. Two British deserters assisted in this attack; Eddie Brown, a police captain who claimed that his brother had been killed by the Irgun, and Peter Madison, an army corporal. They had been recruited by Holy War Army commander Abd al-Qadir al-Husayni.[1540] In revenge, Lehi mined two trains. The first such attack, which took place on 29 February, hit the military coaches of a passenger train north of Rehovot, killing 28 British soldiers and wounding

35. Another attack on 31 March killed 40 people and injured 60. Although there were soldiers on board, all of the casualties were civilians.

The Haganah had previously spared the railway bridge at Rosh HaNikra during their 1946 Night of the Bridges operation. Following the late-1947 announcement that the British would withdraw from Palestine months ahead of schedule, however, the bridge was destroyed by the 21st Battalion[1541] under the Palmach[1542] in late February 1948[1541] to hinder Lebanese arms shipments to Arab forces opposing the UN Partition Plan. As repairs were prohibitively expensive, the tunnels were later completely sealed. This ended the only connection between the European and North African standard gauge railway networks.

In April 1948, the Security Council called upon all governments to prevent fighting personnel or arms from entering Palestine.[1543]

Five and a half months of civil war in Palestine saw a decisive Jewish victory. Jewish forces, led by the Haganah, consolidated their hold on a strip of territory on the coastal plain of Palestine and the Jezreel and Jordan Valleys, and crushed the Palestinian Arab militas. Palestinian society collapsed.[1544]

Aftermath: British policy during the 1948 War

As all the League of Nations mandates were to be taken over by the new United Nations, Britain had declared that it would leave Palestine by 1 August 1948, later setting the date for the termination of the mandate as 15 May; on 14 May 1948 the Zionist leadership announced the Israeli Declaration of Independence. Several hours later, at midnight on 15 May 1948, the British Mandate of Palestine officially expired and the State of Israel came into being.

Hours after the end of the Mandate, contingents of the armies of four surrounding Arab states entered Palestine, setting off the 1948 Arab–Israeli War. As the war progressed, the Israeli forces gained an advantage due to a growing stream of arms and military equipment from Europe that had been clandestinely smuggled or were supplied by Czechoslovakia. In the following months, Israel began to expand the territory under its control.

Throughout the 1948 war, 40 British officers served with the Jordanian Army (then known as the Arab Legion), and the Arab Legion's commander was a British General, John Bagot Glubb.

On 28 May 1948, the United Nations Security Council debated Palestine. The British proposed that the entry of arms and men of military age into Palestine should be restricted. At the request of the United States, the ban was extended to the whole region. A French amendment allowed immigration so long as soldiers were not recruited from immigrants.[1545]

The British had by this time released almost all inmates of the Cyprus internment camps, but continued to hold about 11,000 detainees, mainly military-age males, in the camps.[1546,1547] Authorities in the British, as well as American occupation zones in Germany and Austria imposed restrictions on the emigration of Jews of military age attempting to emigrate during the war.

In October 1948, Israel began a campaign to capture the Negev. In December 1948, Israeli troops made a twenty-mile incursion into Egyptian territory. Under the terms of the Anglo-Egyptian treaty the Egyptians could appeal for British help in the event of an Israeli invasion, however the Egyptians were concerned to avoid any such eventuality. During this period, the Royal Air Force began mounting almost daily reconnaissance missions over Israel and the Sinai, with RAF planes taking off from Egyptian airbases and sometimes flying alongside Egyptian warplanes. On 20 November 1948, the Israeli Air Force shot down a British reconnaissance plane over Israel, killing two airmen.[1548,1549]

On 7 January 1949, Israeli forces shot down five British fighter planes after a flight of RAF planes overflew an Israeli convoy in the Sinai and were mistaken for Egyptian aircraft. Two pilots were killed and one was captured by Israeli troops and briefly detained in Israel. The UK Defence Committee responded to this incident and a Jordanian request by sending two destroyers carrying men and arms to Transjordan.[1550] Israel complained to the UN that these troops were in violation of United Nations Security Council Resolution 50. Britain denied this, claiming the resolution did not apply to Britain and that the troops were not new to the region as they had been transferred from Egypt.[1551] The British also managed to prevent shipments of aviation spirit and other essential fuels from reaching Israel in retaliation.

As the IDF drove into the Negev, the British government launched a diplomatic campaign to prevent Israel from capturing the entire area. Britain viewed the Negev as a strategic land bridge between Egypt and Transjordan that was vital to both British and Western interests in the Middle East, and were anxious to keep it from falling into Israeli hands. On 19 October 1948, Sir Alexander Cadogan, the British representative to the United Nations, pressed for sanctions against Israel. The British believed that it would be in their and the West's strategic interest if they maintained *de facto* control of a land bridge from Egypt to Transjordan, and Foreign Secretary Ernest Bevin tried to persuade the US government to support his position and force Israel to withdraw. In particular, Bevin hoped to restrict Israel's southern border to the Gaza-Jericho-Beersheba road. The British ambassador in Cairo, Sir Ronald Campbell, advocated military intervention against Israel to stop the IDF's drive into the Negev in a January 1949 cable to Bevin. However, the British diplomatic campaign failed to persuade the US government to take action against Israel, with US President

Harry S. Truman referring to the Negev as "a small area not worth differing over". Mounting international and domestic criticism forced an end to Britain's attempts to intervene in the war, and Bevin ordered British forces to stay clear of the Israelis in the Negev.[1552]

The British cabinet ultimately decided that action could be taken to defend Transjordan, but that under no circumstances would British troops enter Palestine.

On 17 January 1949 the Chief of Staff briefed the cabinet on events in the Middle East. Minister of Health, Aneurin Bevan, protested at the decision to send arms to Transjordan, taken by the Defence Committee without cabinet approval. He complained that British policy in Palestine was inconsistent with the spirit and tradition of Labour Party policy and was supported by the Deputy Prime Minister, Herbert Morrison and Chancellor of the Exchequer, Stafford Cripps.[1553]

In January 1949, the British cabinet voted to continue supporting the Arab states, but also voted to recognize Israel and release the last Jewish detainees on Cyprus.[1554] The last detainees began leaving Cyprus in January, and shortly afterward, Britain formally recognized Israel.[1555]

Timeline

1939

- June 12 – A British explosives expert was killed trying to defuse an Irgun bomb near a Jerusalem post office.
- August 26 – Two British police officers, Inspector Ronald Barker and Inspector Ralph Cairns, commander of the Jewish Department of the C.I.D., were killed by an Irgun mine in Jerusalem.

1944

- February 12 – British immigration offices in Jerusalem, Tel Aviv, and Haifa were attacked by Irgun.
- February 14 – Two British constables were shot dead when they attempted to arrest Lehi fighters pasting up wall posters in Haifa.
- February 18 – A police patrol shot and killed a Jewish civilian who had not replied swiftly enough to its challenge.
- February 24 – A British police official and four CID officers were wounded in bombings.
- February 27 – Simultaneous bombing attacks were launched against British income tax offices.

- March 2 – A British constable was shot and severely wounded after coming upon Irgun fighters putting up a poster.
- March 13 – Lehi killed a Jewish CID officer in Ramat Gan.
- March 19 – A Lehi member was shot dead while resisting arrest by the CID in Tel Aviv. Lehi retaliated with an attack in Tel Aviv that killed two police officers and wounded one.
- March 23 – Irgun fighters led by Rahamim Cohen raided and bombed the British intelligence offices and placed explosives. A British soldier and Irgun fighter were killed. An Irgun unit led by Amichai Paglin raided the British intelligence headquarters in Jaffa, and Irgun fighters led by Yaakov Hillel raided the British intelligence offices in Haifa.
- April 1 – A British constable was killed and another wounded.
- July 13 – Irgun fighters broke into and bombed the British intelligence building on Mamilla street in Jerusalem.
- September 29 – A senior British police officer of the Criminal Intelligence Department was assassinated by Irgun in Jerusalem.[1556]
- November 6 – Lehi fighters Eliyahu Bet-Zuri and Eliyahu Hakim assassinated British politician Lord Moyne in Cairo. Moyne's driver was also killed.
- November 1944 to February 1945 – the "Hunting Season": the Haganah actively cooperates with the Mandate authorities in the suppression of the Irgun

1945

- January 27 – A British judge was kidnapped by Irgun and released in exchange for Jewish detainees.
- February/March – end of the so-called "Hunting Season", the Haganah cooperation with the authorities against the Irgun.
- March 22 – Lehi members Eliyahu Bet-Zuri and Eliyahu Hakim were hanged in Cairo.
- August 14 – Irgun fighters overpowered and disarmed two British sentries, and then blew up the Yibne Railway Bridge.[1557]
- October – The Jewish Resistance Movement, a cooperation between the Haganah, Irgun, and Lehi is activated by the Jewish Agency until August, 1946
- October 10 – Haganah fighters raid the Atlit detainee camp, which was being used by the British to hold thousands of illegal Jewish immigrants from Europe, freeing 208 inmates.[1558] The raid was planned by Yitzhak Rabin, commanded by Nahum Sarig, and executed by the Palmach.
- November 1 – Night of the Trains – Haganah fighters sabotaged railroads used by the British, and sank three British guard boats. At the same time, an Irgun unit led by Eitan Livni raided a train station in Lod, destroying

Figure 181: *The King David Hotel after the bombing, photo from The Palestine Post*

a number of buildings and three train engines. One Irgun fighter, two British soldiers, and four Arabs were killed.
- December 27 – Irgun fighters raided and bombed British Intelligence Offices in Jerusalem, killing seven British policemen. Two Irgun fighters were also killed. Irgun also attacked a British Army camp in Northern Tel Aviv. In the exchange of fire, a British soldier and Irgun fighter were killed, and five Irgun fighters were injured.

1946

- January 19 – Jewish fighters destroyed a power station and a portion of the Central Jerusalem Prison with explosives. During the incident, two persons were killed by police.
- January 20 – Palmach attacked the Givat Olga Coast Guard Station. One person was killed and ten were injured during the raid. A Palmach attempt to sabotage the British radar station on Mount Carmel was thwarted. Documents seized by the British indicated that the attacks were retaliation for the seizure of a Jewish immigrant ship two days before.[1559]
- February 22 – Haganah fighters attacked a police Tegart fort with a 200 lb bomb. In the firefight that followed, Haganah suffered casualties.[1560]

Jewish insurgency in Mandatory Palestine

Figure 182: *British paratroopers enforce curfew in Tel Aviv following the King David Hotel bombing, July 1946*

Figure 183: *Zionist leaders arrested during Operation Agatha, in a detention camp in Latrun*

Figure 184: *Jewish civilians guarded by a soldier of the Parachute Regiment wait to be interrogated during a search in Tel Aviv for Jewish militants, July 1946*

- February 23 – Haganah fighters attacked British mobile police forces in Kfar Vitkin, Shfar'am and Sharona.
- February 26 – Irgun and Lehi fighters attacked three British airfields and destroyed dozens of aircraft. One Irgun fighter was killed.
- March 6 – A military truck carrying 30 Irgun fighters disguised as British soldiers approached a British army camp at Sarafand, where the fighters infiltrated into the armoury and stole weaponry. An exchange fire began after the fighters were discovered. The remaining weapons and ammunition in the armoury were destroyed by a mine, and the truck then drove off at high speed. Four Irgun fighters were captured, two of them women. Two of the captured fighters were wounded.
- March 25 – The Jewish immigrant ship *Wingate* was fired on by British police as it docked in Haifa, killing a Palmach member.
- April 2 – Irgun launched a sabotage operation against the railway network in the south, inflicting severe damage. The retreating fighters were surrounded after being spotted by a British reconnaissance aircraft. Two British policemen were killed, and three British soldiers were wounded. Two Irgun fighters were killed, four wounded, and 31 arrested.
- April 23 – Dozens of Irgun fighters disguised as British soldiers and Arab prisoners infiltrated the Ramat Gan police station, then ordered the po-

licemen into the detention cell at gunpoint, blasted open the door to the armoury and looted it. Irgun porters loaded the weapons onto a waiting truck. A British policeman on the upper story shot dead the Irgun Bren gunner covering the raid from a balcony on the building opposite the police station, then fired at the porters, who continued to load weapons under fire. One Irgun member was killed as he ran to the truck, and Irgun commander Dov Gruner was wounded and subsequently captured by the British. After the weapons had been loaded, the truck drove off to an orange grove near Ramat Gan.
- April 25 – Lehi fighters attacked a Tel Aviv car park that was being used by the British Army's 6th Airborne Division, killing seven British soldiers and looting the arms racks they found. They then laid mines and retreated. Some British soldiers retaliated by damaging Jewish property.
- June 16–17 – Night of the Bridges – Haganah carried out a sabotage operation, blowing up ten of the eleven bridges connecting British Mandatory Palestine to the neighbouring countries, while staging 50 diversion ambushes and operations against British forces throughout Palestine. Haganah lost 14 dead and 5 wounded in the operation.[1561] The British responded with raids on Kfar Giladi, Matsuba, and Bet HaArava, encountering only minor resistance. Three Jews were killed, 18 wounded, and 100 detained.
- June 17 – Lehi attacked railroad workshops in Haifa. Eleven Lehi members were killed during the attack.
- June 18 – Irgun fighters took six British officers hostage. They were later released after the death sentences passed on two Irgun fighters were commuted.
- June 20 – British troops searching for the six officers abducted on June 18 killed two Jewish militants.
- June 29 – Operation Agatha – British military and police units began a three-day operation, searching three cities and Jewish settlements throughout Palestine and imposing curfews, arresting 2,718 Jews and seizing numerous arms and munitions which were found unexpectedly. The Jewish Agency building was raided, and numerous documents were confiscated. During the operation, four Jews were killed and 80 injured.
- July 22 – King David Hotel bombing – Irgun fighters bombed the King David Hotel in Jerusalem, which was home to the central offices of the British Mandatory authorities and the headquarters of British forces in Palestine and Transjordan. A total of 91 people were killed, including 28 British soldiers, policemen and civilians. Most of the dead were Arabs. Another 46 people were injured. Irgun suffered two casualties when British soldiers became suspicious and fired at a group of Irgun fighters as they fled from the scene, wounding two. One of them later died from his

injuries.[1562]
- July 29 – British police raided a bomb-making workshop in Tel Aviv.
- July 30 – Tel Aviv was placed under a 22-hour curfew for four days as 20,000 British soldiers conducted house-to-house searches for Jewish militants. The city was sealed off and troops were ordered to shoot curfew violators. British troops detained 500 people for further questioning and seized a large cache of weapons, extensive counterfeiting equipment, as well as $1,000,000 in counterfeit government bonds that was discovered in a raid on the city's largest synagogue.
- August – The Haganah ceases its cooperation with the Irgun, and Lehi (the "Jewish Resistance Movement")
- August 13 – A crowd of about 1,000 Jews attempted to break into the port area of Haifa as two Royal Navy ships departed for Cyprus with 1,300 illegal immigrants on board, and a ship with 600 more was escorted into the port. British soldiers fired on the crowd, killing three and wounding seven.
- August 22 – Palyam frogmen attached a limpet mine to the side of the British cargo ship *Empire Rival*, which had been used to deport Jewish immigrants to Cyprus. A hole was blown in the ship's side.
- August 26 – British troops searched two Jewish coastal villages for three Jews involved in the *Empire Rival* incident. During the operation, 85 persons, including the entire male population of one of the villages, were detained.
- August 30 – British soldiers discovered arms and munitions dumps in Dorot and Ruhama.
- September 8 – Jewish fighters sabotaged railroads in fifty places in Palestine.
- September 9 – Two British officers were killed by an explosion at a public building in Tel Aviv. A British police sergeant, T.G. Martin, who had identified and arrested Lehi leader and future Israeli Prime Minister Yitzhak Shamir, was assassinated near his Haifa home.[1563]
- September 10 – British forces imposed a curfew and searched for militants in Tel Aviv and Ramat Gan, arresting 101 people and wounding four.
- September 15 – Jewish fighters attacked a police station on the coast near Tel Aviv, but were driven off by gunfire.
- September 20 - Bombed Haifa Station
- October 6 – A member of the Royal Air Force was shot and killed.
- October 8 – Two British soldiers were killed when their truck detonated a mine outside Jerusalem. A leading Arab figure was wounded in another mine attack, and mines were also found near government house.

- October 30 – Irgun launched an attack in the Jerusalem Railway Station, killing two British guards.
- October 31 – The British embassy in Rome was damaged by a bomb.
- November 1–2 – Palmach sank three British naval police craft.
- November 9–13 – Jewish underground members launched a series of land mine and suitcase bomb attacks against railroad stations, trains, and streetcars, killing 11 British soldiers and policemen and 8 Arab constables.
- November 17 – Three British policemen and a Royal Air Force sergeant were killed when their truck hit a mine near Lydda.
- November 18 – British police in Tel Aviv attacked Jews on the streets and fired into houses in retaliation for the mine attack that occurred the previous day. Twenty Jews were injured. Meanwhile, a British engineer trying to remove mines planted near an RAF airfield was killed and four other men were injured when one of the mines exploded.
- November 20 – Three people were injured when a bomb exploded in the Jerusalem tax office.
- November 25 – The Jewish immigrant ship *Knesset Israel* was captured by four British destroyers. Efforts to force the Jewish refugees onto deportation ships were met with resistance. Two refugees were killed and 46 wounded. Haganah attacked the Givat Olga police station and the Sydna-Ali coastal patrol station, wounding six British and eight Arab policemen.
- November 26 – The British launched a massive search operation and established a 1,000-man cordon on the Plain of Sharon and in Samaria, looking for the perpetrators of the previous days attacks and illegal weapons. Jewish settlers put up violent resistance to the soldiers. The British reported 65 soldiers and 16 policemen wounded, while the Jews had 8 dead and 75 wounded.
- October 8 – Two British soldiers were killed and three wounded when their truck hit a mine.
- October 31 – The British embassy in Rome was bombed by the Irgun, wounding three.
- December 2–5 – Six British soldiers and four other persons were killed in bomb and mine attacks.
- December 28 – An Irgun prisoner who had been sentenced to 18 years in prison and 18 lashes was whipped.
- December 29 – Night of the Beatings – Irgun fighters kidnapped and flogged six British soldiers. The British responded by ordering their soldiers back into army camps and setting up roadblocks. A car with five armed Irgun men carrying a whip was stopped. British soldiers opened fire, killing one Irgun fighter. The remaining four were arrested.[1564]

Figure 185: *Irgun men in British Army uniforms, preparing to stage the Acre Prison break*

1947

- January 2 – A British soldier was killed when the Bren gun carrier he was riding was hit by a mine. The Irgun also launched a flamethrower attack against a military car park in Tiberias.
- January 8 - Twelve Irgun members were arrested in Rishon LeZion.
- January 5 – Eleven British soldiers were injured in a grenade attack on a train in Banha carrying British troops to Palestine from Egypt.
- January 12 – A Lehi member drove a truck bomb into a police station in Haifa, killing two British and two Arab constables, and wounding 140.
- January 26 – A retired British major, H. Collins, was abducted in Jerusalem, badly beaten, and chloroformed. A British judge was kidnapped the following day. Both men were released when British High Commissioner Alan Cunningham threatened martial law unless the two men were returned unharmed. Collins subsequently died from chloroform poisoning, as the chloroform had been improperly administered by his captors.
- March 1 – Irgun bombed the Officers Club on King George Street in Jerusalem, killing 17 British officers and wounding 27, resulting in martial law that lasted 16 days. Immediately after martial law was declared, two Jews were shot and killed, one of them a four-year-old girl standing on the balcony of her home. During the period of martial law, 78 Jews suspected of membership in the Jewish resistance were arrested.

Figure 186: *A British security zone in Jerusalem, dubbed "Bevingrad" after Ernest Bevin, 1948.*

- March 2 – Three British soldiers were killed by a landmine disguised as a stone that detonated as their vehicle was passing on Mount Carmel.
- March 3 – A mine blew up a British scout car near Tel Aviv, killing three soldiers and injuring one.
- March 4 – Five British soldiers were injured when their truck was wrecked by a mine near Rishon LeZion, and four Arabs were injured when a Royal Air Force vehicle was blown up by a mine near Ramla. A British military office in Haifa was bombed, and a small-scale raid hit an army camp near Hadera.
- March 9 – A British Army camp was attacked in Hadera.
- March 11 – Two British soldiers were killed.
- March 12 – Irgun attacked the Schneller Camp, which was being used as a barracks and office of the Royal Army Pay Corps. One British soldier was killed and eight were wounded. A British camp near Karkur was also raided, shots were fired at the Sarona camp, and a mine exploded near Rishon LeZion.
- March 23 – One British soldier was killed when a train on the Cairo-Haifa line hit a mine in Rehovot.
- March 29 – A British officer was killed when Jewish fighters ambushed a British cavalry party near Ramla.

- April 2 – The *Ocean Vigour*, a British freighter used to transport captured illegal immigrants to Cyprus, was damaged in a bomb attack by Palyam, the naval force of the Palmach.
- April 3 – A British military truck was damaged and blown off the road by a mine in Haifa, injuring two soldiers of the 6th Airborne Division. The British transport ship *Empire Rival* was damaged by a time-bomb while en route from Haifa to Port Said.
- April 7 – A British patrol killed Jewish militant Moshe Cohen.
- April 8 – A British constable was killed in retaliation for Cohen's death. A Jewish boy was also killed by British troops.
- April 13 – The Jewish immigrant ship *Theodor Herzl* was captured by the British. Three Jewish refugees were killed and 27 injured during the takeover.
- April 14 – The Royal Navy captured the Jewish immigrant ship *Guardian*. Two Jews were killed and 14 wounded during the takeover.
- April 17 – The British Army leave centre in Netanya was attacked by three Jewish fighters who shot a sentry dead, tossed three bombs and then escaped.
- April 19 – Four Irgun fighters (Dov Gruner, Yehiel Dresner, Mordechai Alkahi and Eliezer Kashani) were hanged by British authorities. Irgun retaliated with three attacks; a British soldier was killed during a raid on a field dressing station near Netanya, a civilian bystander was killed during an attack on a British armoured car in Tel Aviv, and shots were fired at British troops in Haifa.
- April 21 – Irgun member Meir Feinstein and Lehi member Moshe Barzani killed themselves in prison with grenades smuggled to them in hollowed-out oranges, hours before they were to be hanged.
- April 22 – A British troop train arriving from Cairo was bombed outside Rehovot, killing five soldiers and three civilians, and wounding 39. In a separate incident, two British soldiers were killed in Jerusalem.
- April 25 – Lehi bombed a British police compound, killing five policemen.
- April 26 – A British police official was assassinated.
- May 4 – Acre Prison break – Irgun members working with Jewish prisoners inside Acre Prison managed to blow a hole in the wall, and assault the prison, freeing 28 Jewish prisoners. Nine Irgun and Lehi fighters, including commander Dov Cohen, were killed during the retreat. Five Irgun fighters and eight escapees were later captured.
- May 6 – A British counter-terrorism unit led by Roy Farran abducted 16-year-old Lehi member Alexander Rubowitz, later torturing and killing him.

Figure 187: *The prison wall after the break*

- May 12 – Two British policemen were killed by Jewish fighters in Jerusalem.
- May 15 – Two British soldiers were killed and seven injured by Lehi. A British policeman was also killed in an ambush.
- May 16 – A British constable and a Jewish police superintendent were assassinated.
- June 4 – Eight Lehi Letter bombs addressed to high British government officials, including Prime Minister Clement Attlee, were discovered in London. A British soldier was killed in Haifa.
- June 28 – Lehi fighters opened fire on a line of British soldiers waiting in line outside a Tel Aviv theater, killing three soldiers and wounding two. One Briton was also killed and several wounded in a Haifa hotel. A Jewish fighter was also wounded.
- June 29 – Four British soldiers were wounded in a Lehi attack at a Herzliya beach.
- July 17 – Irgun carried out five mining operations against British military traffic in the vicinity of Netanya, killing one Briton and wounding sixteen.
- July 16 – A British soldier was killed by a vehicle mine near Petah Tikva.
- July 18 – A British soldier was killed.
- July 19 – Irgun attacked four locations in Haifa, killing a British constable and wounding twelve. A British soldier was also killed.

Figure 188: *Clifford Martin and Mervyn Paice killed by the Irgun*

- July 20 – A British soldier was killed.
- July 21 – A Haganah raid knocked out a British radar station in Haifa that was being used to track Aliyah Bet ships. Elsewhere, mortar shells were fired at the headquarters of the British 1st Infantry Division in Tel Litwinsky, a British staff car near Netanya was fired on, and a British soldier was killed when his truck hit a mine near Raanana.
- July 25 – A British soldier was killed and three others were injured when their jeep hit a mine near Netanya. Jewish fighters also blew up railway track near Gaza and damaged a railway bridge near Binyamina.
- July 26 – Two British soldiers were killed by a booby trap.
- July 27 – Seven British soldiers were wounded in an ambush and mine explosions.
- July 29–31 – The Sergeants affair – British authorities hanged Irgun fighters Avshalom Haviv, Yaakov Weiss and Meir Nakar. In retaliation, Irgun hanged British intelligence corps sergeants Mervyn Paice and Clifford Martin, who had previously been abducted and held as hostages, afterwards re-hanging their bodies from trees in a eucalyptus grove near Netanya. A mine laid underneath exploded as one of the bodies was being cut down, injuring a British officer.[1565] In a separate incident, two British soldiers were killed and three wounded by a land mine near Hadera planted by Irgun fighters. British soldiers and policemen reacted

by rampaging in Tel Aviv, breaking windows, overturning cars, stealing a taxi and assaulting civilians. Groups of young Jews then began stoning British foot patrols, causing them to be withdrawn from the city. Upon learning of the stonings, members of mobile police units drove to Tel Aviv in six armored cars, where they smashed windows, raided two cafes and detonated a grenade in the second one, and fired into two crowded buses. Five Jews were killed and fifteen wounded.
- August 1 – An anti-British riot broke out during the funeral procession of the five Jews killed the day before, and 33 Jews were injured. In Jerusalem, an attack by Jewish fighters on a British security zone in Rehavia was repulsed. One attacker was killed and two captured.
- August 5 – Three British police officers were killed by a bomb at the Jerusalem Department of Labor building.[1566]
- August 9 – Irgun bombed a British troop train north of Lydda, killing the Jewish engineer.[1567,1568]
- August 15 - 2 Arabs (including 13-year-old boy) killed in Jaffa, 1 Jew killed in Kfar Saba, 1 Arab killed in [Ramat Gan].[1569]
- August 15 - Orange Grove attack by Haganah: 11 Arabs, including 4 children (3 girls and a 3-year-old boy), their parents and adult sibling were killed in an orange grove outside Tel Aviv. The Haganah claimed responsibility, four workers were killed by machine gun fire and the family of seven when the house they were sleeping in was dynamited.
- August 18 – A British police cadet was killed on Mount Zion.
- August 22 – Two British soldiers were injured when the military truck they were traveling in was hit by a mine.
- September 3 – A postal bomb sent by either Irgun or Lehi exploded in the post office sorting room of the British War Office in London, injuring two.[1570]
- September 21 – A British messenger was killed.
- September 26 – Irgun fighters robbed a bank, killing four British policemen.[1571]
- September 27 – A Jewish illegal immigrant was killed by the British.
- September 29 – 10 killed (4 British policemen, 4 Arab policemen and an Arab couple) and 53 injured in Haifa police headquarters bombing by Irgun. One ton of explosives in a barrel was used for the bombing and Irgun said it was done on the first day of Sukkot to avoid Jewish casualties.[1572,1573,1574]
- September 29 - Irgun bombed the Cairo-Haifa train, twenty miles south of Haifa partially derailing it. One person was hospitalized.
- October 13 – Two British soldiers were killed in Jerusalem.
- November 12 – A total of 21 were killed in British-Jewish clashes.
- November 14 – Four Britons were killed in Tel Aviv and Jerusalem.

- November 17 - 2 Britons (a soldier and a constable) killed and 28 others wounded in bombing/shooting at Jerusalem cafe.
- December 8 - 4 Arabs and 4 Jews (including a woman and a 3 year old) were killed during an Arab attack on Beit Yaakov outside Tel Aviv (this was the first mass Arab attack on a Jewish village).
- December 9 – 7 Jews and 1 Arabs died in clashes in Haifa. A British soldier was also killed in Haifa and another seriously wounded by molotov cocktails thrown at their cars by Jewish insurgents.[1575]
- December 10 – A British soldier was killed and another wounded in Haifa. Two Arabs wounded in an Irgun bombing in Haifa later died.
- December 11 - 11 Jews and 9 Arabs were killed and 46 Arabs and 14 Jews injured, one British soldier wounded died later.(AP reported 41 total deaths, other sources reported 35). Nine of the Jewish deaths along with four injuries occurred during an attack on a bus convoy near Hebron. Four of the Arab deaths and 30 of the wounded were from bombing of a Lebanese-Arab bus in Haifa.[1576]
- December 12 – Jewish underground bombing attacks on buses in Haifa and Ramla killed 2 British soldiers, 20 Arabs and 5 Jews. Thirteen of the Arab deaths occurred during a Jewish attack on the village of Tira near Haifa. One Arab was wounded in another Jewish attack on the village of Shefat. A British Airways bus was attacked and burned near Lydda by Arabs, four people (including one Czech official) were killed.[1577,1578]
- December 13 – Irgun bombings: 3 Arabs killed and 22 wounded (3 critically) by bombs thrown from taxi at Jerusalem's Damascus Gate, the casualties included children. A bomb thrown from a car into a Jaffa cafe killed 6 Arab adults (including an 11-year old) and injured 40 others (three were under 12). 24 armed Jewish men dressed as soldiers attacked the village of Yehudiya near Petah Tikva shooting guns and blowing up houses, 7 Arabs were killed (two women and two children, 3 and 4 years old among them) and 7 others seriously wounded (two women and girl of 4 among them).[1579]
- December 14 - 14 Jews were killed and 9 injured along with 2 British soldiers when troops from the Trans-Jordan Army fired on a bus convoy near Beth Nabala. The Jordanian troops were said to be responding to a grenade attack from the convoy. An 18 month old Arab toddler was killed and a man wounded by a grenade thrown at an Arab bus in Jerusalem. A Jeiwsh policeman was killed near Beersheba[1580]
- December 16 - 2 Jews and one Arab killed near Beersheba. Three Arabs killed near Gaza (reportedly by Arab assailants).[1581]
- December 18 - Haganah attack on [Al-Khisas]: 10 Arabs including five young children were killed when two cars of gunmen drove through the village firing guns and blew up two houses. The raid was ordered

by Haganah as a reprisal attack for the killing of two Jewish settlement policemen.[1582]
- December 24 - 4 Arabs and 2 Jews killed, 26 wounded in shootings on streets and buses in Haifa.[1583]
- December 25 – Lehi members machine-gunned two British soldiers in a Tel Aviv cafe.
- December 29 – Two British constables and 11 Arabs were killed and 32 Arabs wounded when Irgun members threw a bomb from a taxi at Jerusalem's Damascus Gate.[1584]

1948

- February 12 – A British soldier was killed by a sniper in Haifa.
- February 19 – Two British soldiers were killed.
- February 23 – Two British policemen were killed.
- February 29 – As part of the Cairo-Haifa train bombings, Lehi fighters mined a train that included coaches used by British troops north of Rehovot, killing 28 British soldiers and wounding 35.[1585]
- March 3 – A British soldier was killed by a Jewish sniper.
- March 29 – A British soldier was killed by a vehicle mine in Jerusalem.
- April 6 – Irgun fighters led by Ya'akov Meridor raided the British Army camp at Pardes Hanna, killing seven British soldiers.[1586]
- April 20 – Jewish snipers attacked British soldiers and policemen throughout Haifa, wounding two policemen and a soldier. British forces returned fire and killed five snipers.
- April 28 - British troops intervened to stop Operation Hametz, leading to a small battle with the Irgun. The intervention succeeded in preventing a Jewish takeover of Jaffa, while it failed to expel the Irgun from Menashiya due to stiff resistance. To put pressure on Ben-Gurion to rein in the Irgun, British planes flew over Tel Aviv and also bombed Haganah positions in Bat Yam. Eventually the British issued an ultimatum to Ben-Gurion, threatening to bomb Tel Aviv if he didn't stop the Irgun offensive. The next day, an agreement was reached in which Haganah fighters would replace the Irgun in Menashiya, and the Haganah pledged not to attack Jaffa until the end of the Mandate. British troops were allowed to reoccupy the police fort in Menashiya, but the town remained in Jewish hands.[1587]
- May 3 – A Lehi book bomb posted to the parental home of British Major Roy Farran was opened by his brother Rex, killing him.[1588]

Effects

Effect upon mutual British–Arab interests

Anglo-Arab relations were of vital importance to British strategic concerns both during the war and after, notably for their access to oil and to India via the Suez Canal. Britain governed or protected Oman, Sudan, Kuwait, the Arab Emirates, Bahrain and Yemen, had treaties of alliance with Iraq (the Anglo-Iraqi Treaty (1930) and the Anglo-Iraqi Treaty (1948)) and Egypt (Anglo-Egyptian Treaty of 1936). Transjordan was granted independence in 1946 and the Anglo-Jordanian Treaty of 1948 allowed Britain to station troops in Jordan and promised mutual assistance in the event of war.

Effects upon independence movements worldwide

According to the BBC documentary *The Age of Terror: In the Name of Liberation*, the successful Jewish struggle for independence in Palestine inspired numerous violent campaigns for independence in other countries of the world at the time, such as by the Malayan Communist Party in the Malayan Emergency and in Algeria. Political scientist John Bowyer Bell, who studied both the Irgun and the Irish Republican Army, noted that many IRA men whom he interviewed in the 1960s had studied Menachem Begin's memoir *The Revolt*, and used it as a manual for guerilla warfare.[1589] Nelson Mandela had also studied the book, and used it as a guide in planning the ANC's guerrilla campaign against the apartheid government of South Africa.

Books

- Yehuda Bauer, *Out of the Ashes: The Impact of American Jews on Post-Holocaust European Jewry* (Oxford: Pergamon 1989)
- Yehuda Bauer, 'Flight and Rescue: Brichah, *(Random House; New York 1970)*
- Zeev Hadari, *Second Exodus: The Full Story of Jewish Illegal Immigration to Palestine 1945–1948* (London: Valentine Mitchell 1991)
- Arieh Kochavi, *Post-Holocaust Politics: Britain, the United States and Jewish Refugees 1945–1948* (Chapel Hill: University of North Carolina Press 2001)
- Tony Kushner, *The Persistence of Prejudice: Antisemitism in British society during the Second World War* (Manchester: Manchester University Press 1989).
- Miller, Rory, ed. "Britain, Palestine and Empire: The Mandate Years" (2010)

- Roberts, Nicholas E. "Re-Remembering the Mandate: Historiographical Debates and Revisionist History in the Study of British Palestine," *History Compass* (March 2011) 9#3 pp 215–230.

Primary sources

- Menachem Begin, *The Revolt*, 1951.
- Trygve Lie, *In the Cause of Peace, Seven Years with the United Nations* (New York: MacMillan 1954)

References

Bibliography

- Gold, Stephanie (1998), *Israel Guide*, Open Road Publishing<templatestyles src="Module:Citation/CS1/styles.css"></templatestyles>.
- Milstein, Uri; et al. (1998), *Out of Crisis Came Decision, History of the War of Independence*, Vol. IV, University Press of America, ISBN 9780761814894<templatestyles src="Module:Citation/CS1/styles.css"></templatestyles>.

External links

DP conditions: http://bcrfj.revues.org/document269.html Jews on Cyprus: http://news.pseka.net/index.php?module=article&id=8199 DP camps (personal accounts): http://www.virtualmuseum.ca/Exhibitions/orphans/english/themes/pdf/the_dp.pdf

- http://library.thinkquest.org/TQ0312712/Tq03/PAGES%20ONLY/DP%20Good.htm

United Nations Partition Plan for Palestine

<indicator name="pp-default"> 🔒 </indicator>

UN General Assembly Resolution 181 (II)	
 UNSCOP (3 September 1947; see green line) and UN Ad Hoc Committee (25 November 1947) partition plans. The UN Ad Hoc Committee proposal was voted on in the resolution.	
Date	29 November, 1947
Meeting no.	128
Code	A/RES/181(II) (Document[1590])
Voting summary	33 voted for 13 voted against 10 abstained
Result	Recommendation to the United Kingdom, as the mandatory Power for Palestine, and to all other Members of the United Nations the adoption and implementation, with regard to the future government of Palestine, of the Plan of Partition with Economic Union set out in the resolution

 Wikisourcehas original text related to this article:
United Nations General Assembly Resolution 181

The **United Nations Partition Plan for Palestine** was a proposal by the United Nations, which recommended a partition of Mandatory Palestine at the end of the British Mandate. On 29 November 1947, the UN General Assembly adopted the Plan as **Resolution 181 (II)**.

The resolution recommended the creation of independent Arab and Jewish States and a Special International Regime for the city of Jerusalem. The Partition Plan, a four-part document attached to the resolution, provided for the termination of the Mandate, the progressive withdrawal of British armed forces and the delineation of boundaries between the two States and Jerusalem. Part I of the Plan stipulated that the Mandate would be terminated as soon as possible and the United Kingdom would withdraw no later than 1 August 1948. The new states would come into existence two months after the withdrawal, but no later than 1 October 1948. The Plan sought to address the conflicting objectives and claims of two competing movements, Palestinian nationalism and Jewish nationalism, or Zionism.[1591,1592] The Plan also called for Economic Union between the proposed states, and for the protection of religious and minority rights.

The Plan was accepted by the Jewish Agency for Palestine, despite its perceived limitations.[1593] Arab leaders and governments rejected it and indicated an unwillingness to accept any form of territorial division, arguing that it violated the principles of national self-determination in the UN Charter which granted people the right to decide their own destiny.[1594]

Immediately after adoption of the Resolution by the General Assembly, a civil war broke out and the plan was not implemented.

Background

The British administration was formalized by the League of Nations under the Palestine Mandate in 1923, as part of the Partitioning of the Ottoman Empire following World War I. The Mandate reaffirmed the 1917 British commitment to the Balfour Declaration, for the establishment in Palestine of a "National Home" for the Jewish people, with the prerogative to carry it out.[1595] A British census of 1918 estimated 700,000 Arabs and 56,000 Jews.

In 1937, following a six-month-long Arab General Strike and armed insurrection which aimed to pursue national independence and secure the country from foreign control, the British established the Peel Commission. The Commission concluded that the Mandate had become unworkable, and recommended Partition into an Arab state linked to Transjordan; a small Jewish state; and a mandatory zone. To address problems arising from the presence of national minorities in each area, it suggested a land and population transfer[1596] involving the transfer of some 225,000 Arabs living in the envisaged Jewish state and 1,250 Jews living in a future Arab state, a measure deemed compulsory "in the last resort". To address any economic problems, the Plan proposed avoiding interfering with Jewish immigration, since any interference would be liable to produce an "economic crisis", most of Palestine's wealth coming from the Jewish community. To solve the predicted annual budget deficit of the Arab State and reduction in public services due to loss of tax from the Jewish state, it was proposed that the Jewish state pay an annual subsidy to the Arab state and take on half of the latter's deficit.[1597] The Palestinian Arab leadership rejected partition as unacceptable, given the inequality in the proposed population exchange and the transfer of one-third of Palestine, including most of its best agricultural land, to recent immigrants. The Jewish leaders, Chaim Weizmann and David Ben-Gurion, persuaded the Zionist Congress to lend provisional approval to the Peel recommendations as a basis for further negotiations.[1598,1599,1600] In a letter to his son in October 1937, Ben-Gurion explained that partition would be a first step to "possession of the land as a whole".[1601,1602] The same sentiment, that acceptance of partition was a temporary measure beyond which the Palestine would be "redeemed . . in its entirety,"[1603] was recorded by Ben-Gurion on other occasions, such as at a meeting of the Jewish Agency executive in June 1938,[1604] as well as by Chaim Weizmann.[1605]

The British Woodhead Commission was set up to examine the practicality of partition. The Peel plan was rejected and two possible alternatives were considered. In 1938 the British government issued a policy statement declaring that "the political, administrative and financial difficulties involved in the proposal to create independent Arab and Jewish States inside Palestine are so great that this solution of the problem is impracticable". Representatives of Arabs and Jews were invited to London for the St. James Conference, which proved unsuccessful.[1606]

With World War II looming, British policies were influenced by a desire to win Arab world support and could ill afford to engage with another Arab uprising.[1607] The MacDonald White Paper of May 1939 declared that it was "not part of [the British government's] policy that Palestine should become a Jewish State", sought to limit Jewish immigration to Palestine and restricted Arab land sales to Jews. However, the League of Nations commission held that the White Paper was in conflict with the terms of the Mandate as put forth in the past. The outbreak of the Second World War suspended any further deliberations.[1608] The Jewish Agency hoped to persuade the British to restore Jewish immigration rights, and cooperated with the British in the war against Fascism. Aliyah Bet was organized to spirit Jews out of Nazi controlled Europe, despite the British prohibitions. The White Paper also led to the formation of Lehi, a small Jewish organization which opposed the British.

After World War II, in August 1945 President Truman asked for the admission of 100,000 Holocaust survivors into Palestine[1609] but the British maintained limits on Jewish immigration in line with the 1939 White Paper. The Jewish community rejected the restriction on immigration and organized an armed resistance. These actions and United States pressure to end the anti-immigration policy led to the establishment of the Anglo-American Committee of Inquiry. In April 1946, the Committee reached a unanimous decision for the immediate admission of 100,000 Jewish refugees from Europe into Palestine, rescission of the white paper restrictions of land sale to Jews, that the country be neither Arab nor Jewish, and the extension of U.N. Trusteeship. The U.S. endorsed the Commission's findings concerning Jewish immigration and land purchase restrictions,[1610] while The U.K. conditioned their implementation on U.S. assistance in case of another Arab revolt. In effect the British continued to carry out their White Paper policy.[1611] The recommendations triggered violent demonstrations in the Arab states, and calls for a Jihad and an annihilation of all European Jews in Palestine.[1612]

United Nations Special Committee on Palestine (UNSCOP)

League of Nations A-class mandatory territories were to revert to sovereign states on their termination, and after WW2, this is what occurred with the exception of Palestine.[1613,1614] In February 1947, Britain announced its intent to terminate the Mandate for Palestine, referring the matter of the future of Palestine to the United Nations.[1615] The hope was that a binational state would ensue, which meant an unpartitioned Palestine. Ernest Bevin's policy was premised on the idea that an Arab majority would carry the day, which met difficulties with Harry Truman who, sensitive to Zionist electoral pressures in the United States, pressed for a British-Zionist compromise.[1616] In May, the UN formed a Special Committee (UNSCOP) to prepare a report on recommendations for Palestine. The Jewish Agency pressed for Jewish representation and the exclusion of both Britain and Arab countries on the Committee, sought visits to camps where Holocaust survivors were interned in Europe as part of UNSCOP's brief, and in May won representation on the Political Committee.[1617] The Arab states, convinced statehood had been subverted, and that the transition of authority from the League of Nations to the UN was questionable in law, wished the issues to be brought before an International Court, and refused to collaborate with UNSCOP, which had extended an invitation for liaison also to the Arab Higher Committee.[1618] In August, after three months of conducting hearings and a general survey of the situation in Palestine, a majority report of the committee recommended that the region be partitioned into an Arab and a Jewish state, which should retain an economic union. An international regime was envisioned for Jerusalem.

The Arab delegations at the UN had sought to keep separate the issue of Palestine from the issue of Jewish refugees in Europe. During their visit, UNSCOP members were shocked by the extent of Lehi and Irgun violence, then at its apogee, and by the elaborate military presence attested by endemic barb-wire, searchlights, and armoured-car patrols. Committee members also witnessed the SS Exodus affair in Haifa and could hardly have remained unaffected by it. On concluding their mission, they dispatched a subcommittee to investigate Jewish refugee camps in Europe.[1619,1620] The incident is mentioned in the report in relation to Jewish distrust and resentment concerning the British enforcement of the White Paper 1939.

UNSCOP report

On 3 September 1947, the Committee reported to the General Assembly.*CHAPTER V: PROPOSED RECOMMENDATIONS (I)*, Section A of the Report contained eleven proposed recommendations (I - XI) approved unanimously. Section B contained one proposed recommendation approved by a substantial majority dealing with the Jewish problem in general (XI). *CHAPTER VI: PROPOSED RECOMMENDATIONS (II)* contained a *Plan of Partition with Economic Union* to which seven members of the Committee (Canada, Czechoslovakia, Guatemala, the Netherlands, Peru, Sweden and Uruguay), expressed themselves in favour. *CHAPTER VII RECOMMENDATIONS (III)*' contained a comprehensive proposal that was voted upon and supported by three members (India, Iran, and Yugoslavia) for a *Federal State of Palestine*. Australia abstained. In *CHAPTER VIII* a number of members of the Committee expressed certain reservations and observations.

Proposed partition

<templatestyles src="Multiple_image/styles.css" />

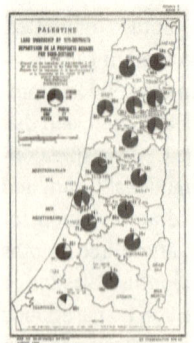

Land ownership

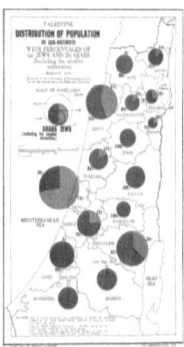

Population distribution

Two maps reviewed by UN Subcommittee 2 in considering partition

The report of the majority of the Committee (CHAPTER VI) envisaged the division of Palestine into three parts: an Arab State, a Jewish State and the City of Jerusalem, linked by extraterritorial crossroads. The proposed Arab State would include the central and part of western Galilee, with the town of Acre, the hill country of Samaria and Judea, an enclave at Jaffa, and the southern coast stretching from north of Isdud (now Ashdod) and encompassing what is now the Gaza Strip, with a section of desert along the Egyptian border. The proposed Jewish State would include the fertile Eastern Galilee, the Coastal Plain, stretching from Haifa to Rehovot and most of the Negev desert, including the southern outpost of Umm Rashrash (now Eilat). The Jerusalem Corpus Separatum included Bethlehem and the surrounding areas.

The primary objectives of the majority of the Committee were political division and economic unity between the two groups. The Plan tried its best to accommodate as many Jews as possible into the Jewish State. In many specific cases,Wikipedia:Citation needed this meant including areas of Arab majority (but with a significant Jewish minority) in the Jewish state. Thus the Jewish State would have an overall large Arab minority. Areas that were sparsely populated (like the Negev desert), were also included in the Jewish state to create room for immigration. According to the plan, Jews and Arabs living in the Jewish state would become citizens of the Jewish state and Jews and Arabs living in the Arab state would become citizens of the Arab state.

By virtue of Chapter 3, Palestinian citizens residing in Palestine outside the City of Jerusalem, as well as Arabs and Jews who, not holding Palestinian citizenship, resided in Palestine outside the City of Jerusalem would, upon the recognition of independence, become citizens of the State in which they were resident and enjoy full civil and political rights.

The Plan would have had the following demographics (data based on 1945).

Territory	Arab and other population	% Arab and other	Jewish population	% Jewish	Total population
Arab State	725,000	99%	10,000	1%	735,000
Jewish State	407,000	45%	498,000	55%	905,000
International	105,000	51%	100,000	49%	205,000
Total	1,237,000	67%	608,000	33%	1,845,000

Data from the Report of UNSCOP: 3 September 1947: CHAPTER 4: A COMMENTARY ON PARTITION[1621]

The land allocated to the Arab State in the final plan included about 43% of Mandatory Palestine[1622][1623][1624] and consisted of all of the highlands, except for Jerusalem, plus one-third of the coastline. The highlands contain the major aquifers of Palestine, which supplied water to the coastal cities of central Palestine, including Tel Aviv.Wikipedia:Citation needed The Jewish State allocated to the Jews, who constituted a third of the population and owned about 7% of the land, was to receive 56% of Mandatory Palestine, a slightly larger area to accommodate the increasing numbers of Jews who would immigrate there.[1625] The Jewish State included three fertile lowland plains – the Sharon on the coast, the Jezreel Valley and the upper Jordan Valley. The bulk of the proposed Jewish State's territory, however, consisted of the Negev Desert, which was not suitable for agriculture, nor for urban development at that time. The Jewish State would also be given sole access to the Sea of Galilee, crucial for its water supply, and the economically important Red Sea.

The committee voted for the plan, 25 to 13 (with 17 abstentions) on 25 November 1947 and the General Assembly was called back into a special session to vote on the proposal. Various sources noted that this was one vote short of the two-thirds majority required in the General Assembly.

Ad hoc Committee

On 23 September 1947 the General Assembly established the Ad Hoc Committee on the Palestinian Question to consider the UNSCOP report. Representatives of the Arab Higher Committee and Jewish Agency were invited and attended.[1626]

During the committee's deliberations, the British government endorsed the report's recommendations concerning the end of the mandate, independence, and Jewish immigration. Wikipedia:Citation needed However, the British did "not feel able to implement" any agreement unless it was acceptable to both

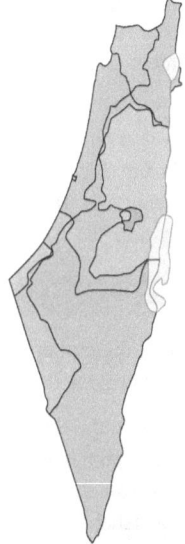

Figure 189:

Boundaries defined in the 1947 UN Partition Plan for Palestine:
Area assigned for a Jewish state
Area assigned for an Arab state
Planned Corpus separatum with the intention
that Jerusalem would be neither Jewish nor Arab

Armistice Demarcation Lines of 1949 (Green Line):
Israeli controlled territory from 1949
Egyptian and Jordanian controlled territory from 1948 until 1967

the Arabs and the Jews, and asked that the General Assembly provide an alternative implementing authority if that proved to be the case.

The Arab Higher Committee rejected both the majority and minority recommendations within the UNSCOP report. They "concluded from a survey of Palestine history that Zionist claims to that country had no legal or moral basis". The Arab Higher Committee argued that only an Arab State in the whole of Palestine would be consistent with the UN Charter.

The Jewish Agency expressed support for most of the UNSCOP recommendations, but emphasized the "intense urge" of the overwhelming majority of Jewish displaced persons to proceed to Palestine. The Jewish Agency criticized the proposed boundaries, especially in the Western Galilee and Western

Jerusalem (outside of the old city), arguing that these should be included in the Jewish state. However, they agreed to accept the plan if "it would make possible the immediate re-establishment of the Jewish State with sovereign control of its own immigration."

Arab states requested representation on the UN ad hoc subcommittees of October 1947, but were excluded from Subcommittee One, which had been delegated the specific task of studying and, if thought necessary, modifying the boundaries of the proposed partition.[1627]

Sub-Committee 2

The Sub-Committee 2, set up on 23 October 1947 to draw up a detailed plan based on proposals of Arab states presented its report within a few weeks.[1628]

Based on a reproduced British report, the Sub-Committee 2 criticised the UNSCOP report for using inaccurate population figures, especially concerning the Bedouin population. The British report, dated 1 November 1947, used the results of a new census in Beersheba in 1946 with additional use of aerial photographs, and an estimate of the population in other districts. It found that the size of the Bedouin population was greatly understated in former enumerations. In Beersheba, 3,389 Bedouin houses and 8,722 tents were counted. The total Bedouin population was estimated at approximately 127,000; only 22,000 of them normally resident in the Arab state under the UNSCOP majority plan. The British report stated:

"It should be noted that the term Beersheba Bedouin has a meaning more definite than one would expect in the case of a nomad population. These tribes, wherever they are found in Palestine, will always describe themselves as Beersheba tribes. *Their attachment to the area arises from their land rights there and their historic association with it.*"

In respect of the UNSCOP report, the Sub-Committee concluded that the earlier population *"estimates must, however, be corrected in the light of the information furnished to the Sub-Committee by the representative of the United Kingdom regarding the Bedouin population. According to the statement, 22,000 Bedouins may be taken as normally residing in the areas allocated to the Arab State under the UNSCOP's majority plan, and the balance of 105,000 as resident in the proposed Jewish State. It will thus be seen that the proposed Jewish State will contain a total population of 1,008,800, consisting of 509,780 Arabs and 499,020 Jews. In other words, at the outset, the Arabs will have a majority in the proposed Jewish State."*

The Sub-Committee 2 recommended to put the question of the Partition Plan before the International Court of Justice (Resolution No. I). In respect of the Jewish refugees due to World War II, the Sub-Committee recommended to request the countries of which the refugees belonged to take them back as much as possible (Resolution No. II). The Sub-Committee proposed to establish a unitary state (Resolution No. III).

Boundary changes

The *ad hoc* committee made a number of boundary changes to the UNSCOP recommendations before they were voted on by the General Assembly.

The predominantly Arab city of Jaffa, previously located within the Jewish state, was constituted as an enclave of the Arab State. The boundary of the Arab state was modified to include Beersheba and a strip of the Negev desert along the Egyptian border, while a section of the Dead Sea shore and other additions were made to the Jewish State. This move increased the Jewish percentage in the Jewish state from 55% to 61%.Wikipedia:Citation needed

The proposed boundaries would also have placed 54 Arab villages on the opposite side of the border from their farm land.Wikipedia:Citation needed In response, the United Nations Palestine Commission was empowered to modify the boundaries "in such a way that village areas as a rule will not be divided by state boundaries unless pressing reasons make that necessary". These modifications never occurred.

The vote

Passage of the resolution required a two-thirds majority of the valid votes, not counting abstaining and absent members, of the UN's then 56 member states. On 26 November, after filibustering by the Zionist delegation, the vote was postponed by three days.[1629] According to multiple sources, had the vote been held on the original set date, it would have received a majority, but less than the required two-thirds. Various compromise proposals and variations on a single state, including federations and cantonal systems were debated (including those previously rejected in committee).[1630,1631] The delay was used by supporters of Zionism in New York to put extra pressure on states not supporting the resolution.

Reports of pressure for and against the Plan

Reports of pressure for the Plan

Zionists launched an intense White House lobby to have the UNSCOP plan endorsed, and the effects were not trivial.[1632] The Democratic Party, a large part of whose contributions came from Jews,[1633] informed Truman that failure to live up to promises to support the Jews in Palestine would constitute a danger to the party. The defection of Jewish votes in congressional elections in 1946 had contributed to electoral losses. Truman was, according to Roger Cohen, embittered by feelings of being a hostage to the lobby and its 'unwarranted interference', which he blamed for the contemporary impasse. When a formal American declaration in favour of partition was given on 11 October, a public relations authority declared to the Zionist Emergency Council in a closed meeting:'under no circumstances should any of us believe or think we had won because of the devotion of the American Government to our cause. We had won because of the sheer pressure of political logistics that was applied by the Jewish leadership in the United States'. State Department advice critical of the controversial UNSCOP recommendation to give the overwhelmingly Arab town of Jaffa, and the Negev, to the Jews was overturned by an urgent and secret late meeting organized for Chaim Weizman with Truman, which immediately countermanded the recommendation. The United States initially refrained from pressuring smaller states to vote either way, but Robert A. Lovett reported that America's U.N. delegation's case suffered impediments from high pressure by Jewish groups, and that indications existed that bribes and threats were being used, even of American sanctions against Liberia and Nicaragua.[1634] When the UNSCOP plan failed to achieve the necessary majority on 25 November, the lobby 'moved into high gear' and induced the President to overrule the State Department, and let wavering governments know that the U.S. strongly desired partition.[1635]

Proponents of the Plan reportedly put pressure on nations to vote yes to the Partition Plan. A telegram signed by 26 US Senators with influence on foreign aid bills was sent to wavering countries, seeking their support for the partition plan. The US Senate was considering a large aid package at the time, including 60 million dollars to China.[1636,1637] Many nations reported pressure directed specifically at them:

- **United States** (Vote: **For**): President Truman later noted, "The facts were that not only were there pressure movements around the United Nations unlike anything that had been seen there before, but that the White House, too, was subjected to a constant barrage. I do not think I ever had as much pressure and propaganda aimed at the White House as I had in this instance. The persistence of a few of the extreme

Zionist leaders—actuated by political motives and engaging in political threats—disturbed and annoyed me."[1638]

- **India** (Vote: **Against**): Indian Prime Minister Jawaharlal Nehru spoke with anger and contempt for the way the UN vote had been lined up. He said the Zionists had tried to bribe India with millions and at the same time his sister, Vijaya Lakshmi Pandit, the Indian ambassador to the UN, had received daily warnings that her life was in danger unless "she voted right". Pandit occasionally hinted that something might change in favour of the Zionists. But another Indian delegate, Kavallam Pannikar, said that India would vote for the Arab side, because of their large Moslem minority, although they knew that the Jews had a case.
- **Liberia** (Vote: **For**): Liberia's Ambassador to the United States complained that the US delegation threatened aid cuts to several countries. Harvey S. Firestone, Jr., President of Firestone Natural Rubber Company, with major holdings in the country, also pressured the Liberian government
- **Philippines** (Vote: **For**): In the days before the vote, Philippines representative General Carlos P. Romulo stated "We hold that the issue is primarily moral. The issue is whether the United Nations should accept responsibility for the enforcement of a policy which is clearly repugnant to the valid nationalist aspirations of the people of Palestine. The Philippines Government holds that the United Nations ought not to accept such responsibility." After a phone call from Washington, the representative was recalled and the Philippines' vote changed.
- **Haiti** (Vote: **For**): The promise of a five million dollar loan may or may not have secured Haiti's vote for partition.
- **France** (Vote: **For**): Shortly before the vote, France's delegate to the United Nations was visited by Bernard Baruch, a long-term Jewish supporter of the Democratic Party who, during the recent world war, had been an economic adviser to President Roosevelt, and had latterly been appointed by President Truman as United States ambassador to the newly created UN Atomic Energy Commission. He was, privately, a supporter of the Irgun and its front organization, the American League for a Free Palestine. Baruch implied that a French failure to support the resolution might block planned American aid to France, which was badly needed for reconstruction, French currency reserves being exhausted and its balance of payments heavily in deficit. Previously, to avoid antagonising its Arab colonies, France had not publicly supported the resolution. After considering the danger of American aid being withheld, France finally voted in favour of it. So, too, did France's neighbours, Belgium, Luxembourg, and the Netherlands.

- **Venezuela** (Vote: **For**): Carlos Eduardo Stolk, Chairman of the Delegation of Venezuela, voted in favor of Resolution 181.[1639]
- **Cuba** (Vote: **Against**): The Cuban delegation stated they would vote against partition "in spite of pressure being brought to bear against us" because they could not be party to coercing the majority in Palestine.[1640]
- **Siam** (Absent): The credentials of the Siamese delegations were cancelled after Siam voted against partition in committee on 25 November.[1641]

There is also some evidence that Sam Zemurray put pressure on several "banana republics" to change their votes.[1642]

Reports of pressure against the Plan

According to Benny Morris, Wasif Kamal, an Arab Higher Committee official, tried to bribe a delegate to the United Nations, perhaps a Russian.

Concerning the welfare of Jews in Arab countries, a number of direct threats were made:

- Jamal Husseini promised, "The blood will flow like rivers in the Middle East". Iraqi Prime Minister Nuri al-Said, said: "We will smash the country with our guns and obliterate every place the Jews seek shelter in".
- Iraq's prime minister Nuri al-Said told British diplomats that if the United Nations solution was not "satisfactory", "severe measures should be taken against all Jews in Arab countries".[1643]

Concerning the welfare of Jews in Arab countries, a number of predictions were made:

- '"On 24 November the head of the Egyptian delegation to the General Assembly, Muhammad Hussein Heykal Pasha, said that "the lives of 1,000,000 Jews in Moslem countries would be jeopardized by the establishment of a Jewish state." At the 29th Meeting of the UN Ad Hoc Committee on Palestine on 24 November 1947, Dr Heykal Pasha, the Egyptian delegate, said, "if the U.N decide to amputate a part of Palestine in order to establish a Jewish state, no force on earth could prevent blood from flowing there... Moreover... no force on earth can confine it to the borders of Palestine itself... Jewish blood will necessarily be shed elsewhere in the Arab world... to place in certain and serious danger a million Jews." Mahmud Bey Fawzi (Egypt) said: "... imposed partition was sure to result in bloodshed in Palestine and in the rest of the Arab world".[1644]

- In a speech at the General Assembly Hall at Flushing Meadow, New York, on Friday, 28 November 1947, Iraq's Foreign Minister, Fadel Jamall, included the following statement: *Partition imposed against the will of the majority of the people will jeopardize peace and harmony in the Middle East. Not only the uprising of the Arabs of Palestine is to be expected, but the masses in the Arab world cannot be restrained. The Arab-Jewish relationship in the Arab world will greatly deteriorate. There are more Jews in the Arab world outside of Palestine than there are in Palestine. In Iraq alone, we have about one hundred and fifty thousand Jews who share with Moslems and Christians all the advantages of political and economic rights. Harmony prevails among Moslems, Christians and Jews. But any injustice imposed upon the Arabs of Palestine will disturb the harmony among Jews and non-Jews in Iraq; it will breed inter-religious prejudice and hatred.*

The Arab states warned the Western Powers that endorsement of the partition plan might be met by either or both an oil embargo and realignment of the Arab states with the Soviet Bloc.

Final vote

On 29 November 1947, the United Nations General Assembly voted 33 to 13, with 10 abstentions and 1 absent, in favour of the modified Partition Plan. The final vote, consolidated here by modern United Nations Regional Groups rather than contemporary groupings, was as follows:

In favour (33 countries, 72% of voting)

Latin American and Caribbean (13 countries):

- Bolivia
- Brazil
- Costa Rica
- Dominican Republic
- Ecuador
- Guatemala
- Haiti
- Nicaragua
- Panama
- Paraguay
- Peru
- Uruguay
- Venezuela

Western European and Others (8 countries):

- ■ Belgium
- ■ Denmark
- ■ France
- ■ Iceland
- ■ Luxembourg
- ■ Netherlands
- ■ Norway
- ■ Sweden

Eastern European (5 countries):

- ■ Byelorussian SSR
- ■ Czechoslovakia
- ■ Poland
- ■ Ukrainian SSR
- ■ Soviet Union

African (2 countries):

- ■ Liberia
- ■ South Africa

Asia-Pacific (3 countries)

- ■ Australia
- ■ New Zealand
- ■ Philippines

North America (2 countries)

- ■ Canada
- ■ United States

Against (13 countries, 28% of voting)

Asia-Pacific (9 countries, primarily Middle East sub-area):

- ■ Afghanistan
- ■ India
- ■ Iran
- ■ Iraq
- ■ Lebanon
- ■ Pakistan
- ■ Saudi Arabia
- ■ Syria
- ■ Yemen

Western European and Others (2 countries):

- ■ Greece

- Turkey

African (1 country):
- Egypt

Latin American and Caribbean (1 country):
- Cuba

Abstentions (10 countries)

Latin American and Caribbean (6 countries):
- Argentina
- Chile
- Colombia
- El Salvador
- Honduras
- Mexico

Asia-Pacific (1 country):
- China

African (1 country):
- Ethiopia

Western European and Others (1 country):
- United Kingdom

Eastern European (1 country):
- Yugoslavia

Absent (1 country)

Asia-Pacific (1 country):
- Thailand

Votes by modern region

If analysed by the modern composition of what later came to be known as the United Nations Regional Groups showed relatively aligned voting styles in the final vote. This, however, does not reflect the regional grouping at the time, as a major reshuffle of regional grouping occurred in 1966. All Western nations voted for the resolution, with the exception of the United Kingdom (the Mandate holder), Greece and Turkey. The Soviet bloc also voted for partition, with the exception of Yugoslavia, which was to be expelled from Cominform the following year. The majority of Latin American nations following Brazilian leadershipWikipedia:Citation needed, voted for partition, with a sizeable minority abstaining. Asian countries (primarily Middle Eastern countries) voted against partition, with the exception of the Philippines.

Regional Group	Members in UNGA181 vote	UNGA181 For	UNGA181 Against	UNGA181 Abstained
African	4	2	1	1
Asia-Pacific	11	1	9	1
Eastern European	6	5	0	1
LatAm and Caribb.	20	13	1	6
Western Eur. & Others	15	12	2	1
Total UN members	56	33	13	10

Reactions

Jews

Most Jews in Palestine and around the world reacted to the UN resolution with satisfaction, but some did not. Jews gathered in Tel Aviv and Jerusalem to celebrate the U.N. resolution during the whole night after the vote. Great bonfires blazed at Jewish collective farms in the north. Many big cafes in Tel Aviv served free champagne. Mainstream Zionist leaders emphasized the "heavy responsibility" of building a modern Jewish State, and committed to working towards a peaceful coexistence with the region's other inhabitants: Jewish units in the United States hailed the action by the United Nations. Most welcomed the Palestine Plan but some felt it did not settle the problem.

Some Revisionist Zionists rejected the partition plan as a renunciation of legitimately Jewish national territory. The Irgun Tsvai Leumi, led by Menachem Begin, and the Lehi (also known as the Stern Group or Gang), the two Revisionist-affiliated underground organisations which had been fighting against both the British and Arabs, stated their opposition. Begin warned that the partition would not bring peace because the Arabs would also attack the small state and that "in the war ahead we'll have to stand on our own, it will be a war on our existence and future."[1645] He also stated that "the bisection of our homeland is illegal. It will never be recognized."[1646] Begin was sure that the creation of a Jewish state would make territorial expansion possible, "after the shedding of much blood."[1647]

Some Post-Zionist scholars endorse Simha Flapan's view that it is a myth that Zionists accepted the partition as a compromise by which the Jewish community abandoned ambitions for the whole of Palestine and recognized the rights of the Arab Palestinians to their own state. Rather, Flapan argued, acceptance was only a tactical move that aimed to thwart the creation of an Arab Palestinian state and, concomitantly, expand the territory that had been assigned by the UN to the Jewish state.[1648,1649,1650,1651,1652] Baruch Kimmerling has said that Zionists "officially accepted the partition plan, but invested all their efforts towards improving its terms and maximally expanding their boundaries while reducing the number of Arabs in them."

Addressing the Central Committee of the Histadrut (the Eretz Israel Workers Party) days after the UN vote to partition Palestine, Ben-Gurion expressed his apprehension, stating:

> *the total population of the Jewish State at the time of its establishment will be about one million, including almost 40% non-Jews. Such a [population] composition does not provide a stable basis for a Jewish State. This [demographic] fact must be viewed in all its clarity and acuteness. With such a [population] composition, there cannot even be absolute certainty that control will remain in the hands of the Jewish majority... There can be no stable and strong Jewish state so long as it has a Jewish majority of only 60%.*[1653]

Ben-Gurion said "I know of no greater achievement by the Jewish people ... in its long history since it became a people."[1654]

Arabs

Arab leaders and governments rejected the plan of partition in the resolution and indicated that they would reject any other plan of partition. The Arab states' delegations declared immediately after the vote for partition that they would not be bound by the decision, and walked out accompanied by the Indian and Pakistani delegates.[1655]

They argued that it violated the principles of national self-determination in the UN charter which granted people the right to decide their own destiny. The Arab delegations to the UN issued a joint statement the day after that vote that stated: "the vote in regard to the Partition of Palestine has been given under great pressure and duress, and that this makes it doubly invalid"[1656]

On 16 February 1948, UN Palestine Commission to the security council reported that: "Powerful Arab interests, both inside and outside Palestine, are defying the resolution of the General Assembly and are engaged in a deliberate effort to alter by force the settlement envisaged therein."[1657] The Arabs were against the establishment of an international regime in Jerusalem too.

Arab states

A few weeks after UNSCOP released its report, Azzam Pasha, the General Secretary of the Arab League, was quoted by an Egyptian newspaper as saying "Personally I hope the Jews do not force us into this war because it will be a war of elimination and it will be a dangerous massacre which history will record similarly to the Mongol massacre or the wars of the Crusades." (This statement from October 1947 has often been incorrectly reported as having been made much later on 15 May 1948.) Pasha told Alec Kirkbride: "We will sweep them [the Jews] into the sea". The Syrian president, Shukri al-Quwatli, told his people: "We shall eradicate Zionism".

The Egyptian king, Farouk, told the American ambassador to Egypt that in the long run the Arabs would soundly defeat the Jews and drive them out of Palestine.[1658]

While Azzam Pasha repeated his threats to forcefully thwart the partition, the first important Arab voice who supported the partition was the influential Egyptian daily "Al Mokattam": "We stand for partition because we believe that it is the best final solution for the problem of Palestine... rejection of partition... will lead to further complications and will give the Zionists another space of time to complete their plans of defense and attack... a delay of one more year which would not benefit the Arabs but would benefit the Jews, especially after the British evacuation."

On 20 May 1948, Azzam told reporters "We are fighting for an Arab Palestine. Whatever the outcome the Arabs will stick to their offer of equal citizenship for Jews in Arab Palestine and let them be as Jewish as they like. In areas where they predominate they will have complete autonomy."[1659]

The Arab League said that some of the Jews would have to be expelled from a Palestinian Arab state.

Abdullah appointed Ibrahim Hashem Pasha as the Military Governor of the Arab areas occupied by troops of the Transjordan Army. He was a former Prime Minister of Transjordan who supported partition of Palestine as proposed by the Peel Commission and the United Nations.

Arabs in Palestine

Haj Amin al-Husseini said in March 1948 to an interviewer in a Jaffa daily *Al Sarih* that the Arabs did not intend merely to prevent partition but "would continue fighting until the Zionists were Annihilated".

Zionists attributed Arab rejection of the plan to mere intransigence. Palestinian Arabs opposed the very idea of partition but reiterated that this partition plan was unfair: the majority of the land (56%) would go to a Jewish state, when

Jews at that stage legally owned only 6-7% of it and remained a minority of the population (33% in 1946).[1660,1661,1662,1663] There were also disproportionate allocations under the plan and the area under Jewish control contained 45% of the Palestinian population. The proposed Arab state was only given 45% of the land, much of which was unfit for agriculture. Jaffa, though geographically separated, was to be part of the Arab state. However, most of the proposed Jewish state was the Negev desert. The plan allocated to the Jewish State most of the Negev desert that was sparsely populated and unsuitable for agriculture but also a "vital land bridge protecting British interests from the Suez Canal to Iraq"[1664,1665]

Few Palestinian Arabs joined the Arab Liberation Army because they suspected that the other Arab States did not plan on an independent Palestinian state. According to Ian Bickerton, for that reason many of them favored partition and indicated a willingness to live alongside a Jewish state.[1666] He also mentions that the Nashashibi family backed King Abdullah and union with Transjordan.[1667]

The AHC demanded that in a Palestinian Arab state, the majority of the Jews should not be citizens (those who had not lived in Palestine before the British Mandate).

According to Musa Alami, the mufti would agree to partition if he were promised that he would rule the future Arab state.

The Arab Higher Committee responded to the partition resolution and declared a three-day general strike in Palestine to begin the following day. On 2 December a large Arab mob, armed with clubs and knives, attacked the Jerusalem New Commercial Center attacking Jewish passersby and shops. The Haganah intelligence identified two AHC officials, as leading the crowd.[1668]

On 4 December a band of 120–150 gunmen from Salame attacked the settlers of the nearby kibbutz Efal, who defended the attack together with Palmah reinforcements.[1669]

British government

When Bevin received the partition proposal, he promptly ordered for it not to be imposed on the Arabs.[1670,1671] The plan was vigorously debated in the British parliament.

In a British cabinet meeting at 4 December 1947, it was decided that the Mandate would end at midnight 14 May 1948, the complete withdrawal by 1 August 1948, and Britain would not enforce the UN partition plan. On 11 December 1947, Britain announced the Mandate would end at midnight 14 May 1948 and its sole task would be to complete withdrawal by 1 August 1948. During the period in which the British withdrawal was completed, Britain refused to share the administration of Palestine with a proposed UN transition regime, to allow the UN Palestine Commission to establish a presence in Palestine earlier than a fortnight before the end of the Mandate, to allow the creation of official Jewish and Arab militias or to assist in smoothly handing over territory or authority to any successor.

United States government

The United States declined to recognize the All-Palestine government in Gaza by explaining that it had accepted the UN Mediator's proposal. The Mediator had recommended that Palestine, as defined in the original Mandate including Transjordan, might form a union.[1672] Bernadotte's diary said the Mufti had lost credibility on account of his unrealistic predictions regarding the defeat of the Jewish militias. Bernadotte noted "It would seem as though in existing circumstances most of the Palestinian Arabs would be quite content to be incorporated in Transjordan."[1673]

Subsequent events

The Partition Plan with Economic Union was not realized in the days following the 29 November 1947 resolution as envisaged by the General Assembly. It was followed by outbreaks of violence in Mandatory Palestine between Palestinian Jews and Arabs known as the 1947–48 Civil War.[1674] After Alan Cunningham, the High Commissioner of Palestine, left Jerusalem, on the morning of 14 May the British army left the city as well. The British left a power vacuum in Jerusalem and made no measures to establish the international regime in Jerusalem.[1675] At midnight on 14 May 1948, the British Mandate expired, and Britain disengaged its forces. Earlier in the evening, the Jewish People's Council had gathered at the Tel Aviv Museum, and approved a proclamation, declaring "the establishment of a Jewish state in Eretz Israel, to be known as the State of Israel".[1676] The 1948 Arab–Israeli War began with the invasion of, or intervention in, Palestine by the Arab States on 15 May 1948.[1677]

Resolution 181 as a legal basis for Palestinian statehood

In 1988, the Palestine Liberation Organization published the Palestinian Declaration of Independence relying on Resolution 181, arguing that the resolution continues to provide international legitimacy for the right of the Palestinian people to sovereignty and national independence.[1678] A number of scholars have written in support of this view.[1679,1680,1681]

A General Assembly request for an advisory opinion, Resolution ES-10/14 (2004), specifically cited resolution 181(II) as a "relevant resolution", and asked the International Court of Justice (ICJ) what are the legal consequences of the relevant Security Council and General Assembly resolutions. Judge Abdul Koroma explained the majority opinion: "The Court has also held that the right of self-determination as an established and recognized right under international law applies to the territory and to the Palestinian people. Accordingly, the exercise of such right entitles the Palestinian people to a State of their own as originally envisaged in resolution 181 (II) and subsequently confirmed."[1682] In response, Prof. Paul De Waart said that the Court put the legality of the 1922 League of Nations Palestine Mandate and the 1947 UN Plan of Partition beyond doubt once and for all.[1683]

Retrospect

In 2011, Mahmoud Abbas stated that the 1947 Arab rejection of United Nations Partition Plan for Palestine was a mistake he hoped to rectify.

References

<templatestyles src="Refbegin/styles.css" />

- Benny Morris (1 October 2008). *1948: A History of the First Arab-Israeli War*[1684]. Yale University Press. ISBN 978-0-300-14524-3. Retrieved 14 July 2013.<templatestyles src="Module:Citation/CS1/styles.css"></templatestyles>
- William Roger Louis (2006). *Ends of British Imperialism: The Scramble for Empire, Suez, and Decolonization*[1685]. I.B.Tauris. ISBN 978-1-84511-347-6. Retrieved 16 August 2013.<templatestyles src="Module:Citation/CS1/styles.css"></templatestyles>
- William Roger Louis (1985). *The British Empire in the Middle East, 1945-1951: Arab Nationalism, the United States, and Postwar Imperialism*[1686]. Oxford University Press. ISBN 978-0-19-822960-5.<templatestyles src="Module:Citation/CS1/styles.css"></templatestyles>

Bibliography

- Bregman, Ahron (2002). *Israel's Wars: A History Since 1947*. London: Routledge.
- Arieh L. Avneri (1984). *The Claim of Dispossession: Jewish Land Settlement and the Arabs, 1878–1948*. Transaction Publishers.

- Fischbach, Michael R. (2003). *Records of Dispossession: Palestinian Refugee Property and the Arab-Israeli Conflict*. Columbia University Press.
- Gelber, Yoav (1997). *Jewish-Transjordanian Relations: Alliance of Bars Sinister*. London: Routledge.
- Khalaf, Issa (1991). *Politics in Palestine: Arab Factionalism and Social Disintegration,*. University at Albany, SUNY.
- Louis, Wm. Roger (1986). *The British Empire in the Middle East,: Arab Nationalism, the United States, and Postwar Imperialism*. Oxford University Press.
- "Palestine"[1687]. Encyclopædia Britannica Online School Edition, 15 May 2006.
- Sicker, Martin (1999). *Reshaping Palestine: From Muhammad Ali to the British Mandate, 1831–1922*. Praeger/Greenwood.

External links

Wikimedia Commons has media related to *United Nations Partition Plan for Palestine*.

Wikisourcehas original text related to this article:
United Nations Special Committee on Palestine Federal State Plan

- UN Resolution 181 (II) A: Future government of Palestine[1688]. On www.un.org. Retrieved 28 July 2018.
- Text of the Resolution at undocs.org[1590]
- Full text of report of Sub-Committee 2 with all appendices, tables and maps[1689]
- JFK in Support of Partition, 1948[1690] Shapell Manuscript Foundation
- Legal Status of West Bank, Gaza and East Jerusalem[1691]
- Maps of Palestine[1692]
- Ivan Rand and the UNSCOP Papers[1693]
- Official Map prepared by UNSCOP[1694]
- 29 November Quiz[1695]
- Firsthand testimonies from the men and women who helped found the State of Israel[1696] on YouTube

Civil War

1947–48 Civil War in Mandatory Palestine

<indicator name="pp-default"> 🔒 </indicator>

Civil War in Palestine (1947–48)
Part of the Intercommunal conflict in Mandatory Palestine, 1948 Palestine War
 Jewish militants at Katamon, Jerusalem.
Date 30 November 1947 – 14 May 1948 (5 months and 2 weeks)
Location Mandatory Palestine
Result <ul><li>Jewish forces overcome Palestinian Arab forces</li><li>Collapse of the Arab society in Palestine</li><li>Beginning of the 1948 Palestinian exodus</li><li>Beginning of the Jewish exodus from Muslim countries</li><li>Israeli Declaration of Independence</li><li>Invasion of Palestine by the Arab League</li></ul>
Belligerents

Jews of Palestine<ul><li>Haganah<ul><li>Palmach</li></ul></li><li>Irgun</li><li>Lehi</li><li>Foreign Volunteers</li><li>Allied Bedouin tribes</li></ul>	Arabs of Palestine<ul><li>Army of the Holy War</li><li>Arab Liberation Army</li></ul>Transjordan<ul><li>Arab Legion</li></ul>	🇬🇧 United Kingdom<ul><li>🇬🇧 United Kingdom military forces in Mandatory Palestine</li></ul>
Commanders and leaders		

David Ben-Gurion Yaakov Dori Yigael Yadin Yigal Allon Menachem Begin	Fawzi al-Qawuqji Abd al-Qadir al-Husayni †	🇬🇧 Gordon MacMillan
Strength		
15,000 (start)[1697] 35,000 (end)	A few thousands	~70,000
Casualties and losses		
1 April : 895[1698] 15 May : ~ 2,000[1699]	1 April : 991	125 dead less than 300 injured[1700]

The **1947–48 Civil War in Mandatory Palestine** was the first phase of the 1948 Palestine war. It broke out after the General Assembly of the United Nations adopted a resolution on 29 November 1947 recommending the adoption of the Partition Plan for Palestine.[1701]

During the civil war, the Jewish and Arab communities of Palestine clashed (the latter supported by the Arab Liberation Army) while the British, who had the obligation to maintain order, organized their withdrawal and intervened only on an occasional basis.

When the British Mandate of Palestine expired on 14 May 1948, and with the Declaration of the Establishment of the State of Israel, the surrounding Arab states—Egypt, Transjordan, Iraq and Syria—invaded what had just ceased to be Mandatory Palestine,[1702] and immediately attacked Israeli forces and several Jewish settlements. The conflict then turned into the 1948 Arab–Israeli War.Wikipedia:Citation needed

Background

Under the control of a British administration since 1920, the area of Palestine found itself the object of a battle between Jewish Zionist nationalists and Palestinian Arab nationalists, who opposed one another just as much as they both opposed the British mandate.

The Palestinian Arab backlash culminated in the 1936–1939 Arab revolt in Palestine. Directed by Palestinian Arab nationalists, the rebels opposed Zionism, the British presence in Palestine and Palestinian Arab politicians who called for pan-Arabic nationalism at the same time. Both the British and the Zionist organizations of the time opposed the revolt; nonetheless, the Palestinian Arab nationalists did obtain from the British a drastic reduction of Jewish immigration, legislated by the 1939 White Paper. However, the consequences of the unsuccessful uprising were heavy. Nearly 5,000 Arabs and 500 Jews died; the various paramilitary Zionist organizations were reinforced, and the majority of the members of the Palestinian Arab political elite exiled themselves, such as Amin al-Husseini, leader of the Arab Higher Committee.

After World War II and The Holocaust, the Zionist movement gained attention and sympathy. In Mandatory Palestine, Zionist groups fought against the British occupation. In the two and a half years from 1945 to June 1947, British law enforcement forces lost 103 dead, and sustained 391 wounded from Jewish militants.[1703] The Palestinian Arab nationalists reorganized themselves, but their organization remained inferior to that of the Zionists. Nevertheless, the weakening of the colonial British Empire reinforced Arab countries and the Arab League.

The Haganah, a Jewish paramilitary organization, was initially involved in the post-war attacks against the British in Palestine but withdrew following the outrage caused by the 1946 Irgun bombing of the British Army Headquarters in the King David Hotel. In May 1946, on the assumption of British neutrality in the future hostilities, a Plan C was formulated that envisaged guidelines for retaliation if and when Palestinian Arab attacks took place on the Yishuv. As the countdown ticked down, the Haganah implemented assaults involving the torching and demolition by explosives against economic infrastructures, the property of Palestinian politicians and military commanders, villages, town neighbourhoods, houses and farms that were deemed to be bases or used by inciters and their accomplices. The killing of armed irregulars and adult males was also foreseen. On 15 August 1947, on suspicion it was a terrorist headquarters, they blew up the house of the Abu Laban family, prosperous Palestinian orange growers, near Petah Tikva. Twelve occupants, including a woman and six children, were killed.[1704] After November 1947, the dynamiting of houses formed a key component of most Haganah retaliatory strikes.[1705]

Diplomacy failed to reconcile the different points of view concerning the future of Palestine. On 18 February 1947, the British announced their withdrawal from the region. Later that year, on 29 November, the General Assembly of the United Nations voted to recommend the adoption and implementation of the partition plan with the support of the big global powers, but not of Britain nor of the Arab States.

Beginning of the Civil War (30 November 1947 – 1 April 1948)

In the aftermath of the adoption of Resolution 181(II) by the United Nations General Assembly recommending the adoption and implementation of the Plan of Partition, the manifestations of joy of the Jewish community were counterbalanced by protests by Arabs throughout the country[1706] and after 1

Figure 190: *Aftermath of the car bomb attack on the Ben Yehuda St., which killed 53 and injured many more.*

December, the Arab Higher Committee enacted a general strike that lasted three days.[1707]

A 'wind of violence'[1708] rapidly took hold of the country, foreboding civil war between the two communities.[1709] Murders, reprisals, and counter-reprisals came fast on each other's heels, resulting in dozens of victims killed on both sides in the process. The impasse persisted as British forces did not intervene to put a stop to the escalating cycles of violence.[1710,1711,1712,1713]

The first casualties after the adoption of Resolution 181(II) by the General Assembly were passengers on a Jewish bus driving on the Coastal Plain near Kfar Sirkin on 30 November. An eight-man gang from Jaffa ambushed the bus killing five and wounding others. Half an hour later they ambushed a second bus, southbound from Hadera, killing two more. Arab snipers attacked Jewish buses in Jerusalem and Haifa.

Irgun and Lehi (the latter also known as the Stern Gang) followed their strategy of placing bombs in crowded markets and bus-stops.[1714] As on 30 December, in Haifa, when members of Irgun, threw two bombs at a crowd of Arab workers who were queueing in front of a refinery, killing 6 of them and injuring 42. An angry crowd massacred 39 Jewish people in revenge, until British soldiers reestablished calm.[1715] In reprisals, some soldiers from the strike force, Palmach and the Carmeli brigade, attacked the village of Balad ash-Sheikh and Hawassa. According to different historians, this attack led to between 21 and 70 deaths.

According to Benny Morris, much of the fighting in the first months of the war took place in and on the edges of the main towns, and was initiated by the Arabs. It included Arab snipers firing at Jewish houses, pedestrians, and traffic, as well as planting bombs and mines along urban and rural paths and roads.[1716]

From January onwards, operations became increasingly militarized.

In all the mixed zones where both communities lived, particularly Jerusalem and Haifa, increasingly violent attacks, riots, reprisals and counter-reprisals followed each other. Isolated shootings evolved into all-out battles. Attacks against traffic, for instance, turned into ambushes as one bloody attack led to another.

On 22 February 1948, supporters of Mohammad Amin al-Husayni organized, with the help of certain British deserters, three attacks against the Jewish community. Using car bombs aimed at the headquarters of the pro-Zionist *Palestine Post* newspaper, the Ben Yehuda St. market and the backyard of the Jewish Agency's offices, they killed 22, 53 and 13 Jewish people respectively, and injured hundreds.[1717,1718] In revenge, Lehi put a landmine on the railroad track in Rehovot on which a train from Cairo to Haifa was travelling, killing 28 British soldiers and injuring 35.[1719] This would be copied on 31 March, close to Caesarea Maritima, which would lead to the death of forty people, injuring 60, who were, for the most part, Arab civilians.[1720]

Having recruited a few thousand volunteers, al-Husayni organized the blockade of the 100,000 Jewish residents of Jerusalem.[1721] To counter this, the Yishuv authorities tried to supply the city with convoys of up to 100 armoured vehicles, but the operation became more and more impractical as the number of casualties in the relief convoys surged. By March, Al-Hussayni's tactic had paid off. Almost all of Haganah's armoured vehicles had been destroyed, the blockade was in full operation, and hundreds of Haganah members who had tried to bring supplies into the city were killed.[1722] The situation for those who dwelt in the Jewish settlements in the highly isolated Negev and North of Galilee was even more critical.

According to the Arab League general Safwat:

> Despite the fact that skirmishes and battles have begun, the Jews at this stage are still trying to contain the fighting to as narrow a sphere as possible in the hope that partition will be implemented and a Jewish government formed; they hope that if the fighting remains limited, the Arabs will

acquiesce in the fait accompli. This can be seen from the fact that the Jews have not so far attacked Arab villages unless the inhabitants of those villages attacked them or provoked them first.

Although a certain level of doubt took hold among Yishuv supporters, their apparent defeats were due more to their wait-and-see policy than to weakness.Wikipedia:Citation needed David Ben-Gurion reorganized Haganah and made conscription obligatory. Every Jewish man and woman in the country had to receive military training.

Allied Powers' policies

This situation caused the United States to withdraw their support for the Partition plan, thus encouraging the Arab League to believe that the Palestinian Arabs, reinforced by the Arab Liberation Army, could put an end to the plan for partition. The British, on the other hand, decided on 7 February 1948, to support the annexation of the Arab part of Palestine by Transjordan.[1723]

Population evacuations

While the Jewish population had received strict orders requiring them to hold their ground everywhere at all costs,[1724] the Arab population was more affected by the general conditions of insecurity to which the country was exposed. Up to 100,000 Arabs, from the urban upper and middle classes in Haifa, Jaffa and Jerusalem, or Jewish-dominated areas, evacuated abroad or to Arab centres eastwards.[1725]

Fighters and arms from abroad

As a consequence of funds raised by Golda Meir which were donated by sympathisers in the United States, and Stalin's decision to support the Zionist cause, the Jewish representatives of Palestine were able to sign very important armament contracts in the East. Other Haganah agents recuperated stockpiles from the Second World War, which helped improve the army's equipment and logistics. Operation Balak allowed arms and other equipment to be transported for the first time by the end of March.

There was an intervention of a number of Arab Liberation Army regiments inside Palestine, each active in a variety of distinct sectors around the different coastal towns. They consolidated their presence in Galilee and Samaria.[1726] Abd al-Qadir al-Husayni came from Egypt with several hundred men of the Army of the Holy War.

German and Bosnian WWII veterans, including former intelligence, Wehrmacht, and Waffen SS officers, were among the 'volunteers' fighting for the Palestinian cause[1727] Veterans of WWII Axis militaries were represented in the ranks of the ALA forces commanded by Fawzi al-Qawuqji (who had been awarded an officer's rank in the Wehrmacht during WWII)[1728] and in the Mufti's forces, commanded by Abd al-Qadir (who had fought with the Germans against the British in Iraq) and Salama (who served as a Waffen SS commando during WWII). Some of the Germans who served the Mufti in his Nablus headquarters were Adolf Schwabe, Albert Grossman, and Rudolf Hoffman.[1729]

Benny Morris writes that the Yishuv was more successful in attracting and effectively deploying foreign military professionals than their Arab adversaries. He concludes that the ex-Nazis and Bosnian Muslims recruited by the Palestinians, Egyptians, and Syrians "proved of little significance" to the outcome of the conflict.[1730]

Death toll

Morris says that by the end of March 1948, the Yishuv had suffered about a thousand dead.[1731] Ilan Pappé estimates that 400 Jews and 1,500 Arabs were killed by January 1948.[1732] In December the Jewish death toll was estimated over 200 and, according to Alec Kirkbride, by 18 January 333 Jews and 345 Arabs were killed while 643 Jews and 877 Arabs were injured.[1733] The overall death toll between December 1947 and January 1948 (including British personnel) was estimated at around 1,000 people, with 2,000 injured.[1734] According to Yoav Gelber, by the end of March there was a total of 2,000 dead and 4,000 wounded. These figures correspond to an average of more than 100 deaths and 200 casualties per week in a population of 2,000,000.

Intervention of foreign forces in Palestine

Violence kept intensifying with the intervention of military units. Although responsible for law and order up until the end of the mandate, the British did not try to take control of the situation, being more involved in the liquidation of the administration and the evacuation of their troops.[1735,1736] Furthermore, the authorities felt that they had lost enough men already in the conflict.

The British either could not or did not want to impede the intervention of foreign forces into Palestine.[1737,1738] According to a special report by the UN Special Commission on Palestine:[1739]

- During the night of 20–21 January, a force of 700 Syrians in battle dress, well-equipped, with mechanized transport, entered Palestine 'via Transjordan.'

Figure 191: *Arab volunteers fighting in Palestine in 1947*

- On 27 January, 'a band of 300 men from outside Palestine, was established in the area of Safed in Galilee and was probably responsible for the intensive heavy weapon and mortar attacks the following week against the settlement of Yechiam.'
- During the night of 29–30 January, a battalion of the Arab Liberation Army, 950 men in 19 vehicles commanded by Fawzi al-Qawuqji, entered Palestine 'via Adam Bridge and dispersed itself around the villages of Nablus, Jenin, and Tulkarem.'

This description corresponds to the entry of Arab Liberation Army troops between 10 January and the start of March:

- The Second regiment of Yarmouk, under the orders of Adib Shishakli[1740] entered Galilee via Lebanon on the night of 11–12 January. The battalion passed through Safed and then settled in the village of Sasa. A third of the regiment's fighters were Palestinian Arabs, and a quarter were Syrian.
- The 1st Yarmouk regiment, commanded by Muhammad Tzafa, entered Palestine on the night of 20–21 January, via the Bridge of Damia from Jordan and dispersed around Samaria, where it established its HQ, in the Northern Samarian city of Tubas. The regiment was composed chiefly of Palestinian Arabs and Iraqis.
- The Hittin regiment, commanded by Madlul Abbas, settled in the west of Samaria with its headquarters in Tulkarem.

- The Hussein ibn Ali regiment provided reinforcement in Haifa, Jaffa, Jerusalem, and several other cities.
- The Qadassia regiment were reserves based in Jab'a.

Fawzi al-Qawuqji, Field Commander of the Arab Liberation Army, arrived, according to his own account, on 4 March, with the rest of the logistics and around 100 Bosniak volunteers in Jab'a, a small village on the route between Nablus and Jenin. He established a headquarters there and a training centre for Palestinian Arab volunteers.

Alan Cunningham, the British High Commissioner in Palestine, thoroughly protested against the incursions and the fact that 'no serious effort is being made to stop incursions'. The only reaction came from Alec Kirkbride, who complained to Ernest Bevin about Cunningham's "hostile tone and threats".[1741]

The British and the information service of Yishuv expected an offensive for 15 February, but it would not take place, seemingly because the Mufti troops were not ready.[1742]

In March, an Iraqi regiment of the Arab Liberation Army came to reinforce the Palestinian Arab troops of Salameh in the area around Lydda and Ramleh, while Al-Hussayni started a headquarters in Bir Zeit, 10 km to the north of Ramallah.[1743] At the same time, a number of North African troops, principally Libyans, and hundreds of members of the Muslim Brotherhood entered Palestine. In March, an initial regiment arrived in Gaza and certain militants among them reached Jaffa.

Morale of the fighters

The Arab combatants' initial victories reinforced morale among them.[1744] The Arab Higher Committee was confident and decided to prevent the set-up of the UN-backed partition plan. In an announcement made to the Secretary-General on 6 February, they declared:[1745]

<templatestyles src="Template:Quote/styles.css"/>

> *The Palestinian Arabs consider any attempt by Jewish people or by whatever power or group of power to establish a Jewish state in an Arab territory to be an act of aggression that will be resisted by force [...]*
> *The prestige of the United Nations would be better served by abandoning this plan and by not imposing such an injustice [...]*
> *The Palestinian Arabs make a grave declaration before the UN, before God and before history that they will never submit to any power that comes to Palestine to impose a partition. The only way to establish a partition is to get rid of them all: men, women, and children.*

At the beginning of February 1948, the morale of the Jewish leaders was not high: "distress and despair arose clearly from the notes taken at the meetings of the Mapai party."[1746] "The attacks against the Jewish settlements and main roads worsened the direction of the Jewish people, who underestimated the intensity of the Arab reaction."[1747] The situation of the 100,000 Jews situated in Jerusalem was precarious, and supplies to the city, already slim in number, were likely to be stopped. Nonetheless, despite the setbacks suffered, the Jewish forces, in particular Haganah, remained superior in number and quality to those of the Arab forces.

First wave of Palestinian refugees

1948 Palestinian exodus
Main Articles
• 1947–48 civil war • 1948 Arab–Israeli War • 1948 Palestine war • Causes of the exodus • Nakba Day • Palestinian refugee • Palestine refugee camps • Palestinian right of return • Palestinian return to Israel • Present absentee • Transfer Committee • Resolution 194
Background
• Mandatory Palestine • Israeli Declaration of Independence • Israeli–Palestinian conflict history • New Historians • Palestine · Plan Dalet • 1947 partition plan · UNRWA
Key incidents

- Battle of Haifa
- Deir Yassin massacre
- Exodus from Lydda and Ramle

Notable writers
• Aref al-Aref · Yoav Gelber • Efraim Karsh · Walid Khalidi • Nur-eldeen Masalha · Benny Morris • Ilan Pappé · Tom Segev • Avraham Sela · Avi Shlaim
Related categories/lists
• List of depopulated villages
Related templates
• Palestinians
• v • t • e[1748]

The high morale of the Arab fighters and politicians was not shared by the Palestinian Arab civilian population. The UN Palestine Commission reported 'Panic continues to increase, however, throughout the Arab middle classes, and there is a steady exodus of those who can afford to leave the country. 'From December 1947 to January 1948, around 70,000 Arabs fled,[1749] and, by the end of March, that number had grown to around 100,000.

These people were part of the first wave of Palestinian refugees of the conflict. Mostly the middle and upper classes fled, including the majority of the families of local governors and representatives of the Arab Higher Committee. Non-Palestinian Arabs also fled in large numbers. Most of them did not abandon the hope of returning to Palestine once the hostilities had ended.[1750]

Policies of foreign powers

Many decisions were made abroad that had an important influence over the outcome of the conflict.

Britain and the Jordanian choice

Britain did not want a Palestinian state led by the Mufti, and opted unofficially instead, on 7 February 1948, to support the annexation of the Arab part of Palestine by Abdullah I of Jordan. At a meeting in London between the commander of Transjordan's Arab Legion, Glubb Pasha, and Secretary of State for Foreign and Commonwealth Affairs, Ernest Bevin, the two parties agreed that they would facilitate the entry of the Arab Legion into Palestine on 15 May and that the Arab part of Palestine be occupied by it. However, they held that the Arab Legion not enter the vicinity of Jerusalem or the Jewish state itself. This option did not envisage a Palestinian Arab state. Although the ambitions of King Abdullah are known, it is not apparent to what extent the authorities of Yishuv, the Arab Higher Committee or the Arab League knew of this decision.

United States turnabout

In mid-March, after the increasing disorder in Palestine and faced with the fear, later judged unfounded, of an Arab petrol embargo,[1751] the US government announced the possible withdrawal of its support for the UN's partition plan and for dispatching an international force to guarantee its implementation. The US suggested that instead Palestine be put under UN supervision.[1752,1753] On 1 April, the UN Security Council voted on the US proposal to convoke a special assembly to reconsider the Palestinian problem; the Soviet Union abstained.[1754] This U-turn by the US caused concern and debate among Yishuv authorities. They thought that after the withdrawal of British troops, the Yishuv could not effectively resist the Arab forces without the support of the US. In this context, Elie Sasson, the director of the Arab section of Jewish Agency, and several other personalities, persuaded David Ben-Gurion and Golda Meyerson to advance a diplomatic initiative to the Arabs. The job of negotiation was delegated to Joshua Palmon, who was prohibited from limiting the Haganah's liberty of action but was authorized to declare that "the Jewish people were ready with a truce."[1755]

Logistical support of the Eastern Bloc

In the context of the embargo imposed upon Palestinian belligerents—Jewish and Arab alike—and the dire lack of arms by the Yishuv in Palestine, Soviet ruler Joseph Stalin's decision to breach the embargo and support the Yishuv with arms exported from Czechoslovakia played a role in the war that was differently appreciated.[1756] However, Syria also bought arms from Czechoslovakia for the Arab Liberation Army, but the shipment never arrived due to Haganah intervention.

Possible motivations for Stalin's decision include his support of the UN Partition plan, and allowing Czechoslovakia to earn some foreign income after being forced to refuse Marshall Plan assistance.[1757]

The extent of this support and the concrete role that it played is up for debate. Figures advanced by historians tend to vary. Yoav Gelber spoke of 'small deliveries from Czechoslovakia arriving by air [...] from April 1948 onwards'[1758] whereas various historians have argued that there was an unbalanced level of support in favor of Yishuv, given that the Palestinian Arabs did not benefit from an equivalent level of Soviet support.[1759] In any case, the embargo that was extended to all Arab states in May 1948 by the UN Security Council caused great problems to them.[1760,1761]

Arab leaders' refusal of direct involvement

Arab leaders did what they possibly could to avoid being directly involved[1762,] in support for the Palestinian cause.[1763]

At the Arab League summit of October 1947, in Aley, the Iraqi general, Ismail Safwat, painted a realist picture of the situation. He underlined the better organization and greater financial support of the Jewish people in comparison to the Palestinians. He recommended the immediate deployment of the Arab armies at the Palestinian borders, the dispatching of weapons and ammunition to the Palestinians, and the contribution of a million pounds of financial aid to them. His proposals were rejected, other than the suggestion to send financial support, which was not followed up on. Nonetheless, a techno-military committee was established to coordinate assistance to the Palestinians. Based in Cairo, it was directed by Sawfat, who was supported by Lebanese and Syrian officers and representatives of the Higher Arab Committee. A Transjordian delegate was also appointed, but he did not participate in meetings.

At the December 1947 Cairo summit, under pressure by public opinion, the Arab leaders decided to create a military command that united all the heads of all the major Arab states, headed by Safwat. They still ignored his calls for financial and military aid, preferring to defer any decision until the end of the Mandate,[1764] but, nevertheless, decide to form the Arab Liberation Army, which would go into action in the following weeks.[1765] On the night of 20–21 January 1948, around 700 armed Syrians entered Palestine via Transjordan.[1766] In February 1948, Safwat reiterated his demands, but they fell on deaf ears: the Arab governments hoped that the Palestinians, aided by the Arab Liberation Army, could manage on their own until the International community renounced the partition plan.

Arms problem

Civil war beginning (until 1 April 1948)

The Arab Liberation Army was, in theory, financed and equipped by the Arab League. A budget of one million pounds sterling had been promised to them,[1767] due to the insistence of Ismail Safwat. In reality, though, funding never arrived, and only Syria truly supported the Arab volunteers in concrete terms. Syria bought from Czechoslovakia a quantity of arms for the Arab Liberation Army but the shipment never arrived due to Hagana force intervention.

Figure 192: *Sten submachine gun*

According to Lapierre & Collins, on the ground, logistics were completely neglected, and their leader, Fawzi al-Qawuqji, envisaged that his troops survive only on the expenses accorded to them by the Palestinian population.[1768] However, Gelber says that the Arab League had arranged the supplies through special contractors. They were equipped with different types of light weapons, light and medium-sized mortars, a number of 75 mm and 105 mm guns, and armoured vehicles but their stock of shells was small.[1769]

The situation that the Army of the Holy War and the Palestinian forces were in was worse. They could not rely on any form of foreign support and had to get by on the funds that Mohammad Amin al-Husayni could raise. The troops' armament was limited to what the fighters already had. To make things even worse, they had to be content with arms bought on the black market or pillaged from British warehouses, and, as a result, did not really have enough arms to wage war.[1770]

Until March, Haganah suffered also a lack of arms. The Jewish fighters benefitted from a number of clandestine factories that manufactured some light weapons,[1771] ammunition and explosives. The one weapon of which there was no shortage was locally produced explosives.[1772] However, they had far less than what was necessary to carry out a war: in November, only one out of every three Jewish combatants was armed, rising to two out of three within Palmach.[1773]

The Hagana sent agents to Europe and to the United States, in order to arm and equip this army. To finance all of this, Golda Meir managed, by the end of December, to collect $25 million through a fundraising campaign set about in the United States to capitalize on American sympathisers to the Zionist cause.[1774] Out of the 129 million US dollars raised between October 1947 and March 1949 for the Zionist cause, more than $78 million, over 60%, were used to buy arms and munition.[1775]

Death toll and analysis

In the last week of March alone, the losses sustained by Haganah were particularly heavy: they lost three large convoys in ambushes, more than 100 soldiers and their fleet of armoured vehicles.

All in all, West Jerusalem was gradually 'choked;' the settlements of Galilee could not be reached in any other way but via the valley of Jordan and the road of Nahariya. This along with the foreseen attack of the Arab states in May and the earlier projected departure date of the British pushed Haganah to the offensive and to apply Plan Dalet from April onwards.

Haganah on the offensive (1 April – 15 May 1948)

A leased transport plane was used for the Operation Balak first arms ferry flight from Czechoslovakia on the end of March 1948. At the beginning of April 1948, a shipment of thousands of rifles and hundreds of machine guns arrived at Tel Aviv harbor. With this big shipment, the Hagana could supply weapons to a concentrated effort, without taking over the arms of other Jewish territory and risking them being with no weapons. The Hagana went into the offensive, although still lacking heavy weapons.

After 15 May 1948

After the Arab states invasion at 15 May, during the first weeks of the 1948 Arab–Israeli War, the arms advantage leant in favour of the Arab states. From June, onwards, there was also a flow of heavy arms. From June, after the first truce, the advantage leant clearly towards the Israelis. This situation's changing was due to the contacts made in November 1947 and afterwards.

The Yishuv purchased rifles, machine guns and munitions from Czechoslovakia,[1776] which were mainly supplied after the British navy blockade was lifted on 15 May 1948, at the end of the British mandate. The Yishuv obtained from Czechoslovakia a supply of Avia S-199 fighter planes too[1777] and, later on in the conflict, Supermarine Spitfires. In the stockpiles left over from World War II, the Yishuv procured all the necessary equipment, vehicles and logistics needed for an army. In France, they procured armoured vehicles despite the ongoing embargo.[1778] The Yishuv bought machines to manufacture arms and munitions, forming the foundations of the Israeli armament industry.[1779]

The Yishuv bought at the United States, bombers and transport aircraft, which during Operation Balak were used to ferry arms and dismantled Avia S-199 fighter planes from Czechoslovakia to Israel, in defiance of the U.N embargo, for 3 months, starting at 12 May 1948.[1780] Some ships were also leased out

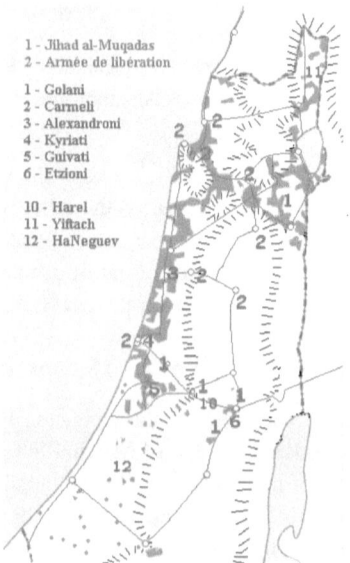

Figure 193: *Theatre of Operation of each Haganah brigade.*

from various European ports so that these goods could be transported by 15 May.

However, for Ben-Gurion, the problem was also constructing an army that was worthy to be a state army.[1781]

Reorganisation of Haganah

After 'having gotten the Jews of Palestine and of elsewhere to do everything that they could, personally and financially, to help Yishuv,' Ben-Gurion's second greatest achievement was his having successfully transformed Haganah from being a clandestine paramilitary organization into a true army.[1782] Ben-Gurion appointed Israel Galili to the position of head of the High Command counsel of Haganah and divided Haganah into 6 infantry brigades, numbered 1 to 6, allotting a precise theatre of operation to each one. Yaakov Dori was named Chief of Staff, but it was Yigael Yadin who assumed the responsibility on the ground as chief of Operations. Palmach, commanded by Yigal Allon, was divided into 3 elite brigades, numbered 10–12, and constituted the mobile force of Haganah.[1783] Ben-Gurion's attempts to retain personal control over the newly formed IDF lead later in July to The Generals' Revolt.

On 19 November 1947, obligatory conscription was instituted for all men and women aged between 17 and 25. By end of March 21,000 people had been

Figure 194: *Map of Jewish settlements and roads in Palestine by 1 December 1947*

conscripted.[1784,1785] On 30 March the call-up was extended to men and single women aged between 26 and 35. Five days later a General Mobilization order was issued for all men under 40.[1786]

"From November 1947, the Haganah, (...) began to change from a territorial militia into a regular army. (...) Few of the units had been well trained by December. (...) By March–April, it fielded still under-equipped battalion and brigades. By April–May, the Haganah was conducting brigade size offensive."[1787]

War of the roads and blockade of Jerusalem

Geographic situation of the Jewish zones

Apart from on the coastline, Jewish yishuvim, or settlements, were very dispersed. Communication between the coastal area (the main area of Jewish settlements) and the peripheral settlements was by road. These road were an easy target for attacks, as most of them passed through or near entirely Arab localities. The isolation of the 100,000 Jewish people in Jerusalem and other Jewish settlements outside the coastal zone, such as kibbutz Kfar Etzion, halfway on the strategic road between Jerusalem and Hebron, the 27 settlements in the

Figure 195: *Abd al-Qadir al-Husayni, prominent military leader during the Palestinian Civil War.*

southern region of Negev[1788] and the settlements to the north of Galilee, were a strategic weakness for the Yishuv.

The possibility of evacuating these difficult to defend zones was considered, but the policy of Haganah was set by David Ben-Gurion. He stated that "what the Jewish people have has to be conserved. No Jewish person should abandon his or her house, farm, kibbutz or job without authorization. Every outpost, every colony, whether it is isolated or not, must be occupied as though it were Tel Aviv itself." No Jewish settlement was evacuated until the invasion of May 1948. Only a dozen kibbutzim in Galilee, and those in Gush Etzion sent women and children into the safer interior zones.[1789]

Ben-Gurion gave instructions that the settlements of Negev be reinforced in number of men and goods, in particular the kibbutzim of Kfar Darom and Yad Mordechai (both close to Gaza), Revivim (south of Beersheba), and Kfar Etzion. Conscious of the danger that weighed upon Negev, the supreme command of Haganah assigned a whole Palmach battalion there.[1790]

Siege of Jerusalem

Jerusalem and the great difficulty of accessing the city became even more critical to its Jewish population, who made up one sixth of the total Jewish pop-

Figure 196: *An Arab road block, at the main road to Jerusalem*

Figure 197: *Palestinian irregulars near a burnt armored Haganah supply truck, the road to Jerusalem, 1948*

Figure 198: *Jerusalem convoy, passing Lifta, April 1948*

Figure 199: *Shielded Jewish convoy during the blockade of Tel Aviv–Jerusalem road*

ulation in Palestine. The long and difficult route from Tel Aviv to Jerusalem, after leaving the Jewish zone at Hulda, went through the foothills of Latrun. The 28-kilometre route between Bab al-Wad and Jerusalem took no less than three hours,[1791] and the route passed near the Arab villages of Saris, Qaluniya, Al-Qastal, and Deir Yassin.[1792]

Abd al-Qadir al-Husayni arrived in Jerusalem with the intent to surround and besiege its Jewish community.[1793] He moved to Surif, a village to the southwest of Jerusalem, with his supporters—around a hundred fighters who were trained in Syria before the war and who served as officers in his army, Jihad al-Muqadas, or Army of the Holy War. He was joined by a hundred or so young villagers and Arab veterans of the British Army.[1794] His militia soon had several thousand men,[1795] and it moved its training quarters to Bir Zeit, a town near Ramallah.

Abd al-Qadir's zone of influence extended down to the area of Lydda, Ramleh, and the Judean Hills where Hasan Salama commanded 1,000 men.[1796] Salama, like Abd al-Qadir, had been affiliated with Mufti Haj Amin al Husseini for years, and had also been a commander in the 1936–1939 Arab revolt in Palestine, participated in the Rashid Ali coup of 1941 and the subsequent Anglo-Iraqi War. Salama had re-entered Palestine in 1944 in Operation Atlas, parachuting into the Jordan Valley as a member of a special German–Arab commando unit of the Waffen SS. He coordinated with al-Husayni to execute a plan of disruption and harassment of road traffic in an attempt to isolate and blockade Western (Jewish) Jerusalem.[1797,1798]

On 10 December, the first organized attack occurred when ten members of a convoy between Bethlehem and Kfar Etzion were killed.

On 14 January, Abd al-Qadir himself commanded and took part in an attack against Kfar Etzion, in which 1,000 Palestinian Arab combatants were involved. The attack was a failure, and 200 of al-Husayni's men died. Nonetheless, the attack did not come without losses of Jewish lives: a detachment of 35 Palmach men who sought to reinforce the establishment were ambushed and killed.[1799]

On 25 January, a Jewish convoy was attacked near the Arab village of al-Qastal. The attack went badly and several villages to the northeast of Jerusalem answered a call for assistance, although others did not, for fear of reprisals.[1800] The campaign for control over the roads became increasingly militaristic in nature, and became a focal point of the Arab war effort. After 22 March, supply convoys to Jerusalem stopped, due to a convoy of around thirty vehicles having been destroyed in the gorges of Bab-el-Wad.[1801]

On 27 March, an important supply convoy from Kfar Etzion was taken in an ambush in south of Jerusalem. They were forced to surrender all of their arms, ammunition and vehicles to al-Husayni's forces. The Jews of Jerusalem requested the assistance of the United Kingdom after 24 hours of combat. According to a British report, the situation in Jerusalem, where a food rationing system was already in application, risked becoming desperate after 15 May.[1802]

The situation in other areas of the country was as critical as the one of Jerusalem. The settlements of Negev were utterly isolated, due to the impossibility of using the Southern coastal road, which passed through zones densely populated by Arabs. On 27 March, a convoy of supplies (the Yehiam convoy) that was intended for the isolated kibbutzim north-west of Galilee was attacked in the vicinity of Nahariya. In the ensuing battle, 42–47 Haganah combatants and around a hundred fighters of the Arab Liberation Army were killed, and all vehicles involved were destroyed.[1803]

Haganah offensive (1 April – 15 May 1948)

The second phase of the war, which began in April, marked a huge change in direction, as Haganah moved to the offensive.

In this stage, Arab forces were composed of around 10,000 men among which between 3,000 and 5,000 foreign volunteers serving in the Arab Liberation Army.[1804,1805,1806] Haganah and Palmach forces were steadily increasing. In March, they aligned around 15,000 men[1807] and in May around 30,000 who were better equipped, trained and organized.[1808,1809,1810]

The armed Palestinian groups were roundly defeated, Yishuv took control of some of the principal routes that linked the Jewish settlements, and as a consequence, Jerusalem was able to receive supplies again. Palestinian society collapsed. Many mixed cities were taken by the Haganah as well as Jaffa. A massive exodus was triggered.

Plan Dalet

Plan Dalet was finalized on 10 March 1948, under the direction of Yigael Yadin. 75 pages long, it laid down the rules and the objects that were to be followed by Haganah during the second phase of the war. Its principal objective was to secure Yishuv's uninterrupted territorial connections, particularly in response to the war of the roads carried out by Al-Hussayni and in preparation for the Arab states' declared intervention. Plan Dalet caused quite a controversy among historians. Some see it as a plan that was primarily defensive and military in nature and a preparation against invasion,[1811] whereas others think that the plan was offensive in nature and aimed at conquering as much of Palestine as possible.

Figure 200: *Yaakov Dori, Haganah's Chief of Staff, and his right-hand man, Yigael Yadin, Chief of Operations.*

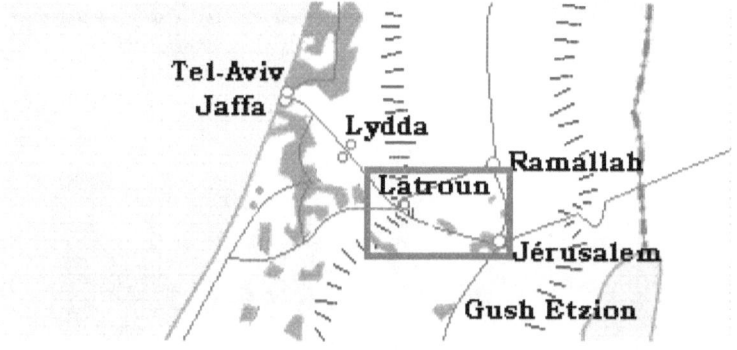

Figure 201: *Theatre of operations*

Operation Nachshon (2–20 April)

At the end of March 1948, Hussayni's troops prevented supply convoys from reaching Jerusalem. The city was besieged and the Jewish population was forced to adhere to a rationing system. Ben-Gurion decided to launch the operation Nachshon to open up the city and provide supplies to Jerusalem.[1812] Operation Nachshon marked the Haganah shift to the offensive, even before launching plan D.

The first orders were given on 2 April 1948 with diversion attacks including Qastel.[1813] Between 5–20 April 1500 men from the Givati and Harel brigades

Figure 202: *Haganah soldier in Al-Qastal on 5 April 1948.*

Figure 203: *Palestinian irregulars of the Holy War Army, approaching al-Qastal village near Jerusalem to take it back from Palmach.*

took control of the road to Jerusalem[1814] and allowed 3 or 4 convoys to reach the city.[1815]

The operation was a military success. All the Arab villages that blocked the route were either taken or destroyed, and the Jewish forces were victorious in all their engagements. Nonetheless, not all the objectives of the operation were achieved, since only 1800 tonnes of the 3,000 envisaged were transported to the city, and two months of severe rationing had to be assumed.[1816]

Abd al-Qadir al-Husayni was killed during the night of 7–8 April, in the midst of the battles taking place in Al-Qastal. The loss of this charismatic Palestinian leader 'disrupted the Arab strategy and organization in the area of Jerusalem.'[1817] His successor, Emil Ghuri, changed tactics: instead of provoking a series of ambushes throughout the route, he had a huge road block erected at Bab al-Wad, and Jerusalem was once again isolated as a consequence.[1818]

Operation Nachshon exposed the poor military organization of the Palestinian paramilitary groups. Due to lack of logistics, particularly food and ammunition, they were incapable of maintaining engagements that were more than a few hours away from their permanent bases.[1819]

Faced with these events, the Arab Higher Committee asked Alan Cunningham to allow the return of the Mufti, the only person capable of redressing the situation. Despite obtaining permission, the Mufti did not get to Jerusalem. His declining prestige cleared the way for the expansion of the influence of the Arab Liberation Army and of Fawzi Al-Qawuqji in the Jerusalem area.

Battle of Mishmar HaEmek (4–15 April)

Mishmar HaEmek is a kibbutz that was founded by Mapam in 1930, in the Jezreel Valley, close to the road between Haifa and Jenin that passes the Megiddo kibbutz. It is situated in a place that Haganah officers considered to be on one of the most likely axes of penetration for a 'major Arab attack' against the Yishuv.[1820,1821]

On 4 April, the Arab Liberation Army launched an attack on the kibbutz with the support of artillery. The attack was fought off by the members of the kibbutz, who were supported by Haganah soldiers. The artillery fire that had almost totally destroyed the kibbutz was stopped by a British column, who arrived on the scene by order of General MacMillan, and, on 7 April, Fawzi Al-Qawuqji accepted a 24-hour ceasefire, but required that the kibbutz be surrendered. The inhabitants of the kibbutz evacuated their children, and, after having consulted Tel Aviv, refused to surrender.[1822]

On 8 or 9 April, Haganah prepared a counter-offensive. Yitzhak Sadeh was put in charge of operations, with the order to 'clean out' the region. The battle

Figure 204: *Women training at Mishmar HaEmek*

Figure 205: *Jewish soldiers at the entry of the Mishmar Ha'emek, 1948*

lasted until 15 April. Sadeh's men besieged all the villages around the kibbutz, and the Arab Liberation Army had to retreat to its bases in Jabba. The majority of the inhabitants of the region fled, but those who did not were either imprisoned or expelled to Jenin. The villages were plundered by some kibbutznikim and razed to the ground with explosives with accordance to Plan Dalet[1823] . [1824]

According to Morris, the Arab Liberation Army soldiers were demoralized by reports of the Deir Yassin massacre and the death of Abd al-Qadir al-Husayni. Throughout battle, they had generally been forced to withdraw and to abandon the people of the villages.[1825] Dominique Lapierre and Larry Collins report that Joshua Palmon, head of a unit of 6 men, failed to seize invaluable pieces of artillery, and they depict the eventsWikipedia:Please clarify as a débâcle for which Fawzi Al-Qawuqji offered extravagant excuses, declaring in particular that the Jewish forces has 120 tanks, six squadrons of fighter and bomber aircraft and that they were supported by a regiment of gentile Russian volunteers.[1826] According to Morris, "according to Ben-Gurion, some 640 Haganah soldiers had faced about twenty-five hundred ALA troops, with superior firepower—and bested them". When the battle finished, Palmach forces continued 'cleaning' operations until 19 April, destroying several villages and forcing those who inhabited them to flee. Some villages were also evacuated under the instruction of Arab authorities.[1827]

In May, Irgun engaged in several operations in the region, razing a number of villages and killing some of their inhabitants, as did some detachments from the Golani and Alexandroni brigades.[1828]

Deir Yassin massacre

Deir Yassin is a village located 5 kilometres west of Jerusalem. On 9 April 1948, independently of operation Nachshon, around 120 Irgun and Lehi men attacked the village. They massacred between 100 and 120 inhabitants of the village, mostly civilians.[1829] The Haganah had approved the attack and assisted in it, but was not involved in the massacre.

The massacre led to indignation from the international community, the more so since the press of the time reported that the death toll was 254. Ben-Gurion roundly condemned it,[1830] as did the principal Jewish authorities: the Haganah, the Great Rabbinate and the Jewish Agency for Israel, who sent a letter of condemnation, apology and condolence to King Abdullah I of Jordan.[1831]

According to Morris, "the most important immediate effect of the atrocity and the media campaign that followed it was how one started to report the fear felt in Palestinian towns and villages, and, later, the panicked fleeing from them."

Another important repercussion was within the Arab population of neighbouring Arab states, which, once again, increased its pressure on the representatives of these states to intervene and come to the aid of the Palestinian Arabs.[1832]

Hadassah medical convoy massacre

On 13 April, partly in revenge for the Deir Yassin massacre, a convoy that was driving towards Jerusalem's Hadassah Hospital on Mount Scopus was attacked by hundreds of Arabs. In the seven-hour battle 79 Jews were killed including doctors and patients. Thirteen British soldiers were present, but they stood by, only putting in a perfunctory attempt at intervention in the last moments of the massacre.[1833]

Lieutenant-Colonel Jack Churchill was present at the scene, and later testified that he had attempted to assist the Hadassah convoy by radioing for support, only for the request to be turned down.[1834]

Battle of Ramat Yohanan and the defection of the Druze

Following the 'fiasco'[1835] of Mishmar HaEmek, Fawzi Al-Qawuqji ordered the Druze regiment of the Arab Liberation Army into action, to carry out diversion operations. Druze soldiers took position in several Arab villages 12 kilometres to the east of Haifa,[1836] whence they occasionally attacked traffic and Jewish settlements, including Ramat Yohanan.

The Kibbutznikim and the Haganah soldiers that supported them forced back their attacks and razed the villages from which they launched their attacks. Having run out of ammunition, the Druze withdrew to their base in Shefa-'Amr, with one hundred casualties.[1837,1838] After an initial failure, a battalion-sized Carmeli force on the night of 15–16 April overran the two villages. The Druze Battalion, on 16 April assaulted the Carmeli positions nine times but the Carmeli troops fought back. By afternoon, the exhausted Druze troops retreated. An Haganah report praised "the well trained and very brave enemy forces."

The Druze had already made contact on several occasions with Yishuv agents and following their defeat at Ramat Yohanan, the Druze officers offered to defect and to join the ranks of Haganah. This proposition was discussed with Yigael Yadin, who refused the proposal but suggested that they could help to carry out sabotage operations behind the backs of the Arabs and to influence their comrades into deserting the army. By the start of May, 212 Wahab soldiers deserted. Taking into account the attitude of his men, Wahab met with Jewish liaison officers on 9 May and agreed to cooperate with Haganah. The two parties avoided clashes, and Wahab created a neutral enclave in the centre of Galilee. Wahab's army did not respond to calls for it to help fight Haganah's

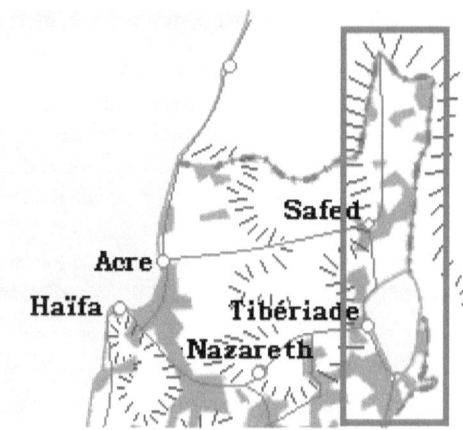

Figure 206: *Theatre of operations*

occupation of Acre, and avoided being present while Haganah occupied the police fortress of Shefa-'Amr during its evacuation by the British.

The position that the Druze took influenced their fate after the war. Given the good relationship between the Druze and Yishuv from 1930 onwards despite their collaboration with the Arab Higher Council and the Arab League, Ben-Gurion insisted that the Druze, as well as the Circassians and the Maronites benefit from a different position to that of the other Arabs.[1839]

Siege of mixed localities

In the context of Plan DaletWikipedia:Citation needed, mixed urban centres, or those on the borders of the Jewish state, were attacked and besieged by Jewish forces. Tiberias was attacked on 10 April and fell six days later; Haifa fell on 23 April, after only one day of combat (Operation Bi'ur Hametz), and Jaffa was attacked on 27 April but fell only after the British abandoned it (Operation Hametz). Safed and Beisan (Operation Gideon) fell on 11 May and 13 May respectively, within the framework of Operation Yitfah, and Acre fell on 17 May, within the framework of Operation Ben-Ami.

The Arab inhabitants of these towns fled or were expelled en masse. In these 6 cities, only 13,000 of the total of 177,000 Arab inhabitants remained by the end of May. This phenomenon ricocheted also in the suburbs and the majority of the zone's Arab villages.

Operation Yiftah (20 April – 24 May)

Galilee Panhandle, a zone in northeastern Galilee, between the Lake Tiberias and Metula, was the Jewish-controlled area that was the most distant and isolated from the area most densely populated by Jews, the coastal plain. The presence of the Lebanese border to the north, the Syrian border to east and the Arab presence in the rest of Galilee made it a probable target for intervention of the Arab armies.[1840] Within the framework of the Dalet plan, Yigael Yadin entrusted Yigal Allon, commander of the Palmach, with the responsibility of managing Operation Yiftah, whose objectives were to control all the aforementioned area and consolidate it ahead of the Arab attack that was planned for 15 May.[1841]

Allon was in charge of the 1st and 3rd Palmach battalions, which had to face the populace of Safed and several dozen Arab villages. The situation was made more problematic by the presence of the British, although they began their evacuation of the area. According to his analysis, it was essential that they empty the zone of any Arab presence to completely protect themselves; the exodus would also encumber the roads that the Arab forces would have to penetrate.[1842]

On 20 April, Allon launched a campaign that mixed propaganda, attacks, seizing control of strongholds that the British had abandoned, and destroying conquered Arab villages. On 1 May, a counter-offensive was launched by Arab militiamen against Jewish settlements but was ultimately unsuccessful. On 11 May, Safed fell, and the operation finished on 24 May after the villages of the valley of Hula were burnt down. Syrian forces' planned offensive in the area failed and, by the end of June, Galilee panhandle from Tiberias to Metula, incorporating Safed, was emptied of all its Arab population.[1843]

Meeting of Golda Meir and King Abdullah I of Jordan (10 May)

On 10 May, Golda Meir and Ezra Danin secretly went to Amman, to the palace of King Abdullah to discuss the situation with him. The situation that Abdullah found himself in was difficult. On one hand, his personal ambitions, the promises made by the Yishuv in November 1947Wikipedia:Citation needed and the British approval of these promises pushed him to consider annexing the Arab part of Palestine without intervening against the future state of Israel. On the other hand, the pressure exerted by his people in reaction to the massacre of Deir Yassin, combined with their feelings with regard to the Palestinian exodus and his agreements with other members of the Arab League pushed him to be more strongly involved in the war against Israel.[1844] He also found himself in a position of power, having the benefit of military support from not only

Figure 207: *Golda Meir in 1943*

the Arab League, but the British. In his diary, Ben-Gurion wrote about Golda Meir's reaction to the meeting:

<templatestyles src="Template:Quote/styles.css"/>

> *We met [on 10 May] amicably. He was very worried and looks terrible. He did not deny that there had been talk and understanding between us about a desirable arrangement, namely that he would take the Arab part [of Palestine]. (...) But Abdullah had said that he could now, on 10 May, only offer the Jews "autonomy" within an enlarged Hashemite kingdom. He added that while he was not interested in invading the areas allocated for Jewish statehood, the situation was volatile. But he voiced the hope that Jordan and the Yishuv would conclude a peace agreement once the dust had settled.*[1845]

Historical analyses of the motivations and conclusions of this meeting differ. According to Dominique Lapierre and Larry Collins – as well as Israeli historiographersWikipedia:Manual of Style/Words to watch#Unsupported attributions[1846] – the intention behind the Yishuv's negotiation was to obtain a peace treaty and avoid an attack by Arab forces. At that time, the balance of power was not favourable for them, but Meir did not manage to convince the King.

According to Morris,[1847] Abdullah 'reconsidered the promises that he made in November to not be opposed to the partition plan,' but left Meir with the

Figure 208: *King Abdullah of Jordan*

impression that he would make peace with the Jewish state once the civil war had finished.

Avi Shlaim spoke of a 'tacit' agreement to prevent the division of Palestine with the Palestinians, arguing the idea that there was a collusion between the Hashemite Kingdom and Yishuv. The historian Yoav Gelber, however, rejected this idea and devoted an entire work to dismounting it.[1848]

Pierre Razoux indicated that 'the majority of experts consider it probable'WP:NOTRS that Ben-Gurion and King Abdullah had an understanding over dividing Palestine, and that only the pressure from the Arab states on Abdullah constrained him from following up on his promise. According to Razoux, this idea explains the attitude of the British, who, following this plan, would thereby fulfill the promises made by Arthur Balfour to the Yishuv and the Hashemite empire at the same time. He states that the presence of Arab Legion troops, before 15 May, near strategic positions held by the British is in this way easy to understand.[1849]

Ilan Pappé[1850] stressed that neither Abdullah's ministers, nor the Arab world itself, seemed to be privy to the discussions held between him and the Yishuv, even if his ambitions on Palestine were widely known. He also stated that Sir Alec Kirkbride and Glubb Pasha thought at the time that, at the very least,

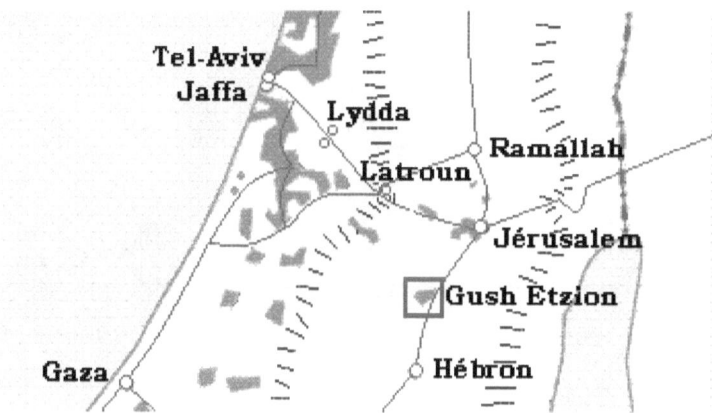

Figure 209: *Theatre of operations*

Azzam Pasha, the Secretary of the Arab League, must have known about Abdullah's double game.

It is certain, on the other hand, that Golda Meir and King Abdullah did not come to an agreement on the status of Jerusalem. On 13 May, the Arab Legion took Kfar Etzion,[1851] strategically located halfway along the road between Hebron and Jerusalem. On 17 May, Abdullah ordered Glubb Pasha, commander of the Arab Legion, to launch an attack against the Holy City.

Kfar Etzion massacre

Kfar Etzion is a group of four settlements established on the strategic route between Hebron and Jerusalem, right in the middle of Arab inhabited territory. It had 400 inhabitants at the end of 1947. After the adoption of Resolution 181(II), it was the object of Arab attacks. Ben-Gurion reinforced it on 7 December, protecting it with a Palmach division, but on 8 January, he authorized the evacuation of the women and children of the settlements.

After 26 March, the last date on which a supply convoy successfully reached it, despite heavy losses of life, the defenders were completely isolated.

On 12 May, Arab Legion units started to attack the settlements. The motivations advanced include their desire to protect one of their last supply convoys before the embargo took effect, which had to travel down the road by Kfar Etzion. Another theory is that the block of settlements obstructed the deployment of the Legion in the area around Hebron, whose attack was one of Abdullah's principal objectives.[1852] External defences fell quickly, and, on 13 May, the first kibbutz was captured, and those who were taken prisoner were massacred; only four survived.[1853,1854] Of the 131 defenders, 127, including 21

Figure 210: *Jewish prisoners taken after the fall of Gush Etzion*

women, were killed, or massacred after they surrendered.[1855] The other three establishments surrendered, and the kibbutzim were first plundered, then razed to the ground. In March 1949 320 prisoners from the Etzion settlements were released from the "Jordan POW camp at Mafrak", including 85 women.[1856]

The events that took place at Kfar Etzion made apparent the limitations of the policy prohibiting evacuation. Although it was effective during civil war, when facing militias, isolated Jewish settlements could not resist the firepower of a regular army, and an evacuation could have made it possible to avoid the captivity or death of those who defended the settlements.

According to Yoav Gelber, the fall and massacre of Kfar Etzion influenced Ben-Gurion's decision to engage the Arab Legion on its way to Jerusalem, although the Haganah General Staff were divided about whether the Legion should be challenged inside Jerusalem itself as such a move could harm the Jews in the city. Ben-Gurion left the final decision to Shaltiel. The battle for Jerusalem was thus set in motion.

Figure 211: *Palmach soldiers attack the San Simon monastery in Katamon, Jerusalem, April 1948 (battle reconstruction)*

Jerusalem: Operations Yevusi and Kilshon ("Pitchfork") (13–18 May)

Operation Yevusi lasted two weeks, from 22 April 1948 to 3 May 1948. Not all objectives were achieved before the British enforced a cease-fire. A Palmach force occupied the strategically located San Simon monastery in Katamon. Arab irregulars attacked the monastery and a heavy battle evolved. Both sides had a lot of wounded and killed fighters. The Palmach considered a retreat while the wounded fighters would blow themselves up, but then it was realized that the Arab force was exhausted and could not continue the fighting. As a result, the Arab residents left the suburb and the southern besieged Jewish suburbs were released.[1857]

The Haganah intended to capture the Old City during the final days of the Mandate.[1858] Its attacks on the seam between East and West Jerusalem from 13–18 May (known as Operation Kilshon) were planned as the initial phase of this conquest.

In Jerusalem, the British held several strategically located security zones named "Bevingrads", at its centre. The city's radio station, telephone exchange and government hospital were located there, along with a number of barracks and the Notre Dame hostel, which dominated the city.[1859] One of

Figure 212: *Bevingrad, centre of the British security zone in Jerusalem*

the main objectives of Operation Kilshon was to take control of these zones of strategic importance while the British withdrew. On 13 May the Haganah extended its control of the Old City's Jewish Quarter and on 14th (having obtained the precise schedule of the evacuation with British complicity) took control of the Bevingrads, including the central post office and the Russian Church compound at 04:00.[1860] They surprised the Arab troops, who offered no resistance.[1861]

A secondary objective of Operation Kilshon was to simultaneously create a continuous frontline between the various isolated Jewish localities. For this aim, Brigadier General David Shaltiel, Haganah's former envoy to Europe, was deployed along with a troop of 400 Haganah soldiers and 600 militia soldiers. Emil Ghuri, the new leader of the Army of the Holy War, also envisaged taking these districts and mobilized 600 soldiers for the mission, but prepared no specific operation.

The secondary aim was also successful. In the North of the city, Jewish forces seized Arab-populated Sheikh Jarrah, made a connection with Mount Scopus, and took the villages surrounding the American colony. In the South, they ensured the connection of the German and Greek colonies with Talpiot and Ramat Rahel, after having taken the Allenby barracks. A Palmach unit even re-established contact with the Jewish district in the Old City via the Zion Gate.[1862]

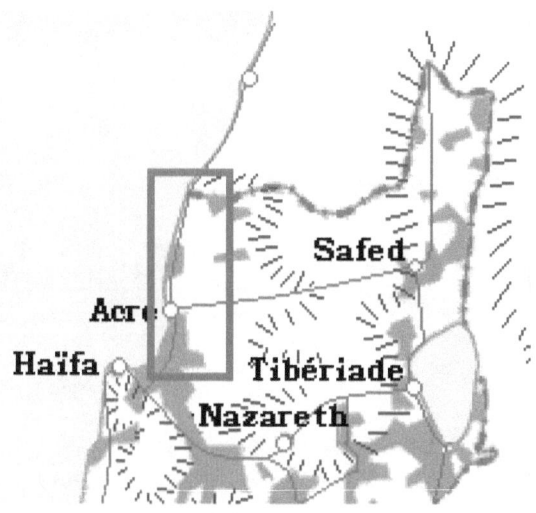

Figure 213: *Theatre of operations*

The irregular Arabic forces were rendered impotent and yielded to panic, calling the situation hopeless and announcing the imminent fall of the city.[1863]

Operation Ben-Ami (13–22 May)

File:RWD 13 - Air dropping supplies to Yehiam, 1948.jpg

Air dropping supplies to besieged Yehiam, 1948

Within the framework of Plan Dalet, Yigael Yadin intended to make a breakthrough in the west of Galilee, wherein a number of isolated Jewish settlements were situated. This zone, which covers the land from Acre all the way to the Lebanese border, was allocated to the Arabs by the Partition plan, but was on the road through which Lebanese forces intended to enter into Palestine.[1864]

The command of this operation was entrusted to Moshe Carmel, head of the Carmeli brigade. It consisted of two phases: the first began on the evening of 13 May, when a column of Haganah's armoured vehicles and lorries advanced along the coast with no resistance. The forces of the Arab Liberation Army fled without entering battle, and the first phase of the operation finished when Acre was taken on 18 May. In the second phase, from 19 May to 21 May, troops went as far as the Yehi'am kibbutz by the Lebanese border, connecting it and conquering and destroying a number of Arab villages on the way.[1865]

Figure 214: *Palestinian Arab refugees in 1948*

Main wave of the Palestinian Arab exodus

Haganah's move to offensive operations during the second phase of the war was accompanied by a huge exodus that involved 350,000 Arab refugees, adding to the 100,000 displaced during the First wave. The term 'Palestinian exodus' is often used to refer to both these and two subsequent waves. These two waves gained a considerable amount of press interest and were widely relayed in the press of the time, more so than most other Palestine-related events.[1866]

The causes of and responsibility for this exodus are highly controversial topics among commentators on the conflict and even historians who specialize in this era. Among the various possible causes, Efraim Karsh attributes the exodus mainly to Arab authorities' instructions to escape,[1867] whereas others argue that a policy of expulsion had been organized by the Yishuv authorities and implemented by Haganah.[1868] Others yet reject these two assumptions and see the exodus as the cumulative effect of all the civil war's consequences.[1869]

Preparations made by the Arab League

During the last meeting of the Arab League in February 1948, the Arab leaders expressed their convictions in the capacity of the Arab Liberation Army to help the Palestinians and to force the international community to give up on the UN-backed partition plan. The following summit took place in Cairo on 10 April, with the situation having clearly developed with the death of Al-Hussayni and the debacle at Mishmar Ha'emek.

Once again, Ismail Safwat called for the immediate deployment of the Arab state armies at the borders of Palestine, and for the need to go beyond the established policy of participating in little more than small-scale raids towards taking part in large-scale operations. For the first time, the Arab leaders discussed the possibility of intervening in Palestine.[1870]

Syria and Lebanon declared themselves ready to intervene immediately, but King Abdullah refused to let the Arab Legion forces intervene immediately in favour of the Palestinians, a move which irritated the Secretary-General of the League, who declared that Abdallah only cedes to the British diktat.

Nonetheless, Abdullah declared himself ready to send the Legion to assist the Palestinian cause after 15 May. In response, Syria insisted that the Egyptian army also take part, and, in spite of the opposition of Egypt's prime minister, King Farouk responded favourably to the Syrian request, but due to his aim of curbing the Jordanians' hegemonic goals rather than his desire to help the Palestinians.

Later on, following the visit of several Palestinian dignitaries in Amman, and despite the opposition of Syria and the Mufti, Haj Amin al-Husseini, Azzam Pasha accepted Abdullah's proposition and sent Ismail Safwat to Amman to organize a coordination between the Arab Liberation Army and Jordan's Arab Legion. It was decided that command over the operations would be reserved for King Abdullah, and that the Iraqis would deploy a brigade in Transjordan to prepare for intervention on 15 May.[1871]

On 26 April, the 'intention to occupy Palestine' was officially announced at the Transjordanian parliament and the Jewish people were 'invited to place themselves beneath King Abdullah's jurisdiction.' The intention to spare their lives was also promised. Yishuv perceived this declaration as being one of war and encourages the Western world to pressure the King, through diplomatic means, to prevent his intervention.[1872]

On 30 April, Jordanians, Egyptians and Iraqis disputed the command of Abdullah. Abdullah received the honorary title of Commander-in-Chief, while the Iraqi general, Aldine Nur Mahmud, was named Chief of Staff. Despite this show of unity, it was agreed that each army would act independent of each other in the theatre of operations.[1873]

On 4 May, the Iraqi task force arrived at Mafraq. It was composed of a regiment of armoured tanks, a regiment of mechanized infantry, and twenty-four artillery weapons, and included 1500 men.[1874] The Egyptians formed two brigades, deploying around 700 men into the Sinai.[1875] The Syrians could not put together a better force, whereas the Lebanese announced that they could not take part in military operations on 10 May.

Figure 215: *Zones controlled by Yishuv by 20 May 1948, with comparison to zones held some five months earlier.*

It was only two days before, on 8 May, that the British Foreign Office was certain of the Arab invasion. Whereas British analysts considered that all Arab armies, except the Arab Legion, were not prepared for the engagements to come,[1876] the Egyptian officers claimed that their advance would be 'a parade with the least risk,' and that their army 'would be in Tel Aviv after just two weeks.'

The state of preparation of the army was such that they did not even have maps of Palestine.[1877] At the time, the final plans of invasion had not even been established yet. British leaders tried in vain to make the Arab leaders reconsider their decision,[1878] and Ismail Safwat resigned in indifference, but the Arab states seemed resolute. On 15 May 1948, the Arab League announced officially that it would intervene in Palestine to guarantee the security and right to self-determination of the inhabitants of Palestine in an independent state.[1879]

Results and aftermath

According to Benny Morris, the result of these five and a half months of fighting was a "decisive Jewish victory". On one side, the "Palestinian Arab military power was crushed" and most of the population in the combat zones was fleeing or had been driven out. On the other side, the "Haganah transformed from a militia into an army" and succeeded "in consolidating its hold on a continuous strip of territory embracing the Coastal Plain, the Jezreel Valley, and the Jordan Valley." The Yishuv proved it had the capability to defend itself, persuading the United States and the remainder of the world to support it and the "victory over the Palestinian Arabs gave the Haganah the experience and self-confidence [...] to confront [...] the invading armies of the Arab states."[1880]

According to Yoav Gelber, during the six weeks between the Haganah offensive on 1 April and the invasion of the Arab armies, the Arabs were defeated in almost every front. The Jewish forces captured four cities (Tiberias, Jaffa, Safed, and Haifa) and 190 villages; most of their residents fled. The refugees flooded Samaria, central Galilee, Mount Hebron region, Gaza region, as well as Transjordan, Lebanon, and southern Syria. With the defeat of the Palestinian forces and the ALA, the Arab League saw no other option than to invade at the end of the British Mandate. The process of deciding to invade and preparing for the attack began two or three weeks before the end of the Mandate, when the level of the defeat was revealed and it was clear the ALA could not prevent it.[1881]

Although the Haganah was a poorly armed ragtag militia, its offensive of the last weeks went well, because Arab villages did not come to the help of their neighboring Arab villages or towns. Moreover, only a few young Arab men from untouched areas (e.g. Nablus, Hebron) participated in the fighting in Jerusalem, Haifa, etc.[1882] Anwar Nusseibeh, a supporter of the Mufti, said the Mufti refused to issue arms to anyone except his political supporters and only recruited his supporters for the forces of the Holy War Army. This partially accounts for the absence of an organized Arab force and for the insufficient amount of arms, which plagued the Arab defenders of Jerusalem.

On 14 May 1948, David Ben-Gurion, on behalf of the Jewish leadership, *declared the establishment of a Jewish state in Eretz Israel, to be known as the State of Israel*.[1883] The 1948 Palestine war entered its second phase with the intervention of the Arab state armies and the beginning of the 1948 Arab–Israeli War.

References

- Elie Barnavi, *Une histoire moderne d'Israël*, Champs / Flammarion, 1988, <templatestyles src="Module:Citation/CS1/styles.css" />ISBN 978-2-08-081246-9* Elie Barnavi, *Une histoire moderne d'Israël*, Champs / Flammarion, 1988, <templatestyles src="Module:Citation/CS1/styles.css" />ISBN 978-2-08-081246-9

- Bickerton, Ian and Hill, Maria (2003). *Contested Spaces: The Arab–Israeli Conflict*. McGraw-Hill. ISBN 978-0-07-471217-7
- Yoav Gelber, *Independence Versus Nakba*; Kinneret–Zmora-Bitan–Dvir Publishing, 2004, ISBN 965-517-190-6 (in Hebrew)
- Yoav Gelber, *Palestine 1948*, Sussex Academic Press, Brighton, 2006, ISBN 978-1-84519-075-0
- Alain Gresh and Dominique Vidal, *Palestine 47, un partage avorté*, Editions Complexe, 1994, ISBN 978-2-87027-521-4.
- Dov Joseph, *The Faithful City – The Siege of Jerusalem 1948*. Library of Congress number 60 10976.
- Efraïm Karsh, *The Arab–Israeli Conflict – The Palestine War 1948*, Osprey Publishing, 2002, ISBN 978-1-84176-372-9
- Jon and David Kimche, *A clash of destinies, The Arab–Jewish War and the founding of the state of Israel*, Praeger, New York, 1960,
- Dominique Lapierre and Larry Collins, *O Jérusalem*, Robert Laffont, 1971, ISBN 978-2-266-10698-6
- Henry Laurens, *Paix et guerre au Moyen-Orient*, Armand Colin, Paris, 2005, ISBN 2-200-26977-3
- Harry Levin. *Jerusalem Embattled – A Diary of the City under Siege*. Cassels, 1997. ISBN 0-304-33765-X.
- Benny Morris, *The Road to Jerusalem: Glubb Pasha, Palestine and the Jews*, I.B.Tauris, 2002, ISBN 978-1-86064-989-9
- Benny Morris, *Histoire revisitée du conflit arabo-sioniste*, Editions complexe, 2003, ISBN 978-2-87027-938-0
- Benny Morris, *The Birth Of The Palestinian Refugee Problem Revisited*, Cambridge University Press, 2004, ISBN 978-0-521-00967-6
- Benny Morris, *1948: A History of the First Arab–Israeli War*, Yale University Press, 2008.
- Ilan Pappé, *La guerre de 1948 en Palestine*, La fabrique éditions, 2000, ISBN 978-2-264-04036-7* Eugène Rogan, Avi Shlaim et al., *La guerre de

Palestine 1948: derrière le mythe, Autrement, 2002, <templatestyles src="Module:Citation/CS1/styles.css" />ISBN 978-2-7467-0240-0
- Yitzhak Rabin, *Mémoires*, Buchet/Chastel, 1980,* Ilan Pappe, *The Ethnic Cleansing of Palestine*, 2006. <templatestyles src="Module:Citation/CS1/styles.css" />ISBN 978-1-85168-555-4.* Pierre Razoux, *Tsahal, nouvelle histoire de l'armée israélienne*, Perrin, 2006, <templatestyles src="Module:Citation/CS1/styles.css" />ISBN 978-2-262-02328-7

Further reading

- Uri Milstein, *History of Israel's War of Independence: A Nation Girds for War*, vol. 1, University Press of America, 1996, <templatestyles src="Module:Citation/CS1/styles.css" />ISBN 978-0-7618-0372-0
- Uri Milstein, *History of Israel's War of Independence: The First Month*, vol. 2, University Press of America, 1997, <templatestyles src="Module:Citation/CS1/styles.css" />ISBN 978-0-7618-0721-6
- Uri Milstein, *History of Israel's War of Independence: The First Invasion*, vol. 3, University Press of America, 1999, <templatestyles src="Module:Citation/CS1/styles.css" />ISBN 978-0-7618-0769-8
- Uri Milstein, *History of Israel's War of Independence: Out of Crisis Came Decision*, vol. 4, University Press of America, 1999, <templatestyles src="Module:Citation/CS1/styles.css" />ISBN 978-0-7618-1489-4
- Salim Tamari, *Jérusalem 1948: Les faubourgs arabes et leur destin durant la guerre*, Institut des études palestiniennes, 2002, <templatestyles src="Module:Citation/CS1/styles.css" />ISBN 978-9953-9001-9-3

Online sources

- Plan Daleth from mideastweb.org[1884]
- United Nations Special Commission, First Special Report to the Security Council: The Problem of Security in Palestine, 16 February 1948, from the United Nations website[1885].
- Palestine remembered[1886] Palestinian view.
- Jewish Virtual Library[1887] Jewish view.

Film

- Elie Chouraqui, *Ô Jérusalem, 2006*.

Arab-Israel War

1948 Arab–Israeli War

<indicator name="pp-default"> 🔒 </indicator>

1948 Arab–Israeli War
Part of 1947–49 Palestine war
 Captain Avraham "Bren" Adan raising the Ink Flag at Umm Rashrash (a site now in Eilat), marking the end of the war.

Date	15 May 1948 – 10 March 1949 (9 months, 3 weeks and 2 days) <small>Final armistice agreement concluded on 20 July 1949</small>
Location	Former British Mandate of Palestine, Sinai Peninsula, southern Lebanon
Result	• Israeli victory • Jordanian partial victory[1890],[1891] • Palestinian Arab defeat • Egyptian defeat • Arab League strategic failure • 1949 Armistice Agreements
Territorial changes	Israel keeps area allotted to it by the Partition Plan and captures ~60% of area allotted to Arab state; Jordanian rule of West Bank, Egyptian occupation of the Gaza Strip

Belligerents

Israel	
Before 26 May 1948 *Paramilitary groups:* • Haganah • Palmach • Irgun • Lehi **After 26 May 1948:** Israel Defense Forces • Minorities Unit **Foreign volunteers:** Mahal	**Irregulars:** Holy War Army Arab Liberation Army **Foreign volunteers:** Muslim Brotherhood Pakistan Sudan[1892]
Commanders and leaders	
Politicians: David Ben-Gurion **Commanders:** Yisrael Galili Yaakov Dori Yigael Yadin Mickey Marcus † Yigal Allon Yitzhak Rabin David Shaltiel Moshe Dayan Shimon Avidan Moshe Carmel Yitzhak Sadeh	**Politicians:** Azzam Pasha King Farouk I King Abdallah I Muzahim al-Pachachi Husni al-Za'im Haj Amin al-Husseini **Commanders:** Ahmed Ali al-Mwawi Muhammad Naguib John Bagot Glubb Habis al-Majali Hasan Salama † Fawzi al-Qawuqji
Strength	
Israel: 29,677 (initially) 117,500 (finally)[1893]</ref>	**Egypt**: 10,000 initially, rising to 20,000Wikipedia:Citation needed **Iraq**: 3,000 initially, rising to 15,000–18,000Wikipedia:Citation needed **Syria**: 2,500–5,000Wikipedia:Citation needed **Transjordan**: 8,000–12,000Wikipedia:Citation needed **Lebanon**: 1,000[1894] **Saudi Arabia**: 800–1,200 (Egyptian command) **Yemen**: 300Wikipedia:Citation needed **Arab Liberation Army**: 3,500–6,000. **Total:** 13,000 (initial) 51,100 (minimal) 63,500 (maximum)[1895]
Casualties and losses	
6,373 killed (about 4,000 fighters and 2,400 civilians)	*Arab armies:* 3,700–7,000 killed *Palestinian Arabs:* 3,000–13,000 killed (both fighters and civilians)[1896]

The **1948 Arab–Israeli War**, or the **Israeli War of Independence**, was fought between the newly declared State of Israel and a military coalition of Arab states over the control of former British Palestine, forming the second and final stage of the 1947–49 Palestine war.Wikipedia:No original research It is also known as the **First Arab–Israeli War**.

There had been tension and conflict between the Arabs and the Jews, and between each of them and the British forces, ever since the 1917 Balfour Declaration and the 1920 creation of the British Mandate of Palestine. British policies dissatisfied both Arabs and Jews. The Arabs' opposition developed into the 1936–1939 Arab revolt in Palestine, while the Jewish resistance developed into the Jewish insurgency in Palestine (1944–1947). In 1947 these ongoing tensions erupted into civil war, following the 29 November 1947 adoption of the United Nations Partition Plan for Palestine, which planned to divide Palestine into three areas: an Arab state, a Jewish state and the Special International Regime for the cities of Jerusalem and Bethlehem.

On 15 May 1948, the ongoing civil war transformed into an inter-state conflict between Israel and the Arab states, following the Israeli Declaration of Independence the previous day. A combined invasion by Egypt, Jordan and Syria, together with expeditionary forces from Iraq, entered Palestine – Jordan having declared privately to Yishuv emissaries on 2 May that it would abide by a decision not to attack the Jewish state.[1897] The invading forces took control of the Arab areas and immediately attacked Israeli forces and several Jewish settlements.[1898,1899] The 10 months of fighting, interrupted by several truce periods, took place mostly on the former territory of the British Mandate and for a short time also in the Sinai Peninsula and southern Lebanon.[1900]

As a result of the war, the State of Israel controlled both the area that the UN General Assembly Resolution 181 had recommended for the proposed Jewish state as well as almost 60% of the area of Arab state proposed by the 1948 Partition Plan,[1901] including the Jaffa, Lydda and Ramle area, Galilee, some parts of the Negev, a wide strip along the Tel Aviv–Jerusalem road, West Jerusalem and some territories in the West Bank. Transjordan took control of the remainder of the former British mandate, which it annexed, and the Egyptian military took control of the Gaza Strip. At the Jericho Conference on 1 December 1948, 2,000 Palestinian delegates called for unification of Palestine and Transjordan as a step toward full Arab unity.[1902] No state was created for the Palestinian Arabs.

The conflict triggered significant demographic change throughout the Middle East. Around 700,000 Palestinian Arabs fled or were expelled from their homes in the area that became Israel, and they became Palestinian refugees in what they refer to as Al-Nakba ("the catastrophe"). In the three years following the war, about 700,000 Jews immigrated to Israel, with many of them having been expelled from their previous countries of residence in the Middle East.[1903]

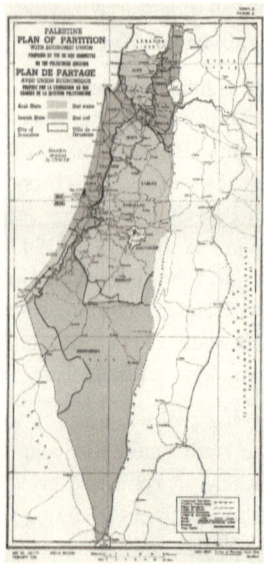

Figure 216: *Proposed separation of Palestine*

Background

Following World War II, the surrounding Arab nations were emerging from mandatory rule. Transjordan, under the Hashemite ruler Abdullah I, gained independence from Britain in 1946 and was called Jordan in 1949, but it remained under heavy British influence. Egypt gained nominal independence in 1922, but Britain continued to exert a strong influence on the country until the Anglo-Egyptian Treaty of 1936 which limited Britain's presence to a garrison of troops on the Suez Canal until 1945. Lebanon became an independent state in 1943, but French troops would not withdraw until 1946, the same year that Syria won its independence from France.

In 1945, at British prompting, Egypt, Iraq, Lebanon, Saudi Arabia, Syria, Transjordan, and Yemen formed the Arab League to coordinate policy between the Arab states. Iraq and Transjordan coordinated policies closely, signing a mutual defence treaty, while Egypt, Syria, and Saudi Arabia feared that Transjordan would annex part or all of Palestine, and use it as a steppingstone to attack or undermine Syria, Lebanon, and the Hijaz.[1904]

On 29 November 1947, the United Nations General Assembly adopted a resolution recommending the adoption and implementation of a plan to partition the British Mandate of Palestine into two states, one Arab and one Jewish, and the City of Jerusalem.[1905]

The General Assembly resolution on Partition was greeted with overwhelming joy in Jewish communities and widespread outrage in the Arab world. In Palestine, violence erupted almost immediately, feeding into a spiral of reprisals and counter-reprisals. The British refrained from intervening as tensions boiled over into a low-level conflict that quickly escalated into a full-scale civil war.[1906,1907,1908,1909,1910,1911]

From January onwards, operations became increasingly militarized, with the intervention of a number of Arab Liberation Army regiments inside Palestine, each active in a variety of distinct sectors around the different coastal towns. They consolidated their presence in Galilee and Samaria.[1912] Abd al-Qadir al-Husayni came from Egypt with several hundred men of the Army of the Holy War. Having recruited a few thousand volunteers, al-Husayni organized the blockade of the 100,000 Jewish residents of Jerusalem.[1913] To counter this, the Yishuv authorities tried to supply the city with convoys of up to 100 armoured vehicles, but the operation became more and more impractical as the number of casualties in the relief convoys surged. By March, Al-Hussayni's tactic had paid off. Almost all of Haganah's armoured vehicles had been destroyed, the blockade was in full operation, and hundreds of Haganah members who had tried to bring supplies into the city were killed.[1914] The situation for those who dwelt in the Jewish settlements in the highly isolated Negev and North of Galilee was even more critical.

While the Jewish population had received strict orders requiring them to hold their ground everywhere at all costs,[1915] the Arab population was more affected by the general conditions of insecurity to which the country was exposed. Up to 100,000 Arabs, from the urban upper and middle classes in Haifa, Jaffa and Jerusalem, or Jewish-dominated areas, evacuated abroad or to Arab centres eastwards.[1916]

This situation caused the United States to withdraw its support for the Partition plan, thus encouraging the Arab League to believe that the Palestinian Arabs, reinforced by the Arab Liberation Army, could put an end to the plan for partition. The British, on the other hand, decided on 7 February 1948, to support the annexation of the Arab part of Palestine by Transjordan.[1917]

Although a certain level of doubt took hold among Yishuv supporters, their apparent defeats were due more to their wait-and-see policy than to weakness. David Ben-Gurion reorganized Haganah and made conscription obligatory. Every Jewish man and woman in the country had to receive military training. Thanks to funds raised by Golda Meir from sympathisers in the United States, and Stalin's decision to support the Zionist cause, the Jewish representatives of Palestine were able to sign very important armament contracts in the East. Other Haganah agents recuperated stockpiles from the Second World War, which helped improve the army's equipment and logistics. Operation Balak

Figure 217: *Palmach M4 Sherman tank leading a convoy.*

allowed arms and other equipment to be transported for the first time by the end of March.

Ben-Gurion invested Yigael Yadin with the responsibility to come up with a plan of offense whose timing was related to the foreseeable evacuation of British forces. This strategy, called Plan Dalet, was readied by March and implemented towards the end of April.[1918] A separate plan, Operation Nachshon, was devised to lift the siege of Jerusalem. 1500 men from Haganah's Givati brigade and Palmach's Harel brigade conducted sorties to free up the route to the city between 5 and 20 April. Both sides acted offensively in defiance of the Partition Plan, which foresaw Jerusalem as a corpus separatum, under neither Jewish nor Arab jurisdiction. The Arabs did not accept the Plan, while the Jews were determined to oppose the internationalization of the city, and secure it as part of the Jewish state.[1919] The operation was successful, and enough foodstuffs to last two months were trucked into Jerusalem for distribution to the Jewish population.[1920] The success of the operation was assisted by the death of al-Husayni in combat. During this time, and independently of Haganah or the framework of Plan Dalet, irregular fighters from Irgun and Lehi formations massacred a substantial number of Arabs at Deir Yassin, an event that, though publicly deplored and criticized by the principal Jewish authorities, had a deep impact on the morale of the Arab population and contributed to generate the exodus of the Arab population.

At the same time, the first large-scale operation of the Arab Liberation Army ended in a debacle, having been roundly defeated at Mishmar HaEmek,[1921] coinciding with the loss of their Druze allies through defection.[1922]

Within the framework of the establishment of Jewish territorial continuity foreseen by Plan Dalet, the forces of Haganah, Palmach and Irgun intended to conquer mixed zones. The Palestinian Arab society was shaken. Tiberias, Haifa, Safed, Beisan, Jaffa and Acre fell, resulting in the flight of more than 250,000 Palestinian Arabs.[1923]

The British had, at that time, essentially withdrawn their troops. The situation pushed the leaders of the neighbouring Arab states to intervene, but their preparation was not finalized, and they could not assemble sufficient forces to turn the tide of the war. The majority of Palestinian Arab hopes lay with the Arab Legion of Transjordan's monarch, King Abdullah I, but he had no intention of creating a Palestinian Arab-run state, since he hoped to annex as much of the territory of the British Mandate for Palestine as he could. He was playing a double-game, being just as much in contact with the Jewish authorities as with the Arab League.

In preparation for the offensive, Haganah successfully launched Operations Yiftah[1924] and Ben-'Ami[1925] to secure the Jewish settlements of Galilee, and Operation Kilshon, which created a united front around Jerusalem. The inconclusive meeting between Golda Meir and Abdullah I, followed by the Kfar Etzion massacre on 13 May by the Arab Legion led to predictions that the battle for Jerusalem would be merciless.

On 14 May 1948, David Ben-Gurion declared the establishment of the State of Israel and the 1948 Palestine war entered its second phase with the intervention of the Arab state armies and the beginning of the 1948 Arab–Israeli War.

Armed forces

By September 1947 the Haganah had "10,489 rifles, 702 light machine-guns, 2,666 submachine guns, 186 medium machine-guns, 672 two-inch mortars and 92 three-inch (76 mm) mortars".

Importing arms

In 1946, Ben-Gurion decided that the Yishuv would probably have to defend itself against both the Palestinian Arabs and neighbouring Arab states and accordingly began a "massive, covert arms acquisition campaign in the West", and acquired many more during the first few months of hostilities.

The Yishuv managed to clandestinely amass arms and military equipment abroad for transfer to Palestine once the British blockade was lifted. In the United States, Yishuv agents purchased three Boeing B-17 Flying Fortress

Figure 218: *An Israeli Avia S-199, in June 1948*

bombers, one of which bombed Cairo in July 1948, some Curtiss C-46 Commando transport planes, and dozens of half-tracks, which were repainted and defined as "agricultural equipment". In Western Europe, Haganah agents amassed fifty 65mm French mountain guns, twelve 120mm mortars, ten H-35 light tanks, and a large number of half-tracks. By mid-May or thereabouts the Yishuv had purchased from Czechoslovakia 25 Avia S-199 fighters (an inferior version of the Messerschmitt Bf-109), 200 heavy machine guns, 5,021 light machine guns, 24,500 rifles, and 52 million rounds of ammunition, enough to equip all units, but short of heavy arms.[1926] The airborne arms smuggling missions from Czechoslovakia were codenamed Operation Balak.

The airborne smuggling missions were carried out by mostly American aviators – Jews and non-Jews – led by ex-U.S. Air Transport Command flight engineer Al Schwimmer.

Schwimmer's operation also included recruiting and training fighter pilots such as Lou Lenart, commander of the first Israeli air assault against the Arabs.

Arms production

The Yishuv also had "a relatively advanced *arms producing* capacity", that between October 1947 and July 1948" produced 3 million 9 mm bullets, 150,000 Mills grenades, 16,000 submachine guns (Sten Guns) and 210 three-inch

(76 mm) mortars", along with a few "Davidka" mortars, which had been indigenously designed and produced. They were inaccurate but had a spectacularly loud explosion that demoralized the enemy. A large amount of the munitions used by the Israelis came from the Ayalon Institute, a clandestine bullet factory underneath kibbutz Ayalon, which produced about 2.5 million bullets for Sten guns. The munitions produced by the Ayalon Institute were said to have been the only supply that was not in shortage during the war. Locally produced explosives were also plentiful. After Israel's independence, these clandestine arms manufacturing operations no longer had to be concealed, and were moved above ground. All of the Haganah's weapons-manufacturing was centralized and later became Israel Military Industries.

Manpower

In November 1947, the Haganah was an underground paramilitary force that had existed as a highly organized, national force, since the Arab riots of 1920–21, and throughout the riots of 1929, Great Uprising of 1936–39,[1927] and World War 2. It had a mobile force, the HISH, which had 2,000 full-time fighters (men and women) and 10,000 reservists (all aged between 18 and 25) and an elite unit, the Palmach composed of 2,100 fighters and 1,000 reservists. The reservists trained three or four days a monthWikipedia:Citation needed and went back to civilian life the rest of the time. These mobile forces could rely on a garrison force, the HIM (*Heil Mishmar*, lit. Guard Corps), composed of people aged over 25. The Yishuv's total strength was around 35,000 with 15,000 to 18,000 fighters and a garrison force of roughly 20,000.[1928]

There were also several thousand men and women who had served in the British Army in World War II who did not serve in any of the underground militias but would provide valuable military experience during the war. Walid Khalidi says the Yishuv had the additional forces of the Jewish Settlement Police, numbering some 12,000, the Gadna Youth Battalions, and the armed settlers.[1929] Few of the units had been trained by December 1947. On 5 December 1947, conscription was instituted for all men and women aged between 17 and 25 and by the end of March, 21,000 had been conscripted.[1930] On 30 March, the call-up was extended to men and single women aged between 26 and 35. Five days later, a General Mobilization order was issued for all men under 40.[1931]

Irgun

The Irgun, whose activities were considered by MI5 to be terrorism, was monitored by the British.

By March 1948, the Yishuv had a numerical superiority, with 35,780 mobilised and deployed fighters for the Haganah,[1932,1933] 3,000 of Stern and Irgun, and a few thousand armed settlers.[1934]

Arab forces

The effective number of Arab combatants is listed at 12,000 by some historians[1935] while others calculate a total Arab strength of approximately 23,500 troops, and with this being more of less or roughly equal to that of the Yishuv. However, as Israel mobilized most of its most able citizens during the war while the Arab troops were only a small percentage of its far greater population, the strength of the Yishuv grew steadily and dramatically during the war.

According to Benny Morris, by the end of 1947, the Palestinians "had a healthy and demoralising respect for the Yishuv's military power" and if it came to battle the Palestinians expected to lose.

Political objectives

Yishuv

Yishuv's aims evolved during the war.[1936] Mobilization for a total war was organized.[1937] Initially, the aim was "simple and modest": to survive the assaults of the Palestinian Arabs and the Arab states. "The Zionist leaders deeply, genuinely, feared a Middle Eastern reenactment of the Holocaust, which had just ended; the Arabs' public rhetoric reinforced these fears". As the war progressed, the aim of expanding the Jewish state beyond the UN partition borders appeared: first to incorporate clusters of isolated Jewish settlements and later to add more territories to the state and give it defensible borders. A third and further aim that emerged among the political and military leaders after four or five months was to "reduce the size of Israel's prospective large and hostile Arab minority, seen as a potential powerful fifth column, by belligerency and expulsion".

Plan Dalet, or Plan D, (Hebrew: ד', תוכנית, Tokhnit dalet) was a plan worked out by the Haganah, a Jewish paramilitary group and the forerunner of the Israel Defense Forces, in autumn 1947 to spring 1948, which was sent to Haganah units in early March 1948. According to the academic Ilan Pappé, its purpose was to conquer as much of Palestine and to expel as many Palestinians as possible,[1938] though according to Benny Morris there was no such intent. In his book *The Ethnic Cleansing of Palestine*, Pappé asserts that Plan Dalet was a "blueprint for ethnic cleansing" with the aim of reducing both rural and urban areas of Palestine.[1939] According to Gelber, the plan specified that in case of resistance, the population of conquered villages was to be expelled outside the borders of the Jewish state. If no resistance was met, the residents could stay put, under military rule.[1940] According to Morris, Plan D called for occupying the areas within the U.N sponsored Jewish state, several concentrations of Jewish population outside those areas (West Jerusalem and Western Galilee), and areas along the roads where the invading Arab armies were expected to attack.[1941]

The intent of Plan Dalet is subject to much controversy, with historians on the one extreme asserting that it was entirely defensive, and historians on the other extreme asserting that the plan aimed at maximum conquest and expulsion of the Palestinians.

The Yishuv perceived the peril of an Arab invasion as threatening its very existence. Having no real knowledge of the Arabs' true military capabilities, the Jews took Arab propaganda literally, preparing for the worst and reacting accordingly."

The Arab League as a whole

The Arab League had unanimously rejected the UN partition plan and were bitterly opposed to the establishment of a Jewish state.

The Arab League before partition affirmed the right to the independence of Palestine, while blocking the creation of a Palestinian government.Wikipedia:Please clarify Towards the end of 1947, the League established a military committee commanded by the retired Iraqi general Isma'il Safwat whose mission was to analyse the chance of victory of the Palestinians against the Jews.[1942] His conclusions were that they had no chance of victory and that an invasion of the Arab regular armies was mandatory. The political committee nevertheless rejected these conclusions and decided to support an armed opposition to the Partition Plan excluding the participation of their regular armed forces.[1943]

In April with the Palestinian defeat, the refugees coming from Palestine and the pressure of their public opinion, the Arab leaders decided to invade Palestine.[1944]

The Arab League gave reasons for its *invasion* in Palestine in the cablegram:

- the Arab states find themselves compelled to intervene in order to restore law and order and to check further bloodshed
- the Mandate over Palestine has come to an end, leaving no legally constituted authority
- *the only solution of the Palestine problem is the establishment of a unitary Palestinian state.*

British diplomat Alec Kirkbride wrote in his 1976 memoirs about a conversation with the Arab League's Secretary-General Azzam Pasha a week before the armies marched: "...when I asked him for his estimate of the size of the Jewish forces, [he] waved his hands and said: 'It does not matter how many there are. We will sweep them into the sea.'"[1945] Approximately six months previously, according to an interview in an 11 October 1947 article of *Akhbar al-Yom*, Azzam said: "I personally wish that the Jews do not drive us to this war, as this will be a war of extermination and a momentous massacre which will be spoken of like the Mongolian massacres and the Crusades".Wikipedia:Neutral point of view#Due and undue weight

According to Yoav Gelber, the Arab countries were "drawn into the war by the collapse of the Palestinian Arabs and the Arab Liberation Army [and] the Arab governments' primary goal was preventing the Palestinian Arabs' total ruin and the flooding of their own countries by more refugees. According to their own perception, had the invasion not taken place, there was no Arab force in Palestine capable of checking the Haganah's offensive".[1946]

King Abdullah I of Jordan

King Abdullah was the commander of the Arab Legion, the strongest Arab army involved in the war according to Rogan and Shlaim in 2007.[1947] However, Morris wrote in 2008 that the Egyptian army was the most powerful and threatening army.[1948] The Arab Legion had about 10,000 soldiers, trained and commanded by British officers.

In 1946–47, Abdullah said that he had no intention to "resist or impede the partition of Palestine and creation of a Jewish state."[1949] Ideally, Abdullah would have liked to annex all of Palestine, but he was prepared to compromise. He supported the partition, intending that the West Bank area of the British Mandate allocated for the Arab state be annexed to Jordan.[1950] Abdullah had secret meetings with the Jewish Agency (at which the future Israeli Prime Minister Golda Meir was among the delegates) that reached an agreement of Jewish non-interference with Jordanian annexation of the West Bank (although Abdullah failed in his goal of acquiring an outlet to the Mediterranean Sea through the Negev desert) and of Jordanian agreement not to attack the area of the Jewish state contained in the United Nations partition resolution (in which Jerusalem was given neither to the Arab nor the Jewish state, but was to be an internationally administered area). In order to keep their support to his plan of annexation of the Arab State, Abdullah promised to the British he would not attack the Jewish State.

The neighbouring Arab states pressured Abdullah into joining them in an "all-Arab military invasion" against the newly created State of Israel, that he used

Figure 219: *King Abdullah outside the Church of the Holy Sepulchre, Jerusalem, 29 May 1948.*

to restore his prestige in the Arab world, which had grown suspicious of his relatively good relationship with Western and Jewish leaders. Jordan's undertakings not to cross partition lines were not taken at face value. While repeating assurances that Jordan would only take areas allocated to a future Arab State, on the eve of war Tawfik Abu al-Huda told the British that were other Arab armies to advance against Israel, Jordan would follow suit.[1951] On 23 May Abdullah told the French consul in Amman that he "was determined to fight Zionism and prevent the establishment of an Israeli state on the border of his kingdom".[1952]

Abdullah's role in this war became substantial. He saw himself as the "supreme commander of the Arab forces" and "persuaded the Arab League to appoint him" to this position.[1953] Through his leadership, the Arabs fought the 1948 war to meet Abdullah's political goals.

The other Arab states

King Farouk of Egypt was anxious to prevent Abdullah from being seen as the main champion of the Arab world in Palestine, which he feared might damage his own leadership aspirations of the Arab world. In addition, Farouk wished to annex all of southern Palestine to Egypt. According to Gamal Abdel Nasser the Egyptian army first communique described the Palestine operations as a merely punitive expedition against the Zionist "gangs", using a term frequent in Haganah reports of Palestinian fighters.[1954]

Nuri as-Said, the strongman of Iraq, had ambitions for bringing the entire Fertile Crescent under Iraqi leadership. Both Syria and Lebanon wished to take certain areas of northern Palestine.

One result of the ambitions of the various Arab leaders was a distrust of all the Palestinian leaders who wished to set up a Palestinian state, and a mutual distrust of each other. Co-operation was to be very poor during the war between the various Palestinian factions and the Arab armies.

Arab Higher Committee of Amin al-Husayni

Following rumours that King Abdullah was re-opening the bilateral negotiations with Israel that he had previously conducted in secret with the Jewish Agency, the Arab League, led by Egypt, decided to set up the All-Palestine Government in Gaza on 8 September under the nominal leadership of the Mufti.[1955] Abdullah regarded the attempt to revive al-Husayni's Holy War Army as a challenge to his authority and all armed bodies operating in the areas controlled by the Arab Legion were disbanded. Glubb Pasha carried out the order ruthlessly and efficiently.[1956,1957]

Initial line-up of forces

Military assessments

Though the state of Israel faced the formidable armies of neighboring Arab countries, yet due to previous battles by the middle of May the Palestinians themselves hardly existed as a military force.[1958] The British Intelligence and Arab League military reached similar conclusions.[1959]

The British Foreign Ministry and C.I.A believed that the Arab States would finally win in case of war.[1960,1961] Martin Van Creveld says that in terms of manpower, the sides were fairly evenly matched.[1962]

In May, Egyptian generals told their government that the invasion will be "A parade without any risks" and Tel Aviv "in two weeks".[1963] Egypt, Iraq, and Syria all possessed air forces, Egypt and Syria had tanks, and all had some modern artillery.[1964] Initially, the Haganah had no heavy machine guns, artillery, armoured vehicles, anti-tank or anti-aircraft weapons, nor military aircraft or tanks. The four Arab armies that invaded on 15 May were far stronger than the Haganah formations they initially encountered.[1965]

On 12 May, three days before the invasion, David Ben-Gurion was told by his chief military advisers (who over-estimated the size of the Arab armies and the numbers and efficiency of the troops who would be committed – much as the Arab generals tended to exaggerate Jewish fighters' strength) that Israel's chances of winning a war against the Arab states were only about even.

Yishuv/Israeli forces

Jewish forces at the invasion: Sources disagree about the amount of arms at the Yishuv's disposal at the end of the Mandate. According to Karsh before the arrival of arms shipments from Czechoslovakia as part of Operation Balak, there was roughly one weapon for every three fighters, and even the Palmach could arm only two out of every three of its active members. According to Collins and LaPierre, by April 1948, the Haganah had managed to accumulate only about 20,000 rifles and Sten guns for the 35,000 soldiers who existed on paper.[1966] According to Walid Khalidi "the arms at the disposal of these forces were plentiful". France authorized Air France to transport cargo to Tel Aviv on 13 May.

Yishuv forces were organised in 9 brigades, and their numbers grew following Israeli independence, eventually expanding to 12 brigades. Although both sides increased their manpower over the first few months of the war, the Israeli forces grew steadily as a result of the progressive mobilization of Israeli society and the influx of an average of 10,300 immigrants each month. By the end of 1948, the Israel Defense Forces had 88,033 soldiers, including 60,000 combat soldiers.[1967]

Brigade	Commander	Size[1968]	Operations
Golani	Moshe Mann	4,500	Dekel, Hiram
Carmeli	Moshe Carmel	2,000	Hiram
Alexandroni	Dan Even	5,200	Latrun, Hametz
Kiryati	Michael Ben-Gal	1,400	Dani, Hametz
Givati	Shimon Avidan	5,000	Hametz, Barak, Pleshet
Etzioni	David Shaltiel		Battle of Jerusalem, Shfifon, Yevusi, Battle of Ramat Rachel
7th Armoured	Shlomo Shamir		Battles of Latrun
8th Armoured	Yitzhak Sadeh		Danny, Yoav, Horev
Oded	Avraham Yoffe		Yoav, Hiram
Harel	Yitzhak Rabin[1969]	1,400	Nachshon, Danny
Yiftach	Yigal Allon	4,500 inc. some Golani	Yiftah, Danny, Yoav, Battles of Latrun
Negev	Nahum Sarig	2,400	Yoav

Figure 220: *Sherman tanks of the Israeli 8th Armoured Brigade, 1948*

After the invasion: France allowed aircraft carrying arms from Czechoslovakia to land on French territory in transit to Israel, and permitted two arms shipments to 'Nicaragua', which were actually intended for Israel.

Czechoslovakia supplied vast quantities of arms to Israel during the war, including thousands of vz. 24 rifles and MG 34 and ZB 37 machine guns, and millions of rounds of ammunition. Czechoslovakia supplied fighter aircraft, including at first ten Avia S-199 fighter planes.

The Haganah readied twelve cargo ships throughout European ports to transfer the accumulated equipment, which would set sail as soon as the British blockade was lifted with the expiration of the Mandate.[1970]

Following Israeli independence, the Israelis managed to build three Sherman tanks from scrap-heap material found in abandoned British ordnance depots.[1971]

The Haganah also managed to obtain stocks of British weapons due to the logistical complexity of the British withdrawal, and the corruption of a number of officials.[1972]

After the first truce: By July 1948, the Israelis had established an air force, a navy, and a tank battalion.

On June 29, 1948, the day before the last British troops left Haifa, two British soldiers sympathetic to the Israelis stole two Cromwell tanks from an arms

1948 Arab–Israeli War

Figure 221: *A Cromwell tank*

depot in the Haifa port area, smashing them through the unguarded gates, and joined the IDF with the tanks. These two tanks would form the basis of the Israeli Armored Corps.

After the second truce: Czechoslovakia supplied Supermarine Spitfire fighter planes, which were smuggled to Israel via an abandoned Luftwaffe runway in Yugoslavia, with the agreement of the Yugoslav government.Wikipedia:Citation needed The airborne arms smuggling missions from Czechoslovakia were codenamed Operation Balak.

Arab forces

At the invasion: In addition to the local irregular Palestinians militia groups, the five Arab states that joined the war were Egypt, Jordan (Transjordan), Syria, Lebanon and Iraq sending expeditionary forces of their regular armies. Additional contingents came from Saudi Arabia and Yemen. On the eve of the war, the available number of Arab troops likely to be committed to war was between 23,500 and 26,500 (10,000 Egyptians, 4,500 Jordanians, 3,000 Iraqis, 3,000–6,000 Syrians, 2,000 ALA volunteers, 1,000 Lebanese, and several hundred Saudis), in addition to the irregular Palestinians already present. Prior to the war, Arab forces had been trained by British and French instructors. This was particularly true of Jordan's Arab Legion under command of Lt Gen Sir John Glubb.

Figure 222: *IDF soldiers of the Samson's Foxes unit advance in a captured Egyptian Bren Gun carrier.*

Syria bought a quantity of small arms for the Arab Liberation Army from Czechoslovakia, but the shipment never arrived due to Haganah force intervention.[1973]

Arab states

Jordan's Arab Legion was considered the most effective Arab force. Armed, trained and commanded by British officers, this 8,000–12,000 strong force was organised in four infantry/mechanised regiments supported by some 40 artillery pieces and 75 armoured cars. Until January 1948, it was reinforced by the 3,000-strong Transjordan Frontier Force. As many as 48 British officers served in the Arab Legion. Glubb Pasha, the commander of the Legion, organized his forces into four brigades as follows:

Military Division	Commander[1974,1975]	Rank	Military Zone of operations
First Brigade, includes: 1st and 3rd regiments	Desmond Goldie	Colonel	Nablus Military Zone
Second Brigade, includes: Fifth and Sixth Regiments	Sam Sidney Arthur Cooke	Brigadier	Support force
Third Brigade, includes: Second and Fourth Regiments	Teel Ashton	Colonel	Ramallah Military Zone

| Fourth Brigade | Ahmad Sudqi al-Jundi | Colonel | Support: Ramallah, Hebron, and Ramla |

The Arab Legion joined the war in May 1948, but fought only in the area that King Abdullah wanted to secure for Jordan: the West Bank, including East Jerusalem.

France prevented a large sale of arms by a Swiss company to Ethiopia, brokered by the U.K foreign office, which was actually destined for Egypt and Jordan, denied a British request at the end of April to permit the landing of a squadron of British aircraft on their way to Transjordan, and applied diplomatic pressure on Belgium to suspend arms sales to the Arab states.

The Jordanian forces were probably the best trained of all combatants. Other combatant forces lacked the ability to make strategic decisions and tactical maneuvers,[1976] as evidenced by positioning the fourth regiment at Latrun, which was abandoned by ALA combatants before the arrival of the Jordanian forces and the importance of which was not fully understood by the Haganah general-staff. In the later stages of the war, Latrun proved to be of extreme importance, and a decisive factor in Jerusalem's fate.

In 1948, **Iraq's** army had 21,000 men in 12 brigades and the Iraqi Air Force had 100 planes, mostly British. Initially the Iraqis committed around 3,000 men[1977] to the war effort, including four infantry brigades, one armoured battalion and support personnel. These forces were to operate under Jordanian guidance[1978] The first Iraqi forces to be deployed reached Jordan in April 1948 under the command of Gen. Nur ad-Din Mahmud.[1979]

In 1948, **Egypt's** army was able to put a maximum of around 40,000 men into the field, 80% of its military-age male population being unfit for military service and its embryonic logistics system being limited in its ability to support ground forces deployed beyond its borders.Wikipedia:Citation needed Initially, an expeditionary force of 10,000 men was sent to Palestine under the command of Maj. Gen. Ahmed Ali al-Mwawi. This force consisted of five infantry battalions, one armoured battalion equipped with British Light Tank Mk VI and Matilda tanks, one battalion of sixteen 25-pounder guns, a battalion of eight 6-pounder guns and one medium-machine-gun battalion with supporting troops.Wikipedia:Citation needed

The Egyptian Air Force had over 30 Spitfires, 4 Hawker Hurricanes and 20 C47s modified into crude bombers.Wikipedia:Citation needed

Syria had 12,000 soldiers at the beginning of the 1948 War, grouped into three infantry brigades and an armoured force of approximately battalion size. The Syrian Air Force had fifty planes, the 10 newest of which were World War II–generation models.

Figure 223: *Vickers light tanks in the desert*

France suspended arms sales to Syria, notwithstanding signed contracts.

Lebanon's army was the smallest of the Arab armies, consisting of only 3,500 soldiers. According to Gelber, in June 1947, Ben-Gurion "arrived at an agreement with the Maronite religious leadership in Lebanon that cost a few thousand pounds and kept Lebanon's army out of the War of Independence and the military Arab coalition."[1980] According to Rogan and Shlaim, a token force of 1,000 was committed to the invasion. It crossed into the northern Galilee and was repulsed by Israeli forces. Israel then invaded and occupied southern Lebanon until the end of the war.[1981]

Arab forces after the first truce: By the time of the second truce, the **Egyptians** had 20,000 men in the field in thirteen battalions equipped with 135 tanks and 90 artillery pieces.[1982]

During the first truce, the **Iraqis** increased their force to about 10,000.[1983] Ultimately, the Iraqi expeditionary force numbered around 18,000 men.[1984]

Saudi Arabia sent hundreds of volunteers to join the Arab forces. In February 1948, around 800 tribesmen had gathered near Aqaba so as to invade the Negev, but crossed to Egypt after Saudi rival King Abdallah officially denied them permission to pass through Jordanian territory.[1985] The Saudi troops were attached to the Egyptian command throughout the war,[1986] and estimates of their total strength ranged up to 1,200.[1987,1988] By July 1948, the Saudis

1948 Arab—Israeli War

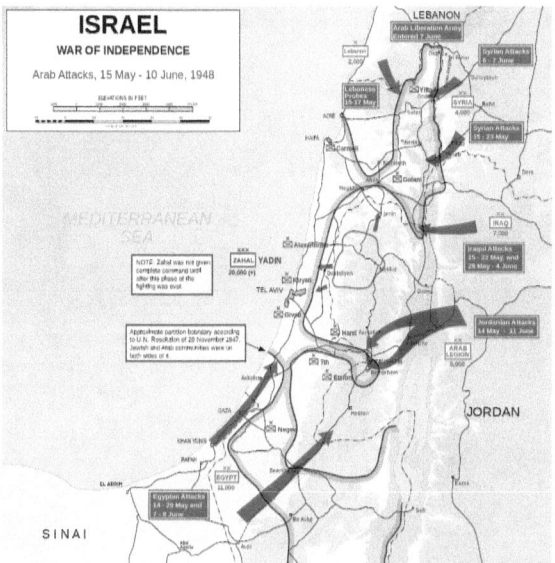

Figure 224: *Arab offensive, 15 May – 10 June 1948*

comprised three brigades within the Egyptian expeditionary force, and were stationed as guards between Gaza city and Rafah.[1989] This area came under heavy aerial bombardment during Operation Yoav in October,[1990] and faced a land assault beginning in late December which culminated in the Battle of Rafah in early January of the new year. With the subsequent armistice of 24 February 1949 and evacuation of almost 4,000 Arab soldiers and civilians from Gaza, the Saudi contingent withdrew through Arish and returned to Saudi Arabia.[1991]

During the first truce, **Sudan** sent six companies of regular troops to fight alongside the Egyptians.[1992] **Yemen** also committed a small expeditionary force to the war effort, and contingents from **Morocco** joined the Arab armies as well.

Course of the war

At the last moment, several Arab leaders, to avert catastrophe – secretly appealed to the British to hold on in Palestine for at least another year.

Figure 225: *A "Butterfly" improvised armored car of the Haganah at Kibbutz Dorot in the Negev, Israel 1948. The armored car is based on CMP-15 truck. The car has brought supply to the kibbutz. The Negev Kibbutz's Wikipedia:Accuracy dispute#Disputed statement children were later evacuated by those cars from their kibbutz, before an expected Egyptian Army attack.*

First phase: 15 May – 11 June 1948

On 14 May 1948, David Ben-Gurion declared the establishment of a Jewish state in Eretz-Israel to be known as the State of Israel, a few hours before the termination of the Mandate. At midnight on 15 May 1948, the British Mandate was officially terminated, and the State of Israel came into being. Several hours later, Iraq and the neighboring Arab states, Egypt, Jordan (Transjordan) and Syria, invaded the newborn state,[1993] and immediately attacked Jewish settlements. What was now Israel had already, from 1 April down to 14 May, conducted 8 of its 13 full-scale military operations outside of the area allotted to a Jewish state by partition, and the operational commander Yigal Allon later stated that had it not been for the Arab invasion, Haganah's forces would have reached 'the natural borders of western Israel.'[1994] Although the Arab invasion was denounced by the United States, the Soviet Union, and UN secretary-general Trygve Lie, it found support from the Republic of China and other UN member states.

The initial Arab plans called for Syrian and Lebanese forces to invade from north while Jordanian and Iraqi forces were to invade from east in order to meet at Nazareth and then to push forward together to Haifa. In the south, the Egyptians were to advance and take Tel Aviv.[1995] At the Arab League meeting in Damascus on 11–13 May, Abdullah rejected the plan, which served Syrian interests, using the fact his allies were afraid to go to war without his army. He proposed that the Iraqis attack the Jezreel valley and the Arab Legion enter Ramallah and Nablus and link with the Egyptian army at Hebron, which was more in compliance with his political objective to occupy the territory allocated to the Arab State by the partition plan and promises not to invade the territory allocated to the Jewish State by the partition plan. In addition, Lebanon decided not to take part in the war at the last minute, due to the still-influential Christians' opposition and due to Jewish bribes.

Intelligence provided by the French consulate in Jerusalem on 12 May 1948 on the Arab armies' invading forces and their revised plan to invade the new state contributed to Israel's success in withstanding the Arab invasion.

The first mission of the Jewish forces was to hold on against the Arab armies and stop them, although the Arabs had enjoyed major advantages (the initiative, vastly superior firepower).[1996] As the British stopped blocking the incoming Jewish immigrants and arms supply, the Israeli forces grew steadily with large numbers of immigrants and weapons, that allowed the Haganah to transform itself from a paramilitary force into a real army. Initially, the fighting was handled mainly by the Haganah, along with the smaller Jewish militant groups Irgun and Lehi. On 26 May 1948, Israel established the Israel Defense Forces (IDF), incorporating these forces into one military under a central command.

Southern front – Negev

The Egyptian force, the largest among the Arab armies, invaded from the south.

On 15 May 1948, the Egyptians attacked two settlements: Nirim, using artillery, armoured cars carrying cannons, and Bren carriers; and Kfar Darom using artillery, tanks and aircraft. The Egyptians attacks met fierce resistance from the few and lightly armed defenders of both settlements, and failed. On 19 May the Egyptians attacked Yad Mordechai, where an inferior force of 100 Israelis armed with nothing more than rifles, a medium machinegun and a PIAT anti-tank weapon, held up a column of 2,500 Egyptians, well-supported by armor, artillery and air units, for five days. The Egyptians took heavy losses, while the losses sustained by the defenders were comparatively light.

One of the Egyptian force's two main columns made its way northwards along the shoreline, through what is today the Gaza Strip and the other column advanced eastwards toward Beersheba.[1997] To secure their flanks, the Egyptians attacked and laid siege to a number of kibbutzim in the Negev, among those

Figure 226: *Israeli soldiers in Nirim*

Figure 227: *Israeli soldiers in Negba*

Kfar Darom, Nirim, Yad Mordechai, and Negba.[1998] The Israeli defenders held out fiercely for days against vastly superior forces, and managed to buy valuable time for the IDF's Givati Brigade to prepare to stop the Egyptian drive on Tel Aviv.

On 28 May the Egyptians renewed their northern advance, and stopped at a destroyed bridge north to Isdud. The Givati Brigade reported this advance but no fighters were sent to confront the Egyptians. Had the Egyptians wished to continue their advance northward, towards Tel Aviv, there would have been no Israeli force to block them.[1999,2000]

From 29 May to 3 June, Israeli forces stopped the Egyptian drive north in Operation Pleshet. In the first combat mission performed by Israel's fledgling air force, four Avia S-199s attacked an Egyptian armored column of 500 vehicles on its way to Isdud. The Israeli planes dropped 70 kilogram bombs and strafed the column, although their machine guns jammed quickly. Two of the planes crashed, killing a pilot. The attack caused the Egyptians to scatter, and they had lost the initiative by the time they had regrouped. Following the air attack, Israeli forces constantly bombarded Egyptian forces in Isdud with *Napoleonchik* cannons, and IDF patrols engaged in small-scale harassment of Egyptian lines. Following another air attack, the Givati Brigade launched a counterattack. Although the counterattack was repulsed, the Egyptian offensive was halted as Egypt changed its strategy from offensive to defensive, and the initiative shifted to Israel.

On 6 June, in the Battle of Nitzanim, Egyptian forces attacked the kibbutz of Nitzanim, located between Majdal (now Ashkelon) and Isdud, and the Israeli defenders surrendered after resisting for five days.

Battles of Latrun

The heaviest fighting occurred in Jerusalem and on the Jerusalem – Tel Aviv road, between Jordan's Arab Legion and Israeli forces. As part of the redeployment to deal with the Egyptian advance, the Israelis abandoned the Latrun fortress overlooking the main highway to Jerusalem, which the Arab Legion immediately seized. The Arab Legion also occupied the Latrun Monastery. From these positions, the Jordanians were able to cut off supplies to Israeli fighters and civilians in Jerusalem.

The Israelis attempted to take the Latrun fortress in a series of battles lasting from 24 May to 18 July. The Arab Legion held Latrun and managed to repulse the attacks. During the attempts to take Latrun, Israeli forces suffered some 586 casualties, among them Mickey Marcus, Israel's first general, who was killed by friendly fire. The Arab Legion also took losses, losing 90 dead and some 200 wounded up to 29 May.[2001]

Building the Burma Road

A bulldozer tows a truck on the "Burma road", June 1948

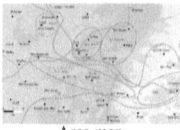
Area map

The besieged Israeli Jerusalem was only saved via the opening of the so-called "Burma Road", a makeshift bypass road built by Israeli forces that allowed Israeli supply convoys to pass into Jerusalem. Parts of the area where the road was built were cleared of Jordanian snipers in May and the road was completed on 14 June. Supplies had already begun passing through before the road was completed, with the first convoy passing through on the night of 1–2 June. The Jordanians spotted the activity and attempted to shell the road, but were ineffective, as it could not be seen. However, Jordanian sharpshooters killed several road workers, and an attack on 9 June left eight Israelis dead. On 18 July, elements of the Harel Brigade took about 10 villages to the south of Latrun to enlarge and secure the area of the Burma Road.

The Arab Legion was able to repel an Israeli attack on Latrun. The Jordanians launched two counterattacks, temporarily taking Beit Susin before being forced back, and capturing Gezer after a fierce battle, which was retaken by two Palmach squads the same evening.[2002]

Jordanian artillery shelling Jerusalem in 1948

Arab Legion soldier standing in ruins of the most sacred Synagogue, the "Hurva", Old City.

Jewish residents of Jerusalem Old City fleeing during the Jordanian offensive

Battle for Jerusalem

The Jordanians in Latrun cut off supplies to western Jerusalem. Though some supplies, mostly munitions, were airdropped into the city, the shortage of food, water, fuel and medicine was acute. The Israeli forces were seriously short of food, water and ammunition.

Figure 228: *Mathematics professor Michael Fekete, the Provost of the Hebrew University of Jerusalem, with his water quota, during the siege of Jerusalem*

King Abdullah ordered Glubb Pasha, the commander of the Arab Legion, to enter Jerusalem on 17 May. The Arab Legion fired 10,000 artillery and mortar shells a day, and also attacked West Jerusalem with sniper fire.

Heavy house-to-house fighting occurred between 19 and 28 May, with the Arab Legion eventually succeeding in pushing Israeli forces from the Arab neighborhoods of Jerusalem as well as the Jewish Quarter of the Old City. The 1,500 Jewish inhabitants of the Old City's Jewish Quarter were expelled, and several hundred were detained. The Jews had to be escorted out by the Arab Legion to protect them against Palestinian Arab mobs that intended to massacre them.[2003] On 22 May, Arab forces attacked kibbutz Ramat Rachel south of Jerusalem. After a fierce battle in which 31 Jordanians and 13 Israelis were killed, the defenders of Ramat Rachel withdrew, only to partially retake the kibbutz the following day. Fighting continued until 26 May, until the entire kibbutz was recaptured. Radar Hill was also taken from the Arab Legion, and held until 26 May, when the Jordanians retook it in a battle that left 19 Israelis and 2 Jordanians dead. A total of 23 attempts by the Harel Brigade to capture Radar Hill in the war failed.

The same day, Thomas C. Wasson, the US Consul-General in Jerusalem and a member of the UN Truce Commission was shot dead in West Jerusalem. It was disputed whether Wasson was killed by the Arabs or Israelis.

Figure 229: *Israeli soldiers in Afula.*

In mid to late October 1948, the Harel Brigade began its offensive in what was known as Operation Ha-Har, to secure the Jerusalem Corridor.

Northern Samaria

An Iraqi force consisting of two infantry and one armoured brigade crossed the Jordan River from northern Jordan, attacking the Israeli settlement of Gesher with little success. Following this defeat, Iraqi forces moved into the strategic triangle bounded by the Arab towns Nablus, Jenin and Tulkarm. On 25 May, they were making their way towards Netanya, when they were stopped. On 29 May, an Israeli attack against the Iraqis led to three days of heavy fighting over Jenin, but Iraqi forces managed to hold their positions. After these battles, the Iraqi forces became stationary and their involvement in the war effectively ended.

Iraqi forces failed in their attacks on Israeli settlements with the most notable battle taking place at Gesher, and instead took defensive positions around Jenin, Nablus, and Tulkarm, from where they could put pressure on the Israeli center.Wikipedia:Citation needed[2004] On 25 May, Iraqi forces advanced from Tulkarm, taking Geulim and reaching Kfar Yona and Ein Vered on the Tulkarm-Netanya road. The Alexandroni Brigade then stopped the Iraqi advance and retook Geulim. On 1 June, the Carmeli and Golani Brigades captured Jenin from Iraqi forces. They were pushed out by an Iraqi counterattack, and lost 34 dead and 100 wounded.

Figure 230: *Syrian R-35 light tank destroyed at Degania Alef.*

Northern front – Lake of Galilee

On 14 May Syria invaded Palestine with the 1st Infantry Brigade supported by a battalion of armoured cars, a company of French R 35 and R 37 tanks, an artillery battalion and other units.[2005] The Syrian president, Shukri al-Quwwatli instructed his troops in the front, "to destroy the Zionists". "The situation was very grave. There aren't enough rifles. There are no heavy weapons," Ben-Gurion told the Israeli Cabinet.[2006,2007] On 15 May, the Syrian forces turned to the eastern and southern Sea of Galilee shores, and attacked Samakh the neighboring Tegart fort and the settlements of Sha'ar HaGolan, Ein Gev, but they were bogged down by resistance. Later, they attacked Samakh using tanks and aircraft, and on 18 May they succeeded in conquering Samakh and occupied the abandoned Sha'ar HaGolan.

On 21 May, the Syrian army was stopped at kibbutz Degania Alef in the north, where local militia reinforced by elements of the Carmeli Brigade halted Syrian armored forces with Molotov cocktails, hand grenades and a single PIAT. One tank that was disabled by Molotov cocktails and hand grenades still remains at the kibbutz. The remaining Syrian forces were driven off the next day by four Napoleonchik mountain guns – Israel's first use of artillery during the war. Following the Syrian forces' defeat at the Deganias a few days later, they abandoned the Samakh village. The Syrians were forced to besiege the kibbutz

Figure 231: *Kaukji, the Arab Liberation Army commander*

rather than advance. One author claims that the main reason for the Syrian defeat was the Syrian soldiers' low regard for the Israelis who they believed would not stand and fight against the Arab army.

On 6 June, nearly two brigades of the Arab Liberation Army and the Lebanese Army took Al-Malkiyya and Qadas in what became the only intervention of the Lebanese army during the war.

On 6 June, Syrian forces attacked Mishmar HaYarden, but they were repulsed. On 10 June, the Syrians overran Mishmar HaYarden and advanced to the main road, where they were stopped by units of the Oded Brigade. Subsequently, the Syrians reverted to a defensive posture, conducting only a few minor attacks on small, exposed Israeli settlements.

Palestinian forces

In the continuity of the civil war between Jewish and Arab forces that had begun in 1947, battles between Israeli forces and Palestinian Arab militias took place, particularly in the Lydda, al-Ramla, Jerusalem, and Haifa areas. On 23 May, the Alexandroni Brigade captured Tantura, south of Haifa, from Arab forces. On 2 June, Holy War Army commander Hasan Salama was killed in a battle with Haganah at Ras al-Ein.

Figure 232: *An Egyptian Spitfire shot down over Tel Aviv on 15 May 1948*

Air operations

All Jewish aviation assets were placed under the control of the *Sherut Avir* (Air Service, known as the SA) in November 1947 and flying operations began in the following month from a small civil airport on the outskirts of Tel Aviv called Sde Dov, with the first ground support operation (in an RWD-13) taking place on 17 December. The Galilee Squadron was formed at Yavne'el in March 1948, and the Negev Squadron was formed at Nir-Am in April. By 10 May, when the SA suffered its first combat loss, there were three flying units, an air staff, maintenance facilities and logistics support. At the outbreak of the war on 15 May, the SA became the Israeli Air Force. With its fleet of light planes it was no match for Arab forces during the first few weeks of the war with their T-6s, Spitfires, C-47s, and Avro Ansons.

On 15 May, with the beginning of the war, four Royal Egyptian Air Force (REAF) Spitfires attacked Tel Aviv, bombing Sde Dov Airfield, where the bulk of Sherut Avir's aircraft were concentrated, as well as the Reading Power Station. Several aircraft were destroyed, some others were damaged, and five Israelis were killed. Throughout the following hours, additional waves of Egyptian aircraft bombed and strafed targets around Tel Aviv, although these raids had little effect. One Spitfire was shot down by anti-aircraft fire, and its pilot was taken prisoner. Throughout the next six days, the REAF would continue to attack Tel Aviv, causing civilian casualties. On 18 May, Egyptian warplanes attacked the Tel Aviv Central Bus Station, killing 42 people and wounding

Figure 233: *Volunteers evacuating a wounded man during Egyptian bombardment of Tel Aviv.*

100. In addition to their attacks on Tel Aviv, the Egyptians also bombed rural settlements and airfields, though few casualties were caused in these raids.[2008]

At the outset of the war, the REAF was able to attack Israel with near impunity, due to the lack of Israeli fighter aircraft to intercept them,[2009] and met only ground fire.

As more effective air defenses were transferred to Tel Aviv, the Egyptians began taking significant aircraft losses. As a result of these losses, as well as the loss of five Spitfires downed by the British when the Egyptians mistakenly attacked RAF Ramat David, the Egyptian air attacks became less frequent. By the end of May 1948, almost the entire REAF Spitfire squadron based in El Arish had been lost, including many of its best pilots.

Although lacking fighter or bomber aircraft, in the first few days of the war, Israel's embryonic air force still attacked Arab targets, with light aircraft being utilized as makeshift bombers, striking Arab encampments and columns. The raids were mostly carried out at night to avoid interception by Arab fighter aircraft. These attacks usually had little effect, except on morale.

The balance of air power soon began to swing in favor of the Israeli Air Force following the arrival of 25 Avia S-199s from Czechoslovakia, the first of which arrived in Israel on 20 May. Ironically, Israel was using the Avia S-199, an

Figure 234: *Avia S-199 Israeli 1st fighter aircraft*

Figure 235: *Israeli Spitfire F Mk*

inferior derivative of the Bf-109 designed in Nazi Germany to counter British-designed Spitfires flown by Egypt. Throughout the rest of the war, Israel would acquire more Avia fighters, as well as 62 Spitfires from Czechoslovakia. On 28 May 1948, Sherut Avir became the Israeli Air Force.

Many of the pilots who fought for the Israeli Air Force were foreign volunteers or mercenaries, including many World War II veterans.

On 3 June, Israel scored its first victory in aerial combat when Israeli pilot Modi Alon shot down a pair of Egyptian DC-3s that had just bombed Tel Aviv. Although Tel Aviv would see additional raids by fighter aircraft, there would be no more raids by bombers for the rest of the war. From then on, the Israeli Air Force began engaging the Arab air forces in air-to-air combat. The first dogfight took place on 8 June, when an Israeli fighter plane flown by Gideon Lichtman shot down an Egyptian Spitfire. By the fall of 1948, the IAF had

Figure 236: *Israeli B-17s in flight*

achieved air superiority and had superior firepower and more knowledgeable personnel, many of whom had seen action in World War II.[2010] Israeli planes then began intercepting and engaging Arab aircraft on bombing missions.

Following Israeli air attacks on Egyptian and Iraqi columns, the Egyptians repeatedly bombed Ekron Airfield, where IAF fighters were based. During a 30 May raid, bombs aimed for Ekron hit central Rehovot, killing 7 civilians and wounding 30. In response to this, and probably to the Jordanian victories at Latrun, Israel began bombing targets in Arab cities. On the night of 31 May/1 June, the first Israeli raid on an Arab capital took place when three IAF planes flew to Amman and dropped several dozen 55 and 110-pound bombs, hitting the King's Palace and an adjacent British airfield. Some 12 people were killed and 30 wounded. During the attack, an RAF hangar was damaged, as were some British aircraft. The British threatened that in the event of another such attack, they would shoot down the attacking aircraft and bomb Israeli airfields, and as a result, Israeli aircraft did not attack Amman again for the rest of the war. Israel also bombed Arish, Gaza, Damascus, and Cairo. Israeli Boeing B-17 Flying Fortress bombers coming to Israel from Czechoslovakia bombed Egypt on their way to Israel.[2011,2012] According to Alan Dershowitz, Israeli planes focused on bombing military targets in these attacks, though Benny Morris wrote that an 11 June air raid on Damascus was indiscriminate.

1948 Arab–Israeli War

Figure 237: *Northland in Greenland circa 1944 which became the Israeli INS Eilat*

Sea battles

At the outset of the war, the Israeli Navy consisted of three former Aliyah Bet ships that had been seized by the British and impounded in Haifa harbor, where they were tied up at the breakwater. Work on establishing a navy had begun shortly before Israeli independence, and the three ships were selected due to them having a military background – one, the INS *Eilat*, was an ex-US Coast Guard icebreaker, and the other two, the INS *Haganah* and INS *Wedgwood*, had been Royal Canadian Navy corvettes. The ships were put into minimum running condition by contractors dressed as stevedores and port personnel, who were able to work in the engine rooms and below deck. The work had to be clandestine to avoid arousing British suspicion. On 21 May 1948, the three ships set sail for Tel Aviv, and were made to look like ships that had been purchased by foreign owners for commercial use. In Tel Aviv, the ships were fitted with small field guns dating to the late 19th century and anti-aircraft guns. After the British left Haifa port on 30 June, Haifa became the main base of the Israeli Navy. In October 1948, a submarine chaser was purchased from the United States. The warships were manned by former merchant seamen, former crewmembers of Aliyah Bet ships, Israelis who had served in the Royal Navy during World War II, and foreign volunteers. The newly refurbished and crewed warships served on coastal patrol duties and bombarded Egyptian coastal installations in and around the Gaza area all the way to Port Said.[2013]

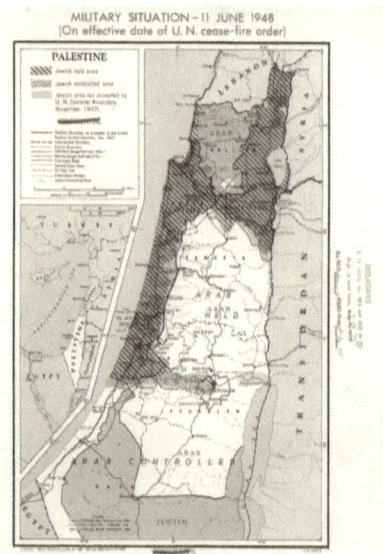

Figure 238: *Palestine Military Situation, June 11, 1948. Truman Papers*

End of the first phase

Throughout the following days, the Arabs were only able to make limited gains due to fierce Israeli resistance, and were quickly driven off their new holdings by Israeli counterattacks.

As the war progressed, the IDF managed to field more troops than the Arab forces. In July 1948, the IDF had 63,000 troops; by early spring 1949, they had 115,000. The Arab armies had an estimated 40,000 troops in July 1948, rising to 55,000 in October 1948, and slightly more by the spring of 1949.

Upon the implementation of the truce, the IDF had control over nine Arab cities and towns or mixed cities and towns: New Jerusalem, Jaffa, Haifa, Acre, Safed, Tiberias, Baysan (Beit She'an), Samakh and Yibna (Yavne). Another city, Jenin, was not occupied but its residents fled. The combined Arab forces captured 14 Jewish settlement points, but only one of them, Mishmar Ha-Yarden, was in the territory of the proposed Jewish State according to Resolution 181. Within the boundaries of the proposed Jewish state, there were twelve Arab villages which opposed Jewish control or were captured by the invading Arab armies, and in addition to them, the Lod Airport and pumping station near Antipatris, which were within the boundaries of the proposed Jewish state, were under the control of the Arabs. The IDF captured about 50 large Arab villages outside of the boundaries of the proposed Jewish State and a larger number of hamlets and Bedouin encampments. 350 square kilometers of the proposed Jewish State were under the control of the Arab forces, while 700 square kilometers of the proposed Arab State were under the control of the IDF. This figure ignores the Negev desert which wasn't under any absolute control of either side.[2014]

In the period between the invasion and the first truce the Syrian army had 315 of its men killed and 400–500 injured; the Iraqi expeditionary force had 200 of its men killed and 500 injured; the Jordanian Arab Legion had 300 of its men killed and 400–500 (including irregulars and Palesinian volunteers fighting under the Jordanians); the Egyptian army had 600 of its men killed and 1,400 injured (including irregulars from the Muslim Brotherhood); the ALA, which returned to fight in early June, had 100 of its men killed or injured. 800 Jews were taken hostage by the Arabs and 1,300 Arabs were taken hostage by the Jews, mostly Palestinians.

First truce: 11 June – 8 July 1948

The UN declared a truce on 29 May, which came into effect on 11 June and lasted 28 days. The truce was designed to last 28 days and an arms embargo was declared with the intention that neither side would make any gains from the truce. Neither side respected the truce; both found ways around the restrictions placed on them. Both the Israelis and the Arabs used this time to improve their positions, a direct violation of the terms of the ceasefire.[2015]

Reinforcements

Israeli Forces 1948[2016]

Initial strength	29,677
4 June	40,825
17 July	63,586
7 October	88,033
28 October	92,275
2 December	106,900
23 December	107,652
30 December	108,300

At the time of the truce, the British view was that "the Jews are too weak in armament to achieve spectacular success". As the truce commenced, a British officer stationed in Haifa stated that the four-week-long truce "would certainly be exploited by the Jews to continue military training and reorganization while the Arabs would waste [them] feuding over the future divisions of the spoils".

Figure 239: *Altalena burning near Tel Aviv beach*

During the truce, the Israelis sought to bolster their forces by massive import of arms. The IDF was able to acquire weapons from Czechoslovakia as well as improve training of forces and reorganization of the army during this time. Yitzhak Rabin, an IDF commander at the time of the war and later Israel's fifth Prime Minister, stated "[w]ithout the arms from Czechoslovakia... it is very doubtful whether we would have been able to conduct the war".

The Israeli army increased its manpower from approximately 30,000–35,000 men to almost 65,000 during the truce due to mobilization and the constant immigration into Israel. It was also able to increase its arms supply to more than 25,000 rifles, 5,000 machine guns, and fifty million bullets. As well as violating the arms and personnel embargo, they also sent fresh units to the front lines, much as their Arab enemies did.

During the truce, Irgun attempted to bring in a private arms shipment aboard a ship called *Altalena*. When they refused to hand the arms to the Israeli government, Ben-Gurion ordered that the arms be confiscated by force if necessary. After meeting with armed resistance, the army was ordered by Ben-Gurion to sink the ship. Several Irgun members and IDF soldiers were killed in the fighting.

UN mediator Bernadotte

The ceasefire was overseen by UN mediator Folke Bernadotte and a team of UN Observers made up of army officers from Belgium, United States, Sweden and France. Bernadotte was voted in by the General Assembly to "assure the safety of the holy places, to safeguard the well being of the population, and to promote 'a peaceful adjustment of the future situation of Palestine'".

Folke Bernadotte reported:

> *During the period of the truce, three violations occurred ... of such a serious nature:*

> 1. *the attempt by ...the Irgun Zvai Leumi to bring war materials and immigrants, including men of military age, into Palestine aboard the ship Altalena on 21 June...*
> 2. *Another truce violation occurred through the refusal of Egyptian forces to permit the passage of relief convoys to Jewish settlements in the Negeb...*
> 3. *The third violation of the truce arose as a result of the failure of the Transjordan and Iraqi forces to permit the flow of water to Jerusalem.*[2017]

> *After the truce was in place, Bernadotte began to address the issue of achieving a political settlement. The main obstacles in his opinion were "the Arab world's continued rejection of the existence of a Jewish state, whatever its borders; Israel's new 'philosophy', based on its increasing military strength, of ignoring the partition boundaries and conquering what additional territory it could; and the emerging Palestinian Arab refugee problem".*

> *Taking all the issues into account, Bernadotte presented a new partition plan. He proposed there be a Palestinian Arab state alongside Israel and that a "Union" "be established between the two sovereign states of Israel and Jordan (which now included the West Bank); that the Negev, or part of it, be included in the Arab state and that Western Galilee, or part of it, be included in Israel; that the whole of Jerusalem be part of the Arab state, with the Jewish areas enjoying municipal autonomy and that Lydda Airport and Haifa be 'free ports' – presumably free of Israeli or Arab sovereignty". Israel rejected the proposal, in particular the aspect of losing control of Jerusalem, but they did agree to extend the truce for another month. The Arabs rejected both the extension of the truce and the proposal.*

Figure 240: *An Egyptian artillery piece captured by battalion 53 of the Givati Brigade.*

Second phase: 8–18 July 1948 ("Ten Day Battles")

On 8 July, the day before the expiration of the truce, Egyptian forces under General Muhammad Naguib renewed the war by attacking Negba.[2018] The following day, Israeli air forces launched a simultaneous offensive on all three fronts, ranging from Quneitra to Arish and the Egyptian air force bombed the city of Tel Aviv.[2019] During the fighting, the Israelis were able to open a lifeline to a number of besieged kibbutzim.

The fighting continued for ten days until the UN Security Council issued the Second Truce on 18 July. During those 10 days, the fighting was dominated by large-scale Israeli offensives and a defensive posture from the Arab side.

Southern front

In the south, the IDF carried out several offensives, including Operation An-Far and Operation Death to the Invader. The task of the 11th Brigades's 1st Battalion on the southern flank was to capture villages, and its operation ran smoothly, with but little resistance from local irregulars. According to Amnon Neumann, a Palmach veteran of the Southern front, hardly any Arab villages in the south fought back, due to the miserable poverty of their means and lack of weapons, and suffered expulsion.[2020] What slight resistance was offered was

Figure 241: *Israeli soldiers in Lod (Lydda) or Ramle.*

quelled by an artillery barrage, followed by the storming of the village, whose residents were expelled and houses destroyed.[2021]

On 12 July, the Egyptians launched an offensive action, and again attacked Negba, which they had previously failed to capture, using three infantry battalions, an armored battalion, and an artillery regiment. In the battle that followed, the Egyptians were repulsed, suffering 200–300 casualties, while the Israelis lost 5 dead and 16 wounded.[2022]

After failing to take Negba, the Egyptians turned their attention to more isolated settlements and positions. On 14 July, an Egyptian attack on Gal On was driven off by a minefield and by resistance from Gal On's residents.[2023]

The Egyptians then assaulted the lightly defended village of Be'erot Yitzhak. The Egyptians managed to penetrate the village perimeter, but the defenders concentrated in an inner position in the village and fought off the Egyptian advance until IDF reinforcements arrived and drove out the attackers. The Egyptians suffered an estimated 200 casualties, while the Israelis had 17 dead and 15 wounded. The battle was one of Egypt's last offensive actions during the war, and the Egyptians did not attack any Israeli villages following this battle.

Figure 242: *Israeli armored vehicles in Lydda airport after the town's capture by Israeli forces.*

Lydda and al-Ramla

On 10 July, Glubb Pasha ordered the defending Arab Legion troops to "make arrangements...for a phony war". Israeli Operation Danny was the most important Israeli offensive, aimed at securing and enlarging the corridor between Jerusalem and Tel Aviv by capturing the roadside cities Lod (Lydda) and Ramle. In a second planned stage of the operation the fortified positions of Latrun – overlooking the Tel Aviv-Jerusalem highway – and the city of Ramallah were also to be captured. Hadita, near Latrun, was captured by the Israelis at a cost of 9 dead.

The objectives of Operation Danny were to capture territory east of Tel Aviv and then to push inland and relieve the Jewish population and forces in Jerusalem. Lydda had become an important military center in the region, lending support to Arab military activities elsewhere, and Ramle was one of the main obstacles blocking Jewish transportation. Lydda was defended by a local militia of around 1,000 residents, with an Arab Legion contingent of 125–300.[2024]

The IDF forces gathered to attack the city numbered around 8,000. It was the first operation where several brigades were involved. The city was attacked from the north via Majdal al-Sadiq and al-Muzayri'a, and from the east via Khulda, al-Qubab, Jimzu and Daniyal. Bombers were also used for the first time in the conflict to bombard the city. The IDF captured the city on 11 July.

1948 Arab–Israeli War

Figure 243: *Arab forces surrender to the victorious Israelis in Ramla.*

Up to 450 Arabs and 9–10 Israeli soldiers were killed. The next day, Ramle fell. The civilian populations of Lydda and Ramle fled or were expelled to the Arab front lines, and following resistance in Lydda, the population there was expelled without provision of transport vehicles; some of the evictees died on the long walk under the hot July sun.

On 15–16 July, an attack on Latrun took place but did not manage to occupy the fort. A desperate second attempt occurred on 18 July by units from the Yiftach Brigade equipped with armored vehicles, including two Cromwell tanks, but that attack also failed. Despite the second truce, which began on 18 July, the Israeli efforts to conquer Latrun continued until 20 July.

Jerusalem

Operation Kedem's aim was to secure the Old City of Jerusalem, but fewer resources were allocated. The operation failed.[2025] Originally the operation was to begin on 8 July, immediately after the first truce, by Irgun and Lehi forces. However, it was delayed by David Shaltiel, possibly because he did not trust their ability after their failure to capture Deir Yassin without Haganah assistance.

Irgun forces commanded by Yehuda Lapidot were to break through at the New Gate, Lehi was to break through the wall stretching from the New Gate to the Jaffa Gate, and the Beit Horon Battalion was to strike from Mount Zion.

Figure 244: *Beit Horon Battalion soldiers in the Russian Compound in Jerusalem, 1948*

The battle was planned to begin on the Shabbat, at 20:00 on 16 July, two days before the second ceasefire of the war. The plan went wrong from the beginning and was postponed first to 23:00 and then to midnight. It was not until 02:30 that the battle actually began. The Irgun managed to break through at the New Gate, but the other forces failed in their missions. At 05:45 on 17 July, Shaltiel ordered a retreat and to cease hostilities.

On 14 July 1948, Irgun occupied the Arab village of Malha after a fierce battle. Several hours later, the Arabs launched a counterattack, but Israeli reinforcements arrived, and the village was retaken at a cost of 17 dead.

Southern Galilee

The second plan was Operation Dekel, which was aimed at capturing the Lower Galilee including Nazareth. Nazareth was captured on 16 July, and by the time the second truce took effect at 19:00 18 July, the whole Lower Galilee from Haifa Bay to the Sea of Galilee was captured by Israel.

Eastern Galilee

Operation Brosh was launched in a failed attempt to dislodge Syrian forces from the Eastern Galilee and the Benot Yaakov Bridge. During the operation, 200 Syrians and 100 Israelis were killed. The Israeli Air Force also bombed Damascus for the first time.

Second truce: 18 July – 15 October 1948

At 19:00 on 18 July, the second truce of the conflict went into effect after intense diplomatic efforts by the UN.

On 16 September, Count Folke Bernadotte proposed a new partition for Palestine in which the Negev would be divided between Jordan and Egypt, and Jordan would annex Lydda and Ramla. There would be a Jewish state in the whole of Galilee, with the frontier running from Faluja northeast towards Ramla and Lydda. Jerusalem would be internationalized, with municipal autonomy for the city's Jewish and Arab inhabitants, the Port of Haifa would be a free port, and Lydda Airport would be a free airport. All Palestinian refugees would be granted the right of return, and those who chose not to return would be compensated for lost property. The UN would control and regulate Jewish immigration.

The plan was once again rejected by both sides. On the next day, 17 September, Bernadotte was assassinated in Jerusalem by the militant Zionist group Lehi. A four-man team ambushed Bernadotte's motorcade in Jerusalem, killing him and a French UN observer sitting next to him. Lehi saw Bernadotte as a British and Arab puppet, and thus a serious threat to the emerging State of Israel, and feared that the provisional Israeli government would accept the plan, which it considered disastrous. Unbeknownst to Lehi, the government had already decided to reject it and resume combat in a month. Bernadotte's deputy, American Ralph Bunche, replaced him.[2026,2027,2028]

On 22 September 1948, the Provisional State Council of Israel passed the Area of Jurisdiction and Powers Ordnance, 5708–1948. The law officially added to Israel's size by annexing all land it had captured since the war began. It also declared that from then on, any part of Palestine captured by the Israeli army would automatically become part of Israel.

Little triangle pocket

The Arab villagers of the area known as the "Little Triangle" south of Haifa, repeatedly fired at Israeli traffic along the main road from Tel Aviv to Haifa and were supplied by the Iraqis from northern Samaria. The sniping at traffic continued during the Second Truce. The poorly planned assaults on 18 June and 8 July had failed to dislodge Arab militia from their superior positions. The Israelis launched Operation Shoter on 24 July in order to gain control of the main road to Haifa and to destroy all the enemy in the area. Israeli assaults on 24 and 25 July were beaten back by stiff resistance. The Israelis then broke the Arab defenses with an infantry and armour assault backed by heavy artillery shelling and aerial bombing. Three Arab villages surrendered, and most of the inhabitants fled before and during the attack. The Israeli soldiers and aircraft struck

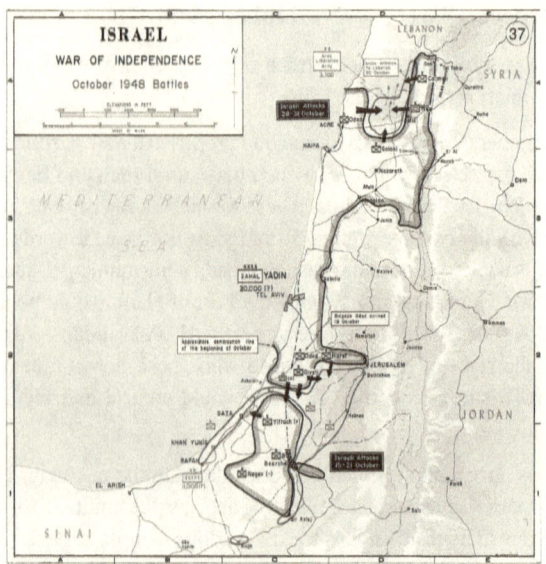

Figure 245: *October battles*

at one of the Arab retreat routes, killing 60 Arab soldiers.Wikipedia:Accuracy dispute#Disputed statement. Most of the inhabitants fled before and during the attack, reaching northern Samaria; hundreds were forcibly expelled during the following days. At least a hundred militiamen and civilians were killed.

The Arabs claimed that the Israelis had massacred Arab civilians, but the Israelis rejected the claims.Wikipedia:Accuracy dispute#Disputed statement A United Nations investigation found no evidence of a massacre. Following the operation, the Tel Aviv-Haifa road was open to Israeli military and civilian traffic, and Arab roadblocks along the route were removed. Traffic along the Haifa-Hadera coastal railway was also restored.

Third phase: 15 October 1948 – 10 March 1949

Israel launched a series of military operations to drive out the Arab armies and secure the northern and southern borders of Israel.

Northern front – Galilee

On 22 October, the third truce went into effect.[2029] Irregular Arab forces refused to recognize the truce, and continued to harass Israeli forces and settlements in the north. On the same day that the truce came into effect, the Arab Liberation Army violated the truce by attacking Manara, capturing the

Figure 246: *An Israeli mortar team outside Safsaf in October 1948.*

Figure 247: *Israeli soldiers attack Sasa during Operation Hiram, October 1948.*

strongpoint of Sheikh Abed, repulsing counterattacks by local Israeli units, and ambushed Israeli forces attempting to relieve Manara. The IDF's Carmeli Brigade lost 33 dead and 40 wounded.[2030] Manara and Misgav Am were totally cut off, and Israel's protests at the UN failed to change the situation.

On 24 October, the IDF launched Operation Hiram and captured the entire upper Galilee area, driving the ALA and Lebanese Army back to Lebanon, and ambushing and destroying an entire Syrian battalion. The Israeli force of four infantry brigades was commanded by Moshe Carmel. The entire operation lasted just 60 hours, during which numerous villages were captured, often after locals or Arab forces put up resistance. Arab losses were estimated at 400 dead and 550 taken prisoner, with low Israeli casualties.

Some prisoners were reportedly executed by the Israeli forces. An estimated 50,000 Palestinian refugees fled into Lebanon, some of them fleeing ahead of the advancing forces, and some expelled from villages which had resisted, while the Arab inhabitants of those villages which had remained at peace were allowed to remain and became Israeli citizens. The villagers of Iqrit and Birim were persuaded to leave their homes by Israeli authorities, who promised them that they would be allowed to return. Israel eventually decided not to allow them to return, and offered them financial compensation, which they refused to accept.

At the end of the month, the IDF had captured the whole of Galilee, driven all Lebanese forces out of Israel, and had advanced 5 miles (8.0 km) into Lebanon to the Litani River, occupying thirteen Lebanese villages. In the village of Hula, two Israeli officers killed between 35 and 58 prisoners as retaliation for the Haifa Oil Refinery massacre. Both officers were later put on trial for their actions.

Negev

Israel launched a series of military operations to drive out the Arab armies and secure the borders of Israel. However, invading the West Bank might have brought into the borders of the expanding State of Israel a massive Arab population it could not absorb. The Negev desert was an empty space for expansion, so the main war effort shifted to Negev from early October.[2031] Israel decided to destroy or at least drive out the Egyptian expeditionary force since the Egyptian front lines were too vulnerable as permanent borders.

On 15 October, the IDF launched Operation Yoav in the northern Negev. Its goal was to drive a wedge between the Egyptian forces along the coast and the Beersheba-Hebron-Jerusalem road and ultimately to conquer the whole Negev. This was a special concern on the Israeli part because of a British diplomatic campaign to have the entire Negev handed over to Egypt and Jordan, and which

Figure 248: *Israeli troops occupying abandoned Egyptian trenches at Huleiqat, October 1948.*

Figure 249: *IDF forces in Beersheba during Operation Yoav.*

Figure 250: *IDF artillery unit in the Negev*

Figure 251: *IDF forces near Bayt Nattif (near Hebron) after it was captured. Oct 1948.*

thus made Ben-Gurion anxious to have Israeli forces in control of the Negev as soon as possible.

Operation Yoav was headed by the Southern Front commander Yigal Allon. Committed to Yoav were three infantry and one armoured brigades, who were given the task of breaking through the Egyptian lines. The Egyptian positions were badly weakened by the lack of a defense in depth, which meant that once the IDF had broken through the Egyptian lines, there was little to stop them. The operation was a huge success, shattering the Egyptian ranks and forcing the Egyptian Army from the northern Negev, Beersheba and Ashdod.

In the so-called "Faluja Pocket", an encircled Egyptian force was able to hold out for four months until the 1949 Armistice Agreements, when the village was peacefully transferred to Israel and the Egyptian troops left. Four warships of the Israeli Navy provided support by bombarding Egyptian shore installations in the Ashkelon area, and preventing the Egyptian Navy from evacuating retreating Egyptian troops by sea.

On 19 October, Operation Ha-Har commenced in the Jerusalem Corridor, while a naval battle also took place near Majdal (now Ashkelon), with three Israeli corvettes facing an Egyptian corvette with air support. An Israeli sailor was killed and four wounded, and two of the ships were damaged. One Egyptian plane was shot down, but the corvette escaped. Israeli naval vessels also shelled Majdal on 17 October, and Gaza on 21 October, with air support from the Israeli Air Force. The same day, the IDF captured Beersheba, and took 120 Egyptian soldiers prisoner. On 22 October, Israeli naval commandos using explosive boats sank the Egyptian flagship *Emir Farouk*, and damaged an Egyptian minesweeper.

On 9 November 1948, the IDF launched Operation Shmone to capture the Tegart fort in the village of Iraq Suwaydan. The fort's Egyptian defenders had previously repulsed eight attempts to take it, including two during Operation Yoav. Israeli forces bombarded the fort before an assault with artillery and airstrikes by B-17 bombers. After breaching the outlying fences without resistance, the Israelis blew a hole in the fort's outer wall, prompting the 180 Egyptian soldiers manning the fort to surrender without a fight. The defeat prompted the Egyptians to evacuate several nearby positions, including hills the IDF had failed to take by force. Meanwhile, IDF forces took Iraq Suwaydan itself after a fierce battle, losing 6 dead and 14 wounded.

From 5 to 7 December, the IDF conducted Operation Assaf to take control of the Western Negev. The main assaults were spearheaded by mechanized forces, while Golani Brigade infantry covered the rear. An Egyptian counterattack was repulsed. The Egyptians planned another counterattack, but it failed after Israeli aerial reconnaissance revealed Egyptian preparations,

Figure 252: *An Israeli convoy in the Negev during Operation Horev*

and the Israelis launched a preemptive strike. About 100 Egyptians were killed, and 5 tanks were destroyed, with the Israelis losing 5 killed and 30 wounded.Wikipedia:Citation needed

On 22 December, the IDF launched Operation Horev (also called Operation Ayin). The goal of the operation was to drive all remaining Egyptian forces from the Negev, destroying the Egyptian threat on Israel's southern communities and forcing the Egyptians into a ceasefire. During five days of fighting, the Israelis secured the Western Negev, expelling all Egyptian forces from the area.

Israeli forces subsequently launched raids into the Nitzana area, and entered the Sinai Peninsula on 28 December. The IDF captured Umm Katef and Abu Ageila, and advanced north towards Al Arish, with the goal of encircling the entire Egyptian expeditionary force. Israeli forces pulled out of the Sinai on 2 January 1949 following joint British-American pressure and a British threat of military action. IDF forces regrouped at the border with the Gaza Strip. Israeli forces attacked Rafah the following day, and after several days of fighting, Egyptian forces in the Gaza Strip were surrounded. The Egyptians agreed to negotiate a ceasefire on 7 January, and the IDF subsequently pulled out of Gaza. According to Morris, *"the inequitable and unfair rules of engagement: the Arabs could launch offensives with impunity, but international interventions always hampered and restrained Israel's counterattacks."*[2032]

Figure 253: *The funeral of a Royal Air Force pilot killed during a clash with the Israeli Air Force.*

On 28 December, the Alexandroni Brigade failed to take the Falluja Pocket, but managed to seize Iraq el-Manshiyeh and temporarily hold it. The Egyptians counterattacked, but were mistaken for a friendly force and allowed to advance, trapping a large number of men. The Israelis lost 87 soldiers.Wikipedia:Citation needed

On 5 March, Operation Uvda was launched following nearly a month of reconnaissance, with the goal of securing the Southern Negev from Jordan. The IDF entered and secured the territory, but did not meet significant resistance along the way, as the area was already designated to be part of the Jewish state in the UN Partition Plan, and the operation meant to establish Israeli sovereignty over the territory rather than actually conquer it. The Golani, Negev, and Alexandroni brigades participated in the operation, together with some smaller units and with naval support.

On 10 March, Israeli forces secured the Southern Negev, reaching the southern tip of Palestine: Umm Rashrash on the Red Sea (where Eilat was built later) and taking it without a battle. Israeli soldiers raised a hand-made Israeli flag ("The Ink Flag") at 16:00 on 10 March, claiming Umm Rashrash for Israel. The raising of the Ink Flag is considered to be the end of the war.

Anglo-Israeli air clashes

As the fighting progressed and Israel mounted an incursion into the Sinai, the Royal Air Force began conducting almost daily reconnaissance missions over Israel and the Sinai. RAF reconnaissance aircraft took off from Egyptian airbases and sometimes flew alongside Royal Egyptian Air Force planes. High-flying British aircraft frequently flew over Haifa and Ramat David Airbase, and became known to the Israelis as the "shuftykeit."

On 20 November 1948, an unarmed RAF photo-reconnaissance De Havilland Mosquito of No. 13 Squadron RAF was shot down by an Israeli Air Force P-51 Mustang flown by American volunteer Wayne Peake as it flew over the Galilee towards Hatzor Airbase. Peake opened fire with his cannons, causing a fire to break out in the port engine. The aircraft turned to sea and lowered its altitude, then exploded and crashed off Ashdod. The pilot and navigator were both killed.[2033]

Just before noon on 7 January 1949, four Spitfire FR18s from No. 208 Squadron RAF on a reconnaissance mission in the Deir al-Balah area flew over an Israeli convoy that had been attacked by five Egyptian Spitfires fifteen minutes earlier. The pilots had spotted smoking vehicles and were drawn to the scene out of curiosity. Two planes dived to below 500 feet altitude to take pictures of the convoy, while the remaining two covered them from 1,500 feet.[2034]

Israeli soldiers on the ground, alerted by the sound of the approaching Spitfires and fearing another Egyptian air attack, opened fire with machine guns. One Spitfire was shot down by a tank-mounted machine gun, while the other was lightly damaged and rapidly pulled up. The remaining three Spitfires were then attacked by patrolling IAF Spitfires flown by Slick Goodlin and John McElroy, volunteers from the United States and Canada respectively. All three Spitfires were shot down, and one pilot was killed.

Two pilots were captured by Israeli soldiers and taken to Tel Aviv for interrogation, and were later released. Another was rescued by Bedouins and handed over to the Egyptian Army, which turned him over to the RAF. Later that day, four RAF Spitfires from the same squadron escorted by seven Hawker Tempests from No. 213 Squadron RAF and eight from No. 6 Squadron RAF went searching for the lost planes, and were attacked by four IAF Spitfires. The Israeli formation was led by Ezer Weizman. The remaining three were manned by Weizman's wingman Alex Jacobs and American volunteers Bill Schroeder and Caesar Dangott. The Tempests found they could not jettison their external fuel tanks, and some had non-operational guns. Schroeder shot down a British Tempest, killing pilot David Tattersfield, and Weizman severely damaged a British plane flown by Douglas Liquorish. Weizman's plane and two other

British aircraft also suffered light damage during the engagement. The battle ended after the British wiggled their wings to be more clearly identified, and the Israelis eventually realized the danger of their situation and disengaged, returning to Hatzor Airbase.

Israeli Prime Minister David Ben-Gurion personally ordered the wrecks of the RAF fighters that had been shot down to be dragged into Israeli territory. Israeli troops subsequently visited the crash sites, removed various parts, and buried the other aircraft. However, the Israelis did not manage to conceal the wrecks in time to prevent British reconnaissance planes from photographing them. An RAF salvage team was deployed to recover the wrecks, entering Israeli territory during their search. Two were discovered inside Egypt, while Tattersfield's Tempest was found north of Nirim, four miles inside Israel. Interviews with local Arabs confirmed that the Israelis had visited the crash sites to remove and bury the wrecks. Tattersfield was initially buried near the wreckage, but his body was later removed and reburied at the British War Cemetery in Ramla.[2035]

In response, the RAF readied all Tempests and Spitfires to attack any IAF aircraft they encountered and bomb IAF airfields. British troops in the Middle East were placed on high alert with all leave cancelled, and British citizens were advised to leave Israel. The Royal Navy was also placed on high alert. At Hatzor Airbase, the general consensus among the pilots, most of whom had flown with or alongside the RAF during World War II, was that the RAF would not allow the loss of five aircraft and two pilots to go without retaliation, and would probably attack the base at dawn the next day. That night, in anticipation of an impending British attack, some pilots decided not to offer any resistance and left the base, while others prepared their Spitfires and were strapped into the cockpits at dawn, preparing to repel a retaliatory airstrike. However, despite pressure from the squadrons involved in the incidents, British commanders refused to authorize any retaliatory strikes.[2036]

The day following the incident, British pilots were issued a directive to regard any Israeli aircraft infiltrating Egyptian or Jordanian airspace as hostile and to shoot them down, but were also ordered to avoid activity close to Israel's borders. Later in January 1949, the British managed to prevent the delivery of aviation spirit and other essential fuels to Israel in retaliation for the incident. The British Foreign Office presented the Israeli government with a demand for compensation over the loss of personnel and equipment.[2037]

UN Resolution 194

In December 1948, the UN General Assembly passed Resolution 194. It called to establish a UN Conciliation Commission to facilitate peace between Israel and Arab states. However, many of the resolution's articles were not fulfilled, since these were opposed by Israel, rejected by the Arab states, or were overshadowed by war as the 1948 conflict continued.

Weapons

Largely leftover World War II era weapons were used by both sides. Egypt had some British equipment; the Syrian army had some French. German, Czechoslovak and British equipment was used by Israel.

Type	Arab armies	IDF
Tanks	Matilda tanks, R-39s, FT-17s, R35s, Panzer IVs (dug in and used as stationary gun emplacements by Egypt), Fiat M13/-40, Sherman M4, M-22, Vickers MK-6.	Cromwell tanks, H39s, M4 Sherman
APCs/-IFVs	British World War II era trucks, Humber Mk III & IV, Automitrailleuses Dodge/-Bich type, improvised armored cars/-trucks, Marmon-Herrington Armoured Cars, Universal Carriers, Lloyd Towing Carriers	British World War II era trucks, improvised armored cars/trucks, White M3A1 Scout Cars, Daimler Armoured Cars, M3 Half-tracks, IHC M14 Half-tracks, M5 Half-tracks
Artillery	Mortars, 15 cm sIG33 auf Pz IIs, 25 mm anti-tank guns on Bren carriers, improvised self-propelled guns used by Syrians in 1948–49, 65 mm mountain guns on Lorraine 38L *chenillettes*, 2-pounder anti-tank guns, 6-pounder anti-tank guns	Mortars, 2-inch (51 mm) British mortars, 65 mm French howitzers (*Napoleonchiks*), 120 mm French mortars, Davidka mortars
Aircraft	Spitfires, T-6 Texans, C-47 Dakotas, Hawker Hurricanes, Avro Ansons	Spitfires, Avia S-199s, B-17 Flying Fortresses, P-51 Mustangs, C-47 Dakotas
Small Arms	Lee–Enfield rifles, Bren Guns, Sten guns, MAS 36s	Sten guns, Mills grenades, Karabiner 98k (Czech copies), Bren Guns, MG-34 Machine guns, Thompson submachine guns, Lee–Enfield rifles, Molotov cocktails, PIAT anti-tank infantry weapon

Aftermath

1949 Armistice Agreements

In 1949, Israel signed separate armistices with Egypt on 24 February, Lebanon on 23 March, Jordan on 3 April, and Syria on 20 July. The Armistice Demarcation Lines, as set by the agreements, saw the territory under Israeli control encompassing approximately three-quarters of the prior British administered Mandate as it stood after Transjordan's independence in 1946. Israel controlled territories of about one-third more than was allocated to the Jewish State under the UN partition proposal.[2038] After the armistices, Israel had control over 78% of the territory comprising former Mandatory Palestine or some 8,000 square miles (21,000 km^2), including the entire Galilee and Jezreel Valley in the north, whole Negev in south, West Jerusalem and the coastal plain in the center.

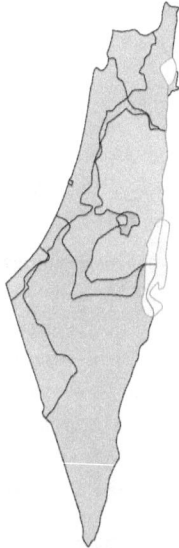

Figure 254:

Boundaries defined in the 1947 UN Partition Plan for Palestine:
Area assigned for a Jewish state
Area assigned for an Arab state
*Planned Corpus separatum with the intention
that Jerusalem would be neither Jewish nor Arab*

Armistice Demarcation Lines of 1949 (Green Line):
Israeli controlled territory from 1949
Egyptian and Jordanian controlled territory from 1948 until 1967

The armistice lines were known afterwards as the "Green Line". The Gaza Strip and the West Bank (including East Jerusalem) were occupied by Egypt and Jordan respectively. The United Nations Truce Supervision Organization and Mixed Armistice Commissions were set up to monitor ceasefires, supervise the armistice agreements, to prevent isolated incidents from escalating, and assist other UN peacekeeping operations in the region.

Just before the signing of the Israel-Jordan armistice agreement, general Yigal Allon proposed to conquer the West Bank up to the Jordan River as the natural, defensible border of the state. Ben-Gurion refused, although he was aware that the IDF was militarily strong enough to carry out the conquest. He feared the reaction of Western powers and wanted to maintain good relations with the

United States and not to provoke the British. More, the results of the war were already satisfactory and Israeli leaders had to build a nation.

Casualties

Israel lost 6,373 of its people, about 1% of its population at the time, in the war. About 4,000 were soldiers and the rest were civilians. Around 2,000 were Holocaust survivors.

The exact number of Arab casualties is unknown. One estimate places the Arab death toll at 7,000, including 3,000 Palestinians, 2,000 Egyptians, 1,000 Jordanians, and 1,000 Syrians. In 1958, Palestinian historian Aref al-Aref calculated that the Arab armies' combined losses amounted to 3,700, with Egypt losing 961 regular and 200 irregular soldiers and Jordan losing 362 regulars and 200 irregulars. According to Henry Laurens, the Palestinians suffered double the Jewish losses, with 13,000 dead, 1,953 of whom are known to have died in combat situations. Of the remainder, 4,004 remain nameless but the place, tally and date of their death is known, and a further 7,043, for whom only the place of death is known, not their identities nor the date of their death. According to Laurens, the largest part of Palestinian casualties consisted of non-combatants and corresponds to the successful operations of the Israelis.[2039]

Demographic outcome

Palestinian Arabs

1948 Palestinian exodus

Main Articles
• 1947–48 civil war
• 1948 Arab–Israeli War
• 1948 Palestine war
• Causes of the exodus
• Nakba Day
• Palestinian refugee
• Palestine refugee camps
• Palestinian right of return
• Palestinian return to Israel

• Present absentee
• Transfer Committee
• Resolution 194
Background
• Mandatory Palestine
• Israeli Declaration of Independence
• Israeli–Palestinian conflict history
• New Historians
• Palestine · Plan Dalet
• 1947 partition plan · UNRWA
Key incidents
• Battle of Haifa • Deir Yassin massacre • Exodus from Lydda and Ramle
Notable writers
• Aref al-Aref · Yoav Gelber • Efraim Karsh · Walid Khalidi • Nur-eldeen Masalha · Benny Morris • Ilan Pappé · Tom Segev • Avraham Sela · Avi Shlaim
Related categories/lists
• List of depopulated villages
Related templates
• Palestinians
• v • t • e[2040]

During the 1947–1948 Civil War in Mandatory Palestine and the 1948 Arab–Israeli War that followed, around 750,000 Palestinian Arabs fled or were expelled from their homes, out of approximately 1,200,000 Arabs living in former British Mandate of Palestine. In 1951, the UN Conciliation Commission for Palestine estimated that the number of Palestinian refugees displaced from Israel was 711,000.[2041]

This number did not include displaced Palestinians inside Israeli-held territory. More than 400 Arab villages, and about ten Jewish villages and neighborhoods, were depopulated during the Arab–Israeli conflict, most of them during 1948. According to estimate based on earlier census, the total Muslim population in Palestine was 1,143,336 in 1947.[2042] The causes of the 1948 Palestinian exodus are a controversial topic among historians.[2043] After the war, around 156,000 Arabs remained in Israel and became Israeli citizens.

Displaced Palestinian Arabs, known as Palestinian refugees, were settled in Palestinian refugee camps throughout the Arab world. The United Nations established UNRWA as a relief and human development agency tasked with providing humanitarian assistance to Palestinian refugees. Arab nations refused to absorb Palestinian refugees, instead keeping them in refugee camps while insisting that they be allowed to return.

Refugee status was also passed on to their descendants, who were also largely denied citizenship in Arab states, except in Jordan. The Arab League instructed its members to deny Palestinians citizenship "to avoid dissolution of their identity and protect their right of return to their homeland." More than 1.4 million Palestinians still live in 58 recognized refugee camps, while more than 5 million Palestinians live outside Israel and the Palestinian territories.

The Palestinian refugee problem and debate about the Palestinian right of return are also major issues of the Arab–Israeli conflict. Palestinians and their supporters have staged annual demonstrations and commemorations on 15 May of each year, which is known to them as "Nakba Day". The popularity and number of participants in these annual Nakba demonstrations has varied over time. During the Second Intifada after the failure of the Camp David 2000 Summit, the attendance at the demonstrations against Israel increased.

Jews

Jewish exodus from Arab and Muslim countries
Communities

• Mizrahi
  • Persian
  • Baghdadi
• Sephardi

Background

• Jews under Muslim rule
  • Ottoman
  • Old Yishuv
• Antisemitism in the Arab World
  • The Holocaust in Libya
  • Farhud
• Zionism
• Arab–Israeli conflict
  • 1948 Arab–Israeli War
  • Suez Crisis
  • Six-Day War
• Algerian War

Main events
• Magic Carpet (Yemen) • Ezra and Nehemiah (Iraq) • Lebanese exodus • Egyptian exodus • Moroccan exodus   • Operation Yachin • Pied-Noir (Algeria) • Day of Revenge (Libya) • Exodus of Iran's Jews
Resettlement

• Aliyah
• HIAS • Mossad LeAliyah Bet • JDC
   • Mizrahi Jews in Israel
• Iranian • Iraqi • Kurdish • Moroccan
• Syrian • Turkish • Yemenite
   • Transition camps
   • Immigrant camps
   • Development towns
   • Austerity
• North African Jews in France

Advocation
• Remembrance Day • JIMENA • JJAC • WOJAC • *The Forgotten Refugees*
Related topics
• Arab Jews • Musta'arabi • Maghrebi Jews • Berber Jews
• v • t • e[2044]

During the 1948 War, around 10,000 Jews were forced to evacuate their homes from Arab dominated parts of former Mandatory Palestine. But in the three years from May 1948 to the end of 1951, 700,000 Jews settled in Israel, mainly along the borders and in former Arab lands, doubling the Jewish population there. Of these, upwards of 300,000 arrived from Asian and North African nations.[2045],[2046] Among them, the largest group (over 100,000) was from Iraq. The remaining came mostly from Europe, including 136,000 from the 250,000 displaced Jews of World War II living in refugee camps and urban centers in Germany, Austria, and Italy,[2047] and more than 270,000 coming from Eastern Europe,[2048] mainly Romania and Poland (over 100,000 each). On the establishment of the state, a top priority was given to a policy for the "ingathering of exiles", and the Mossad LeAliyah Bet gave key assistance to the Jewish Agency to organize immigrants from Europe and the Middle East, and arrange for their transport to Israel. For Ben-Gurion, a fundamental defect of the State was that 'it lacked Jews'.[2049]

Jewish immigrants from Arab and Muslim countries left for numerous reasons. The war's outcome had exacerbated Arab hostilities to local Jewish communities. News of the victory aroused messianic expectations in Libya and Yemen; Zionism had taken root in many countries; active incentives for making aliyah formed a key part of Israeli policy; and better economic prospects and security were to be expected from a Jewish state. Some Arab governments, Egypt, for example, held their Jewish communities hostage at times. Persecution, political instability, and news of a number of violent pogroms also played a role. Some 800,000–1,000,000 Jews eventually left the Arab world over the next three decades as a result of these various factors. Approximately 680,000 of them immigrated to Israel; the rest mostly settled in Europe (mainly France) or the Americas.

Israel initially relied on Jewish Agency-run tent camps known as immigrant camps to accommodate displaced Jews from Europe and Muslim nations. In the 1950s, these were transformed into transition camps ("Ma'abarot"), where living conditions were improved and tents were replaced with tin dwellings. Unlike the situation in the immigrant camps, when the Jewish Agency provided for immigrants, residents of the transition camps were required to provide for themselves. These camps began to decline in 1952, with the last one closing in 1963. The camps were largely transformed into permanent settlements known as development towns, while others were absorbed as neighborhoods of the towns they were attached to, and the residents were given permanent housing in these towns and neighborhoods.

Most development towns eventually grew into cities. Some Jewish immigrants were also given the vacant homes of Palestinian refugees. There were also attempts to settle Jewish refugees from Arab and Muslim countries in moshavim (cooperative farming villages), though these efforts were only partially successful, as they had historically been craftsmen and merchants in their home countries, and did not traditionally engage in farm work.

Historiography

After the war, Israeli and Palestinian historiographies differed on the interpretation of the events of 1948:[2050] in the West the majority view was of a tiny group of vastly outnumbered and ill-equipped Jews fighting off the massed strength of the invading Arab armies; it was also widely believed that the Palestinian Arabs left their homes on the instruction of their leaders.[2051]

From 1980, with the opening of the Israeli and British archives, some Israeli historians have developed a different account of the period. In particular, the role played by Abdullah I of Jordan, the British government, the Arab aims during the war, the balance of force and the events related to the Palestinian exodus have been nuanced or given new interpretations. Some of them are still hotly debated among historians and commentators of the conflict today.[2052]

In popular culture

A 2015 PBS documentary, *A Wing and a Prayer*, depicts the Al Schwimmer-led airborne smuggling missions to arm Israel.

The film *Cast a Giant Shadow* tells the story of an American colonel who was instrumental in the Israeli victory.

Maps

- Operation Sinai 22 December 1948 – 7 January 1949[2053]

Notes

References

<templatestyles src="Refbegin/styles.css" />

- Adrian, Nathan (2004). *Britain, Israel and Anglo-Jewry 1949–57*. Routledge
- Bickerton, Ian and Hill, Maria (2003). *Contested Spaces: The Arab-Israeli Conflict*. McGraw-Hill. <templatestyles src="Module:Citation/CS1/styles.css" />ISBN 978-0-07-471217-7
- Black, Ian (1992). *Israel's Secret Wars: A History of Israel's Intelligence Services*. Grove Press. <templatestyles src="Module:Citation/CS1/styles.css" />ISBN 978-0-8021-3286-4
- Bowyer Bell, John (1996). *Terror Out of Zion: The Fight For Israeli Independence*. Transaction Publishers. <templatestyles src="Module:Citation/CS1/styles.css" />ISBN 978-1-56000-870-5
- Bregman, Ahron (2002). *Israel's Wars: A History Since 1947*. London: Routledge. <templatestyles src="Module:Citation/CS1/styles.css" />ISBN 978-0-415-28716-6
- Brown, Judith and Louis, Roger (1999). *The Oxford History of the British Empire*. Oxford: Oxford University Press. <templatestyles src="Module:Citation/CS1/styles.css" />ISBN 978-0-19-820564-7

- Cragg, Kenneth. *Palestine. The Prize and Price of Zion*. Cassel, 1997. <templatestyles src="Module:Citation/CS1/styles.css" />ISBN 978-0-304-70075-2
- van Creveld, Martin (2004). *Moshe Dayan*. Weidenfeld & Nicolson. <templatestyles src="Module:Citation/CS1/styles.css" />ISBN 978-0-297-84669-7
- Collins, Larry and Lapierre, Dominique (1973). *O Jerusalem!"*, Pan Books. <templatestyles src="Module:Citation/CS1/styles.css" />ISBN 978-0-330-23514-3
- El-Nawawy, Mohammed (2002), *The Israeli-Egyptian Peace Process in the Reporting of Western Journalists*, Ablex/Greenwood, <templatestyles src="Module:Citation/CS1/styles.css" />ISBN 978-1-56750-544-3
- Geddes, Charles L. (1991). *A Documentary History of the Arab-Israeli Conflict*. Praeger. <templatestyles src="Module:Citation/CS1/styles.css" />ISBN 978-0-275-93858-1
- Gelber, Yoav (1997). *Jewish-Transjordanian Relations 1921–48: Alliance of Bars Sinister*. London: Routledge. <templatestyles src="Module:Citation/CS1/styles.css" />ISBN 978-0-7146-4675-6
- Gelber, Yoav (2004). *Israeli-Jordanian Dialogue, 1948–1953: Cooperation, Conspiracy, or Collusion?*. Sussex Academic Press.
- Gelber, Yoav (2004) "*Independence Versus Nakba*"; Kinneret Zmora-Bitan Dvir Publishing, <templatestyles src="Module:Citation/CS1/styles.css" />ISBN 965-517-190-6
- Gelber, Yoav (2006). *Palestine 1948. War, Escape and the Emergence of the Palestinian Refugee Problem*. Sussex Academic Press. <templatestyles src="Module:Citation/CS1/styles.css" />ISBN 978-1-84519-075-0
- Gershoni, Haim (1989). *Israel: The Way it was*. Associated University Presses.
- Gilbert, Martin (1998). *Israel: A History*[2054]. Black Swan. <templatestyles src="Module:Citation/CS1/styles.css" />ISBN 978-0-552-99545-0
- Gold, Dore (2007), *The Fight for Jerusalem: Radical Islam, the West, and the Future of the Holy City*, Regnery Publishing, <templatestyles src="Module:Citation/CS1/styles.css" />ISBN 978-1-59698-029-7
- Israel Foreign Ministry, Foreign Ministry of the Russian Federation, Israel State Archives, Russian Federal Archives, Cummings Center for Russian Studies Tel Aviv University, Oriental Institute (2000). *Documents on Israeli Soviet Relations, 1941–53*. London: Routledge. <templatestyles src="Module:Citation/CS1/styles.css" />ISBN 978-0-7146-4843-9
- Joseph, Dov. *The Faithful City – The Siege of Jerusalem, 1948*. Simon & Schuster, 1960. Congress # 60 10976
- Kaniuk, Yoram (2001). *Commander of the Exodus*. Grove Press. <templatestyles src="Module:Citation/CS1/styles.css" />ISBN 978-0-8021-

3808-8
- Karsh, Efraim (2002), *The Arab-Israeli Conflict. The Palestine War 1948*, Osprey, ISBN 978-1-84176-372-9<templatestyles src="Module:Citation/CS1/styles.css"></templatestyles>
- Fischbach, Michael R. 'Land'. In Philip Mattar (ed.) *Encyclopedia of the Palestinians,* Infobase Publishing. 2005. pp. 291–98
- Flint, Colin. *Introduction to Geopolitics,* Routledge 2012
- Heller, Joseph. *The Birth of Israel, 1945–1949: Ben-Gurion and His Critics*, University Press of Florida, 2001
- Karsh, Inari & Karsh, Efraim (1999). *Empires of the Sand: The Struggle for Mastery in the Middle East, 1789–1923*. Harvard University Press. <templatestyles src="Module:Citation/CS1/styles.css" />ISBN 978-0-674-00541-9
- Katz, Sam (1988). *Israeli Units Since 1948.* Osprey Publishing. <templatestyles src="Module:Citation/CS1/styles.css" />ISBN 978-0-85045-837-4
- Khalaf, Issa *Politics in Palestine: Arab Factionalism and Social Disintegration, 1939–1948.* SUNY Press, 1991
- Khalidi, Rashid (2001). "The Palestinians and 1948: the underlying causes of failure." In Eugene Rogan and Avi Shlaim (eds.). *The War for Palestine* (pp. 12–36). Cambridge: Cambridge University Press. <templatestyles src="Module:Citation/CS1/styles.css" />ISBN 978-0-521-79476-3
- Khalidi, Rashid (2006). *The Iron Cage:The Story of the Palestinian Struggle for Statehood.* Boston, MA:Beacon Press. <templatestyles src="Module:Citation/CS1/styles.css" />ISBN 978-0-8070-0309-1
- Khalidi, Walid (1987). *From Haven to Conquest: Readings in Zionism and the Palestine Problem Until 1948*[2055]. Institute for Palestine Studies. <templatestyles src="Module:Citation/CS1/styles.css" />ISBN 978-0-88728-155-6
- Khalidi, Walid (ed.) (1992). *All that remains.* Institute for Palestine Studies. <templatestyles src="Module:Citation/CS1/styles.css" />ISBN 978-0-88728-224-9
- Krämer, Gudrun, *A History of Palestine: From the Ottoman Conquest to the Founding of the State of Israel,* Princeton UP 2011.
- Kurzman, Dan (1970), *Genesis 1948 – the first Arab-Israeli war*, New American Library, New York, Library of Congress CCN: 77-96925
- Levenberg, Haim (1993). *Military Preparations of the Arab Community in Palestine: 1945–1948.* London: Routledge. <templatestyles src="Module:Citation/CS1/styles.css" />ISBN 978-0-7146-3439-5
- Levin, Harry. *Jerusalem Embattled – A Diary of the City under Siege.* Cassels, 1997. <templatestyles src="Module:Citation/CS1/styles.css"

/>ISBN 9780304337651
- Lockman, Zachary. *Comrades and Enemies: Arab and Jewish Workers in Palestine, 1906–1948*. University of California Press, 1996
- Makdisi Saree, *Palestine Inside Out: An Everyday Occupation*, W.W. Norton & Company 2010
- Morris, Benny (1988), *The Birth of the Palestinian Refugee Problem, 1947–1949*, Cambridge Middle East Library
- Morris, Benny (1994), *1948 and after; Israel and the Palestinians*
- Morris, Benny (2001). *Righteous Victims: A History of the Zionist-Arab Conflict, 1881–2001*. Vintage Books. <templatestyles src="Module:Citation/CS1/styles.css" />ISBN 978-0-679-74475-7
- Morris, Benny (2004), *The Birth of the Palestinian Refugee Problem Revisited*, Cambridge University Press, Cambridge UK, <templatestyles src="Module:Citation/CS1/styles.css" />ISBN 978-0-521-81120-0
- Morris, Benny (2008), *1948: The First Arab-Israeli War*[2056], Yale University Press, New Haven, <templatestyles src="Module:Citation/CS1/styles.css" />ISBN 978-0-300-12696-9
- Oring, Elliott (1981). *Israeli Humor – The Content: The Content and Structure of the Chizbat of the Palmah*. SUNY Press. <templatestyles src="Module:Citation/CS1/styles.css" />ISBN 978-0-87395-512-6
- Oren, Michael, *Six Days of War*, Random House Ballantine Publishing Group, (New York 2003, <templatestyles src="Module:Citation/CS1/styles.css" />ISBN 0-345-46192-4
- Pappe, Ilan (2006), *The Ethnic Cleansing of Palestine*, Oneworld Publications, Oxford, England, <templatestyles src="Module:Citation/CS1/styles.css" />ISBN 978-1-85168-467-0
- Penkower, Monty Noam (2002). *Decision on Palestine Deferred: America, Britain and Wartime Diplomacy, 1939–1945*. London: Routledge. <templatestyles src="Module:Citation/CS1/styles.css" />ISBN 978-0-7146-5268-9
- Pollack, Kenneth (2004). *Arabs at War: Military Effectiveness, 1948–1991*. University of Nebraska Press. <templatestyles src="Module:Citation/CS1/styles.css" />ISBN 978-0-8032-8783-9
- Richelson, Jeffrey T. (1997). *A Century of Spies: Intelligence in the Twentieth Century*. Oxford: Oxford University Press. <templatestyles src="Module:Citation/CS1/styles.css" />ISBN 978-0-19-511390-7
- Rogan, Eugene L. and Avi Shlaim, eds. *The War for Palestine: Rewriting the History of 1948*. Cambridge: Cambridge UP, 2001
- Rogan, Eugene L. and Avi Shlaim, eds. *The War for Palestine: Rewriting the History of 1948*. 2nd edition. Cambridge: Cambridge UP, 2007
- Rogan, Eugene L. "Jordan and 1948: the persistence of an official history." Rogan and Shlaim. *The War for Palestine*. pp. 104–24

- Sadeh, Eligar (1997). *Militarization and State Power in the Arab-Israeli Conflict: Case Study of Israel, 1948–1982.* Universal Publishers. <templatestyles src="Module:Citation/CS1/styles.css" />ISBN 978-0-9658564-6-1
- Sachar, Howard M. (1979). *A History of Israel,* New York: Knopf. <templatestyles src="Module:Citation/CS1/styles.css" />ISBN 978-0-679-76563-9
- Sayigh, Yezid (2000). *Armed Struggle and the Search for State: The Palestinian National Movement, 1949–1993.* Oxford: Oxford University Press. <templatestyles src="Module:Citation/CS1/styles.css" />ISBN 978-0-19-829643-0
- Sela, Avraham. "Abdallah Ibn Hussein." *The Continuum Political Encyclopedia of the Middle East.* Ed. Avraham Sela. New York: Continuum, 2002. pp. 13–14.
- Shapira, Anita (1992). *Land and Power: Zionist Resort to Force, 1881–1948.* Oxford University Press. <templatestyles src="Module:Citation/CS1/styles.css" />ISBN 978-0-19-506104-8
- Shlaim, Avi (2001). "Israel and the Arab Coalition." In Eugene Rogan and Avi Shlaim (eds.). *The War for Palestine* (pp. 79–103). Cambridge: Cambridge University Press. <templatestyles src="Module:Citation/CS1/styles.css" />ISBN 978-0-521-79476-3
- Sicker, Martin (1999). *Reshaping Palestine: From Muhammad Ali to the British Mandate, 1831–1922.* Praeger/Greenwood. <templatestyles src="Module:Citation/CS1/styles.css" />ISBN 978-0-275-96639-3
- Stearns, Peter N. Citation[2057] from *The Encyclopedia of World History* Sixth Edition, Peter N. Stearns (general editor), 2001 Houghton Mifflin Company, at Bartleby.com.
- Tripp, Charles. "Iraq and the 1948 War: mirror of Iraq's disorder." in Rogan and Shlaim. *The War for Palestine.* pp. 125–50.

Further reading

History

- Aloni, Shlomo (2001). *Arab-Israeli Air Wars 1947–82.* Osprey Publishing. <templatestyles src="Module:Citation/CS1/styles.css" />ISBN 978-1-84176-294-4
- Beckman, Morris (1999). *The Jewish Brigade: An Army With Two Masters, 1944–45.* Sarpedon Publishers. <templatestyles src="Module:Citation/CS1/styles.css" />ISBN 978-1-86227-423-5
- Ben-Ami, Shlomo (2006). *Scars of War, Wounds of Peace: The Israeli-Arab Tragedy.* Oxford University Press. <templatestyles src="Module:Citation/CS1/styles.css" />ISBN 978-0-19-518158-6

- Benvenisti, Meron (2002). *Sacred Landscape*. University of California Press. <templatestyles src="Module:Citation/CS1/styles.css" />ISBN 978-0-520-23422-2
- Flapan, Simha (1987), *The Birth of Israel: Myths and Realities*, Pantheon Books, New York.
- Gilbert, Martin (1976). *The Arab-Israeli Conflict: Its History in Maps* Weidenfeld & Nicolson. <templatestyles src="Module:Citation/CS1/styles.css" />ISBN 978-0-297-77241-5
- Landis, Joshua. "Syria and the Palestine War: fighting King 'Abdullah's 'Greater Syria plan.'" Rogan and Shlaim. *The War for Palestine*. 178–205.
- Masalha, Nur (1992). *Expulsion of the Palestinians: The Concept of 'Transfer' in Zionist Political Thought, 1882–1948*, Institute for Palestine Studies, <templatestyles src="Module:Citation/CS1/styles.css" />ISBN 978-0-88728-235-5
- Pappe, Ilan (2006), *The Ethnic Cleansing of Palestine*, Oneworld Publications, Oxford, England, <templatestyles src="Module:Citation/CS1/styles.css" />ISBN 978-1-85168-467-0
- Reiter, Yitzhak, "National Minority, Regional Majority: Palestinian Arabs Versus Jews in Israel" (*Syracuse Studies on Peace and Conflict Resolution*), (2009) Syracuse Univ Press (Sd). <templatestyles src="Module:Citation/CS1/styles.css" />ISBN 978-0-8156-3230-6
- Sheleg, Yair (2001). "A Short History of Terror[2058]" *Haaretz*.
- Zertal, Idith (2005). *Israel's Holocaust and the Politics of Nationhood*. Cambridge: Cambridge University Press. <templatestyles src="Module:Citation/CS1/styles.css" />ISBN 978-0-521-85096-4

Fiction

- *The Hope* by Herman Wouk, a historical novel that includes a fictionalized version of Israel's War of Independence.

External links

 Wikimedia Commons has media related to *1948 Arab-Israeli War*.

- One of last surviving founders of IAF recalls mission that stopped Egypt from advancing on Tel Aviv.[2059]
- Pictorial History: Air Force Volunteers.[2060]
- Overview of The 1948 Israeli War of Independence (documentary)[2061] on YouTube
- Video footage of the Israeli Independence War[2062] on YouTube

- About the War of Independence[2063]
- United Nations: System on the Question of Palestine[2064]
- Summary of Arab-Israeli wars[2065]
- History of Palestine, Israel and the Israeli-Palestinian Conflict[2066]
- Palestinian viewpoint concerning the context of the 1948 war[2067] at the Library of Congress Web Archives (archived 2002-09-13)
- The BBC on the UN Partition Plan[2068]
- The BBC on the Formation of Israel[2069]
- Israeli War of Independence: an autobiographical account by a South African participant[2070]
- Israel and the Arab Coalition in 1948[2071]
- "I Have Returned"[2072]. *Time Magazine*. 15 March 1948. Retrieved 31 October 2009.<templatestyles src="Module:Citation/CS1/styles.css"></templatestyles>
- "War for Jerusalem Road"[2073]. *Time Magazine*. 19 April 1948. Retrieved 31 October 2009.<templatestyles src="Module:Citation/CS1/styles.css"></templatestyles>

Appendix

References

[1] //en.wikipedia.org/w/index.php?title=Template:History_of_Israel&action=edit
[2] //en.wikipedia.org/w/index.php?title=Template:History_of_Palestine&action=edit
[3] James Serpell, The domestic dog: its evolution, behaviour, and interactions with people, pp 10-12. Cambridge University Press, 1995, see also [Haaretz http://www.haaretz.com/travel-in-israel/tourist-tip-of-the-day/tourist-tip-237-the-prehistoric-man-museum-at-ma-ayan-baruch.premium-1.524213]
[4] Bright, John (2000)"A History of Israel" (John Knox Press Westminster)
[5] Albright, William F. "From Abraham to Ezra"
[6] See http://www.ancientneareast.net/wares_kerak.html
[7] https://web.archive.org/web/20070615144724/http://www.hindunet.org/saraswati/html/urseals.htm
[8] http://www.edwardtbabinski.us/biblical_archaeology/stone_to_bronze.html
[9] http://www.archaeowiki.org/Archaeology_of_the_Southern_Levant
[10] //en.wikipedia.org/w/index.php?title=Template:History_of_Israel&action=edit
[11] //en.wikipedia.org/w/index.php?title=Template:Jews_and_Judaism_sidebar&action=edit
[12] King & Stager 2001, p. xxiii.
[13] Miller 1986, p. 36.
[14] Coogan 1998, pp. 4–7.
[15] Finkelstein 2001, p. 78.
[16] Killebrew 2005, pp. 38–39.
[17] Cahill in Vaughn 1992, pp. 27–33.
[18] Kuhrt 1995, p. 317.
[19] Killebrew 2005, pp. 10–6.
[20] Golden 2004b, pp. 61–62.
[21] McNutt 1999, p. 47.
[22] Golden 2004a, p. 155.
[23] Stager in Coogan 1998, p. 91.
[24] Dever 2003, p. 206.
[25] McNutt 1999, p. 35.
[26] McNutt 1999, pp. 46–47.
[27] McNutt 1999, p. 69.
[28] Miller 1986, p. 72.
[29] Killebrew 2005, p. 13.
[30] Edelman in Brett 2002, pp. 46–47.
[31] Finkelstein and Silberman (2001) Free Press, New York, p. 107,
[32] Avraham Faust, "How Did Israel Become a People? The Genesis of Israelite Identity", *Biblical Archaeology Review* 201 (2009): 62–69, 92–94.
[33] Finkelstein and Silberman (2001), p. 107
[34] Compare:
[35] Thompson 1992, p. 408.
[36] Mazar in Finkelstein 2007, p. 163.
[37] Lemche 1998, p. 85.
[38] Grabbe 2008, pp. 225–26.
[39] Lehman in Vaughn 1992, p. 149.
[40] David M. Carr, *Writing on the Tablet of the Heart: Origins of Scripture and Literature*, Oxford University Press, 2005, 164.
[41] First Impression: What We Learn from King Ahaz's Seal (#m1) http://www.archaeological-center.com/en/monographs/m1, by Robert Deutsch, Archaeological Center.
[42] Thompson 1992, pp. 410–11.
[43] Grabbe 2004, p. 28.

44. Lemaire in Blenkinsopp 2003, p. 291.
45. Davies 2009.
46. Lipschits 2005, p. 48.
47. Blenkinsopp in Blenkinsopp 2003, pp. 103–05.
48. Blenkinsopp 2009, p. 228.
49. Middlemas 2005, pp. 1–2.
50. Miller 1986, p. 203.
51. Middlemas 2005, p. 2.
52. Middlemas 2005, p. 10.
53. Middlemas 2005, p. 17.
54. Bedford 2001, p. 48.
55. Barstad 2008, p. 109.
56. Albertz 2003a, p. 92.
57. Albertz 2003a, pp. 95–96.
58. Albertz 2003a, p. 96.
59. Blenkinsopp 1988, p. 64.
60. Lipschits in Lipschits 2006, pp. 86–89.
61. Grabbe 2004, pp. 29–30.
62. Nodet 1999, p. 25.
63. Davies in Amit 2006, p. 141.
64. Niehr in Becking 1999, p. 231.
65. Wylen 1996, p. 25.
66. Grabbe 2004, pp. 154–55.
67. Soggin 1998, p. 311.
68. Miller 1986, p. 458.
69. Blenkinsopp 2009, p. 229.
70. Albertz 1994, pp. 437–38.
71. Kottsieper in Lipschits 2006, pp. 109–10.
72. Becking in Albertz 2003b, p. 19.
73. Davies 1992, pp. 149–50.
74. Philip R. Davies in *The Canon Debate*, p. 50: "With many other scholars, I conclude that the fixing of a canonical list was almost certainly the achievement of the Hasmonean dynasty."
75. Ben-Sasson 1976, p. 246.
76. Tubbs, Jonathan (2006)"The Canaanites" (BBC Books)
77. Van der Toorn 1996, p. 4.
78. Van der Toorn 1996, pp. 181–82.
79. Smith 2002, p. 57.
80. Dever (2005), p.
81. Van der Toorn 1999, p. 911–13.
82. Dunn and Rogerson, pp. 153–54
83. Avery Peck, p. 58
84. Grabbe (2004), pp. 243–44
85. Avery Peck, p. 59
86. https://books.google.com/books?id=yvZUWbTftSgC&pg=RA1-PA145&lpg=RA1-PA145&dq=History+of+Israelite+Religion,+Volume+1++Albertz#v=onepage&q&f=false
87. https://books.google.com/books?id=exjyhvRy7YUC&dq=Albertz+a+history+of+israelite+religion&printsec=frontcover#v=onepage&q&f=false
88. https://books.google.com/books?id=Xx9YzJq2B9wC&dq=Rainer+Albertz,+%22Israel+in+exile%22&printsec=frontcover#v=onepage&q&f=false
89. https//books.google.com
90. https//books.google.com
91. https//books.google.com
92. https//books.google.com
93. https//books.google.com
94. https//books.google.com

[95] https://books.google.com/books?id=MOd320e710IC&printsec=frontcover&dq=Osarsiph&cad=1#v=onepage&q&f=false
[96] https://books.google.com/books?id=3PvirfZkfvQC&printsec=frontcover&dq=Ezra-Nehemiah:+A+Commentary++By+Joseph+Blenkinsopp#v=onepage&q&f=false
[97] https://books.google.com/books?id=R65fhpcUFcgC&printsec=frontcover&dq=Judah+and+the+Judeans+in+the+neo-Babylonian+period#v=onepage&q&f=false
[98] https://books.google.com/books?id=m1V1DeBS6P0C&printsec=frontcover&dq=Judaism,+the+first+phase:+the+place+of+Ezra+and+Nehemiah#v=onepage&q&f=false
[99] https://books.google.com/books?id=Z0wawEnu0UkC&pg=PA43&dq=Hebrew+Bible&cad=3#v=onepage&q&f=false
[100] https//books.google.com
[101] https://books.google.com/books?id=0VG67yLs-LAC&printsec=frontcover&dq=Bright+History+of+Israel#v=onepage&q&f=false
[102] https://books.google.com/books?id=zFhvECwNQD0C&dq=The+Oxford+History+of+the+Biblical+World&printsec=frontcover#v=onepage&q&f=false
[103] https://books.google.com/books?id=nlb1PQAACAAJ&dq=A+brief+introduction+to+the+old+testament+coogan
[104] https://books.google.com/books?id=pMcM8GGO_n8C&printsec=frontcover&dq=Philip+Davies+In+search+of+Ancient+Israel#v=onepage&q=&f=false
[105] https://web.archive.org/web/20080528230034/http://www.arts.ualberta.ca/JHS/Articles/article_47.htm
[106] http://www.arts.ualberta.ca/JHS/Articles/article_47.htm
[107] https://books.google.com/books?id=y-gfwlltlRwC&printsec=frontcover&dq=Yahweh+and+the+gods+and+goddesses+of+Canaan#v=onepage&q&f=false
[108] https//books.google.com
[109] https//books.google.com
[110] https//books.google.com
[111] https//books.google.com
[112] https//books.google.com
[113] https//books.google.com
[114] https://books.google.com/books?id=jpbngoKHg8gC&dq=The+quest+for+the+historical+Israel:&printsec=frontcover#v=onepage&q=&f=false
[115] https//books.google.com
[116] https//books.google.com
[117] https//books.google.com
[118] https://books.google.com/books?id=VSJWkrXfbLQC&dq=Family+religion+in+Babylonia,+Syria,+and+Israel&printsec=frontcover#v=onepage&q&f=false
[119] https//books.google.com
[120] https//books.google.com
[121] https://books.google.com/books?id=VtAmmwapfVAC&printsec=frontcover&dq=Biblical+peoples+and+ethnicity:+an+archaeological#v=onepage&q&f=false
[122] https//books.google.com
[123] https://books.google.com/books?id=V_sfMzRPTgoC&printsec=frontcover&dq=Am%C3%A9lie+Kuhrt+The+ancient+Near+East#v=onepage&q&f=false
[124] https://books.google.com/books?id=JIoY7PagAOAC&dq=lemche+the+israelites+in+history+and+tradition&printsec=frontcover#v=onepage&q=&f=false
[125] https://books.-google.com/books?id=-etsKv-4V2oC&printsec=frontcover&dq=The+archaeology+of+society+in+the+Holy+Land++Thomas+E.+Levy#v=onepage&q&f=false
[126] https://books.google.com/books?id=78nRWgb-rp8C&printsec=frontcover&dq=Lipschitz,+Oded+fall+and+rise#v=onepage&q&f=false
[127] https://books.google.com/books?id=6NsxZRnxE70C&pg=PA75&lpg=PA75&dq=Lipschits+Yehud#v=onepage&q=Lipschits%20Yehud&f=false
[128] https://books.google.com/books?id=smPZ-ou74EwC&printsec=frontcover&dq=Phoenicians++Glenn+Markoe#v=onepage&q&f=false
[129] https//books.google.com
[130] https//books.google.com

[131] https://books.google.com/books?id=Jrpx-op_-XkC&printsec=frontcover&dq=lester+grabbe+1995&cad=1#v=onepage&q&f=false
[132] https//books.google.com
[133] https://books.google.com/books?id=Gtm7NtK87poC&printsec=frontcover&dq=Chieftains+of+the+highland+clans#v=onepage&q=&f=false
[134] https://books.google.com/books?id=Qjkz_8EMoaUC&printsec=frontcover
[135] https//books.google.com
[136] https://web.archive.org/web/20110717120935/http://www.tyndalehouse.com/tynbul/library/TynBull_2004_55_2_01_Pitkanen_EthnicityIsraelSettlement.pdf
[137] http://www.tyndalehouse.com/tynbul/library/TynBull_2004_55_2_01_Pitkanen_EthnicityIsraelSettlement.pdf
[138] https://books.google.com/books?id=qX7r2lAQdFkC&pg=PA238&lpg=PA238&dq=hesse+wapnish#v=onepage&q=hesse%20wapnish&f=false
[139] https://books.google.com/books?id=1yM3AuBh4AsC&printsec=frontcover&dq=Smith+Early+History+of+God#v=onepage&q&f=false
[140] https//books.google.com
[141] https//books.google.com
[142] https://books.google.com/books?id=yCkRz5pfxz0C&printsec=frontcover&dq=Dictionary+of+Deities#v=onepage&q&f=false
[143] https//books.google.com
[144] https//books.google.com
[145] https://books.google.com/books?id=db4hr55j0yYC&pg=PA1&dq=The+religion+of+ancient+Israel++By+Patrick+D.+Miller&cad=4#v=onepage&q&f=false
[146] https//books.google.com
[147] https//books.google.com
[148] http://dannyreviews.com/h/Creation_of_History_in_Ancient_Israel.html
[149] https//books.google.com
[150] https//books.google.com
[151] https//books.google.com
[152] https//books.google.com
[153] https//books.google.com
[154] http://www.jpost.com/Home/Article.aspx?id=8467
[155] https//books.google.com
[156] https//books.google.com
[157] https//books.google.com
[158] https//books.google.com
[159] https//books.google.com
[160] https//books.google.com
[161] https//books.google.com
[162] https//books.google.com
[163] https//books.google.com
[164] //en.wikipedia.org/w/index.php?title=Template:Jews_and_Judaism_sidebar&action=edit
[165] [[Strong's Exhaustive Concordance of the Bible http://www.blueletterbible.org/lang/lexicon/lexicon.cfm?strongs=H5680] #5680]
[166] Step Bible http://www.stepbible.org/?q=strong=H5680|version=ESV&options=HVNUG&qFilter=H5680
[167] Eerdmans Dictionary of the Bible https://books.google.co.uk/books?id=qRtUqxkB7wkC&pg=PA567#v=onepage&q&f=false, p.567, "Hebrew, Hebrews... A non-ethnic term"
[168] Collapse of the Bronze Age https://books.google.co.uk/books?id=fuczEUuOt6UC&pg=PA266#v=onepage&q&f=false, p.266, quote: "Opinion has sharply swung away from the view that the Apiru were the earliest Israelites in part because Apiru was not an ethnic term nor were Apiru an ethnic group."
[169] The Electronic Pennsylvania Sumerian Dictionary s.v. SA-GAZ. The Assyrian Dictionary of the Oriental Institute of the University of Chicago volume H (1956) p. 13 & p. 84; volume Š/1 (1989) p. 70. http://psd.museum.upenn.edu/epsd/

[170] Thayer's Lexicon http://www.blueletterbible.org/lang/lexicon/lexicon.cfm?Strongs=G1445&t=NKJV
[171] //en.wikipedia.org/w/index.php?title=Hebrews&action=edit
[172] http://www.mechon-mamre.org/p/pt/pt0110.htm#21
[173] Jewish Encyclopedia article on Eber http://www.jewishencyclopedia.com/view.jsp?letter=E&artid=17
[174] entry in britannica.com http://www.britannica.com/EBchecked/topic/259033/Hebrew
[175] William David. Reyburn - Euan McG. Fry - A handbook on Genesis - New York - United Bible Societies - 1997
[176] https://www.biblegateway.com/passage/?search=Gen.+14%3A13&version=NRSV
[177] Hebrews entry in Jewish Encyclopedia http://www.jewishencyclopedia.com/articles/7445-hebrew
[178] entry in thefreedictionary.com http://www.thefreedictionary.com/Hebrews
[179] Encyclopædia Britannica: Hebrews, Epistle to the http://encyclopedia.jrank.org/HAN_HEG/HEBREWS_EPISTLE_TO_THE.html
[180] http://www.jewishencyclopedia.com/
[181] http://www.jewishhistory.huji.ac.il/
[182] //en.wikipedia.org/w/index.php?title=Template:Tribes_of_Israel&action=edit
[183] "Israelite" http://dictionary.reference.com/browse/israelite. *Random House Webster's Unabridged Dictionary.*
[184] Finkelstein, Israel. "Ethnicity and origin of the Iron I settlers in the Highlands of Canaan: Can the real Israel stand up?." The Biblical archaeologist 59.4 (1996): 198–212.
[185] Finkelstein, Israel. The archaeology of the Israelite settlement. Jerusalem: Israel Exploration Society, 1988.
[186] Finkelstein, Israel, and Nadav Na'aman, eds. From nomadism to monarchy: archaeological and historical aspects of early Israel. Yad Izhak Ben-Zvi, 1994.
[187] Finkelstein, Israel. "The archaeology of the United Monarchy: an alternative view." Levant 28.1 (1996): 177–87.
[188] Finkelstein, Israel, and Neil Asher Silberman. The Bible Unearthed: Archaeology's New Vision of Ancient Israel and the Origin of Sacred Texts. Simon and Schuster, 2002.
[189] K. L. Noll, *Canaan and Israel in Antiquity: An Introduction,* https://books.google.com/books?id=2rnyjxLHy-QC&pg=PA164 A&C Black, 2001 p. 164: "It would seem that, in the eyes of Merneptah's artisans, Israel was a Canaanite group indistinguishable from all other Canaanite groups." "It is likely that Merneptah's Israel was a group of Canaanites located in the Jezreel Valley."
[190] Tubb, 1998. pp. 13–14
[191] Mark Smith in "The Early History of God: Yahweh and Other Deities of Ancient Israel" states "Despite the long regnant model that the Canaanites and Israelites were people of fundamentally different culture, archaeological data now casts doubt on this view. The material culture of the region exhibits numerous common points between Israelites and Canaanites in the Iron I period (c. 1200–1000 BCE). The record would suggest that the Israelite culture largely overlapped with and derived from Canaanite culture... In short, Israelite culture was largely Canaanite in nature. Given the information available, one cannot maintain a radical cultural separation between Canaanites and Israelites for the Iron I period." (pp. 6–7). Smith, Mark (2002) "The Early History of God: Yahweh and Other Deities of Ancient Israel" (Eerdman's)
[192] Rendsburg, Gary (2008). "Israel without the Bible". In Frederick E. Greenspahn. The Hebrew Bible: New Insights and Scholarship. NYU Press, pp. 3–5
[193] Robert L.Cate, "Israelite", in Watson E. Mills, Roger Aubrey Bullard, *Mercer Dictionary of the Bible,* https://books.google.com/books?id=goq0VWw9rGIC&pg=PA420 Mercer University Press, 1990 p. 420.
[194] (855 KB), Hum Mutat 24:248–260, 2004.
[195] Yohanan Aharoni, Michael Avi-Yonah, Anson F. Rainey, Ze'ev Safrai, *The Macmillan Bible Atlas*, 3rd Edition, Macmillan Publishing: New York, 1993, p. 115. A posthumous publication of the work of Israeli archaeologist Yohanan Aharoni and Michael Avi-Yonah, in collaboration with Anson F. Rainey and Ze'ev Safrai.
[196] The Samaritan Update http://www.thesamaritanupdate.com/ Retrieved 1 January 2017.

[197] Ann E. Killebrew, Biblical Peoples and Ethnicity. An Archaeological Study of Egyptians, Canaanites, Philistines and Early Israel 1300–1100 B.C.E. (Archaeology and Biblical Studies) https://books.google.com/books/about/Biblical_Peoples_and_Ethnicity.html?id= VtAmmwapfVAC&redir_esc=y, Society of Biblical Literature, 2005

[198] * "In the broader sense of the term, a Jew is any person belonging to the worldwide group that constitutes, through descent or conversion, a continuation of the ancient Jewish people, who were themselves the descendants of the Hebrews of the Old Testament." • "The Jewish people as a whole, initially called Hebrews ('Ivrim), were known as Israelites (Yisre'elim) from the time of their entrance into the Holy Land to the end of the Babylonian Exile (538 BC)." Jew http://www.britannica.com/EBchecked/topic/303358/Jew at Encyclopædia Britannica http://www.britannica.com/

[199] "Israelite, in the broadest sense, a Jew, or a descendant of the Jewish patriarch Jacob" Israelite http://www.britannica.com/EBchecked/topic/296891/Israelite at Encyclopædia Britannica http://www.britannica.com/

[200] "Hebrew, any member of an ancient northern Semitic people that were the ancestors of the Jews." Hebrew (People) http://www.britannica.com/EBchecked/topic/259033/Hebrew at Encyclopædia Britannica http://www.britannica.com/

[201] Natural History 102:11 (November 1993): 12–19.

[202] Yesaahq ben 'Aamraam. *Samaritan Exegesis: A Compilation Of Writings From The Samaritans*. 2013. Benyamim Tsedaka, at 1:24 https://www.youtube.com/watch?v=y8WsR5lpUyE

[203] John Bowman. Samaritan Documents Relating to Their History, Religion and Life (Pittsburgh Original Texts and Translations Series No. 2). 1977.

[204] Strong's Exhaustive Concordance G2474

[205] Brown Drivers Briggs H3478

[206] http://www.mechon-mamre.org/p/pt/pt0132.htm#29

[207] Scherman, Rabbi Nosson (editor), *The Chumash*, The Artscroll Series, Mesorah Publications, LTD, 2006, pp. 176–77

[208] Kaplan, Aryeh, "Jewish Meditation", Schocken Books, New York, 1985, p. 125

[209] Caroline Johnson Hodge, *If Sons, Then Heirs: A Study of Kinship and Ethnicity in the Letters of Paul*, https://books.google.com/books?id=Kd6ImHYoNUsC&pg=PA53 Oxford University Press, 2007 pp. 52–55.

[210] Markus Cromhout, *Jesus and Identity: Reconstructing Judean Ethnicity in Q*, https://books.google.com/books?id=apHXBgAAQBAJ&pg=PA122 James Clarke & Co, 2015 pp. 121ff.

[211] Daniel Lynwood Smith, *Into the World of the New Testament: Greco-Roman and Jewish Texts and Contexts*, https://books.google.com/books?id=Yi7aBAAAQBAJ&pg=PA124 Bloomsbury Publishing, 2015 p. 124.

[212] Stephen Sharot, *Comparative Perspectives on Judaisms and Jewish Identities*, https://books.google.com/books?id=EAMLEM4lYlAC&pg=PA146 Wayne State University Press 2011 p. 146.

[213] *Settings of silver: an introduction to Judaism*, Stephen M. Wylen, Paulist Press, 2000, , p. 59

[214] //en.wikipedia.org/w/index.php?title=Template:History_of_Israel&action=edit

[215] Israel Finkelstein, Neil Asher Silberman, *The Bible Unearthed*, Simon and Schuster 2002, p. 104.

[216] K. van der Toorn, *Family Religion in Babylonia, Ugarit and Israel: Continuity and Changes in the Forms of Religious Life* https://books.google.com/books?id=VSJWkrXfbLQC&pg=PA282, BRILL 1996 pp. 181, 282.

[217] Alan Mittleman, "Judaism: Covenant, Pluralism and Piety", in Bryan S. Turner (ed.) *The New Blackwell Companion to the Sociology of Religion* https://books.google.com/books?id=RheC7rG9u6gC&pg=PA345, John Wiley & Sons, 2010 pp. 340–63, 346.

[218] Richard A. Gabriel, *The Military History of Ancient Israel* https://books.google.com/books?id=72ZR9KCh9lUC&pg=PA63. Greenwood Publishing Group, 2003 p. 63: The ethnically mixed character of the Israelites is reflected even more clearly in the foreign names of the group's leadership. Moses himself, of course, has an Egyptian name. But so do Hophni, Phinehas, Hur, and Merari, the son of Levi.

[219]

[220] Stefan Paas, *Creation and Judgement: Creation Texts in Some Eighth Century Prophets* https://books.google.com/books?id=lfF31IAuBtAC&pg=PA114. Brill, 2003 pp. 110–21, 144.

[221] Grabbe 2008, p. 75

[222] McNutt 1999, p. 70.

[223] Joffe pp. 440ff.

[224] Davies, 1992, pp. 63–64.

[225] Joffe pp. 448–49.

[226] Joffe p. 450.

[227] Finkelstein & Silberman 2001, The Bible Unearthed p. 221.

[228] Sefer Devariam Pereq לד; ב: Deuteronomy 34, 2, Sefer Yehoshua Pereq ב; ז Joshua 20, 7, Sefer Yehoshua Pereq לב, כא: Joshua 21, 32, Sefer Melakhim Beth Pereq טו; כט Second Kings 15, 29, Sefer Devrei Ha Yamim Aleph Pereq ו; סא First Chronicles 6, 76

[229] See File:12 Tribes of Israel Map.svg

[230] Josephus, *Antiquities of the Jews* XVIII.7.2. Josephus, *War of the Jews* II.8.11, II.13.7, II.14.4, II.14.5

[231] http://www.mechon-mamre.org/p/pt/pt0148.htm#1

[232] *The Jews in the time of Jesus: an introduction* p. 18 https://books.google.com/books?id=SHgiy-k_wsUC&lpg=PA18&pg=PA18#v=onepage&q&f=false Stephen M. Wylen, Paulist Press, 1996, 215 pages, pp. 18–20

[233] http://www.mechon-mamre.org/p/pt/pt0135.htm#22

[234] Bereshith, Genesis

[235] Shemoth; Exodus 1 and 2

[236] Shemoth; Exodus 3 and 4

[237] English translation of the papyrus. A translation also in R. B. Parkinson, *The Tale of Sinuhe and Other Ancient Egyptian Poems*. Oxford World's Classics, 1999. http://www.reshafim.org.il/ad/egypt/texts/ipuwer.htm

[238] Shemoth; Exodus 5 through 15

[239] Shemoth; Exodus 15, 19, and 20

[240] Bereshith; Genesis 1

[241] *The Hidden Face of God: Science Reveals the Ultimate Truth* by Gerald L. Schroeder PhD (May 9, 2002)

[242] Shemoth; Exodus 24

[243] Tehillim; Psalms 106, 19–20

[244] Shemoth; Exodus 21 through 32

[245] Shemoth; Exodus, 34, 6–7

[246] Shemoth; Exodus 34

[247] Wayiqra; Leviticus 26

[248] Shemoth; Exodus 35 through 40, Wayiqra; Leviticus, Bamidhbar; Numbers, Devariam; Deuteronomy

[249] Devariam; Deuteronomy 28 and 29 and 30

[250] Devariam; Deuteronomy

[251] Yehoshua; Joshua, Shoftim; Judges, Shmuel; Samuel, Melakhim; Kings

[252] Melakhim; Kings, Divrei HaYamim; Chronicles

[253] Daniel, Ezra, Nehemiah

[254] Genesis 11:31

[255] Judith 5:6

[256] World Book Encyclopedia. Chaldea. John A. Brinkman. Chicago. World Book, Inc. 2006

[257] 30.^ Jump up to: a b c d e f g "N. Al-Zahery et al. "Y-chromosome and mtDNA polymorphisms in Iraq, a crossroad of the early human dispersal and of post-Neolithic migrations" (2003)" (PDF). Retrieved 2010-12-10. https://www.familytreedna.com/sign-in?ReturnUrl=%2Fpdf%2FAl_Zahery.pdf

[258] 13.^ Jump up to: a b c d e f g h Hammer MF, Redd AJ, Wood ET, et al. (June 2000). "Jewish and Middle Eastern non-Jewish populations share a common pool of Y-chromosome biallelic haplotypes". Proceedings of the National Academy of Sciences of the United States of America. 97 (12): 6769–6774. Bibcode:2000PNAS...97.6769H. doi:10.1073/pnas.100115997. PMC 18733 Freely accessible.

[259] 14.^ Jump up to: a b c d e f g h i Nebel, Almut; Filon, Dvora; Brinkmann, Bernd; Majumder, Partha P.; Faerman, Marina; Oppenheim, Ariella (November 2001). "The Y Chromosome Pool of Jews as Part of the Genetic Landscape of the Middle East". The American Journal of Human Genetics. 69 (5): 1095–112. doi:10.1086/324070. PMC 1274378 Freely accessible.
[260] https://books.google.com/books?id=yvZUWbTftSgC&pg=RA1-PA145&lpg=RA1-PA145&dq=History+of+Israelite+Religion,+Volume+1++Albertz#v=onepage&q&f=false
[261] https://books.google.com/books?id=exjyhvRy7YUC&dq=Albertz+a+history+of+israelite+religion&printsec=frontcover#v=onepage&q&f=false
[262] https://books.google.com/books?id=Xx9YzJq2B9wC&dq=Rainer+Albertz,+%22Israel+in+exile%22&printsec=frontcover#v=onepage&q&f=false
[263] https//books.google.com
[264] https//books.google.com
[265] https//books.google.com
[266] https//books.google.com
[267] https//books.google.com
[268] https//books.google.com
[269] https://books.google.com/?id=MOd320e710IC&printsec=frontcover&dq=Osarsiph#v=onepage&q&f=false
[270] https://books.google.com/books?id=3PvirfZkfvQC&printsec=frontcover&dq=Ezra-Nehemiah:+A+Commentary++By+Joseph+Blenkinsopp#v=onepage&q&f=false
[271] https://books.google.com/books?id=R65fhpcUFcgC&printsec=frontcover&dq=Judah+and+the+Judeans+in+the+neo-Babylonian+period#v=onepage&q&f=false
[272] https://books.google.com/books?id=m1V1DeBS6P0C&printsec=frontcover&dq=Judaism,+the+first+phase:+the+place+of+Ezra+and+Nehemiah#v=onepage&q&f=false
[273] https//books.google.com
[274] https://books.google.com/books?id=0VG67yLs-LAC&printsec=frontcover&dq=Bright+History+of+Israel#v=onepage&q&f=false
[275] https://books.google.com/books?id=zFhvECwNQD0C&dq=The+Oxford+History+of+the+Biblical+World&printsec=frontcover#v=onepage&q&f=false
[276] https://books.google.com/books?id=nlb1PQAACAAJ&dq=A+brief+introduction+to+the+old+testament+coogan
[277] https://books.google.com/books?id=pMcM8GGO_n8C&printsec=frontcover&dq=Philip+Davies+In+search+of+Ancient+Israel#v=onepage&q=&f=false
[278] https://web.archive.org/web/20080528230034/http://www.arts.ualberta.ca/JHS/Articles/article_47.htm
[279] http://www.arts.ualberta.ca/JHS/Articles/article_47.htm
[280] https://books.google.com/books?id=y-gfwlltlRwC&printsec=frontcover&dq=Yahweh+and+the+gods+and+goddesses+of+Canaan#v=onepage&q&f=false
[281] https//books.google.com
[282] https//books.google.com
[283] https//books.google.com
[284] https//books.google.com
[285] https//books.google.com
[286] https//books.google.com
[287] https://books.google.com/books?id=jpbngoKHg8gC&dq=The+quest+for+the+historical+Israel:&printsec=frontcover#v=onepage&q=&f=false
[288] https//books.google.com
[289] https//books.google.com
[290] https//books.google.com
[291] https://books.google.com/books?id=VSJWkrXfbLQC&dq=Family+religion+in+Babylonia,+Syria,+and+Israel&printsec=frontcover#v=onepage&q&f=false
[292] https//books.google.com
[293] https//books.google.com
[294] https://books.google.com/books?id=DaVjGgPmmCsC&pg=PA269&dq=Formation+of+the+Pentateuch#v=onepage&q=Formation%20of%20the%20Pentateuch&f=false
[295] https://books.google.com/books?id=jH4MkEQH7M8C&pg=PA238

[296] https//docs.google.com
[297] https://books.google.com/books?id=VtAmmwapfVAC&printsec=frontcover&dq=Biblical+peoples+and+ethnicity:+an+archaeological#v=onepage&q&f=false
[298] https//books.google.com
[299] https://books.google.com/books?id=V_sfMzRPTgoC&printsec=frontcover&dq=Am%C3%A9lie+Kuhrt+The+ancient+Near+East#v=onepage&q&f=false
[300] https://books.google.com/books?id=JIoY7PagAOAC&dq=lemche+the+israelites+in+history+and+tradition&printsec=frontcover#v=onepage&q=&f=false
[301] https://books.google.com/books?id=-etsKv-4V2oC&printsec=frontcover&dq=The+archaeology+of+society+in+the+Holy+Land++Thomas+E.+Levy#v=onepage&q&f=false
[302] https://books.google.com/books?id=78nRWgb-rp8C&printsec=frontcover&dq=Lipschitz,+Oded+fall+and+rise#v=onepage&q&f=false
[303] https://books.google.com/books?id=6NsxZRnxE70C&pg=PA75&lpg=PA75&dq=Lipschits+Yehud#v=onepage&q=Lipschits%20Yehud&f=false
[304] https://books.google.com/books?id=smPZ-ou74EwC&printsec=frontcover&dq=Phoenicians++Glenn+Markoe#v=onepage&q&f=false
[305] https//books.google.com
[306] https//books.google.com
[307] https://books.google.com/?id=Jrpx-op_-XkC&printsec=frontcover&dq=lester+grabbe+1995#v=onepage&q&f=false
[308] https//books.google.com
[309] https://books.google.com/books?id=Gtm7NtK87poC&printsec=frontcover&dq=Chieftains+of+the+highland+clans#v=onepage&q=&f=false
[310] https//books.google.com
[311] https://web.archive.org/web/20110717120935/http://www.tyndalehouse.com/tynbul/library/TynBull_2004_55_2_01_Pitkanen_EthnicityIsraelSettlement.pdf
[312] http://www.tyndalehouse.com/tynbul/library/TynBull_2004_55_2_01_Pitkanen_EthnicityIsraelSettlement.pdf
[313] https://books.google.com/books?id=qX7r2lAQdFkC&pg=PA238&lpg=PA238&dq=hesse+wapnish#v=onepage&q=hesse%20wapnish&f=false
[314] https://books.google.com/books?id=1yM3AuBh4AsC&printsec=frontcover&dq=Smith+Early+History+of+God#v=onepage&q&f=false
[315] https//books.google.com
[316] https//books.google.com
[317] https://books.google.com/books?id=yCkRz5pfxz0C&printsec=frontcover&dq=Dictionary+of+Deities#v=onepage&q&f=false
[318] https://books.google.com/?id=GH-n4ctvlDYC&pg=PA40&dq=The+Canaanites+and+Their+Land#v=onepage&q=The%20Canaanites%20and%20Their%20Land&f=false
[319] https//books.google.com
[320] https://books.google.com/?id=SHgiy-k_wsUC&printsec=frontcover&dq=An+introduction+to+early+Judaism++By+James+C.+VanderKam#v=onepage&q&f=false
[321] https://books.google.com/books?id=db4hr55j0yYC&pg=PA1&dq=The+religion+of+ancient+Israel++By+Patrick+D.+Miller#v=onepage&q&f=false
[322] //en.wikipedia.org/w/index.php?title=Template:Judges&action=edit
[323] (sing. Hebrew: שֹׁפֵט šōpêṭ/shofet, pl. שֹׁפְטִים šōpəṭîm/shoftim)
[324] Boling & Nelson 2006.
[325] Gordon 1962, pp. 296–297.
[326] Coogan 2009, p. 178.
[327] Malamat 1971, p. 129.
[328] Kitchen 2003.
[329] Thompson 2000, p. 96.
[330] Payne 1996, pp. 630–631.
[331] Arnold & Williamson 2005, p. 590.
[332] Brettler 2002, p. 107; Davies 2006, p. 26; Thompson 2000, p. 96.
[333] Exodus 18:13–26.
[334] Hauser 1975.

[335] //doi.org/10.2307%2F3265729
[336] //www.worldcat.org/issn/0021-9231
[337] This article uses the term "Israelite" as defined by *The Encyclopedia of the Jewish Religion*: The name . . signifies the people composed of [Jacob's] descendants (the "children of Israel"), being applied (a) to the whole people (including Judah) . . [but] (b) with the division of the kingdom after the death of Solomon, to the Northern Kingdom only."<ref name= "werblowskiwigoder1966">
[338] //en.wikipedia.org/w/index.php?title=Template:History_of_Israel&action=edit
[339] Lemaire, Andre. "King Saul." http://www.myjewishlearning.com/history/Ancient_and_Medieval_History/2500_BCE-539_BCE/Social_History/Sauls_United_Kingdom.shtml?p=2 *My Jewish Learning*. 27 May 2014.
[340] Kenneth Kitchen, How We Know When Solomon Ruled: Israel's Kings, BAR September/October 2001
[341] http://www.mediasense.com/athena/jerusalem.htm
[342] https://www.jewishvirtuallibrary.org/jsource/History/Kings.html
[343] http://www.newadvent.org/cathen/08193a.htm
[344] //en.wikipedia.org/w/index.php?title=Template:History_of_Israel&action=edit
[345] Finkelstein, Israel; Silberman, Neil Asher (2002) *The Bible Unearthed : Archaeology's New Vision of Ancient Israel and the Origin of Its Sacred Texts*, Simon & Schuster,
[346] * Zechariah 10:6 http://www.biblegateway.com/passage/?search=Zechariah%2010:6;&version=49;
[347] * II Samuel 2:10 http://www.biblegateway.com/passage/?book_id=10&chapter=2&verse=10&version=31&context=verse
[348] 1 Kings 22:51 http://www.biblegateway.com/passage/?search=1%20Kings%2022:51;&version=9; and many subsequent passages
[349] https://www.biblica.com/bible/?osis=niv:2_Kings.17:5–17:5
[350] See Yohanan Aharoni, et al. (1993) *The Macmillan Bible Atlas*, p. 94, Macmillan Publishing: New York; and Amihai Mazar (1992) *The Archaeology of the Land of the Bible: 10,000 – 586 B.C.E*, p. 404, New York: Doubleday, see pp. 406-410 for discussion of archaeological significance of Shomron (Samaria) under Omride Dynasty.
[351] https://www.biblica.com/bible/?osis=niv:2_Kings.16:9–16:9
[352] https://www.biblica.com/bible/?osis=niv:2_Kings.15:29–15:29
[353] Considered to be a contemporary of the Assyrian King Shalmaneser III (858–824 BC) to whom he paid tribute. This is based on an inscription on The Black Obelisk of Shalmaneser III showing "Yaua" son of Omri paying tribute, dated to 841 BCE.
[354] Paid tribute to the Assyrian King Shalmaneser V (727–722 BCE) but rebelled in 725 BCE. Shalmaneser besieged the capital, Samaria, but died shortly before the fall of the city. His brother Sargon II (722–705 BCE) completed the siege with success in 722. Some of the population of the Northern Kingdom was exiled to other parts of the Assyrian Empire and new population groups were resettled in the new Assyrian province of Samaria. A small group of people fled south to take refuge in Judah.
[355] http://www.mechon-mamre.org/p/pt/pt09a16.htm#31
[356] Jonathan S. Greer (2015) "The Sanctuaries at Dan and Bethel" http://www.bibleodyssey.org/en/places/related-articles/sanctuaries-at-dan-and-bethel.aspx
[357] http://www.mechon-mamre.org/p/pt/pt09a12.htm#29
[358] "Israelite Temple" http://teldan.wordpress.com/israelite-temple/, Tel Dan Excavations
[359] http://www.mechon-mamre.org/p/pt/pt09a12.htm#26
[360] http://www.aboutisrael.co.il
[361] http://www.dinur.org/resources/resourceCategoryDisplay.aspx?categoryID=411&rsid=478
[362] http://www.complete-bible-genealogy.com/judah_israel_kings.htm
[363] Moore & Kelle 2011, p. 302.
[364] //en.wikipedia.org/w/index.php?title=Template:History_of_Israel&action=edit
[365] , Emory University, 1997
[366] //en.wikipedia.org/w/index.php?title=Template:Kings_of_Judah&action=edit
[367] http://www.mechon-mamre.org/p/pt/pt1030.htm#1
[368] http://www.mechon-mamre.org/p/pt/pt1036.htm#5
[369] http://www.mechon-mamre.org/p/pt/pt09b18.htm#13

[370] http://www.mechon-mamre.org/p/pt/pt09b18.htm#14
[371] James B. Pritchard, ed., *Ancient Near Eastern Texts Related to the Old Testament* (Princeton, NJ: Princeton University Press, 1965) 287–88.
[372] http://www.mechon-mamre.org/p/pt/pt09b18.htm#17
[373] No 24 WA21946, The Babylonian Chronicles, The British Museum
[374] http://www.mechon-mamre.org/p/pt/pt09b24.htm#14
[375] http://www.mechon-mamre.org/p/pt/pt09b25.htm#26
[376] http://www.mechon-mamre.org/p/pt/pt1143.htm#5
[377] http://www.mechon-mamre.org/p/pt/pt1144.htm#1
[378] http://www.mechon-mamre.org/p/pt/pt35a06.htm#15
[379] https://books.google.com/books?id=yvZUWbTftSgC&pg=PA145#v=onepage&q&f=false
[380] https://books.google.com/books?id=exjyhvRy7YUC
[381] https://books.google.com/books?id=Xx9YzJq2B9wC
[382] https://books.google.com/books?id=hwExATCqwvwC&pg=PA7#v=snippet&q=%22attention%20to%20the%20interesting%20fact%22&f=false
[383] https://books.google.com/books?id=Ku4OKVrEd4MC&pg=PA467#v=onepage&q&f=false
[384] http://www.jhsonline.org/Articles/article_47.htm
[385] https://books.google.com/books?id=zqJxkKy-cMMC
[386] https://books.google.com/books?id=MOd320e710IC&q=Osarsiph
[387] https://books.google.com/books?id=3PvirfZkfvQC
[388] https://books.google.com/books?id=R65fhpcUFcgC
[389] https://books.google.com/books?id=R65fhpcUFcgC&pg=PR5#v=onepage&q=%22Bethel%20in%20the%20Neo-Babylonian%20Period%22&f=false
[390] https://books.google.com/books?id=m1V1DeBS6P0C
[391] https://books.google.com/books?id=RfFRhC4FpZkC&pg=PA45#v=onepage&q=Finkelstein%20haser-style%20layout&f=false
[392] https://books.google.com/books?id=0VG67yLs-LAC
[393] https://books.google.com/books?id=zFhvECwNQD0C
[394] https://books.google.com/books?id=pMcM8GGO_n8C
[395] https://web.archive.org/web/20080528230034/http://www.arts.ualberta.ca/JHS/Articles/article_47.htm
[396] http://www.arts.ualberta.ca/JHS/Articles/article_47.htm
[397] https://books.google.com/books?id=6-VxwC5rQtwC
[398] https://books.google.com/books?id=8WkbUkKeqcoC
[399] https://books.google.com/books?id=2Vo-11umIZQC&pg=PA153#v=onepage&q=John%20W.%20Rogerson%20Deuteronomy&f=false
[400] https://books.google.com/books?id=bua2dMa9fJ4C
[401] https://books.google.com/books?id=lu6ywyJr0CMC
[402] https://books.google.com/books?id=jpbngoKHg8gC
[403] https://books.google.com/books?id=EResmS5wOnkC
[404] https://books.google.com/books?id=yTMzJAKowyEC&pg=PA62#v=onepage&q=Late%20Bronze%20collapse%20in%20Canaan&f=false
[405] https://books.google.com/books?id=VtAmmwapfVAC
[406] https://books.google.com/books?id=OtOhypZz_pEC
[407] https://books.google.com/books?id=V_sfMzRPTgoC
[408] https://books.google.com/books?id=JIoY7PagAOAC
[409] https://books.google.com/books?id=-etsKv-4V2oC
[410] https://books.google.com/books?id=78nRWgb-rp8C
[411] https://books.google.com/books?id=6NsxZRnxE70C&pg=PA75#v=onepage&q=Lipschits%20Yehud&f=false
[412] https://books.google.com/books?id=hd28MdGNyTYC&pg=PA33#v=onepage&q=&f=false
[413] https://books.google.com/books?id=Jrpx-op_-XkC&dq=lester+grabbe+1995&source=gbs_similarbooks_s
[414] https://books.google.com/books?id=uDijjc_D5P0C
[415] https://books.google.com/books?id=Gtm7NtK87poC

[416] https://books.google.com/books?id=Qjkz_8EMoaUC&pg=PA19#v=snippet&q=Thompson+%22Van+Seters%22&f=false
[417] https://web.archive.org/web/20110717120935/http://www.tyndalehouse.com/tynbul/library/TynBull_2004_55_2_01_Pitkanen_EthnicityIsraelSettlement.pdf
[418] http://www.tyndalehouse.com/tynbul/library/TynBull_2004_55_2_01_Pitkanen_EthnicityIsraelSettlement.pdf
[419] https://books.google.com/books?id=qX7r2lAQdFkC&pg=PA238#v=onepage&q=hesse%20wapnish&f=false
[420] https://books.google.com/books?id=Dzw_H5GhkfYC
[421] https://books.google.com/books?id=VSJWkrXfbLQC
[422] https://books.google.com/books?id=db4hr55j0yYC
[423] Jewish Encyclopedia: Rome: Early Settlement in Rome http://jewishencyclopedia.com/view.jsp?artid=352&letter=R&search=rome#1005
[424] Benjamin Isaac *The Near East under Roman Rule: Selected Papers* (Leiden: Brill 1998)
[425] H.H. Ben-Sasson, *A History of the Jewish People*, Harvard University Press, 1976, , *The Crisis Under Gaius Caligula*, pages 254-256: "The reign of Gaius Caligula (37-41) witnessed the first open break between the Jews and the Julio-Claudian empire. Until then — if one accepts Sejanus' heyday and the trouble caused by the census after Archelaus' banishment — there was usually an atmosphere of understanding between the Jews and the empire ... These relations deteriorated seriously during Caligula's reign, and, though after his death the peace was outwardly re-established, considerable bitterness remained on both sides. .. Caligula ordered that a golden statue of himself be set up in the Temple in Jerusalem. .. Only Caligula's death, at the hands of Roman conspirators (41), prevented the outbreak of a Jewish-Roman war that might well have spread to the entire East."
[426] Jewish Encyclopedia: BAR KOKBA AND BAR KOKBA WAR: Publius Marcellus http://jewishencyclopedia.com/view.jsp?artid=237&letter=B&search=Bar%20Kokba#762: "...and thus about fifty strongholds and 985 undefended towns and villages fell into their hands (Dio Cassius, lxix. 14)."
[427] Jewish Encyclopedia: Galilee http://jewishencyclopedia.com/view.jsp?artid=32&letter=G&search=Galilee: "After the fall of the Jewish state a new period of prosperity set in for Galilee; and it gradually became the center of Jewish life in Palestine."
[428] H.H. Ben-Sasson, *A History of the Jewish People*, Harvard University Press, 1976, , page 334: "In an effort to wipe out all memory of the bond between the Jews and the land, Hadrian changed the name of the province from Iudaea to Syria-Palestina, a name that became common in non-Jewish literature."
[429] http://www.jewishpress.com/sections/books/a-jewish-slave-in-rome/2017/07/24/
[430] Abrahamson et al. The Persian conquest of Jerusalem in 614 compared with Islamic conquest of 638.
[431] Rosenwein, Barbara H. (2004). A Short History of the Middle Ages. Ontario. pp. 71–72.
[432] Frank McLynn, "Richard and John: Kings at War," chapter 5, page 118.
[433] //en.wikipedia.org/w/index.php?title=Template:History_of_Israel&action=edit
[434] Benjamin Z. Kedar, "Samaritan History: The Frankish Period", in Alan David Crown (ed.), *The Samaritans* (Tübingen: J. C. B. Mohr, 1989), pp. 82–94.
[435] The First Crusade is extensively documented in primary and secondary sources. See for example Thomas Asbridge, *The First Crusade: A New History* (Oxford: 2004); Christopher Tyerman, *God's War: A New History of the Crusades* (Penguin: 2006); Jonathan Riley-Smith, *The First Crusade and the Idea of Crusading* (Pennsylvania: 1991); and the lively but outdated Steven Runciman, *A History of the Crusades: Volume 1, The First Crusade and the Foundation of the Kingdom of Jerusalem* (Cambridge: 1953).
[436] William of Tyre, *A History of Deeds Done Beyond the Sea*, trans. E.A. Babcock and A.C. Krey, Columbia University Press, 1943, vol. 1, bk. 9, ch. 9.
[437] Riley-Smith (1979), "The Title of Godfrey of Bouillon", *Bulletin of the Institute of Historical Research* **52**, pp. 83–86.
[438] Murray, Alan V. (1990), "The Title of Godfrey of Bouillon as Ruler of Jerusalem", *Collegium Medievale* **3**, pp. 163–178.
[439] Asbridge, pg. 326.

[440] William of Tyre, vol. 1, bk. 9, ch. 16, pg. 404.
[441] Tyerman, pp. 201–202.
[442] Hans Eberhard Mayer, *The Crusades*, 2nd ed., trans. John Gillingham (Oxford: 1988), pp. 171–76.
[443] William of Tyre, vol. 1, bk. 11, ch. 27, pp. 507–508.
[444] Thomas Madden, *The New Concise History of the Crusades* (Rowman and Littlefield, 2005), pp. 40–43.
[445] Madden, pg. 43.
[446] Mayer, pp. 71–72.
[447] Mayer, pp. 72–77.
[448] Tyerman, pp. 207–208.
[449] Mayer, pp. 83–85.
[450] Mayer, pp. 83–84.
[451] William of Tyre, vol. II, bk. 14, ch. 18, pg. 76.
[452] Mayer, pp. 86–88.
[453] Mayer, pg. 92.
[454] Jonathan Phillips, *The Second Crusade: Extending the Frontiers of Christendom* (Yale University Press, 2007), pp. 216–227.
[455] Tyerman, pp. 344–345.
[456] Mayer, 108–111.
[457] Mayer, pg. 112
[458] Madden, pp. 64–65.
[459] William of Tyre, vol. II, bk. 18 ch. 16, pg. 265.
[460] Tyerman, pp. 347–348; Mayer, pg. 118–119.
[461] Mayer, pp. 119–120.
[462] Tyerman, pg. 350.
[463] Marshall W. Baldwin, "The Decline and Fall of Jerusalem, 1174–1189", in *A History of the Crusades* (gen. ed. Kenneth M. Setton), vol. 1: The First Hundred Years (ed. Marshall W. Baldwin, University of Wisconsin Press, 1969), pg. 592ff.
[464] Steven Runciman, *A History of the Crusades*, vol. 2: The Kingdom of Jerusalem and the Frankish East (Cambridge University Press, 1952), pg. 404.
[465] Hans E. Mayer, *The Crusades* (trans. John Gillingham, 1972; 2nd ed., Oxford University Press, 1988), pp. 127–128.
[466] Peter W. Edbury, "Propaganda and faction in the Kingdom of Jerusalem: the background to Hattin", in *Crusaders and Moslems in Twelfth-Century Syria* (ed. Maya Shatzmiller, Leiden: Brill, 1993), pg. 174.
[467] Hamilton pg. 158.
[468] Hamilton, pg. 93.
[469] Hamilton, pp. 105–106.
[470] Hamilton, pg. 101.
[471] Hamilton, pg. 115.
[472] Hamilton, pg. 118.
[473] Hamilton, pp. 122–130.
[474] Hamilton, pp. 132–136.
[475] Hamilton, pp. 150–158.
[476] Hamilton, pg. 161.
[477] Hamilton, pp. 162–163; Edbury and Rowe, "William of Tyre and the Patriarchal election of 1180", *The English Historical Review* 93 (1978), repr. *Kingdoms of the Crusaders: From Jerusalem to Cyprus* (Aldershot: Ashgate, Variorum Collected Series Studies, 1999), pp. 23–25.
[478] Hamilton, pp. 170–171.
[479] Hamilton, pp. 174–183.
[480] Hamilton, pp. 186–192.
[481] Hamilton, pp. 192–196.
[482] Hamilton, pp. 202–203.
[483] Hamilton, pp. 204–210.

[484] Hamilton, pp. 212-216.
[485] Hamilton, pp. 216-223.
[486] Hamilton, pp. 223-231.
[487] Peter W. Edbury, *The Kingdom of Cyprus and the Crusades, 1191-1374* (Cambridge: Cambridge University Press, 1991), pp. 4-5.
[488] Edbury, *Kingdom of Cyprus and the Crusades*, pp. 25-26.
[489] Stark, *God's Battalions*
[490] Edbury, *Kingdom of Cyprus and the Crusades*, pp. 26-29.
[491] Edbury, *Kingdom of Cyprus and the Crusades*, pp. 31-33.
[492] Riley-Smith, *The Crusades: A History* (2nd ed., Yale University Press, 2005), pp. 146-147.
[493] Riley-Smith, *The Crusades: A History*, p. 150.
[494] Humphreys, pp. 111-122
[495] Riley-Smith, *The Crusades: A History*, pp. 153-160.
[496] Edbury, *Kingdom of Cyprus and the Crusades*, pp. 40-41.
[497] Edbury, *Kingdom of Cyprus and the Crusades*, p. 48.
[498] James M. Powell, *Anatomy of a Crusade: 1213-1221* (University of Pennsylvania Press, 1986), pp. 128-135.
[499] Thomas C. Van Cleve, "The Fifth Crusade", in *A History of the Crusades* (gen. ed. Kenneth M. Setton), vol. 2: The Later Crusades, 1189-1311 (ed. R.L. Wolff and H.W. Hazard, University of Wisconsin Press, 1969), pp. 394-395.
[500] Powell, pp. 137-195.
[501] Edbury, *Kingdom of Cyprus and the Crusades*, pp. 55-56.
[502] Edbury, *Kingdom of Cyprus and the Crusades*, pp. 57-64.
[503] Riley-Smith, *The Crusades: A History*, 2nd ed., pp. 180-182.
[504] Riley-Smith, *The Crusades: A History*, 2nd ed., p. 182.
[505] Tyerman, *God's War*, pp. 725-726.
[506] Michael Lower, *The Barons' Crusade: A Call to Arms and its Consequences* (University of Pennsylvania Press, 2005), pp. 159-177.
[507] Tyerman, *God's War*, pp. 770-771.
[508] Tyerman, *God's War*, pp. 784-803.
[509] Edbury, *Kingdom of Cyprus and the Crusades*, pp. 81-85.
[510] Steven Runciman, "The Crusader States, 1243-1291", in History of the Crusades, vol. 2, pp. 568-570.
[511] Runciman, "The Crusader States, 1243-1291", pp. 570-575.
[512] Edbury, *Kingdom of Cyprus and the Crusades*, pp. 85-90.
[513] Edbury, *Kingdom of Cyprus and the Crusades*, pp. 92-99.
[514] William of Tyre, vol. 1, bk. 9, ch. 19, pg. 408.
[515] Fulcher of Chartres, *A History of the Expedition to Jerusalem*, trans. Frances Rita Ryan, University of Tennessee Press, 1969, bk. III, ch. XXXVII.3. pg. 271 (available online http://www.fordham.edu/halsall/source/fulk3.html).
[516] Fulcher, bk. III, ch. XXXVII.4, pg. 271.
[517] Many chronicles of individual pilgrims are collected together in the Palestine Pilgrims' Text Society (London, 1884–); "Recueil de voyages et mémoires", published by the Société de Géographie (Paris, 1824–66); "Recueil de voyages et de documents pour servir à la géographie" (Paris, 1890–).
[518] Ronnie Ellenblum, Frankish Rural Settlement in the Latin Kingdom of Jerusalem (Cambridge University Press, 1998), pp. 3–4, 10–11.
[519] Joshua Prawer, *The Crusaders' Kingdom: European Colonialism in the Middle Ages* (Praeger, 1972), pg. 60; pp. 469–470; and throughout.
[520] Ellenblum, pp. 5–9.
[521] Ellenblum, pp. 26–28.
[522] Ellenblum, pp. 36–37.
[523] Prawer, Crusader Institutions, pp. 197, 205.
[524] Hans Mayer, "Latins, Muslims, and Greeks in the Latin Kingdom of Jerusalem", History 63 (1978), pg. 175; reprinted in *Probleme des lateinischen Königreichs Jerusalem* (Variorum, 1983).

[525] Mayer calls them "chattels of the state"; Hans Mayer, "Latins, Muslims, and Greeks in the Latin Kingdom of Jerusalem", History 63 (1978), pg. 177; reprinted in *Probleme des lateinischen Königreichs Jerusalem* (Variorum, 1983).

[526] Prawer, Crusader Institutions, pg. 207; Jonathan Riley-Smith, "Some lesser officials in Latin Syria" (English Historical Review, vol. 87, no. 342 (Jan., 1972)), pp. 1–15.

[527] Pernoud *The Crusaders* pg. 172.

[528] Prawer, Crusader Institutions, pg. 202.

[529] Jonathan Riley-Smith, The Feudal Nobility, pp. 62–63.

[530] Yvonne Friedman, *Encounter between Enemies: Captivity and Ransom in the Latin Kingdom of Jerusalem*. Brill, 2002, throughout.

[531] Prawer, Crusader Institutions, pg. 209.

[532] Prawer, Crusader Institutions, pg. 214.

[533] Tyerman, God's War, pg 230.

[534] Tyerman, God's War, pg 231.

[535] Tyerman, God's War, pg 234.

[536] Tyerman, God's War, pg 235.

[537] Tyerman, God's War, pg 237-8.

[538] Josiah C. Russell, "Population of the Crusader States", in Setton, ed. Crusades, vol. 5, pg. 108.

[539] Benjamin Z. Kedar, "The Subjected Muslims of the Frankish Levant", in *Muslims Under Latin Rule, 1100–1300*, ed. James M. Powell, Princeton University Press, 1990, pg. 148; reprinted in *The Crusades: The Essential Readings*, ed. Thomas F. Madden, Blackwell, 2002, pg. 244. Kedar quotes his numbers from Joshua Prawer, *Histoire du royaume latin de Jérusalem*, tr. G. Nahon, Paris, 1969, vol. 1, pp. 498, 568–72.

[540] Benjamin Z. Kedar, "The Subjected Muslims of the Frankish Levant", in *Muslims Under Latin Rule, 1100–1300*, ed. James M. Powell, Princeton University Press, 1990, pg. 148–149; reprinted in *The Crusades: The Essential Readings*, ed. Thomas F. Madden, Blackwell, 2002, pg. 244. Kedar quotes his numbers from Joshua Prawer, *Histoire du royaume latin de Jérusalem*, tr. G. Nahon, Paris, 1969, vol. 1, pp. 498, 568–72.

[541] Ellenblum, pg. 31.

[542] William of Tyre, vol. 2, bk. 22, ch. 23, pp. 486–488.

[543] According to Ludolph of Suchem (which seems exaggeration): "In Acre and the other places nearly a hundred and six thousand men were slain or taken, and more than two hundred thousand escaped from thence. Of the Saracens more than three hundred thousand were slain, as is well known even to this day." —From Ludolph of Suchem, p. 268-272

[544] Michaud, *The History of the Crusades*, Vol. 3, p. 18 ; available in full at Google Books https://books.google.com/books?id=mAcMAAAAYAAJ. Note that in a footnote Michaud claims reliance on "the chronicle of Ibn Ferat" (Michaud, Vol.3, p.22) for much of the information he has concerning the *Mussulmans*.

[545] Hans E. Mayer, "Guillaume de Tyr à l'école", in *Kings and Lords in the Latin Kingdom of Jerusalem* (Variorum, 1994), pg. V.264; originally published in Mémoires de l'Académie des sciences, arts et belles-lettres de Dijon 117 (1985–86).

[546] Note the famous example of William of Tyre, *Willemi Tyrensis Archiepiscopi Chronicon*, ed. R. B. C. Huygens, Corpus Christianorum, Continuatio Medievalis, vol. 38 (Turnhout: Brepols, 1986), bk. 19, ch. 12, pp. 879–881. This chapter was discovered after the publication of Babcock and Krey's translation and is not included in the English edition.

[547] For example, King Baldwin III "was fairly well educated", and "particularly enjoyed listening to the reading of history..." (William of Tyre, vol. 2, bk. 16, ch. 2, pg. 138.) King Amalric I "was fairly well educated, although much less so than his brother" Baldwin III; he "was well skilled in the customary law by which the kingdom was governed", and "listened eagerly to history and preferred it to all other kinds of reading." (William of Tyre, vol. 2, bk. 19, ch. 2, pg. 296.)

[548] William of Tyre, introduction by Babcock and Krey, pg. 16.

[549] Benjamin Z. Kedar, *On the origins of the earliest laws of Frankish Jerusalem: The canons of the Council of Nablus, 1120* (*Speculum* 74, 1999), pp. 330–331; Marwan Nader, *Burgesses and Burgess Law in the Latin Kingdoms of Jerusalem and Cyprus (1099–1325)* (Ashgate: 2006), pg. 45.

[550] Nader, pp. 28–30.

[551] Nader, pp. 158–170
[552] Nader, pp. 170–77.
[553] https://books.google.com/books?id=YdzpSO1_Pm8C&pg
[554] http://libtext.library.wisc.edu/HistCrusades/
[555] http://www.newadvent.org/cathen/08361a.htm
[556] Corrected population for Mortality Level=8.
[557] Abu-Manneh 1999, p. 36.
[558] The 1915 *Filastin Risalesi* ("Palestine Document") is a country survey of the VIII Corps of the Ottoman Army, which identified Palestine as a region including the sanjaqs of Akka (the Galilee), the Sanjaq of Nablus, and the Sanjaq of Jerusalem (Kudus Sherif), see Ottoman Conceptions of Palestine-Part 2: Ethnography and Cartography, Salim Tamari http://www.palestine-studies.org/sites/default/files/jq-articles/48_Shifting_Ottoman_2.pdf
[559] Abu-Manneh 1999, p. 43.
[560] Abu-Manneh 1999, p. 39.
[561] , pp. 369–370
[562] Abu-Manneh 1999, p. 43–44.
[563] https://books.google.com/books?id=OjuKhNEmFvoC
[564] //en.wikipedia.org/w/index.php?title=Template:History_of_Israel&action=edit
[565] //en.wikipedia.org/w/index.php?title=Template:History_of_Palestine&action=edit
[566] During its existence the territory was known simply as *Palestine*, but, in later years, a variety of other names and descriptors have been used, including *Mandatory* or **Mandate Palestine**, the **British Mandate of Palestine** and **British Palestine**.
[567] Allenby to Robertson 25 January 1918 in Hughes 2004, p. 128
[568] Article 22, The Covenant of the League of Nations http://avalon.law.yale.edu/20th_century/leagcov.asp#art22 and "Mandate for Palestine," *Encyclopedia Judaica*, Vol. 11, p. 862, Keter Publishing House, Jerusalem, 1972
[569] Marjorie M. Whiteman, *Digest of International Law*, vol. 1, US State Department (Washington, DC: U.S. Government Printing Office, 1963) pp. 650–652
[570] *Official Records of the Second Session of the General Assembly*, Supplement No. 11, United Nations Special Committee on Palestine, Report to the General Assembly, Volume 1. Lake Success, NY, 1947. A/364, 3 September 1947, Chapter II.C.68. https://unispal.un.org/UNISPAL.NSF/0/FB6DD3F0E9535815852572DD006CC607
[571] Ira M. Lapidus, *A History of Islamic Societies*, 2002: "The first were the nationalists, who in 1918 formed the first Muslim-Christian associations to protest against the Jewish national home" p.558
[572] Tessler, *A History of the Israeli-Palestinian Conflict, Second Edition*, 2009: "An All-Palestine Congress, known also as the First Congress of the Muslim-Christian Societies, was organised by the MCA and convened in Jerusalem in February 1919." p.220-221
[573] The Palestine Chronicle
[574] Shamir, Ronen (2013) *Current Flow: The Electrification of Palestine* Stanford: Stanford University Press
[575] Caplan, Neil. *Palestine Jewry and the Arab Question, 1917 – 1925*. London and Totowa, NJ: F. Cass, 1978. pp. 148–161.
[576] "It was not scholarly religious credentials that made Hajj Amin an attractive candidate for president of the SMC in the eyes of colonial officials. Rather, it was the combination of his being an effective nationalist activist and a member of one of Jerusalem's most respected notable families that made it advantageous to align his interests with those of the British administration and thereby keep him on a short tether." Weldon C. Matthews, *Confronting an Empire, Constructing a Nation: Arab Nationalists and Popular Politics in Mandate Palestine*, I.B.Tauris, 2006 pp. 31–32
[577] For details see Yitzhak Reiter, *Islamic Endowments in Jerusalem under British Mandate*, Frank Cass, London Portland, Oregon, 1996
[578] Excluding funds for land purchases. Sahar Huneidi, *A Broken Trust: Herbert Samuel, Zionism and the Palestinians 1920–1925*, I.B. Tauris, London and New York, 2001 p. 38. The 'Jewish Agency', mentioned in article 4 of the Mandate only became the official term in 1928. At the time the organisation was called the Palestine Zionist Executive.

[579] 1922 Palestine Order in Council https://unispal.un.org/UNISPAL.NSF/0/C7AAE196F41AA055052565F50054E656
[580] Legislative Council (Palestine) http://www.answers.com/topic/legislative-council-palestine Answers.com
[581]
[582] League of Nations, *Official Journal*, October 1923, p. 1217.
[583] : The Jewish Settlement Police were created and equipped with trucks and armoured cars by the British working with the Jewish Agency.
[584] William Roger Louis, Ends of British Imperialism: The Scramble for Empire, Suez, and Decolonization https://books.google.com/books/about/Ends_of_British_Imperialism.html?id=NQnpQNKeKKAC&redir_esc=y, 2006, p. 391
[585] Benny Morris, *One State, Two States: Resolving the Israel/Palestine Conflict*, 2009, p. 66
[586] Benny Morris, The Birth of the Palestinian Refugee Problem Revisited https://books.google.com/books/about/The_Birth_of_the_Palestinian_Refugee_Pro.html?id=uM_kFX6edX8C&redir_esc=y, p. 48; p. 11 "while the Zionist movement, after much agonising, accepted the principle of partition and the proposals as a basis for negotiation"; p. 49 "In the end, after bitter debate, the Congress equivocally approved—by a vote of 299 to 160—the Peel recommendations as a basis for further negotiation."
[587] 'Zionists Ready To Negotiate British Plan As Basis', *The Times* Thursday, 12 August 1937; p. 10; Issue 47761; col B.
[588] Eran, Oded. "Arab-Israel Peacemaking." *The Continuum Political Encyclopedia of the Middle East*. Ed. Avraham Sela. New York: Continuum, 2002, p. 122.
[589] Letter from David Ben-Gurion to his son Amos, written 5 October 1937 http://www.palestineremembered.com/download/B-G%20LetterTranslation.pdf, Obtained from the Ben-Gurion Archives in Hebrew, and translated into English by the Institute of Palestine Studies, Beirut
[590] Quote: "No Zionist can forgo the smallest portion of the Land Of Israel. [A] Jewish state in part [of Palestine] is not an end, but a beginning ..... Our possession is important not only for itself ... through this we increase our power, and every increase in power facilitates getting hold of the country in its entirety. Establishing a [small] state .... will serve as a very potent lever in our historical effort to redeem the whole country"
[591] Quote from a meeting of the Jewish Agency executive in June 1938: "[I am] satisfied with part of the country, but on the basis of the assumption that after we build up a strong force following the establishment of the state, we will abolish the partition of the country and we will expand to the whole Land of Israel." in
; and
[592] From a letter from Chaim Weizmann to Arthur Grenfell Wauchope, High Commissioner for Palestine, while the Peel Commission was convening in 1937: "We shall spread in the whole country in the course of time ..... this is only an arrangement for the next 25 to 30 years."
[593] Why Italian Planes Bombed Tel-Aviv? http://www.isracast.com/article.aspx?ID=470&t=Why-Italian-Planes-Bombed-Tel-Aviv?
[594] How the Palmach was formed http://www.historycentral.com/Israel/1941PalmachFormed.html (History Central)
[595] Secret World War II documents released by the UK in July 2001, include documents on Operation ATLAS (See References: KV 2/400–402 http://www.nationalarchives.gov.uk/documents/july2001.pdf. A German task force led by Kurt Wieland parachuted into Palestine in September 1944. This was one of the last German efforts in the region to attack the Jewish community in Palestine and undermine British rule by supplying local Arabs with cash, arms and sabotage equipment. The team was captured shortly after landing.
[596] Corrigan, Gordon. *The Second World War* Thomas Dunne Books, 2011 p. 523, last paragraph
[597] The "Hunting Season" (1945) https://www.jewishvirtuallibrary.org/jsource/History/season.html by Yehuda Lapidot (Jewish Virtual Library)
[598] UN Doc A/364 Add. 1 of 3 September 1947 https://unispal.un.org/UNISPAL.NSF/0/FB6DD3F0E9535815852572DD006CC607
[599] *American Jewish History*, Jeffrey S. Gurock, American Jewish Historical Society, p. 243
[600] Article 11 of the United Nations Charter

[601] "Palestine" http://school.eb.com/eb/article-45071. Encyclopædia Britannica Online School Edition, 2006. 15 May 2006.
[602] See *Mandates, Dependencies and Trusteeship*, by H. Duncan Hall, Carnegie Endowment, 1948, pp. 266–267.
[603] *The British Empire in the Middle East, 1945–1951* https://books.google.com/books?id= ATQQ0FMS1FQC&pg=PA348, p. 348. William Roger Louis, Clarendon Press, 1984
[604] Herzog, Chaim and Gazit, Shlomo: *The Arab-Israeli Wars: War and Peace in the Middle East from the 1948 War of Independence to the Present*, p. 46
[605] U.N. Resolution 181 (II). Future Government of Palestine, Part 1-A, Termination of Mandate, Partition and Independence http://www.yale.edu/lawweb/avalon/un/res181.htm .
[606] Israel Ministry of Foreign Affairs: *Declaration of Establishment of State of Israel: 14 May 1948*: Retrieved 10 April 2012 http://www.mfa.gov.il/MFA/Peace+Process/Guide+to+the+ Peace+Process/Declaration+of+Establishment+of+State+of+Israel.htm
[607] Bier, Aharon, & Slae, Bracha,*For the sake of Jerusalem*, Mazo Publishers, 2006, p. 49
[608] *Declaration of the Establishment of the State of Israel*, 14 May 1948.
[609] Masalha, Nur (1992). "Expulsion of the Palestinians." Institute for Palestine Studies, this edition 2001, p. 175.
[610] "In 1948 half of Palestine's... Arabs were uprooted from their homes and became refugees"
[611] Appendix IX-B, 'The Arab Expeditionary Forces to Palestine, 15/5/48, Khalidi, 1971, p. 867.
[612] Bayliss, 1999, p. 84.
[613] League of Nations, Permanent Mandate Commission, Minutes of the Ninth Session http://domino.un.org/unispal.nsf/9a798adbf322aff38525617b006d88d7/ 1504facc47efbe05052565f0006b70bb?OpenDocument (Arab Grievances), Held at Geneva from 8 to 25 June 1926
[614] League of Nations, Permanent Mandate Commission, Minutes of the Ninth Session https:// unispal.un.org/DPA/DPR/unispal.nsf/0/1504FACC47EFBE05052565F0006B70BB (Arab Grievances), Held at Geneva from June 8th to 25th, 1926,
[615] See Papers relating to the foreign relations of the United States
[616] See Defending the Rights of Others, by Carol Fink, Cambridge University, 2006, , p. 28
[617] See the Statement of the Principal Accredited Representative, Hon. W. Ormsby-Gore, C.330.M.222, Mandate for Palestine – Minutes of the Permanent Mandates Commission/League of Nations 32nd session, 18 August 1937 http://domino.un.org/UNISPAL. NSF/0145a8233e14d2b585256cbf005af141/fd05535118aef0de052565ed0065ddf7? OpenDocument
[618] See the Judgment in "Legal Consequences of the Construction of a Wall in the Occupied Palestinian Territory" http://www.icj-cij.org/docket/files/131/1681.pdf (PDF)
[619] See paragraphs 49, 70, and 129 of the International Court of Justice Advisory Opinion, Legal Consequences of the Construction of a Wall in the Occupied Palestinian Territory PDF http://www.icj-cij.org/docket/files/131/1671.pdf and PAUL J. I. M. DE WAART (2005). "International Court of Justice Firmly Walled in the Law of Power in the Israeli–Palestinian Peace Process." *Leiden Journal of International Law*, 18, pp. 467–487,
[620] https://web.archive.org/web/20140916132453/http://unispal.un.org/UNISPAL.NSF/0/ C7AAE196F41AA055052565F50054E656
[621] "Palestine. The Constitution Suspended., Arab Boycott Of Elections., Back To British Rule" *The Times*, 30 May 1923, p. 14, Issue 43354
[622] See Foreign relations of the United States, 1947. The Near East and Africa Volume V, p. 1033
[623] In June of 1947, the British Mandate Government of Palestine had published the following statistics: "It is estimated that over a quarter of the Jewish population in Palestine are Sephardic Jews of whom some 60,000 were born of families resident in Palestine for centuries. The bulk of the Sephardic community, however, consists of oriental Jews emanating from Syria, Egypt, Persia, Iraq, Georgia, Bokhara and other Eastern countries. They are confined mainly to the larger towns ..." (From: *Supplement to Survey of Palestine - Notes compiled for the information of the United Nations Special Committee on Palestine - June 1947*, Gov. Printer Jerusalem, pp. 150–151)
[624] *Palestine Jewry and the Arab Question, 1917–1925*, by Caplan, Neil. London and Totowa, NJ: F. Cass, 1978. pp. 161–165.

[625] p. 210: "Arab illegal immigration is mainly ... casual, temporary and seasonal". pp. 212: "The conclusion is that Arab illegal immigration for the purpose of permanent settlement is insignificant".

[626] *Supplement to Survey of Palestine - Notes compiled for the information of the United Nations Special Committee on Palestine - June 1947*, Gov. Printer Jerusalem, p. 18

[627] See History of Zionism (1600–1918), Volume I, Nahum Sokolow, 1919 Longmans, Green, and Company, London, pp. xxiv–xxv

[628] See the report of the United Nations Special Committee on Palestine, UN Document A/364, 3 September 1947

[629] Memorandum By The Secretary of State for the Colonies, "PALESTINE: HIGH COMMISSIONERS VIEWS ON POLICY", March 1930, UK National Archives Cabinet Paper CAB/24/211, formerly C.P. 108 (30)

[630] See Partner to Partition: The Jewish Agency's Partition Plan in the Mandate Era, by Yossi Katz, Routledge, 1998,

[631] See *Letters to Paula and the Children*, David Ben Gurion, translated by Aubry Hodes, University of Pittsburgh Press, 1971 pp. 153–157

[632] See *Righteous Victims: A History of the Zionist–Arab Conflict, 1881–1999*, by Benny Morris, Knopf, 1999, , p. 138

[633] See *Scars of war, Wounds of Peace: The Israeli–Arab Tragedy*, by Shlomo Ben-Ami, Oxford University Press, USA, 2006, , p. 17

[634] See Foreign relations of the United States, 1946, The Near East and Africa Volume VII, pp. 692–693

[635] "Land Ownership in Palestine," CZA, KKL5/1878. The statistics were prepared by the Palestine Lands Department for the Anglo-American Committee of Inquiry, 1945, ISA, Box 3874/file 1. See

[636] Lorenzo Kamel (2014), "Whose Land? Land Tenure in Late Nineteenth- and Early Twentieth-Century Palestine", *British Journal of Middle Eastern Studies*, pp. 230–242. http://www.tandfonline.com/doi/pdf/10.1080/13530194.2013.878518 http://www.tandfonline.com/doi/pdf/10.1080/13530194.2013.878518%20

[637] Land Ownership of Palestine http://domino.un.org/maps/m0094.jpg – Map prepared by the Government of Palestine on the instructions of the UN Ad Hoc Committee on the Palestine Question.

[638] Table 2 showing Holdings of Large Jewish Lands Owners as of December 31st, 1945, British Mandate: A Survey of Palestine: Volume I – Page 245. Chapter VIII: Land: Section 3., prepared by the British Mandate for the United Nations http://www.palestineremembered.com/Articles/A-Survey-of-Palestine/Story6686.html Survey of Palestine Retrieved 4 July 2015

[639] Ownership of land in Palestine, Share of Palestinan Arabs and Jews as of 1 April 1943, prepared by the British Mandate for the United Nations http://www.palestineremembered.com/Acre/Articles/Story1000.html Survey of Palestine Retrieved 25 August 2014

[640] *ibid*, Supplement p30.

[641] *A Survey of Palestine* (Prepared in December 1945 and January 1946 for the information of the Anglo-American Committee of Inquiry), vol. 1, chapter VIII, section 7, Government Printer of Jerusalem, pp. 260–262 http://www.palestineremembered.com/Articles/A-Survey-of-Palestine/Story6703.html

[642] Mills, E. *Census of Palestine, 1931" (UK government, 1932), Vol I, pp. 61–65.*

[643] The Political History of Palestine under British Administration https://web.archive.org/web/20150908182126/http://unispal.un.org/UNISPAL.NSF/0/16B8C7CC809B7E5B8525694B0071F3BD, Memorandum to the United Nations Special Committee

[644] The Palestine Order in Council, 10 August 1922, article 11 https://unispal.un.org/UNISPAL.NSF/0/C7AAE196F41AA055052565F50054E656 : "The High Commissioner may, with the approval of a Secretary of State, by Proclamation divide Palestine into administrative divisions or districts in such manner and with such subdivisions as may be convenient for purposes of administration describing the boundaries thereof and assigning names thereto."

[645] Shamir, Ronen (2013). *Current Flow: The Electrification of Palestine*. Stanford: Stanford University Press.

[646] https://books.google.com/books?id=zAJZCKAwtPMC&pg=PR5&cad=0_1#PPA1,M1

[647] https://books.google.com/books?id=zAJZCKAwtPMC
[648] https://books.google.com/books?id=xp3MQavDxjIC
[649] https://books.google.com/books?id=h3EOJGiBBpQC&pg=PR5&cad=0_1#PPA12,M1
[650] https://books.google.com/books?id=h3EOJGiBBpQC
[651] https://books.google.com/books?id=qSpIAAAAMAAJ
[652] https://books.google.com/books?id=ZawVAQAACAAJ
[653] https://books.google.com/books?id=GVaG4WGKj9MC
[654] https://books.google.com/books?id=jC9MbKNh8GUC
[655] //doi.org/10.1017%2Fs0020818300025534
[656] https://books.google.com/books?id=XvT8CWv2DakC&pg=PA127
[657] https://books.google.com/books?id=XvT8CWv2DakC
[658] https://books.google.com/books?id=hpvnNILnO3kC
[659] https://books.google.com/books?id=Wn6gAAAAMAAJ
[660] https://books.google.com/books?id=h4K06WBjCrAC
[661] https://books.google.com/books?id=8Teb4dKHQcoC
[662] https://books.google.com/books?id=nrc3EUh9cyUC
[663] https://books.google.com/books?id=ekQOAAAAQAAJ
[664] https://www.jstor.org/stable/2142128
[665] http://babel.hathitrust.org/cgi/pt?id=mdp.39015004891787;view=1up;seq=1
[666] //tools.wmflabs.org/geohack/geohack.php?pagename=Jewish_Agency_for_Israel&params=31.777_N_35.216_E_
[667] " Board of Governors http://www.jewishagency.org/content/43391". *Jewish Agency for Israel*. Retrieved June 17, 2018.
[668]
[669] http://www.jewishagency.org
[670] //en.wikipedia.org/w/index.php?title=Jewish_Agency_for_Israel&action=edit
[671] //en.wikipedia.org/w/index.php?title=Template:Aliyah&action=edit
[672] http://www.jewishagency.org/experience-israel/program/283 (Accessed 2013-12-8)
[673] http://www.onwardisrael.com/
[674] http://www.onwardisrael.com/ (Accessed 2013-12-8)
[675] https://israeltechallenge.com/
[676] http://jewishagency.org/israel-in-your-community (Accessed 2013-12-8)
[677] http://www.hillel.org/jewish/hillel-israel/jewish-agency-israel-fellows (Accessed 2013-12-8)
[678] (Accessed 29 August 2013)
[679] http://www.jafi.org/NR/rdonlyres/5E7223DA-91C8-4FD0-9E12-ED1E87ABD175/0/YouthAliyahVillages_ProgramProposal_708.pdf (Accessed 2013-12-8)
[680] "New Jewish Agency program for high school graduates launches today" http://ejewishphilanthropy.com/new-jewish-agency-program-for-high-school-graduates-launches-today/, EJewish Philanthropy (Accessed 2013-12-8)
[681] https//web.archive.org
[682] http://www.amigour.com/
[683] http://jewishagency.org/aliyah/program/455 (Accessed 2013-12-8)
[684] http://jewishagency.org/aliyah (Accessed 2013-12-8)
[685] http://jewishagency.org/aliyah/program/456 (Accessed 2013-12-8)
[686] http://jewishagency.org/aliyah/program/302 (Accessed 2013-12-8)
[687] http://jewishagency.org/aliyah/program/300 (Accessed 2013-12-8)
[688] http://www.jafi.org/NR/rdonlyres/8DF7FC52-2B91-49DA-941C-CE9FDB5FC277/0/TAKA_ProgramBrief_708.pdf (Accessed 2013-12-8)
[689] http://jafi.org/JewishAgency/English/About/Updates/Personal+Stories/Archive/2009/dec21.htm (Accessed 2013-12-8)
[690] The Jewish Agency for Israel Social Activism Unit, "Our Work With Minorities," pamphlet distributed at Board of Governors meetings October 2015.
[691] League of Nations, *Mandate for Palestine and Memorandum by the British Government Relating to Its Application to Transjordan, Approved by the Council of the League of Nations on September 16th, 1922.* Published in Geneva, Switzerland on September 2, 1926. Document #

C.P.M 466 [C.529.M.314.1922.VI] [C.667.M.396.1922.VI]. Page 2, Article 4. Copy available upon request from the League of Nations Archives in Geneva.

[692] Walter Laqueur, *A History of Zionism*, p. 153

[693] https://www.gutenberg.org/files/25282/25282-h/25282-h.htm (Accessed 14.8.2013)

[694] Gordon, Hayim. *Israel Today* p157

[695] https://www.jewishvirtuallibrary.org/jsource/History/ww1.html (Accessed 12.8.2013)

[696] https://www.jewishvirtuallibrary.org/jsource/History/ww1.html (Accessed 12.8.2013)

[697] Plans Zionist Commission https://timesmachine.nytimes.com/timesmachine/1918/02/13/102668924.pdf, *The New York Times*, Feb. 13, 1918

[698] *History of Zionism, 1600–1918* by Nahum Sokolow

[699] *The Zionist Commission (Va'ad HaTzirim)* https://web.archive.org/web/20061002040541/http://www.jafi.org.il/education/jafi75/history/commission.html. Jewish Agency for Israel, archived on 02-10-2006

[700] *The Palestine Chronicle*: Palestine Through History: A Chronology (I) http://www.palestinechronicle.com/view_article_details.php?id=14037

[701] *Israel Pocket Library* (IPL), "Zionism". Keter, 1973. p. 76

[702] *Timeline 1921* https://web.archive.org/web/20040824193249/http://www.jafi.org.il/education/jafi75/timeline1b.html#1. Jewish Agency for Israel, archived on 24-08-2004

[703] *Palestine Jewry and the Arab Question, 1917–1925*, Neil Caplan, London and Totowa, New Jersey: F. Cass, 1978.

[704] Caplan, Neil. "Palestine Jewry and the Arab Question, 1917–1925." London and Totowa, NJ: F. Cass, 1978

[705] Central Office of the Zionist Organisation, "Resolutions of the 16th Zionist Congress, Zurich, July 28 – August 11th, 1929, with a Summary Report of the Proceedings," London, 1930. Viewed at http://www.bjpa.org/Publications/details.cfm?PublicationID=18204 on November 19, 2014.

[706] ART. 4. of the Mandate for Palestine http://avalon.law.yale.edu/20th_century/palmanda.asp#art4. *Emphasis added.* "The Zionist organization, so long as its organization and constitution are in the opinion of the Mandatory appropriate, shall be recognised as such agency. It shall take steps in consultation with His Britannic Majesty's Government **to secure the co-operation of all Jews who are willing to assist in the establishment of the Jewish national home.**

[707] Anglo-American Committee of Inquiry – Chapter III http://avalon.law.yale.edu/20th_century/angch03.asp, 1946

[708] Ganin, Zvi. *An Uneasy Relationship: American Jewish Leadership and Israel, 1948–1957* p. 20.

[709] Tessler Mark, *A History of the Israeli-Palestinian Conflict*, p. 194

[710]

[711] *Israel Pocket Library*, Keter 1973, p. 142.

[712] "Israel Pocket Library", Keter 1973, pp. 104, 165, 175, 249.

[713] *Israel Pocket Library*, Keter 1973, p. 213.

[714] *Israel Pocket Library*, Keter 1973, p. 168.

[715] https://www.jewishvirtuallibrary.org/jsource/zionism/zionman.html (Accessed 12 August 2013)

[716] https://www.knesset.gov.il/vip/bengurion/eng/BenGurion Bioframe eng.html (Accessed 12 August 2013)

[717] *Israel Pocket Library*, Keter 1973, pp. 107–08.

[718] *Israel Pocket Library*, Keter 1973, p. 142.

[719] *Timeline 1947* https://web.archive.org/web/20040824193321/http://www.jafi.org.il/education/jafi75/timeline3h.html#1. The Jewish Agency for Israel

[720] Friedman, Saul S. *A History of the Middle East*. 2004, p. 249

[721] *Jerusalem The new city comes of age: Architecture in the British Mandate Period* (21) (Accessed 8 August 2013)

[722] "Help Me Get Home, Brother," *Jerusalem Post* (22) (Accessed 8 August 2013)

[723] Naor, Mordechai. *Zionism: The First 120 Years* (Hebrew). Zionist Library. 2002. p. 34.

[724] Halamish, Aviva. *The Exodus Affair: Holocaust Survivors and the Struggle for Palestine*. Syracuse University Press. 1998

[725] Rotbard, Sharon. *Wall and Tower – The Mold of Israeli Adrikalut*. In: *Territories*, KW Institute for Contemporary Art, Berlin, 2003, p. 162.
[726] https://www.jewishvirtuallibrary.org/jsource/judaica/ejud_0002_0008_0_08075.html (Accessed 6 September 2014)
[727] http://www.jweekly.com/article/full/19954/youth-aliyah-marks-70-years-of-rescuing-children-at-risk/ (Accessed 8 August 2013)
[728] https://www.jewishvirtuallibrary.org/jsource/Immigration/youth aliyah.html (Accessed 8 August 2013)
[729] Hacohen, Dr. Dvora, *Children of the Times: Youth Aliyah 1933–1938* (Hebrew), Published by Yad Ben Zvi, Yad Vashem, and Ben Gurion University, 2012
[730] http://veterans.haifa.ac.il/index.php?option=com_content&view=article&id=190&Itemid=26 (accessed January 16, 2014)
[731] http://www.palyam.org/English/Hahapala/mainpage (Accessed 12 August 2013)
[732] http://www.palyam.org/English/HaMossad/mainpage (Accessed 12 August 2013)
[733] https://www.jewishvirtuallibrary.org/jsource/History/resist.html (Accessed 8 August 2013)
[734] Clarke, Thurston, *By Blood and Fire*, Putnam, 1981, Ch. 6.
[735] Sager, Samuel. "Israel's Provisional State Council and Government." *Middle Eastern Studies* Vol 14 No 1 (Jan 1978) pp. 91–101.
[736] "Zionists Proclaim New State of Israel, Truman Recognizes it and Hopes for Peace", *New York Times*, 15 May 1948
[737] HaCohen, Dvora. *Immigrants in Turmoil: Mass Immigration to Israel and its Repercussions in the 1950s and After*, Syracuse University Press, 2003. p. 99
[738] http://www.jafi.org.il/Jewish Agency/English/About/History (Accessed 12 August 2013)
[739] https://www.jewishvirtuallibrary.org/jsource/talking/jew refugees.html (Accessed 8 August 2013)
[740] London, Yaron: *Du-Siach Biographi* (Hebrew), Ma'ariv, Tel Aviv 1993
[741] https://www.jewishvirtuallibrary.org/jsource/Zionism/wzo.html (Accessed 12 August 2013)
[742] http://www.israellawresourcecenter.org/israellaws/fulltext/jewishagencystatuslaw.html (Accessed 12 August 2013)
[743] See the full text of the law at http://www.israellawresourcecenter.org/israellaws/fulltext/jewishagencystatuslaw.htm.
[744] http://www.jafi.org.il/JewishAgency/English/About/History/#t8 (Accessed 20 January 2014)
[745] http://www.jewishagency.org/Jewish Agency/English/About/History (Accessed 12 August 2013)
[746] http://www.wzo.org.il/index.php?dir=site&page=article&op=item&cs=3212&langpage=eng&category=3096 (Accessed 8 August 2013)
[747] Israel Pocket Library, Keter 1973, p. 144.
[748] "US Completes Operation Moses", Doyle McManus, The Courier (LA Times) March 24, 1985
[749] Brinkley, Joel (May 26, 1991). "Ethiopian Jews and Israelis Exult as Airlift Is completed". *The New York Times*
[750] http://www.jafi.org.il/Jewish Agency/English/About/Press+Room/Aliyah+Statistics (Accessed 12 August 2013)
[751] Khanin, Vladimir. "Aliyah From the Former Soviet Union: Contribution to the National Security Balance." 2010 p.6.
[752] http://p2g.jewishagency.org/ (Accessed 12 August 2013)
[753] http://www.masaisrael.org/
[754] http://www.jpost.com/Jewish-World/Jewish-News/Jewish-Agency-to-change-focus (Accessed 29 August 2013)
[755] http://www.jpost.com/Jewish-World/Jewish-News/Jewish-Agency-approves-new-mission (Accessed 12 August 2013)
[756] http://ejewishphilanthropy.com/the-new-jewish-agency-approach-peoplehood-for-survival (Accessed 12 August 2013)
[757] Israel Pocket Library "Zionism". p. 104. Bianchini: killed in an attack on a train on the Syrian border. Eder: "returned to London". Kisch: "nine difficult years". Arlosoroff: assassinated.
[758] https://www.knesset.gov.il/mk/eng/mk_eng.asp?mk_individual_id_t=545

[759] Natan Sharansky Elected Chairman of the Executive http://www.jafi.org/JewishAgency/English/About/Press+Room/Press+Releases/2009/jun26.htm Press Release
[760] *Israel Pocket Library* (IPL), "Zionism". Keter, 1973. p. 142
[761] http://birthrightisrael.com
[762] http://www.myisraelsummer.com/
[763] http://www.tenprogram.org/
[764] http://p2g.jewishagency.org/
[765] http://connectlv.com
[766] http://makomisrael.org/
[767] http://www.jpppi.org.il/
[768] http://www.zionistarchives.org.il/en/Pages/Default.aspx
[769] http://www.masaisrael.org
[770] //en.wikipedia.org/w/index.php?title=Template:Aliyah&action=edit
[771] Israeli government site on the Fifth Aliyah http://www.moia.gov.il/Moia_en/AboutIsrael/aliya5.htm
[772] Yoav Gelber, "The Historical Role of Central European Immigration to Israel," *Leo Baeck Institute Year Book* 38 (1993), p. 327.
[773] Yoav Gelber, "The Historical Role of Central European Immigration to Israel," *Leo Baeck Institute Year Book* 38 (1993), p. 326 n. 6.
[774] http://epa.oszk.hu/01500/01536/00013/pdf/UJ_1984_1985_075-115.pdf footnote on page 90
[775] Macartney 1956, pp. 439–42.
[776] Macartney 1956, p. 441, n. 3.
[777] Jelínek 1971, p. 255.
[778] Miller 1975, p. 33.
[779] Miller 1975, p. 34.
[780] Miller 1975, p. 38.
[781] Miller 1975, p. 45.
[782] Kolanović 2006, p. 473.
[783] Weinberg 1994, pp. 199–202.
[784] DiNardo 1996, p. 713.
[785] Chinvanno 1992, p. 13.
[786] Flood 1970, p. 989.
[787] China's Declaration of War Against Japan, Germany and Italy http://www.jvl.leverage.it/chinas-declaration-of-war-against-japan-germany-and-italy-december-1941 at the Jewish Virtual Library.
[788] Boog et al. 2001.
[789] //doi.org/10.2307%2F2943163
[790] https://books.google.com/books?id=e9znk7vMS-0C
[791] //doi.org/10.2307%2F2944662
[792] //doi.org/10.1017%2Fs0008938900015363
[793] //doi.org/10.1080%2F14690760600963248
[794] https://www.youtube.com/watch?v=k0ZPS2fhDNM
[795] Hughes, M. (2009) The Banality of Brutality: British Armed Forces and the Repression of the Arab Revolt in Palestine, 1936–39 https://web.archive.org/web/20160221163210/http://v-scheiner.brunel.ac.uk/bitstream/2438/7251/4/The%20banality%20of%20brutality.pdf, *English Historical Review* Vol. CXXIV No. 507, pp. 314–354.
[796] Black, 2006, p. 128.
[797] Swedenberg, 2003, p. 220.
[798] Kimmerling & Migdal, 2003, p. 103.
[799] Millman, 1998, p. 22.
[800] Bowyer Bell, 1996, p. 44.
[801] Morris, 1999, p. 145.
[802] Levenberg, 1993, pp. 74–76.
[803] Morris, 1999, pp. 159–160.
[804] Kelly 2017, p. 2.
[805]

[806] Norris, 2008, pp. 25, 45.
[807] Kelly 2017, p. 5.
[808] Khalidi, 2002, pp. 21, 35.
[809] Patai, 1971, p. 59.
[810] Morris, 1999, p. 160.
[811] Morris, 1999, p. 159.
[812] Gilbert 1998, p. 80.
[813] Matthews, 2006, p. 237.
[814] Krämer, 2008, p. 263.
[815] Krämer, 2008, pp. 262–263.
[816] Krämer, 2008, pp. 239–240.
[817] 'Nablus Bandits Seen as Izz ed Din's followers' http//www.jpress.org.il, *Palestine Post*, Friday, 17 April 1936.
[818] 'Yesterday in Palestine' http//www.jpress.org.il, *Palestine Post*, Thursday, 30 April 1936.
[819] Highwaymen's Second Victim Dead' http//www.jpress.org.il, *Palestine Post*, Tuesday, 21 April 1936.
[820] 'Turk Killed by Hold-up Men' http//www.jpress.org.il, *Palestine Post*, Thursday, 16 April 1936
[821] Gilbert, 1998, p. 80.
[822] Bar-On, 2004, p. 23.
[823] 'Little Change in Situation' http//www.jpress.org.il, *Palestine Post*, Thursday, 23 April 1936.
[824] Yazbak, M. (2000). From Poverty to Revolt: Economic Factors in the Outbreak of the 1936 Rebellion in Palestine. *Middle Eastern Studies*, 36(3), pp. 93–113.
[825] Krämer, 2008, p. 273.
[826] Krämer, 2008, p. 239.
[827] Krämer, 2008, p. 254.
[828] Khalidi, 2001, p. 25.
[829] Krämer, 2008, pp. 256–259.
[830] Krämer, 2008, pp. 2656–266.
[831] Krämer, 2008, p. 264.
[832] Commins, 2004, p. 113.
[833] Thomas, 2007, p. 295.
[834] Morewood, 2004, pp. 86–96.
[835] Tripp, 2002, pp. 71–75.
[836] Morris, 1999, p. 129.
[837] Horne, 2003, p. 208.
[838] Peel Commission Report Cmd. 5479, 1937, p. 96.
[839] Krämer, 2008, p. 272.
[840] Peel Commission Report Cmd. 5479, 1937, p. 97.
[841] 'The Funeral http//www.jpress.org.il, *Palestine Post*, Tuesday, 21 April 1936.
[842] 'Funeral of Nine Jewish Dead' http//www.jpress.org.il, *Palestine Post*, Tuesday, 21 April 1936.
[843] Kayyālī, 1978, p. 193.
[844] Peel Commission Report Cmd. 5479, 1937, p. 100.
[845] C. Townshend, The defence of Palestine: insurrection and public security, 1936–1939. *The English Historical Review*, Vol. 103 (1988) 917-949.
[846] Peel Commission Report Cmd. 5479, 1937, pp. 100–102.
[847] Krämer, 2008, p. 274.
[848] Krämer, 2008, p. 291.
[849] Kayyālī, 1978, p. 196.
[850] Segev, 2000, p. 423.
[851] Horne, 2003, p. 213.
[852] Kayyālī, 1978, p. 197.
[853] Krämer, 2008, p. 278.
[854] Horne, 2003, pp. 210, 218.
[855] Peel Commission Report Cmd. 5479, 1937, pp. 99, 104–105.
[856] Segev, 2000, p. 401.
[857] Wasserstein, 2004, pp. 106–114

[858] Morris, 1999, pp. 138–144.
[859] Statement by His Majesty's Government in the United Kingdom, Presented by the Secretary of State for the Colonies to Parliament by Command of His Majesty November 1938.
[860] Cohen, 2009, p. 125.
[861] Anglo-American Committee of Inquiry – Appendix IV http://avalon.law.yale.edu/20th_century/angap04.asp Palestine: Historical Background
[862]
[863] Horne, 2003, p. 239.
[864] Segev, 2000, p. 417.
[865] Cabinet Papers, 30 July 1946, CAB 128/6 http://www.nationalarchives.gov.uk/catalogue/displaycataloguedetails.asp?CATLN=6&CATID=776442&SearchInit=4&SearchType=6&CATREF=CAB+128/6.
[866] See also WO 32/9618 Emergency Regulations 1936. Palestine Martial Law (Defence) Order in Council 1936.
[867] Segev, 2000, p. 399.
[868] Palestine, 1938 Allegations Against British Troops, CAB 24/282 http://www.nationalarchives.gov.uk/catalogue/displaycataloguedetails.asp?CATLN=6&CATID=775828&SearchInit=4&SearchType=6&CATREF=CAB+24/282#summary, p. 4.
[869] Segev, 2000, p. 42.
[870] Segev, 2000, p. 425.
[871] Horne, 2003, pp. 235–236.
[872] Thomas, 2008, p. 254.
[873] Benjamin-Grob-Fitzgibbon,'Britain's small wars: the challenge to Empire,' in Randall D. Law, *The Routledge History of Terrorism*, https://books.google.com/books?id=3ZCsBwAAQBAJ&pg=PA181 Routledge, 2015, pp. 177–189, 181.
[874] Bruce Hoffman, *Anonymous Soldiers: The Struggle for Israel, 1917–1947*, Knopf, 2015, p. 73.
[875] Segev, 2000, p. 428.
[876] Morris, 1999, p. 150.
[877] Segev, 2000, p. 416.
[878] Omissi, 1990, pp. 74–76.
[879] Rotter, 2008, p. 51.
[880] Gilmour, Ian and Andrew. "Terrorism Review." *Journal of Palestine Studies*, Volume 17, Issue 2, 1988, p. 131.
[881] Omissi, 1990, p. 158.
[882] Ben-Ami, 2005, p. 11.
[883] Harris, 1998, p. 30.
[884] Thomas, 2008, p. 246.
[885] Black and Morris, 1991, p. 16.
[886] Harouvi, 1999, p. 33.
[887] Stewart, 2002, pp. 7–10.
[888] Krämer, 2008, p. 293.
[889] Ferrier and Bamberg, 1994, p. 165.
[890] Thomas, 2008, pp. 244–246.
[891] Harouvi, 1999, pp. 32–34.
[892] Frilling, 2005, p. 279.
[893] Adelman, 2008, p. 154.
[894] Frilling, 2005, p. 28.
[895] Kaniuk, 2001, p. 101.
[896] Laffin, 1979, p. 80.
[897] Kimmerling, 1989, p. 38.
[898] Swedenburg, 2003, p. 220.
[899] Morris, 1999, p. 132.
[900] Cleveland, 2000, p. 255.
[901] Sacharov, 2004, p. 23.
[902] Adelman, 2008, p. 156.
[903] Krämer, 2008, p. 292.

904 Segev, 2000, p. 427.
905 Segev, 2000, p. 426.
906 Morris, 1999, p. 149.
907 Johnson, 2010, p. 807.
908 Krämer, 2008, p. 242.
909 Bajohr, 2002, p. 122.
910 Segev, 1991, pp. 22, 29.
911 Nicosia, 2008, p. 99.
912 Ben-Ami, 2005, p. 14.
913 Segev, 2000, pp. 386–387.
914 Morris, 1999, p. 147.
915 Morris, 1999, p. 133.
916 Arielli, 2010, pp. 109–132.
917 Gettleman and Schaar, 2003, p. 181.
918 Morris, 1999, p. 153.
919 Morris, 1999, pp. 153–154.
920 Horne, 2003, pp. 237–238.
921 Cohen, 2009, p. 198.
922 Cohen, 2009, p. 167.
923 Swedenberg, 2003, p. 125.
924 Sayigh, p. 669.
925 Swedenberg, 2003, p. 139.
926 Horne, 2003 p. 228.
927
928 Horne, 2003, pp. 224, 238.
929 'Situation in Brief: Official Reports' http//www.jpress.org.il, *Palestine Post*, Monday, 3 October 1938.
930 Horne, 2003, pp. 224–226, 239.
931 Swedenburg, 2003, p. 88.
932 LeVine, 2012, p. 149.
933 LeVine, 2012, p. 153.
934 Swedenburg, 2003, p. 87.
935 Swedenburg, 2003, p. 30.
936 Frisch, 2008, p. 23.
937 Cohen, 2009, p. 152.
938 LeVine, 2012, p. 154.
939 Horne, 2003, pp. 224, 226, 228, 239–240.
940 Swedenburg, 2003, p. 121.
941 Fry, MacKereth & Rabinovich, 1985, p. 172.
942 Horne, 2003, pp. 225, 228–230.
943 Horne, 2003, pp. 225, 235, 238.
944 *Jewish Spectator*, 1937, Volume 3, p. 8.
945 Parsons, ed. Schayegh, 2015, p. 395.
946 Krämer, 2008, p. 295.
947 Segev, 2000, p. 388.
948 Shapira, 1999, p. 250.
949 Segev, 2000, p. 449.
950 Segev, 2000, p. 439; 459.
951 Segev, 2000, pp. 450–451.
952 Morris, 1999, p. 121.
953 Nashif, 2008, p. 24.
954 Segev, 2000, pp. 436–441.
955 Segev, 2000, p. 443.
956 Segev, 2000, p. 442.
957 Swedenburg, 2003, pp. xxii, 13–15.
958 Segev, 2000, p. 433.

[959] https://web.archive.org/web/20120127035141/http://unispal.un.org/UNISPAL.NSF/0/88A6BF6F1BD82405852574CD006C457F

[960] https://unispal.un.org/UNISPAL.NSF/0/EB5B88C94ABA2AE585256D0B00555536

[961] http://www.zionism-israel.com/dic/Arab_Revolt.htm

[962] http://www.historytoday.com/charles-townshed/first-intifada-rebellion-palestine-1936-39

[963] Debate and vote on 23 May 1939; Hansard. Downloaded 10 December 2011 http://hansard.millbanksystems.com/commons/1939/may/23/palestine#S5CV0347P0_19390523_HOC_302

[964] Occasionally also known as the **MacDonald White Paper** (e.g. Caplan, 2015, p.117) after Malcolm MacDonald, the British Colonial Secretary who presided over its creation.

[965] Hansard, HC Deb 22 May 1939 vol 347 cc1937-2056 http://hansard.millbanksystems.com/commons/1939/may/22/palestine-1 and HC Deb 23 May 1939 vol 347 cc2129-97 http://hansard.millbanksystems.com/commons/1939/may/23/palestine; "Resolved, That this House approves the policy of His Majesty's Government relating to Palestine as set out in Command Paper No. 6019."

[966] by 268 votes to 179.

[967] Hansard, HC Deb 18 February 1947 vol 433 cc985-94 http://hansard.millbanksystems.com/commons/1947/feb/18/palestine-conference-government-policy: "We have, therefore, reached the conclusion that the only course now open to us is to submit the problem to the judgment of the United Nations ...
Mr. Janner Pending the remitting of this question to the United Nations, are we to understand that the Mandate stands. and that we shall deal with the situation of immigration and land restrictions on the basis of the terms of the Mandate, and that the White Paper of 1939 will be abolished? ...
Mr. Bevin No, Sir. We have not found a substitute yet for that White Paper, and up to the moment, whether it is right or wrong, the House is committed to it. That is the legal position. We did, by arrangement and agreement, extend the period of immigration which would have terminated in December, 1945. Whether there will be any further change, my right hon. Friend the Colonial Secretary, who, of course, is responsible for the administration of the policy, will be considering later."

[968] Caplan 2015, p. 114: "As it had been made clear from the start, the absence of agreement at the St James's Conference meant that the British were left, after March 17th 1939, to finalise and to enforce their new Palestine policy unilaterally. A White Paper, first drafted in late March, was not published until early May, thus affording Arabs and Jews further opportunities to continue their efforts at influencing the final terms of the proposed British policy."

[969] *A Survey of Palestine - prepared in December 1945 and January 1946 for the information of the Anglo-American Committee of Inquiry.* Reprinted 1991 by The Institute of Palestine Studies, Washington. Volumes One: . p.54.

[970] Khalaf 1991, p. 66: "The White Paper was never to be implemented, initially because of Cabinet opposition and then because of preoccupation with the war effort. However, 1939 and the first two years of the war saw a quiet, low key dialogue between the government and Palestinians who were ready to accept the White Paper. But the government's intention was to keep the Arabs placated, encourage the moderates, and continue to talk but promise very little, particularly on the constitutional provisions contained in the White Paper."

[971] King Husain and the Kingdom of Hejaz, Randall Baker, Oleander Press, 1979 https://books.google.com/books?id=n706ShSYt-sC&pg=PA221&dq=&ei=VaM7SeidLKPCM-2J5L8D&client=#PPA54,M1, , page 54

[972] Statement by His Majesty's Government in the United Kingdom, Presented by the Secretary of State for the Colonies to Parliament by Command of His Majesty November, 1938.

[973] Anglo-American Committee of Inquiry - Appendix IV http://avalon.law.yale.edu/20th_century/angap04.asp Palestine: Historical Background

[974] Hilberg, Raul, *The Destruction of the European Jews*, (1961) New Viewpoints, New York 1973 p.716

[975] *A Survey of Palestine - prepared in December 1945 and January 1946 for the information of the Anglo-American Committee of Inquiry.* Reprinted 1991 by The Institute of Palestine Studies, Washington. Volume one. p.54.

[976] House of Commons Debates, Volume 347 column 1984 http://hansard.millbanksystems.com/commons/1939/may/22/palestine-1#column_1984
[977] Hilberg, Raul, *The Destruction of the European Jews,* (1961) New Viewpoints, New York 1973 p.717 n.7
[978] Khalif 1991, p. 283.
[979] Morris, Benny, "The Tangled Truth", *The New Republic,* May '07, '08 https://newrepublic.com/article/books/the-tangled-truth
[980] Cohen 2014, p. 367: "In July 1940, Colonel S.F. Newcombe. an Arabist who had served with T.E. Lawrence during World War One, made a Middle East tour sponsored by the British Council. His mission was to improve Arab public opinion about Britain. The government agreed that he should stop over in Baghdad to try unofficially, with the help of Nuri al-Said, to obtain the Mufti's endorsement of the While Paper. On his way Newcombe was briefed in Jerusalem by the High Commissioner. He was instructed to meet only with Nuri al-Said and with two prominent Palestinians. Jamal Husayni the Multi's cousin, and Musa Alami, but not with the Mufti himself. Newcombe stayed in Baghdad for 2 weeks."
[981] Buheiry, Marwan R. (1989) *The Formation and Perception of the Modern Arab World. Studies by Marwan R Buheiry.* Edited by Lawrence I. Conrad. Darwin Press, Princeton. p.177
[982] Kayyali, Abdul-Wahhab Said (no date) *Palestine. A Modern History* Croom Helm. p.221.
[983] Zev Golan: *Free Jerusalem: Heroes, Heroines and Rogues who Created the State of Israel*
[984] Penkower, Monty Noam: Decision on Palestine Deferred: America, Britain and Wartime Diplomacy, 1939-1945
[985] The Brigade by Howard Blum, p.5. In 1946, a Yiddish song published in the *Yishuv* by Jacob Jacobs ad Isadore Lilian included these lyrics: *Tserisn muz vern dos vayse papir, In der fremd viln mir mer nit zayn. Habeyt mishomyim ureey, Groyser got kuk arop un ze, Vi men yogt undz, vi men plot undz, Got, her oys undzer geshrey.* "They don't care about Jewish anguish, The White Paper must be torn, We don't want to be away from our home anymore." (As described in "Palestine in Song," YIVO News No. 204, Winter 2008, p.15
[986] Survey. p.56.
[987] Anglo-American Committee of Inquiry - Appendix IV copy at http://avalon.law.yale.edu/20th_century/angap04.asp
[988] Ofer, Dalia, *Escaping the Holocaust* (1990) pages 218ff, 290.
[989] Ofer, Dalia, *Escaping the Holocaust* (1990) page 219
[990] Ofer, Dalia, *Escaping the Holocaust* (1990) page 290
[991] Ovendale, R, "The Palestine Policy of the British Labour Government 1945-1946", *International Affairs,* Vol. 55, pages 409-431.
[992] Hilberg, Raul *The Destruction of the European Jews,* (1971) New Viewpoints ed. New York, 1973 p.729
[993] *Report of the Anglo-American Committee* (1946) Cmd.6808 pp.65-66
[994] *New York Times* 11/08/46 pg 35, UK Foreign Office document 371/52651
[995] https://books.google.com/books?id=9pRvIDxE5jAC&pg=PA283
[996] https://books.google.com/books?id=MZhhCQAAQBAJ&pg=PA117
[997] https://books.google.com/books?id=DLPpAgAAQBAJ&pg=PA368
[998] http://hansard.millbanksystems.com/lords/1939/may/23/palestine
[999] https://web.archive.org/web/20160421094344/http://www.yale.edu/lawweb/avalon/mideast/brwh1939.htm
[1000] https://www.jewishvirtuallibrary.org/jsource/History/peel1.html
[1001] //en.wikipedia.org/w/index.php?title=Template:The_Holocaust_sidebar&action=edit
[1002] "Unter der NS-Herrschaft ermordete Juden nach Land." / "Jews by country murdered under Nazi rule." https://www.bpb.de/fsd/centropa/ermordete_juden_nach_land.php Bundeszentrale für politische Bildung / Federal Agency for Civic Education (Germany), April 29th 2018
[1003] Gilbert, Martin. *Kristallnacht: Prelude to Destruction.* Harper Collins, 2006, p. 30.
[1004] Trudy Alexy, *The Mezuzah in the Madonna's Foot,* Simon & Schuster, 1993. p. 74.
[1005] "Jewish Soldiers in the Allied Armies" http://www.yadvashem.org/holocaust/about/combat-resistance/jewish-soldiers. Yad Vashem.
[1006] *The Hebrew Impact on Western Civilization,* Dagobert D. Runes

[1007] Noah Klieger (11 September 2006), Army was Polish, soldiers were Jews. http://www.ynetnews.com/articles/0,7340,L-3302233,00.html Exhibition set to open next week salutes anonymous Jewish fighters who fought with Poland's armies.

[1008] Yad Vashem, The Holocaust: Combat and Resistance. Jewish Soldiers in the Allied Armies. http://www.yadvashem.org/yv/en/holocaust/about/07/jewish_soldiers.asp

[1009] http://www1.yadvashem.org/yv/en/holocaust/about/index.asp?WT.mc_id=wiki

[1010] Gray 2015, p. 8.

[1011] Niewyk & Nicosia 2000, p. 52.

[1012] The broadest definition would include the Jews, Porajmos (genocide of the Roma); Aktion T4 (Germany's eugenics program); the persecution of homosexuals; Slavs; the German mistreatment of Soviet prisoners of war; the murder of political opponents; and the persecution of Jehovah's Witnesses.<ref name="FOOTNOTENiewykNicosia200047–51">Niewyk & Nicosia 2000, pp. 47–51.

[1013] Niewyk & Nicosia 2000, p. 45.

[1014] Hebrew: הַשּׁוֹאָה, *HaShoah*, "the catastrophe"

[1015] United States Holocaust Memorial Museum: "Six million Jews died in the Holocaust. ... According to the *American Jewish Yearbook*, the Jewish population of Europe was about 9.5 million in 1933. ... By 1945, most European Jews—two out of every three—had been killed."<ref> "Jewish Population of Europe in 1945" https://www.ushmm.org/wlc/en/article.php?ModuleId=10005687, *Holocaust Encyclopedia*, United States Holocaust Memorial Museum. Retrieved 9 October 2017.

[1016] Landau 2016, p. 3.

[1017] For one example of historians who include the Roma and disabled in their definition of "the Holocaust", see .

[1018] Donald Niewyk and Francis Nicosia (*The Columbia Guide to the Holocaust*, 2000): "The Holocaust is commonly defined as the mass murder of more than 5,000,000 Jews by the Germans during World War II. Not everyone finds this a fully satisfactory definition. The Nazis also killed millions of people belonging to other groups: Gypsies, the physically and mentally handicapped, Soviet prisoners of war, Polish and Soviet citizens, political prisoners, religious dissenters, and homosexuals. Can it be said that any of these groups were treated in the same way as the Jews and for the same reasons and hence deserve to be included in the history of the Holocaust? A positive answer to this question would require a broader definition of the Holocaust and acknowledging as many as 17,000,000 victims. A more expansive view might also induce us to push the start of the Holocaust back from 1941 to 1939 (if we include the handicapped) or even to 1933 (if we assume that the whole thing was premeditated)."<ref name="FOOTNOTENiewykNicosia200043">Niewyk & Nicosia 2000, p. 43.

[1019] "Encyclopedia of Camps and Ghettos, 1933–1945" https://www.ushmm.org/research/publications/encyclopedia-camps-ghettos, United States Holocaust Memorial Museum.

[1020] //en.wikipedia.org/w/index.php?title=Template:The_Holocaust_sidebar&action=edit

[1021] Dawidowicz 1986, p. xxxvii.

[1022] *Oxford Dictionaries* (2017): "from Old French holocauste, via late Latin from Greek holokauston, from holos 'whole' + kaustos 'burnt' (from kaiein 'burn')".<ref name=OED>

[1023] The definition continued: "Figuratively, a great slaughter or sacrifice of life, as by fire or other accident, or in battle".<ref name=Whitney>

[1024] Fischel 2010, p. 115.

[1025] Meltzer, Julian (23 May 1943). "Palestine Zionists Find Outlook Dark" https://www.nytimes.com/1943/05/23/archives/palestine-zionists-find-outlook-dark-they-see-little-hope-now-for.html, *The New York Times*.

[1026] Lustigman & Lustigman 1994, p. 111.

[1027] Black 2016, p. 201.

[1028] The Hebrew word *churban* is used by many Orthodox Jews to refer to the Holocaust.<ref name="FOOTNOTEFischel199846">Fischel 1998, p. 46.

[1029] Berenbaum 2006, p. xix.

[1030]

[1031] Gilbert 1985, p. 18.

[1032] Hayes 2015, p. xiii–xiv.

1033. Hilberg 2003, p. 1133.
1034. Marrus 2015, p. vii.
1035. Snyder 2010, p. 412.
1036. Berenbaum 2006, p. 103.
1037. Arad 1987, pp. 154–159.
1038. Fischel 1998, p. 167.
1039. United States Holocaust Memorial Museum 1996, p. 7.
1040. Crowe 2008, p. 447.
1041. Evans 2015, p. 385.
1042. Gellately & Stoltzfus 2001, p. 216.
1043. Eberhard Jäckel (1986): "The National Socialist killing of the Jews was unique in that never before had a state with the authority of its responsible leader decided and announced that a specific human group, including its aged, its women, its children and infants, would be killed as quickly as possible, and then carried through this resolution using every possible means of state power."<ref>, citing Jäckel, Eberhard (12 September 1986). "Die elende Praxis der Untersteller. Das Einmalige der nationalsozialistischen Verbrechen lässt sich nicht leugnen". *Die Zeit*.
1044. Bauer 2002, p. 49.
1045. Friedländer 2007, pp. 51–52.
1046. Bloxham 2009, p. 130.
1047. , citing
1048. Friedländer 2007, p. xxi.
1049. Gilbert 2001, p. 289.
1050. Niewyk & Nicosia 2000, pp. 229–230.
1051. Fisher 2001, pp. 410–414.
1052. Hanauske-Abel 1996, p. 1453.
1053. Müller-Hill 1999, p. 338.
1054. Friedländer 2007, p. 505.
1055. Müller-Hill 1999, pp. 340–342.
1056. The full extent of Mengele's work is unknown because records he sent to Otmar von Verschuer are assumed to have been destroyed.<ref name="FOOTNOTEMüller-Hill1999348">Müller-Hill 1999, p. 348.
1057. Lifton 2000, p. 358.
1058. Harran 2000, p. 384.
1059. Jones 2006, p. 148.
1060. Bergen 2016, pp. 14–17.
1061. Fischer 2002, pp. 47–49.
1062. Evans 1989, pp. 69–70.
1063. Friedlander 1994, pp. 495–496.
1064. Evans 2004, pp. 377–378.
1065. The party was originally formed after World War I as the *Deutsche Arbeiterpartei* or DAP (German Workers' Party) and changed its name in April 1920 to the *Nationalsozialistische Deutsche Arbeiterpartei* or NDAP (National Socialist German Workers' Party, or Nazi Party).<ref name="FOOTNOTESnyder197663">Snyder 1976, p. 63.
1066. Peukert 1994, p. 289.
1067. Snyder 1976, p. 63.
1068. Fischer 2002, p. 47.
1069. Yahil 1990, pp. 41–43.
1070. Kershaw 1998, p. 60.
1071. Bergen 2016, pp. 52–54.
1072. Bergen 2016, p. 56.
1073. Fritzsche 2009, pp. 38–39.
1074. Noakes & Pridham 1983, p. 499.
1075. Wachsmann 2015, pp. 28–30.
1076. Wachsmann 2015, pp. 32–38.
1077. Gilbert 1985, p. 32.
1078. Longerich 2012, p. 155.

[1079] Wachsmann 2015, pp. 84–86.
[1080] Peukert 1987, p. 214.
[1081] Friedländer 1997, p. 33.
[1082] Evans 2004, pp. 434–435.
[1083] Burleigh & Wippermann 1991, p. 78.
[1084] Friedländer 1997, pp. 32–33.
[1085] Friedländer 1997, p. 29.
[1086] Friedländer 1997, p. 134.
[1087] Evans 2005, pp. 158–159, 169.
[1088] Hanauske-Abel 1996, p. 1459.
[1089] Lifton 2000, p. 21.
[1090] Hanauske-Abel 1996, p. 1457.
[1091] Proctor 1988, pp. 101–103.
[1092] Tolischus, Otto D. (21 December 1933). "400,000 Germans to be sterilized" https://query.nytimes.com/gst/abstract.html?res=9C0CE6DC1531E333A25752C2A9649D946294D6CF, *The New York Times*.
[1093] Hanauske-Abel 1996, p. 1458.
[1094] Proctor 1988, pp. 106–108.
[1095] Burleigh & Wippermann 1991, pp. 142–149.
[1096] Kershaw 2000, pp. 252–261.
[1097] Bloxham 2009, p. 171.
[1098] Lifton 2000, p. 142.
[1099] Niewyk & Nicosia 2000, p. 48.
[1100] Strous 2007.
[1101] Lifton 2000, pp. 90–95.
[1102] Hanauske-Abel 1996, pp. 1458–1459.
[1103] Arad, Gutman & Margaliot 2014, p. 78.
[1104]
[1105] Gilbert 2001, p. 285.
[1106] Fischel 1998, p. 20.
[1107] Friedländer 1997, p. 1.
[1108] Friedländer 1997, p. 12.
[1109] Evans 2005, p. 16.
[1110] Cesarani 2016, pp. 147–150.
[1111] Cesarani 2016, pp. 153–155.
[1112] Evans 2005, pp. 659–661.
[1113] Niewyk & Nicosia 2000, p. 200.
[1114] Cesarani 2016, pp. 181.
[1115] The French had planned to try Grynszpan for murder, but the German invasion in 1940 interrupted the proceedings. Grynszpan was handed over to the Germans and his fate is unknown.<ref name="FOOTNOTEFriedländer1997301–302">Friedländer 1997, pp. 301–302.
[1116] Cesarani 2016, p. 183.
[1117] Evans 2005, pp. 581–582.
[1118] Evans 2005, pp. 583–584.
[1119] Bloxham 2009, p. 168.
[1120] Cesarani 2016, pp. 184–185.
[1121] Cesarani 2016, p. 184, 187.
[1122] Evans 2005, p. 591.
[1123] Cesarani 2016, p. 200.
[1124] Evans 2005, pp. 595–596.
[1125] Ben-Rafael, Glöckner & Sternberg 2011, pp. 25–26.
[1126] Friedländer 1997, pp. 224–225.
[1127] Friedländer 1997, pp. 62–63.
[1128] Browning 2001.
[1129] Cesarani 2016, p. 382.
[1130] Fischel 2010, p. 264.

1131 Chase 1999, p. xiii.
1132 Naimark 2001, p. 73.
1133 Browning 2004, pp. 81–85.
1134 Browning 2004, p. 88.
1135 Hildebrand 1984, p. 70.
1136 Crowe 2008, pp. 158–159.
1137 Bergen 2016, pp. 136–137.
1138 Black 2016, p. 29.
1139 Browning 2004, pp. 111–113.
1140 Black 2016, pp. 29–30.
1141 Bergen 2016, p. 146.
1142 Black 2016, p. 31.
1143 After the invasion of Poland, the Germans planned to set up a Jewish reservation in southeast Poland around the transit camp in Nisko, but the "Nisko Plan" failed, in part because it was opposed by Hans Frank, the new Governor-General of the General Government territory.<ref name="FOOTNOTEBlack201631">Black 2016, p. 31.
1144 Cesarani 2016, p. 264.
1145 Cesarani 2004, pp. 77–79.
1146 Cesarani 2004, pp. 259–260, 280, 288.
1147 Cesarani 2016, pp. 261–263.
1148 Cesarani 2004, p. 266.
1149 Longerich 2010, pp. 156-159.
1150 Edelheit 1994, p. 52.
1151 Cesarani 2016, p. 262.
1152 Bergen 2016, p. 169.
1153 McKale 2002, p. 162.
1154 McKale 2002, p. 161.
1155 McKale 2002, pp. 162–163.
1156 McKale 2002, p. 164.
1157 McKale 2002, pp. 165–166.
1158 Zuccotti 1993, p. 52.
1159 McKale 2002, pp. 192–193.
1160 Black 2016, p. 134.
1161 Black 2016, pp. 137–139.
1162 Bauer 2001, pp. 256–257.
1163 Black 2016, p. 140.
1164 Black 2016, p. 141.
1165 Black 2016, pp. 131–133.
1166 Friling, Ioanid & Ionesc 2004, pp. 125–126.
1167 Black 2016, pp. 134–135.
1168 Rozett & Spector 2013, p. 161.
1169 Black 2016, pp. 136–137.
1170 Black 2016, p. 135.
1171 ;.
1172 Rozett & Spector 2013, p. 274.
1173 Rees 2005.
1174 Baumel 2001, p. 135.
1175 Fischel 2010, pp. 50–52.
1176 Wachsmann 2015, pp. 287–288.
1177 Longerich 2010, pp. 314–320.
1178 Black 2016, p. 76.
1179 Black 2016, p. 104.
1180 Rozett 1990, p. 1222.
1181 Wachsmann 2015, p. 347.
1182 Harran 2000, p. 461.
1183 Wachsmann 2015, pp. 125–127, 623.

[1184] Yahil 1990, p. 134.
[1185] Wachsmann 2015, p. 119.
[1186] Browning 1986, pp. 345–348.
[1187] Hilberg 2003, pp. 216–7.
[1188] Yahil 1990, p. 166.
[1189] Yahil 1990, p. 169.
[1190] Longerich 2010, p. 161.
[1191] Longerich 2010, p. 167.
[1192] Yahil 1990, p. 165.
[1193] Bergen 2016, p. 148.
[1194] Longerich 2010, p. 166.
[1195] Trunk 1996, pp. 1–6.
[1196] Hilberg 1993, p. 106.
[1197] Hilberg 1993, p. 170.
[1198] Bergen 2016, pp. 150–152.
[1199] Hilberg 1980, p. 104.
[1200] Bergen 2016, pp. 150–151.
[1201] Berenbaum 2006, pp. 81–83.
[1202] Hilberg 1993, p. 109.
[1203] Berenbaum 2006, pp. 79–81.
[1204] Hilberg 2003, p. 1111.
[1205] Snyder 2010, p. 285.
[1206] Berenbaum 2006, p. 114.
[1207] Dwork & van Pelt 2003, p. 239.
[1208] Dwork & van Pelt 2003, pp. 242–243.
[1209] Yahil 1990, p. 378.
[1210] Yahil 1990, pp. 378–380.
[1211] Yahil 1990, pp. 382–385.
[1212] Yahil 1990, pp. 474–478.
[1213] Berenbaum 2006, pp. 175–177.
[1214] Yahil 1990, pp. 163, 258.
[1215] Bergen 2016, p. 195.
[1216] Dwork & van Pelt 2003, pp. 267–269.
[1217] Some scholars say they were orchestrated by the Organization of Ukrainian Nationalists,<ref name="FOOTNOTEAmar201599">Amar 2015, p. 99.
[1218] Longerich 2010, p. 194.
[1219] Longerich 2010, p. 196.
[1220] The exact details of who killed whom and when are murky and have led to much debate in Poland.<ref name="FOOTNOTELongerich2010196">Longerich 2010, p. 196.
[1221] Evans 1989, p. 59.
[1222] Burleigh 2001, pp. 512, 526–527.
[1223] Matthäus 2004, p. 268.
[1224] Matthäus 2004, p. 275.
[1225] Matthäus 2004, pp. 275–276.
[1226] Matthäus 2004, pp. 270–271.
[1227] Browning 2004, pp. 224–225.
[1228] Hilberg 2003, p. 291.
[1229] Fischel 2010, p. 67.
[1230] Bergen 2016, pp. 199–200.
[1231] Evans 2008, pp. 226–227.
[1232] The Germans continued to use the ravine for mass killings throughout the war, and the total killed there could have been as high as 100,000.<ref name="FOOTNOTEBergen2016199">Bergen 2016, p. 199.
[1233] McKale 2002, p. 203.
[1234] Fritz 2011, pp. 102–104.
[1235] Bergen 2016, p. 200.

1236. Fischel 1998, pp. 42–43.
1237. Bergen 2016, p. 160.
1238. Gerlach 2016, p. 74.
1239. Cesarani 2016, p. 513.
1240. Arad 2009, p. 138.
1241. Gerlach 1998, p. 759.
1242. "Wannsee Conference and the 'Final Solution'" https://www.ushmm.org/wlc/en/article.php?ModuleId=10005477, *Holocaust Encyclopedia*, United States Holocaust Memorial Museum. Retrieved 8 October 2017.
1243. Gerlach 1998, p. 764.
1244. Gerlach 2016, p. 80.
1245. Goebbels noted: "Regarding the Jewish question, the Fuhrer is determined to clear the table. He warned the Jews that if they were to cause another world war, it would lead to their own destruction. Those were not empty words. Now the world war has come. The destruction of the Jews must be its necessary consequence. We cannot be sentimental about it. It is not for us to feel sympathy for the Jews. We should have sympathy rather with our own German people. If the German people have to sacrifice 160,000 victims in yet another campaign in the east, then those responsible for this bloody conflict will have to pay for it with their lives."<ref name="FOOTNOTEGerlach1998122">Gerlach 1998, p. 122.
1246.
1247. Roseman 2003.
1248. Longerich 2010, p. 306.
1249. Gerlach 2016, pp. 84–85.
1250. Longerich 2010, p. 307.
1251. Wannsee-Protokoll: "Diese Aktionen sind jedoch lediglich als Ausweichmöglichkeiten anzusprechen, doch werden hier bereits jene praktischen Erfahrungen gesammelt, die im Hinblick auf die kommende Endlösung der Judenfrage von wichtiger Bedeutung sind."<ref>
1252. Longerich 2010, p. 308.
1253. Jones 2006, p. 153.
1254. Gerlach 2016, p. 99.
1255. Gerlach 2016, p. 99, note 165.
1256. Montague 2012, pp. 14–16, 64–65.
1257. Black 2016, pp. 70–71.
1258. Fischel 2010, pp. 57–58.
1259. Fischel 1998, p. 81.
1260. Longerich 2010, p. 282.
1261. Fischel 1998, pp. 81–85.
1262. Black 2016, pp. 69–70.
1263. Crowe 2008, p. 243.
1264. Arad 1987, p. 98.
1265. Fischel 1998, pp. 81–82.
1266. Bauer 1994, p. 156.
1267. Dwork & van Pelt 2003, pp. 287–288.
1268. Piper 1998b, p. 173.
1269. Montague 2012, pp. 76–85.
1270. Piper 1998b, p. 162.
1271. Piper 1998b, p. 157.
1272. Piper 1998b, p. 170.
1273. Piper 1998b, p. 163.
1274. Piper 1998b, pp. 170–171.
1275. Piper 1998b, p. 172.
1276. Piper 1998b, pp. 163–164.
1277. Fischel 1998, pp. 83–84.
1278. Fischel 1998, pp. 84–85.
1279. Longerich 2010, pp. 330.
1280. Arad 1987, pp. 170–171.

[1281] Longerich 2010, pp. 340–341.
[1282] Hilberg 2003, pp. 1112–1128.
[1283] Henri Michel argues that resistance consisted not only of physical opposition but of any activity that gave the Jews dignity and humanity in humiliating and inhumane conditions. Bauer defines resistance as actions that in any way opposed the German directives, laws, or conduct.<ref name="FOOTNOTEBauer1997117">Bauer 1997, p. 117.
[1284] Hilberg 1996, pp. 126–137.
[1285] Snyder 2010, p. 283.
[1286] Longerich 2010, p. 341.
[1287] Black 2016, pp. 82–85.
[1288] Black 2016, pp. 83–84.
[1289] According to Polish and Jewish accounts, hundreds or thousands of Germans were killed,<ref name="FOOTNOTEGutman1994243">Gutman 1994, p. 243.
[1290] Bergen 2016, p. 269.
[1291] About 7000 died during the fighting and around 7000 sent to Treblinka.<ref name="FOOTNOTECesarani2016616">Cesarani 2016, p. 616.
[1292] Cesarani 2016, p. 636.
[1293] Arad 1987, pp. 286, 293–294.
[1294] Fischel 1998, p. 99.
[1295] Fischel 1998, pp. 95–96.
[1296] Fischel 1998, p. 98.
[1297] Arad 1987, p. 337.
[1298] Arad 1987, p. 341.
[1299] Rees 2005, pp. 256–257.
[1300] Kennedy 2007, p. 780.
[1301] Fischel 1998, pp. 100–101.
[1302] Cesarani 2016, p. 648.
[1303] Tec 2001, p. 546.
[1304] Snyder 2010, p. 302.
[1305] French Jews were active in the French Resistance.<ref name="FOOTNOTEBergen2016273">Bergen 2016, p. 273.
[1306] Zuccotti 1993, p. 274.
[1307] Zuccotti 1993, p. 275.
[1308] Laqueur 2001, pp. 351.
[1309] Fleming 2014a, p. 35.
[1310] Spector 1990, p. 158.
[1311] Wachsmann 2015, pp. 532–533.
[1312] Crowe 2008, p. 354.
[1313] Niewyk & Nicosia 2000, p. 183.
[1314] Some reports have Karski infiltrating Bełżec disguised as a guard,<ref name="FOOTNOTELukas2012159">Lukas 2012, p. 159.
[1315] Fleming 2014b, p. 144.
[1316] Fleming 2014a, p. 35–36.
[1317] Zimmerman 2015, p. 181.
[1318] Zimmerman 2015, pp. 181–182.
[1319] Zimmerman 2015, p. 182.
[1320] Novick 2000, p. 23.
[1321] Novick 2000, pp. 27–28.
[1322] Dwork & van Pelt 2003, pp. 256–257.
[1323] Longerich 2010, pp. 330–339, 375–379.
[1324] The only exception was Lodz Ghetto, which was not liquidated until mid-1944.<ref name="FOOTNOTEDworkvan Pelt2003256-257">Dwork & van Pelt 2003, pp. 256-257.
[1325] Longerich 2010, pp. 360–373, 386–389, 390–396.
[1326] Longerich 2010, pp. 345–353.

[1327] One exception was the area around Bialystok, where over 100,000 Jews were deported to extermination camps, most to Treblinka but a few to Auschwitz.<ref name="FOOTNOTELongerich2010352–353">Longerich 2010, pp. 352–353.
[1328] Yahil 1990, pp. 376–378.
[1329] Kwiet 2004, pp. 61, 69–71, 76–77.
[1330] Kwiet 2004, pp. 77–78.
[1331] Fischer 1998, pp. 536–538.
[1332] Black 2016, pp. 108.
[1333] Evans 2002, p. 95.
[1334] Braham 2011, p. 45.
[1335] Braham (2011) and the USHMM give the figure as 440,000, Longerich (2010) as 437,000.<ref name="FOOTNOTEBraham201145">Braham 2011, p. 45.
[1336] Longerich 2010, p. 408.
[1337] "Deportation of Hungarian Jews" https://www.ushmm.org/learn/timeline-of-events/1942-1945/deportation-of-hungarian-jews, United States Holocaust Memorial Museum. Retrieved 5 October 2017.
[1338] Fischel 2010, pp. 31, 76–77.
[1339] Löb 2009, p. 69, citing "A Monstrous 'Offer'", *The Times*, 20 July 1944.
[1340] Black 2016, pp. 107–109.
[1341] Weinberg 2001, p. 219.
[1342] Polonsky 2001, p. 488.
[1343] Longerich 2012, p. 695.
[1344] Bergen 2016, pp. 290–292.
[1345] Longerich 2010, pp. 410–412.
[1346] Friedländer 2007, pp. 648–650.
[1347] Niewyk & Nicosia 2000, p. 165.
[1348] Longerich 2010, p. 411.
[1349] Hitchcock 2008, p. 283.
[1350] Hitchcock 2008, p. 297.
[1351] Hitchcock 2008, p. 340.
[1352] Gilbert 1985, p. 798.
[1353] Wachsmann 2015, p. 577.
[1354] Gilbert 1985, pp. 808–809.
[1355] Gilbert 1985, p. 810.
[1356] Cesarani 2016, p. 762.
[1357] Hitchcock 2008, p. 289.
[1358] Bell 2017, p. 100.
[1359] Dimbleby, Richard (15 April 1945). "Liberation of Belsen" http://news.bbc.co.uk/1/hi/in_depth/4445811.stm. BBC News. Retrieved September 2012. "Richard Dimbleby reporting from Bergen-Belsen", part 1/2 https://www.youtube.com/watch?v=2hLYavpMSFs, part 2/2 https://www.youtube.com/watch?v=opn15-59L1I, BBC News, courtesy of YouTube.
[1360] Hayes 2015, p. xii.
[1361] Berenbaum 2006, p. 125.
[1362] Berenbaum 2006, p. 126.
[1363] Milton 2001, p. 350.
[1364] Lichtblau 2013.
[1365] Michman 2012, p. 197.
[1366] Bauer & Rozett 1990, p. 1797.
[1367] Dawidowicz 1986, p. 403.
[1368] Bauer & Rozett 1990, p. 1799.
[1369] Gilbert 2001, p. 245.
[1370] "Children during the Holocaust" https://www.ushmm.org/wlc/en/article.php?ModuleId=10005142, *Holocaust Encyclopedia*, United States Holocaust Memorial Museum. Retrieved 8 October 2017.
[1371] Gilbert 2001, p. 291.
[1372] Fischel 1998, p. 87.

[1373] Bauer & Rozett 1990, pp. 1799–1802.
[1374] Niewyk & Nicosia 2000, pp. 221–222.
[1375] Rhodes 2002, p. 274.
[1376] Black 2016, pp. 29–31.
[1377] Piper 1998a, p. 62.
[1378] Niewyk & Nicosia 2000, p. 47.
[1379] Bauer 1998, p. 453.
[1380] Longerich 2010, p. 50.
[1381] Evans 2015, pp. 378–379.
[1382] Hancock 2004, pp. 383–96.
[1383] Huttenbach 2016, p. 31.
[1384] Longerich 2010, pp. 418–421.
[1385] Bloxham 2009, p. 119.
[1386] Bloxham 2009, p. 114.
[1387] Bauer 1998, pp. 445–446.
[1388] Evans 2008, pp. 174–175.
[1389] Snyder 1976, p. 359.
[1390] Longerich 2012, pp. 450–452.
[1391] Fritz 2011, p. 23.
[1392] Mazower 2008, p. 204-205.
[1393] Mazower 2008, pp. 208–211.
[1394] Rummel 1992, p. 18.
[1395] Gellately 2001, p. 153.
[1396] Berghahn 1999, pp. 32–33.
[1397] Bloxham 2009, p. 112.
[1398] Gellately 2001, p. 154.
[1399] Evans 2008, pp. 173-174.
[1400] Piotrowski 1998, p. 295.
[1401] Szafranski 1960, p. 43.
[1402] Szafranski 1960, p. 49.
[1403] Half the death toll were Jews.<ref name="FOOTNOTEKochanski2012532">Kochanski 2012, p. 532.
[1404] Kochanski 2012, p. 532.
[1405] Lukas 2012, pp. 25–27.
[1406] Bergen 2016, pp. 186–192.
[1407] Fritz 2011, pp. 333–334.
[1408] Bergen 2016, pp. 214–215.
[1409] Snyder 2010, pp. 250–251.
[1410] Wachsmann 2015, p. 125.
[1411] Fischel 2010, p. 184.
[1412] Harran 2000, p. 108.
[1413] Steakley 1974.
[1414] Longerich 2012, p. 237.
[1415] Giles 1992, pp. 45–7.
[1416] Milton 2001, pp. 346–349.
[1417] Garbe 2001, p. 251.
[1418] Lusane 2003, pp. 97–8.
[1419] Buchheim 1968, p. 381.
[1420] Buchheim 1968, pp. 386–7.
[1421] Browning 1998, p. 57.
[1422] Marrus 1987, pp. 89–91.
[1423] Evans 1989, p. 71.
[1424] Marrus 1987, p. 92.
[1425] Marrus 1987, p. 93.
[1426] Biddiss 2001, p. 643.
[1427] Snyder 1976, p. 255.

[1428] Two of the indictments were dropped before the end of the trial. Robert Ley committed suicide in prison, and Gustav Krupp was judged unfit for trial.<ref name="FOOTNOTEBiddiss2001643">Biddiss 2001, p. 643.
[1429] Biddiss 2001, pp. 643–644.
[1430] Conot 1984, p. 495.
[1431] Biddiss 2001, p. 646.
[1432] Crowe 2008, p. 412.
[1433] Crowe 2008, pp. 430-433.
[1434] Zweig 2001, pp. 531–532.
[1435] Bazyler 2005, p. 173.
[1436] Samuels 2009, p. 259.
[1437] Novick 2000, p. 9.
[1438] Stone 2010, pp. 211–212.
[1439] https://books.google.com/books?id=j6VCNno2DVMC&pg=PA15
[1440] //doi.org/10.1017%2Fs0008938900011158
[1441] //www.jstor.org/stable/4546081
[1442] https://books.google.com/books?id=4LQWAQAAIAAJ&q=Lublin-Lipowa+reservation
[1443] https://books.google.ca/books?id=nIUFQGN2y4EC&q=Volksgemeinschaft+idea
[1444] //doi.org/10.1093%2Fhgs%2Fdcu014
[1445] //doi.org/10.2307%2F1431896
[1446] //www.jstor.org/stable/1431896
[1447] http://www.inshr-ew.ro/ro/files/Raport%20Final/Final_Report.pdf
[1448] //doi.org/10.1086%2F235167
[1449] //doi.org/10.1177%2F002200949202700103
[1450] //www.jstor.org/stable/260778
[1451] //doi.org/10.1136%2Fbmj.313.7070.1453
[1452] //www.jstor.org/stable/29733730
[1453] //doi.org/10.1177%2F000271628045000109
[1454] //www.jstor.org/stable/1042561
[1455] https://www.nytimes.com/2013/03/03/sunday-review/the-holocaust-just-got-more-shocking.html
[1456] //doi.org/10.7152%2Facro.v5i1.1378
[1457] //www.jstor.org/stable/23332180
[1458] http://www.hawaii.edu/powerkills/NAZIS.CHAP1.HTM
[1459] http://www.fordham.edu/halsall/pwh/steakley-nazis.html
[1460] //doi.org/10.1093%2Fhgs%2F5.2.157
[1461] http://www.annals-general-psychiatry.com/content/6/1/8
[1462] //doi.org/10.1186%2F1744-859X-6-8
[1463] //www.ncbi.nlm.nih.gov/pmc/articles/PMC1828151
[1464] //www.ncbi.nlm.nih.gov/pubmed/17326822
[1465] http://www.science.co.il/jewish/Holocaust-museums.php
[1466] https://www.h-net.org/~holoweb/
[1467] http://eisenhower.archives.gov/research/online_documents/holocaust.html
[1468] http://www.wienerlibrary.co.uk/
[1469] http://www.ushmm.org/educators/teaching-about-the-holocaust/common-questions
[1470] http://avalon.law.yale.edu/imt/wannsee.asp
[1471] https://www.youtube.com/watch?v=-w5GLwBwN-0&index=94&list=PL06DE3D4B636D50C9
[1472] https://www.youtube.com/watch?v=n_4WoQfz-N0&index=95&list=PL06DE3D4B636D50C9
[1473] https://www.youtube.com/watch?v=knCKIny5NPU&index=96&list=PL06DE3D4B636D50C9
[1474] https://www.youtube.com/watch?v=QtRDt6uAB0U
[1475] http://www.holocaustchronicle.org/index.html
[1476] http://www.holocaustresearchproject.org/
[1477] https://books.google.com/books?id=5kkEAAAAMBAJ&pg=PA81

[1478] //en.wikipedia.org/w/index.php?title=Template:Aliyah&action=edit
[1479] Ofer and Weiner (1996) "Dead-End Journey - The Tragic Story of the Kladovo-Sabac Group", pp 29-34.
[1480] //en.wikipedia.org/wiki/Aliyah_Bet#endnote_Named_after_Enzo_Sereni
[1481] //en.wikipedia.org/wiki/Aliyah_Bet#endnote_Named_after_Ord_Charles_Wingate
[1482] *Unalga* 1912, Cutters, Craft & U.S. Coast Guard-Manned Army & Navy Vessels, U.S. Coast Guard Historian's Office
[1483] http://www.israelvets.com/
[1484] https://www.jewishvirtuallibrary.org/jsource/Immigration/Aliyah_during_war.html
[1485] http://www.ushmm.org/wlc/article.php?lang=en&ModuleId=10005776
[1486] http://www.paulsilverstone.com/immigration/Primary/index.html
[1487] http://www1.yadvashem.org/yv/en/education/educational_materials/shapira_survivors.asp?WT.mc_id=wiki
[1488] Charters, David A. *The British army and Jewish insurgency in Palestine, 1945-47*. Springer, 1989, p. X
[1489] Hoffman, Bruce. *Inside Terrorism*. Colombia University Press, New York, pp. 49-51
[1490] Benjamin Grob-Fitzgibbon: *Imperial Endgame: Britain's Dirty Wars and the End of Empire*, p. 100
[1491] Cesarani, David. "One hundred years of Zionism in England." European Judaism: A Journal for the New Europe 25, no. 1 (1992): 40-47.
[1492] Benjamin Grob-Fitzgibbon. *Imperial Endgame: Britain's Dirty Wars and the End of Empire*. p.12. https//books.google.com
[1493] French, D. *The British Way in Counter-Insurgency, 1945–1967*. Oxford University Press, 2011: p48.
[1494] *Jewish Chronicle* 8/8/47 and 22/8/47, both p. 1. See also Bagon, Paul (2003). "The Impact of the Jewish Underground upon Anglo Jewry: 1945–1947". St Antony's College, University of Oxford M-Phil thesis (mainly the conclusion) http://users.ox.ac.uk/~metheses/Bagon.html Retrieved on 2008-10-25.
[1495] http://www1.yadvashem.org/odot_pdf/Microsoft%20Word%20-%206312.pdf
[1496] Fraser, T. G., "A crisis of leadership: Weizmann and the Zionist reactions to the Peel Commission's proposals, 1937–38", *Journal of Contemporary History* (Oct. 1988) Vol. 23, No. 4, p. 657.
[1497] Text of Cmnd 5893 on the United Nations website, downloaded October 2011 https://unispal.un.org/UNISPAL.NSF/0/4941922311B4E3C585256D17004BD2E2
[1498] Shabtai Teveth, 1985, *Ben-Gurion and the Palestinian Arabs*, p. 200
[1499] Donald L. Niewyk and Francis R. Nicosia: *The Columbia Guide to the Holocaust* (2013)
[1500] ["Irgun Zeva'i Le'umi—"The National Military Organization"] (Etzel, I.Z.L.)". Jewishvirtuallibrary.org. Retrieved 2013-08-12.
[1501] Colin Shindler (1995). *The land beyond promise: Israel, Likud and the Zionist dream*. I.B. Tauris.
[1502] "Stern Gang" The Oxford Companion to World War II. Ed. I. C. B. Dear and M. R. D. Foot. Oxford University Press, 2001.
[1503] *The Mauritian shekel: the story of the Jewish detainees in Mauritius, 1940–1945* by Geneviève Pitot, Donna Edouard, Helen Topor, 1998
[1504] Ovendale, R, "The Palestine Policy of the British Labour Government 1945–1946", International Affairs, Vol. 55, pages 409–431.
[1505] *One Palestine Complete: Jews and Arabs under the British Mandate* by Tom Segev p. 482, Abacus 2001
[1506] Louis, William Roger: *Ends of British Imperialism: The Scramble for Empire, Suez, and Decolonization*, p. 419-422
[1507] Weiler, Peter: *Ernest Bevin*, p. 170
[1508] *Flight and Rescue: Brichah*, written by Yehuda Bauer, published by Random House; New York, 1970
[1509] Marrus, Michael Robert; Aristide R. Zolberg (2002). *The Unwanted: European Refugees from the First World War Through the Cold War*. Temple University Press. p. 336.

[1510] Aleksiun, Natalia. "Beriḥah" http://www.yivoencyclopedia.org/printarticle.aspx?id=219. YIVO. "Suggested reading: Arieh J. Kochavi, "Britain and the Jewish Exodus...," Polin 7 (1992): pp. 161–175"
[1511] Jeffery, Keith: *The Secret History of MI6* (2010)
[1512] *The Times* 3/8/1946 p. 4.
[1513] Ted Gottfried, *Displaced persons: the liberation and abuse of Holocaust survivors*, p. 25
[1514] A. Kochavi, *Post-Holocaust Politics: Britain, the United States and Jewish Refugees 1945–1948* (Chapel-Hill: University of North Carolina Press 2001), pp 45–56. Y. Bauer, *Out of the Ashes: The Impact of American Jews on Post-Holocaust European Jewry* (Oxford: Pergamon 1989) chapter 2.
[1515] Inquiry Report yale.edu http://www.yale.edu/lawweb/avalon/anglo/angch02.htm chapter II paragraph 12
[1516] Y. Bauer, *Out of the Ashes: The Impact of American Jews on Post-Holocaust European Jewry* (Oxford: Pergamon 1989) p. 86, Z. V. Hadari, *Second Exodus: The Full Story of Jewish Illegal Immigration to Palestine 1945–1948* (London: Valentine Mitchell 1991) p. 18. In reality less wanted to go to Palestine but DP's responded to Zionist requests that they write Palestine.
[1517] Benson, Michael T. *Harry S. Truman and the Founding of Israel*
[1518] New York Times 11/08/46, PG 35. UK Foreign Office document 371/52651
[1519] Bell, Bowyer J.: *Terror out of Zion* (1976),
[1520] Colin Shindler, *The Land Beyond Promise: Israel, Likud and the Zionist Dream*, https://books.google.com/books?id=7VBoVr089GwC&pg=PA32 I.B.Tauris, 2002 pp.31–32.
[1521] *Foundations of Civil and Political Rights in Israel and the Occupied Territories*, Yvonne Schmidt, GRIN 2001, p. 312
[1522] M. Begin, *The Revolt: Memoirs of the Commander of the National Military Organization* (Tel-Aviv: 1984 in Hebrew), chapter 8.
[1523] *The Palestine triangle: the struggle for the Holy Land, 1935–48* by Nicholas Bethell p. 267 1979
[1524] *One Palestine Complete: Jews and Arabs under the British Mandate* by Tom Segev pp. 479–480, Abacus 2001
[1525] *One Palestine Complete: Jews and Arabs under the British Mandate* by Tom Segev p. 480, Abacus 2001
[1526] Horne, Edward (1982). A Job Well Done (Being a History of The Palestine Police Force 1920–1948). The Anchor Press. pp. 272, 288, 289
[1527] Brendon, Piers: *The Decline And Fall of the British Empire. 1781–1997*
[1528] Andrew, Christopher (2009) The Defence of the Realm. The Authorized History of MI5. Allen Lane. Page 922. Note 39. Pages 355–359.
[1529] Eshel, Aryeh (1990). The Breaking of the Gallows. Zmora Beitan. pp. 307–312.
[1530]
[1531] *Jewish Chronicle* 8/8/47 and 22/8/47, both p. 1. For a discussion of antisemitism in Britain see T. Kushner, *The Persistence of Prejudice: Antisemitism in British society during the Second World War* (Manchester: Manchester University Press 1989). See workersliberty.org http://www.workersliberty.org/node/6351 for an eye witness account of the Manchester riot.
[1532] See *Post-Holocaust Politics Britain, the United States, and Jewish Refugees, 1945–1948* by Arieh J. Kochavi, North Carolina 2001.
[1533] see the House of Commons Debates (Hansard), Volume 427 Column 1682 23/10/46
[1534] Weiler, Peter: *Ernest Bevin*, p. 172
[1535] Jewish Telegraphic Agency 7/1/48, *The Times* 19/12/46 p. 3 and 27/2/47 p. 5.
[1536] Kochavi, Arieh J.: *Post-Holocaust Politics: Britain, the United States, and Jewish Refugees, 1945–1948*
[1537] UN resolution 181 section 1A. yale.edu http://www.yale.edu/lawweb/avalon/un/res181.htm
[1538] *The Times* 22/1/48 p. 4, Trygve Lie, *In the Cause of Peace, Seven Years with the United Nations* (New York: MacMillan 1954) p. 163
[1539] Gelber 2006, p. 137
[1540] Lapierre, Dominique and Collins, Larry: *O! Jerusalem!* (page 192)
[1541] Milstein et al. (1998), p. 87.
[1542] Gold (1998), p. 254.

[1543] Security Council Resolution 46 (1948) 17/4/48
[1544] Benny Morris, *1948*, p. 179
[1545] Security Council Resolution 50 (1948), clauses 2–4 in Index to resolutions of the Security Council : 1946–1991 (New York: United Nations 1992).
[1546] Tucker, Spencer C.: The Encyclopedia of the Arab-Israeli Conflict: A Political, Social, and Military History (2008)
[1547] Arieh Kochavi (1998). "The Struggle against Jewish Immigration to Palestine". Middle Eastern Studies 34: 146–167.
[1548] *The Times* January 5, 1949 "No Intention of Intervening"
[1549] *The Times* 20 January 1949 p. 4 "Urgent Need for Information"
[1550] *The Times* January 10, 1949 p. 3 "British Force Sent to Akaba"
[1551] *The Times* 10/1/1949 p. 4 "British Troops in Transjordan"
[1552] Cohen, Michael Joseph: *Fighting World War Three from the Middle East: Allied Contingency Plans, 1945–1954*, p. 114
[1553] *The Observer* 23/1/49
[1554] *The Times* 25/1/49 "Last detainees leaving Cyprus"
[1555] *The Times* 31/1/49 p. 4 "Israeli view of recognition"
[1556] Martin Gilbert – *Churchill and the Jews*
[1557] Yehuda Lapidot – *Besieged*
[1558]
[1559] http://www.palmach.org.il/show_item.asp?levelId-42858&itemId-8708&itemType=0
[1560] Horne, pp. 295–296
[1561] Silver, p. 64
[1562] Thurston Clarke, *By Blood and Fire* (1981)
[1563] Marton, Kati: *A Death in Jerusalem*
[1564] *Time, Un-British* (1948)
[1565] Segev, Tom (2001). *One Palestine, Complete; Jews and Arabs under the British Mandate*
[1566] 35 Zionist Leaders Detained as Bomb Kills 3 Constables http://timesmachine.nytimes.com/timesmachine/1947/08/06/104326626.html?pageNumber=1 NY Times, August 6, 1947
[1567] Terrorists Wreck Haifa Troop Train http://timesmachine.nytimes.com/timesmachine/1947/08/10/87799583.html?pageNumber=1 NY Times, August 10, 1947
[1568] Trial of Two Jews Begin http://timesmachine.nytimes.com/timesmachine/1947/11/18/104376392.html?pageNumber=21 NY Times, November 18, 1947
[1569] Haganah Kills 11 in Palestine Hunt for Arab Gunmen http://timesmachine.nytimes.com/timesmachine/1947/08/16/87806964.html?pageNumber=1 NY Times, August 16, 1947
[1570] *The Sunday Times*, Sept 24 1972, p. 8
[1571] Donald Neff, *Hamas: A pale image of the Jewish Irgun and Lehi Gangs*. Washington Report on Middle East Affairs.
[1572] Terrorists Strike in Palestine Again http://timesmachine.nytimes.com/timesmachine/1947/10/01/104341366.html?pageNumber=14 NY Times, September 30, 1947
[1573] Blast Set by Irgun to Speed Army Exit http://timesmachine.nytimes.com/timesmachine/1947/09/30/282546022.html?pageNumber=15 NY Times, September 30, 1947
[1574] Donald Neff, Hamas: A Pale Image of the Jewish Irgun And Lehi Gangs http://www.wrmea.com/archives/May-June_2006/0605014.html, Washington Report on Middle East Affairs, May/June 2006, p. 14-15.
[1575]
[1576] 35 Deaths in Day Set Palestine Peak http://timesmachine.nytimes.com/timesmachine/1947/12/12/87564627.html?pageNumber=1 NY Times, December 12, 1947
[1577] http://www.timripley.co.uk/terrorism/terrorism1.htm
[1578] Jews Carry Fight to Arabs: Palestine Adds 28 to Dead http://timesmachine.nytimes.com/timesmachine/1947/12/13/99279874.html?pageNumber=1 *New York Times*, December 13, 1947
[1579]
[1580] Arab Legion Force in Palestine Kills 14 Jews in Convoy http://timesmachine.nytimes.com/timesmachine/1947/12/15/104390132.html?pageNumber=1 NY Times, December 15, 1947

[1581] Phantom Vehicle Alerts Jerusalem: Day's Toll is 6 Dead http://timesmachine.nytimes.com/timesmachine/1947/12/17/104391601.html?pageNumber=21 NY TImes, December 17, 1947
[1582]
[1583] 6 Dead, 26 Injured in Haifa Fighting http://timesmachine.nytimes.com/timesmachine/1947/12/25/87567080.html?pageNumber=4 NY Times, December 25, 1947
[1584] Pope Brewer, Sam. IRGUN BOMB KILLS 11 ARABS, 2 BRITONS http://timesmachine.nytimes.com/timesmachine/1947/12/30/104398952.html?pageNumber=1. *The New York Times*. December 30, 1947.
[1585] *The Times* – 1 March 1948
[1586] *The Scotsman* – 7 April 1948
[1587] Morris, Benny: *1948: A History of the First Arab-Israeli War*, pgs 151-152
[1588]
[1589] https://www.telegraph.co.uk/news/obituaries/1444118/John-Bowyer-Bell.html "During the course of his research he discovered that the Irgun saw the Irish War of Independence as a role model, and he began to explore the history of the IRA as background. (He would later get to know IRA men who studied Menachem Begin's memoir *The Revolt* as a manual of guerrilla warfare.)"
[1590] https://undocs.org/A/RES/181(II)
[1591] William B. Quandt, Paul Jabber, Ann Mosely Lesch *The Politics of Palestinian Nationalism*, https://books.google.com/books?id=gwika-Y-ghwC&pg=PA7 University of California Press, 1973 p.7.
[1592] Part II. – Boundaries recommended in UNGA Res 181 https://books.google.com/books?id=hQaDrfuGw1YC&pg=PA78 Molinaro, Enrico *The Holy Places of Jerusalem in Middle East Peace Agreements* Page 78
[1593] *The Question of Palestine*: Brochure DPI/2517/Rev.1: Chapter 2, *The Plan of Partition and end of the British Mandate* https://www.un.org/Depts/dpi/palestine/ch2.pdf
[1594] Sami Hadawi, *Bitter Harvest: A Modern History of Palestine*, https://books.google.com/books?id=ghf_OBksgykC&pg=PA76 Olive Branch Press, (1989)1991 p.76.
[1595] The Palestine Mandate http://avalon.law.yale.edu/20th_century/palmanda.asp "the Mandatory should be responsible for putting into effect the [Balfour] declaration originally made on November 2nd, 1917"
[1596] Palestine Royal Commission report, 1937, 389–391 https://unispal.un.org/pdfs/Cmd5479.pdf
[1597] Mandated Landscape: British Imperial Rule in Palestine 1929-1948
[1598] William Roger Louis, Ends of British Imperialism: The Scramble for Empire, Suez, and Decolonization https://books.google.com/books/about/Ends_of_British_Imperialism.html?id=NQnpQNKeKKAC&redir_esc=y, 2006, p.391
[1599] Benny Morris, One state, two states: resolving the Israel/Palestine conflict, 2009, p. 66
[1600] Partner to Partition: The Jewish Agency's Partition Plan in the Mandate Era, Yosef Kats, Chapter 4, 1998 Edition, Routledge,
[1601] Letter from David Ben-Gurion to his son Amos, written 5 October 1937 http://www.palestineremembered.com/download/B-G%20LetterTranslation.pdf, Obtained from the Ben-Gurion Archives in Hebrew, and translated into English by the Institute of Palestine Studies, Beirut
[1602] Quote: "No Zionist can forgo the smallest portion of the Land Of Israel. [A] Jewish state in part [of Palestine] is not an end, but a beginning ..... Our possession is important not only for itself ... through this we increase our power, and every increase in power facilitates getting hold of the country in its entirety. Establishing a [small] state .... will serve as a very potent lever in our historical effort to redeem the whole country"
[1603] Jerome Slater, 'The Significance of Israeli Historical revisionism' in Russell A. Stone, Walter P. Zenner(eds.) *Critical Essays on Israeli Social Issues and Scholarship,* https://books.google.it/books?id=sLbGOXe5B6YC&pg=PA182 Vol.3 SUNY Press, 1994 pp.179-199 p.182.
[1604] Quote from a meeting of the Jewish Agency executive in June 1938: "[I am] satisfied with part of the country, but on the basis of the assumption that after we build up a strong force following the establishment of the state, we will abolish the partition of the country and we will expand to the whole Land of Israel." in

and
[1605] From a letter from Chaim Weizmann to Arthur Grenfell Wauchope, High Commissioner for Palestine, while the Peel Commission was convening in 1937: "We shall spread in the whole country in the course of time ..... this is only an arrangement for the next 25 to 30 years."
[1606] Palestine. Statement by His Majesty's Government in the United Kingdom. Presented by the Secretary of State for the Colonies to Parliament by Command of His Majesty. November, 1938. Cmd. 5893.
[1607] Hilberg, Raul, *The Destruction of the European Jews*, (1961) New Viewpoints, New York 1973 p.716
[1608] Anglo-American Committee of Inquiry - Appendix IV http://avalon.law.yale.edu/20th_century/angap04.asp Palestine: Historical Background
[1609] William roger louis, 1985, p.386
[1610] Morris, 2008, p.34
[1611] Gurock, Jeffrey S. *American Jewish History* American Jewish Historical Society, page 243
[1612] Morris, 2008, p.35
[1613] Nele Matz, 'Civilization and the Mandate System under the League of Nations,' in Armin Von Bogdandy, Rüdiger Wolfrum, Christiane E. Philipp (eds.) *Max Planck Yearbook of United Nations Law*, https://books.google.com/books?id=EHpHKjM5HnUC&pg=PA87 Martinus Nijhoff Publishers 2005 pp.47-96, p.87:'those mandated territories that had been classified as A mandates, with the exception of Palestine, werre finally granted full independence in addition to the already established structures for provisional self-governance,'
[1614] Baylis Thomas, *How Israel was Won: A Concise History of the Arab-Israeli Conflict*, https://books.google.com/books?id=6T_Ff6Ra57sC&pg=PA47 Lexington Books 1999 p.47.
[1615] David D. Newsom, *The Imperial Mantle: The United States, Decolonization, and the Third World*, https://books.google.com/books?id=vv559P5d7m8C&pg=PA77 Indiana University Press, p.77.
[1616] William Roger Louis, *Ends of British Imperialism: The Scramble for Empire, Suez, and Decolonization*, https://books.google.com/books?id=NQnpQNKeKKAC&pg=PA437 Palgrave/Macmillan 2006, pp.404,429-437.
[1617] Daniel Mandel, *H V Evatt and the Establishment of Israel: The Undercover Zionist*, https://books.google.com/books?id=ikGQAgAAQBAJ&pg=PA83 Routledge 2004 pp.73,81. The liaison officers with Aubrey Eban and David Horowitz.(p.83)
[1618] Daniel Mandel, *H V Evatt and the Establishment of Israel: The Undercover Zionist*, https://books.google.com/books?id=ikGQAgAAQBAJ&pg=PA83 Routledge 2004 p.88.
[1619] Morris, 2008, p. 43
[1620] Howard Sachar, *A History of the Jews in the Modern World*, https://books.google.com/books?id=TLxA9W7q74sC&pg=PT671 Random House, 2007 p.671.
[1621] https//web.archive.org
[1622] UN Partition Plan http://www.merip.org/palestine-israel_primer/un-partition-plan-pal-isr.html at Merip.
[1623] Colbert C. Held, John Thomas Cummings, https://books.google.com/books?id=vcxVDgAAQBAJ&pg=PT287 *Middle East Patterns: Places, People, and Politics*, 6th ed. Hachette UK, 2013 p.255: It called for three entities: a Jewish state with 56 percent of Mandate Palestine; an Arab state, 43 percent.'
[1624] Abdel Monem Said Aly, Shai Feldman, Khalil Shikaki, *Arabs and Israelis: Conflict and Peacemaking in the Middle East*, https://books.google.com/books?id=sgk8BQAAQBAJ&pg=PT71 PalgraveMacmillan 2013 p.50: 'a year before the UN adoption of the Resolution, the Arab population of Palestine comprised 68 percent of the total and owned about 85 percent of the land; the Jewish population comprised about one-third of the total and owned about 7 percent of the land.
[1625] Palestine Division Wins in Committee 25 to 13, 17 Abstain http://timesmachine.nytimes.com/timesmachine/1947/11/26/104381572.html?pageNumber=1, NY Times, 26 November 1947
[1626] Yearbook of The United Nations 1947–48 https://unispal.un.org/unispal.nsf/9a798adbf322aff38525617b006d88d7/5ce900d2de34aadf852562bd007002d2?OpenDocument

[1627] Baylis Thomas, *How Israel was Won: A Concise History of the Arab-Israeli Conflict,* https://books.google.com/books?id=6T_Ff6Ra57sC&pg=PA47 Lexington Books 1999 p.57 n.6.

[1628] *Report of Sub-Committee 2* https://unispal.un.org/pdfs/AAC1432.pdf (doc.nr. A/AC.14/32). 10 November 1947; on https://unispal.un.org/UNISPAL.NSF/0/ba8f82c57961b9fc85257306007096b8

For the Bedouin issue, see par. 61-73 on pp. 39-46 and Appendix 3: *Note on the Bedouin population of Palestine presented by the representative of the United Kingdom* d.d. 1 November 1947 on pp. 65-66

[1629] Assembly Delays Vote on Palestine http://timesmachine.nytimes.com/timesmachine/1947/11/27/issue.html, NY Times, 27 November 1947

[1630] U.N. Puts off Vote on Palestine a Day: Compromise is Aim http://timesmachine.nytimes.com/timesmachine/1947/11/29/104382303.html?pageNumber=2, NY Times, 29 November 1947

[1631] Unitary Palestine Fails in Committee http://timesmachine.nytimes.com/timesmachine/1947/11/25/104380046.html?pageNumber=1, NY Times, 25 November 1947

[1632] John J. Mearsheimer, Stephen M. Walt, *The Israel Lobby and US Foreign Policy,*(2007) Penguin Books 2008 p.371, n.8. Truman also remarked:'In all of my political experience I don't ever recall the Arab vote swinging a close election'.(p.142).

[1633] Michael Joseph Cohen, *Truman and Israel,* https://books.google.com/books?id=0sWRpKFjvbEC&pg=PA157 University of California Press 1990 p.162.

[1634] Michael Joseph Cohen, *Truman and Israel,* https://books.google.com/books?id=0sWRpKFjvbEC&pg=PA157 University of California Press 1990 161-163

[1635] Michael Joseph Cohen (1990) *Truman and Israel* University of California Press. pp.163-154 https://books.google.com/books?id=0sWRpKFjvbEC&pg=PA157: "Greece, the Philippines, and Haiti - three countries utterly dependent on Washington - suddenly came out one after another against its declared policy ...Abba Hillel Silver reported to the American Zionist Emergency Council: 'During this time, we marshalled our forces, Jewish and non-Jewish opinion, leaders and masses alike, converged on the Government and induced the President to assert the authority of his Administration to overcome the negative attitude of the State Department which persisted to the end, and persists today. The result was that our Government made its intense desire for the adoption of the partition plan to the wavering governments.'"

[1636] Chinese Put Needs at Several Billion http://timesmachine.nytimes.com/timesmachine/1947/11/30/87561706.html?pageNumber=33, *New York Times,* 30 November 2015

[1637] House, Debating Aid, Veers to Attacks on U.S. Policies http://timesmachine.nytimes.com/timesmachine/1947/12/05/104387411.html?pageNumber=1, NY Times, 5 December 1947

[1638] , p. 28 https://books.google.com/books?id=o9y6AAAAIAAJ&q=disturbed+and+annoyed+me#search_anchor, cite, Harry S. Truman, *Memoirs 2,* p. 158.

[1639] Benton Harbor *News-Palladium,* Friday, 25 October 1946, p. 6.

[1640] Palestine Vote Delayed http//find.galegroup.com *Times of London,* 29 Nov 1947

[1641] Political Issues Delay Asia Talks http://timesmachine.nytimes.com/timesmachine/1947/11/27/87561086.html?pageNumber=18, NY Times, 27 November 1947

[1642] Rich Cohen. *The Fish That Ate the Whale.* New York, NY: Farrar Straus Giroux, 2012.

[1643] Morris 2008, p. 412

[1644] 29th Meeting of the Ad Hoc Committee on Palestine: 24 November 1947: Retrieved 31 December 2013 https://unispal.un.org/UNISPAL.NSF/5ba47a5c6cef541b802563e000493b8c/49e8cf7b046bf55b85256a7200671a8e/$FILE/gapal83.pdf

[1645] Begin, Menachem (1978) *The Revolt.* p. 412.

[1646] Begin, Menachem (1977) *In The Underground: Writings and Documents.* Vol 4, p. 70.

[1647] Aviezer Golan and Shlomo Nakdimon (1978) *Begin* p. 172, cited in Simha Flapan, *The Birth of Israel,* Pantheon Books, New York, 1988. p. 32

[1648] Simha Flapan, *The Birth of Israel: Myths and Realities,* Pantheon, 1988, , pages 8–9

[1649] Sean F. McMahon, *The Discourse of Palestinian-Israeli Relations* https://books.google.com/books?id=Xq6MAgAAQBAJ&pg=PA40, Routledge 2010 p. 40.

[1650] P. J. I. M. De Waart, *Dynamics of Self-determination in Palestine* https://books.google.com/books?id=8bfkImTG1MgC&pg=PA138, BRILL 1994 p. 138

[1651] Mehran Kamrava, *The Modern Middle East: A Political History since the First World War* https://books.google.com/books?id=CkLHZCzMEJkC&pg=PA83, 2nd edition University of California Press 2011 p. 83

[1652] Shourideh C. Molavi, *Stateless Citizenship: The Palestinian-Arab Citizens of Israel* https://books.google.com/books?id=eMNkMYmqkdwC&pg=PA126, BRILL 2014 p. 126

[1653] Jamal K Kanj (2010) *Children of Catastrophe*

[1654] Morris 2008, p. 65

[1655] Palestine Partition Approved by U.N. http://search.proquest.com/hnptimesofindia/docview/346416099/pageviewPDF/1622F56DC3634BA5PQ/3?accountid=147304, Times of India, 1 December 1947

[1656] Arab Leaders Call Palestine Vote "Invalid" http://timesmachine.nytimes.com/timesmachine/1947/11/30/87561776.html?pageNumber=54, NY Times, 30 November 1947

[1657] UNITED NATIONS PALESTINE COMMISSION https://unispal.un.org/UNISPAL.NSF/0/FDF734EB76C39D6385256C4C004CDBA7 First Special Report to the Security Council

[1658] Morris 2008, p. 410

[1659] *Palestine Post*, 21 May 1948, p. 3.

[1660] Sean F. McMahon, *The Discourse of Palestinian-Israeli Relations: Persistent Analytics and Practices*, https://books.google.it/books?id=Q8eLAgAAQBAJ&pg=PT90 Routledge, 2009 .p.90

[1661] Youssef M. Choueiri, *A Companion to the History of the Middle East*, https://books.google.it/books?id=lioTXW3316AC&pg=PA281 Blackwell 2005 p.281

[1662] William B. Quandt, Paul Jabber, Ann Mosely Lesch, *The Politics of Palestinian Nationalism*, https://books.google.it/books?id=gwika-Y-ghwC&pg=PA46 Rand Corporation/University of California Press, 1973 pp.46-7.

[1663] John B. Quigly, *The Case for Palestine: An International Law Perspective*, https://books.google.it/books?id=VaUvqHNd6m0C&pg=PA36 Duke University Press, 2005 p.36.

[1664] Anita Shapira, *Yigal Allon, Native Son: A Biography*, University of Pennsylvania Press, 2004, p.239.

[1665] Itzhak Galnoor, *The Partition of Palestine: Decision Crossroads in the Zionist Movement*, State University of New York Press, 1994, p.195.

[1666] Bickerton, Ian J., Klausner, Carla L. (2001) *A Concise History of the Arab-Israeli Conflict*, 4th edition, Prentice Hall, , page 88.

[1667] Bickerton & Klausner (2001), page 103

[1668] Morris, 2008, p. 76, 77

[1669] Morris, 2008, p. 102

[1670] Morris 2008, p. 73

[1671] Louis 2006, p. 419

[1672] See memo from Acting Secretary Lovett to Certain Diplomatic Offices, Foreign relations of the United States, 1949. The Near East, South Asia, and Africa, Volume VI, pages 1447–48

[1673] See Folke Bernadotte, "To Jerusalem", Hodder and Stoughton, 1951, pages 112–13

[1674]

[1675] Yoav Gelber, *Independence Versus Nakba*; Kinneret–Zmora-Bitan–Dvir Publishing, 2004, , p.104

[1676] Declaration of Establishment of State of Israel: 14 May 1948 http://www.mfa.gov.il/MFA/Peace+Process/Guide+to+the+Peace+Process/Declaration+of+Establishment+of+State+of+Israel.htm

[1677] Cablegram from the Secretary-General of the League of Arab States to the Secretary-General of the United Nations 15 May 1948: Retrieved 4 May 2012

[1678] See

[1679] See The Palestine Declaration To The International Criminal Court: The Statehood Issue and Silverburg, Sanford R. (2002), "Palestine and International Law: Essays on Politics and Economics", Jefferson, N.C: McFarland & Co, , pages 37–54

[1680] See Chapter 5 "Israel (1948–1949) and Palestine (1998–1999): Two Studies in the Creation of States", in Guy S. Goodwin-Gill, and Stefan Talmon, eds., The Reality of International Law: Essays in Honour of Ian Brownlie (Oxford: Clarendon Press, 1999)

[1681] Sourcebook on public international law, by Tim Hillier, Routledge, 1998, , page 217; and Prof. Vera Gowlland-Debbas, "Collective Responses to the Unilateral Declarations of Independence of Southern Rhodesia and Palestine, An Application of the Legitimizing Function of the United Nations", The British Yearbook of International Law, 1990, pp.l35-l53

[1682] See paragraph 5, Separate opinion of Judge Koroma http://www.icj-cij.org/docket/files/131/1679.pdf

[1683] See De Waart, Paul J.I.M., "International Court of Justice Firmly Walled in the Law of Power in the Israeli–Palestinian Peace Process", *Leiden Journal of International Law*, 18 (2005), pp. 467–487

[1684] https://books.google.com/books?id=CC7381HrLqcC&pg=PA332

[1685] https://books.google.com/books?id=NQnpQNKeKKAC&pg=PA420

[1686] https://books.google.com/books?id=ATQQ0FMS1FQC&pg=PA474

[1687] http://school.eb.com/eb/article-45071

[1688] http://www.un.org/en/ga/search/view_doc.asp?symbol=A/RES/181(II)

[1689] http://www.mlwerke.de/NatLib/Pal/UN1947_Palestine-Minority-Report_start.htm

[1690] http://www.shapell.org/manuscript.aspx?jfk-partition-plan-1948-truman

[1691] http://www.globalpolitician.com/articleshow.asp?ID=3309&cid=2&sid=72

[1692] http://www.passia.org/palestine_facts/MAPS/1947-un-partition-plan-reso.html

[1693] https://web.archive.org/web/20050308151232/http://www.cdn-friends-icej.ca/un/unscop.html

[1694] https://web.archive.org/web/20090124212115/http://domino.un.org/maps/m0103_1b.gif

[1695] http://www.jcpa.org/quiz/November29.html

[1696] https://www.youtube.com/watch?v=QrIjzUK0FKg

[1697] T.G Fraser, 'The Arab Israeli Conflict', (Basingstoke, Palgrave Mcmillan, 2004), pp.40, 41.

[1698] Yoav Gelber (2006), p. 85

[1699] Benny Morris, *The Birth of the Palestinian Refugee Problem Revisited*, 2004, p. 35

[1700] Yoav Gelber (2004) p. 104

[1701] Resolution 181 (II). Future government of Palestine A/RES/181(II)(A+B) 29 November 1947 http://daccess-dds-ny.un.org/doc/RESOLUTION/GEN/NR0/038/88/IMG/NR003888.pdf?OpenElement

[1702] Benny Morris (2008), p. 180 and further

[1703] Henry Laurens, *La Question de Palestine*, volume 2, Fayard, Paris 2002 pp.571-572.

[1704] Walid Khalidi. "Before their Diaspora." IPS 1984. p. 253. Benny Morris, *The Birth of the Palestinian refugee problem, 1947–1949*, 2004 p. 343. Morris gives no precise date or number of casualties but describes the house as "suspected of being an Arab terrorist headquarters." He also states that on 20 May 1947 the Palamach blew up a coffee house in Fajja after the murder of two Jews in Petah Tikva.

[1705] Morris 2004 p.343:9 December 1947, the Givati brigade blew up a house in the village of Karatiyya; on 11 December a house was blown up in Haifa's Wadi Rishmiya neighbourhood. On 18 December 1947, two houses were destroyed by the Palmach in a raid on Khisas in the Galilee; On 19 December, the house of the mukhtar of Qazaza was partially demolished to revenge the murder of a Jew; On December 26, several houses were blown up in Silwan; on 27 December 3 houses were blown up in Yalu; On 4 January 1948 Etzioni blew up the Christian-owned Semiramis Hotel in Jerusalem's Katamon quarter.

[1706] Extracts from Time Magazine of that time http://www.time.com/time/archive/preview/0,10987,934119,00.html

[1707] Yoav Gelber (2006), p. 17

[1708] This expression is taken from Ilan Pappé (2000), p. 111

[1709] Benny Morris (2003), p. 65

[1710] Ilan Pappé (2000), p. 111

[1711] Morris 2008, p. 76

[1712] Efraïm Karsh (2002), p. 30

[1713] Benny Morris (2003), p. 101

[1714] B. Morris, 2004, *The Birth of the Palestinian refugee problem revisited*, p. 66

[1715] *The Palestine Post* of 31 December 1947: Archives of the newspaper http://www.jpress.org.il/Default/Skins/TAUEn/Client.asp?Skin=TAUEn&enter=true&sPublication=PLS&Publication=PLS&Hs=advanced&AW=1291929116843&AppName=2

[1716] Benny Morris (2008), p. 101
[1717] Yoav Gelber (2006), p. 24
[1718] Efraïm Karsh (2002), p. 36
[1719] *The Times*, 1 March 1948
[1720] Newspapers of the time: *The Palestine Post*, 1 April 1948 and *The Times*, on the same day, attribute the incident to Lehi.
[1721] Dominique Lapierre et Larry Collins (1971), chap. 7, pp. 131–153
[1722] Benny Morris (2003), p. 163
[1723] Henry Laurens (2005), p. 83
[1724] Dominique Lapierre et Larry Collins (1971), p. 163
[1725] Benny Morris (2003), p. 67
[1726] Yoav Gelber (2006), pp. 51–56
[1727] Benny Morris 2008, p.85"
[1728] "Ruhmloses Zwischenspiel: Fawzi al-Qawuqji in Deutschland, 1941–1947," by Gerhard Höpp in Peter Heine, ed., Al-Rafidayn: Jahrbuch zu Geschichte und Kultur des modernen Iraq (Würzburg: Ergon Verlag, 1995), (http://www.zmo.de/biblio/nachlass/hoepp/01_30_064.pdf) p.16
[1729] Benny Morris 2008 p.435
[1730] Benny Morris 2008, p.403"
[1731] Benny Morris (2008), p. 112
[1732] Ilan Pappe (2006), p. 72.
[1733] Yoav Gelber (2004), p. 67
[1734] Special UN report https://unispal.un.org/UNISPAL.NSF/0/FDF734EB76C39D6385256C4C004CDBA7 by the United Nations Special Commission (16 February 1948), § II.5
[1735] United Nations Special Commission (16 February 1948), § II.9.c
[1736] Dominique Lapierre and Larry Collins (1971), p. 185
[1737] This policy would change; at the end of the mandate, the High Commissioner, Alan Cunningham, opposed the deployment of Arab Legion troops into the territory and threatened the Arab states with RAF intervention if they grouped their forces around the border or crossed it. (Yoav Gelber (2006), p. 115)
[1738] L. Carl Brown, *Diplomacy in the Middle East: The International Relations of Regional and Outside powers*, I.B.Tauris, 2004, pp. 26-27.
[1739] United Nations Special Commission (16 February 1948), § II.7
[1740] Shishakli would seize the power in Syria between 29 October 1951 and 25 February 1954 (Henry Laurens (2005), pp. 115–116)
[1741] Yoav Gelber (2006), p. 51
[1742] Yoav Gelber (2006), p. 55
[1743] Yoav Gelber (2006), p. 56
[1744] United Nations Special Commission (16 February 1948), § II.7.3
[1745] United Nations Special Commission (16 February 1948), § II.6
[1746] Ilan Pappé (2000), p. 113
[1747] Ilan Pappé (2000), p. 113, quoting Milstein, Milhemet, vol. 2, p. 47
[1748] //en.wikipedia.org/w/index.php?title=Template:Nakba&action=edit
[1749] Ilan Pappé (2000), p. 125
[1750] Yoav Gelber (2006), p.77
[1751] Henry Laurens (2005), p. 84
[1752] Yoav Gelber (2006), p.71
[1753] Benny Morris (2003), p. 13
[1754] See the entry at 1 April 1948 http://indaily.net/?p=1299
[1755] Yoav Gelber (2006), pp. 71–73
[1756] See here
[1757] For a discussion of the motivation of Czech aid, see L'aide militaire tchèque à Israël, 1948 http://www.persee.fr/web/revues/home/prescript/article/receo_0035-1415_1974_num_5_1_1180
[1758] Yoav Gelber (2006), p. 14

[1759] See for example the résumé of an article by Arnold Krammer L'aide militaire tchèque à Israël, 1948 http://www.persee.fr/web/revues/home/prescript/article/receo_0035-1415_1974_num_5_1_1180.
[1760] Yoav Gelber (2006), p. 13
[1761] 17 April 1948 resolution https://www.jewishvirtuallibrary.org/jsource/UN/unres46.html
[1762] This term is important. Pappé underlined that they were not ready 'to have their own troops intervene' in the conflict, but that they would rather follow other solutions, such as delegating the task to a voluntary force, like the Arab Liberation Army, that they financed.
[1763] Ilan Pappé (2000), p. 146
[1764] Ilan Pappé (2000), p. 147
[1765] Yoav Gelber (2006), p. 5
[1766] UN Security Council 270th meeting report https://unispal.un.org/unispal.nsf/9a798adbf322aff38525617b006d88d7/d3bc8aaa0231aae0802564ad003974d2?OpenDocument&Highlight=0,S%2FAgenda,270
[1767] Dominique Lapierre et Larry Collins (1971), p. 137
[1768] Dominique Lapierre et Larry Collins (1971), p. 305
[1769] Benny Morris (2008), p.90.
[1770] Yoav Gelber (2006), p. 38
[1771] http://www.שומרחה-ליח-תתומע.co.il/?section=217#_ftn19 produced sten sub machine guns, 2" and 3" mortars and ammunition
[1772] Dov Joseph, *The Faithful City – The Siege of Jerusalem 1948*. Library of Congress number 60 10976. p. 8: "For example, all the land mines used against Rommel came from Jewish factories in Palestine."
[1773] Efraïm Karsh (2002), p. 25
[1774] Dominique Lapierre et Larry Collins (1971), Chap. 12
[1775] Benny Morris (2003), p. 240
[1776] Dominique Lapierre et Larry Collins (1971), et pp. 108–109
[1777] Walid Khalidi, *Before Their Diaspora*, Institute for Palestine Studies, Washington DC, 1991, p. 316 rapporté par Issa Fahel by Gary D. Keenan http://www.canpalnet-ottawa.org/canpalissafahel.html
[1778] Pierre Razoux (2006), p.79 et p. 523
[1779] Dominique Lapierre et Larry Collins (1971), pp. 109–113
[1780] Dominique Lapierre et Larry Collins (1971), pp. 375–376
[1781] Pierre Razoux (2006), pp. 96, 575
[1782] Ilan Pappé (2000), p.79
[1783] Efraïm Karsh (2002), p. 31
[1784] Joseph, pp. 23, 38. Gives the date of the call-up as 5 December.
[1785] Ilan Pappé (2000), p. 80
[1786] Levin, pp. 32, 117. Pay £P2 per month. c.f. would buy 2 lbs. of meat in Jerusalem, April 1948. p. 91.
[1787] Benny Morris (2003), pp. 16–17
[1788] Efraïm Karsh (2002), p. 34
[1789] Yoav Gelber (2006), p. 8
[1790] Yoav Gelber (2006), p. 28
[1791] Dominique Lapierre et Larry Collins (1971), p. 214
[1792] Dominique Lapierre et Larry Collins (1971), pp. 122–123
[1793] Dominique Lapierre et Larry Collins (1971), p. 7
[1794] Yoav Gelber (2006), pp. 36–37
[1795] Efraïm Karsh (2002), p. 27
[1796] Yoav Gelber (2006), p. 37
[1797] Yoav Gelber (2006), p. 26
[1798] Efraïm Karsh (2002), p. 26
[1799] Efraïm Karsh (2002), p. 38
[1800]
[1801] Pierre Razoux (2006), p. 66
[1802] Efraïm Karsh (2002), p. 40

[1803] Benny Morris (2003), p. 254
[1804] Benny Morris, in the *Birth revisited*, 2003, p. 34.
[1805] Yoav Gelber, *Palestine 1948*, 2006, p. 51
[1806] Ilan Pappe, *The ethnic cleansing of Palestine*, 2006, p. 44
[1807] David Tal, *War in Palestine 1948*, 2004, p. 362
[1808] Benny Morris, in the *Birth revisited*, 2003, p. 16.
[1809] Yoav Gelber, *Palestine 1948*, 2006, p.73.
[1810] Ilan Pappe, *The ethnic cleansing of Palestine*, 2006, p. 44 gives the number of 50,000 with 30,000 fighting forces.
[1811] Plan D – Master Defense Plan of the Hagana http://www.mideastweb.org/pland.htm
[1812] Dominique Lapierre et Larry Collins (1971), p. 369
[1813] Yoav Gelber 2006, p. 83
[1814] Dominique Lapierre et Larry Collins (1971), p. 372
[1815] Benny Morris (Benny Morris (2003), p. 236) speaks of 3 resupply convoys but Lapierre and Collins (Dominique Lapierre et Larry Collins (1971), p. 456) speak of a fourth convoy of 300 lorries that left Kfar Biou on the dawn of 20 April.
[1816] Dominique Lapierre et Larry Collins (1971), p. 457
[1817] Dominique Lapierre et Larry Collins (1971), p. 455
[1818] Dominique Lapierre et Larry Collins (1971), p. 456
[1819] Yoav Gelber (2006), p. 89
[1820] Yoav Gelber (2006), p. 403
[1821] Benny Morris (2003), p. 240
[1822] Dominique Lapierre et Larry Collins (1971), p. 426
[1823] Benny Morris (2003), pp. 242–243
[1824] Benny Morris (2003), *The destruction of the Arab villages*, pp. 342-360.
[1825] Benny Morris (2003), p. 242
[1826] Dominique Lapierre et Larry Collins (1971), p. 427
[1827] Benny Morris (2003), pp. 243–244
[1828] Benny Morris (2003), p. 244
[1829] Yoav Gelber, *Palestine 1948*, Appendix II http://www.ee.bgu.ac.il/~censor/katz-directory/05-12-14gelber-palestine-1948-appendix-II-what-happened-in-deir-ypssin-english.pdf
[1830] Yoav Gelber (2006), p. 317
[1831] Benny Morris (2003), p. 239
[1832] Dominique Lapierre et Larry Collins (1971), p. 528
[1833] Dominique Lapierre et Larry Collins (1971), p. 429–442
[1834] Robert Barr Smith, *Fighting Jack Churchill Survived: A Wartime Odyssey Beyond Compare* World War Two History, Profiles Column, July 2005
[1835] This word is from Yoav Gelber (Yoav Gelber (2006), p. 93)
[1836] Shafa 'Amr, Khirbet Kasayir et Hawsha
[1837] Yoav Gelber (2006), p. 93
[1838] Benny Morris (2003), p. 245
[1839] Yoav Gelber (2006), pp. 225–226
[1840] Yoav Gelber (2006), pp. 134–135
[1841] Benny Morris (2003), p. 248
[1842] Benny Morris (2003), pp. 248–250
[1843] Benny Morris (2003), pp. 249–252
[1844] Ilan Pappé (2000), p. 167
[1845] *War Diary 1948–1949*, ed. Elhanan Orren and Gershon Rivlin, Israël Defence Ministry Press, Tel Aviv, 1982, p. 409
[1846] Dominique Lapierre et Larry Collins (1971), pp. 525–530
[1847] Benny Morris (1881), p. 221
[1848] Both theses are developed in Avi Shlaim, *Collusion Across the Jordan: King Abdullah, the Zionist movement and the Partition of Palestine*, Columbia University Press, 1988 and in Yoav Gelber, *Israeli-Jordanian dialogue, 1948–1953: cooperation, conspiracy or collusion*, Sussex Academic Press, 2004.
[1849] Pierre Razoux (2006), p. 523

[1850] Ilan Pappé (2000), pp. 168–169
[1851] Efraïm Karsh (2002), p. 51
[1852] Yoav Gelber (2006), p. 95
[1853] Yoav Gelber (2006), p. 96
[1854] Official site of the kibbutz http://www.kfar-etzion.co.il/History/tabid/228/articleType/ArticleView/articleId/9/PageID/57/History-of-the-Etzion-Bloc1.aspx
[1855] Benny Morris, *The road to Jerusalem*, p. 139
[1856] Moshe Dayan, 'The Story of My Life'. Page 130. Out of a total of 670 prisoners released.
[1857] Benni Morris (2008), p. 131
[1858] Benny Morris (2002), pp. 155–156.
[1859] Dominique Lapierre et Larry Collins (1971), p. 576
[1860] Dominique Lapierre et Larry Collins (1971), pp. 580–582
[1861] Dominique Lapierre et Larry Collins (1971), pp. 575–576
[1862] According to this Israeli site http://daat.ac.il/daat/english/history/lapidot/27.htm with confirmation from this map from the Passia organization http://www.passia.org/palestine_facts/MAPS/images/jer_maps/UNPartition.html
[1863] Yoav Gelber (2006), p. 140
[1864] Yoav Gelber (2006), pp. 134–135 Although the last (the Lebanese) ultimately would not engage in combat
[1865] Benny Morris (2003), pp. 252–254
[1866] See, for example, in *The New York Times* archives: : Despair is voiced by arab refugees https://pqasb.pqarchiver.com
[1867] Karsh, Efraim, *The Arab-Israeli Conflict: The Palestine War 1948*. Osprey Publishing, 2002, pp. 87–92
[1868] Ilan Pappe, *The Ethnic cleansing of Palestine*, pp. xii–xiii.
[1869] Benny Morris, *The Birth of the Palestinian Refugee Problem Revisited*, Oxford University Press, 2004, Conclusions.
[1870] Yoav Gelber (2006), p. 120
[1871] Yoav Gelber (2006), pp. 122–123
[1872] Yoav Gelber (2006), pp. 124–125
[1873] Yoav Gelber (2006), p. 127
[1874] Yoav Gelber (2006), p. 126
[1875] Yoav Gelber (2006), p. 128
[1876] Yoav Gelber (2006), pp. 126, 132
[1877] Dominique Lapierre et Larry Collins (1971), pp. 453–454
[1878] Dominique Lapierre et Larry Collins (1971), p. 133
[1879] Arab League Declaration, 15 May 1948 https://www.jewishvirtuallibrary.org/jsource/History/arab_invasion.html from jewishvirtuallibrary.com. Retrieved 26 September 2007.
[1880] Benny Morris, *1948*, p. 179.
[1881] Yoav Gelber (2004) p. 118
[1882] Morris 2008 p. 400
[1883] Israel Ministry of Foreign Affairs: *Declaration of Establishment of State of Israel: 14 May 1948*. http://www.mfa.gov.il/MFA/Peace+Process/Guide+to+the+Peace+Process/Declaration+of+Establishment+of+State+of+Israel.htm
[1884] http://www.mideastweb.org/pland.htm
[1885] https://www.webcitation.org/5v5sZ1pPb?url=http://unispal.un.org/UNISPAL.NSF/0/FDF734EB76C39D6385256C4C004CDBA7
[1886] http://www.palestineremembered.com/
[1887] https://www.jewishvirtuallibrary.org/jsource/History/1948toc.html
[1888] Oren 2003, p. 5.
[1889] Morris, Benny (2008), *1948: The First Arab-Israeli War* https://books.google.com/books?id=CC7381HrLqcC&pg=PA332&lpg=PA332, Yale University Press, p.205, New Haven, .
[1890] Anita Shapira, *L'imaginaire d'Israël : histoire d'une culture politique* (2005), Latroun : la mémoire de la bataille, Chap. III. 1 l'événement pp. 91–96
[1891] Benny Morris (2008), p. 419.
[1892] Morris, 2008, p. 332.

[1893] This includes the entire military personnel count – both combat units and logistical units.<ref name = "Gelber12">Gelber (2006), p. 12.
[1894] Pollack, 2004; Sadeh, 1997
[1895] At maximum, not half of the forces of the Israelis but these numbers include only the combat units sent to the former mandate-territory of Palestine, not the entire military strength. UNIQ-ref-0-5d4cfb4109fe789c-QINU
[1896] Morris 2008, pp. 404–06.
[1897] David Tal, *War in Palestine, 1948: Israeli and Arab Strategy and Diplomacy*, p. 153.
[1898] Benny Morris (2008), p. 401.
[1899] Zeev Maoz, *Defending the Holy Land*, University of Michigan Press, 2009 p. 4: 'A combined invasion of a Jordanian and Egyptian army started ... The Syrian and the Lebanese armies engaged in a token effort but did not stage a major attack on the Jewish state.'
[1900] Rogan and Shlaim 2007 p. 99.
[1901] Cragg 1997 pp. 57, 116.
[1902] Benvenisti, Meron (1996), *City of Stone: The Hidden History of Jerusalem*, University of California Press, . p. 27
[1903] Morris, 2001, pp. 259–60.
[1904] Morris, 2008, pp. 66–69
[1905] UNITED NATIONS: General Assembly: A/RES/181(II): 29 November 1947: *Resolution 181 (II). Future government of Palestine*. http://domino.un.org/unispal.nsf/0/7f0af2bd897689b785256c330061d253
[1906] Greg Cashman, Leonard C. Robinson, *An Introduction to the Causes of War: Patterns of Interstate Conflict from World War 1 to Iraq*, https://books.google.com/books?id=x7K2GYnXRngC&pg=PA165 Rowman & Littlefield 2007 p. 165.
[1907] Benjamin Grob-Fitzgibbon, *Imperial Endgame: Britain's Dirty Wars and the End of Empire*, https://books.google.com/books?id=NUeYAAAAQBAJ&pg=PT57 Palgrave/Macmillan 2011 p. 57
[1908] Ilan Pappé (2000), p. 111
[1909] Morris 2008, p. 76
[1910] Efraïm Karsh (2002), p. 30
[1911] Benny Morris (2003), p. 101
[1912] Yoav Gelber (2006), pp. 51–56
[1913] Dominique Lapierre et Larry Collins (1971), chap. 7, pp. 131–53
[1914] Benny Morris (2003), p. 163
[1915] Dominique Lapierre et Larry Collins (1971), p. 163
[1916] Benny Morris (2003), p. 67
[1917] Henry Laurens (2005), p. 83
[1918] David Tal, *War in Palestine, 1948: Israeli and Arab Strategy and Diplomacy,* Routledge 2004 p. 89.
[1919] David Tal, pp. 89–90.
[1920] Dominique Lapierre et Larry Collins (1971), pp. 369–81
[1921] Benny Morris (2003), pp. 242–43
[1922] Benny Morris (2003), p. 242
[1923] Henry Laurens (2005), pp. 85–86
[1924] Benny Morris (2003), pp. 248–52
[1925] Benny Morris (2003), pp. 252–54
[1926] Martin Van Creveld, *Sword and the Olive: A Critical History of the Israeli Defense Force*, Public Affairs (1998) 2002 p. 78
[1927]
[1928] Gelber, p. 73; Karsh 2002, p. 25.
[1929] W. Khalidi, 'Plan Dalet: Master Plan for the Conquest of Palestine', J. Palestine Studies 18(1), pp. 4–33, 1988 (reprint of a 1961 article)
[1930] Joseph, Dov. "The Faithful City – The Siege of Jerusalem, 1948." Simon and Suchster, 1960. Congress # 60 10976. pp. 23, 38.
[1931] Levin, Harry. "Jerusalem Embattled – A Diary of the City under Siege." Cassels, 1997. pp. 32, 117. Pay £P2 per month. c.f. would buy 2lb of meat in Jerusalem, April 1948. p. 91.

[1932] Benny Morris (2004), p. 16
[1933] Gelber (2006), p. 73
[1934] D. Kurzman, "Genesis 1948", 1970, p. 282.
[1935] Henry Laurens, *La Question de Palestine*, vol.3, Fayard 2007 p. 70
[1936] Morris, 2008, pp. 397–98.
[1937] Moshe Naor,*Social Mobilization in the Arab/Israeli War of 1948: On the Israeli Home Front*, Routledge 2013 p. 15.
[1938] Pappe, Ilan. *The Ethnic Cleansing of Palestine*.
[1939] Pappé, 2006, pp.xii, 86–126
[1940] Gelber 2006 p. 306
[1941] Morris 2008 p. 119
[1942] Gelber (2006), p. 11
[1943] Henry Laurens, *La Question de Palestine*, Fayard, 2007 p. 32.
[1944] Gelber (2006), p. 11.
[1945] Morris 2008 p. 187; quoting p. 24 of Kirkbride's memoirs https://books.google.com/books?id=i8FcAgAAQBAJ&pg=PA24
[1946]
[1947] Rogan and Shlaim 2007 p. 110.
[1948] Morris, 2008, p. 310
[1949] Sela, 2002, p. 14.
[1950] Morris (2008), pp. 190–92
[1951] Tal,*War in Palestine, 1948: Israeli and Arab Strategy and Diplomacy*, p. 154.
[1952] Zamir, 2010, p. 34
[1953] Tripp, 2001, p. 137.
[1954] Morris, 2004 pp. 76, 82, 104, 126, 130, 202, 253
[1955] Shlaim, 2001, p. 97.
[1956] Shlaim, 2001, p. 99.
[1957] Benny Morris (2003), p. 189.
[1958] Martin Van Creveld,*Sword and the Olive: A Critical History of the Israeli Defense Force,*, Public Affairs (1998) 2002 p. 75
[1959] Morris (2003), pp. 32–33.
[1960] Morris (2008), p. 81.
[1961] Benny (2008), p. 174.
[1962] Martin Van Creveld, *Sword and the Olive: A Critical History of the Israeli Defense Force*, https://books.google.com/books?id=baa0OKb51rIC&pg=PA80, Public Affairs (1998) 2002 p. 78
[1963] Morris 2008 p. 185
[1964] Morris, 2003, p. 35.
[1965] Morris, 2008, p. 401
[1966] Collins and LaPierre, 1973 p. 355
[1967] Morgan, Michael L.:*The Philosopher as Witness: Fackenheim and Responses to the Holocaust*, p. 182
[1968] Ben Gurion, David *War Diaries, 1947–1949*. Arabic edition translated by Samir Jabbour. Institute of Palestine Studies, Beirut, 1994. p. 303.
[1969] Later, in the midst of the war, Yitzhak Rabin was succeeded by Joseph Tebenkin who led Operation Ha-Har.
[1970] Morris, 2008: pp. 176–77
[1971] Laffin, John: *The Israeli Army in the Middle East Wars 1948–73*, p. 8
[1972] Laurens, vol. 3 p. 69.
[1973] Gelber (2006), p. 50.
[1974] Ma'an Abu Nawar, *The Jordanian-Israeli war, 1948–1951: a history of the Hashemite Kingdom of Jordan*, p. 393.
[1975] Benny Morris, *Victimes : histoire revisitée du conflit arabo-sioniste*, 2003, pp. 241, 247–55.
[1976] Pollack 2004, p. ?.
[1977] D. Kurzman, 'Genesis 1948', 1972, p. 382.
[1978] I. Pappe, "The ethnic cleansing of Palestine", 2006, p. 129.

[1979] Pollack, 2002, pp. 149–55.
[1980] Yoav Gelber, 2006, "Sharon's Inheritance" http://www.aisisraelstudies.org/2006papers/Gelber%20Yoav%202006.pdf
[1981] Rogan and Shlaim 2001, p. 8.
[1982] Pollack, 2002, pp. 15–27.
[1983] D. Kurzman, "Genesis 1948", 1972, p. 556.
[1984] Pollack, 2002, p. 150.
[1985] Gelber, p. 55
[1986] Morris, 2008, pp. 322 and 326.
[1987] Uthman Hasan Salih. *DAWR AL-MAMLAKA AL-'ARABIYYA AL-SA'UDIYYA FI HARB FI-LASTIN 1367H/1948* (The role of Saudi Arabia in the Palestine war of 1948), Revue d'Histoire Maghrébine [Tunisia] 1986 13(43–44): 201–21.
[1988] Morris, 2008, p. 205; cites British diplomatic communications.
[1989] Gelber, p. 200
[1990] Gelber, p. 203
[1991] Gelber, p. 239
[1992] Morris, 2008, p. 269.
[1993] Yoav Gelber, *Palestine 1948*, 2006 – Chap. 8 "The Arab Regular Armies' Invasion of Palestine".
[1994] Sean F. McMahon,*The Discourse of Palestinian-Israeli Relations: Persistent Analytics and Practices,* Routledge 2010 p. 37: "If it wasn't for the Arab invasion there would have been no stop to the expansion of the forces of Haganah who could have, with the same drive, reached the natural borders of western Israel". Walid Khalidi, "Plan Dalet: Master Plan for the Conquest of Palestine," *Journal of Palestine Studies*, Vol. 18, No. 1, Special Issue: Palestine 1948, (Autumn,1988), pp. 4–33, p. 19.
[1995] Yoav Gelber (2006), p. 130.
[1996] Morris, 2008, p. 263
[1997] Wallach et al. (Volume 2, 1978), p. 29
[1998] Tal, 2004, p. 179
[1999] Morris, 2008, p. 239
[2000] tal 2004 p. 182
[2001] *War in Palestine, 1948: Israeli and Arab Strategy and Diplomacy.* David Tal.
[2002] Morris, 2008, pp. 229–30
[2003] (Benny (2008), "1948: The First Arab-Israeli War", Yale University Press, New Haven,).Mordechai Weingarten
[2004] *The Palestine Post: State of Israel is Born* (1948)
[2005] Pollack 2002, pp. 448–57
[2006] Morris, 2008, pp. 253–54
[2007] Tal, 2004, pp. 251
[2008] Morris (2008), p. 261
[2009] Morris, 2008, p. 235
[2010] Morris, 2001, pp. 217–18.
[2011] Morris, 2008, p. 262.
[2012] Aloni, 2001, pp. 7–11.
[2013] Gershoni, pp. 46–47
[2014] Gelber, 2004, Kinneret, p.220
[2015] Morris, 2008, pp. 269–71
[2016] Bregman, 2002, p. 24 citing Ben Gurion's diary of the war
[2017] Security Council, S/1025, 5 October 1948, REPORT BY THE UNITED NATIONS, MEDIATOR ON THE OBSERVATION OF THE TRUCE IN, PALESTINE DURING THE PERIOD FROM 11 JUNE, TO 9 JULY 1948 https://unispal.un.org/UNISPAL.NSF/0/7D468BBE932AC79C802564C00037B882 , During the period of the truce, three violations occurred ... of such a serious nature... the *Altalena* incident, the Negeb convoys, and the question of the water supply to Jerusalem.... 1. the attempt by ...the Irgun Zvai Leumi to bring war materials and immigrants, including men of military age, into Palestine aboard the ship *Altalena* on 21 June... 2. Another truce violation occurred through the refusal of Egyptian forces to

permit the passage of relief convoys to Jewish settlements in the Negeb... 3. The third violation of the truce arose as a result of the failure of the Transjordan and Iraqi forces to permit the flow of water to Jerusalem.

[2018] Alfred A. Knopf. *A History of Israel from the Rise of Zionism to Our Time.* New York. 1976. p. 330.

[2019] Gelber, 2006, Kinneret, p.226

[2020] Gideon Levy and Alex Levac, 'Drafting the blueprint for Palestinian refugees' right of return,' http://www.haaretz.com/weekend/twilight-zone/1.550550 at Haaretz 4 October 2013: 'In all the Arab villages in the south almost nobody fought. The villagers were so poor, so miserable, that they didn't even have weapons ... The flight of these residents began when we started to clean up the routes used by those accompanying the convoys. Then we began to expel them, and in the end they fled on their own.'

[2021] David Tal, *War in Palestine, 1948: Israeli and Arab Strategy and Diplomacy,* Routledge 2004 p. 307.

[2022] Herzog and Gazit, 2005, p. 86

[2023] Lorch, Netanel (1998). *History of the War of Independence*

[2024] Kadish, Alon, and Sela, Avraham. (2005) "Myths and historiography of the 1948 Palestine War revisited: the case of Lydda," *The Middle East Journal,* 22 September 2005; and Khalidi, Walid. (1998) Introduction to Munayyer, Spiro. The fall of Lydda https://web.archive.org/web/20110718144237/http://www.palestine-studies.org/enakba/Memoirs/Munayyer,%20The%20Fall%20of%20Lydda.pdf. *Journal of Palestine Studies,* Vol. 27, No. 4, pp. 80–98.

[2025] Map of the Attacks http://www.allthatremains.com/Maps/IsraeliMiliteryDuringTheTruce07-08-48-To-07-18-48.jpg.

[2026] A. Ilan, *Bernadotte in Palestine,* 1948 (Macmillan, 1989) p. 194

[2027] J. Bowyer Bell, Assassination in International Politics, *International Studies Quarterly,* vol. 16, March 1972, pp. 59–82.

[2028] Review of Kati Marton's biography.

[2029] Shapira, Anita. Yigal Allon; Native Son; A Biography Translated by Evelyn Abel, University of Pennsylvania Press p. 247

[2030] Gelber, 2006, p. 33

[2031] Shlomo Ben-Ami (Shlomo Ben-Ami (2006), pp. 41–42)

[2032] Morris 2008, p. 404

[2033] Aloni, 2001, p. 18.

[2034] Aloni, 2001, p. 22.

[2035] Cohen, Michael Joseph: *Truman and Israel* (1990)

[2036] Adrian, p. 7

[2037] Adrian, p. 59

[2038] L. Carl Brown (2013), p. 126.

[2039]

[2040] //en.wikipedia.org/w/index.php?title=Template:Nakba&action=edit

[2041] General Progress Report and Supplementary Report of the United Nations Conciliation Commission for Palestine, Covering the Period from 11 December 1949 to 23 October 1950 https://unispal.un.org/UNISPAL.NSF/0/93037E3B939746DE8525610200567883 , published by the United Nations Conciliation Commission, 23 October 1950. (U.N. General Assembly Official Records, 5th Session, Supplement No. 18, Document A/1367/Rev. 1)

[2042] Government of Palestine, *A Survey of Palestine,* Supplement, p. 10 (1946)

[2043] http://www.history.ac.uk/reviews/paper/hughesMatthew.html The War for Palestine. Rewriting the History of 1948 by Eugene L. Rogan and Avi Shlaim . Retrieved 8 August 2009. Archived https://www.webcitation.org/5iwzyIK8U?url=http://www.history.ac.uk/reviews/paper/hughesMatthew.html 11 August 2009.

[2044] //en.wikipedia.org/w/index.php?title=Template:Jewish_exodus_from_Arab_and_Muslim_countries&action=edit

[2045] Sachar, pp. 395–403.

[2046] Devorah Hakohen, *Immigrants in Turmoil: Mass Immigration to Israel and Its Repercussions in the 1950s and after,* https://books.google.com/books?id=fYOiPrm-6PsC&pg=PA292 Syracuse University Press 2003 p.267

[2047] Displaced Persons http://www.ushmm.org/wlc/article.php?lang=en&ModuleId=10005462 retrieved on 29 October 2007 from the U.S. Holocaust Museum.
[2048] Tom Segev, *1949. The First Israelis*, Owl Books, 1986, p. 96.
[2049] Devorah Hakohen, *Immigrants in Turmoil: Mass Immigration to Israel and Its Repercussions in the 1950s and after*, https://books.google.com/books?id=fYOiPrm-6PsC&pg=PA292 Syracuse University Press 2003 pp. 24, 31, 42, 45.
[2050] Avi Shlaim, *The Debate about 1948* http://users.ox.ac.uk/~ssfc0005/The%20Debate%20About%201948.html, International Journal of Middle East Studies, 27:3, 1995, pp. 287–304.
[2051] Avi Shlaim, "The Debate about 1948", *International Journal of Middle East Studies*, Vol. 27, No. 3 (Aug. 1995), pp. 287–304.
[2052] Benny Morris, "Benny Morris on fact, fiction, & propaganda about 1948", *The Irish Times*, 21 February 2008, reported by Jeff Weintraub http://jeffweintraub.blogspot.com/2008/02/benny-morris-on-fact-fiction-propaganda.html
[2053] https://www.jewishvirtuallibrary.org/jsource/images/maps/1948war2.jpg
[2054] https://books.google.com/books?id=Wn6gAAAAMAAJ
[2055] https://books.google.com/books?id=qSpIAAAAMAAJ
[2056] https://books.google.com/books?id=CC7381HrLqcC&pg=PA332&lpg=PA332
[2057] https://web.archive.org/web/20060629024035/http://www.bartleby.com/67/3770.html
[2058] https://web.archive.org/web/20051204222100/http://www.haaretzdaily.com/hasen/pages/ShArt.jhtml?itemNo=101419
[2059] http://www.jpost.com/Defense/Article.aspx?id=277611
[2060] http://www.israelvets.com/pictorialhist_air_force.html
[2061] https://www.youtube.com/watch?v=HHmBiATUono
[2062] https://www.youtube.com/watch?v=yUDcL4y0R1I
[2063] https://www.knesset.gov.il/holidays/eng/independence_day_war.htm
[2064] http://domino.un.org/UNISPAL.NSF/
[2065] http://www.historyguy.com/arab_israeli_wars.html
[2066] http://www.mideastweb.org/briefhistory.htm
[2067] http://webarchive.loc.gov/all/20020913220119/http://www.zmag.org/shalom-meqa.htm
[2068] http://news.bbc.co.uk/1/hi/in_depth/middle_east/israel_and_the_palestinians/key_documents/1681322.stm
[2069] http://news.bbc.co.uk/1/shared/spl/hi/middle_east/03/v3_ip_timeline/html/1948.stm
[2070] http://israeliwarofindependence.blogspot.com/
[2071] http://users.ox.ac.uk/~ssfc0005/Israel%20and%20the%20Arab%20Coalition%20in%2019481.html
[2072] http://www.time.com/time/magazine/article/0,9171,779710,00.html
[2073] http://www.time.com/time/magazine/article/0,9171,798381,00.html

Article Sources and Contributors

The sources listed for each article provide more detailed licensing information including the copyright status, the copyright owner, and the license conditions.

Prehistory of the Levant *Source:* https://en.wikipedia.org/w/index.php?oldid=850752120 *License:* Creative Commons Attribution-Share Alike 3.0 *Contributors:* Againme, Al-Andalus, Archaeogenetics, BD2412, Brenont, Cattus, Chris the speller, DMacks, Davehi1, Debresser, Dmitri Lytov, Doug Weller, Drsmoo, Emmette Hernandez Coleman, Fayenatic london, Gilabrand, Goustien, Hugo999, IZAK, Jheald, Joe Roe, Johan Jönsson, John D. Croft, John Hyams, JonHarder, Keith McClary, Kuratowski's Ghost, Kwamikagami, L0st H0r!z0ns, Laurel Lodged, Legalize, Look2See1, Madalibi, Marcocapelle, Mmcannis, Natg 19, Niceguyedc, Nøkkenbuer, Onceinawhile, PiCo, R'n'B, Rjwilmsi, SeriouslySerious, Sheila1988, Sumerophile, TheCuriousGnome, Triggerhippie4, Tzimtzum1, WikiTryHardDieHard, Woohookitty, ZMatskevich, 24 anonymous edits 1

History of ancient Israel and Judah *Source:* https://en.wikipedia.org/w/index.php?oldid=859319818 *License:* Creative Commons Attribution-Share Alike 3.0 *Contributors:* 9898Username9898, Againme, Angelsi 1989, Arado, Arminden, Axelwa, BD2412, Backarn, Beauty School Dropout, Bender235, Bgwhite, Caballero1967, Calatayudboy, Chewings72, Chris troutman, Christian75, ClueBot NG, Damiens.rf, Dane, DaoXan, Debresser, Dimadick, Dirkbb, Doug Weller, Dsarah3, EdJohnston, Editor2020, Enthusiast01, Epicgenius, Excirial, Fences and windows, Frietjes, Gilded Snail, Greyshark09, Hairy Dude, Hsennett, I dream of horses, ISavedPvtRyan, Ian.thomson, IcePanN, InformationvsInjustice, IronGargoyle, Jandalhandler, JerryRussell, Jianhui67, Jobas, John of Reading, JosephusOfJerusalem, JudeccaXIII, Jytdog, K6ka, Kuru, LouisAlain, Marcocapelle, Marek69, Mark Arsten, MarnetteD, Materialscientist, Money money tickle parsnip, Monochrome Monitor, Musashiaharon, Music314812813478, MusikAnimal, Naviguessor, NawlinWiki, Neo-Jay, Nurg, Nuriah Jaconiah, Ogress, Onceinawhile, Onel5969, Oshwah, Paul2520, PiCo, Place Clichy, ProfGray, Prohibited Area, QuackGuru, Qwertyus, REDSAW123, Rarevogel, Saxophilist, Shellwood, Shrike, Simon Wtekni, Simplexity22, Smalljim, Speravir, Srich32977, StAnselm, Steve03Mills, Student7, Sylvain1972, TAnthony, Tahc, Tgeorgescu, Therealswaggyp, Therf3003, Theroadislong, Torvalu4, Triggerhippie4, TrollTool, Wrestlingring, Zero0000, Zuormak, יניב יבריב, חורון, 185 anonymous edits 9

Hebrews *Source:* https://en.wikipedia.org/w/index.php?oldid=863237177 *License:* Creative Commons Attribution-Share Alike 3.0 *Contributors:* 78.26, AK456, Achowat, Aetheling, AjaxSmack, Al Qurashi, AlanUS, Alexander Schatz, Alexf, Aminul027, Angel ivanov angelov, Angelsi 1989, Arjayay, Ashurbanippal, Bailey51415, Bejnar, Belson 303, Bender235, Bumm13, Calatayudboy, CarlosKni, ChrisGualtieri, Citation bot 1, ClueBot NG, Crystallizedcarbon, DXRD, Dalai lama ding dong, Davemck, DavidLeighEllis, Dbachmann, Dcirovic, Dejvid, Denisarona, Doug Weller, El C, Epbr123, Esc2003, Ewan2, Excirial, Fayenatic london, Felida97, Fkjms73, Future Perfect at Sunrise, Gadget593, GarthHempel, Greenknight dv, Gul e, Harsimaja, Hertz1888, Hmains, IZAK, Infantom, IronGargoyle, Jayjg, Jfdwolff, Jpadula, Jprg1966, Jsonitsac, Jytdog, KDTW Flyer, Kade 123, Kaldari, Kbseah, Khazar2, Kwamikagami, Ladislav Demeter, Largoplazo, Le Fedora Man, Lotje, LuK3, MadGuy7023, Malik Shabazz, Marek69, Mark Arsten, Markbelinsky, Maryester, Materialscientist, Mogism, NFD9001, NawlinWiki, Neuroforever, NewEnglandYankee, Nikosgreencookie, Nite-Sirk, Nitsansh, Oceanyam, Ogress, Onceinawhile, Orr-Stav, PaulYtaak, Peacedance, PlyrStar93, Predachron, Prinsgezinde, Queen Geedorah88, RayneVanDunem, Reaper Eternal, Recordstraight83, Rich Janis, Rich Smith, Rjwilmsi, RolandR, Seaphoto, Seraphim System, Shadowowl, Singaporian, Snow Blizzard, Spirit-RC, Squids and Chips, StAnselm, Stephenb, Teacherbrock, Thanatos666, Thane, The Mark of the Beast, TheRealTuna7, Tide rolls, Titodutta, Tiusonritchil, Tjsummerschool, Tom.Reding, Truth Alone, ValiantStag, WNYY98, Walter Görlitz, Wayne Slam, Wbm1058, Wolfman12405, XAshurukinx, Yaphehm'odh, Yarenn Šagor, Yaron Livne, YehudaMizrahi, Yuvn86, Zad68, יהודה, אריה גור 160 anonymous edits 31

Israelites *Source:* https://en.wikipedia.org/w/index.php?oldid=862203743 *License:* Creative Commons Attribution-Share Alike 3.0 *Contributors:* 1Tolasona, Adavidb, Agtx, Al-Andalus, Alexb102072, Ali69eh, AmirSurfLera, Arado, Arminden, Averysoda, BD2412, Backendgaming, Bender235, Bgwhite, BobKilcoyne, Broilinglegs, Bus stop, Caballero1967, Catlemur, Chhandama, Chris the speller, ChronoFrog, ClueBot NG, Comfr, Cuchullain, Dannouk, DaoXan, DavidLeighEllis, Debresser, Dimadick, DisillusionedBitterAndKnackered, Doug Weller, Download, Dxrd, E.M.Gregory, Eagleash, EamonnPKeane, EdJohnston, Editguy111, Editor2020, Emir of Wikipedia, Enthusiast01, Fuortu, GenoV84, GermanJoe, Glacier2009, Greyshark09, Hazhk, Hertz1888, HistoneSebas, IZAK, Ibadibam, Isambard Kingdom, Jackfork, Jacob D, Joaopaulopontes, Jodosma, Joefromrandb, John of Reading, Johnmcintyre1959, Jon Ace, JosephusOfJerusalem, Jprg1966, Jytdog, LilyWilliamsxoxo, LindsayH, Loopy30, MShabazz, Maczkopeti, MagicatthemovieS, Malik Shabazz, Mandruss, MarnetteD, Materialscientist, Maureendepresident, Mike Rosoft, Monochrome Monitor, MusenInvincible, MusikAnimal, Neo-Jay, Newmancbn, Niceguyedc, NickCT, Nishidani, Nitpicking polish, No More Mr Nice Guy, Nurg, Nxavar, Ogress, Omnipaedista, Onceinawhile, Penguins Are Animals 5327, Philip Trueman, Pwldnvthailand, Qed237, Qwertyus, Rich Farmbrough, Rrburke, Shamecca53, Shintaraguru, Shrike, Sitush, Sleepless80, Soniapanel, Srich32977, StAnselm, Tajotep, The Human Trumpet Solo, Thine Antique Pen, Thomas Paine1776, Tiki2134, Trappist the monk, Triggerhippie4, Tritomex, TypoBoy, Unreal7, Velella, Wafitzge, WarKosign, Welsh, WereSpielChequers, Wiae, Widr, William Allen Simpson, Wtmitchell, Ymblanter, Yseaursk23, Zozoulia, ԱշոտՏՆՂ, יהודה, אריה גור 97 anonymous edits 35

Biblical judges *Source:* https://en.wikipedia.org/w/index.php?oldid=863418692 *License:* Creative Commons Attribution-Share Alike 3.0 *Contributors:* 110TT011, A Fellow Editor, A.J.Chesswas, A8UDI, Adamlance, Agrumer, Alansohn, Aldy, Alephb, Anna Lincoln, Appraiser, Ar2332, Barticus88, Baruchim, BeeArkKey, Ben Ammi, Bermicourt, Bgwhite, BobKilcoyne, Boing! said Zebedee, Brandmeister, CambridgeBayWeather, Carminowe of Hendra, Clarince63, Clinkophonist, ClueBot NG, Courcelles, Cush, Dampinograaf, Davepape, Dbachmann, Debbiesw, ELApro, Eaefremov, Eliyak, Enthusiast01, Excirial, FDuffy, Fastifex, GHcool, Gedaliaf, GeoffreyT2000, Ghelae, Gilliam, Hairy Dude, Imeriki al-Shimoni, Ivanov id, J.delanoy, Jerm729, Jim1138, Jordi Roqué, Jovrtn, JustBerry, Jytdog, Lacrimosus, Lazulilasher, LilHelpa, MASQUERAID, Manul, MarcoLittel, MarcoTolo, Maureendepresident, Meieimatai, Metallurgist, Minister Kay, Mlambros, Mo1nathan, Morethom, Multi67, Mweisenfeld, Narky Blert, Nehrams2020, Niceguyedc, OlEnglish, Onesius, Pastordavid, Phillaw, Physicistjedi, PiCo, Pierpietro, Pochsad, Quest for Truth, Radagast83, Renigyas, Robin S, Rrostrom, Sandstein, Septrillion, Serols, Shaun, Sheila1988, StAnselm, Storkk, Summer Song, Thirdright, Tombomp, Topbanana, TreasuryTag, Vanished user ewfisn2348tui2f8n2fio2utjfeoi210r39jf, Vlmastra, WikHead, WikiFlier, Willking1979, Woohookitty, Xoloz, Zapzooma, Zarcademan123456, 139 anonymous edits 55

Kingdom of Israel (united monarchy) *Source:* https://en.wikipedia.org/w/index.php?oldid=865606379 *License:* Creative Commons Attribution-Share Alike 3.0 *Contributors:* AbuMohammad84, AmirSurfLera, Angelsi 1989, Aquillion, Arjayay, Asum991, Bearkat7000, BedrockPerson, Bender235, Beyond My Ken, BibleScholar, BobKilcoyne, Braganza, CLCStudent, CataracticPlanets, CleverRoz, ClueBot NG, Cyberbot II, Daniel Klimovich, DaoXan, Debresser, Deisenbe, Dimadick, Doug Weller, Editor2020, Emir of Wikipedia, Enthusiast01, Entropyandvodka, FDRMRZUSA, Favonian, Fayenatic london, Freepress2122, FutureTrillionaire, GHcool, GLOOOm9, GünniX, Hertz1888, Hijiri88, I dream of horses, Ian.thomson, Isambard Kingdom, JUSTINLEUII, Javert2113, Jim1138, John of Reading, Johnmcintyre1959, Jonney2000, Jprg1966, JudeccaXIII, Jytdog, K6ka, KH-1, Kaobear, KingSkyLord, Look2See1, MShabazz, Malik Shabazz, Marcocapelle, Marek69, Marselan, Materialscientist, Maximajorian Viridio, Migeo, Monochrome Monitor, Moogsi, Navops47, Nederlandse Leeuw, Nonstopdrivel, Nuts like your mom, Oajmar, Orangemike, Oshwah, Ottawagalz, Pepper, Pixarkid101, Pmokeefe, Qwertyus, Ricky81682, Rodw, Romesdealt, SamiSLEEM, Scott Illini, Shellwood, Shrike, Simon Adler, Sjö, Smeat75, StAnselm, Stesmo, Stickee, StjJackson, Tajotep, Tgeorgescu, Triggerhippie4, William Allen Simpson, Wing gundam, Winsocker, Zzuuzz, יניב יבריב, חורון, 低端人口 , 145 anonymous edits . 61

Kingdom of Israel (Samaria) *Source:* https://en.wikipedia.org/w/index.php?oldid=865606135 *License:* Creative Commons Attribution-Share Alike 3.0 *Contributors:* *DuckundWeg*, 1990'sguy, 3primetime3, Acroterion, AddMore-III, AmYisroelChai, American Starkiller, Andrewa, Angel ivanov angelov, Armbrust, Arminden, Auntof6, Auric, Averysoda, Bazuz, BedrockPerson, Bennylin, Bgpaulus, Binksternet, C.Fred, CLCStudent, Cornelhac9, Craig Pemberton, DXRD, DaoXan, Darkjudah, Davshul, Debresser, Deisenbe, Dimadick, Discographer, Do not collect, Don4of4, Doug Weller, Drmies, Ecthelion83, Editor2020, El C, Enthusiast01, Entropyandvodka, Erik9, Fayenatic london, Feline Hymnic, Finn Bjørklid, Fixer88, Gabriel Kielland, General Ization, Gilgamesh∼enwiki, GodenDaeg, Good Olfactory, Greyjoy, Greyshark09, Guns of brixham, Hadarot, Harvzsf, Hilmorel, Hmains, Hmainsbot1, Infantom, IntoThinAir, J04n, JackintheBox, Jandalhandler, Jauerback, Jim1138, Jlapidus, John "Hannibal" Smith, John Hyams, JonHarder, Joshua Segal, Jprg1966, JudeccaXIII, Junze.09, Kibi78704, Kiore, Koavf, Kuratowski's Ghost, L293D, LilHelpa, Lisa, LordGorval, MShabazz, Magister Scienta, Malik Shabazz, Malus Catulus, Marcocapelle, Marselan, Martis II, Maureendepresident, Midrashah, Mike Rosoft, Mike hayes, Mistakefinder, Mohammed Awny Dabbour, Monochrome Monitor, Muhammad Umair Mirza, Navops47, NawlinWiki, Neddyseagoon, Nederlandse Leeuw, Ninja247, Omnipaedista, Onceinawhile, Oshwah, Paracel63, Philarete∼enwiki, ProKro, R'n'B, Reign of Toads, Rich Farmbrough, Rjwilmsi, Rmaad Daamr, RoyYa, SJ Defender, SchreiberBike, Shellwood, Shibo77, Shrike, SimonP, StAnselm, Str1977, TAnthony, Tahir mq, Tajotep, Thecrookedcoinlessjew, Tide rolls, Triggerhippie4, Tritomex, Twillisjr, Uberhill, Unreal7, Vanished user ewfisn2348tui2f8n2fio2utjfeoi210r39jf, Viking Rollo, Von Altringen, WereSpielChequers, Weyd, When Other Legends Are Forgotten, Woohookitty, Xuxalliope, Yahnatan, Yaron Livne, Zoeperkoe, יניב, חורון, ששש.מ.ל 131 anonymous edits 71

Kingdom of Judah *Source:* https://en.wikipedia.org/w/index.php?oldid=865606559 *License:* Creative Commons Attribution-Share Alike 3.0 *Contributors:* ---, 1990'sguy, AddMore-III, All Rows4, American Starkiller, Andrewman327, Armbrust, Arminden, Auric, Avusi nabusi, BartPR, BedrockPerson, Ben Ben, Bender235, Beukford, CambridgeBayWeather, Chowbok, Choy4311, ClueBot NG, Crapapple, Crowtow849, Dailycare, Daniel Klimovich, DaoXan, Darlene Hutchins, David.moreno72, Daylight15, Debresser, Deisenbe, Do not collect, Don4of4, Doug Weller, Drsmoo, Dtr1604, Durfels, Editor2020, Egeymi, Eharding, Emmette Hernandez Coleman, Enthusiast01, Entropyandvodka, Fab1uk, Fayenatic london, Finavon, Flyer22 Reborn, Frietjes, Geagea, Gilliam, Guns of brixham, Guy355, Hairy Dude, HammerFilmFan, Happysailor, Hertz1888, Hiberniantears, Hmains, Hmainsbot1, ISavedPvtRyan, Infantom, Infotryman, IronMaidenRocks, Isambard Kingdom, Jaliscan, Jason Quinn, Jheald, Jnate19, Johnmcintyre1959, Jonesey95, Jprg1966, JudeccaXIII, Jytdog, Khazar2, Klemen Kocjancic, Lfdder, Lightlowemon, Look2See1, MB298, MShabazz, Magioladitis, Malik Shabazz, Marcocapelle, Marselan, Materialscientist, MediaKill13, Midrashah, Monochrome Monitor, Naomi.piquette, Narky Blert, Natureguy1980, Navops47, Neo-Jay, Ogress, OmnipotentEntity, Onceinawhile, Ost316, Peacedance, PiCo, Ponyo, Professor alacarte, Qwertyus, Rivalitaet, Serols, Srich32977, StAnselm, Steel1943, Student7,

TAnthony, Tahir mq, Telpardec, Tgeorgescu, Theredheifer, Triggerhippie4, Velella, Wikieditor101, Winsocker, Wlglunight93, XtinaS, יניב, הורין, ששש.מ.ל, 135 anonymous edits 83

History of the Jews in the Roman Empire *Source:* https://en.wikipedia.org/w/index.php?oldid=863562813 *License:* Creative Commons Attribution-Share Alike 3.0 *Contributors:* 72, A.amitkumar, Againme, Agtx, Arminden, Bluevenge, Bongwarrior, CASSIOPEIA, Calarcon, CaptainLepton, Chesdovi, ClueBot NG, Cplakidas, Cynwolfe, DVdm, DarkKing Rayleigh, DuckeggAlex, Editor2020, Egsan Bacon, Enthusiast01, Eurodyne, Excirial, Fluffernutter, Gary123, GermanJoe, Ginsuloft, Glane23, HickoryOughtShirt?4, Hieroglyph albert, I dream of horses, IZAK, IntoThinAir, Jackson Peebles, Jandkas, Jason.nlw, Johnbod, JosephusOfJerusalem, Judy Somerville, KylieTastic, Makecat, Marcocapelle, Mdanaher, Melcous, Menchi, Narky Blert, Narrowusername561, Novusuna, Omnipaedista, Owais Khursheed, Pavel Krupička, Pavel Vozenilek, Pedro8790, Piledhighandeep, Porschia2, Qwertyus, R'n'B, Reconsider the static, RetroCraft314, Russian Rocky, Serols, Shellwood, Simplexity22, Smeat75, Stesmo, Stvnkir, SuperHamster, Ulric1313, Uncle Dick, Webclient101, WilliamDigiCol, Woohookitty, יניב, הורין, ‎Ÿ, 143 anonymous edits 99

Kingdom of Jerusalem *Source:* https://en.wikipedia.org/w/index.php?oldid=862912731 *License:* Creative Commons Attribution-Share Alike 3.0 *Contributors:* A. Parrot, Adam Bishop, AjaxSmack, Al Ameer son, Al.xonder, Ala.foum, Alessadri, Alphathon, Andrei Iosifovich, Antidiskriminator, Arminden, Auntof6, BD2412, Bankster, Bellroth, Bender235, Blanche of King's Lynn, Blaue Max, Blue520, Borsoka, CalicoCatLover, Certes, Charles Matthews, Chewings72, Chicbyaccident, Choess, Chris the speller, Cirflow, ClueBot NG, Colonies Chris, CommonsDelinker, Cplakidas, Cracker.please88, DA1, Darkstar8799, Dbachmann, Debgerish, Dianaalsadi123, Donner60, Dragovit, Editor2020, Egsan Bacon, Eleman, Excirial, Fayenatic london, Frietjes, Fæ, Gilabrand, Glide08, GoingBatty, Governor Sheng, Greyshark09, Hayden120, Hayk.arabaget, HeneralVicente23, Hmains, Hmainsbot1, I Feel Tired, I dream of horses, Ian Rose, Icairns, Infantom, Intakhab, Iridescent, Ixfd64, JacBourg, Jack Bufalo Head, Jack Upland, Jacob D, Jan Kentink, Joy, JudeccaXIII, Kansas Bear, Kgrad, Khazar2, Klemen Kocjancic, Krakkos, Ktr101, Laurel Lodged, LiamKasbar, LionSunne, Look2See1, Lotje, Lugia2453, Lylefor, Mabdul, Magioladitis, Malik Shabazz, Marcocapelle, Marcusaurelius161, Marek69, Martin1225, MeanMotherJr, Medizinball, Michael Cockrell, Migeo, MikhaëlO, Mitchell.robbins, Moagim, Mukogodo, Nihlus1, Omnipaedista, Onceinawhile, Onel5969, OwenBlacker, Pagony, Pandukht, Pariah24, Per Honor et Gloria, Pktlaurence, Plastikspork, R'n'B, RR, Radman2020, Realpoetamagna, Royfixedit, RudolfRed, SMC, SQGibbon, Sageo, SamuelTheGhost, Sandsoftblue, Seonookim, ShelleyAdams, Shellwood, Sigehelmus, Sir Arbalest, Smack, Sorabino, Srnec, StAnselm, Steinsplitter, StevenJ81, StjJackson, Thomas Courtenay, Earl of Devon, Tobby72, Toby Bartels, Tom-L, Tzahy, Ucucha, Uishaki, Ulric1313, Unother, Urselius, Uspzor, Villevalloworms, Vmavanti, WTMitchell3, Winsocker, Winterst, Woohookitty, אריה גור, יהודה, ייהלייזושמר, باسم, سوسو العربية, გიო ოქროპ, 142 anonymous edits 109

Mutasarrifate of Jerusalem *Source:* https://en.wikipedia.org/w/index.php?oldid=843372899 *License:* Creative Commons Attribution-Share Alike 3.0 *Contributors:* Al Ameer son, Androoox, Arminden, Ayeff, BD2412, Bearcat, Bender235, Bolter21, CarolOfTheForest, Comnenus, DH85868993, Dcirovic, Dreamsarenotreal, E.M.Gregory, Editor2020, Elie plus, Enthusiast01, Gilabrand, Gotipe, Greyshark09, Huldra, Ithinkicahn, Jacob D, JamesBWatson, Johnpacklambert, Jonesey95, Lectonar, MB, Marcocapelle, Michael Cockrell, Mumbo-jumbophobe, Newimpartial, Omnipaedista, Onceinawhile, Qualitatis, RH Swearengin, RickinBaltimore, Rjwilmsi, Roscelese, Sean.hoyland, Sidoroff-B, Squids and Chips, Supreme Deliciousness, SwisterTwister, Tabletop, Tanbircdq, The Anomebot2, Tim!, Triggerhippie4, Ultimate Destiny, Underlying lk, WhisperToMe, Widefox, Xact, Y, Zero0000, 49 anonymous edits 153

Mandatory Palestine *Source:* https://en.wikipedia.org/w/index.php?oldid=865621503 *License:* Creative Commons Attribution-Share Alike 3.0 *Contributors:* 7uperWkipedan, A2soup, Acroterion, AlexEng, Alexlange, AmirSurfLera, Andy M. Wang, Anonymous from the 21st century, Arminden, Averysoda, BD2412, BedrockPerson, BeenAroundAWhile, Bender235, Benjamin.1209, Biblioworm, Bjarlin, Bolter21, Born2bgratis, BreakfastJr, CasualObserver'48, Cawhee, Cliftonian, ClueBot NG, CommonsDelinker, Corriebertus, Dan Pelleg, DanDanT, Danny lost, DaoXan, Davidbena, DeFacto, Deborahjay, Debresser, Deii nk, Delores Moghadam, DemocraticLuntz, DiverDave, Dont belittle245, Dormskirk, DrFrench, Editor2020, Emir of Wikipedia, Eric Pode lives, Etan J. Tal, Eztransmission, FeatherPluma, Felix r, Finnusertop, Flinders Petrie, Frietjes, Frmorrison, GGranddad, Gertiu32, Gilliam, Gilo1969, Global Cerebral Ischemia, Greyshark09, Grolltech, HJ Mitchell, Hertz1888, Huldra, Hummingbird, Ianblair23, Ibarabi, Icewhiz, ImTheIP, Iridescent, J 1982, JB82, JJMC89, JackintheBox, JamesBWatson, Jandalhandler, Jd22292, Jgrantduff, John90jacobson, Johnmcintyre1959, Jprg1966, KylieTastic, Levitetribe, Litalbn1, Look2See1, MAlexanderNoble, MShabazz, Magnolia677, Majora, Makeandtoss, Malik Shabazz, Mannerheimo, Marcocapelle, Marek69, Markunator, Materialscientist, Matthew Proctor, McSly, Mccapra, Mdann52, Methestes, Metropolitan90, MisterMorton, Moto53, Mr. Dodo'sss, Mumbo-jumbophobe, Mx. Granger, NSH002, Nableezy, Naraht, Natg 19, No More Mr Nice Guy, Notthebestusername, Omnipaedista, Onceinawhile, Peter Chastain, Plucas58, Pluto2012, Primefac, R'n'B, Reenem, RekishiEJ, Richard Keatinge, RichardWeiss, Rjwilmsi, Robert Brukner, Robochrist, Rothorpe, Rrostrom, Salbers, Sangdeboeuf, SantiLak, Sdittman, Sean.hoyland, Selfstudier, SheriffIsInTown, Shrike, ShulMaven, Simonpratt, Sokuya, SpanishSnake, Srich32977, Stefanomione, Sudhamarang, Sue Douglasss, Supreme Deliciousness, Swingoswingo, Tango303, Tarook97, Tassedethe, Tobby72, Tritomex, Tzadikv, ValarianB, WOSlinker, Werldwayd, When Other Legends Are Forgotten, Wikiliki, Williamteoh97, Willschmut, Wlglunight93, Ykantor, Ynhockey, Yoav95179, Yunis, ZScarpia, Zero0000, Zozoulia, X, יניב, הורין 80 anonymous edits 163

Jewish Agency for Israel *Source:* https://en.wikipedia.org/w/index.php?oldid=862510681 *License:* Creative Commons Attribution-Share Alike 3.0 *Contributors:* Adi Kayam, Aimeeweiss, Akisch, Anomalocaris, Arado, Arminden, Atbannett, BD2412, Bearcat, Bender235, Bensin, Bgwhite, Biosketch, CN3777, CasualObserver'48, Catlemur, Chaimpesach, Closedmouth, ClueBot NG, Cmr08, Colonies Chris, CommonsDelinker, CyberXRef, Davidchoen, Debresser, Dimension31, Dpi659, Dsp13, Eat me, I'm an azuki, Enthusiast01, Epicgenius, Etan J. Tal, Ethantblack, Evenshushan2000, Eytan1928, Fayenatic london, Gilabrand, Happy138, Headbomb, Hibernian, Hmains, IRISZOOM, Ijon, Israelforlife, Jacob D, JamesAM, Jeff G., Jersey92, John of Reading, Jon Kolbert, Jonesey95, Josve05a, Jpgordon, Jprg1966, Jtaifeld, JustAGal, Lapkis∼enwiki, Lotje, Magioladitis, Malik Shabazz, Marcocapelle, Materialscientist, Michipedian, Midrashah, Mkativerata, MuhannadDarwish, Muneeb abid mehmood, My Chemistry romantic, Odder, Onceinawhile, PLNR, Padres Hana, Parkwells, Perplexed566, PiMaster3, Place Clichy, Quackslikeaduck, Qualitatis, Quidam65, R. S. Shaw, Rachel Kops, Rbwriter, Robert Brukner, Rodw, Sarah Bronson, Scriberius, Srich32977, Srnec, Steinsplitter, Stemonitis, Stephen G. Brown, Stirmysoultogigglemode, Tafkira2, TaraIngrid, Triggerhippie4, Udidoll, Wavelength, Zero0000, דן, ווולבו 40 anonymous edits 213

Fifth Aliyah *Source:* https://en.wikipedia.org/w/index.php?oldid=857886897 *License:* Creative Commons Attribution-Share Alike 3.0 *Contributors:* Acidburn24m, Arnavchaudhary, BD2412, Chesdovi, Egosi124, EivindJ, Epearl, Etan J. Tal, Faigl.ladislav, Fatal!ty, Ganacka, Gilliam, Jimhoward72, King of the fourth, Marcocapelle, Michael Cockrell, Number 57, Plot Spoiler, Poldy Bloom, Polylerus, Rakoon, Reenem, Rjwilmsi, Shellwood, Squash Racket, Steinsplitter, Superpie, TaBOT-zerem, Tewfik, TheCuriousGnome, TrickyH, Xaxes, Του Δημήτρη, 55דוד יניב, הורין 18 anonymous edits 249

Tripartite Pact *Source:* https://en.wikipedia.org/w/index.php?oldid=863165665 *License:* Creative Commons Attribution-Share Alike 3.0 *Contributors:* 23 editor, A Werewolf, Akinkhoo, Andrwsc, Axxxion, BeenAroundAWhile, Bender235, Binksternet, BokicaK, Bukubku, CAPTAIN RAJU, Chanceharrah, Chrisahn, ClueBot NG, Cymru.lass, DH85868993, DavidBrooks, Dcirovic, Denver20, Devin, Dimadick, Donner60, Dzenanz, Eastlaw, Ed-Johnston, Edokter, El cid, el campeador, Fat&Happy, George yo wiki, Good Olfactory, Gorthian, GregorB, Gujuguy, HIDECCHI001, Hilmorel, Howcheng, IamSoStupidBecauseIamPoo, IronGargoyle, J 1982, J Milburn, Javanx3d, Jdaloner, Jonesey95, Joy, Khajidha, King Of The Moas, Kintetsubuffalo, Klemen Kocjancic, Kostja, Kyauk, Lajbi, Letdemsay, Lt.Specht, LuigiPortaro29, MPS1992, Mandruss, Materialscientist, Mentatus, Mikko H., Mogism, Mrodowicz, My Chemistry romantic, My name is not dave, NYBrook098, Narky Blert, NeroN BG, Niceguyedc, Nsaa, Nyttend, Opa-un, Outriggr, Owain Knight, Pavlor, Peacemaker67, Pelaisse, Per Honor et Gloria, PinkOrangeCat, Polylerus, Propatriamori, Ptbotgourou, Pudeo, RA0808, RelativeQuantumTheory, Repdetect117, Rich Farmbrough, Rjwilmsi, Rodw, Romanov loyalist, Rrostrom, Sangjinhwa, Sardanaphalus, Semi-Lobster, Senjuto, Setawut, Shoshui, SindreKA, Srnec, TAnthony, THEWULFMAN, Tec15, TheBlueMapper, TheMagnificent101, Thecheesykid, Thommy9, Tide rolls, Tim!, Trurle, TwinkleMore, Vanobamo, Wavelength, Whiskey, Widr, Wwheaton, Yaush, YellowMonkey, Yerpo, Zoupan, ÄDA - DÄP, Δ, Ÿ, 221 anonymous edits 253

1936–1939 Arab revolt in Palestine *Source:* https://en.wikipedia.org/w/index.php?oldid=850623292 *License:* Creative Commons Attribution-Share Alike 3.0 *Contributors:* 8HGasma, Againme, AhmadArabi, Al Ameer son, Al-Andalusi, AmirSurfLera, AndresHerutJaim, Applodion, Arado, Arminden, Arpose, AustralianRupert, Averysoda, Azcolvin429, BD2412, Bahaa.pal, Bender235, Bgwhite, Blue-bi-bear, Bongwarrior, Brigade Piron, Cambalachero, Candido, Charles Essie, Chris the speller, ChrisGualtieri, Chrism, Clpo13, ClueBot NG, CommonsDelinker, Cyberbot II, Dabbler, Dana3780, DePiep, Denis MacEoin, Dl2000, Donner60, Drsmoo, E.M.Gregory, Eastfarthingan, Edward, Elockid, Emir of Wikipedia, Enthusiast01, Eyal Rubin, Faizan, Fayenatic london, Fconaway, Galatz, Gilabrand, Gob Lofa, GraemeLeggett, Greyshark09, Hanay, HandsomeFella, Headbomb, Historylover4, Hugo999, Huldra, IRISZOOM, Icewhiz, Ijon, Infantom, InverseHypercube, IranitGreenberg, Iwant2write, Jabotito48, Jarmunn, Jesse V., Jim.henderson, John of Reading, Joseon Empire, JustAGal, Keith-264, Khazar2, Kingbird1, Kingsindian, Ks0stm, Kyuko, Lectonar, Look2See1, Lotje, LoveFerguson, MShabazz, Magioladitis, Mark Schierbecker, Mayumashu, MelissaLond, Mhroe, Michael Demiurgos, Mild Bill Hiccup, Monochrome Monitor, Mr Stephen, MusikAnimal, Nableezy, Natg 19, Niceguyedc, Nishidani, No More Mr Nice Guy, Notreallydavid, Number 57, Ohconfucius, Onceinawhile, PLNR, Padres Hana, Philip Trueman, Pluto2012, Professor alacarte, Quinton Feldberg, R. S. Shaw, Ronreisman, Rpawson, Russ3Z, Sakiv, Sherira, ShimonChai, Shrike, Sonntagsbraten, Srich32977, Star77∼enwiki, Stumink, Sunmist, Sunny Xmas, TAnthony, Taurniul, Taurui01, TheCuriousGnome, Topbanana, TruPepitoM, Tutangamon, Uishaki, WPGA2345, WQUlrich, Wlglunight93, Ykantor, Ynhockey, ZScarpia, Zero0000, Zzuuzz, أبو عمر الفلسطيني, 81 anonymous edits ??

White Paper of 1939 *Source:* https://en.wikipedia.org/w/index.php?oldid=857803530 *License:* Creative Commons Attribution-Share Alike 3.0 *Contributors:* Arminden, Averysoda, BD2412, Baatarsaikan, Bellerophon5685, Bender235, Bradeos Graphon, Breno, Caiaffa, Cartographile, ClueBot NG, Cmichael, Deror avi, El C, Elan26, Elfelix, Encyclopedia77, Faigl.ladislav, Fayenatic london, Fikolitetroup, Funnyhat, Galatz, Garamond Lethe, Good Olfactory, GraemeLeggett, Ground Zero, Guy Montag, HG1, HamburgerRadio, HandsomeFella, Harlan wilkerson, Hmains, Huldra, IRISZOOM, IZAK, Iadmc, Ian Pitchford, Iridescent, J.delanoy, J04n, Jbeans, Joe in Australia, Joelouis98, Jprg1966, Jsolinsky, Jweiss11, KantElope, Keira1992, Keith D, Khazar2, L.Willms, Lacrimosus, Legobot II, Luwilt, MALLUS, Marcocapelle, Mike Schwartz, MikeyTMNT, Miszatomic, Monochrome Monitor, Motacilla, Mtsmallwood, Mufka, NSH001, Nishidani, Onceinawhile, Optakeover, PLNR, Padres Hana, Peter cohen, Plastikspork, Rbwik, Recognizance, Reenem, Richard Keatinge, Rjakew, Robert Brukner, Robofish, SJP, Satualm, SchreiberBike, Scientizzle, Scott Adler, Scott Paeth, Selfstudier, Shrike, Skier Dude, Sm8900, SoLando, Stemonitis, Str1977, Telaviv1, Tewfik, Textorus, Thecurran, Tiggerjay, Tim!, Timrollpickering, Tom Lapper, Troop350, Uishaki, Ulflarsen, Uriber, UrukHaiLoR, Vladmirfish, Wfraga, Wikimag74, Wingman417, YUL89YYZ, Yash2017, Yasya, Ykantor, Ykauyn78, ZScarpia, Zero0000, יניב, הורין, 105 anonymous edits 312

History of the Jews during World War II *Source:* https://en.wikipedia.org/w/index.php?oldid=864368738 *License:* Creative Commons Attribution-Share Alike 3.0 *Contributors:* -), 1234567890blob, 16@r, 3 of Diamonds, 72, Abcdukil, Alan Liefting, AnnaFrance, Archiloc, ArnoldReinhold, BD2412,

Barkeep, Bgwhite, Blanchardb, Bobo192, Bongwarrior, Bouncebyour, Brambleclawx, CASSIOPEIA, Camw, CaroleHenson, Chris the speller, Ckruschke, ClueBot NG, Crystallizedcarbon, Dac04, Dan Koehl, Daonguyen95, Darkwind, Darth Panda, Dcirovic, Dirkbb, Discospinster, Doug Weller, Dysepsion, Editor2020, EdmundT, El bot de la dieta, Epbr123, Faithlessthewonderboy, Frostbitejoe, Geni, Gilliam, Glane23, Hannahbydal, Hello71, Hghyux, Hmains, IZAK, Iridescent, IronGargoyle, J.delanoy, JMMuller, Jacurek, Jasonanaggie, Jeff G., John K, John254, JustBerry, Kanebckuu, Kicker Aha, Klundarr, KylieTastic, Lairor, LuK3, Lugia2453, MMS2013, Marc87, Marcocapelle, MarnelteD, Materialscientist, MattWade, Mdann52, Mechanical digger, Mild Bill Hiccup, Mimihitam, Monopoly31121993, MusicalKnight, My Chemistry romantic, Natg 19, Nezzadar, Nocheats, Onebravemonkey, Orphan Wiki, Oshwah, Oxfordwang, Patrick Dempsey (Holocaust), Person who formerly started with "216", Pessimist2006, Philip Trueman, Pinkfloyd100, Poeticbent, Radon210, Reenem, Rich Farmbrough, Rjd0060, Rrburke, S251572, Sardanaphalus, Shellwood, Shirik, Silverhorse, Sjö, Snow Blizzard, SoLando, Sosthenes12, Supreme Dragon, Thatguyflint, The PIPE, TheFreeWorld, Tide rolls, Tim1357, Triggerhippie4, Triwbe, TyA, Ubiquity, VoABot II, WarburgerII, Wayne Slam, Widr, WikiHead, Wikid77, Wikipelli, Yamaguchi先生, Викизавр, חורון ינב׳, 227 anonymous edits 325
The Holocaust *Source:* https://en.wikipedia.org/w/index.php?oldid=865230615 *License:* Creative Commons Attribution-Share Alike 3.0 *Contributors:* 344917661X, 5belldaniel, Acroterion, Aditya Mishra H1N1, Antandrus, Anthony22, AssadistDEFECTOR, BD2412, Bear-rings, Beauty School Dropout, Beland, Birkeen, CapLiber, Capt Jim, Catriona, Citizen Canine, ClueBot NG, Dan Koehl, DangerousJXD, Dick Shane, DocWatson42, Doug Weller, Ealdgyth, Educator57, Edwin trinh14, Ehn, ExRat, GizzyCatBella, Godthegod, Governor Jerjerrod, Hijuecutivo, Hmains, Hohum, Hotspur23, Ian.thomson, Icewhiz, Jhertel, Joe K., Joel Mc, Joey Steel, John of Reading, JohnGDallman, Jontel, Jurassicjae, K.e.coffman, KHMELNYTSKYIA, Kablammo, KarndenmcLean, Karl.i.biased, Keiiri, Kierzek, Laszlo Panaflex, LeoC12, LittleJerry, MagicMatador, Malik Shabazz, Metoody, MyMoloboaccount, Mzajac, Narcissus14, Obenritter, Onel5969, Oranjelo100, Orr, Paul Siebert, Pauli133, Paulinho28, Poeticbent, Prinsgezinde, Raulpenaranda, Rich Farmbrough, Rivertorch, Rjwilmsi, Robby.is.on, Roderickslily, Rreagan007, Ryan1783, Seraphim System, Shaded0, ShadowHawk555, Skipfortyfour, Skylax30, SlimVirgin, Southenddave, SquidHomme, Surtsicna, The Man in Question, TheFreeWorld, ThurnerRupert, Tobby72, Vihelik, Yabti, Yamb, Yatzhek, .62ינב׳ ,חורון, 56 anonymous edits 330
Aliyah Bet *Source:* https://en.wikipedia.org/w/index.php?oldid=863660056 *License:* Creative Commons Attribution-Share Alike 3.0 *Contributors:* Acidburn24m, Adrian two, Aieff, Alexf, Asa Zernik, BD2412, Backendgaming, Bender235, Bimbigoli, Brackenheim, Brewcrewer, Brycehughes, Chefallen, Chronus, ClueBot NG, Colonies Chris, DagosNavy, Davidcannon, Dawkeye, Deborahjay, Deror avi, Dodo19～enwiki, Donama, Dormskirk, EIFY, Edie Vanja, Edwardx, Ehudamir, Ekrodg, El C, Eldad, Faigl.ladislav, Fatal!ty, Former user 2, Fpetran, Gareth Griffith-Jones, George100, Gilabrand, Greyshark09, HantsAV, Helix84, Herrbeerrt, Historicist, Hmains, I dream of horses, IZAK, Ian Pitchford, J.delanoy, JHistory, Jamie9897, Jeff3000, Jeneme, Jethro B, Jimhoward72, Jonel, Jpallan, Jweiss11, Keilana, Kyuko, LFaraone, Leifern, Linuxbeak, Livna-Maor, Lotje, MBisanz, MPerel, Manxruler, McZusatz, Mimihitam, Mogism, Motacilla, MrOllie, Nableezy, Nahumm, Nfl2007guy, Noswald, Number 57, Outback the koala, Pearle, Place Clichy, Poeticbent, Poliocretes, Popper12, Prgefen, Proofreader, Quitehelpful, Reenem, Reinyday, Renamed user 5695569576f6b340, Rjwilmsi, Rms125a@hotmail.com, Robert Brukner, Roland zh, Rrostrom, SZAgassi, Samee, Sarah Bronson, Sarahj2107, Sbryen, Sean.hoyland, Sonntagsbraten, Steinsplitter, StevenBirnam, Sue Gardner, Tazmaniacs, Tewfik, Textorus, TheDragonhunter, Thecurran, USHMMwesthem, Wavelength, Wayne Slam, WereSpielChequers, Wolfman, Wronkiew, Xyl 54, Yanas girl, Ynhockey, Zero0000, ציוב׳ ,קודיקד פארוני, דיוד׳, 41 anonymous edits 397
Jewish insurgency in Mandatory Palestine *Source:* https://en.wikipedia.org/w/index.php?oldid=860634056 *License:* Creative Commons Attribution-Share Alike 3.0 *Contributors:* $1LENCE D00600D, AddWittyNameHere, AmirSurfLera, Arminden, Ashashyou, AustralianRupert, Averysoda, BD2412, BU Rob13, Bender235, Berserker276, Bolter21, British want Judah Judenfrei, Chris the speller, ClueBot NG, Cnwilliams, CommonsDelinker, Cplakidas, DagosNavy, Dan100, Darian2009, Dedpan1, Dreddis Rules, Drsmoo, Dlockid, Euryalus, Fayenatic london, Flyer22 Reborn, Frosty, FutureTrillionaire, Gfcan777, Greyshark09, Ground Zero, Hlackyboy, Hertz1888, Hmains, Huldra, IRISZOOM, Infantom, Iridescent, Ironhoids, Iwant2write, Jenks24, Jodosma, Johnmcintyre1959, JonaQwer, Jprg1966, Katangais, Keith D, La katz79, LilHelpa, LlywelynII, Loki51, Lord of Mirkwood, Lotje, Magioladitis, Makeandtoss, Malik Shabazz, Marcocapelle, MelissaLond, Mikrobølgeovn, Monochrome Monitor, Nableezy, NawlinWiki, Nishidani, Onceinawhile, PLNR, Par Ah Dux, Pluto2012, RandomScholar30, Reenem, Robert Brukner, Sean.hoyland, Sgn45t, Shiribaz, Sobreira, Subir-Grewal, Supreme Deliciousness, Swazzo, TheGracefulSlick, Tom.Reding, UnbiasedVictory, Wavelength, Wikipadoh, Wikipelli, Wlglunight93, XavierItzm, Yikkayaya, Ykantor, ZScarpia, Zero0000, השמשיינב׳ ,דירוד׳, 41 anonymous edits 413
United Nations Partition Plan for Palestine *Source:* https://en.wikipedia.org/w/index.php?oldid=857956027 *License:* Creative Commons Attribution-Share Alike 3.0 *Contributors:* 331dot, AManWithNoPlan, Abhinav, Alpha3031, AmirSurfLera, Anders Feder, Andre.bittar, AnonMoos, Arius1988, Arminden, BD2412, Backendgaming, Bad Dryer, BeenAroundAWhile, Beland, Bender235, Bgwhite, Bolter21, Brandmeister, BreakfastJr, Brentworks, Brewcrewer, Cengime, Chewings72, Chris the speller, Cliftonian, ClueBot NG, Correctorbetus, DadaNeem, Dailycare, Dan653, DanielRHarris, Di2000, Dlv999, ElHef, EtienneDolet, Faceless Enemy, Fayenatic london, Fourathkoury75, Galatz, Ged UK, GeneralizationsAreBad, Good Olfactory, GünniX, Haldraper, Horseford, Hotshot977, Howcheng, Huldra, IRISZOOM, IkeBanet, Igorp jj, Itsmejudith, IZAK2, Jdaloner, Jennica, Jmg38, John of Reading, Jon Kolbert, KahnJohn27, Klots888, L.Willms, LahmacunKebab, LilHelpa, Loop202, Lord Bolingbroke, M.ye86, Magioladitis, Maile66, Makeandtoss, Malercoster, Mannerheimo, Marcocapelle, Materialscientist, Methestes, Mild Bill Hiccup, Mumbo-jumbophobe, Mx. Granger, Newyorkadam, Nishidani, No More Mr Nice Guy, Onceinawhile, Orenburg1, PLNR, Pabkothepenguin, PalaceGuard008, Pluto2012, Rich Farmbrough, Rollinmoss, Rrostrom, Sakiv, Sammy1857, Shrike, Sluzzelin, Smerus, Snargle1, Srednuas Lenoroc, Stumink, SubirGrewal, Supreme Dragon, Trahelliven, Uglemat, Valenciano, Wavelength, Welsh, WereSpielChequers, Wickey-nl, Wlglunight93, Wrestlingring, Yb2, Ykantor, ZScarpia, Zenomax, Zero0000, 78 anonymous edits 452
1947–48 Civil War in Mandatory Palestine *Source:* https://en.wikipedia.org/w/index.php?oldid=865100835 *License:* Creative Commons Attribution-Share Alike 3.0 *Contributors:* 1exec1, Alfie Gandon, AmirSurfLera, Anaod, Arminden, Aua, Averysoda, BD2412, BU Rob13, Bender235, Best blogeerer, Billy Hathorn, Bolter21, Booboo29, Brewcrewer, Bus stop, Cannolis, Catriona, Ceosad, Certes, Charles Essie, Choess, Chris the speller, Citizen Canine, ClueBot NG, CommonsDelinker, Crainedmeipait, Denisrodmann88, Diannaa, Diblidabliduu, Dhombsen8, EdJohnston, EzA+lSeb Nnakari, Fayenatic london, Frederico1234, GenQuest, Glovacki, Gob Lofa, Good Olfactory, GreenC, Greyshark09, Grubemeister, Hdll00, Hertz1888, Hmains, Holdoffhunger, Hugo999, Huldra, IRISZOOM, Illegitimate Barrister, IranitGreenberg, Itsmejudith, JFG, Jbarta, Jbeck8924, Jd22292, Jim118, Jmj713, Jonney2000, Joshua Rowe, Jprg1966, Keiiri, Keith-264, Khazar2, Kintetsubuffalo, Lightlowemon, Lothar von Richthofen, Lyndaship, MShabazz, MX44, Marcocapelle, Mark Schierbecker, Materialscientist, Mediolic, MelbourneStar, MelissaLond, Mogism, MusikAnimal, Nableezy, Never white-out, Niceguyede, Nihiltres, Nishidani, Octopus1066, PLNR, Padres Hana, Petebutt, Philip Cross, Pluto2012, ProudIrishAspie, QueenCake, Rebutcher, Redrose64, Ronreisman, Rrostrom, Sean.hoyland, Sonntagsbraten, Steverci, TAnthony, Takinginterest01, The Devil's Advocate, Trahelliven, Trefork, TrickyH, Uishaki, UnbiasedVictory, Volunteer Marek, Welsh, Wickey-nl, WikiPoun, Wlglunight93, Ykantor, Ynhockey, Zero0000, MAXIMuM HOT, חורון ינב׳ ,47 anonymous edits ....??
1948 Arab–Israeli War *Source:* https://en.wikipedia.org/w/index.php?oldid=865100424 *License:* Creative Commons Attribution-Share Alike 3.0 *Contributors:* A D Monroe III, A.h. king, Adapad, Aexon79, Airplaneman, Al-Andalusi, AmirSurfLera, Amphicoelias, Anders Feder, Andrwsc, AntanO, Anticitizen 98, Antillarum, Arjayay, Arminden, AsceticRose, Ashurbanippal, Averysoda, Axeman89, BD2412, Banedon, Bender235, BethNaught, Bgwhite, Bolter21, Calthinus, CapLiber, Catriona, Certes, Chewings72, Chipperdude15, Chymicus, Codrinb, CopperSquare, CsikosLo, Cyberbot II, Dan Koehl, Dan100, Daniel1212, Davidbena, Dawnseeker2000, De wafelenbak, Dewritech, Dreddis Rules, E.M.Gregory, Eggishorn, Egsan Bacon, Ekips39, Equinox, Eric Knaalen, Eudialytos, Expokerer, Faceless Enemy, Fayenatic london, Funnyhat, GabrielF, Gadget850, Gfcan777, Grant65, GregKaye, GünniX, Haakonsson, Hairy Dude, Heavenlyblue, Hertz1888, Hohum, Howcheng, Huldra, IRISZOOM, Icewhiz, Iwant2write, J 1982, Jd22292, Joehedaya1, John of Reading, Johnmcintyre1959, Jon Kolbert, Jonesey95, Jonney2000, Jprg1966, Jweiss11, Kahtar, Kaltenmeyer, Klemen Kocjancic, Kndimov, Kollserp, Kombucha, Kritikos99, Krosshair1, Kumdano9, Lemnaminor, LightandDark2000, Lisa, Lollipopolollipopolollipop, MacAuslan, Makeandtoss, Malayedit, Malik Shabazz, Markunator, Markus1423, MarneltleD, Mikeblas, Mikrobølgeovn, Mogism, Monochrome Monitor, Monopoly31121993, Mortense, Murph9000, Natg 19, NiD.29, Niceguyede, Nick3069, Nishidani, Novis-M, Octopus1066, Onceinawhile, Otutusaus, Padres Hana, Paine Ellsworth, Paul K., Phantomsnake, Pluto2012, Pppery, QueenCake, R'n'B, Reenem, Rgeb893, Rhododendrites, Rigadoun, Rjwilmsi, Rogerob, Rmmanm, SUM1, Sct72, Sean.hoyland, Sefarkas, Seraphim System, Sfan00 IMG, Simbagraphix, Sirich32977, Steinsplitter, Steverci, TAnthony, Tanbircdq, That's Pretty Good, The PIPE, TheIntroverted-Dude, Trahelliven, Trappist the monk, Ulf Heinsohn, Valenciano, Varnent, Vasyaivanov, Wayfarer, Whoop whoop pull up, Wikiliki, Wingedsubmariner, Winterst, Wlglunight93, Xezbeth, Ykantor, Yossimgim, ZScarpia, Zero0000, Zyxw, חורון ינב׳, ...??

646

Image Sources, Licenses and Contributors

The sources listed for each image provide more detailed licensing information including the copyright status, the copyright owner, and the license conditions.

Image *Source:* https://en.wikipedia.org/w/index.php?title=File:Kotel_Israel.jpg *License:* Creative Commons Attribution-Sharealike 3.0 *Contributors:* SuperJew 1

Image *Source:* https://en.wikipedia.org/w/index.php?title=File:Flag_of_Israel.svg *License:* Public Domain *Contributors:* "The Provisional Council of State Proclamation of the Flag of the State of Israel" of 25 Tishrei 5709 (28 October 1948) 2

Image *Source:* https://en.wikipedia.org/w/index.php?title=File:Israel-2013(2)-Jerusalem-Temple_Mount-Dome_of_the_Rock_(SE_exposure).jpg *License:* Attribution *Contributors:* User:Godot13 2

Image *Source:* https://en.wikipedia.org/w/index.php?title=File:Flag_of_Palestine.svg *License:* Public Domain *Contributors:* Orionist, previous versions by Makaristos, Mysid, etc. 3

Image *Source:* https://en.wikipedia.org/w/index.php?title=File:Padlock-silver.svg *Contributors:* AzaToth, BotMultichill, BotMultichillT, Gurch, Jarekt, Kallerna, Multichill, Perhelion, Rd232, Riana, Sarang, Siebrand, Steinsplitter, 4 anonymous edits 9

Figure 1 *Source:* https://en.wikipedia.org/w/index.php?title=File:Kingdoms_of_Israel_and_Judah_map_830.svg *License:* GNU Free Documentation License *Contributors:* Oldtidens_Israel_&_Judea.svg: FinnWikiNo derivative work: Richardprins (talk) 11

Image *Source:* https://en.wikipedia.org/w/index.php?title=File:Star_of_David.svg *License:* Public Domain *Contributors:* ABF, Aamsse, CMBJ, Cathy Richards, Cirt, Dbc334, DenisKrivosheev, Ekeb, Erin Silversmith, Fibonacci, Fs, Gjyaj, Huhsunqu, Humus sapiens∼commonswiki, Knochen, Korg, Madden, Margriet, Mormegil, Nagy, Nickjbor∼commonswiki, Ogre, Pd4u, Penguins Are Animals 5327, Pessimist2006, Ricordisamoa, Rocket000, Rugby471, Sarang, Shalom, Stratford490, The Evil IP address, Thivierr, Tom-L, Waldir, Wildfeuer, Zscout370, 46 anonymous edits 11

Figure 2 *Source:* https://en.wikipedia.org/w/index.php?title=File:Merenptah_Israel_Stele_Cairo.jpg *License:* Creative Commons Attribution-Sharealike 3.0 *Contributors:* Webscribe 14

Figure 3 *Source:* https://en.wikipedia.org/w/index.php?title=File:Baal_Ugarit_Louvre_AO17330.jpg *License:* Public Domain *Contributors:* User:Jastrow 15

Figure 4 *Source:* https://en.wikipedia.org/w/index.php?title=File:A_reconstructed_israelite_house,_Monarchy_period3.jpg *License:* Public Domain *Contributors:* User:Talmoryair 16

Figure 5 *Source:* https://en.wikipedia.org/w/index.php?title=File:Fotothek_df_ps_0002470_Innenräume_^_Ausstellungsgebäude.jpg *License:* Creative Commons Attribution-Share Alike 3.0 Germany *Contributors:* A. Wagner, Common Good, Hadhuey, Jbribeiro1, MB-one 18

Figure 6 *Source:* https://en.wikipedia.org/w/index.php?title=File:Hasmoneese_rijk.PNG *License:* GNU Free Documentation License *Contributors:* () 21

Figure 7 *Source:* https://en.wikipedia.org/w/index.php?title=File:Canaanites_and_Shasu_Leader_captives_from_Ramses_III's_tile_collection;_By_Niv_Lugassi.png *Contributors:* User:Wolfman12405 32

Figure 8 *Source:* https://en.wikipedia.org/w/index.php?title=File:Chaldean_soldiers_with_Hebrew_captives.jpg *Contributors:* Atlasowa, CarlosKni 33

Figure 9 *Source:* https://en.wikipedia.org/w/index.php?title=File:Dura_Europos_fresco_Jews_cross_Red_Sea.jpg *License:* Public Domain *Contributors:* made by photographer Becklectic 34

Image *Source:* https://en.wikipedia.org/w/index.php?title=File:Commons-logo.svg *License:* logo *Contributors:* Anomie, Callanecc, CambridgeBayWeather, Jo-Jo Eumerus, RHaworth 35

Figure 10 *Source:* https://en.wikipedia.org/w/index.php?title=File:Mosaic_Tribes.jpg *License:* Public Domain *Contributors:* Ori229 37

Image *Source:* https://en.wikipedia.org/w/index.php?title=File:1695_Eretz_Israel_map_in_Amsterdam_Haggada_by_Abraham_Bar-Jacob.jpg *License:* Public Domain *Contributors:* user:Humus sapiens 35

Figure 11 *Source:* https://en.wikipedia.org/w/index.php?title=File:Merneptah_Israel_Stele_Cairo.JPG *Contributors:* - 38

Figure 12 *Source:* https://en.wikipedia.org/w/index.php?title=File:The_map_of_the_Holy_Land_by_Marino_Sanudo_(drawn_in_1320).jpg *License:* Public Domain *Contributors:* Marino Sanuto the Elder (c. 1260 – 1338); Pietro Vesconte 43

Figure 13 *Source:* https://en.wikipedia.org/w/index.php?title=File:Stiftshuette_Modell_Timnapark.jpg *License:* Creative Commons Attribution-Sharealike 3.0,2.5,2.0,1.0 *Contributors:* Ruk7 44

Figure 14 *Source:* https://en.wikipedia.org/w/index.php?title=File:12_Tribes_of_Israel_Map.svg *License:* Creative Commons Attribution-ShareAlike 3.0 Unported *Contributors:* Translated by Kordas by user:'יוס' by user:Janz derivative work: 46

Figure 15 *Source:* https://en.wikipedia.org/w/index.php?title=File:Speculum_Darmstadt_2505_31r_Sangor.jpg *License:* Public Domain *Contributors:* FA2010 56

Figure 16 *Source:* https://en.wikipedia.org/w/index.php?title=File:Biblical_judges.png *License:* Public Domain *Contributors:* User:Cush 57

Figure 17 *Source:* https://en.wikipedia.org/w/index.php?title=File:Kingdom_of_Israel_1020_map.svg *License:* Creative Commons Attribution-ShareAlike 3.0 Unported *Contributors:* Regno di Davide.svg: RobertoReggi 12 Tribes of Israel Map.svg: Richardprins 12_tribus_de_Israel.svg: Translated by Korda 62

Figure 18 *Source:* https://en.wikipedia.org/w/index.php?title=File:Kingdoms_of_Israel_and_Judah_map_830.svg *License:* GNU Free Documentation License *Contributors:* Oldtidens_Israel_&_Judea.svg: FinnWikiNo derivative work: Richardprins (talk) 67

Figure 19 *Source:* https://en.wikipedia.org/w/index.php?title=File:Qeiyafa_city_wall1.jpg *License:* Creative Commons Attribution-Sharealike 3.0 *Contributors:* Skyview Photography Ltd 70

Image *Source:* https://en.wikipedia.org/w/index.php?title=File:Human_headed_winged_bull_facing.jpg *License:* Public Domain *Contributors:* User:Jastrow 71

Image *Source:* https://en.wikipedia.org/w/index.php?title=File:Flag_of_Jordan.svg *License:* Public Domain *Contributors:* User:SKopp 72

Image *Source:* https://en.wikipedia.org/w/index.php?title=File:Flag_of_Lebanon.svg *License:* Public Domain *Contributors:* Traced based on the CIA World Factbook with some modification done to the colours based on information at Vexilla mund 72

Image *Source:* https://en.wikipedia.org/w/index.php?title=File:Flag_of_Syria.svg *License:* Public Domain *Contributors:* see below 72

Figure 20 *Source:* https://en.wikipedia.org/w/index.php?title=File:Deportation_of_Jews_by_Assyrians.svg *License:* GNU Free Documentation License *Contributors:* Joelholdsworth 76

Figure 21 *Source:* https://en.wikipedia.org/w/index.php?title=File:Genealogy_of_the_kings_of_Israel_and_Judah.svg *License:* Public Domain *Contributors:* Genealogy_of_the_kings_of_Israel_and_Judah.png: User:Mr. Absurd derivative work: Jon C (talk) 77

Image *Source:* https://en.wikipedia.org/w/index.php?title=File:Nebukadnessar_II.jpg *License:* Public Domain *Contributors:* User Hedning on sv.wikipedia 83

Figure 22 *Source:* https://en.wikipedia.org/w/index.php?title=File:Mesha_stele.jpg *License:* Public Domain *Contributors:* Chamberi, DopefishJustin, JMCC1, Lord van Tasm, Mmcannis∼commonswiki, Oreus, Sumerophile∼commonswiki, Tintazul, ישראל ,קרול 2 anonymous edits 84

Figure 23 *Source:* https://en.wikipedia.org/w/index.php?title=File:Stamped-bulla_seal-side.jpg *License:* Public Domain *Contributors:* Funhistory 90

Figure 24 *Source:* https://en.wikipedia.org/w/index.php?title=File:PLATE4CX.jpg *License:* Public Domain *Contributors:* THE HISTORY OF COSTUME By Braun & Schneider 92

Figure 25 *Source:* https://en.wikipedia.org/w/index.php?title=File:Dura_Europos_fresco_holy_man.jpg *License:* Public Domain *Contributors:* made by photographer Becklectic 100

Figure 26 *Source:* https://en.wikipedia.org/w/index.php?title=File:Siege_and_destruction_of_Jerusalem_(f._155v)_Cropped.jpg *License:* Creative Commons Zero *Contributors:* Jason.nlw, Shakko, Sic19, Soerfm 101

Figure 27 *Source:* https://en.wikipedia.org/w/index.php?title=File:Arch_of_Titus_Menorah.png *License:* Creative Commons Attribution 3.0 *Contributors:* derivative work: Steerpike (talk) Arc_de_Triumph_copy.jpg: user: חשלום בית 102

Figure 28 *Source:* https://en.wikipedia.org/w/index.php?title=File:2nd_century_Rome_gold_goblet_shows_Jewish_ritual_objects.jpg *License:* Public Domain *Contributors:* Bibi Saint-Pol, Clio20, DenghiùComm, Djampa, G.dallorto, Humus sapiens∼commonswiki, NicoScribe, Roomba, Wst, Xenophon, 3 anonymous edits 103

Figure 29 *Source:* https//en.wikipedia.org *License:* Attribution *Contributors:* user:G.dallorto 104

Figure 30 *Source:* https//en.wikipedia.org *License:* Public Domain *Contributors:* File Upload Bot (Magnus Manske), JuTa, Leyo, Léna, Wheeke 106

Image *Source:* https://en.wikipedia.org/w/index.php?title=File:Vexillum_Regni_Hierosolymae.svg *License:* Creative Commons Attribution 3.0 *Contributors:* Ec.Domnowall 109

Image *Source:* https://en.wikipedia.org/w/index.php?title=File:Arms_of_the_Kingdom_of_Jerusalem.svg *License:* Creative Commons Attribution-Sharealike 3.0 *Contributors:* User:Heralder, User:Katepanomegas 109

Image *Source:* https://en.wikipedia.org/w/index.php?title=File:Map_Crusader_states_1135-en.svg *License:* GNU Free Documentation License *Contributors:* User:MapMaster 110

Image *Source:* https://en.wikipedia.org/w/index.php?title=File:Blank.png *License:* Public Domain *Contributors:* Bastique, BrandonXLF, Chlewey, ChrisDHDR, Ghouston, It Is Me Here, Jed, Paradoctor, Patrick, Penubag, Perhelion, Rocket000, Roomba, Sarang, Timeroot, Tintazul 111
Image *Source:* https://en.wikipedia.org/w/index.php?title=File:Flag_of_Ayyubid_Dynasty.svg *License:* Public Domain *Contributors:* Ch1902 111
Image *Source:* https://en.wikipedia.org/w/index.php?title=File:Mameluke_Flag.svg *License:* Public Domain *Contributors:* Alkari, Anime Addict AA, AnonMoos, Ashashyou, Bobrayner, CommonsDelinker, Cycn, Dbachmann, Homo lupus, JMCC1, Latebird, Lliura, Ryucloud∼commonswiki, Sarang, SiBr4, TRAJAN 117, Takabeg, Tom-L, 1 anonymous edits 111
Image *Source:* https://en.wikipedia.org/w/index.php?title=File:Flag_of_Cyprus.svg *License:* Public Domain *Contributors:* User:Vzb83 111
Image *Source:* https://en.wikipedia.org/w/index.php?title=File:Flag_of_Egypt.svg *License:* Public Domain *Contributors:* Open Clip Art 111
Figure 31 *Source:* https://en.wikipedia.org/w/index.php?title=File:Godefroi1099.jpg *License:* Public Domain *Contributors:* Acoma, Dahlfred, Dbachmann, Guise, Mel22, Shakko, 2 anonymous edits 115
Figure 32 *Source:* https://en.wikipedia.org/w/index.php?title=File:Funeral_of_Baldwin_I.jpg *License:* Public Domain *Contributors:* Sebastien Mamerot 117
Figure 33 *Source:* https://en.wikipedia.org/w/index.php?title=File:Croisés.jpg *License:* Public Domain *Contributors:* Epìdosis, Santosga, Shizhao, 2 anonymous edits 119
Figure 34 *Source:* https://en.wikipedia.org/w/index.php?title=File:Tower_of_david_jerusalem.jpg *License:* Creative Commons Attribution 2.0 *Contributors:* AndreasPraefcke, Jgritz∼commonswiki, Longbomb, Ronaldino, Talmoryair, Wst, עדירל 121
Figure 35 *Source:* https://en.wikipedia.org/w/index.php?title=File:Manuelcomnenus.jpg *License:* Public Domain *Contributors:* Flamarande∼commonswiki, G.dallorto, KirmiziAdam, NeverDoING, Saperaud∼commonswiki, Shakko, 竹麦魚 (Searobin) 122
Figure 36 *Source:* https://en.wikipedia.org/w/index.php?title=File:Jan_Lievens-_King_Guy_of_Lusignan_and_King_Saladin.tif *License:* Public Domain *Contributors:* 2A02A03F, BeatrixBelibaste, Bjh21, Bukk, Funck77, Mattes, Shakko, Sixflashphoto, Vincent Steenberg, Wellink, Wieralee, Wmpearl, 3 anonymous edits 127
Figure 37 *Source:* https://en.wikipedia.org/w/index.php?title=File:Crusader_States_1190.svg *Contributors:* - 128
Figure 38 *Source:* https://en.wikipedia.org/w/index.php?title=File:Al-Kamil_Muhammad_al-Malik_and_Frederick_II_Holy_Roman_Emperor.jpg *License:* Public Domain *Contributors:* User:Chris 73 131
Figure 39 *Source:* https://en.wikipedia.org/w/index.php?title=File:JanBrienne.jpg *License:* Public Domain *Contributors:* Acoma, Mel22 134
Figure 40 *Source:* https://en.wikipedia.org/w/index.php?title=File:KrakDesChevaliers.jpg *License:* Public Domain *Contributors:* User:Disdero 139
Figure 41 *Source:* https://en.wikipedia.org/w/index.php?title=File:Crusader_coin_Acre_1230.jpg *License:* Creative Commons Attribution-Sharealike 3.0 *Contributors:* PHGCOM 142
Figure 42 *Source:* https://en.wikipedia.org/w/index.php?title=File:Crusader_coin_Acre_circa_1230.jpg *License:* Creative Commons Attribution-Sharealike 3.0 *Contributors:* PHGCOM 142
Figure 43 *Source:* https://en.wikipedia.org/w/index.php?title=File:Crusader_coins_of_the_Kingdom_of_Jerusalem.jpg *License:* Creative Commons Attribution-Sharealike 3.0 *Contributors:* User:PHGCOM 147
Figure 44 *Source:* https://en.wikipedia.org/w/index.php?title=File:Holy_sepulchre_exterior.jpg *License:* Creative Commons Attribution 2.0 *Contributors:* Wayne McLean, user jgritz 148
Figure 45 *Source:* https://en.wikipedia.org/w/index.php?title=File:Melisende-Psalter_f9v.jpg *License:* Public Domain *Contributors:* GDK, Io Herodotus, Jheald, Shakko, Wst 149
Image *Source:* https://en.wikipedia.org/w/index.php?title=File:Ottoman_Flag.svg *Contributors:* - 153
Image *Source:* https://en.wikipedia.org/w/index.php?title=File:Flag_of_the_United_Kingdom.svg *License:* Public Domain *Contributors:* Anomie, Good Olfactory, Jo-Jo Eumerus, MSGJ, Mifter 153
Image *Source:* https://en.wikipedia.org/w/index.php?title=File:CUINET(1896)_LA_SYRIE.jpg *Contributors:* Avery Jensen, INeverCry, Metilsteiner 153
Figure 46 *Source:* https://en.wikipedia.org/w/index.php?title=File:Ottoman_map_of_the_Mutasarrifate_of_Jerusalem,_from_1882-83_(1300_AH).jpg *License:* Public Domain *Contributors:* Ciaurlec, Mapmarks, Onceinawhile 156
Figure 47 *Source:* https://en.wikipedia.org/w/index.php?title=File:Ottoman_Syria,_1893_map.jpg *License:* Public Domain *Contributors:* Look2See1, Mapmarks, OgreBot 2, Onceinawhile, باسم, عمرو بن كلثوم, 1 anonymous edits 156
Figure 48 *Source:* https://en.wikipedia.org/w/index.php?title=File:1889_Modern_Palestine,_shewing_Turkish_provinces.jpg *License:* Public Domain *Contributors:* Danny lost, Geagea 156
Figure 49 *Source:* https://en.wikipedia.org/w/index.php?title=File:Map_of_the_Jerusalem_Sanjak.jpg *License:* Public Domain *Contributors:* Onceinawhile 157
Figure 50 *Source:* https://en.wikipedia.org/w/index.php?title=File:Jerusalem_Sanjak_—_Memalik-i_Mahruse-i_Shahane-ye_Mahsus_Mukemmel_ve_Mufassal_Atlas_(1907).jpg *License:* Public Domain *Contributors:* Mehmed Nasrullah, Mehmed Rüşdi, Mehmed Eşref 157
Figure 51 *Source:* https//en.wikipedia.org *License:* Public Domain *Contributors:* Bekpashi Mehmed Nasrullah, Mehmed Rüşdi, Mehmed Eşref (بيكباشي محمد نصر الله وآخرون) 158
Figure 52 *Source:* https://en.wikipedia.org/w/index.php?title=File:1913_Ottoman_Geography_Textbook_Showing_the_Sanjak_of_Jerusalem_and_Palestine.jpeg *License:* Public Domain *Contributors:* Onceinawhile 158
Image *Source:* https://en.wikipedia.org/w/index.php?title=File:Padlock-blue.svg *Contributors:* User:AzaToth, User:Eleassar 163
Image *Source:* https://en.wikipedia.org/w/index.php?title=File:Public_Seal_of_High_Commissioner_of_Palestine.svg *License:* Creative Commons Attribution-Sharealike 3.0 *Contributors:* Oren neu dag (talk) 163
Image *Source:* https://en.wikipedia.org/w/index.php?title=File:Map_of_Mandatory_Palestine_in_1946_with_major_cities_(in_English).svg *Contributors:* User:Bolter21 163
Image *Source:* https://en.wikipedia.org/w/index.php?title=File:Flag_of_Hejaz_1917.svg *License:* Public domain *Contributors:* () 164
Image *Source:* https://en.wikipedia.org/w/index.php?title=File:Flag_of_Hamas.svg *License:* Public Domain *Contributors:* Guilherme Paula, Oren neu dag 164
Figure 53 *Source:* https://en.wikipedia.org/w/index.php?title=File:A_world_in_perplexity_(1918)_(14780310121).jpg *Contributors:* Cathy Richards, FlickreviewR 2, Fæ, Geagea, Kilom691, Magnolia677, Wieralee, ביקורת 169
Figure 54 *Source:* https://en.wikipedia.org/w/index.php?title=File:Samuelarrival.jpg *Contributors:* American Colony (Jerusalem). Photo Dept., photographer. 169
Figure 55 *Source:* https://en.wikipedia.org/w/index.php?title=File:Palestinian_delegation_1929.jpg *Contributors:* Aviados, Bürgerentscheid, Ceedjee∼commonswiki, Movieevery, N. Wadid, Netanel h, Stewi101015 170
Figure 56 *Source:* https://en.wikipedia.org/w/index.php?title=File:Palest_against_british.gif *License:* Creative Commons Attribution-Sharealike 3.0 *Contributors:* hanini 171
Figure 57 *Source:* https//en.wikipedia.org *Contributors:* Matson Photo Service, photographer 173
Figure 58 *Source:* https//en.wikipedia.org *License:* Creative Commons Attribution 2.0 *Contributors:* Tom Beazley, published by aussiejeff 174
Figure 59 *Source:* https://en.wikipedia.org/w/index.php?title=File:JB_HQ.jpg *License:* Public Domain *Contributors:* After Midnight, Epson291, Humus sapiens, Sfan00 IMG 176
Figure 60 *Source:* https://en.wikipedia.org/w/index.php?title=File:VE_day_Jerusalem_1945.jpg *Contributors:* Matson Photo Service, photographer 177
Figure 61 *Source:* https://en.wikipedia.org/w/index.php?title=File:UN_Partition_Plan_For_Palestine_1947.svg *License:* Public Domain *Contributors:* U.S. Central Intelligence Agency 178
Figure 62 *Source:* https://en.wikipedia.org/w/index.php?title=File:BritsLvHaifa3061948.jpg *License:* Creative Commons Attribution-Sharealike 3.0 *Contributors:* Geagea, OgreBot 2, Poliocretes, צחוב קודקוד 181
Figure 63 *Source:* https//en.wikipedia.org *License:* Creative Commons Attribution-Sharealike 3.0 *Contributors:* Geagea, Man vyi, Matanya, Steinsplitter 182
Image *Source:* https://en.wikipedia.org/w/index.php?title=File:Palestine_stamp.jpg *License:* Public Domain *Contributors:* stamp by Fred Taylor for United Kingdom Government 183
Image *Source:* https://en.wikipedia.org/w/index.php?title=File:عملة_فلسطينية_معدنية.jpg *License:* Creative Commons Attribution 3.0 *Contributors:* Arabmuslim12 183
Image *Source:* https://en.wikipedia.org/w/index.php?title=File:Stamp_palestine_10_mils.jpg *License:* Public Domain *Contributors:* David Bjorgen 184
Image *Source:* https://en.wikipedia.org/w/index.php?title=File:Mill_(British_Mandate_for_Palestine_currency,_1927).jpg *License:* Creative Commons Attribution-Sharealike 3.0 *Contributors:* Arabmuslim12. 184
Image *Source:* https://en.wikipedia.org/w/index.php?title=File:British_Mandate_Palestinian_passport.jpg *License:* Creative Commons Attribution-Sharealike 3.0 *Contributors:* وسام زقوت 185
Image *Source:* https://en.wikipedia.org/w/index.php?title=File:2011-07-04_09.41.jpg *License:* Creative Commons Attribution 3.0 *Contributors:* Asad112 185
Figure 64 *Source:* https://en.wikipedia.org/w/index.php?title=File:Palestine_1930.jpg *License:* Public Domain *Contributors:* Jarekt, Makeandtoss, TMagen 187

Figure 65 *Source:* https://en.wikipedia.org/w/index.php?title=File:Jewish_immigration_to_Mandatory_Palestine_(1920-1945).jpg *Contributors:* User:Paasikivi ... 189

Figure 66 *Source:* https://en.wikipedia.org/w/index.php?title=File:Palestine_Land_ownership_by_sub-district_(1945).jpg *License:* UN map *Contributors:* JHistory, JorgeGG, Judithcomm, Onceinawhile, Timeshifter ... 193

Figure 67 *Source:* https://en.wikipedia.org/w/index.php?title=File:WhitePaper.jpg *License:* Public Domain *Contributors:* JHistory, Jeff G., Zero0000 ... 196

Figure 68 *Source:* https://en.wikipedia.org/w/index.php?title=File:Palestine_Distribution_of_Population_1947_UN_map_no_93(b).jpeg *License:* UN map *Contributors:* Bravo Charlie Delta, JorgeGG, Judithcomm, Natuur12, Onceinawhile, Oompahloompah2016, Timeshifter ... 197

Figure 69 *Source:* https://en.wikipedia.org/w/index.php?title=File:Ymca_boys_jeru.jpg *Contributors:* Matson Photo Service, photographer. .. 198

Figure 70 *Source:* https://en.wikipedia.org/w/index.php?title=File:Barclays_building_Jerusalem_1939.JPG *License:* Public Domain *Contributors:* Catsmeat, Drkup(IMJ), Geagea, Kaganer, Matanya, Netanel h ... 200

Figure 71 *Source:* https://en.wikipedia.org/w/index.php?title=File:Palestine-WW1-3.jpg *License:* Public Domain *Contributors:* Department of Military Art and Engineering, at the U.S. Military Academy (West Point). ... 202

Figure 72 *Source:* https://en.wikipedia.org/w/index.php?title=File:Field_Marshal_Allenby_British_troops_Jerusalem_dec_11_1917.jpg *License:* Public Domain *Contributors:* Bjarlin, Netanel h, OttawaAC, Varlaam ... 202

Figure 73 *Source:* https://en.wikipedia.org/w/index.php?title=File:Big_Gen_Watson_Mayor_Jerusalem_Dec_1917.jpg *License:* Public Domain *Contributors:* Netanel h, OttawaAC, Rcbutcher, Vysotsky ... 203

Figure 74 *Source:* https://en.wikipedia.org/w/index.php?title=File:Ottoman_surrender_of_Jerusalem_restored.jpg *License:* Public Domain *Contributors:* American Colony (Jerusalem) ... 203

Figure 75 *Source:* https://en.wikipedia.org/w/index.php?title=File:GPO,_Jerusalem.jpg *License:* Creative Commons Attribution-Sharealike 3.0 *Contributors:* The Matson Photo service, Jerusalem, Palestine. ... 204

Figure 76 *Source:* https://en.wikipedia.org/w/index.php?title=File:Rockefeller_Tower_Jerusalem.jpg *License:* Creative Commons Attribution 2.5 *Contributors:* Gila Brand, aka Gilabrand at en.wikipedia ... 204

Figure 77 *Source:* https://en.wikipedia.org/w/index.php?title=File:Central_Post_Office_in_Yaffo.JPG *License:* Attribution *Contributors:* Avi1111 dr. avishai teicher ... 204

Figure 78 *Source:* https://en.wikipedia.org/w/index.php?title=File:Anglo-Palestine_Bank.jpg *License:* Public Domain *Contributors:* User:מתניה 205

Figure 79 *Source:* https://en.wikipedia.org/w/index.php?title=File:Western_Wall_Jerusalem_1933.jpg *License:* Public Domain *Contributors:* Geagea, Oyoyoy ... 205

Figure 80 *Source:* https://en.wikipedia.org/w/index.php?title=File:British_Mandate_tribunal_building.jpg *License:* Creative Commons Attribution 3.0 *Contributors:* File Upload Bot (Magnus Manske), Kelly, OgreBot 2, Ymblanter ... 206

Figure 81 *Source:* https://en.wikipedia.org/w/index.php?title=File:PikiWiki_Israel_612_YMCA_א.ק.מ.י..JPG *License:* Creative Commons Attribution 2.5 *Contributors:* זמיר זאב ... 206

Figure 82 *Source:* https://en.wikipedia.org/w/index.php?title=File:Bevingrad2.jpg *License:* Creative Commons Attribution-Sharealike 2.5 *Contributors:* American Colony Photographers ... 207

Figure 83 *Source:* https://en.wikipedia.org/w/index.php?title=File:British_mailbox_Jerusalem.jpg *License:* Attribution *Contributors:* he:משתמש:דויר1845 ... 207

Figure 84 *Source:* https://en.wikipedia.org/w/index.php?title=File:Palestine1941.jpg *License:* Creative Commons Attribution-Sharealike 3.0 *Contributors:* User:Arabmuslim12 ... 208

Figure 85 *Source:* https://en.wikipedia.org/w/index.php?title=File:CurfewPalestine_01.jpg *License:* Creative Commons Attribution-Sharealike 3.0 *Contributors:* Etan J. Tal ... 208

Figure 86 *Source:* https://en.wikipedia.org/w/index.php?title=File:Hamosadot_Haleumiyim_Rehavia.JPG *License:* Attribution *Contributors:* Neta 214

Image *Source:* https://en.wikipedia.org/w/index.php?title=File:PikiWiki_Israel_20841_The_Palmach.jpg *License:* Public Domain *Contributors:* Geagea, Pikiwikisrael, י יעל ... 215

Figure 87 *Source:* https://en.wikipedia.org/w/index.php?title=File:Rabot_-_Torah.JPG *License:* Creative Commons Attribution-Sharealike 3.0 *Contributors:* User:גוטליב חמי ... 220

Figure 88 *Source:* https://en.wikipedia.org/w/index.php?title=File:Umm_al-Fahm,_2013.jpg *License:* Creative Commons Attribution-Sharealike 3.0 *Contributors:* User:Moataz1997 ... 224

Figure 89 *Source:* https://en.wikipedia.org/w/index.php?title=File:Flickr_-_Israel_Defense_Forces_-_Druze_"Herev"_Battalion_Training.jpg *License:* Creative Commons Attribution-Sharealike 2.0 *Contributors:* Israel Defense Forces ... 226

Figure 90 *Source:* https://en.wikipedia.org/w/index.php?title=File:Bomb_shelter_-_Sderot.jpg *License:* Public Domain *Contributors:* Import.export ... 227

Figure 91 *Source:* https://en.wikipedia.org/w/index.php?title=File:Second_aliyah_Pioneers_in_Migdal_1912_in_kuffiyeh.jpg *License:* Public Domain *Contributors:* Avin, Cnyborg, Croquant, Geagea, Humus sapiens∼commonswiki, Jonund, Lx 121, Matanya, Mattes, Nizzan Cohen, Svajcr, TVJunkie, Talmoryair, עדירל, יוסי, 1 anonymous edits ... 228

Figure 92 *Source:* https://en.wikipedia.org/w/index.php?title=File:PikiWiki_Israel_44384_Haim_Weizman.jpg *License:* Public Domain *Contributors:* OgreBot 2, Pikiwikisrael, Wouterhagens, יעקב ... 229

Figure 93 *Source:* https://en.wikipedia.org/w/index.php?title=File:Mandate_for_Palestine_(legal_instrument).png *Contributors:* User:Oncenawhile 230

Figure 94 *Source:* https://en.wikipedia.org/w/index.php?title=File:Palestine_immigrant_certificate.jpg *License:* GNU Free Documentation License *Contributors:* Etan J. Tal ... 231

Figure 95 *Source:* https://en.wikipedia.org/w/index.php?title=File:Ben_Gurion_1959.jpg *License:* Public Domain *Contributors:* Calliopejen1, CyberXRef, Geagea, J.-H. Janßen, Oyoyoy, Yann ... 233

Figure 96 *Source:* https://en.wikipedia.org/w/index.php?title=File:Jewish_Agency_bombing.jpg *License:* Public Domain *Contributors:* OgreBot 2, Padres Hana, Poliocretes ... 234

Figure 97 *Source:* https://en.wikipedia.org/w/index.php?title=File:RehaFreier1964.jpg *License:* Creative Commons Attribution-Sharealike 3.0 *Contributors:* Etan J. Tal ... 235

Figure 98 *Source:* https://en.wikipedia.org/w/index.php?title=File:19450715_Buchenwald_survivors_arrive_in_Haifa.jpg *License:* Public Domain *Contributors:* 1989, BotMultichill, Catsmeat, Ellywa, Hidro, JHistory, Jarekt, Kaganer, Pessimist2006, Pikiwikisrael, Schekinov Alexey Victorovich, Steinsplitter, עדירל יעקב, י, יעל ... 236

Figure 99 *Source:* https://en.wikipedia.org/w/index.php?title=File:Declaration_of_State_of_Israel_1948.jpg *License:* Public Domain *Contributors:* Addy Rozenbaum, Alan, Aviados, Bensin, Bukvoed, David Shay, Elya, Faigl.ladislav, Geagea, HG1, Huyme, Iluvatar, J.-H. Janßen, J.delanoy, Jdx, Jkelly, Nard the Bard, Ondrejk, Ramaksoud2000, Schekinov Alexey Victorovich, Six 7 8∼commonswiki, Talmoryair, Thuresson, Triggerhippie4, Yonatanh, Yuval Y, עדירל, 8 anonymous edits ... 237

Figure 100 *Source:* https://en.wikipedia.org/w/index.php?title=File:4X-ADN_Operation_Magic_Carpet.jpg *License:* Public Domain *Contributors:* BotAdventures, Geagea, Oyoyoy, Pikiwikisrael, VN-B468, 1 anonymous edits ... 238

Figure 101 *Source:* https://en.wikipedia.org/w/index.php?title=File:Flickr_-_Government_Press_Office_(GPO)_-_Ethiopian_immigrants_coming_off_a_Boeing_jet.jpg *License:* Creative Commons Attribution-Sharealike 3.0 *Contributors:* Dobie80, Geagea, Matanya, Pikiwikisrael, Steinsplitter, ליאור ... 240

Figure 102 *Source:* https://en.wikipedia.org/w/index.php?title=File:Grupo_de_Taglit.JPG *License:* Creative Commons Attribution-Sharealike 3.0 *Contributors:* User:Luqux ... 241

Figure 103 *Source:* https://en.wikipedia.org/w/index.php?title=File:Natan_Sharansky_2016.jpg *License:* Creative Commons Attribution 3.0 *Contributors:* Atbannett, Hanay, Ldorfman ... 244

Figure 104 *Source:* https://en.wikipedia.org/w/index.php?title=File:AlanHoffman.jpg *License:* Creative Commons Attribution-Sharealike 2.0 *Contributors:* Jewish Agency for Israel ... 246

Figure 105 *Source:* https://en.wikipedia.org/w/index.php?title=File:Binyan_Hamosadot_Haleumiyim_RD.JPG *License:* Attribution *Contributors:* Rotem Danzig ... 247

Figure 106 *Source:* https://en.wikipedia.org/w/index.php?title=File:Palestine_immigrant_certificate.jpg *License:* GNU Free Documentation License *Contributors:* Etan J. Tal ... 252

Image *Source:* https://en.wikipedia.org/w/index.php?title=File:Signing_ceremony_for_the_Axis_Powers_Tripartite_Pact;.jpg *License:* Public Domain *Contributors:* 37ophiuchi, Beao, Calmer Waters, D6, Damiens.rf, Diannaa, Enkyo2, IxK85, J Milburn, Kelisi, Kintetsubuffalo, Mosedschurte, Niceguyedc, Nyttend, Petri Krohn, Rjensen, SchuminWeb, Sfan00 IMG ... 253

Image *Source:* https://en.wikipedia.org/w/index.php?title=File:Flag_of_German_Reich_(1935–1945).svg *Contributors:* - ... 253

Image *Source:* https://en.wikipedia.org/w/index.php?title=File:Flag_of_Italy_(1861-1946)_crowned.svg *License:* Creative Commons Attribution-Sharealike 2.5 *Contributors:* F l a n k e r ... 253

Image *Source:* https://en.wikipedia.org/w/index.php?title=File:Merchant_flag_of_Japan_(1870).svg *Contributors:* - ... 253

Image *Source:* https://en.wikipedia.org/w/index.php?title=File:Flag_of_Hungary_(1915-1918,_1919-1946).svg *License:* Creative Commons Zero *Contributors:* User:Zscout370, colour correction: User:R-41, current version: Thommy ... 253

Image *Source:* https://en.wikipedia.org/w/index.php?title=File:Flag_of_Romania.svg *Contributors:* AdiJapan ... 253
Image *Source:* https://en.wikipedia.org/w/index.php?title=File:Flag_of_First_Slovak_Republic_1939-1945.svg *Contributors:* - ... 253
Image *Source:* https://en.wikipedia.org/w/index.php?title=File:Flag_of_Bulgaria.svg *License:* Public Domain *Contributors:* SKopp ... 253
Image *Source:* https://en.wikipedia.org/w/index.php?title=File:Flag_of_Yugoslavia_(1918–1943).svg *Contributors:* - ... 253
Image *Source:* https://en.wikipedia.org/w/index.php?title=File:Flag_of_Independent_State_of_Croatia.svg *License:* Public domain *Contributors:* public domain by User:Zscout370 ... 253
Figure 107 *Source:* https://en.wikipedia.org/w/index.php?title=File:Tripartite_Pact_27_September_1940.jpg *License:* Creative Commons Attribution-Sharealike 3.0 *Contributors:* World Imaging ... 254
Figure 108 *Source:* https://en.wikipedia.org/w/index.php?title=File:Bundesarchiv_Bild_183-L09218,_Berlin,_Japanische_Botschaft.jpg *License:* Creative Commons Attribution-Sharealike 3.0 Germany *Contributors:* BotMultichill, Duch, Kintetsubuffalo, Leit, Lx 121, Prüm ... 256
Figure 109 *Source:* https://en.wikipedia.org/w/index.php?title=File:Protokol-1.03.1941.jpg *License:* Creative Commons Attribution 3.0 *Contributors:* Bogdan Filow, Ioachim Ribbentrop, Ciano, Hiroshi Oshima ... 259
Figure 110 *Source:* https://en.wikipedia.org/w/index.php?title=File:Thai-German_in_Berlin_1943.png *License:* Creative Commons Attribution 2.5 *Contributors:* OgreBot 2, Setawut, Tvcccp, 4 anonymous edits ... 262
Figure 111 *Source:* https://en.wikipedia.org/w/index.php?title=File:1941_Chinese_War_Declaration_vs_Germany_and_Italy.jpg *License:* Public Domain *Contributors:* BotMultichill, Chenspec, Jusjih, KTo288, Mogelzahn, MtBell, Zaccarias ... 263
Image *Source:* https://en.wikipedia.org/w/index.php?title=File:Train_hostages.jpg *License:* Public Domain *Contributors:* Chaim Kahanov and Zecharia Oryon ... 266
Image *Source:* https://en.wikipedia.org/w/index.php?title=File:Flag_of_the_British_Army.svg *License:* Public Domain *Contributors:* Created in Adobe Illustrator CS2, based off the above sources, by Philip Ronan ... 266
Image *Source:* https://en.wikipedia.org/w/index.php?title=File:Haganah_Symbol.svg *License:* Creative Commons Attribution-Sharealike 3.0 *Contributors:* User:Meronim ... 266
Image *Source:* https://en.wikipedia.org/w/index.php?title=File:Flag_of_Ladonia.svg *License:* Public Domain *Contributors:* User:Quilbert ... 266
Image *Source:* https://en.wikipedia.org/w/index.php?title=File:Ensign_of_the_Royal_Air_Force.svg *Contributors:* - ... 267
Image *Source:* https://en.wikipedia.org/w/index.php?title=File:Naval_Ensign_of_the_United_Kingdom.svg *License:* Public Domain *Contributors:* Alkari, Allforrous, AnonMoos, Avicennasis, Bender235, Benzoyl, Cathy Richards, Cycn, Dancingwombatsrule, Ec.Domnowall, Fry1989, Homo lupus, Illegitimate Barrister, Pumbaa80, SiBr4, Stunteltje, Xiengyod~commonswiki, Yaddah, 6 anonymous edits ... 267
Image *Source:* https://en.wikipedia.org/w/index.php?title=File:Skull_and_crossbones.svg *Contributors:* Andux, Andy0101, AnselmiJuan, Bayo, BotMultichill, BotMultichillT, Coyau, D0ktorz, Derbeth, Eugenio Hansen, OFS, Franzenshof, Ies, J.delanoy, JMCC1, Jahoe, Jdx, Juliancolton, Karelj, MarianSigler, Natr, Sarang, Shuhazmir, Sidpatil, Silsor, Stas1995, Stepshep, Str4nd, Sven Manguard, SweetCanadianMullet, The Evil IP address, Tiptoety, Túrelio, W!B:, Wknight94, 25 anonymous edits ... 267
Figure 112 *Source:* https://en.wikipedia.org/w/index.php?title=File:PikiWiki_Israel_12857_Events_in_Israel.jpg *License:* Public Domain *Contributors:* Geagea, Hanay, Netanel h, Pikiwikisrael, יעקב ... 269
Figure 113 *Source:* https://en.wikipedia.org/w/index.php?title=File:Remains_of_a_burnt_Jewish_passenger_bus,_Result_of_terrorist_acts.jpg *License:* Public Domain *Contributors:* PD-USGov https://www.loc.gov/pictures/resource/matpc.18606/ ... 270
Figure 114 *Source:* https://en.wikipedia.org/w/index.php?title=File:Tarab_Abd_al-Hadi.jpg *License:* Public Domain *Contributors:* BotMultichill, Cathy Richards, File Upload Bot (Magnus Manske), Rafic.Mufid, Sarah Canbel, Trijnstel, بدارين ... 272
Figure 115 *Source:* https://en.wikipedia.org/w/index.php?title=File:Wauchope_1936_and_Allenby_1917_Cartoon_in_Falastin_June_1936.jpeg *License:* Public Domain *Contributors:* Onceinawhile ... 274
Figure 116 *Source:* https://en.wikipedia.org/w/index.php?title=File:Khalil_Sakakini.jpg *License:* Public Domain *Contributors:* ملكية عامة ... 275
Figure 117 *Source:* https://en.wikipedia.org/w/index.php?title=File:David_BG.jpg *License:* Public Domain *Contributors:* Faigl.ladislav, Geagea, Ingsoc ... 276
Figure 118 *Source:* https://en.wikipedia.org/w/index.php?title=File:Arab_strike_1936._Car_with_brooms_to_sweep_away_tacks_thrown_by_strikers.jpg *License:* Public Domain *Contributors:* Monopoly31121993, Mr.Shoval ... 277
Figure 119 *Source:* https://en.wikipedia.org/w/index.php?title=File:Lord_Peel_arrives.jpg *License:* Public Domain *Contributors:* Matson Photo Service, photographer ... 279
Figure 120 *Source:* https://en.wikipedia.org/w/index.php?title=File:PikiWiki_Israel_297_Kibutz_Gan-Shmuel_sk1-_38_גן-שמואל_-_אש_בשדות_1936-9.jpg *License:* Creative Commons Attribution 2.5 *Contributors:* Daniel1, Geagea, Netanel h, Pikiwikisrael ... 279
Figure 121 *Source:* https://en.wikipedia.org/w/index.php?title=File:Palest_against_british.gif *License:* Creative Commons Attribution-Sharealike 3.0 *Contributors:* hanini ... 282
Figure 122 *Source:* https://en.wikipedia.org/w/index.php?title=File:Havlagah_bus_during_1936-1939_Arab_revolt-British_Mandate_of_Palestine.jpg *Contributors:* Abu badali~commonswiki, Brakeet, Christophe cagé, Geagea, Humus sapiens~commonswiki, Netanel h, Roland zh, SC96, Talmoryair, יעקב ... 282
Figure 123 *Source:* https://en.wikipedia.org/w/index.php?title=File:Jews_evacuate_the_Old_City,_1936.jpg *License:* Public Domain *Contributors:* Chesdovi, Geagea, Justinien 03, OgreBot 2 ... 283
Figure 124 *Source:* https://en.wikipedia.org/w/index.php?title=File:Opstand_tegen_Britten_in_Palestina_-_Arabs_revolt_against_the_English_authority.jpg *Contributors:* Nationaal Archief ... 283
Figure 125 *Source:* https://en.wikipedia.org/w/index.php?title=File:Latrun-Police-Building.jpg *License:* Creative Commons Attribution 2.5 *Contributors:* User:Bukvoed ... 287
Figure 126 *Source:* https://en.wikipedia.org/w/index.php?title=File:Almog_IL15_Pillboxgoren.jpg *License:* Public Domain *Contributors:* Almog 288
Figure 127 *Source:* https://en.wikipedia.org/w/index.php?title=File:HMS_Malaya.jpg *License:* Public Domain *Contributors:* UK Government 289
Figure 128 *Source:* https://en.wikipedia.org/w/index.php?title=File:Reuven_Shiloah.jpg *License:* Public Domain *Contributors:* BotMultichill, Geagea, Hovev, Mstislavl, Pessimist2006, Smat, Альма, חובבשירה ש', דוד ... 291
Figure 129 *Source:* https://en.wikipedia.org/w/index.php?title=File:PikiWiki_Israel_6918_Wingates_Special_Night.jpg *License:* Public Domain *Contributors:* Netanel h, Pikiwikisrael ... 293
Figure 130 *Source:* https://en.wikipedia.org/w/index.php?title=File:Ghaffis_in_Nesher_2.jpg *License:* Creative Commons Attribution-Sharealike 3.0 *Contributors:* Geagea, Hanay, OgreBot 2, 1 anonymous edits ... 293
Figure 131 *Source:* https://en.wikipedia.org/w/index.php?title=File:Palestinian_rebels_1937.jpg *License:* Public Domain *Contributors:* Al Ameer son, 1 anonymous edits ... 298
Figure 132 *Source:* https://en.wikipedia.org/w/index.php?title=File:Abd_al-Rahim_Hajj_Muhammad_portrait,_cropped.jpg *License:* Public Domain *Contributors:* Al Ameer son, 1 anonymous edits ... 299
Figure 133 *Source:* https://en.wikipedia.org/w/index.php?title=File:Farhan_Sa'di_arrested_by_British.jpg *License:* Public Domain *Contributors:* Al Ameer son, Sarah Canbel ... 300
Figure 134 *Source:* https://en.wikipedia.org/w/index.php?title=File:WhitePaper1939riot.jpg *Contributors:* Matson Photo Service, photographer 302
Figure 135 *Source:* https://en.wikipedia.org/w/index.php?title=File:WhitePaper1939Poster.jpg *Contributors:* American Colony (Jerusalem). Photo Dept., photographer ... 303
Figure 136 *Source:* https://en.wikipedia.org/w/index.php?title=File:LondonConference1939.jpg *License:* Public Domain *Contributors:* FSII, Faigl.ladislav, File Upload Bot (Magnus Manske), Geagea, Hohum, Huldra, N. Wadid, OgreBot 2, TheRealHuldra ... 305
Image *Source:* https://en.wikipedia.org/w/index.php?title=File:1939_White_Paper_cmd_6019.djvu *License:* Public Domain *Contributors:* Onceinawhile, Poliocretes ... 312
Figure 137 *Source:* https://en.wikipedia.org/w/index.php?title=File:LondonConference1939.jpg *License:* Public Domain *Contributors:* FSII, Faigl.ladislav, File Upload Bot (Magnus Manske), Geagea, Hohum, Huldra, N. Wadid, OgreBot 2, TheRealHuldra ... 313
Figure 138 *Source:* https://en.wikipedia.org/w/index.php?title=File:WhitePaper.jpg *License:* Public Domain *Contributors:* JHistory, Jeff G., Zero0000 ... 316
Figure 139 *Source:* https//en.wikipedia.org *Contributors:* Matson Photo Service, photographer ... 318
Figure 140 *Source:* https://en.wikipedia.org/w/index.php?title=File:Demonstration_in_Tel_Aviv_against_the_British_mandate_policy_H_ih_038.JPG *License:* Public Domain *Contributors:* Geagea, National Library of Israel, עדירל יעקב ... 319
Figure 141 *Source:* https://en.wikipedia.org/w/index.php?title=File:Demonstration_in_Tel_Aviv_against_the_British_mandate_policy_H_ih_037.JPG *License:* Public Domain *Contributors:* National Library of Israel ... 319
Image *Source:* https://en.wikipedia.org/w/index.php?title=File:Bundesarchiv_Bild_183-N0827-318,_KZ_Auschwitz,_Ankunft_ungarischer_Juden.jpg *License:* Creative Commons Attribution-Sharealike 3.0 Germany *Contributors:* AdamBMorgan, BotMultichill, Catsmeat, Davidplan66, Gertsam, Goesseln, Hannolans, Jarekt, LudwigSebastianMicheler, Man vyi, Mtsmallwood, Rowanwindwhistler, SlimVirgin, Svajcr, Tom5551, Yarl, 5 anonymous edits ... 325
Figure 142 *Source:* https://en.wikipedia.org/w/index.php?title=File:Rosh_Hashanah_Evening_(6158254119).jpg *Contributors:* FlickreviewR 2, Fæ, עדירל ... 329
Image *Source:* https://en.wikipedia.org/w/index.php?title=File:Selection_Birkenau_ramp.jpg *Contributors:* Unknown. Several sources believe the photographer to have been Ernst Hoffmann or Bernhard Walter of the SS ... 330
Image *Source:* https://en.wikipedia.org/w/index.php?title=File:World_War_II_in_Europe,_1942.svg *Contributors:* User:Goran tek-en ... 334

Image *Source:* https://en.wikipedia.org/w/index.php?title=File:WW2-Holocaust-Europe.png *License:* Creative Commons Attribution 3.0 *Contributors:* User:Dna-Dennis ... 334
Figure 143 *Source:* https://en.wikipedia.org/w/index.php?title=File:Doctors'_trial,_Nuremberg,_1946–1947.jpg *License:* Public Domain *Contributors:* US Army photographers ... 336
Figure 144 *Source:* https://en.wikipedia.org/w/index.php?title=File:Bundesarchiv_Bild_102-14469,_Berlin,_Boykott-Posten_vor_jüdischem_Warenhaus.jpg *License:* Creative Commons Attribution-Sharealike 3.0 Germany *Contributors:* BotMultichill, Falcorian, Innotata, Martin H., Ras67, Robert Weemeyer, Rybak∼commonswiki, Watchduck ... 339
Figure 145 *Source:* https://en.wikipedia.org/w/index.php?title=File:Neues_Volk_eugenics_poster,_c._1937_(brightened).jpeg *License:* Public Domain *Contributors:* OgreBot 2, SlimVirgin ... 340
Figure 146 *Source:* https://en.wikipedia.org/w/index.php?title=File:Jewish_refugees_at_Croydon_airport_1939.jpg *License:* anonymous-EU *Contributors:* AP/World Wide Photos (see "Illustrations", London 2000, p. viii.) ... 342
Figure 147 *Source:* https://en.wikipedia.org/w/index.php?title=File:Burning_Synagoge_Kristallnacht_1938.jpg *License:* anonymous-EU *Contributors:* Apdency, Chefallen, DarwIn, Mtsmallwood, Nyakanyaka, Tasja∼commonswiki, Ulf Heinsohn, 4 anonymous edits ... 343
Figure 148 *Source:* https://en.wikipedia.org/w/index.php?title=File:Germany1941.png *License:* GNU Free Documentation License *Contributors:* Morty, Mackler, Lucius1976 ... 345
Figure 149 *Source:* https://en.wikipedia.org/w/index.php?title=File:German_J_stamped_passport_used_to_escape_Europe_in_1940.jpg *Contributors:* User:Huddyhuddy ... 346
Figure 150 *Source:* https://en.wikipedia.org/w/index.php?title=File:מורנים_'ישאי'_5.jpg *License:* Public Domain *Contributors:* An unknown journalist ... 348
Figure 151 *Source:* https://en.wikipedia.org/w/index.php?title=File:Bundesarchiv_Bild_192-269,_KZ_Mauthausen,_Häftlinge_im_Steinbruch.jpg *License:* Creative Commons Attribution-Sharealike 3.0 Germany *Contributors:* Alonso de Mendoza, Daniel Baránek, Diannaa, Herzi Pinki, John commons, Lechthaler, Mtsmallwood, Tm, Tom5551, 1 anonymous edits ... 349
Figure 152 *Source:* https://en.wikipedia.org/w/index.php?title=File:Stroop_Report_-_Warsaw_Ghetto_Uprising_06b.jpg *License:* Public Domain *Contributors:* AKA MBG, AVRS, Adambro, AndreasPraefcke, Andy Dingley, Arria Belli, Ascaron, Berrucomons, Beyond My Ken, Blackcat, Blurpeace, BotMultichill, Clpo13, Daczor, Daniel*D, Diego pmc, Dmitri Lytov, Docu, Dsmurat, Durova, Faigl.ladislav, Foroa, France05alpes, Fredy.00, Gorgo, Imartin6, Jarekt, Jeanot, Julia W, Kekator, Kozuch, Kramer Associates, Lupo, M11rtinb, Mario modesto, Marrante, Mattes, Mattia Luigi Nappi, Mtsmallwood, Mywood, Nagy, NatanFlayer, Nauticashades, Neukoln, Paris 16, Pinar, Pouyana, Ras67, Schekinov Alexey Victorovich, Starscream, Syujhtrrdy, Takabeg, Thierry Caro, Tom5551, Tonchino, Uaauaa, Vanmeetin, Waldir, Westborder, XDaniX, Yann, Yatzhek, א, 17 anonymous edits ... 351
Figure 153 *Source:* https://en.wikipedia.org/w/index.php?title=File:Zwłoki_dzieci_getto_warszawskie_05.jpg *License:* Public Domain *Contributors:* Boston9, OgreBot 2 ... 352
Figure 154 *Source:* https://en.wikipedia.org/w/index.php?title=File:Lviv_pogrom_(June_-_July_1941).jpg *License:* Public Domain *Contributors:* Butko, Darekm135, Dd1495, Poeticbent ... 353
Figure 155 *Source:* https://en.wikipedia.org/w/index.php?title=File:Einsatzgruppe_shooting.jpg *License:* Public Domain *Contributors:* Gustav Hille 354
Figure 156 *Source:* https://en.wikipedia.org/w/index.php?title=File:Liepaja_December_1941_massacres_01.jpeg *License:* Public Domain *Contributors:* generally ascribed to Carl Strott (Nazi war criminal), but some sources differ. ... 355
Figure 157 *Source:* https://en.wikipedia.org/w/index.php?title=File:Wannsee_Conference_-_List_of_Jews_in_European_countries.JPG *License:* Public domain *Contributors:* User:LeonardoG ... 356
Figure 158 *Source:* https://en.wikipedia.org/w/index.php?title=File:Auschwitz-birkenau-main_track.jpg *License:* GNU Free Documentation License *Contributors:* Bontenbal, Chmee2, Ikar.us, Kameraad Pjotr, LtPowers, MGA73bot2, Makthorpe, Mtsmallwood, Ronaldino, Sebastian Wallroth, Stunter∼commonswiki, Trycatch, Ultratomio ... 358
Figure 159 *Source:* https://en.wikipedia.org/w/index.php?title=File:Auschwitz_Resistance_282_cropped.JPG *Contributors:* Alex, Aleko or Alekos, a member of the Sonderkommando from Greece, often named as Alberto, Albert or Alex Errera, a Gree ... 359
Figure 160 *Source:* https://en.wikipedia.org/w/index.php?title=File:Stroop_Report_-_Warsaw_Ghetto_Uprising_13.jpg *License:* Public Domain *Contributors:* Andros64, BomBom, BotMultichill, Catrìona, Howcheng, Jarekt, Lotje, Movieevery, Nizzan Cohen, Pieter Kuiper, Poeticbent, 1 anonymous edits ... 361
Figure 161 *Source:* https://en.wikipedia.org/w/index.php?title=File:The_Black_Book_of_Poland_(21–24).jpg *License:* Public Domain *Contributors:* Ministry of Information of the Polish government-in-exile ... 364
Image *Source:* https://en.wikipedia.org/w/index.php?title=File:May_1944_-_Jews_from_Carpathian_Ruthenia_arrive_at_Auschwitz-Birkenau.jpg *Contributors:* Unknown. Several sources believe the photographer to have been Ernst Hoffmann or Bernhard Walter of the SS ... 364
Figure 162 *Source:* https://en.wikipedia.org/w/index.php?title=File:Dachau_Death_Train.jpeg *License:* Public Domain *Contributors:* Eric Schwab 366
Figure 163 *Source:* https://en.wikipedia.org/w/index.php?title=File:The_Liberation_of_Bergen-belsen_Concentration_Camp,_April_1945_BU4260.jpg *License:* Public Domain *Contributors:* Ain92, Deanlaw, Figure19, Fæ, Labattblueboy, Mehlauge, Monopoly31121993, Rcbutcher, Robert Weemeyer, Túrelio, Viloris, Wolfmann, 5 anonymous edits ... 367
Figure 164 *Source:* https://en.wikipedia.org/w/index.php?title=File:Bundesarchiv_R_165_Bild-244-48,_Asperg,_Deportation_von_Sinti_und_Roma.jpg *License:* Creative Commons Attribution-Sharealike 3.0 Germany *Contributors:* BotMultichill, HerrAdams, Lx 121, Mtsmallwood, Olahus, Softwarehistorian, Themightyquill, WhisperToMe, 1 anonymous edits ... 371
Figure 165 *Source:* https://en.wikipedia.org/w/index.php?title=File:Czeslawa_Kwoka_-_Brasse.jpg *License:* Public Domain *Contributors:* Wilhelm Brasse (attributed) ... 372
Figure 166 *Source:* https://en.wikipedia.org/w/index.php?title=File:Execution_of_Poles_by_German_Einsatzkomanndo_Oktober1939.jpg *Contributors:* - ... 373
Figure 167 *Source:* https://en.wikipedia.org/w/index.php?title=File:Bundesarchiv_Bild_192-208,_KZ_Mauthausen,_Sowjetische_Kriegsgefangene.jpg *License:* Creative Commons Attribution-Sharealike 3.0 Germany *Contributors:* Auric, Bdell555, BotMultichill, Bundesarchiv-B6, Lechthaler, Monopoly31121993, Mtsmallwood, Quibik, Ruff tuff cream puff, SunOfErat, XenonX3, 4 anonymous edits ... 374
Figure 168 *Source:* https://en.wikipedia.org/w/index.php?title=File:Gedenktafel_Rosa_Winkel_Nollendorfplatz.jpg *License:* Creative Commons Attribution-Sharealike 3.0 *Contributors:* Manfred Brueckels ... 375
Figure 169 *Source:* https://en.wikipedia.org/w/index.php?title=File:Obersalzberg_meeting_-_May_1939.png *License:* Public Domain *Contributors:* Eva Braun ... 377
Figure 170 *Source:* https://en.wikipedia.org/w/index.php?title=File:Defendants_in_the_dock_at_the_Nuremberg_Trials.jpg *License:* Public Domain *Contributors:* Beao, BotMultichill, Brian Ammon, Cloclob∼commonswiki, Cookie, Drdoht, EugeneZelenko, Evrik, Felix Stember, GT1976, Gkml, Howard61313, Jarekt, Jatkins, Joshuashearn, Jörg Zägel, Klemen Kocjancic, Leyo, Madmax32, Mogelzahn, O (bot), PDD, PMG, Paul.Matthies, Petronas, Schaengel89∼commonswiki, Siebrand, Steinsplitter, Torsade de Pointes, Ukas, Viiictorrr, Zzyzx11, 11 anonymous edits ... 378
Figure 171 *Source:* https://en.wikipedia.org/w/index.php?title=File:Group_14_Aliyah_Beth_1947.png *License:* Creative Commons Attribution 2.5 *Contributors:* User:Helix84 ... 400
Figure 172 *Source:* https://en.wikipedia.org/w/index.php?title=File:Buchenwald_concentration_camp_survivors_sailing_to_Haifa,_June_1945.jpg *License:* Public Domain *Contributors:* Brackenheim, Ceedjee∼commonswiki, Deborahjay, Faigl.ladislav, Geagea, JHistory, Ldorfman, Netanel h, O (bot), Place Clichy, Poliocretes, Ravit, Wini, עדירל, יעקב, 2 anonymous edits ... 404
Figure 173 *Source:* https://en.wikipedia.org/w/index.php?title=File:Hagana_Ship_-_Jewish_State_at_Haifa_Port_(1947).jpg *License:* Public Domain *Contributors:* Aviados, BotMultichill, Catsmeat, Geagea, Hanay, JHistory, Magister, Mattes, Pessimist2006, Roland zh, Steinsplitter, יעל י ... 407
Figure 174 *Source:* https://en.wikipedia.org/w/index.php?title=File:Exodus_1947_ship.jpg *License:* Public Domain *Contributors:* self-scanned from collection of uploader, JGHowes ... 407
Figure 175 *Source:* https://en.wikipedia.org/w/index.php?title=File:Bundesarchiv_Bild_183-R68235,_Naharija,_Landung_jüdischer_Auswanderer.jpg *License:* Creative Commons Attribution-Sharealike 3.0 Germany *Contributors:* ALE!, Bukvoed, De728631, Duch, Finavon, G.dallorto, Geagea, JHistory, Monopoly31121993, Netanel h, Pessimist2006, Smiley.toerist, Stunteltje, יעל חובבשירה י ... 408
Figure 176 *Source:* https://en.wikipedia.org/w/index.php?title=File:Ha'apala_After_The_World_War_II_-_en.webm *Contributors:* User:JHistory 410
Figure 177 *Source:* https://en.wikipedia.org/w/index.php?title=File:PikiWiki_Israel_12118_monument_to_the_victims_on_immigrants_ship_salvado.jpg *License:* Creative Commons Attribution 2.5 *Contributors:* ד"ר אבישי טייכר ... 411
Image *Source:* https://en.wikipedia.org/w/index.php?title=File:PalestineRailways-1946-sabotage-JaffaJerusalem-1.jpg *License:* Creative Commons Zero *Contributors:* Altona, Ashashyou, Catsmeat, Ingolfson, Motacilla, TheGrappler ... 413
Figure 178 *Source:* https://en.wikipedia.org/w/index.php?title=File:PeelMap.png *License:* Public Domain *Contributors:* Geagea, Zero0000 ... 415
Figure 179 *Source:* https://en.wikipedia.org/w/index.php?title=File:Etzel002.jpg *License:* Public Domain *Contributors:* Irgun ... 422
Figure 180 *Source:* https//en.wikipedia.org *License:* Public Domain *Contributors:* Jeff G., Onceinawhile, Poliocretes ... 424
Figure 181 *Source:* https://en.wikipedia.org/w/index.php?title=File:KD_1946.JPG *License:* Public Domain *Contributors:* Bukk, Christophe cagé, Deror avi, Drork, Enricopedia, Faigl.ladislav, Geagea, Kaganer, Liftarn, Netanel h, Pieter Kuiper, Poliocretes, PxMa, Shizhao, Valleyofdawn, א. חומר 436
Figure 182 *Source:* https://en.wikipedia.org/w/index.php?title=File:Curfew_in_Tel_Aviv_H_ih_039.JPG *License:* Public Domain *Contributors:* Photographer: Haim Fain ... 437

Figure 183 *Source:* https://en.wikipedia.org/w/index.php?title=File:Latrun_detention_camp.jpg *License:* Public Domain *Contributors:* Avin, BotMultichill, Bukvoed, Geagea, Mzungu, Netanel h, Nudve∼commonswiki, O (bot), Place Clichy, Poliocretes, Robert Weemeyer, 1 anonymous edits . 437

Figure 184 *Source:* https://en.wikipedia.org/w/index.php?title=File:Jewish_civilians_waiting_to_be_interrogated_July_1946.jpg *License:* Public Domain *Contributors:* No 1 Army Film & Photographic Unit Turner W R H (Sergeant) 438

Figure 185 *Source:* https://en.wikipedia.org/w/index.php?title=File:Irgun_men_in_costume.jpg *License:* Public Domain *Contributors:* Ashashyou, BotMultichill, Christophe cagé, Geagea, Nudve∼commonswiki, א. תומר 442

Figure 186 *Source:* https://en.wikipedia.org/w/index.php?title=File:Bevingrad.jpg *License:* Public Domain *Contributors:* Unknown - not relevant for the licence 443

Figure 187 *Source:* https://en.wikipedia.org/w/index.php?title=File:The_Acre_prison_after_the_break,_1947.jpg *License:* Public Domain *Contributors:* Aviados, BotMultichill, Bukvoed, Christophe cagé, Geagea, Hidro, Lotje, Netanel h, Nudve∼commonswiki, Poliocretes, א. תומר 445

Figure 188 *Source:* https://en.wikipedia.org/w/index.php?title=File:Hanged_sergeants.jpg *License:* Public Domain *Contributors:* Ashashyou, Aviados, BotMultichill, Christophe cagé, Geagea, Ingolfson, JHistory, Jakednb, Liftarn, Lotje, Nudve∼commonswiki, Poliocretes, א. תומר 446

Image *Source:* https://en.wikipedia.org/w/index.php?title=File:UN_Palestine_Partition_Versions_1947.jpg *License:* UN map *Contributors:* User:Zero0000 452

Image *Source:* https://en.wikipedia.org/w/index.php?title=File:Wikisource-logo.svg *License:* Creative Commons Attribution-Sharealike 3.0 *Contributors:* ChrisiPK, Guillom, INeverCry, Jarekt, JuTa, Leyo, Lokal Profil, MichaelMaggs, NielsF, Rei-artur, Rocket000, Romaine, Steinsplitter 452

Figure 189 *Source:* https://en.wikipedia.org/w/index.php?title=File:1947-UN-Partition-Plan-1949-Armistice-Comparison.svg *License:* Public Domain *Contributors:* AnonMoos 459

Image *Source:* https://en.wikipedia.org/w/index.php?title=File:Flag_of_the_United_States_(1912-1959).svg *License:* Public Domain *Contributors:* Created by jacobolus using Adobe Illustrator. 462

Image *Source:* https://en.wikipedia.org/w/index.php?title=File:Flag_of_India.svg *License:* Public Domain *Contributors:* Anomie, Jo-Jo Eumerus, Mifter 463

Image *Source:* https://en.wikipedia.org/w/index.php?title=File:Flag_of_Liberia.svg *License:* Public Domain *Contributors:* Government of Liberia 463

Image *Source:* https://en.wikipedia.org/w/index.php?title=File:Flag_of_the_Philippines_(navy_blue).svg *License:* Creative Commons Attribution-Sharealike 2.5 *Contributors:* Alkari, Billinghurst, FakirNL, FreshCorp619, Jeenim, Kurrop, Ljmajer, Lokal Profil, MGA73bot2, Mabuhay1946, Mattes, Patstuart, SiBr4, Tcfc2349, User 50, 2 anonymous edits 463

Image *Source:* https://en.wikipedia.org/w/index.php?title=File:Flag_of_Haiti_(1859-1964).svg *Contributors:* - 463

Image *Source:* https://en.wikipedia.org/w/index.php?title=File:Flag_of_France_(1794-1815).svg *Contributors:* - 463

Image *Source:* https://en.wikipedia.org/w/index.php?title=File:Flag_of_Venezuela_(1930–1954).svg *License:* Creative Commons Attribution-Sharealike 3.0 *Contributors:* Bodhisattwa, Cycn, FXXX, Fry1989, Illegitimate Barrister, Sangjinhwa, Shadowxfox, Tcfc2349, 6 anonymous edits . 464

Image *Source:* https://en.wikipedia.org/w/index.php?title=File:Flag_of_Cuba.svg *License:* Public Domain *Contributors:* Anime Addict AA, Beao, Benzoyl, Cathy Richards, Charlesjsharp, Cycn, Dbenbenn, Denelson83, DerBorg, EclecticArkie, Emijrp, F l a n k e r, FreshCorp619, Fry1989, Homo lupus, Huhsunqu, J.delanoy, Jdx, Klemen Kocjancic, Ludger1961, MAXXX-309, Madden, Mattes, Neq00, NeverDoING, Persiana, Ricordisamoa, SKopp, Sarang, SiBr4, Spacebirdy, TFerenczy, ThomasPusch, Torstein, Túrelio, Zscout370, 10 anonymous edits 464

Image *Source:* https://en.wikipedia.org/w/index.php?title=File:Flag_of_Thailand.svg *Contributors:* Achim55, Andy Dingley, Chaddy, Denelson83, Dfddtdt, Duduziq, Emerentia, Fry1989, Gabbe, Giro720, Gurch, Hedwig in Washington, Homo lupus, Illegitimate Barrister, Jo Shigeru, Juiced lemon, Kimjiho2015, Klemen Kocjancic, Mattes, Neq00, Paul 012, Perhelion, Rugby471, Sahapon-krit hellokitty, Siebrand, TOR, Teetaweepo, Xiengyod∼commonswiki, Yann, Ytoyoda, Zscout370, Δ, 28 anonymous edits 464

Image *Source:* https://en.wikipedia.org/w/index.php?title=File:Flag_of_Bolivia.svg *License:* Public Domain *Contributors:* Anakin∼commonswiki, Avala, Cathy Richards, Cesar david rodriguez, Cycn, Dbenbenn, Fred J, Fry1989, GoldenRainbow, Hedwig in Washington, HoheHoffnungen, Homo lupus, Huhsunqu, Klemen Kocjancic, Koefbac, Mattes, Neq00, Pixeltoo, Reisio, Richard Melo da Silva, Rocket000, Rodejong, Rojk∼commonswiki, SKopp, Sarang, SiBr4, Smaug the Golden, Spiritia, Srtxg, ThomasPusch, Torstein, UberHalogen, Zscout370, 7 anonymous edits 465

Image *Source:* https://en.wikipedia.org/w/index.php?title=File:Flag_of_Brazil.svg *License:* Public Domain *Contributors:* Anomie, Jo-Jo Eumerus 465

Image *Source:* https://en.wikipedia.org/w/index.php?title=File:Flag_of_Costa_Rica.svg *License:* Public Domain *Contributors:* Drawn by User:SKopp, rewritten by User:Gabbe 465

Image *Source:* https://en.wikipedia.org/w/index.php?title=File:Flag_of_the_Dominican_Republic.svg *License:* Public Domain *Contributors:* User:Nightstallion 465

Image *Source:* https://en.wikipedia.org/w/index.php?title=File:Flag_of_Ecuador.svg *License:* Public Domain *Contributors:* President of the Republic of Ecuador, Zscout370 465

Image *Source:* https://en.wikipedia.org/w/index.php?title=File:Flag_of_Guatemala.svg *License:* Public Domain *Contributors:* User:K21edgo .465

Image *Source:* https://en.wikipedia.org/w/index.php?title=File:Flag_of_Nicaragua.svg *License:* Public Domain *Contributors:* C records, Ecemaml, MICOMANDANTESEQUEDA, RobertBDurham, Shervinafshar, SiBr4, Tacsipacsi, 1 anonymous edits 465

Image *Source:* https://en.wikipedia.org/w/index.php?title=File:Flag_of_Panama.svg *License:* Public Domain *Contributors:* -xfi-, Addicted04, Alkari, Bast64∼commonswiki, Benzoyl, Blackcat, Cathy Richards, CemDemirkartal, Comandante777, Cycn, Duduziq, Fadi the philologer, FreshCorp619, Fry1989, Geagea, Golden Bosnian Lily, Huhsunqu, Hystrix, Joshbaumgartner, Klemen Kocjancic, Liftarn, Mattes, NicoScribe, Nightstallion, Ninane, Pumbaa80, Reisio, Rfc1394, Sangjinhwa, SiBr4, TFCforever, TFerenczy, Taichi, Thomas81, ThomasPusch, Zscout370, Ö, Фёдор Гусляров, 28 anonymous edits 465

Image *Source:* https://en.wikipedia.org/w/index.php?title=File:Flag_of_Paraguay_(1842-1954).svg *License:* Public Domain *Contributors:* Kaiser Torikka 465

Image *Source:* https://en.wikipedia.org/w/index.php?title=File:Flag_of_Peru_(1825-1950).svg *License:* Creative Commons Attribution-Sharealike 2.5 *Contributors:* User:Huhsunqu 465

Image *Source:* https://en.wikipedia.org/w/index.php?title=File:Flag_of_Uruguay.svg *License:* Public Domain *Contributors:* User:Reisio (original author) 465

Image *Source:* https://en.wikipedia.org/w/index.php?title=File:Flag_of_Belgium_(civil).svg *License:* Public Domain *Contributors:* Allforrous, Andres gb.ldc, Bean49, Cathy Richards, David Descamps, Dbenbenn, Denelson83, Evanc0912, FreshCorp619, Fry1989, Gabriel trzy, Howcome, IvanOS, Jdx, Mimich, Ms2ger, Nightstallion, Oreo Priest, Pitke, Ricordisamoa, Rocket000, Rodejong, Sarang, SiBr4, Sir Iain, ThomasPusch, Warddr, Zscout370, ייהלייזיושמר, 15 anonymous edits 466

Image *Source:* https://en.wikipedia.org/w/index.php?title=File:Flag_of_Denmark.svg *License:* Public Domain *Contributors:* Madden 466

Image *Source:* https://en.wikipedia.org/w/index.php?title=File:Flag_of_France.svg *License:* Public Domain *Contributors:* Anomie, Fastily, Jo-Jo Eumerus 466

Image *Source:* https://en.wikipedia.org/w/index.php?title=File:Flag_of_Iceland.svg *License:* Public Domain *Contributors:* ALE!, ArniDagur, Benzoyl, Cathy Richards, Duduziq, Enbéká, F l a n k e r, F. F. Fjodor, Fry1989, GeMet, GoldenRainbow, Homo lupus, Iketsi, IvanOS, Jarekt, Juetho, Klemen Kocjancic, Liambaker98, Lirion, MAXXX-309, Magasjukur2, Mattes, Peeperman, RainbowSilver2ndBackup, S.Örvarr.S, Sarang, SiBr4, Superzerocool, ThomasPusch, Yarl, Zscout370, Ævar Arnfjörð Bjarmason, 8 anonymous edits 466

Image *Source:* https://en.wikipedia.org/w/index.php?title=File:Flag_of_Luxembourg.svg *License:* Public Domain *Contributors:* User:SKopp .466

Image *Source:* https://en.wikipedia.org/w/index.php?title=File:Flag_of_the_Netherlands.svg *License:* Public Domain *Contributors:* Zscout370 466

Image *Source:* https://en.wikipedia.org/w/index.php?title=File:Flag_of_Norway.svg *License:* Public Domain *Contributors:* Dbenbenn 466

Image *Source:* https://en.wikipedia.org/w/index.php?title=File:Flag_of_Sweden.svg *License:* Public Domain *Contributors:* Anomie, Jo-Jo Eumerus, Mr. Stradivarius 466

Image *Source:* https://en.wikipedia.org/w/index.php?title=File:Flag_of_the_Byelorussian_SSR_(1940).svg *Contributors:* - 466

Image *Source:* https://en.wikipedia.org/w/index.php?title=File:Flag_of_the_Czech_Republic.svg *License:* Public Domain *Contributors:* -xfi-, Alkari, Andres gb.ldc, AwOc, Benzoyl, Bjankuloski06en, C41n, Cycn, Denelson83, Denniss, Dzordzm, EZBELLA, Er Komandante, Fedor204, Fibonacci, FreshCorp619, Fry1989, Future Perfect at Sunrise, Gumruch, Homo lupus, JuTa, Klemen Kocjancic, Leyo, Li-sung, MAXXX-309, Madden, Miraceti, NeverDoING, Nightstallion, Pfctdayelise, Phlegmatic, Pseudomoi, Pumbaa80, Ratatosk, Ricordisamoa, Saibo, Sangjinhwa, Sarang, Shybird, SiBr4, Stephanie∼commonswiki, V-ball, Wiki-vr, علی المزارقه, 43 anonymous edits 466

Image *Source:* https://en.wikipedia.org/w/index.php?title=File:Flag_of_Poland.svg *License:* Public Domain *Contributors:* Anomie, Jo-Jo Eumerus, Mifter 466

Image *Source:* https://en.wikipedia.org/w/index.php?title=File:Flag_of_the_Ukrainian_SSR_(1927-1937).svg *Contributors:* - 466

Image *Source:* https://en.wikipedia.org/w/index.php?title=File:Flag_of_the_Soviet_Union_(1936–1955).svg *License:* GNU Free Documentation License *Contributors:* User:Rotemliss 466

Image *Source:* https://en.wikipedia.org/w/index.php?title=File:Flag_of_South_Africa_(1928–1982).svg *License:* Public Domain *Contributors:* Parliament of South Africa (Vector graphics image by Denelson83) 466

Image *Source:* https://en.wikipedia.org/w/index.php?title=File:Flag_of_Australia.svg *License:* Public Domain *Contributors:* Anomie, Jo-Jo Eumerus, Mifter 466

Image *Source:* https://en.wikipedia.org/w/index.php?title=File:Flag_of_New_Zealand.svg *License:* Public Domain *Contributors:* Achim1999, Adabow, Adambro, Arria Belli, Avenue, Bawolff, Bjankuloski06en, ButterStick, Cycn, Denelson83, Denniss, Donk∼commonswiki, Duduziq, EugeneZelenko, Fred J, FreshCorp619, Fry1989, George Ho, GoldenRainbow, Hugh Jass, Ibagli, Jusjih, Klemen Kocjancic, MAXXX-309, Mamndassan, Mattes,

Mindmatrix, Nightstallion, O, Ozgurnarin, Peeperman, Pembe karadeniz, Poco a poco, Poromiami, Reisio, Rfc1394, Salvabl, Salvaeditor, Sarang, Shizhao, SiBr4, Steinsplitter, Tabasco~commonswiki, TintoMeches, Transparent Blue, Voyager, Väsk, Xufanc, Yann, Zscout370, 43 anonymous edits 466

Image *Source:* https://en.wikipedia.org/w/index.php?title=File:Canadian_Red_Ensign_(1921–1957).svg *License:* Public Domain *Contributors:* User:Denelson83 466

Image *Source:* https://en.wikipedia.org/w/index.php?title=File:Flag_of_Afghanistan_(1931–1973).svg *License:* Public Domain *Contributors:* at en.wikipedia. 466

Image *Source:* https://en.wikipedia.org/w/index.php?title=File:State_Flag_of_Iran_(1925).svg *Contributors:* - 466

Image *Source:* https://en.wikipedia.org/w/index.php?title=File:Flag_of_Iraq_(1921–1959).svg *License:* Public Domain *Contributors:* Antemister, Ashashyou, Ashrf1979, Burts, FreshCorp619, Illegitimate Barrister, J. Patrick Fischer, Madden, Mathonius, MrPenguin20, R-41~commonswiki, Sportsguy17, Takabeg, Zscout370, Ранко Николић, 4 anonymous edits 466

Image *Source:* https://en.wikipedia.org/w/index.php?title=File:Flag_of_Pakistan.svg *License:* Public Domain *Contributors:* User:Zscout370 466

Image *Source:* https://en.wikipedia.org/w/index.php?title=File:Flag_of_Saudi_Arabia_(1938–1973).svg *License:* Public domain *Contributors:* FDRMRZUSA, FreshCorp619, Illegitimate Barrister, JuTa, OgreBot 2, Sangjinhwa, 4 anonymous edits 466

Image *Source:* https://en.wikipedia.org/w/index.php?title=File:Flag_of_Syria_(1932-1958;_1961-1963).svg *License:* Public Domain *Contributors:* User:AnonMoos 466

Image *Source:* https://en.wikipedia.org/w/index.php?title=File:Flag_of_the_Mutawakkilite_Kingdom_of_Yemen.svg *License:* Public Domain *Contributors:* User:Urmas 466

Image *Source:* https://en.wikipedia.org/w/index.php?title=File:Flag_of_Greece_(1822-1978).svg *License:* Public Domain *Contributors:* (of code) User:Makaristos 466

Image *Source:* https://en.wikipedia.org/w/index.php?title=File:Flag_of_Turkey.svg *License:* Public Domain *Contributors:* User:Dbenbenn 467

Image *Source:* https://en.wikipedia.org/w/index.php?title=File:Flag_of_Egypt_(1922–1958).svg *License:* Public Domain *Contributors:* Alkari, AnonMoos, Billinghurst, BomBom, Burts, Cycn, Dharmadhyaksha, F l a n k e r, Faris knight, FreshCorp619, Herbythyme, JMCC1, Jdx, Kajk, Kookaburra, Mattes, Mysid, Nagy, Oren neu dag, Rotemliss, Sangjinhwa, Sarang, SiBr4, Urmas, Ранко Николић, زكريا, 9 anonymous edits 467

Image *Source:* https://en.wikipedia.org/w/index.php?title=File:Flag_of_Argentina.svg *Contributors:* ALE!, Alkari, Allforrous, Barcex, Bencmq, Bobika, Cambalachero, Cathy Richards, Courcelles, Dbenbenn, Denelson83, Eugenio Hansen, OFS, Fanghong, Fma12, FreshCorp619, Fry1989, Geger54, Golden Bosnian Lily, GoldenRainbow, Hambrientino, HoheHoffnungen, Huhsunqu, INeverCry, Jarould, Jdx, Juliancolton, Klemen Kocjancic, Kved, Kwpolska, Lankiveil, LechitaPL, MAXXX-309, Maks Stirlitz, Nagy, Neq00, Nickitoolivares, NicoScribe, Niridya, Odder, Philosophenschule des Platon, Prev, Pumbaa80, Reisio, Richardkiwi, Sarang, SiBr4, Smaug the Golden, Steinsplitter, TFerenczy, TigerTjäder, Yaddah, ZooFari, Zscout370, 28 anonymous edits 467

Image *Source:* https://en.wikipedia.org/w/index.php?title=File:Flag_of_Chile.svg *License:* Public Domain *Contributors:* Alkari, Andres gb.ldc, B1mbo, Benzoyl, BotMultichill, Cathy Richards, Cycn, David Newton, Dbenbenn, Denelson83, Er Komandante, Fibonacci, File Upload Bot (Magnus Manske), FreshCorp619, Fry1989, GoldenRainbow, Herbythyme, Huhsunqu, Kallerna, Kanonkas, Klemen Kocjancic, Kwasura, Kyro, LechitaPL, Leyo, MAXXX-309, Mattes, McZusatz, Mozzan, Nagy, Nightstallion, Perhelion, Piastu, Pixeltoo, Pumbaa80, SKopp, Sangjinhwa, Sarang, SiBr4, Smaug the Golden, Srtxg, Sterling.M.Archer, Str4nd, Tcfc2349, Ultratomio, VulpesVulpes42, Vzb83~commonswiki, Xarucoponce, Yakoo, Yonatanh, Zscout370, 55 anonymous edits 467

Image *Source:* https://en.wikipedia.org/w/index.php?title=File:Flag_of_Colombia.svg *License:* Public Domain *Contributors:* SKopp 467

Image *Source:* https://en.wikipedia.org/w/index.php?title=File:Flag_of_El_Salvador.svg *License:* Public Domain *Contributors:* user:Nightstallion 467

Image *Source:* https://en.wikipedia.org/w/index.php?title=File:Flag_of_Honduras.svg *License:* Public Domain *Contributors:* Cathy Richards, D1990, Denelson83, ECanalla, Feydey, FixFixer, Fred J, FreshCorp619, GoldenRainbow, Homo lupus, JMCC1, Klemen Kocjancic, Mattes, Matthew hk, Neq00, Oak27, Pumbaa80, Rocket000, RubiksMaster110, SKopp, SiBr4, Siebrand, Steinsplitter, ThomasPusch, Tocino, Vzb83~commonswiki, Yuval Madar, ZooFari, Zscout370, 10 anonymous edits 467

Image *Source:* https://en.wikipedia.org/w/index.php?title=File:Flag_of_Mexico_(1934–1968).png *License:* Public Domain *Contributors:* AtomicIce, Fry1989, Illegitimate Barrister, Kimdime, とある白い猫, 1 anonymous edits 467

Image *Source:* https://en.wikipedia.org/w/index.php?title=File:Flag_of_the_Republic_of_China.svg *License:* Public Domain *Contributors:* User:SKopp 467

Image *Source:* https://en.wikipedia.org/w/index.php?title=File:Flag_of_Ethiopia_(1897-1936;_1941-1974).svg *Contributors:* Oren neu dag 467

Image *Source:* https://en.wikipedia.org/w/index.php?title=File:Flag_of_Yugoslavia_(1946-1992).svg *License:* Public Domain *Contributors:* Flag designed by Đorđe Andrejević-KunSVG coding: Zscout370 467

Image *Source:* https://en.wikipedia.org/w/index.php?title=File:Katamon.jpg *License:* Public Domain *Contributors:* Israeli GPO photographer 475

Figure 190 *Source:* https://en.wikipedia.org/w/index.php?title=File:Ben_Yehuda_22_fev_1948.jpg *License:* Public Domain *Contributors:* Ceedjee~commonswiki, Chesdovi, Christophe cagé, Netanel h, Talmoryair, 2 anonymous edits 478

Figure 191 *Source:* https://en.wikipedia.org/w/index.php?title=File:Arab_volunteers.jpg *License:* Public Domain *Contributors:* Abdulrazzaq Badran (Photo Journalist to Egyptian Dar El Hilal magazine) 482

Image *Source:* https://en.wikipedia.org/w/index.php?title=File:Man_see_school_nakba.jpg *License:* Public Domain *Contributors:* Adnanmuf~commonswiki, BotMultichill, EChastain, SpacemanSpiff, Timeshifter, 1 anonymous edits 484

Figure 192 *Source:* https://en.wikipedia.org/w/index.php?title=File:Smg_sten_MK_IIS_01.jpg *License:* Public Domain *Contributors:* Hohum, Nemo5576 488

Figure 193 *Source:* https://en.wikipedia.org/w/index.php?title=File:Ordre_de_bataille_Palestine_avril_48.gif *License:* GNU Free Documentation License *Contributors:* Ceedjee contact 490

Figure 194 *Source:* https://en.wikipedia.org/w/index.php?title=File:Jewish_zones_12147.PNG *License:* Creative Commons Attribution-ShareAlike 3.0 Unported *Contributors:* It's-is-not-a-genitive 491

Figure 195 *Source:* https://en.wikipedia.org/w/index.php?title=File:Husayni.jpg *License:* Public Domain *Contributors:* Arian Writing, BotMultichill, Ceedjee~commonswiki, Christophe cagé, Dcoetzee, EPO, Kjetil r, Korrigan, Padres Hana, Producer, Thib Phil, عماد الدين المقدسي, 4 anonymous edits 492

Figure 196 *Source:* https://en.wikipedia.org/w/index.php?title=File:Machsom.jpg *License:* Public Domain *Contributors:* BokicaK, Brühl, Geagea, Netanel h 493

Figure 197 *Source:* https://en.wikipedia.org/w/index.php?title=File:PikiWiki_Israel_20804_The_Palmach.jpg *License:* Public Domain *Contributors:* Brakeet, Movieevery, Netanel h, Pikiwikisrael, 1 anonymous edits 493

Figure 198 *Source:* https://en.wikipedia.org/w/index.php?title=File:Jerusalem_convoy.jpg *License:* Public Domain *Contributors:* Geagea, Hohum, Padres Hana, 1 anonymous edits 494

Figure 199 *Source:* https://en.wikipedia.org/w/index.php?title=File:Convois_2.JPG *License:* Public Domain *Contributors:* Brakeet, Bukvoed, Ceedjee~commonswiki, Christophe cagé, Rama, 2 anonymous edits 494

Figure 200 *Source:* https://en.wikipedia.org/w/index.php?title=File:Dori_and_Yadin.JPG *License:* GNU Free Documentation License *Contributors:* BotMultichill, Ceedjee~commonswiki, Drork, MGA73bot2, Matanya, יעקב 497

Figure 201 *Source:* https://en.wikipedia.org/w/index.php?title=File:Nachshon.GIF *License:* GNU Free Documentation License *Contributors:* Bloody-libu, File Upload Bot (Magnus Manske), MGA73bot2, Magog the Ogre 497

Figure 202 *Source:* https://en.wikipedia.org/w/index.php?title=File:Fall_of_Qastel_on_April_5_1948.jpg *License:* Public Domain *Contributors:* Unknown - not relevant for the licence in Israel. The date is important (see below). 498

Figure 203 *Source:* https://en.wikipedia.org/w/index.php?title=File:Kastal.jpg *License:* Public Domain *Contributors:* Padres Hana, TheRealHuldra 498

Figure 204 *Source:* https://en.wikipedia.org/w/index.php?title=File:Mishmar_HaEmek.JPG *License:* Public Domain *Contributors:* Hashomer Hatzair 500

Figure 205 *Source:* https://en.wikipedia.org/w/index.php?title=File:MishmarHaemek2.jpg *License:* Public Domain *Contributors:* Alonr, Bukk, Ceedjee~commonswiki, Christophe cagé, Geagea, Rama, TheRealHuldra, 2 anonymous edits 500

Figure 206 *Source:* https://en.wikipedia.org/w/index.php?title=File:Yiftah.GIF *License:* GNU Free Documentation License *Contributors:* AnonMoos, BotMultichillT, It's-is-not-a-genitive~commonswiki, Timeshifter 503

Figure 207 *Source:* https://en.wikipedia.org/w/index.php?title=File:Golda_Meir_1943.jpg *License:* Public Domain *Contributors:* OgreBot 2, Sonntagsbraten 505

Figure 208 *Source:* https://en.wikipedia.org/w/index.php?title=File:Kingabdullahbinhussein.jpg *Contributors:* Albertomos, Ashrf1979, Bontenbal, Bubuka, Ceedjee~commonswiki, Davepape, Dbenbenn, Greenshed, Gryffindor, Guety, Gugganij, Herbythyme, SteveStrummer, Takabeg, Thuresson, Trijnstel, 4 anonymous edits 506

Figure 209 *Source:* https://en.wikipedia.org/w/index.php?title=File:Gush_Etzion.GIF *License:* GNU Free Documentation License *Contributors:* It's-is-not-a-genitive~commonswiki, MGA73bot2, OgreBot 2, Timeshifter 507

Figure 210 *Source:* https://en.wikipedia.org/w/index.php?title=File:Etzion_Tal_Prisoners.jpg *License:* Public Domain *Contributors:* BotMultichill, Ceedjee~commonswiki, Kippi70, Netanel h, Padres Hana 508

Figure 211 *Source:* https://en.wikipedia.org/w/index.php?title=File:PikiWiki_Israel_20755_The_Palmach.jpg *License:* Public Domain *Contributors:* Chesdovi, Netanel h, Pikiwikisrael 509

Figure 212 *Source:* https://en.wikipedia.org/w/index.php?title=File:Bevingrad.jpg *License:* Public Domain *Contributors:* Unknown - not relevant for the licence 510
Figure 213 *Source:* https://en.wikipedia.org/w/index.php?title=File:Ben'Ami.GIF *License:* GNU Free Documentation License *Contributors:* Bot-MultichillT, Christophe cagé, It's-is-not-a-genitive~commonswiki, Timeshifter 511
Figure 214 *Source:* https://en.wikipedia.org/w/index.php?title=File:Palestinian_refugees.jpg *License:* Public Domain *Contributors:* Fred Csasznik 512
Figure 215 *Source:* https://en.wikipedia.org/w/index.php?title=File:Zones_controlled_by_Yishuv_by_the_20may48.GIF *License:* GNU Free Documentation License *Contributors:* File Upload Bot (Magnus Manske), Innotata, OgreBot 2 514
Image *Source:* https://en.wikipedia.org/w/index.php?title=File:Raising_the_Ink_Flag_at_Umm_Rashrash_(Eilat).jpg *License:* Creative Commons Attribution-Sharealike 3.0 *Contributors:* AnonMoos, Geagea, Hanay, Jaredzimmerman (WMF), LLs, Matanya, Neukoln, Poliocretes, Ran Ayase, Ranbar, Steinsplitter, Triggerhippie4, Wieralee, Yann, علي المزارع 519
Image *Source:* https://en.wikipedia.org/w/index.php?title=File:Badge_of_the_Israel_Defense_Forces.svg *License:* Creative Commons Attribution-Sharealike 3.0 *Contributors:* Flag_of_the_Israel_Defence_Forces.svg: Meronim derivative work: User:Zscout370 (Return fire) 520
Image *Source:* https://en.wikipedia.org/w/index.php?title=File:Flag_of_Druze.svg *License:* Public Domain *Contributors:* Copyright (c) 2005 Verdy p (also fr:User:Verdy_p) (attribution line, when needed) 520
Image *Source:* https://en.wikipedia.org/w/index.php?title=File:Arab_Liberation_Army_(bw).svg *License:* Creative Commons Attribution-Sharealike 3.0 *Contributors:* Valleeyofdawn, modified by Zscout370 520
Image *Source:* https://en.wikipedia.org/w/index.php?title=File:Flag_of_the_Muslim_Brotherhood.gif *License:* Public Domain *Contributors:* Cathy Richards, Denniss, Jeff G., Mikrobølgeovn, Ratatosk 520
Image *Source:* https://en.wikipedia.org/w/index.php?title=File:Flag_of_Anglo-Egyptian_Sudan.svg *License:* Creative Commons Attribution-Sharealike 3.0 *Contributors:* User:Abjiklam 520
Image *Source:* https://en.wikipedia.org/w/index.php?title=File:Flag_of_the_Arab_League.svg *License:* Public Domain *Contributors:* Flad 520
Figure 216 *Source:* https://en.wikipedia.org/w/index.php?title=File:UN_Palestine_Partition_Versions_1947.jpg *License:* UN map *Contributors:* User:Zero0000 522
Figure 217 *Source:* https://en.wikipedia.org/w/index.php?title=File:PikiWiki_Israel_21221_The_Palmach.jpg *License:* Public Domain *Contributors:* Articseahorse, Crazy Ivan, Netanel h, Pikiwikisrael 524
Figure 218 *Source:* https://en.wikipedia.org/w/index.php?title=File:Avia_S-199_in_June_1948_(Israeli_Air_Force).jpeg *License:* Public Domain *Contributors:* Articseahorse, Joshbaumgartner, NeverDoING, Poliocretes, Steinsplitter, Wieralee, Ynhockey, 2 anonymous edits 526
Figure 219 *Source:* https://en.wikipedia.org/w/index.php?title=File:King_Abdullah,_Jerusalem,_29_May_1948.jpg *License:* Public Domain *Contributors:* John Roy Carlson 531
Figure 220 *Source:* https://en.wikipedia.org/w/index.php?title=File:Tanks_of_the_Israeli_8th_Armoured_Brigade_(1948).jpg *License:* Public Domain *Contributors:* Joram Field 534
Figure 221 *Source:* https://en.wikipedia.org/w/index.php?title=File:The_British_Army_in_the_United_Kingdom_1939-45_H37168.jpg *License:* Public Domain *Contributors:* Ain92, Aiexpl, Fæ, Labattblueboy, Rcbutcher 535
Figure 222 *Source:* https://en.wikipedia.org/w/index.php?title=File:BrenCarrierShualeiShimshon.png *License:* Public Domain *Contributors:* Ashashyou, Brakeet, Ynhockey, חובבשירה, 1 anonymous edits 536
Figure 223 *Source:* https://en.wikipedia.org/w/index.php?title=File:The_British_Army_in_North_Africa_1940_E443.2.jpg *License:* Public Domain *Contributors:* Ain92, Fæ, Gunbirddriver2, HantsAV, Labattblueboy 538
Figure 224 *Source:* https://en.wikipedia.org/w/index.php?title=File:1948_Arab_Israeli_War_-_May_15-June_10.svg *License:* Public Domain *Contributors:* Mr. Edward C. Krasonborski and Mr. Frank Martini, Department of History, U.S. Military Academy Honza.havlicek (talk) 539
Figure 225 *Source:* https://en.wikipedia.org/w/index.php?title=File:Butterfly_Armored-car_Gvar-Am-israel1948.jpg *License:* Creative Commons Attribution-Sharealike 3.0 *Contributors:* Brakeet, Geagea, Hanay, Poliocretes, Ykantor 540
Figure 226 *Source:* https://en.wikipedia.org/w/index.php?title=File:Nirim1948_1.jpg *License:* Public Domain *Contributors:* Geagea, Ynhockey 542
Figure 227 *Source:* https://en.wikipedia.org/w/index.php?title=File:Negba1948Defenses.jpg *License:* Public Domain *Contributors:* Geagea, Ynhockey 542
Image *Source:* https://en.wikipedia.org/w/index.php?title=File:Handasa-burma001.jpg *License:* Public Domain *Contributors:* File Upload Bot (Magnus Manske), Netanel h, OgreBot 2, Wieralee, Yuval Y 544
Image *Source:* https://en.wikipedia.org/w/index.php?title=File:Burma_Road_1948.jpg *License:* Public Domain *Contributors:* Original uploaded by Golf Bravo) 544
Image *Source:* https://en.wikipedia.org/w/index.php?title=File:Latroun_(11_juin).png *License:* Creative Commons Attribution-Sharealike 3.0 *Contributors:* Ceedjee 544
Image *Source:* https://en.wikipedia.org/w/index.php?title=File:1948-Jordanian_artillery_shelling_Jerusalem.jpg *Contributors:* Bobamortioppois, File Upload Bot (Magnus Manske), OgreBot 2, חובבשירה 544
Image *Source:* https://en.wikipedia.org/w/index.php?title=File:Arab_Legion_soldier_in_ruins_of_Hurva.jpg *License:* Public Domain *Contributors:* John Roy Carlson 544
Image *Source:* https://en.wikipedia.org/w/index.php?title=File:Jewish_Quarter_Refugees.jpg *Contributors:* Chesdovi, Daniel Baránek, Pessimist2006, Talmoryair, עידו־ל 544
Figure 228 *Source:* https://en.wikipedia.org/w/index.php?title=File:Prof_Fekete_Rector_Heb_Uni-water-allocation.jpg *License:* Public Domain *Contributors:* Alan, Geagea, Kopiersperre, Mjrmtg, Ramaksoud2000, Yann, Ykantor 545
Figure 229 *Source:* https://en.wikipedia.org/w/index.php?title=File:Afulahagana.jpg *License:* Public Domain *Contributors:* ידי על מסרק יודע לא אמיר. אברהם 546
Figure 230 *Source:* https://en.wikipedia.org/w/index.php?title=File:Deganiatank1.jpg *License:* GNU Free Documentation License *Contributors:* Almog, Articseahorse, BotAdventures, Bukvoed, Gandvik, MGA73bot2, 1 anonymous edits 547
Figure 231 *Source:* https://en.wikipedia.org/w/index.php?title=File:PikiWiki_Israel_20772_The_Palmach.jpg *License:* Public Domain *Contributors:* Netanel h, Pikiwikisrael 548
Figure 232 *Source:* https://en.wikipedia.org/w/index.php?title=File:Egyptian_Plane_TA_1948.jpg *License:* Public Domain *Contributors:* Articseahorse, Ashashyou, Cobatfor, Geagea, PeterWD, Poliocretes, YoavR, חובבשירה, 3 anonymous edits 549
Figure 233 *Source:* https://en.wikipedia.org/w/index.php?title=File:Egyptian_bombing_1948.jpg *License:* Public Domain *Contributors:* Ashashyou, Geagea, Poliocretes, Sonntagsbraten, YoavR 550
Figure 234 *Source:* https://en.wikipedia.org/w/index.php?title=File:Avia-S-199-IAF-101Sqn-Tel-Nof-Israel-1948-01.jpg *License:* Public Domain *Contributors:* Articseahorse, Joshbaumgartner, OgreBot 2, Wieralee 551
Figure 235 *Source:* https://en.wikipedia.org/w/index.php?title=File:Spitfire-MkIX-hatzerim-1-2.jpg *License:* Creative Commons Attribution 2.5 *Contributors:* User:Bukvoed 551
Figure 236 *Source:* https://en.wikipedia.org/w/index.php?title=File:Israeli_B-17Gs_01011953.JPG *License:* Public Domain *Contributors:* CyberXRef, Flayer, Geagea, Joshbaumgartner, MK-3B-NBN, Poliocretes 552
Figure 238 *Source:* https://en.wikipedia.org/w/index.php?title=File:Northland_Color_1.jpg *License:* Public Domain *Contributors:* Aschroet, BotMultichill, FSV, KTo288, KudzuVine 553
Figure 238 *Source:* https://en.wikipedia.org/w/index.php?title=File:Palestine_Military_Situation,_June_11,_1948,_Truman_Papers.jpg *License:* Public Domain *Contributors:* Onceinawhile 554
Figure 239 *Source:* https://en.wikipedia.org/w/index.php?title=File:Altalena_off_Tel-Aviv_beach.jpg *License:* Public Domain *Contributors:* Bukk, Christophe cagé, Faigl.ladislav, Geagea, Matanya, Mattes, Netanel h, Stuntelje, חומר, א, 1 anonymous edits 556
Figure 240 *Source:* https://en.wikipedia.org/w/index.php?title=File:6pdr-Aibdis.jpg *License:* Public Domain *Contributors:* Ain92, Ashashyou, Matanya, Netanel h, OgreBot 2 558
Figure 241 *Source:* https://en.wikipedia.org/w/index.php?title=File:IDFSoldierInLyddaOrRamla.png *License:* Public Domain *Contributors:* Brakeet, Bukvoed, NatanFlayer, Ynhockey, 1 anonymous edits 559
Figure 242 *Source:* https://en.wikipedia.org/w/index.php?title=File:LyddaAirportCapture.png *License:* Public Domain *Contributors:* Brakeet, Bukvoed, Ori~, Ronaldino, Ynhockey, 1 anonymous edits 560
Figure 243 *Source:* https://en.wikipedia.org/w/index.php?title=File:Ramla_prisoners_of_war,_July_12-13,_1948.png *License:* Public Domain *Contributors:* Geagea, J 1982, Ori~, Schekinov Alexey Victorovich, Ynhockey 561
Figure 244 *Source:* https://en.wikipedia.org/w/index.php?title=File:PikiWiki_Israel_2184_1948_war_תחלוה_תואמצעה.jpg *License:* Creative Commons Attribution 2.5 *Contributors:* Netanel h, Pikiwikisrael, Ynhockey, 2 anonymous edits 562
Figure 245 *Source:* https://en.wikipedia.org/w/index.php?title=File:1948_arab_israeli_war_-_Oct.jpg *License:* Public Domain *Contributors:* 1989, Humus sapiens~commonswiki, Talmoryair, Timeshifter 564
Figure 246 *Source:* https://en.wikipedia.org/w/index.php?title=File:Zionist_mortar_team_outside_Zafzaf_in_October_1948.png *Contributors:* Palestine Remembered 565
Figure 247 *Source:* https://en.wikipedia.org/w/index.php?title=File:Israeli_soldiers_in_battle_with_the_Arab_village_of_Sassa.jpg *License:* Creative Commons Attribution-Sharealike 3.0 *Contributors:* Geagea, Huldra, Marcus Cyron, Matanya, Poliocretes, Steinsplitter 565
Figure 248 *Source:* https://en.wikipedia.org/w/index.php?title=File:Israelis_at_Faluja.jpg *License:* Public Domain *Contributors:* Ashashyou, Huldra, Masur, Padres Hana, Ynhockey 567

Figure 249 *Source:* https://en.wikipedia.org/w/index.php?title=File:Beersheba_1948.jpg *License:* Public Domain *Contributors:* Alonr, Amirki, BotMultichill, Brakeet, Bukvoed, Daniel Baránek, Geagea, Hidro, Hovev, NatanFlayer, Poliocretes, Wieralee, 2 anonymous edits 567
Figure 250 *Source:* https://en.wikipedia.org/w/index.php?title=File:Negev_Brigade_soldiers_1948.jpg *License:* Public Domain *Contributors:* Geagea, Poliocretes, Sonntagsbraten 568
Figure 251 *Source:* https://en.wikipedia.org/w/index.php?title=File:Beit_Natif_1948.jpg *License:* Public Domain *Contributors:* Israeli GPO photographer 568
Figure 252 *Source:* https://en.wikipedia.org/w/index.php?title=File:Operation_Horev.jpg *License:* Public Domain *Contributors:* Israeli GPO photographer 570
Figure 253 *Source:* https://en.wikipedia.org/w/index.php?title=File:Ramle_Funeral_1949.jpg *License:* Public Domain *Contributors:* Geagea, Nirvi, יעקב חובמשירה 571
Figure 254 *Source:* https://en.wikipedia.org/w/index.php?title=File:1947-UN-Partition-Plan-1949-Armistice-Comparison.svg *License:* Public Domain *Contributors:* AnonMoos 575
Image *Source:* https://en.wikipedia.org/w/index.php?title=File:Yemenites_go_to_Aden.jpg *License:* Public Domain *Contributors:* Akamol, Alonr, BDaniel, Blackcat, Chenspec, G.dallorto, Geagea, Kippi70, MGA73bot2, Matanya, Mcapdevila, Tomer T, Túrelio, דוד, ש, 1 anonymous edits 578

License

Creative Commons Attribution-Share Alike 3.0
//creativecommons.org/licenses/by-sa/3.0/

Index

Aaron, 39, 45
Abba Hillel Silver, 632
Abba Kovner, 419
Abbasid, 113
Abbasid Caliphate, 3, 166
Abdallah al-Asbah, 267, 299
Abd al-Qadir al-Husayni, 267, 273, 431, 476, 480, 492, 495, 499, 501, 523
Abd al-Rahim al-Hajj Muhammad, 267, 299
Abdon (Judges), 55, 58
Abdul Khallik, 267
Abdul Koroma, 473
Abdullah I of Jordan, 169, 191, 485, 501, 520, 522, 581
Abdul Rahman Hassan Azzam, 470, 507, 520, 530
Abijah, 88
Abijah of Judah, 87, 88
Abimelech (Judges), 55, 64
Ablex Publishing, 582
Abraham, 33, 34, 36
Absalom, 65
Abu Ageila, 570
Abu Ibrahim al-Kabir, 267, 299
Abwein, 160
Achaemenid Empire, 3, 12, 19, 93, 166
Acheulian, 4
Acre (city), 525
Acre, Israel, 110, 112, 172, 194, 225, 270, 503, 511, 554
Acre Prison, 294, 444
Acre Prison break, 427, 442, 444
Acre Sanjak, 154
Acre Subdistrict, Mandatory Palestine, 199
Activism, 243
Acts of the Apostles, 103
Adad-nirari III, 81
Adam Bridge, 482
Adar, 91
Adelaide del Vasto, 117
Ad hoc, 64
Ad Hoc Committee on the Palestinian Question, 452, 458
Adib Shishakli, 482

Administrative detention, 281
Admiral, 267
Admiralty, 150
Adolf Eichmann, 342, 344, 357, 402
Adolf Erik Nordenskiöld, 43
Adolf Hitler, 253, 297, 328, 331, 379, 418
Adolf Hitlers rise to power, 314, 331
Adonijah, 66
Aegean Sea, 259, 402
Aelia Capitolina, 99, 102
Aerial bombing of cities, 288
Afghanistan, 466
African Group, 466
African National Congress, 450
After the Holocaust, 322
Afula, 546
Agnes of Courtenay, 123
Ahab, 16, 75, 78, 80, 89
Ahaz, 17, 75, 88
Ahaziah of Israel, 78, 89
Ahaziah of Judah, 87, 89
Ahmad Mohamad Hasan, 267
Ahmed Ali al-Mwawi, 520, 537
Ahron Bregman, 581, 641
Aimery of Jerusalem, 130
Air Commodore, 267, 288
Air France, 533
Air Officer Commanding, 267, 288
Air superiority, 552
Air Vice-Marshall, 276
Ajalon, 527
Akkadian Empire, 7
Akko, 114, 457
Aktion T4, 330, 331, 334, 335, 359, 368, 617
Al-Abbasiyya, 448
Al-Adil I, 130
Al-Adil II, 134
Al-Afdal ibn Salah ad-Din, 130
Al-Afdal Shahanshah, 115, 116
Alan Cunningham, 182, 413, 431, 442, 472, 483, 635
Al-Andalus, 144
Alan Dershowitz, 552
Alan G. Cunningham, 164

Alan Hoffmann, 245
Alan Millard, 59
Al-Ashraf, 132
Al-Ashraf Khalil, 113, 140
Al-Aziz Uthman, 130
Albania, 327, 328
Al-Bassa, 284
Albert Einstein, 232, 341
Albert Hourani, 310
Albert of Aix, 141
Alec Kirkbride, 470, 481, 506, 530
Aleph, 184
Aleph (Hebrew), 398
Aleppo, 114, 119
Alexander Cadogan, 433
Alexander the Great, 12, 19, 20, 93
Alexander Tsankov, 259
Alexander von Falkenhausen, 346
Alexandria, 100
Alexandrian Crusade, 150
Alexandroni Brigade, 533, 546, 548, 571
Aley, 487
Al-Faluja, 159
Alfonso V of Aragon, 151
Alfred A. Knopf, 210
Alfred Jodl, 379
Alfred Rosenberg, 338, 379
Algeria, 450
Algerian War, 578
Al-Husayni, 170, 297
Alice of Antioch, 118
Alice of Champagne, 132
Ali Ekrem Bolayır, 161
Aliya Bet, 176
Aliyah, 213, 215, 223, 242, 243, 249, 268, 397, 398, 579
Aliyah and Yishuv during World War I, 215, 249, 397
Aliyah Bet, 174, 215, 234, 235, 249, 322, 397, **397**, 416, 419, 454, 553
Aliyah from Ethiopia, 216, 249, 397
Aliyah from Latin America in the 2000s, 216, 249, 397
Al-Jazira, Mesopotamia, 130
Al-Kamil, 130, 131
Al Karak, 130
Al-Karak, 89
Al-Khisas, 634
Al-Lajjun, 301
Allenby Bridge, 159
Allied-occupied Germany, 399
Allies of World War I, 154, 155, 257
Allies of World War II, 261, 362, 379, 402, 417
All-Palestine Government, 168, 532
All-Palestine Protectorate, 3, 164, 167
Alltagsgeschichte, 377

Al-Malkiyya, 548
Al-Mansurah, 131
Al-Mansur Ibrahim, 135
Al-Midan, 301
Al-Muazzam, 130
Al-Mulayha, 159
Al-Mustali, 115
Al-Muzayria, 560
Alphabet, 42
Alphonse of Poitiers, 136
Al-Qasemi Academic College of Education, 225
Al-Qastal, 495, 498, 499
Al Qastal, Palestine, 498
Al-Qubab, 560
Alsace-Lorraine, 347
Al Schwimmer, 526
Altalena Affair, 556
Al-Tira, Haifa, 225, 448
Amalric II of Jerusalem, 124
Amalric I of Jerusalem, 120
Amalric, Prince of Tyre, 140
Amariah, 58
Amaury VI of Montfort, 134
Amaziah of Judah, 88
Amélie Kuhrt, 69
American Jewish Joint Distribution Committee, 579
Amichai Paglin, 413, 435
Amigour, 215
Amin al-Husayni, 170, 320
Amin al-Husseini, 267, 417, 477
Amman, 6, 504, 513, 552
Ammon, 16, 34, 41, 66, 91
Ammon (nation), 62
Amon of Judah, 88
Amoraim, 104
Amorites, 7
Amos (prophet), 81
Amud Cave, 4
Am Yisrael Foundation, 216, 250, 398
Anachronism, 62
Anathema, 65
Anatolia, 6, 114
Ancient Canaanite religion, 22
Ancient Egypt, 13, 33, 44, 91
Ancient Greek, 32
Ancient Israel, 36
Ancient Judaism (book), 35
Ancient Mesopotamian religion, 71, 83
Ancient Near East, 36
Ancient Rome, 99
Ancient Semitic-speaking peoples, 31, 36
Ancient world, 39
Anders Army, 329
André Lemaire, 24, 590

Andrew II of Hungary, 130
Aneurin Bevan, 434
Angel, 23
Angel Bakeries, 201
Angevin Empire, 118
Anglo-American Committee, 607
Anglo-American Committee of Enquiry, 421
Anglo-American Committee of Inquiry, 177, 179, 322, 454, 616
Anglo-Egyptian Sudan, 520
Anglo-Egyptian Treaty of 1936, 274, 450, 522
Anglo-Iraqi Treaty (1930), 450
Anglo-Iraqi Treaty (1948), 450
Anglo-Iraqi War, 495
Anglo-Israeli air clashes, 433
Anglo-Jordanian Treaty of 1948, 450
Anglo-Palestine Bank, 205
Anita Shapira, 210, 310, 585
Annals of the American Academy of Political and Social Science, 388
An-Nasir Dawud, 133
Anointing, 65
Anschluss, 342
Anthony Eden, 363
Anti-Comintern Pact, 255, 261
Antigonus I Monophthalmus, 3, 166
Anti-imperialism, 306
Anti-Jewish violence in Eastern Europe, 1944–1946, 421
Anti-Judaism in the pre-Christian Roman Empire, 99
Antiochus IV Epiphanes, 20
Antipatris, 554
Antisemitism, 337
Anti-Semitism, 189
Antisemitism in the Arab world, 578
Anti-Zionist, 171, 269
Anwar Nusseibeh, 515
Apostasy, 56
Apries, 91
Aqaba, 159, 538
Aqedah, 43
Arabah, 13
Arab citizens of Israel, 221, 222, 224, 577
Arab Emirates, 450
Arab–Israeli conflict, 2, 10, 41, 64, 73, 86, 112, 165, 578
Arab general strike (Mandatory Palestine), 268
Arab Higher Committee, 266, 268, 275, 280, 320, 455, 458, 464, 471, 478, 483, 485, 486, 499
Arabia, 147, 313
Arabian Desert, 12, 66
Arabic language, 109, 110, 141, 154, 159–161, 163, 167
Arab Investigation Centres, 287

Arab Jews, 579
Arab League, 180, 470, 477, 479, 480, 486, 487, 503, 504, 514, 522, 523, 529, 532, 578
Arab Legion, 301, 413, 432, 475, 485, 507, 513, 525, 530, 536, 543, 544, 560, 635
Arab Liberation Army, 475, 476, 480, 482, 486, 487, 496, 501, 502, 512, 513, 520, 523, 535, 536, 548, 564
Arab nationalist, 170
Arab people, 115, 144
Arabs, 89, 476
Arab states, 520
Arab world, 580
Arad, Israel, 221, 222, 225
Aram (biblical region), 75
Aram Damascus, 16
Aram-Damascus, 66, 89
Archaeoastronomy, 5
Archaeology, 36
Archaeology of Israel, 2, 10, 41, 64, 73, 86, 112, 165
Archbishop of Tyre, 141
Archibald Wavell, 1st Earl Wavell, 267
Arch of Titus, 102
Arda of Armenia, 117
Aref al-Aref, 485, 576, 577
Aren Maeir, 69
Argentina, 467
Arieh Dulzin, 245
Arieh Kochavi, 450
Arif Abd al-Raziq, 267
Arish, 159, 539, 552, 558, 570
Aristobulus II, 100
Arkady Sobolev, 258
Ark of the Covenant, 45
Armee Juive, 362
Armenian Kingdom of Cilicia, 113
Armenian language, 32, 34
Armia Krajowa, 362
Armistice, 574
Armor, 62
Armored Corps (Israel), 535
Armored personnel carrier, 574
Arms shipments from Czechoslovakia to Israel 1947–1949, 556
Arms shipments from Czechoslovakia to Israel 1947–49, 432, 534
Army of the Holy War, 475, 480, 488, 495, 520, 523
Arnold Krammer, 636
Arraba, Jenin, 301
Arrow Cross Party, 349
Arsuf, 133, 140
Arthur Balfour, 506

Arthur Grenfell Wauchope, 251, 267, 271, 274, 605, 631
Arthur Ruppin, 228, 244
Arthur Seyss-Inquart, 346
Artillery, 532, 538
Artisan, 580
Artuqids, 115
Aryanization (Nazism), 326
Aryan race, 337
Asa of Judah, 74, 87, 88
Ashdod, 457, 543, 569, 572
Asher, 44
Asherah, 22, 87
Ashkalon, 18
Ashkelon, 42, 89, 92, 114, 116, 160, 543, 569
Ashlar, 66
Ashurbanipal, 90
Ashur-uballit II, 90
Asia, 250
Asia Minor, 6, 99
Asia-Pacific Group, 466
Asperg, 371
As-Salih Ayyub, 134
As-Salih Ismail, Emir of Damascus, 134
Assassination, 65, 68, 563
Assembly of Representatives election, 1920, 168
Assembly of Representatives (Mandate Palestine), 168, 201
Assizes of Jerusalem, 150
Associated University Presses, 582
Assyria, 74, 75, 87, 89
Assyrian cuneiform, 84
Assyrian Empire, 67, 76
Assyrian exile, 71
Assyrian people, 90
Assyrian Siege of Jerusalem, 89
Atabeg, 114
Athaliah, 75, 87, 89
Atlit detainee camp, 400, 420, 435
Attack on Pearl Harbour, 357
Aubrey Eban, 631
Augustus, 21, 99, 101
Auja al-Hafir, 159, 277
Auschwitz Album, 330
Auschwitz concentration camp, 326, 328, 335, 336, 359, 360, 370
Austerity in Israel, 216, 250, 398, 579
Australia, 466
Austria-Hungary, 337
Avalon Project, 358, 396
Avia S-199, 489, 526, 534, 543, 550, 574
Avi Shlaim, 485, 516, 577, 584, 585, 637, 643
Avraham Adan, 519
Avraham Burg, 245
Avraham Sela, 485, 577, 585, 605

Avraham Stern, 321, 418
Avraham Yoffe, 533
Avro Anson, 549, 574
Avshalom Haviv, 446
A Wing and a Prayer (film), 581
Awni Abdul Hadi, 305
Axis powers, 175, 297, 330, 331, 335, 480
Aybak, 136
Ayyubid, 113
Ayyubid dynasty, 2, 3, 10, 40, 64, 72, 86, 111, 112, 165, 166
Azzam Pasha, 470
Azzam Pasha quotation, 530

B-17 Flying Fortress, 574
Baal, 15, 22, 80, 87
Baal cycle, 80
Baasha (king), 78
Baasha of Israel, 89
Bab al-Wad, 495
Babi Yar, 355
Babylon, 18, 47, 99
Babylonia, 92, 93
Babylonian captivity, 42, 69, 91
Babylonian Chronicles, 82, 91
Babylonian Empire, 91
Babylonian exile, 46, 84
Bad Reichenhall, 399
Baghdad, 113
Baghdadi Jews, 578
Bagrut, 218
Bahai Faith, 164
Bahrain, 450
Baibars, 113, 136
Bailiffs, 123
Bakar, 405
Balad al-Shaykh massacre, 479
Baldwin III of Jerusalem, 118, 147
Baldwin II of Jerusalem, 118
Baldwin I of Jerusalem, 110, 116, 117
Baldwin of Ibelin, 124, 127
Baldwin V of Jerusalem, 124, 126
Balfour Declaration, 167, 168, 320, 453, 521
Balfour Declaration, 1917, 314
Balfour Declaration of 1917, 190, 229, 233, 273, 304, 415
Balian Grenier, 132, 134
Balian of Arsuf, 139
Balian of Beirut, 133, 136
Balian of Ibelin, 124, 127
Banana republic, 464
Bangkok, 261
Banha, 442
Bantam Books, 211
Bar Kochba revolt, 43
Bar Kokhba revolt, 102, 105

Barnett Janner, Baron Janner, 615
Barons Crusade, 134
Baruch Kimmerling, 309, 469
Basileus, 56
Basle program, 190
Bat Galim, 406
Bathsheba, 68
Battalion, 504
Battle, 479
Battle for Jerusalem (1948), 543
Battle near Majdal, 569
Battle of Ager Sanguinis, 118
Battle of Agridi, 133
Battle of Ain Jalut, 138
Battle of al-Babein, 122
Battle of al-Mansurah, 136
Battle of al-Sannabra, 117
Battle of Arsuf, 129
Battle of Ascalon, 116
Battle of Ascalon (1153), 121
Battle of Azaz (1125), 118
Battle of Beersheba (1948), 569
Battle of Belvoir Castle (1182), 125
Battle of Carchemish, 91
Battle of Casal Imbert, 133
Battle of Cresson, 127
Battle of Fariskur, 136
Battle of France, 344, 346
Battle of Greece, 260, 347
Battle of Haifa (1948), 181, 485, 577
Battle of Harim, 122
Battle of Hattin, 128, 273
Battle of Inab, 120
Battle of Jaffa (1192), 129
Battle of Jerusalem (1917), 203
Battle of Jerusalem (1948), 533
Battle of July 12, 558
Battle of Megiddo (609 BC), 90
Battle of Montgisard, 110, 124
Battle of Mount Zemaraim, 88
Battle of Myriokephalon, 124
Battle of Nirim, 541
Battle of Nitzanim, 543
Battle of Nur Shams, 277, 288
Battle of Qarqar, 16
Battle of Rafah (1948), 570
Battle of Rafah (1949), 539
Battle of Ramat Rachel, 533
Battle of Ramla (disambiguation), 117
Battle of the Netherlands, 346
Battle of Yad Mordechai, 541
Battle of Zephath, 88
Battles of Kfar Darom, 541
Battles of Latrun, 533
Battles of Latrun (1948), 552
Battles of the Kinarot Valley, 547

Battles of the Sinai (1948), 570
Bat Yam, 449
Baysan, 554
Bayt Itab, 160
Bayt Jibrin, 160
Bayt Nattif, 568
BBC, 450
Beacon Press, 209, 583
Bedfordshire and Hertfordshire Regiment, 277
Bedouin, 126, 143, 475, 572
Beerot Yitzhak, 559
Beersheba, 154, 159, 194, 195, 197, 199, 225, 448, 461, 492, 541, 566, 567, 569
Beersheba Subdistrict, Ottoman Empire, 159
Before Christ, 77
Beirut, 113, 117
Beisan, 172, 194, 199, 270, 503, 525
Beit Jala, 160
Beit Jann, 225
Beit Susin, 544
Beit Yaakov, 448
Belarus, 373
Belarusian Auxiliary Police, 326
Belgium, 466
Belzec extermination camp, 328, 335, 359
Bełżec extermination camp, 360, 370
Ben-Ami, 642
Ben Gurion International Airport, 563
Ben-Hadad I, 89
Benjamin, 44
Benjamin of Tudela, 114, 141
Benjamin Z. Kedar, 146, 152
Benno Müller-Hill, 391
Benny Morris, 210, 309, 320, 479, 485, 501, 514, 516, 577, 584, 616, 629, 634, 637, 638, 640
Bensheim, 343
Ben Yehuda Street bombings, 479
Ben Yehuda Street (Jerusalem), 431
Beraita, 104
Berber Jews, 579
Bergen Belsen, 425
Bergen-Belsen concentration camp, 367
Berghof (residence), 377
Berihah, 175
Berlin, 253
Berlin Philharmonic, 341
Berl Locker, 245
Bermuda Conference, 332
Bernard Avishai, 35
Bernard Baruch, 463
Bernard Law Montgomery, 1st Viscount Montgomery of Alamein, 267, 285
Bernard Wasserstein, 311
Beta Israel, 176
Betar, 402

Bet HaArava, 439
Bethel, 18
Bethlehem, 47, 115, 154, 160, 457, 495, 521
Beth Shean, 6
Bet (letter), 398
Bezalel, 45
Bezant, 111, 147
Bf-109, 551
Białystok Ghetto, 350
Białystok Ghetto Uprising, 362
Biblical archaeology, 38, 73
Biblical Archeology, 14
Biblical Hebrew, 38
Biblical judges, 55, **55**, 64
Biblical Minimalism, 85
Biblical Mount Sinai, 45
Biblical patriarch, 38
Bibliotheca Sacra, 27
Bielski partisans, 329, 362
Bilad al-Sham, 2, 10, 40, 64, 72, 86, 112, 165
Bilbeis, 122
Bilhah, 44
Biltmore Conference, 192
Binational state, 455
Binyanei HaUma, 239
Birkenau, 330
Bir Zeit, 495
Black Hand (Palestine), 171, 188, 269
Black market, 488
Black Obelisk, 598
Black Obelisk of Shalmaneser III, 81
Black Sea, 176, 402
Black Sunday, 1937, 280
Black Swan (imprint), 582
Black Watch, 297
Bloodlands: Europe Between Hitler and Stalin, 393
Blood libel, 337
BMW, 380
Bnot Yaakov Bridge, 4
Board of Deputies of British Jews, 232
Board of Governors, 213
Boeing B-17 Flying Fortress, 525, 552
Bogdan Filov, 259
Bohemond III of Antioch, 122, 124
Bohemond VI of Antioch, 137
Bohemund IV of Antioch, 133
Bolivia, 465
Booby trap, 446
Book of Ezekiel, 19
Book of Isaiah, 19, 74
Book of Jeremiah, 19, 91, 93
Book of Joshua, 22, 55
Book of Judges, 22, 55, 56, 58, 64
Book of Lamentations, 19
Book of Tobit, 76

Books of Chronicles, 88
Books of Kings, 19, 22, 93
Books of Samuel, 22, 55
Border, 511
Boris III of Bulgaria, 258, 348
Bosniaks, 483
Bosphorus, 403
Boycott, 171
Bratislava, 402
Brazil, 465
Bren carrier, 541
Bren Gun, 574
Bricha, 215, 236, 249, 397, 399
Brigantine, 406
British Armed Forces, 329, 413
British Army, 266, 268, 406, 408, 413, 417, 495
British Burma, 261
British Empire, 167, 291, 294, 305, 453
British–Zionist conflict, 477
British government, 312
British House of Commons, 318, 616
British Library, 149
British Malaya, 261
British Mandate for Palestine (legal instrument), 167, 230, 414, 452, 453
British parliament, 471
British Petroleum, 290
British Raj, 430
British withdrawal from Palestine, 432
British Zionist Federation, 229
Broad Wall (Jerusalem), 17
Bruno Walter, 341
Buchenwald, 366
Buchenwald concentration camp, 336, 343, 404
Budapest Ghetto, 350
Buffs (Royal East Kent Regiment), 417
Bulgaria, 403
Bulgarian Communist Party, 259
Bulgarian language, 32
Bulgarian Orthodox Church, 348
Bulla (seal), 17
Burgas, 403
Burma Road (Israel), 544
Burning bush, 45
Byblos, 6
Byelorussian Soviet Socialist Republic, 466
Byzantine art, 148
Byzantine Emperor, 122
Byzantine Empire, 100, 113, 114
Byzantine–Sasanian War of 602–628, 105

C-47, 549
C-47 Dakota, 574
C-47 Skytrain, 537

Caesarea, 133, 403, 406
Caesarea Maritima, 114, 130, 479
Caesars Civil War, 99, 100
Cairo, 177, 180, 433, 435, 444, 479, 487, 552
Cairo–Haifa train bombings 1948, 479
Cairo-Haifa train bombings 1948, 431, 449
Calibrated years, 4
Caliph, 115
Cambridge University Press, 152, 209, 583–586, 602
Cambyses, 19
Camel, 62
Camel train, 147
Camp David 2000 Summit, 578
Canaan, 1, 3, 9, 13, 34, 36, 40, 57, 63, 72, 85, 111, 164, 166
Canaanite languages, 36
Canaanite pantheon, 36
Canaanite people, 32
Canaanite Religion, 71, 83
Canaanites, 15
Canada, 466
Canadian Military Pattern truck, 540
Canon de 65 M (montagne) modele 1906, 543
Capital punishment, 427
Car bomb, 479
Carden Loyd tankette, 574
Cardiff, 428
Carlile Aylmer Macartney, 265
Carlos Eduardo Stolk, 464
Carlos P. Romulo, 463
Carmeli brigade, 479, 533, 546, 547, 566
Carole Hillenbrand, 152
Carpathian Ruthenia, 364
Cast a Giant Shadow, 581
Castration, 375
Category:Aliyah, 215, 249, 397
Category:History of Israel, 1, 9, 40, 63, 72, 85, 111, 164
Category:History of Palestine (region), 2, 166
Category:Jews and Judaism, 12, 31
Category:The Holocaust, 325, 331
Catholic Church, 110, 116
Catholic Encyclopedia, 59
Catholicism, 337
Causes of the 1948 Palestinian exodus, 484, 576, 577
Cavalry, 62
Ceasefire, 499, 557
Cement Incident, 269
Census of Quirinius, 102, 600
Central Agency for Jewish Emigration in Vienna, 342
Central Committee of National Jihad in Palestine, 266, 299
Central European History, 383

Century Dictionary, 332
Chaim Rumkowski, 351
Chaim Weizman, 462
Chaim Weizmann, 173, 174, 191, 229, 280, 454
Chalcolithic, 5
Chancery (medieval office), 148
Chapter 7, 595
Chapter VI, 457
Chariotry, 62
Charisma, 64
Charles George Herbermann, 59
Charles of Anjou, 136
Charles R. H. Tripp, 585
Charles S. Maier, 390
Charles Tegart, 286, 287
Charles Townshend (historian), 311
Chartres, 141
Château Pèlerin, 131
Chelmno concentration camp, 328
Chełmno extermination camp, 335, 356, 359, 360, 370
Chemosh, 84
Chief Justice, 284
Chieftain, 61, 68
Children of Israel, 598
Chile, 467
Chloroform, 442
Christian Era, 99
Christian Gerlach, 357, 387
Christianity, 164
Christian symbols, 147
Christopher Browning, 377, 383
Christopher Tyerman, 600
Chronology of Aliyah in modern times, 215, 249, 397
Churban Europa, 332
Church of the Holy Sepulchre, 115, 148, 531
C.I.A, 532
Circa, 4
Circassians, 197, 503
Cisco Systems, 222, 242
Citation missing title, 23–29
CITEREFAbu-Manneh1999, 604
CITEREFAmar2015, 621
CITEREFArad1987, 618, 622, 623
CITEREFArad2009, 622
CITEREFAradGutmanMargaliot2014, 619
CITEREFArnoldWilliamson2005, 597
CITEREFBauer1994, 622
CITEREFBauer1997, 623
CITEREFBauer1998, 625
CITEREFBauer2001, 620
CITEREFBauer2002, 618
CITEREFBauerRozett1990, 624, 625
CITEREFBaumel2001, 620

665

CITEREFBazyler2005, 626
CITEREFBell2017, 624
CITEREFBen-RafaelGlöcknerSternberg2011, 619
CITEREFBerenbaum2006, 617, 618, 621, 624
CITEREFBergen2016, 618, 620–625
CITEREFBerghahn1999, 625
CITEREFBiddiss2001, 625, 626
CITEREFBlack1991, 172
CITEREFBlack2016, 617, 620, 622–625
CITEREFBloxham2009, 618, 619, 625
CITEREFBolingNelson2006, 597
CITEREFBoogRahnStumpfWegner2001, 611
CITEREFBraham2011, 624
CITEREFBrettler2002, 597
CITEREFBrowning1986, 621
CITEREFBrowning1998, 625
CITEREFBrowning2001, 619
CITEREFBrowning2004, 620, 621
CITEREFBuchheim1968, 625
CITEREFBurleigh2001, 621
CITEREFBurleighWippermann1991, 619
CITEREFCaplan2015, 615
CITEREFCesarani2004, 620
CITEREFCesarani2016, 619, 620, 622–624
CITEREFChase1999, 620
CITEREFChinvanno1992, 611
CITEREFCohen2014, 616
CITEREFConot1984, 626
CITEREFCoogan2009, 597
CITEREFCrowe2008, 618, 620, 622, 623, 626
CITEREFDavies2006, 597
CITEREFDawidowicz1986, 617, 624
CITEREFDiNardo1996, 611
CITEREFDworkvan Pelt2003, 621–623
CITEREFEdelheit1994, 620
CITEREFEvans1989, 618, 621, 625
CITEREFEvans2002, 624
CITEREFEvans2004, 618, 619
CITEREFEvans2005, 619
CITEREFEvans2008, 621, 625
CITEREFEvans2015, 618, 625
CITEREFFischel1998, 617–619, 622–624
CITEREFFischel2010, 617, 619–622, 624, 625
CITEREFFischer1998, 624
CITEREFFischer2002, 618
CITEREFFisher2001, 618
CITEREFFleming2014a, 623
CITEREFFleming2014b, 623
CITEREFFlood1970, 611
CITEREFFriedlander1994, 618
CITEREFFriedländer1997, 619
CITEREFFriedländer2007, 618, 624
CITEREFFrilingIoanidIonesc2004, 620
CITEREFFritz2011, 621, 625
CITEREFFritzsche2009, 618
CITEREFGarbe2001, 625
CITEREFGellately2001, 625
CITEREFGellatelyStoltzfus2001, 618
CITEREFGerlach1998, 622
CITEREFGerlach2016, 622
CITEREFGilbert1985, 617, 618, 624
CITEREFGilbert1998, 172
CITEREFGilbert2001, 618, 619, 624
CITEREFGiles1992, 625
CITEREFGold1998, 628
CITEREFGordon1962, 597
CITEREFGray2015, 617
CITEREFGutman1994, 623
CITEREFHanauske-Abel1996, 618, 619
CITEREFHancock2004, 625
CITEREFHarran2000, 618, 620, 625
CITEREFHauser1975, 597
CITEREFHayes2015, 617, 624
CITEREFHilberg1980, 621
CITEREFHilberg1993, 621
CITEREFHilberg1996, 623
CITEREFHilberg2003, 618, 621, 623
CITEREFHildebrand1984, 620
CITEREFHitchcock2008, 624
CITEREFHuttenbach2016, 625
CITEREFJelínek1971, 611
CITEREFJones2006, 618, 622
CITEREFKelly2017, 611, 612
CITEREFKennedy2007, 623
CITEREFKershaw1998, 618
CITEREFKershaw2000, 619
CITEREFKhalaf1991, 615
CITEREFKhalidi2001, 172
CITEREFKhalidi2006, 172, 187
CITEREFKhalif1991, 616
CITEREFKingStager2001, 589
CITEREFKitchen2003, 597
CITEREFKochanski2012, 625
CITEREFKolanović2006, 611
CITEREFKwiet2004, 624
CITEREFLandau2016, 617
CITEREFLaqueur2001, 623
CITEREFLichtblau2013, 624
CITEREFLifton2000, 618, 619
CITEREFLöb2009, 624
CITEREFLongerich2010, 620–625
CITEREFLongerich2012, 618, 624, 625
CITEREFLukas2012, 623, 625
CITEREFLusane2003, 625
CITEREFLustigmanLustigman1994, 617
CITEREFMacartney1956, 611
CITEREFMalamat1971, 597
CITEREFMarrus1987, 625
CITEREFMarrus2015, 618
CITEREFMatthäus2004, 621

CITEREFMazower2008, 625
CITEREFMcKale2002, 620, 621
CITEREFMichman2012, 624
CITEREFMiller1975, 611
CITEREFMilstein et al.1998, 628
CITEREFMilton2001, 624, 625
CITEREFMontague2012, 622
CITEREFMooreKelle2011, 598
CITEREFMorris2001, 187
CITEREFMüller-Hill1999, 618
CITEREFNaimark2001, 620
CITEREFNiewykNicosia2000, 617–619, 623–625
CITEREFNoakesPridham1983, 618
CITEREFNovick2000, 623, 626
CITEREFPayne1996, 597
CITEREFPeukert1987, 619
CITEREFPeukert1994, 618
CITEREFPiotrowski1998, 625
CITEREFPiper1998a, 625
CITEREFPiper1998b, 622
CITEREFPollack2004, 640
CITEREFPolonsky2001, 624
CITEREFProctor1988, 619
CITEREFRees2005, 620, 623
CITEREFRhodes2002, 625
CITEREFRoseman2003, 622
CITEREFRozett1990, 620
CITEREFRozettSpector2013, 620
CITEREFRummel1992, 625
CITEREFSamuels2009, 626
CITEREFSegev2000, 187
CITEREFShapira1992, 172
CITEREFSnyder1976, 618, 625
CITEREFSnyder2010, 618, 621, 623, 625
CITEREFSpector1990, 623
CITEREFSteakley1974, 625
CITEREFStone2010, 626
CITEREFStrous2007, 619
CITEREFSzafranski1960, 625
CITEREFTec2001, 623
CITEREFThompson2000, 597
CITEREFTrunk1996, 621
CITEREFUnited States Holocaust Memorial Museum1996, 618
CITEREFWachsmann2015, 618–621, 623–625
CITEREFWeinberg1994, 611
CITEREFWeinberg2001, 624
CITEREFYahil1990, 618, 621, 624
CITEREFZimmerman2015, 623
CITEREFZuccotti1993, 620, 623
CITEREFZweig2001, 626
City-state, 66
Civil and political rights, 185
Civil society, 273
Civil war, 66
Claimants to the throne of Jerusalem, 140
Clarence Lusane, 390
Classical Antiquity, 36, 71
Claude Cahen, 143
Clement Attlee, 421, 427, 445
Cleromancy, 62
Client state, 12, 21, 66, 101
Clifford Martin (soldier), 446
Close air support, 287
Coele-Syria, 1, 9, 40, 63, 72, 86, 111, 165
Coldstream Guards, 283, 297
Collaboration with the Axis Powers, 330, 331
Collateral (finance), 222
Collective punishment, 286
Colombia, 467
Colony, 291
Columbia University Press, 151, 474, 600
Commander-in-chief, 267, 513
Command paper, 312
Commissar, 374
Commissar Order, 374
Common Era, 77
Commons:Category:1936–1939 Arab revolt in Palestine, 311
Commons:Category:1948 Arab-Israeli War, 586
Commons:Category:British Mandate of Palestine, 212
Commons:Category:Fifth Aliyah, 252
Commons:Category:Haapala, 412
Commons:Category:Hebrews, 35
Commons:Category:Jewish Agency for Israel, 247
Commons:Category:Jews in World War II, 330
Commons:Category:Kingdom of Jerusalem, 151
Commons:Category:Kingdom of Judah, 93
Commons:Category:Tripartite Pact, 266
Commons:Category:United Nations Partition Plan for Palestine, 474
Commune of Acre, 133
Community ransom, 295
Concentration camp, 280, 327
Concession (politics), 268
Condé Benoist Pallen, 59
Condominium (international law), 167
Confederated Tribes of Israel, 64
Conference on Jewish Material Claims Against Germany, 379
Confessional community, 200
Conquest of Canaan, 15
Conrad III of Germany, 119
Conradin, 136
Conrad IV of Germany, 132
Conrad of Montferrat, 128

Conscription, 490, 527
Conservative Judaism, 219
Conspiracy (crime), 379
Constance of Antioch, 118
Constanţa, 401, 403
Constantine the Great, 99
Constantinople, 99, 128, 154
Constantius Gallus, 104
Constantius II, 104
Consulate General of France in Jerusalem, 541
Consulate General of the United States, Jerusalem, 545
Consul (representative), 292
Continuation War, 261
Continuum Publishing, 585
Conversion of Constantine, 105
Convoy of 35, 495
Corpus separatum (Jerusalem), 179, 183, 455, 459, 524, 575
Costa Rica, 465
Cotton, 146
Council of Acre, 119
Council of Clermont, 114
Council of Jamnia, 102
Council of Nablus, 118, 150
Count of Champagne, 134
Count of Jaffa, 120
County of Edessa, 113
County of Jaffa, 116
County of Tripoli, 113
Coup détat, 75
Court History of David, 65
Covenant of the League of Nations, 186
Crematoria, 335
Crete, 405
Crime against peace, 379
Criminal Investigation Department, 281, 292, 434
Criminal Investigations Department, 435
Cromwell tank, 534, 561, 574
Crossing the Red Sea, 45
Crown of thorns, 116
Croydon airport, 342
Cruiser, 289
Crusade, 113
Crusade of 1101, 116
Crusade of 1197, 130
Crusader invasions of Egypt, 122
Crusader Red Sea raids, 125
Crusader state, 112, 117
Crusader states, 113
Crusades, 118, 147
Cuba, 467
Cult (religious practice), 36
Cultural exogamy, 13
Culture hero, 43

Curtiss C-46 Commando, 526
Cyprus, 111, 236, 400, 405, 420, 440, 444
Cyprus internment camps, 322, 400, 420, 433
Cyrus H. Gordon, 56, 59
Cyrus the Great, 12, 19, 20, 47
Czechoslovakia, 179, 327, 328, 466, 486, 487, 489, 526, 533, 536, 550, 552
Czesława Kwoka, 372

Dachau concentration camp, 336, 338, 366
Dahlem (Berlin), 337
Daimbert of Pisa, 116
Daimler Armoured Car, 574
Damascus, 6, 75, 114, 117, 119, 120, 154, 292, 552, 562
Damascus Eyalet, 2, 10, 40, 64, 73, 86, 112, 151, 153, 165
Damascus Gate, 449
Damietta, 122, 131
Dan (Bible), 44
Daniel Kievsky, 141
Daniyal, 560
Danube, 402
Darius the Great, 19
David, 37, 47, 61, 68, 87
David Ben Gurion, 245
David Ben-Gurion, 173, 191, 214, 232, 233, 244, 276, 280, 306, 321, 415, 417, 425, 454, 476, 480, 520, 523, 525, 547, 573
David Cesarani, 343, 384
David Horowitz (economist), 631
Davidic dynasty, 18
Davidic line, 42, 68, 74, 87
Davidka, 527, 574
David M. Kennedy, 389
David Petrie, 286
David Raziel, 417
David Shaltiel, 520, 533, 561
Davids Palace, 66
David Tal (historian), 637
Day of Revenge, 579
Day to mark the departure and expulsion of Jews from the Arab countries and Iran, 579
Dead Sea, 13, 159, 461
Death, 105
Death squads, 331
Deborah, 55, 58
Declaration by United Nations, 363
Declaration of Independence (Israel), 183
Defence (Emergency) Regulations, 281
Defense in depth, 569
Degania Alef, 547
De Havilland Mosquito, 572
Deir al-Balah, 572
Deir Yassin, 495, 501, 561

Deir Yassin massacre, 485, 501, 524, 577
Democracy, 243
Demographic history of Jerusalem, 111
Demographic history of Palestine (region), 216, 250, 398
Demographics, 578
Demon, 23
Demonym, 42
Denailing, 287
Denmark, 466
Dennis Ross, 220
Derby, 428
Destroyer, 289
Destruction of the kingdom, 65
Determinative, 42
Detlev Peukert, 392
Deuteronomist, 22
Deuteronomistic history, 22
Deuteronomy, 19, 47, 63
Deutsche Allgemeine Zeitung, 256
Deutsche Bank, 380
Deutsches Afrika Korps, 297
Deutsches Ärzteblatt, 339
Deutsches Nachrichtenbüro, 256
Development of the Hebrew Bible canon, 21
Development town, 216, 250, 398, 579, 580
Dhekelia Cantonment, 400
Diadochi, 12
Diaspora, 39, 103, 218
Dietrich Eckart, 338
Diocese of the East, 1, 3, 9, 40, 63, 72, 86, 111, 165, 166
Direk Jayanama, 261
Disbarment, 339
Displaced persons, 399, 420
Displaced persons camp, 409
Displaced persons camps in post-World War II Europe, 579
Disputed statement, 42, 43, 231, 245, 268, 424, 540, 564
Districts of Mandatory Palestine, 194, 199
Divine retribution, 56
Division of the land .28chapters 13.E2.80.9321.29, 46
Doberman Pinscher, 287
Doctors trial, 336
Dodecanese, 402
Dog, 4
Domestication, 4
Döme Sztójay, 257
Dominican Republic, 465
Dominion of India, 463
Dominique Lapierre, 501, 516, 582
Donald Wiseman, 59
Dore Gold, 582
Dorot, 440, 540

Doubleday (publisher), 210
Dov Gruner, 439, 444
Dov Yosef, 237, 582
Downfall, 626–605 BC, 84
Dragiša Cvetković, 260
Dr. Josef Bühler, 328
Druze, 143, 155, 164, 197, 297, 502, 525
Druze in Israel, 221, 225
Druzism, 110
Dudley Pound, 267, 290
Due and undue weight, 530
Dunam, 192, 271
Duqaq, 114
Dura-Europos, 34
Dušan Simović, 260

Earl G. Harrison, 421
Early Bronze Age, 7
Early Christianity, 12
Eastern European Group, 466
Eastern Front (World War II), 314, 356, 373
Eastern Mediterranean, 12, 84, 101
Eastern Orthodox Church, 110, 116
Eastern Roman Empire, 105, 600
East Jerusalem, 225, 575
Eber, 32–34, 39
Eberhard Jäckel, 335, 618
Eberhard Karl University, 341
Ebla, 7
Ecbatana, 76
Ecuador, 465
Edict of Milan, 99
Edict of Thessalonica, 100
Edmund Allenby, 167
Edmund Allenby, 1st Viscount Allenby, 274
Edom, 22, 41, 66, 89, 91, 99
Edomites, 34
Edward A. Pace, 59
Edward Bernard Raczyński, 363
Edward I of England, 139
Edward Wood, 1st Earl of Halifax, 305, 313
Edwin R. Thiele, 68, 77
Efraim Karsh, 485, 577, 583, 638
Egged (company), 303
Egypt, 6, 33, 88–91, 111, 113, 116, 154, 274, 315, 430, 442, 450, 467, 535
Egyptian Air Force, 572
Egyptian Expeditionary Force, 167
Egyptian military, 521
Egyptian Navy, 569
Egyptian pound, 164
Egypt (Roman province), 99
Ehud, 55, 58
Eilat, 6, 457, 519, 571
Ein Gev, 547
Einsatzgruppen, 331, 354, 371

669

Einsatzkommando, 326, 373
Ein Vered, 546
Eitan Livni, 413, 435
El Al, 216, 239, 250, 398
El Amir Farouq, 569
El Arish, 550
El (god), 22, 39
Eliahu Sacharoff, 310
Eli (Bible), 58
Eli (biblical figure), 55
Eliezer Kashani, 444
Elijah, 81
Elisha, 81
Eliyahu Bet Zuri, 177
Eliyahu Bet-Zuri, 435
Eliyahu Golomb, 267, 303
Eliyahu Hakim, 177, 435
Elon (Judges), 55, 58
El Salvador, 467
Embriaco family, 137
Emergency Quota Act, 251
Emirate of Transjordan, 167, 233, 268, 277, 278, 288, 301, 314, 453
Empire of Japan, 253, 347
Enclave and exclave, 154
Encyclopædia Britannica, 474
Encyclopedia of the Holocaust, 369
En:Digital object identifier, 59, 210, 265, 383, 386–388, 390, 394
End of World War II in Europe, 331
English, 36
English Channel, 427
English Historical Review, 603
English language, 163
En:International Standard Serial Number, 59
En:JSTOR, 383, 386–388, 391
En:PubMed Central, 394
Entrepreneurship, 222
Ephraim, 44, 76
Ephraim and Judah, 74
Ephraim Kishon, 239
Epic Cycle, 63
Epi-Palaeolithic, 4
Epistle to the Hebrews, 34
Eponym, 39, 44
Eretz Israel, 183, 515
Eretz Israel Museum, 16
Eretz Yisrael, 167, 184
Eretz Yisrael Office, 228
Ernest Benjamin, 176
Ernest Bevin, 322, 419, 422, 427, 430, 433, 443, 455, 471, 483, 485, 615
Ernst Toller, 337
Ernst vom Rath, 343
Ernst von Weizsäcker, 257
Erwin Rommel, 174, 297

Esarhaddon, 89, 90
Es Skhul, 4
Estonia, 327
Estonian Auxiliary Police, 326
Ethiopia, 88, 467
Ethiopian Empire, 296
Ethiopian Jews in Israel, 222, 223, 226
Ethnarch, 21
Ethnic cleansing, 330, 380
Ethnic group, 36
Ethnolinguistics, 39
Ethnonym, 31, 34
Ethnoreligious group, 38
Etzioni Brigade, 533, 561, 562
Euphrates, 90
Euphrates River, 66
Europe, 250, 328
European Jew, 330
European Jews, 330, 415
Eusebius, 74
Eustace III of Boulogne, 118
Eva Braun, 377
Evelyn Barker, 413, 425
Events leading to the attack on Pearl Harbor, 263

Évian Conference, 315, 342, 416

Exile, 65
Exodus of Irans Jews, 579
Exonym and endonym, 39
Expulsion of the Palestinians: The Concept of Transfer in Zionist Political Thought, 1882–1948, 586
Extermination camp, 328, 331, 335, 358
Extermination through labour, 350
Extraterritorial crossroad, 457
Eyalet, 154
Ezekiel, 20, 91
Ezer Weizman, 572
Ezion-Geber, 89
Ezra, 20, 47

Facebook, 219
Fakhr al-Mulk Radwan, 114
Fakhri Abd al-Hadi, 267
Falastin (newspaper), 274
Fall of Ruad, 151
Fall of Tripoli (1289), 146
Faluja Pocket, 569
Famagusta, 400
Family history, 13
Farhan al-Sadi, 267, 300
Farhud, 578
Farming, 5
Farouk of Egypt, 531

Fascist, 258
Fatimid, 113, 116
Fatimid Caliphate, 3, 111, 115, 166
Fawzi al-Qawukji, 277
Fawzi al-Qawuqji, 267, 299, 476, 481, 499, 501, 520
Federal Agency for Civic Education, 326
Federated Malay States, 200
Felipe VI of Spain, 151
Fellahin, 271
Ferramonti di Tarsia, 402
Feudalism, 110, 141
Fief, 150
Fifth Aliyah, 215, 249, **249**, 397, 417
Fifth column, 528
Fifth Crusade, 131
File:RWD 13 - Air dropping supplies to Yehiam, 1948.jpg, 511
Final Solution, 326, 328, 331, 357
Final Solution to the Jewish Question, 332
Financial crisis and famine, 102
Financial endowment, 213
Finland, 327
Firestone Natural Rubber Company, 463
First Aliyah, 215, 249, 397
First Book of Chronicles, 58
First Book of Samuel, 58
First British census of Palestine, 197
First Council of Lyon, 136
First Crusade, 110, 112
First Jewish–Roman War, 12, 43, 102, 105
First skirmishes and battle of June 2, 543
First Temple Period, 42
First World War, 167
Fiscus Judaicus, 99, 103
Flag of Israel, 176
Flag of Mandatory Palestine, 163
Flag of the Ottoman Empire, 153
Flogging, 427
Flooding of the Nile, 132
Folke Bernadotte, 178, 557, 563
Folk hero, 69
Folk religion, 71, 83
Food cooperative, 225
Foot whipping, 287
Forced disappearance, 374
Forced labour, 345
Forced labour under German rule during World War II, 380
Ford, 380
Foreign and Commonwealth Office, 573
Former Soviet Union, 223, 240
Fortification, 69, 290
Fosh (Haganah unit), 266, 295
Foundation Remembrance, Responsibility and Future, 380

Fourteen Points, 186
Fourth Aliyah, 215, 249, 250, 397
Fourth Crusade, 130
Fourth Lateran Council, 130
France, 114, 314, 405, 422, 427, 466, 533, 534
Francis of Assisi, 131
Franciszek Piper, 392
Franco-Mongol alliance, 137
Franco-Syrian Treaty of Independence (1936), 273
Frankfurt Auschwitz Trials, 376
Frankincense, 6
Franks, 140
Frederick I, Holy Roman Emperor, 124, 128
Frederick II, Holy Roman Emperor, 113, 131
Frederick II of Hohenstaufen, 113
Frederick Kisch, 244, 292
French Algeria, 347
French denier, 147
French Fourth Republic, 463
French Jews, 623
French Madagascar, 344
French people, 113
French protectorate in Morocco, 347
French Protectorate of Tunisia, 347
French Resistance, 623
Friendly fire, 543
Frigyes Villani, 257
Fr:Problématique du matériel lors de la guerre de Palestine de 1948, 635
FT-17, 574
Fulcher of Chartres, 140, 151
Fulk of Jerusalem, 118

Gad (son of Jacob), 44
Galeazzo Ciano, 253
Galilee, 13, 42, 102, 242, 457, 480, 482, 492, 502, 504, 511, 515, 521, 523, 525, 563, 572, 574
Galilee Man, 4
Galilee Panhandle, 504
Galilee Squadron, 549
Gal On, 559
Gamal Abdel Nasser, 531
Gan Shmuel, 279
Gas chamber, 335
Gas van, 356
Gath (city), 69
Gathering of Israel, 47, 215, 249, 397
Gay bar, 375
Gaza City, 6, 114, 154, 159, 160, 194, 199, 408, 483, 492, 515, 532, 552, 553, 569
Gaza District, 195
Gaza Strip, 168, 457, 519, 521, 541, 570, 575
Gaza Subdistrict, Ottoman Empire, 159
Geba (city), 89

Gedaliah, 92
Gefen Publishing House, 412
Gelber, 634–639
Gelber2004, 634, 635, 638
Gelignite, 284
Gemara, 38
Genealogy, 13
General Government, 327, 328, 330, 344, 345, 365
General Officer Commanding, 267
Generalplan Ost, 372
General strike, 172, 478
General Zionists, 278
Genesis creation narrative, 45
Genoa, 133
Genocide, 328, 330
Gentile, 501
Gentile Christians, 31
Geoffrey Megargee, 368
Geoffrey of Sergines, 136
Geoffrey Salmond, 169
Geoffrey V of Anjou, 118
Geographic coordinate system, 213
Geopolitical entity, 167
George Antonious, 305
George Antonius, 306, 425
Gerald of Lausanne, 133
Gerald Reitlinger, 369
Gerald Schroeder, 595
Gerar, 88
Gerhard Weinberg, 265
German AB-Aktion in Poland, 372
German Air Force, 260
German Army (Wehrmacht), 260, 418
German declaration of war against the United States (1941), 264, 357
German empire, 337
German federal election, March 1933, 338
German invasion of Denmark (1940), 346
German mistreatment of Soviet prisoners of war, 331, 617
German occupation of Czechoslovakia, 258
German-occupied Europe, 330, 331, 334
German-occupied Poland, 335
German resistance, 378
German resistance to Nazism, 331
German Studies Review, 386
German Workers Party, 618
Germany, 422, 426
Gershon Galil, 68, 77
Gesher, Israel, 546
Gestapo, 379
Geulim, 546
Gezer, 42, 66
Gezer (kibbutz), 544
Ghassulian, 3, 5, 166

Ghetto, 331
Ghettos in German-occupied Europe (1939–1944), 335
Ghettos in Nazi-occupied Europe, 345
Ghetto uprising, 353
Gibeah, 66
Gideon, 55, 58
Gideon Levy, 642
Gilbert Mackereth, 286, 301
Gilead, 16, 76
Giovanni Villani, 131
Givat Ada, 269
Givati Brigade, 533, 543, 558
Glasgow, 428
Glubb Pasha, 485, 532, 536, 560
Gnaeus Cornelius Scipio Hispanus, 100
Gobekli Tepe, 5
God, 39, 65
Godfrey of Bouillon, 112, 115
God in Judaism, 37, 45
Golan Heights, 72
Golani Brigade, 533, 546, 569
Golda Meir, 480, 486, 488, 504, 523, 525, 530
Golden Age, 62
Golden Calf, 45
Gold glass, 103
Goliath, 69
Gondar, 221
Gordon MacMillan, 476
Gordon MacMillan (British Army officer), 413
Goren, 288
Gorge, 495
Gothic architecture, 148
Governance of the Gaza Strip, 164
Government of the Soviet Union, 260
Grand Master of the Teutonic Knights, 132
Grand Mufti of Jerusalem, 170, 268
Grand Vizier, 154
Great Britain, 229, 260
Great Depression, 337
Great Seljuk Empire, 114
Great Seljuq Empire, 111
Great Syrian Revolt, 301
Greece, 328, 466
Greek language, 32, 34, 38, 141, 332
Greek Orthodox, 114, 143
Greenland, 553
Green Line (Israel), 459, 575
Greenwood Publishing, 582, 585
Greenwood Publishing Group, 323
Grojanowski Report, 363
Guarantors, 226
Guard Corps (Haganah), 295
Guatemala, 465
Gudrun Krämer, 583
Guillaume de Beaujeu, 140

Gun running, 289
Gush Etzion, 508
Gush Etzion Convoy, 495
Gustav Hertz, 342
Gustav Krupp, 626
Guy of Ibelin, constable of Cyprus, 136
Guy of Lusignan, 124, 127

Haaretz, 586, 642
Haavara Agreement, 251, 296, 344
Haazinu, 47
Habiru, 33, 41
Habis al-Majali, 520
Hachette UK, 631
Hadassah medical convoy massacre, 502
Hadera, 443, 446, 478, 564
Hadita, 560
Hadrian, 99, 106
Hadrian in Judea, 102
Haganah, 175–177, 181, 188, 231, 266–269, 292, 303, 399, 401, 402, 407, 409, 413, 414, 423, 432, 435, 436, 439, 471, 475, 477, 484, 492, 496–499, 501, 509, 520, 523, 525–527, 532, 534
Haifa, 116, 172, 174, 181, 194, 196, 199, 201, 269, 293, 402, 404, 420, 434, 435, 438, 439, 442–444, 448, 449, 457, 479, 483, 499, 503, 515, 525, 548, 553–555, 563, 572
Haifa Oil Refinery massacre, 478, 566
Haim Arlosoroff, 244, 296, 406
Haiti, 179
Haj Amin al-Husseini, 268, 280, 417, 470, 520
Haj Amin Husseini, 312
Hajj Amin al-Husseini, 187
Halhul, 284
Hama, 124, 301
Hamad Saab, 301
Hamburg, 422
Hamid Suleiman Mardawi, 267
Hamossad Lealiyah Bet, 236
Hamoukar, 6
Hanging, 268
Hannah Szenes, 236
Hansard, 323
Hans Eberhard Mayer, 601
Hans E. Mayer, 123, 601
Hans Frank, 620
Har Adar, 545
Haredi Judaism, 221, 226
Harel Brigade, 533, 544–546
Harold MacMichael, 267, 413
Harold W. Attridge, 58
Harran, 90
Harry Herbert Trusted, 200
Harry S Truman, 179, 182, 462

Harry S. Truman, 177, 421, 429, 434
Harry Truman, 455
Harvard University Press, 309, 583
Harvey S. Firestone, Jr., 463
Hasan Salama, 267, 483, 495, 520, 548
Hashemite, 167, 313
Hashemites, 522
Hashshashin, 129
Hasmonean, 21, 100
Hasmonean Civil War, 100
Hasmonean dynasty, 1, 3, 9, 12, 40, 63, 72, 86, 111, 165, 166
Hasmonean kingdom, 42
Hatzor Airbase, 572
Haute Cour of Jerusalem, 110, 150
Havlagah, 280, 296, 303
Hawker Hurricane, 537, 574
Hawker Tempest, 572
Hayim Nahman Bialik, 232
Hazzan, 239
Hebraization of surnames, 216, 250, 398
Hebrew, 32, 34, 71, 83, 239
Hebrew alphabet, 398
Hebrew Bible, 31, 33, 37, 39, 55, 58, 61, 62, 73, 74, 80, 83, 87
Hebrew calendar, 2, 10, 41, 64, 73, 86, 105, 112, 165, 183
Hebrew language, 31, 32, 36, 39, 45, 56, 61, 73, 83, 109, 163, 167, 213, 250, 292, 306, 332, 398, 597, 617
Hebrew-language, 215
Hebrews, **31**, 37, 39, 45
Hebrew University, 545
Hebrew University of Jerusalem, 201
Hebron, 6, 66, 83, 154, 160, 194, 199, 491, 537, 566
Hebron Subdistrict, Ottoman Empire, 160
HeHalutz, 416
Heinrich Himmler, 175, 377, 379
Heinrich Müller (Gestapo), 357
Hejaz, 197
Hellenistic civilization, 103
Hellenistic Judaism, 21, 103
Helmut Krausnick, 384
Helvis of Ramla, 120
Henotheism, 22
Henrietta Szold, 235
Henri Michel, 623
Henry Friedlander, 386
Henry Holt and Company, 210
Henry II, Count of Bar, 134
Henry II of Champagne, 129
Henry II of Cyprus, 110
Henry II of England, 118, 124, 126
Henry II of Jerusalem, 139, 151
Henry I of Cyprus, 132, 136

Henry IV, Duke of Limburg, 132
Henry IV of England, 151
Henry Laurens, 516
Henry Laurens (scholar), 576, 640
Henry Mond, 2nd Baron Melchett, 232
Henry of Antioch, 138
Henry VI, Holy Roman Emperor, 130
Herbert Morrison, 434
Herbert Samuel, 232, 278
Herbert Samuel, 1st Viscount Samuel, 164, 168, 169
Hermann Göring, 378
Hermann Neubacher, 258
Hermann of Salza, 132
Herman Wouk, 586
Herodian dynasty, 1, 9, 12, 21, 40, 63, 72, 86, 111, 165
Herodian kingdom, 1, 3, 9, 40, 63, 72, 86, 111, 165, 166
Herodian Tetrarchy, 1, 9, 40, 63, 72, 86, 111, 165
Herods Temple, 600
Herod the Great, 21, 99, 101
Hero of the Soviet Union, 328
Herschel Grynszpan, 343
Herut, 231
Herzliya, 445
Hethum I, King of Armenia, 137
Hezekiah, 17, 76, 77, 87–89
HIAS, 579
Hieroglyph, 42
High Commissioner, 317, 483
High Commissioner of Palestine, 472
High Commissioners for Palestine and Transjordan, 164, 199, 267, 268, 605, 631
High Commissioners of Palestine, 168
High Middle Ages, 110
Hijaz, 167, 522
Hillel Cohen, 307
Hillel II, 105
Hillel: The Foundation for Jewish Campus Life, 218, 241
Hish (Haganah corps), 295, 527
Histadrut, 201, 287, 423
Historical Jewish population comparisons, 216, 250, 398
Historiography, 505
History, 3, 167
History of ancient Egypt, 74
History of ancient Israel and Judah, 1, 3, 9, **9**, 36, 40, 63, 72, 85, 111, 164, 166
History of Israel, 1, 9, 40, 63, 72, 85, 111, 164
History of Israeli nationality, 2, 10, 41, 64, 73, 86, 112, 165
History of Jerusalem, 2, 10, 41, 64, 73, 86, 112, 165

History of Jerusalem during the Middle Ages, 1, 9, 40, 63, 72, 86, 111, 165
History of Palestine, 2, 166
History of the ancient Levant, 12
History of the Israeli–Palestinian conflict, 484, 577
History of the Jews and Judaism in the Land of Israel, 2, 10, 41, 64, 73, 86, 112, 165, 216, 250, 398
History of the Jews during World War II, **325**
History of the Jews in Argentina, 220
History of the Jews in Brazil, 220
History of the Jews in Egypt, 99
History of the Jews in France, 223
History of the Jews in Germany, 219, 332
History of the Jews in Greece, 220
History of the Jews in Italy, 99
History of the Jews in Libya, 347
History of the Jews in Poland, 328
History of the Jews in South Africa, 220
History of the Jews in the Czech Republic, 326
History of the Jews in the Ottoman Empire, 578
History of the Jews in the Roman Empire, **99**
History of the Jews in the Soviet Union, 219
History of the Jews in Ukraine, 223
History of the Jews under Muslim rule, 578
History of the Philippines (1946–65), 463
History of Zionism, 2, 10, 41, 64, 73, 86, 112, 165
Hitler, 251
Hitlers Chancellery, 340
HMS Ajax (22), 409
HMS Brissenden (L79), 405
HMS Chaplet (R52), 406
HMS Charity (R29), 408
HMS Chequers (R61), 405
HMS Cheviot (R90), 408, 410
HMS Chevron (R51), 404
HMS Chieftain (R36), 406
HMS Childers (R91), 406, 410
HMS Chivalrous (R21), 406
HMS Emerald (D66), 290
HMS Espiegle (J126), 406
HMS Haydon (L75), 406
HMS Hood (51), 290
HMS Jervis (F00), 405
HMS Malaya, 284, 289
HMS Mauritius (80), 410
HMS Mermaid (U30), 410
HMS Moon (J329), 406
HMS Octavia (J290), 406
HMS Peacock (U96), 404
HMS Pelican (L86), 411
HMS Phoebe (43), 410
HMS Providence (J325), 409
HMS Repulse (1916), 290

HMS Rowena (J384), 406
HMS Saumarez (G12), 405
HMS St Austell Bay (K634), 406
HMS St Brides Bay (K600), 408
HMS Talybont (L18), 404
HMS Venus (R50), 405
HMS Verulam (R28), 410
HMS Virago (R75), 405
HMS Warspite (03), 290
HMS Welfare (J356), 406
Hodierna of Tripoli, 118
Holocaust, 176, 239, 328, 454, 528
Holocaust survivors, 398
Holocaust train, 335
Holocaust trains, 331, 352
Holocaust (TV miniseries), 332
Holy Land, 43, 114
Holy of Holies, 46
Holy Roman Emperor, 113
Holy Sepulchre, 147
Holy Temple in Jerusalem, 47
Holy War Army, 431, 498, 515
Homeland for the Jewish people, 215, 249, 397
Homer, 56
Homo, 4
Homo sapiens, 4
Homs, 301
Honduras, 467
Horites, 7
Horticulture, 5
Hosea, 81
Hoshea, 80
Hotchkiss H35, 526, 574
Houghton Mifflin Company, 585
House of Bourbon, 151
House of Commons of the United Kingdom, 312, 426
House of Courtenay, 123
House of Habsburg, 151
House of Joseph, 42, 74
House of Lords, 318
House of Saul, 68
Houston Stewart Chamberlain, 337
Howard Morley Sachar, 585
Howard M. Sachar, 631
Howitzer, 289
Hugh G. M. Williamson, 57, 58
Hugh III of Burgundy, 124
Hugh III of Cyprus, 138
Hugh II of Cyprus, 136
Hugh II of Jaffa, 118
Hugh Mackintosh Foot, Baron Caradon, 294
Hugh of Brienne, 138
Hulagu Khan, 138
Hula, Lebanon, 566
Huleiqat, 567

Human Development Index, 201
Human sacrifice, 89
Humber Armoured Car, 574
Humphrey II of Toron, 120
Humphrey IV of Toron, 124
Hungarian Jews, 330
Hungary, 328
Hunter-gatherers, 5
Hurfeish, 225
Hurrians, 7
Hurva Synagogue, 544
Husayni, 273
Husni al-Zaim, 520
Hussein-McMahon Correspondence, 313
Hydrogen cyanide, 360
Hyrcanus II, 100

Ian Black (journalist), 307, 581
Ian Hancock, 370, 388
Ian Kershaw, 377, 389, 395
Iași pogrom, 327, 348
Iași pogrom, 353
Ibelin (castle), 119, 148
Ibelin family, 120, 125
Ibn Jubayr, 141, 144
Ibrahim Hakki Pasha, 161
Ibrahim Nassar, 267
I.B.Tauris, 209
I.B. Tauris, 310
Ibzan, 55, 58
Iceland, 466
Identification in Nazi camps, 350
IDF Sword Battalion, 520
Idolatry, 87
Idumea, 21
I. F. Stone, 400
IG Farben Trial, 258
IHC M14 Half-track, 574
I. Howard Marshall, 59
Ilan Pappe, 517, 637, 638
Ilan Pappé, 209, 481, 485, 516, 528, 577, 584, 586
Illuminated manuscript, 148
Imad ad-Din Zengi, 119
Immanuel Löw, 232
Immediate consequences and exile, 47
Immigrant Absorption Minister of Israel, 239
Immigrant camps (Israel), 216, 250, 398, 579, 580
Imperial Japanese Army, 262
Imperial Japanese Navy, 262
Improvised explosive devices, 426
Inari Karsh, 583
Independence, 522
Independence Party (Palestine), 188, 273, 292

Independent State of Croatia, 253, 260, 347, 354
India, 466
Indian National Congress, 273
Infantry, 490
Infantry fighting vehicle, 574
Ink Flag, 519, 571
Institute for Palestine Studies, 209, 583, 586
Institute of Palestine Studies, 605, 630
Insurrection, 65
Intelligenzaktion, 372
Intercommunal conflict in Mandatory Palestine, 475
Intercommunal violence in Mandatory Palestine, 266
Interdict, 133
Intergovernmental Committee on Refugees, 342
International Court of Justice, 186, 460
International Standard Book Number, 24, 26, 28, 35, 48–55, 58, 59, 93–96, 162, 209–211, 264, 265, 306–311, 323, 381–395, 412, 451, 473, 515–517, 581–586
Interpellation (politics), 259
Interwar period, 164
In the Tanakh, 23
Invasion of Poland, 331, 344
Invasion of Yugoslavia, 253, 347
Ion Antonescu, 258
Ioudaioi, 39
Ioveta of Bethany, 118
Iqrit, 566
Iqta, 143
Iran, 179, 466
Iranian Jews in Israel, 579
Iraq, 278, 315, 450, 466
Iraqi Air Force, 537
Iraqi Jews in Israel, 579
Iraqi people, 482
Iraq Suwaydan, 569
Irgun, 172, 177, 180, 189, 237, 266, 270, 280, 296, 321, 408, 413, 414, 417, 422, 423, 425, 431, 435, 455, 463, 468, 475, 477, 478, 501, 520, 524, 527, 541, 561
Irgun and Lehi internment in Africa, 423
Irish Republican Army, 450
Irish War of Independence, 286
Iron Age, 36, 42, 69, 83
Iron Guard, 258
Iron Wall (essay), 296
Isaac, 34, 36
Isaac Herzog, 213, 245
Isabella II of Jerusalem, 130
Isabella of Cyprus, 138
Isabella of Ibelin, Queen of Cyprus, 139
Isabella of Jerusalem, 123

Ish-boseth, 68
Ish-bosheth, 65
Ishmaelites, 34
Ishtar Gate, 18
Islam, 110, 164
Islamic art, 148
ISO 259-3, 31
ISO 3166, 71
ISO 3166-2:IL, 71
Israel, 2, 10, 39, 41, 42, 44, 64, 72, 73, 83, 86, 111–113, 154, 164, 165, 168, 214, 288, 306, 379, 414, 432, 489, 519, 520, 535, 540, 579
Israel Antiquities Authority, 69
Israel Defense Forces, 175, 221, 224, 225, 490, 520, 533, 536, 541
Israel Finkelstein, 14, 69, 76
Israel Galili, 490
Israel Gutman, 382, 393
Israeli Air Force, 433, 549, 551, 562, 569, 571, 572
Israeli Antiquities Authority, 85
Israeli Civil Administration, 3, 167
Israeli coastal plain, 574
Israeli Declaration of Independence, 2, 10, 41, 64, 73, 86, 112, 164, 165, 306, 432, 475, 476, 484, 520, 521, 540, 577
Israeli Military Governorate, 3, 167
Israeli naval campaign in Operation Yoav, 569
Israeli Navy, 553, 569
Israeli Prime Minister, 530
Israelis, 39
Israelite, 55, 64, 74
Israelite highland settlement, 42
Israelite period, 12
Israelites, 1, 9, 31, 34, **35**, 36, 40, 61, 63, 72, 75, 85, 87, 111, 164
Israel Military Industries, 527
Israel (name), 36
Israel Prize, 217, 247
Israels Secret Wars: A History of Israels Intelligence Services, 210, 581
Issa Battat, 267, 301
Issachar, 44
Istanbul, 403
Is the Holocaust Unique?, 380, 393
István Csáky, 257
Italian bombings on Palestine in World War II, 174
Italian Campaign (World War II), 176, 418
Italian city-states, 113
Italian declaration of war on the United States, 264
Italian language, 32, 34, 109, 110
Italian Libya, 347
Italic peoples, 140

Italo-Greek War, 259
Iudaea Province, 21, 101, 102
Ivan Popov (diplomat), 258
Izz ad-Din al-Qassam, 171, 267, 269
Izzat Darwaza, 267

Jack Churchill, 502
Jacob, 34, 36, 38, 43, 598
Jacob Lestschinsky, 369
Jacob wrestling with the angel, 39
Jaffa, 6, 116, 154, 194, 195, 199, 205, 269, 276, 284, 303, 435, 447, 449, 457, 461, 462, 470, 483, 496, 503, 515, 521, 525, 554
Jaffa Electric Company, 201
Jaffa Gate, 561
Jaffa, Israel, 148
Jaffa riots, 188, 189, 527
Jaffa Road, 204, 296
Jaffa Subdistrict, Ottoman Empire, 160
Jair, 55, 58
Jamal al-Husseini, 188, 305, 313, 320
Jamal Husseini, 464
James Armand de Rothschild, 318
Jan Karski, 363
Jan Lievens, 127
Janoah, 75
Japanese declaration of war on the United States and the British Empire, 254
Japanese invasion of Thailand, 261
Jasenovac concentration camp, 371
Jawaharlal Nehru, 463
J. Bowyer Bell, 307, 450, 581, 628, 642
J. C. Hurewitz, 323
Jean Ancel, 369
Jean I de Grailly, 140
Jebel Qafzeh remains, 4
Jeconiah, 88, 91, 93
Jedwabne pogrom, 353
Jeffrey T. Richelson, 584
Jehoahaz of Israel, 79
Jehoahaz of Judah, 88, 91
Jehoash of Israel, 79
Jehoash of Judah, 88
Jehoiachin, 20
Jehoiakim, 88, 91
Jehoram of Israel, 78, 89
Jehoram of Judah, 75, 87, 89
Jehoshaphat, 75, 87, 89
Jehovahs Witnesses, 350, 376
Jehu, 75, 79
Jenin, 194, 199, 300, 482, 483, 499, 546, 554
Jephthah, 55, 58
Jeremiah, 91, 92
Jeremy Black (historian), 307, 345
Jericho, 3, 166

Jeroboam, 74, 78, 80, 88
Jeroboam II, 79
Jeroboams Revolt, 71, 83, 88
Jerusalem, 6, 7, 13, 17, 43, 66, 75, 80, 83, 110, 113, 121, 140, 147, 153, 154, 160, 181, 187, 194, 199, 200, 202, 203, 213, 225, 247, 281, 411, 424, 434, 435, 440, 447, 452, 457, 459, 468, 471, 475, 479, 483, 484, 491, 493, 495, 496, 509, 521, 544, 545, 554, 560, 563, 575
Jerusalem Corridor, 546, 569
Jerusalem cross, 109
Jerusalem in Judaism, 102
Jerusalem Post, 479
Jerusalem Subdistrict, Ottoman Empire, 160
Jerusalem Talmud, 104, 105
Jerusalem temple, 101
Jesse, 47
Jethro (Bible), 45, 58
Jetur, 75
Jewish, 213
Jewish Agency, 170, 174, 314, 406, 455, 486
Jewish Agency for Israel, **213**, 216, 250, 321, 398, 403, 416, 423, 424, 439, 501, 580, 605
Jewish Agency for Palestine, 188, 251, 453, 454
Jewish Agency International Development, 246
Jewish Bolshevism, 337, 338
Jewish Brigade, 175, 362, 418, 616
Jewish Christian, 31
Jewish Christians, 34
Jewish diaspora, 43, 99, 213, 215, 217, 249, 397
Jewish Encyclopedia, 34, 100
Jewish exodus from Arab and Muslim countries, 215, 238, 249, 397, 475, 578, 579
Jewish exodus from Arab lands, 521
Jewish Federations of North America, 216, 244, 246
Jewish–Roman wars, 99
Jewish history, 2, 10, 41, 64, 73, 86, 112, 165
Jewish identity, 11, 23, 31, 220, 221, 242, 243
Jewish insurgency in Mandatory Palestine, **413**
Jewish insurgency in Palestine, 168, 177, 521
Jewish law, 38
Jewish Migration from Lebanon Post-1948, 215, 249, 397, 579
Jewish military history, 2, 10, 41, 64, 73, 86, 112, 165
Jewish National Council, 201, 237, 266
Jewish National Fund, 194, 216, 229, 238, 250, 271, 398
Jewish Parachutists of Mandate Palestine, 418
Jewish partisans, 329, 419
Jewish people, 39, 105

Jewish peoplehood, 11, 31
Jewish People Policy Institute, 220
Jewish Peoples Council, 472
Jewish Quarter (Jerusalem), 545
Jewish question, 215, 249, 397
Jewish refugees, 216, 250, 342, 398
Jewish Resistance Movement, 178, 414, 423, 435, 454
Jewish resistance under Nazi rule, 417
Jewish revolt against Constantius Gallus, 1, 9, 40, 64, 72, 86, 111, 165
Jewish revolt against Gallus, 104
Jewish revolt against Heraclius, 1, 10, 40, 64, 72, 86, 105, 112, 165
Jewish-Roman wars, 102
Jewish Settlement Police, 266, 292, 295, 605
Jewish state, 530
Jewish Supernumerary Police, 266, 294, 295
Jewish tradition, 37
Jewish Virtual Library, 323, 412, 605
Jews, 11, 31, 36, 37, 39, 99, 100, 114, 143, 213, 215, 249, 326, 330, 397, 398
Jews as a chosen people, 46
Jews during the Fascist era, 326
Jews in British camps on Cyprus, 178, 322, 400
Jews under the Nazis (1933-45), 326
Jew (word), 11, 31, 39
Jezebel, 80
Jezreel Valley, 16, 90, 196, 458, 499, 574
Jezreel Valley Regional Council, 225
Jihad, 120, 313
JIMENA, 579
Jimzu, 560
J. I. Packer, 59
JNF, 229
Joachim von Ribbentrop, 253, 379
Joel Brand, 365
John Bagot Glubb, 183, 432, 506, 507, 520, 545
John Dill, 267, 277
John Gillingham, 601
John Hyrcanus, 43
John II Comnenus, 119
John II of Beirut, 137
John II of Jerusalem, 139
John J. Mearsheimer, 632
John Laffin, 309
John of Arsuf, 134, 137
John of Brienne, 130, 134
John of Ibelin (jurist), 136, 146
John of Ibelin, the Old Lord of Beirut, 130
John Rymer-Jones, 413
John Vereker, 6th Viscount Gort, 413
Joint Declaration by Members of the United Nations, 363
Jonah, 79, 81

Jonathan (1 Samuel), 65
Jonathan Riley-Smith, 152, 600, 603
Jordan, 72, 111, 113, 154, 439, 475, 476, 480, 481, 485, 489, 513, 515, 521, 522, 535, 540, 574
Jordanian annexation of the West Bank, 3, 164, 167, 168, 459, 519, 521, 575
Jordan Rift Valley, 4
Jordan River, 13, 65, 167, 275
Jordan Valley (Middle East), 458
Joscelin III of Edessa, 123
Josef Mengele, 336
Josef Stalin, 480
Joseph Goebbels, 343, 357, 379
Joseph (Hebrew Bible), 44
Joseph Klausner, 294
Joseph Stalin, 486, 523
Josephus, 74, 595
Joshua, 47, 55, 57
Joshua Landis, 586
Joshua Palmon, 501
Joshua Prawer, 143, 146, 152, 603
Josiah, 22, 87, 88, 90
Jotham of Judah, 17, 88
Journal of Contemporary History, 387
Journal of Hebrew Scriptures, 25
Journal of Palestine Studies, 641, 642
Józefów, Biłgoraj County, 377
Jozef Tiso, 258
JSTOR, 211
Judaea (Roman province), 99
Judah (Bible), 44
Judah haNasi, 104
Judaism, 11, 31, 38, 83, 99, 110, 164
Judaizers, 31
Judea, 42, 99, 105, 457
Judean, 17
Judea (Roman province), 1, 3, 9, 12, 31, 40, 63, 72, 86, 111, 165, 166
Judenrat, 351
Judenrein, 418
Judges, 59
Judith M. Brown, 581
Julian Grenier, 137
Julian the Apostate, 105
Julio-Claudian, 600
Julius Caesar, 99, 101
Julius Hallervorden, 341
Jund al-Urdunn, 2, 3, 10, 40, 64, 72, 86, 112, 165, 166
Jund Filastin, 2, 3, 10, 40, 64, 72, 86, 112, 165, 166
Juris Zarins, 5
Justice for Jews from Arab Countries, 579

Kadesh Barnea, 6

Kadesh (Syria), 6
Kaiser Wilhelm Institute of Anthropology, Human Heredity, and Eugenics, 337
Kaiser Wilhelm Society, 341
Kamil al-Husayni, 170
Kankaanpää, 261
Karabiner 98k, 574
Karatiyya, 634
Kareah, 92
Karl Brandt, 340
Karl Wolff, 377
Karsh, 634–636, 638, 639
Kassam rocket, 227
Katamon, 475, 509, 634
Katy Antonius (Jerusalem), 425
Kaunas pogrom, 327
Kebara Cave, 4
Kenites, 22
Kenneth Kitchen, 57, 59, 69, 77, 598
Kenneth Pollack, 584
Kenneth Setton, 152
Kenneth W. Stein, 210
Kenya, 430
Kerak, 119, 126, 148
Kerbogha, 114
Keren Hayesod, 216, 234, 238, 241, 244, 246
Kfar Darom, 492
Kfar Etzion, 491, 492, 495, 507
Kfar Etzion massacre, 525
Kfar Giladi, 439
Kfar Saba, 447
Kfar Sirkin, 478
Kfar Tavor, 293
Kfar Vitkin, 438
Kfar Yona, 546
Khabur (Euphrates), 75
Khalil al-Sakakini, 275
Khan Yunis, 160
Khedivate of Egypt, 154, 155
Khirbet Kerak, 7
Khirbet Qeiyafa, 69, 70, 85
Khulda, 495, 560
Khwarazmian dynasty, 113, 135
Kibbutz, 216, 218, 224, 250, 398, 471, 492, 496, 499, 501, 540, 541
Kibbutz Harduf, 221
Kibbutzim, 229
Kibbutz Ulpan, 224
Kiev, 355
Kilij Arslan I, 114
Killed in action, 267, 476, 520
King Ahab, 67
King Ahazs seal, 17
King David Hotel, 436, 439
King David Hotel bombing, 178, 414, 424, 439, 477

Kingdom of Bulgaria, 253, 258, 327
Kingdom of Cyprus, 113, 129, 151
Kingdom of Egypt, 288, 476, 521, 522, 540
Kingdom of Hungary (1920–1946), 253, 257
Kingdom of Hungary (1920–46), 253
Kingdom of Iraq, 268, 417, 476, 521, 535, 540
Kingdom of Israel (Samaria), 1, 9, 11, 12, 37, 39, 40, 61, 63, 67, **71**, 72, 85, 87, 88, 111, 164
Kingdom of Israel (united monarchy), 1, 9, 31, 40, 43, 47, 57, **61**, 63, 71–74, 83, 85, 87, 111, 164
Kingdom of Italy, 253
Kingdom of Jerusalem, 2, 3, 10, 40, 64, 72, 86, **109**, 112, 165, 166
Kingdom of Judah, 1, 9, 11, 12, 17, 37–40, 42, 47, 61, 63, 67, 72–74, 80, **83**, 85, 111, 164
Kingdom of Naples, 151
Kingdom of Romania, 253, 257
Kingdom of Samaria, 42, 47
Kingdom of Yugoslavia, 253, 260
King Elah, 78
King Farouk, 513
King Farouk I, 520
King George Street (Jerusalem), 442
King Hiram I, 66
King of Jerusalem, 110, 116, 151
King of Judah, 75
King of Navarre, 134
Kings Highway (ancient), 6
Kings of Cyprus, 151
Kings of Italy, 151
Kings of Judah, 87
Kings of Spain, 151
Kinneret Zmora-Bitan Dvir, 582
Kiryati Brigade, 533
Kiryat Shmuel, Jerusalem, 206
Kitab al itibar, 141, 151
Kitbuqa, 137
Kitos War, 102
Kladovo, 402
Klaus Hildebrand, 388
Knight, 141
Knights Hospitaller, 118, 133
Knights Templar, 118, 133, 149
Knopf Publishing, 585
Kohanim, 38
Kohen, 39
Kovno Ghetto, 350
Krak des Chevaliers, 139
Kraków Ghetto, 350
Kristallnacht, 327, 334, 343, 349
Kufic, 147
Kunst-Werke Institute for Contemporary Art, 610

Kurdish Jews in Israel, 579
Kurdish language, 32
Kurkh Monoliths, 81
Kurt Weitzmann, 107
Kurt Wieland, 605
Kuwait, 450

Labor Zionism, 278
Labour Party (UK), 322, 419
Ladislaus Löb, 390
Lake Tiberias, 275
Land Lottery, 47
Land of Canaan, 37, 46
Land of Israel, 2, 10, 12, 15, 41, 64, 73, 86, 99, 112, 165, 184, 215, 249, 397, 540
Lapierre collins, 635–639
Lapis lazuli, 45
Large Stone Structure, 85
Larry Collins (writer), 501, 516, 582
La Spezia, 405
Late Bronze Age, 42
Late Bronze Age collapse, 13, 31, 63
Latin, 32, 110
Latin American and Caribbean Group, 465
Latin Emperor of Constantinople, 134
Latin language, 109, 147
Latin Patriarch of Jerusalem, 116
Latrun, 237, 287, 437, 495, 537, 544, 560
Latvia, 327, 328, 355
Latvian Auxiliary Police, 326
Laupheim, 343
Laurens, 635, 639
Law for the Prevention of Hereditarily Diseased Offspring, 340
Law for the Restoration of the Professional Civil Service, 339
Law of Return, 215, 223, 249, 397
Layperson, 38
Leader, 32
Leaders of the tribes of Israel, 36
League of Nations, 167, 179, 230, 274, 314, 432, 453, 455
League of Nations mandate, 163, 167, 455, 522
Leah, 36, 44
Lebanese Armed Forces, 548
Lebanese people, 301
Lebanon, 72, 111, 113, 287, 290, 299, 401, 406, 466, 482, 511, 513, 515, 535, 566
Lebensraum, 338, 372
Lee–Enfield rifle, 574
Lehigh University, 237
Lehi (group), 174, 177, 321, 413, 414, 418, 423, 425, 431, 435, 439, 442, 454, 455, 468, 475, 478, 479, 501, 520, 524, 541, 561, 563
Leib Yaffe, 234

Leipheim, 399
Lekh Lekha, 33
Leon Blum, 232
Leopold VI, Duke of Austria, 130
Leslie Hore-Belisha, 1st Baron Hore-Belisha, 320
Leszno, 373
Letter bomb, 445
Levant, 4, 12, 91, 167
Levee-en-masse, 124
Levi, 44
Levites, 38, 39
Lewis Yelland Andrews, 280
Liberal Party (UK), 318
Liberia, 463, 466
Library of Congress, 332, 587
Library of the Arsenal, 106
Libya, 430, 483
Licinius, 99
Liepāja massacres, 355
Life unworthy of life, 340
Lifta, 494
Light tank, 547
Light Tank Mk VI, 537, 574
Limassol, 132
Limpet mine, 440
List of Adolf Hitlers directives, 260
List of Arab towns and villages depopulated during the 1948 Palestinian exodus, 485, 577
List of countries by population, 154
List of Irgun attacks during the 1930s, 172
List of Israeli museums, 2, 10, 41, 64, 73, 86, 112, 165
List of Jewish leaders in the Land of Israel, 2, 10, 41, 64, 73, 86, 112, 165
List of titles and honours of the Spanish Crown, 151
List of villages depopulated during the Arab–Israeli conflict, 577
List of years in Israel, 2, 10, 41, 64, 73, 86, 112, 165
Litani River, 566
Lithuania, 327, 328
Lithuanian Activist Front, 327
Lithuanian Auxiliary Police Battalions, 326
Liverpool, 428
Lloyd George, 318
LMLK seal, 17
Lod, 115, 160, 225, 435, 447, 483, 495, 521, 560, 563
Lod Airport, 554, 560
Lodz Ghetto, 623

Łódź Ghetto, 350

London, 428, 445
London Conference (1939), 174, 305, 312, 315, 320, 416, 454
Lone soldiers, 224
Lord Moyne, 177, 414, 423
Lorraine 37L, 574
Louis Arie Pincus, 245
Louis IX of France, 136
Louis VII of France, 119
Lou Lenart, 526
Louvre, 15
Low Countries, 370
Lower Galilee, 562
Lower Palaeolithic, 4
Luang Wichitwathakan, 262
Lublin reservation, 345
Lubya, 296
Lucy Dawidowicz, 369, 384
Luftwaffe, 535
Lunisolar, 105
Lusignan, 113
Lusignan dynasty, 132
Lutheranism, 337
Luxembourg, 327, 466
Lviv Ghetto, 327
Lviv pogroms, 327, 353
Lwów Ghetto, 350

M22 Locust, 574
M3 Half-track, 574
M3 Scout Car, 574
M4 Sherman, 524, 534, 574
M5 Half-track, 574
Maabarot, 216, 239, 250, 398, 579, 580
Maan, 289
Maccabean Revolt, 21
MacDonald White Paper, 454
Machine gun, 489
Machon Ayalon, 527
Machon Le Madrichim, 218
Madagascar, 344
Madoff scandal, 246
Mafraq, 513
Maghrebi Jews, 579
Mahal (Israel), 475, 520, 551
Mahanaim, 66
Mahmoud Abbas, 473
Mahmud Nedim Pasha, 154
Majdal al-Sadiq, 560
Majdanek, 328
Majdanek concentration camp, 335, 359, 360, 367, 370
Malayan Communist Party, 450
Malayan Emergency, 450
Malcolm Hoenlein, 220
Malcolm MacDonald, 305, 313, 615

Malha, 562
Malik az-Zahir, 130
Malik-Shah I, 114
Maly Trostenets extermination camp, 359, 360
Mamilla, 435
Mamluk, 112, 113, 149
Mamluk Sultanate (Cairo), 2, 3, 10, 40, 64, 72, 86, 111, 112, 136, 165, 166
Manara, Israel, 564
Manasseh of Judah, 87–89
Manasseh (tribal patriarch), 44
Manasses of Hierges, 119
Manchester, 428
Manchester Regiment, 286
Mandate Palestine, 214
Mandatory Palestine, 2, 3, 10, 40, 64, 73, 86, 112, 154, 155, **163**, 165, 167, 266, 267, 288, 312, 329, 344, 362, 398, 413–415, 452, 475, 476, 484, 519–521, 525, 574, 577
Mandatory Palestine passport, 183
Manna, 45
Manuel I Comnenus, 121, 122
Mapai, 296
Mapam, 499
March 1947 martial law in Mandatory Palestine, 442
Marc Zvi Brettler, 58
Maresha, 88
Maria Komnene, Queen consort of Jerusalem, 122
Maria of Antioch, 121, 138
Maria of Montferrat, 130, 134
Maritsa, 259
Mark Mazower, 391
Marmon-Herrington Armoured Car, 574
Maronites, 503
Marqab, 139
Marshall Plan, 486
Marshall W. Baldwin, 123
Martial law, 268, 281, 442
Martin Bell, 382
Martin C. Dean, 368
Martin Gilbert, 210, 308, 332, 369, 387, 582, 586, 616
Martinus Nijhoff Publishers, 210
Martin Van Creveld, 582, 640
Marxism, 338
Mary of Antioch, 151
MAS 36, 574
Masa Israel Journey, 214, 217
Masoretic text, 56
Mateh Asher Regional Council, 225
Matilda II tank, 537, 574
Mauritius, 176, 400, 402, 418
Mauthausen concentration camp, 374

Mauthausen-Gusen concentration camp, 349, 359
Max Heiliger, 335
Max Weber, 35
McGraw-Hill, 581
McMahon–Hussein Correspondence, 167
M. D. Eder, 244
Mecca, 125
Mechina, 221, 225
Medes, 3, 76, 166
Media event, 422
Medieval art, 148
Medieval commune, 133
Medieval Greek, 110
Medieval Greek language, 109
Medieval university, 147
Medina, 125
Mediterranean, 66, 290
Mediterranean and Middle East theatre of World War II, 417
Mediterranean Fleet, 267, 290
Mediterranean Sea, 66, 113, 399
Megiddo (kibbutz), 499
Megiddo (place), 90
Mehmet Cavit Bey, 161
Mehmet Tevfik Biren, 161
Meir Feinstein, 444
Melisende of Jerusalem, 118
Melisende of Lusignan, 138
Melisende Psalter, 148, 149
Member of Parliament, 318
Menachem Begin, 180, 413, 423, 451, 468, 476
Menahem, 79
Menashiya, 449
Menorah (Temple), 102
Mercenary, 147
Merchant, 580
Meribah, 47
Merneptah, 39, 42
Merneptah Stele, 13, 14, 38, 39, 42
Meron Benvenisti, 143, 146, 586
Merovingian, 105
Mervyn Paice, 446
Mesha, 75, 84, 89
Mesha Stele, 16, 75, 84
Mesopotamia, 6
Messerschmitt Bf-109, 526
Metonic cycle, 105
Metonym, 300
Metula, 504
Mexico, 467
MG 34, 534
MG-34, 574
MI5, 286, 527
Miar, 284

Michael Berenbaum, 335, 381, 392
Michael Burleigh, 384
Michael Coogan, 59
Michael Fekete, 545
Michael Fleming (historian), 362
Michael Marrus, 333
Michael McDonnell, 200, 284
Michal, 65
Mickey Marcus, 520, 543
Microgrant, 222
Microlith, 4
Middle Ages, 337
Middle Bronze Age, 7
Middle East, 313, 466
Middle East Command, 288
Middle Eastern megaliths, 5
Middle Palaeolithic, 4
Midian, 22, 58
Midianites, 22, 34
Midrash, 104
Migdol, 92
Migration of Moroccan Jews to Israel, 215, 249, 397, 579
Miklós Horthy, 257
Miles of Plancy, 123
Milestone, 426
Milgram experiment, 377
Military alliance, 253
Military order (society), 118
Military tribunal, 379
Millet (Ottoman Empire), 199
Millo, 64
Mills bomb, 526, 574
Ministry of Aliyah and Integration, 216, 250, 398
Ministry of Education (Israel), 223
Minsk ghetto, 356
Misgav Am, 566
Mishkan, 43–45
Mishmar HaEmek, 500, 525
Mishmar HaYarden, 548, 554
Mishna, 39
Mishnah, 38, 103, 104
Mithridates VI of Pontus, 101
Mixed Armistice Commissions, 575
Mizocz Ghetto, 354
Mizpah in Benjamin, 18, 89, 92
Mizrachi (religious Zionism), 278
Mizrahi Jews, 578
Mizrahi Jews in Israel, 579
Mizwa, 47
Moab, 16, 41, 66, 84, 89, 91
Moabites, 34
Mobile Guards, 295
Mobile units (Haganah unit), 295
Modern archaeology, 62

Modern Hebrew, 31, 39, 73
Modern history, 2, 10, 40, 64, 72, 86, 112, 165
Modern Israel, 74
Modern Orthodox Judaism, 219
Modi Alon, 551
Mohammad Amin al-Husayni, 297, 479, 488
Mohammad Amin al-Husseini, 170, 175
Mohammad Mahmoud Ranaan, 267
Mohammed Saleh al-Hamad, 267
Molotov cocktail, 448, 547, 574
Molotov–Ribbentrop Pact, 255
Monarchy, 71, 83, 110
Money laundering, 335
Möngke Khan, 138
Mongol, 113
Mongols, 135
Monolatrism, 22, 36, 71
Monopoli, 403
Monotheism, 22, 36, 71, 87
Montfort Castle, 132
Montreal (Crusader castle), 148
Mordechai Alkahi, 444
Mordechai Weingarten, 641
Moroccan Jews in Israel, 579
Morphia of Melitene, 118
Morris 1948, 634, 635, 638
Morris Beckman (writer), 585
Morris birth, 634–639
Morrisglubb, 638
Morrison-Grady Plan, 192
Morris victims fr, 636, 637
Mortar (weapon), 482, 574
Moses, 44, 58
Moshav, 580
Moshavim, 229
Moshe Barzani, 444
Moshe Carmel, 520, 533, 566
Moshe Dayan, 520, 582
Moshe Sharett, 237, 245, 294, 295, 303
Moshe Shertok, 232, 244
Moshe Sneh, 413
Moslem, 463
Mossad, 291, 292, 379
Mossad LeAliyah Bet, 176, 216, 234, 250, 295, 398, 399, 424, 579, 580
Mosul, 114, 117
Mosul–Haifa oil pipeline, 275
Mount Carmel, 13, 297, 436, 443
Mount Gerizim, 43
Mount Hebron, 297, 515
Mount Herzl, 411
Mount Lebanon, 13
Mount Moriah, 43
Mount Scopus, 510
Mount Seir, 41
Mount Sinai, 45

Mount Tabor, 130
Mount Zion, 447, 561
Mousterian, 4
Mufti, 485
Muhammad al-Ashmar, 267, 301
Muhammad Naguib, 520, 558
Mukhtar, 284
Munhata, 5
Murray Greenfield, 401, 412
Musa al-Alami, 320
Musa Alami, 305, 313, 471
Musa al-Husayni, 170
Musa al-Husseini, 187
Muslim Brotherhood, 483, 520, 555
Muslim-Christian Associations, 168
Muslim conquest of the Levant, 3, 166
Muslim conquests, 105
Muslim history in Palestine, 3, 166
Mustaarabi Jews, 579
Mustafa Osta, 267
Mutasarrifate of Jerusalem, 2, 10, 40, 64, 73, 86, 112, **153**, 165
Mutasarrifates of the Ottoman Empire, 153
Mutawakkilite Kingdom of Yemen, 268
Muzahim al-Pachachi, 520
MV Mefküre, 176, 403
MV Struma, 176, 403
Mytilene, 402

NAALE Program, 218
Nablus, 114, 126, 149, 172, 194, 199, 270, 285, 482, 483, 536, 546
Nablus Sanjak, 154
Nacht und Nebel, 374
Nadab of Israel, 78
Nahariya, 404, 408, 410, 489, 496
Nahum, 81
Nahum Sokolow, 232, 609
Nakba Day, 484, 576, 578
Naphish, 75
Naphtali, 44
Napoleonchik, 547, 574
Naram-Sin of Akkad, 7
Naseer Aruri, 210
Nashashibi, 172, 273, 297, 417
Nashashibi clan, 268
Natan Sharansky, 220, 242, 244, 245
Nathan Israel Department Store, 339
Nathan Stoltzfus, 387
Nathan Yellin-Mor, 413
National Assembly (Bulgaria), 259
National Bloc (Palestine), 273
National capital, 66
National Cyber Bureau, 217
National Defence Party (Palestine), 273

National Defense Party (Mandatory Palestine), 266, 268
National god, 22, 80
National home for the Jewish people, 190, 232
National Library of Israel, 319
National Museum of Rome, 104
National myth, 36
National Socialist German Workers Party, 338
Natufian, 5
Natufian culture, 1, 3, 9, 40, 63, 72, 85, 111, 164, 166
Natzweiler concentration camp, 336
Naval blockade, 420
Nazareth, 194, 199, 225, 297, 562
Nazareth Capitals, 149
Nazareth District, 299
Nazareth Subdistrict, Ottoman Empire, 154, 161
Nazi boycott of Jewish businesses, 339
Nazi collaborators, 420
Nazi concentration camp badge, 350
Nazi concentration camps, 331, 358
Nazi crimes against the Polish nation, 326, 331
Nazi Germany, 175, 250, 251, 253, 296, 305, 326, 330, 331, 379, 398, 399, 417, 551
Nazi ghettos, 331
Nazi Party, 251, 331, 340
Nazism, 328, 379
Nazism and race, 175
NBC, 332
Neanderthal, 4
Near East, 5
Near East timeline, 12
Nebi Musa, 273
Nebuchadnezzar II of Babylon, 91
Necho II, 90
Nefesh BNefesh, 216, 250, 398
Negation of the Diaspora, 215, 249, 397
Negba, 542, 559
Negev, 6, 180, 225, 242, 277, 433, 479, 492, 521, 523, 538, 540, 541, 563, 574
Negev Bedouin, 221, 225
Negev Brigade, 533, 571
Negev Desert, 155, 457, 458, 461
Nehemiah, 20
Neil Asher Silberman, 69, 76
Nelson Mandela, 450
Neo-Assyrian Empire, 12, 17, 71, 73, 90
Neo-Babylonian Empire, 12, 17, 68, 80, 84, 87, 90
Neolithic, 5
Neolithic period, 5
Neolithic revolution, 5
Nesher, 293
Net, 242
Netanya, 409, 427, 444–446, 546

Netherlands, 328, 466
Neuengamme concentration camp, 336
Neues Volk, 340
Neville Chamberlain, 305, 312, 313
New American Library, 583
New Gate, 561
New Historians, 484, 577
New Testament, 103
New York Times, 616, 629
New Zealand, 466
Nicaragua, 465, 534
Nicholas Bethell, 211
Nicosia, 400
Night of the Beatings, 427, 441
Night of the Bridges, 424, 432, 439
Night of the Trains, 423, 435
Nile, 44
Nilin, 160
Nimrud Slab, 81
Nimrud Tablet K.3751, 84
Nineveh, 79
Niqqud, 104
Nir-Am, 549
Nirim, 542, 573
Nisko, 620
Nitzana, Israel, 570
Nitzanim, 543
No. 13 Squadron RAF, 572
No. 208 Squadron RAF, 572
No. 213 Squadron RAF, 572
No. 6 Squadron RAF, 572
Noah, 32
Nobility, 147
Nodab, 75
Nollendorfplatz, 375
Nomad, 14, 31
Nomadic pastoralism, 5
Noph, 92
Norman Naimark, 391
North Africa, 409
North African Campaign, 417
North American Group, 466
Northern Kingdom, 598
Northern Levant, 5
Norway, 327, 466
Norwegian Campaign, 346
Notrim, 293
Nuova Cronica, 131
Nur ad-Din Zangi, 113, 120
Nur-eldeen Masalha, 485, 577, 586, 606
Nuremberg, 379
Nuremberg Laws, 314, 331, 341, 415
Nuremberg trials, 336, 379
Nuri al-Said, 464
Nuri as-Said, 274, 320, 532

O

O Jerusalem, 628
Oaxaca, 221
Obergruppenführer, 356
Occupation of Poland (1939–1945), 353, 356
Occupation of the Gaza Strip by Egypt, 3, 167, 459, 519, 521, 575
Occupied Enemy Territory Administration, 2, 10, 40, 64, 73, 86, 112, 153–155, 164, 165, 167, 168
Occupied Europe, 335
Occupied Poland, 353
Ocean Vigour, 444
Oded Brigade, 533, 548
Oded Lipschits, 68
Odessa, 348
Odilo Globocnik, 345
Odo Poilechien, 139
Office of Racial Policy, 340
Officers of the Kingdom of Jerusalem, 141, 149
Oilfield, 290
O Jerusalem, 582
O Jerusalem (film), 517
Old City (Jerusalem), 297, 544
Old City of Jerusalem, 283
Old French, 114
Old French language, 109, 110
Old Yishuv, 2, 10, 40, 64, 73, 86, 112, 165, 215, 249, 397, 578
Olei Hagardom, 427
Olim, 223
Oman, 450
Omri, 17, 74, 75, 78, 81
Omrides, 73
One-state solution, 35, 304
Oneworld Publications, 584, 586
Onward Israel, 214
Opel, 380
Operation Agatha, 237, 424, 437, 439
Operation An-Far, 558
Operation Assaf, 569
Operation ATLAS, 605
Operation Atlas (Mandatory Palestine), 495
Operation Balak, 480, 489, 523, 526, 533, 535
Operation Barak, 533
Operation Barbarossa, 260, 261, 326, 327, 331, 345, 348
Operation Biur Hametz, 503
Operation Compass, 297
Operation Danny, 533, 560
Operation Death to the Invader, 558
Operation Dekel, 533, 562
Operation Ezra and Nehemiah, 215, 249, 397, 579
Operation Gideon, 503
Operation Ha-Har, 546, 569, 640
Operation Hametz, 449, 503, 533
Operation Harvest Festival, 365
Operation Hiram, 533, 566
Operation Horev, 533, 539, 570
Operation Joshua, 240
Operation Kedem, 561
Operation Kilshon, 183, 525
Operation Magic Carpet (Yemen), 215, 238, 249, 397, 579
Operation Margarethe, 365
Operation Moses, 240
Operation Nachshon, 497, 524, 533
Operation Pillar of Defense, 223
Operation Pleshet, 533, 543
Operation Reinhard, 331, 335, 359
Operation Retribution (1941), 260
Operation Shfifon, 533
Operation Shmone, 569
Operation Shoter, 563
Operation Solomon, 240
Operation Tannenberg, 326
Operation Uvda, 571
Operation Velvetta, 535
Operation Yachin, 579
Operation Yevusi, 509, 533
Operation Yiftah, 525, 533
Operation Yoav, 533, 539, 566, 567
Ophir, 89
Oral history, 370
Oral law, 104
Orange (fruit), 146
Orde Charles Wingate, 172
Orderic Vitalis, 141
Order in Council, 170, 281
Orde Wingate, 293
Ordnance QF 6 pounder, 537
Organization of Ukrainian Nationalists, 621
Orpo battalions, 326, 377
Orthodox Jews, 617
Osprey Publishing, 583, 585
Othniel, 55, 58
Otmar von Verschuer, 337, 618
Ottoman Army, 301
Ottoman Empire, 154, 199, 228, 271, 313
Ottoman Parliament, 155
Ottoman Syria, 2, 10, 40, 64, 73, 86, 112, 155, 165, 167, 188
Ottoman Turkish language, 154, 159–161
Ottoman Wars in Europe, 150
Otton de Grandson, 140
Otto von Habsburg, 151
Oultrejordain, 116, 130, 148
Outline of Judaism, 11, 31
Outremer, 140
Oxford University Press, 152, 210, 474, 581, 584, 585

Ox goad, 56
Oyneg Shabbos (group), 363

P-51 Mustang, 572, 574
Pactum Warmundi, 118, 147
Pakistan, 466, 520
Palaestina Prima, 1, 3, 9, 40, 63, 72, 86, 111, 165, 166
Palaestina Secunda, 1, 3, 9, 40, 63, 72, 86, 111, 165, 166
Paleo-Hebrew alphabet, 45
Palestine Airways, 201
Palestine Arab Congress, 168
Palestine Arab Party, 268
Palestine Electric Company, 201
Palestine Jewish Colonisation Association, 194
Palestine Liberation Organization, 472
Palestine Pilgrims Text Society, 602
Palestine police, 171, 269, 300, 404
Palestine Police Force, 181, 183, 266, 268, 290, 413
Palestine Post, 633
Palestine pound, 164
Palestine Railway, 413
Palestine refugee camps, 484, 576, 577
Palestine Regiment, 417
Palestine (region), 146, 154, 167, 184, 188, 228, 250, 314, 476, 484, 504, 528, 529, 577
Palestine War, 537
Palestinian Arab, 189, 268
Palestinian Arab Party, 273
Palestinian Declaration of Independence, 472
Palestinian flag, 298
Palestinian general strike, 291
Palestinian Jews, 268
Palestinian Legislative Council election, 1923, 171, 186
Palestinian National Authority, 3, 167
Palestinian nationalism, 453
Palestinian people, 475, 476
Palestinian refugee, 484, 521, 563, 576, 577
Palestinian return to Israel, 484, 576
Palestinian right of return, 484, 576, 578
Palestinian Scout Association, 273
Palestinian territories, 578
PalgraveMacmillan, 631
Palmach, 175, 295, 403, 404, 413, 420, 423, 432, 435, 436, 444, 475, 479, 492, 496, 501, 504, 509, 520, 524, 527, 558
Palmah, 471
Palyam, 440, 444
Panama, 465
Pan-Arabism, 292
Pantheon Books, 586
Panzer IV, 574

Papal legate, 116
Pappé, 634–638
Pappep72, 635
Parachute Regiment (United Kingdom), 438
Paraguay, 465
Paramilitary, 490
Parczew partisans, 329
Pardes Hanna, 449
Pardes Hanna-Karkur, 443
Paris, France, 155
Partitioning of the Ottoman Empire, 453
Partition of the Ottoman Empire, 151, 167
Partition (politics), 452
Partnership 2gether, 219
Partnership2Gether, 214, 241, 243
Passfield white paper, 232
Passover, 47
Pastoralism, 14
Pathros, 92
Patria disaster, 402, 403
Patriarch (Bible), 43
Patriarchs (Bible), 36
Patrick Domville, 289
Paul de Lagarde, 337
Pauline epistles, 103
Peel Commission, 172, 191, 233, 278, 312, 314, 415, 453
Pekah, 75, 80
Pekahiah, 79
Pelagius of Albano, 131
Pentateuch, 19
Penuel, 71
Permanent Mandates Commission, 320
Persecution of homosexuals in Nazi Germany and the Holocaust, 331, 617
Persecution of Jehovahs Witnesses in Nazi Germany, 331, 617
Persecution of Jews, 361
Persian Jews, 578
Peru, 179, 465
Perushim, 215, 249, 397
Petah Tikva, 270, 445, 448, 477
Peter Hayes (historian), 333, 369, 388
Peter I, Duke of Brittany, 134
Peter II of Yugoslavia, 260
Peter Longerich, 358, 361, 390
Peter Novick, 380
Peter N. Stearns, 585
Peter W. Edbury, 123
Peulot Meyuhadot, 266, 295, 296
Pharaoh, 34, 88, 90
Philip I, Count of Flanders, 124
Philip II of France, 126, 128
Philip K. Hitti, 151
Philip Mattar, 304, 583
Philip of Milly, 120

Philip of Montfort, Lord of Tyre, 133
Philipp Bouhler, 340
Philippines, 466
Philip R. Davies, 59
Philistia, 3, 66, 90, 166
Philistine, 6
Philistines, 13, 62, 65, 66, 89
Phoenicia, 3, 13, 31, 66, 166
Phoenician alphabet, 75
Phoenicians, 6
PIAT, 541, 547, 574
Pied-Noir, 579
Pietro Vesconte, 43
Pillar of Cloud, 45
Pillar of Fire (theophany), 45
Pinhas Rutenberg, 168, 201
Pinhas Sapir, 245
Pisa, 133
Pithos, 14
Plaek Phibunsongkhram, 261
Plain of Sharon, 441
Plaisance of Antioch, 136
Plan D, 497
Plan Dalet, 192, 484, 489, 511, 528, 577
Plaster cast, 104
Ploieşti, 257
Pogrom, 327, 337, 343
Poitou, 124
Poland, 416, 419, 466
Polemic, 65
Poles, 372
Police state, 426
Polish areas annexed by Nazi Germany, 344, 345
Polish Armed Forces in the West, 329
Polish government-in-exile, 362, 364
Polish Jews, 351, 353
Polish September Campaign, 326
Political moves and Assyrian invasion, 84
Political Science Quarterly, 211
Politics of Israel, 71
Pompey, 12, 21
Pompey in the East, 99
Pompey the Great, 101
Pope Gregory IX, 132
Pope Innocent IV, 136
Pope Urban II, 114
Pope Urban IV, 137
Population growth, 199
Population transfer, 17
Porajmos, 330, 331, 370, 617
Portal:Israel, 2, 10, 41, 64, 73, 87, 112, 165
Portal: Judaism, 12, 31
Portal:Palestine, 3, 167
Port-de-Bouc, 409
Port of Haifa, 563

Port Said, 444, 553
Postwar, 579
Post-War, 579
Post-World War II: North African Jewish migration, 579
Post-Zionist, 468
Pottery Neolithic, 5
Pound sterling, 429, 487
PPNA, 5
PPNB, 5
Praeger Publishers, 582, 585
Prehistory of the Levant, 1, **1**, 2, 9, 40, 63, 72, 85, 111, 164, 166
Pre-Modern Aliyah, 215, 249, 397
Pre-Pottery Neolithic, 3, 166
Pre-Roman history of ancient Israel and Judah, 102
Present absentee, 484, 577
Presidencies and provinces of British India, 286
President of the United States, 421
Priestly source, 19
Primary, secondary and tertiary sources, 185
Primus inter pares, 150
Principality of Antioch, 113
Principality of Galilee, 116
Proconsul, 101
Promised Land, 215, 249, 397
Proselytes, 102
Proselytization, 103
Protectorate of Bohemia and Moravia, 345
Province, 101
Provisional State Council, 563
Provost (education), 545
Pro-Wailing Wall Committee, 295
Prussian Academy of Sciences, 341
Psamtik I, 90
Ptolemaic Kingdom, 99
Ptolemy I, 20
Public Seal of Mandatory Palestine, 163
PubMed Identifier, 394
Putti, 104

Qadas, 548
Qadi, 187
Qahtanites, 34
Qalawun, 139
Qalqilyah, 273
Qalunya, 495
Qazaza, 634
QF 25 pounder, 537
QF 2 pounder naval gun, 289
Quincy Wright, 211
Quneitra, 558
Quran, 277
Qutuz, 138

Raanana, 446
Rabbi, 104
Rabbinic Judaism, 12
Rabigh, 125
Race (human categorization), 337
Rachel, 36, 44
Radiocarbon dated, 69
RAF Intelligence, 289, 292
RAF Regiment, 289
Rages, 76
Raghib al-Nashashibi, 170, 187, 267, 297
Ralph Bunche, 563
Ralph Cairns, 281, 434
Ramallah, 160, 194, 199, 495, 536, 560
Ramat David Airbase, 181, 550, 572
Ramat Efal, 471
Ramat Gan, 435, 438, 440
Ramat Rachel, 545
Ramat Yohanan, 502
Ramla, 115, 160, 225, 443, 448, 561, 563, 573
Ramle, 194, 199, 521, 560
Ramleh, 483, 495
Ramoth-Gilead, 89
Randolph L. Braham, 383
Random checkpoint, 426
Random House Websters Unabridged Dictionary, 593
Ran (Haganah unit), 292, 295
Raphael Patai, 310
Rapport special, 635
Ras al-Ein, 548
Rashid Ali, 495
Rashid Khalidi, 186, 209, 308, 583
Rashidun Caliphate, 3, 166
Ratification, 312
Raul Hilberg, 315, 333, 361, 369, 388, 615, 631
Ravensbrück concentration camp, 336, 367
Raymond III of Tripoli, 122, 123
Raymond IV of Toulouse, 115
Raymond of Poitiers, 118
Raynald of Châtillon, 124, 125
Razoux, 636, 637
Reading Power Station, 549
Rebecca, 36
Recent African origin of modern humans, 4
Recha Freier, 235
Red Army, 328, 362, 363
Red Sea, 13, 34, 45, 66, 125, 458, 571
Reformation, 337
Reform Judaism, 219
Reform Party (Palestine), 273
RefWallach2, 641
Reginald of Sidon, 128
Régine Pernoud, 152
Regnery Publishing, 582

Rehavia, 234, 447
Rehoboam, 47, 61, 67, 74, 87, 88
Rehovot, 431, 443, 444, 449, 457, 479, 552
Reich Central Office for the Combating of Homosexuality and Abortion, 375
Reich Main Security Office, 356
Reichmark, 343
Reich Ministry of Public Enlightenment and Propaganda, 357
Reich Security Main Office, 344
Reichskommissar, 346
Reichskommissariat Ostland, 359
Reichsleiter, 340
Reichsmark, 340
Reinhard Heydrich, 328, 344, 356, 377
Rekhesh, 295
Relations between Nazi Germany and the Arab world, 417
Relief, 102
Religio licita, 102
Religions of the ancient Near East, 22
Renaissance, 147
Renault R35, 547, 574
Renault R40, 574
René Grousset, 141
Repressions, 326
Republic of China (1912–1949), 467, 540
Republic of Cuba (1902–1959), 464
Republic of Genoa, 113
Republic of Haiti (1859–1957), 463, 465
Republic of Venice, 113, 118
Reserve Police Battalion 101, 377
Resolution 181, 180
Return to Zion, 215, 249, 397
Reuben (Bible), 44
Reuven Shiloah, 291, 292
Revisionist Maximalism, 295
Revisionist Zionism, 231, 278, 296, 399, 468
Revival of the Hebrew language, 216, 250, 398
Revivim, 492
Revolution, 291
Rezin, 75
Rheims, 141
Rhodes, 402
Richard, 1st Earl of Cornwall, 135
Richard A. Gabriel, 594
Richard Dimbleby, 367, 624
Richard D. Nelson, 58
Richard Filangieri, 132
Richard I of England, 128
Richard J. Evans, 380, 385
Richard OConnor, 297
Richard Peirse, 276
Riga Ghetto, 350
Right of return, 563
Riots in Palestine of 1929, 527

Rise of monotheism, 83
Rise of the Ottoman Empire, 150
Rishon LeZion, 442, 443
River Jordan, 159
Roadblock (barrier), 289
Robert A. Lovett, 462
Robert Gellately, 387
Robert Haining, 267
Robert Jay Lifton, 390
Robert Ley, 626
Robert of Artois, 136
Robert the Monk, 116
Rocket, 226
Roderic Hill, 267
Roger de Flor, 140
Roger II of Sicily, 117
Roger of San Severino, 139
Rolls-Royce Armoured Car, 284
Roman Catholicism, 143
Roman colony, 99
Roman empire, 21, 31, 99, 101, 103, 105
Roman Ghetto, 101
Romania, 326, 402
Romanian language, 32, 34
Romani genocide, 334, 368
Romani people, 370, 617
Roman Senate, 21, 99
Roman triumph, 102
Rome, 427, 441
Ronald Ian Campbell, 433
Ronnie Ellenblum, 146
Rosh HaNikra Crossing, 432
Rosh Hashanah, 329
Routledge, 210, 211, 581–584
Royal Air Force, 287, 329, 413, 433, 440, 443, 571, 572, 635
Royal Artillery, 418
Royal Canadian Navy, 553
Royal Commission, 278, 314
Royal Dutch Shell, 290
Royal Egyptian Air Force, 549
Royal Engineers, 285
Royal Marines, 290, 413, 420
Royal Navy, 176, 289, 329, 400, 401, 413, 418, 440, 553, 573
Royal Northumberland Fusiliers, 297
Royal Ulster Rifles, 284
Roy Farran, 444, 449
Rudolf Höss, 360
Rudolph Rummel, 372
Ruhama, 229, 440
Russian Compound, 207, 562
Russian language, 32
Russian SFSR, 326
RWD-13, 549

Sabra (person), 216, 250, 398
Saburō Kurusu, 253
Sachsenhausen concentration camp, 336, 343
Sack of Jerusalem (10th century BC), 88
Saewulf, 141
Safad, 194, 199, 273, 299
Safed, 482, 503, 504, 515, 525, 554
Saffa, Ramallah, 160
Safsaf, 565
Said al-As, 267, 301
Saint Sabas, 137
Saladin, 112, 113, 122, 127, 273
Salah (biblical figure), 33
Salama, Jaffa, 471
Salim Tamari, 517
Sallai Meridor, 245
Salt March and civil disobedience, 188
Samakh, Tiberias, 547, 554
Samaria, 6, 21, 42, 67, 99, 441, 457, 480, 482, 515, 523
Samaria (ancient city), 16, 61, 71, 73, 74, 76, 598
Samaritan, 19
Samaritanism, 110
Samaritan revolts, 1, 10, 40, 64, 72, 86, 112, 165
Samaritans, 36, 37, 39, 114, 143
Samosata, 130
Samson, 55, 58
Samsons Foxes, 536
Samuel, 55, 58
Samuel (Bible), 62
Sam Zemurray, 464
Sanhedrin, 105
Sanitation, 281
Sanjak, 155
Sanjak of Acre, 154
Sanjak of Nablus, 154
San Remo Conference, 185, 230, 314
Sanur, Jenin, 300
Sapir College, 227
Sarah, 36
Saree Makdisi, 584
Sargon II, 76, 82, 598
Sargon II of Assyria, 75
Sargon of Akkad, 7
Saris, 495
Sarona (colony), 443
Sassanid Empire, 105
Saudi Arabia, 268, 315, 466, 522, 535
Saul, 47, 61, 62, 68, 87
Saul Friedländer, 335, 386
S:Cablegram from the Secretary-General of the League of Arab States to the Secretary-General of the United Nations, 529, 633

Scars of War, Wounds of Peace: The Israeli-Arab Tragedy, 307, 585
Schloss Hartheim, 341
Schneller Orphanage, 443
Schooner, 176
Schutzmannschaft, 326
Schutzstaffel, 331, 343, 379
Science and technology in Israel, 242
Scientific racism, 337
Scriptorium, 148
S:Declaration of Independence (Israel), 606
Sde Dov Airport, 549
Sderot, 225, 226, 229
Sea of Galilee, 458, 504, 547, 562
Sea of Marmara, 403
Sebastian Haffner, 328
Second Aliyah, 215, 229, 249, 397
Second Book of Chronicles, 58
Second Book of Samuel, 65
Second British census of Palestine, 197
Second Council of Lyon, 139
Second Crusade, 119
Second Intifada, 578
Second Italo-Abyssinian War, 290
Second Polish Republic, 328
Second Temple period, 1, 9, 22, 40, 43, 63, 72, 86, 111, 164
Second Vienna Award, 257
Secretary-General, 513
Secretary of State for Foreign and Commonwealth Affairs, 485
Secretary of State for the Colonies, 615
Secretary of State for War, 320
Secret Intelligence Service, 419
Sectarian conflict in Mandatory Palestine, 413
Security Council, 432
Security Division (Wehrmacht), 331
Sedentism, 5
Sefer Torah, 45
Sejanus, 102, 600
Seleucid Empire, 12, 99
Seleucids, 20
Seleucus I Nicator, 3, 166
Self-determination, 306, 453, 469
Seljuk Turks, 114
Selvino children, 175
Semeia, 25, 50, 94
Semiramis Hotel bombing, 634
Semitic languages, 5
Sennacherib, 17, 84, 89
Sephardi Jews, 578
Sepphoris, 104
Serbia, 347
Serbian language, 32

Şerif Mehmed Rauf Paşa, 161

Service-learning, 221
Seventh Crusade, 136
Sextus Julius Severus, 102
Seychelles, 280
S. F. Newcombe, 320
Shaar HaGolan, 547
Shabbat, 23, 562
Shabtai Teveth, 627
Shai (Haganah unit), 292, 295
Shallum of Israel, 79
Shalmaneser III, 16, 81, 598
Shalmaneser V, 75, 82, 598
Shamash, 22
Shamgar, 55, 56, 58
Shanghai, 347
Shanty town, 271
Shapira, 638
Shariah, 170
Sharona, 438
Sharon, Israel, 458
Sharon plain, 90
Shasu, 31, 33, 41
Shaul Avigur, 295
Shavuoth, 47
Shawar, 122
Shchuka-class submarine, 176, 403
Shebna, 17
Shechem, 6, 43, 61, 64, 67, 71, 73, 74
Shefa-Amr, 438, 502
Shefat, 448
Shefayim, 403, 404
Sheikh Abed, 566
Shem, 32
Sherit ha-Pletah, 399, 411, 421
Sherman tank, 574
Sherut Avir, 549
Shfela, 13
Shia, 114, 143
Shia Islam, 115
Shiloh (Biblical), 66
Shiloh (Biblical city), 6
Shimon Avidan, 520, 533
Shimon Peres, 220
Shirkuh, 122
Shishak, 16, 88
Shlichim, 218
Shlomo Ben-Ami, 307, 585, 642
Shlomo Shamir, 533
Shmita, 46
Shmuel Katz (politician), 211
Shoah, 332
Sholem Asch, 232
Shomer Shabbat, 46
Shoshenq I, 16
Shukri al-Quwatli, 470
Shukri al-Quwwatli, 547

Siberia, 344
Sibylla of Jerusalem, 123
Sicherheitsdienst, 379
Sicilian Vespers, 139
Sidon, 117, 132
Sidon Sea Castle, 132
Siegen, 343
Siege of Acre (1189–1191), 128
Siege of Acre (1291), 111, 112, 114, 140, 146
Siege of Aleppo (1260), 137
Siege of Antioch (1268), 138, 146
Siege of Baghdad (1258), 137
Siege of Constantinople (1204), 130
Siege of Damascus (1148), 120
Siege of Edessa, 119
Siege of Jerusalem (1099), 110, 115
Siege of Jerusalem (1187), 110, 128
Siege of Jerusalem (1244), 110, 135
Siege of Jerusalem (1948), 492, 524
Siege of Jerusalem (587 BC), 83, 87, 91
Siege of Jerusalem (597 BC), 91
Siege of Jerusalem (63 BC), 12, 99
Siege of Jerusalem (70), 99, 102
Siege of Jerusalem (70 AD), 43
Siege of Kerak, 126
Siege of Malta (World War II), 263
Siege of Ruad, 140
Siege of Tripoli (1271), 138
Siege of Tripoli (1289), 140
Siemens, 380
Sigmund Freud, 342
Sigurd I of Norway, 117
Silat al-Harithiya, 300
Silesia, 339
Silk, 146
Siloam, 76
Siloam inscription, 17
Siloam tunnel, 17
Silwan, 634
Simeon (Hebrew Bible), 44
Simha Dinitz, 245
Simha Flapan, 468, 586
Simon Bar Kochba, 21
Simon & Schuster, 582
Sinai, 159, 513
Sinai and Palestine Campaign, 154, 167
Sinai Desert, 45, 113
Sinai Peninsula, 12, 519, 521
Sir Arthur Harris, 1st Baronet, 267, 288
Six-Day War, 239, 578
Sixth Crusade, 110, 113, 132
Skype, 219
Slav, 372
Slave labour, 374
Slavery, 103
Slavery in medieval Europe, 144

Slavic languages, 34
Slavs, 331, 617
Slick Goodlin, 572
Slovak-Hungarian War, 258
Slovak invasion of Poland, 258
Slovak Republic (1939–1945), 253, 258
Smyrniote crusades, 151
SNCF, 380
Sobibor extermination camp, 335, 359
Sobibór extermination camp, 328, 360, 370
Social entrepreneurship, 222, 225
Socialist Federal Republic of Yugoslavia, 467
Society for the Defense of Palestine, 266
Society of Biblical Literature, 594
Sodom and Gomorrah, 7
Solel Boneh, 287
Solomon, 47, 61, 66, 68, 74, 87, 598
Solomons Temple, 66, 89
Sonderkommando, 360, 362
Sonderkommando photographs, 359
Source criticism (biblical studies), 61
South Africa, 450, 466
Southern Dobruja, 257
Southern Lebanon, 519, 521
Southern Levant, 4, 36, 83, 112
Southern Syria, 3, 167, 184
Soviet bloc, 467
Soviet occupation of Bessarabia and Northern Bukovina, 258
Soviet occupation of Poland, 1939–1941, 344
Soviet partisans, 362
Soviet submarine Shch-213, 403
Soviet submarine Shch-215, 403
Soviet Union, 179, 240, 258, 260, 335, 466, 486
Spanish Civil War, 278
Special Interrogation Group, 417
Special Night Squads, 172, 266, 293–295
Speculum (journal), 603
Spice trade, 146
Spitfire, 549
Split of early Christianity and Judaism, 99
Spring 1945 offensive in Italy, 176, 418
SS Athena (1893), 406
SS Atlantic (1885), 402
SS Exodus, 400, 407, 409, 421, 428, 455
SS Milos (1878), 402
SS Pacific (1880), 402
SS Patria (1913), 176, 402, 403
Stab-in-the-back myth, 337
Stafford Cripps, 434
Stalinism, 380
Start-up Nation, 2, 10, 41, 64, 73, 86, 112, 165
State church of the Roman Empire, 100, 105
Statement of Information Relating to Acts of Violence, 424

State of Israel, 175, 183, 238, 515, 520, 521, 525
State of Israel (1948–present), 3, 167
State of Palestine, 3, 111, 113, 154, 164, 167
State-owned enterprise, 216
State University of New York Press, 210
Sten, 488, 526, 574, 636
Stephen M. Walt, 632
Stepped Stone Structure, 85
Stern Gang, 189, 527
Steven Runciman, 123, 152, 600, 601
St. Jamess Palace, 305
Stone tool, 4
Streams of Zionism, 229
Struma disaster, 176, 403
Struma (river), 259
Sturmabteilung, 327, 339, 343, 379
Stutthof, 359
Submarine chaser, 553
Sudan, 450
Suez Canal, 175, 274, 450, 522
Suez Crisis, 578
Suffolk Regiment, 290
Sufi, 143
Sugar, 146
Sukkot, 447
Sukkoth, 47
Sultanate of Rûm, 114
Sultan of Egypt, 123
Sunni, 114, 143
SUNY Press, 584
Supermarine Spitfire, 489, 535, 537, 549, 572, 574
Supreme Muslim Council, 170, 278
Surety, 222
Surif, 495
Sussex Academic Press, 582
Suzerainty, 117, 129
Sweden, 466
Switzerland, 232
Sykes–Picot Agreement, 167
Sykes-Picot Agreement, 314
Synagogue, 23, 327, 343
Synagogue of Dura-Europos, 100
Syria, 6, 72, 90, 91, 113, 114, 139, 278, 287, 313, 466, 487, 495, 513, 515, 535
Syriac Orthodox, 114, 116, 143
Syrian Air Force, 537
Syrian people, 481, 482
Syrian Republic (1946–63), 476, 521, 540
Syria Palaestina, 1, 3, 9, 21, 40, 63, 72, 86, 102, 111, 165, 166
Syria-Palaestina, 184
Syria (Roman province), 99, 101
Syria Vilayet, 155
Szlama Ber Winer, 363

T-6 Texan, 549, 574
Taas, 294, 295
Tabun Cave, 4
Tadeusz Piotrowski (sociologist), 392
Taglit, 217
Taglit-Birthright Israel, 217, 241
Tahpanhes, 92
Tahunian, 3, 166
Talent (measurement), 91
Talmud, 103
Tammuz (Hebrew month), 74
Tanakh, 36
Tannaim, 104
Tantura, 548
Tanzimat, 155
Tarab Abdul Hadi, 272, 273
Tarnovo Constitution, 259
Tarvisio, 175
Taurus Mountains, 12
Tawfik Abu al-Huda, 531
Tax, 74
Taxpayer Identification Number, 213
Tayibe, 301
Technion, 201
Tegart fort, 287, 295, 436, 547, 569
Tegarts wall, 288, 295
Tel Aviv, 174, 181, 224, 225, 270, 303, 401, 434, 436, 440, 444, 447, 448, 468, 492, 521, 532, 543, 549, 563, 572
Tel Aviv Central Bus Station, 549
Tel Aviv University, 69
T. E. Lawrence, 169, 313
Tel Hazor, 6, 7, 57, 66
Tel Megiddo, 6, 66
Tel Nof Airbase, 552
Template:Aliyah, 216, 250, 398
Template:History of Israel, 2, 10, 41, 64, 73, 87, 112, 166
Template:History of Palestine, 4, 167
Template:Jewish exodus from Arab and Muslim countries, 579
Template:Jews and Judaism sidebar, 12, 31
Template:Judges, 55
Template:Kings of Judah, 88
Template:Nakba, 485, 577
Template:Palestinians, 485, 577
Template talk:Aliyah, 216, 250, 398
Template talk:History of Israel, 2, 10, 41, 64, 73, 87, 112, 166
Template talk:History of Palestine, 4, 167
Template talk:Jewish exodus from Arab and Muslim countries, 579
Template talk:Jews and Judaism sidebar, 12, 31
Template talk:Judges, 55
Template talk:Kings of Judah, 88
Template talk:Nakba, 485, 577

Template talk:The Holocaust sidebar, 325, 332
Template talk:Tribes of Israel, 36
Template:The Holocaust sidebar, 325, 332
Template:Tribes of Israel, 36
Temple, 105
Temple in Jerusalem, 31, 43, 80, 102
Temple Mount, 149
Temple of Jerusalem, 91
Ten Commandments, 45
Ten Lost Tribes, 36, 75
Ten plagues of Egypt, 45
Territories and regions, 467
Teutonic Knights, 132, 133
Textile, 146
Textual critic, 62
Textual criticism, 73
TGWU, 419
Thailand, 464, 467
The American Hebrew, 332
The Arab General Strike and armed insurrection, 453
The Bible Unearthed, 14, 69, 76, 594, 595
The Black Book of Poland, 364
The Bloody Day in Jaffa, 270
The Destruction of the European Jews, 333
The Encyclopedia of the Jewish Religion, 598
The Encyclopedia of World History, 585
The English Historical Review, 601
The Ethnic Cleansing of Palestine, 584, 586
The Exodus, 15, 45, 47
The Forgotten Refugees, 579
The Generals Revolt, 490
The Holocaust, 223, 325, 326, **330**, 331, 418, 477, 576
The Holocaust in Albania, 326
The Holocaust in Austria, 326
The Holocaust in Belarus, 326
The Holocaust in Belgium, 326
The Holocaust in Estonia, 326
The Holocaust in France, 326
The Holocaust in Italian Libya, 326
The Holocaust in Latvia, 326
The Holocaust in Lithuania, 326
The Holocaust in Luxembourg, 326
The Holocaust in Norway, 326
The Holocaust in occupied Poland, 326
The Holocaust in Poland, 326
The Holocaust in Russia, 326
The Holocaust in Serbia, 326
The Holocaust in the Independent State of Croatia, 326
The Holocaust in Ukraine, 326
The Hope (novel), 586
The Hunting Season, 177, 414, 423, 435
The Jerusalem Post, 30, 436
The Jewish question, 228

The Jews of Libya during the Holocaust, 578
The New Republic, 616
Theobald I of Navarre, 134
Theodora Komnene, Queen of Jerusalem, 121
Theodore Herzl, 228
The Ottoman Empire, 153
The Palestine Post, 634, 635, 641
The Queens Own Royal West Kent Regiment, 290
Theresienstadt, 352
Theresienstadt concentration camp, 367
The Revolt, 450, 451
The Scotsman, 630
The Sergeants affair, 427, 446
The Sunday Times, 629
The Times, 430, 630, 635
Think tank, 220
Third Aliyah, 215, 249, 397
Third Crusade, 110, 112, 128
Third Intermediate Period of Egypt, 33
Third Mithridatic War, 101
Third Reich, 378
Third Temple, 105
Thirteen Attributes of Mercy, 46
Thomas Asbridge, 600
Thomas Becket, 126
Thomas C. Wasson, 545
Thomas F. Madden, 117, 601
Thomas Haycraft, 200
Thomas Joseph Shahan, 59
Thompson submachine gun, 574
Tiber, 101
Tiberian vocalization, 31, 73
Tiberias, 104, 116, 127, 194, 199, 224, 442, 503, 515, 525, 554
Tiergarten, Berlin, 341
Tiergartenstraße, 341
Tiglath-Pileser III, 75, 76, 81, 82
Tigris, 7
Timeline of deportations of French Jews to death camps, 380
Timeline of Israeli history, 2, 10, 41, 64, 73, 86, 112, 165
Time (magazine), 629
Timna Park, 44
Timothy D. Snyder, 333, 393
Tirzah (ancient city), 71, 73, 74
Tisha BAv, 103
Tito–Stalin split, 467
Titus, 43, 102
Tnuva, 201
Tola (Bible), 55
Tola (biblical figure), 58
Tolidah, 114
Tom Segev, 210, 310, 485, 577, 629
Tony Kushner (academic), 450

Toponym, 42
Torah, 19, 20, 43, 45
Toron, 144
Tosefta, 104
Tower and stockade, 295
Tower of David, 120, 121, 149, 169
Trade route, 6
Traditional story, 22
Transaction Publishers, 210, 581
Transfer Committee, 484, 577
Transhumance, 5
Transjordan Frontier Force, 536
Transjordan memorandum, 314
Trans-Jordan memorandum, 180
Transjordan (region), 36
Transnistria, 348
Transylvania, 257
Treaty of Berlin (1878), 186
Treaty of Craiova, 259
Treaty of Ramla, 129
Treblinka extermination camp, 328, 335, 348, 352, 359, 360, 370
Triangle (Israel), 563
Tribe of Asher, 36, 74, 77
Tribe of Benjamin, 36, 38, 74, 75, 87, 88
Tribe of Dan, 36, 74
Tribe of Ephraim, 36, 39, 42, 74, 75, 77
Tribe of Gad, 36, 74–76
Tribe of Issachar, 36, 74, 77
Tribe of Joseph, 36
Tribe of Judah, 36–39, 42, 74, 75, 87, 598
Tribe of Levi, 36, 38, 39, 75
Tribe of Manasseh, 36, 39, 74–77
Tribe of Naphtali, 36, 42, 74, 75, 89
Tribe of Reuben, 36, 74–76
Tribe of Simeon, 36, 74, 75
Tribe of Zebulun, 36, 74, 77
Tribes of Israel, 57
Tripartite Pact, **253**
Truman trusteeship proposal, 182
Trygve Lie, 451, 540, 628
Tubas, 64, 482
Tulcea, 402
Tulkarem, 482
Tulkarm, 194, 199, 270, 273, 299, 546
Tunis, 138
Turanshah, 136
Turcopoles, 147
Turkey, 467
Turkish Jews in Israel, 579
Turkish language, 159–161
Turkish people, 143
Tutush I, 114
Twelve Tribes of Israel, 35, 37, 598
Twenty-sixth Dynasty of Egypt, 84
Twin towns and sister cities, 241

Tyndale Bulletin, 28, 54, 96
Typhoid fever, 352
Typhus, 367
Tyre, Lebanon, 66, 110, 118
Tzipi Livni, 220
Tzrifin, 438

Ubeidiya, 4
Ugarit, 80
Ukrainian Auxiliary Police, 326
Ukrainian Soviet Socialist Republic, 466
Ulpan, 216, 223, 239, 250, 398
Ulpan Etzion, 224
Umayyad Caliphate, 3, 166
Umm al-Fahm, 225
U.N, 489
UN charter, 469
Underground to Palestine, 400
UNESCO World Heritage Site, 139
Union Flag, 176
United Israel Appeal, 241, 244
United Jewish Appeal, 430
United Jewish Communities, 241
United Kingdom, 163, 413, 467, 475, 615
United Kingdom–United States relations, 429
United Kingdom general election, 1945, 419
United Nations, 429, 430, 432, 433, 452, 455, 476
United Nations Charter, 453
United Nations Conciliation Commission, 573, 642
United Nations General Assembly, 452, 465, 476, 477, 522, 573
United Nations General Assembly Resolution 194, 484, 573, 577
United Nations Palestine Commission, 461
United Nations Partition Plan for Palestine, 179, 186, 312, 430, 432, **452**, 459, 476, 477, 484, 519, 521, 523, 554, 575, 577
United Nations Regional Groups, 465, 467
United Nations Relief and Works Agency for Palestine Refugees in the Near East, 484, 577
United Nations resolution, 452
United Nations Security Council, 432
United Nations Security Council Resolution 50, 433
United Nations Special Committee on Palestine, 430, 455
United Nations Truce Supervision Organization, 575
United Partisan Organization, 329, 361
United States, 254, 328, 399, 414, 462, 466, 480, 525
United States Armed Forces, 362
United States Coast Guard, 553

United States Congress, 428
United States Holocaust Memorial Museum, 334, 368, 396, 617
United States of Venezuela, 464
United States Senate, 462
Universal Carrier, 442, 536, 574
University at Albany, SUNY, 474
University of California Press, 586
University of Nebraska Press, 584
University of North Carolina Press, 210
UN Partition Plan, 237
UNRRA, 399
UNRWA, 578
UNSCOP, 179, 452
UN Security Council, 486
Unsupported attributions, 328, 505
Untermenschen, 354, 372
Upper Galilee, 299, 566
Upper Palaeolithic, 4
Urbanization, 69
Uri Milstein, 517
Ursicinus (Roman general), 104
Uruguay, 179, 465
Uruk, 6
Usamah ibn Munqidh, 141
Usamah ibn-Munqidh, 151
USCGC Gresham (WPG-85), 408
USCGC Northland (WPG-49), 409
USCGC Unalga (WPG-53), 406
U.S. dollar, 246
Ustaše, 371
Ustaše militia, 354
Ustashe, 347
Uzziah, 88

Vassals of the Kingdom of Jerusalem, 116, 149
Vassal state, 17, 66
VE Day, 177
Venezuela, 465
Vespasian, 43, 102
Viacheslav Molotov, 362
Via Maris, 6, 90
Vichy France, 327
Vichy regime, 347
Vickers, 574
Vienna, 402
VIII Corps (Ottoman Empire), 604
Vijaya Lakshmi Pandit, 463
Vilayet, 155
Vilayet of Beirut, 154
Village Statistics, 1945, 193
Vilna Ghetto, 350
Vintage Books, 584
Vital Cuinet, 153
Vizier, 115
Vojtech Tuka, 258

Volker Berghahn, 383
Völkischer Beobachter, 338
Völkisch movement, 337
Volksdeutsche, 345
Volksgemeinschaft, 338
Volkswagen, 380
Vyacheslav Molotov, 260
Vz. 24, 534

Wadi, 13
Waffen SS, 480
Waldemar Erfurth, 261
Walid Khalidi, 209, 268, 309, 485, 577, 583, 641
Walter Edward Guinness, 1st Baron Moyne, 177
Walter Guinness, 1st Baron Moyne, 435
Walter IV of Brienne, 134
Walter Laqueur, 609
Wannsee, 357
Wannsee conference, 328, 331, 335, 356, 622
Waqf, 170, 187
War crime, 379
War of aggression, 379
War of Saint Sabas, 137
War of the Jews, 595
War of the Lombards, 110, 113, 133
War of the Spanish Succession, 151
Warsaw Ghetto, 350, 352, 361, 370
Warsaw Ghetto Uprising, 329, 351, 361
Warsaw uprising, 329, 362, 373
Warthegau, 345
War with Judah, 17
Washington Report on Middle East Affairs, 629
Wasif Kamal, 267
Waterboarding, 287
Water supply and sanitation in Israel, 458
Wehrmacht, 371, 480
Weidenfeld & Nicolson, 582, 586
West Bank, 72, 83, 168, 519, 521, 575
Western Aramaic, 110
Western Desert Campaign, 417
Western European and Others Group, 465
Western Wall, 206
West Germany, 379
West Jerusalem, 545, 574
White paper, 312, 616
White Paper of 1939, 172, 176, 198, 302, 304, **312**, 398, 414, 416, 419
Who is a Jew?, 11, 31
Wikipedia:Avoid weasel words, 33
Wikipedia:Citation needed, 34, 62, 63, 65–68, 168, 175, 180, 184, 193, 217, 251, 302, 320, 399, 400, 403, 405, 457, 458, 461, 467, 476, 480, 503, 504, 520, 527, 535, 537, 546, 570, 571

Wikipedia:Citing sources, 56–58
Wikipedia:Identifying reliable sources, 64, 66
Wikipedia:Link rot, 82
Wikipedia:No original research, 521
Wikipedia:Please clarify, 216, 314, 501, 529
Wikisource, 452, 474
Wikisource:United Nations General Assembly Resolution 181, 452
Wikisource:United Nations Special Committee on Palestine Federal State Plan, 474
Wiktionary:massacre, 326
Wilhelm Keitel, 379
William B. Quandt, 630
William F. Albright, 68, 77
William James Fitzgerald (jurist), 200
William of Malmesbury, 141
William of Montferrat, Count of Jaffa and Ascalon, 124
William of Tyre, 140, 141, 151, 600
William Ormsby-Gore, 4th Baron Harlech, 606
William Peel, 1st Earl Peel, 191, 279, 415
William Roger Louis, 581
William V of Montferrat, 126
Winneba, 221
Winston Churchill, 177, 318, 363, 403, 429
Winter War, 261
With Egypt, 539
Wolfgang Benz, 369
Woodhead Commission, 280, 314, 416, 454
Wool, 146
World Organization of Jews from Arab Countries, 579
World War I, 154, 155, 229, 313, 337, 453
World War II, 164, 250, 321, 326, 328, 330, 344, 379, 399, 416, 417, 429, 454, 551
World War II.2C Resistance and the Holocaust, 326
World War II and the Holocaust, 326
World Zionist Congress, 173, 191, 280, 454
World Zionist Organization, 216, 218, 228, 244, 250, 398
WP:NOTRS, 506
Wyndham Deedes, 169
WZO, 239

Xylotymbou, 400

Yaakov Dori, 476, 497, 520
Yaakov Meridor, 449
Yabad, 171, 269
Yad Mordechai, 492
Yad Vashem, 330, 369, 384, 616
Yahweh, 17, 22, 36, 37, 41, 71, 80, 87
Yale University, 323
Yale University Press, 584, 601, 638
Yalo, 634

Yaqub al-Ghusayn, 313
Yarka, 225
Yarkon River, 159, 410
Yarmouk River, 482
Yatta, Hebron, 297
Yavne, 554
Yavneel, 549
Yawl, 406
Yehiam, 511
Yehiel Dresner, 444
Yehuda Arazi, 292
Yehuda Bauer, 369, 381, 382, 450
Yehuda Lapidot, 561, 629
Yehuda Leib Maimon, 233
Yehud (Babylonian province), 1, 9, 40, 63, 72, 83–85, 92, 111, 164
Yehud Medinata, 1, 3, 9, 12, 18–20, 40, 63, 72, 86, 93, 111, 165, 166
Yemen, 6, 450, 466, 522, 535
Yemenite Jews, 176
Yemenite Jews in Israel, 579
Yenoam, 42
Yerida, 216, 250, 398
Yezid Sayigh, 585
Yibna, 196, 554
Yiddish language, 616
Yiftach Brigade, 533, 561
Yigael Yadin, 67, 476, 496, 497, 502, 504, 511, 520, 524
Yigal Allon, 476, 490, 504, 520, 533, 540, 569
Yigal Alon, 172
Yishuv, 32, 168, 174, 216, 250, 266, 268, 271, 398, 411, 413, 428, 475, 476, 479, 486, 489–491, 504, 512, 521, 523, 528, 616
Yisrael Galili, 413, 520
Yisrael Gutman, 381, 392
Yisrael Meir Lau, 404
Yitzak Arad, 369
Yitzak Shamir, 178
Yitzhak Arad, 381
Yitzhak Gruenbaum, 234
Yitzhak Rabin, 435, 517, 520, 533, 556
Yitzhak Sadeh, 499, 520, 533
Yitzhak Shamir, 413, 440
YMCA, 198, 207
Yoav Gelber, 485, 506, 515, 516, 530, 577, 582, 633, 637, 641
Yodh, 184
Yom HaAliyah, 216, 250, 398
Yoram Kaniuk, 582
Yosef Almogi, 245
Yosef Garfinkel, 85
Young Communities, 222
Younger Dryas, 5
Young Mens Muslim Association, 188, 272
Young Turk Revolution, 155, 161

Youth Aliyah, 216, 235, 250, 398
Youth Congress Party, 272
Youth Futures, 215, 221, 242
Youth village, 215, 216, 221, 250, 398
YouTube, 266, 474, 586
Yugoslav accession to the Tripartite Pact, 253
Yugoslav coup détat, 253, 260
Yugoslavia, 175, 179, 327, 328, 402, 535
Yusuf Abu Durra, 267, 300
Yusuf Hamdan, 267, 301

Zagros Mountains, 7
Zalman Shazar, 245
Zebadiah, 58
Zebulun, 44
Zechariah of Israel, 79
Zedekiah, 88, 91
Zeev Bielski, 245
Zeev Hadari, 450
Zeev Jabotinsky, 231, 296, 321
Zeev Safrai, 593
Zerah, 88
Zerubbabel, 93
Zikhron Yaakov, 196
Zilpah, 44
Zimri (king), 78
Zion Gate, 510
Zionism, 2, 10, 40, 64, 73, 86, 112, 165, 170, 215, 249, 362, 397, 453, 476, 480, 523, 578
Zionist Commission, 168, 230
Zionist Congress, 232
Zionist Federation of Germany, 344
Zionist movement, 399, 477
Zionist Organisation, 232
Zionists, 229
Zionist youth movement, 218
Zion Square, 302
Ziony Zevit, 29, 55, 97
Zipporah, 45
Zobah, 66
Zurich, 232
Zuttiyeh Cave, 4
Zyklon-B, 360

www.ingramcontent.com/pod-product-compliance
Lightning Source LLC
Chambersburg PA
CBHW021412300426
44114CB00010B/464